BIRDS AND BIRDING AT CAPE MAY

Clay and Pat Sutton

STACKPOLE BOOKS

For those who came before us,
mentors, scribes, and conservationists alike,
and with gratitude to those who will choose to follow after.
May the magic of bird migration at Cape May never cease,
nor cease to amaze.

Copyright © 2006 by Stackpole Books

Published by
STACKPOLE BOOKS
5067 Ritter Road
Mechanicsburg, PA 17055
www.stackpolebooks.com

Printed in the United States of America

10 9 8 7 6 5 4 3 2 1

First edition

Cover photos by Jerry Liguori (Peregrine Falcon) and Clay and Pat Sutton (lighthouse)
Cover design by Wendy Reynolds
All photographs by Clay and Pat Sutton unless otherwise indicated

Library of Congress Cataloging-in-Publication Data
Sutton, Clay, 1949–
  Birds and birding at Cape May / Clay and Pat Sutton
    p. cm.
  Includes index.
  ISBN-13: 978-0–8117-3134–8
  ISBN-10: 0-8117-3134-0
    1. Birds—New Jersey—Cape May. 2. Bird watching—New Jersey—Cape May.
  I. Sutton, Patricia, 1951– II. Title

QL684.N5S88 2006
598.072'3474998—dc22
                                                                    2006004775

Contents

Foreword

It began as a romance, the book you hold in your hands.

In 1975 a young woman from suburban Pennsylvania met a young man from the Jersey Shore. He taught her birds (while he learned them better himself), they fell in love, and a partnership was born.

For more than thirty years, Pat and Clay Sutton have been exploring southern New Jersey's forests, fields, salt marshes, swamps, bogs, beaches, and backyards, observing and documenting the wildlife, collecting and sharing information with other dedicated scientists and naturalists, and fighting the good fight to publicize and preserve what can be saved. And now they have given us this rich and wonderful book—the where, when, how, and why of the birds of the Cape May area.

You may know of the most celebrated of Cape May's natural phenomena—the autumn raptor migration at the Point, the spring spectacle of the Red Knots and other long-distance migrant shorebirds on the Delaware Bayshore, the Higbee Beach morning songbird flights, and the Avalon seabird watch (where a *million* migrant birds can be seen in a single fall season!). Open this book, however and, no matter what your level of expertise, you will learn them better. Along the way you will learn also about lesser-known places and phenomena—the kite fest at the Beanery, the winter staging of scoters on the Bay, the recovery of the Osprey, the fall of the Bobwhite, the puzzling disappearance of the Evening Grosbeak, the record of waterfowl and shorebird abundance reflected in duck decoy collections—and much, much more.

Even readers who know Cape May very well might find themselves shaking their heads at the wonder of it all, presented in such careful, first-person detail here. Where else on the East Coast can you find (count 'em!) *eight* Western Kingbirds lined up on a single fence? Away from the borderlands, where else in North America can you hope to spot (as a handful of sharp observers have over the years) *seventeen* species of diurnal raptors in a single day? What other birding hot spot anywhere on Planet Earth can claim records for Whiskered Tern, Eurasian Kestrel, Rock Wren, Mongolian Plover, and Mountain Bluebird? Where else can the sighting of a Dovekie from the northernmost Atlantic Ocean be eclipsed a few minutes later by a Fork-tailed Flycatcher from the South American tropics?

Among the historical perspectives compiled here, you will find David Pietersen De Vries on the flocks of Passenger Pigeons he observed at Cape May in 1633; Thomas Nuttall on his first view of the great, green forests of the Delaware Bay in 1808; Roger Tory Peterson and Robert P. Allen on the gunning of robins, flickers, herons, hawks, and other birds in Cape May in the 1930s; Edwin Way Teale on the clouds of swallows he observed at the Point in 1950 while compiling notes for the book that became *Autumn Across America;* Philadelphia newspaper columnist Dale Rex Coman on an Osprey shot at its nest during the dark years of raptor decimation in the 1960s; Cape May painter and conservationist Al Nicholson on his discovery of the Mississippi Kite at the Point in 1976; Pete Dunne on his first days at the Cape May Bird Observatory hawkwatch later that same year; and Paul Lehman on what might have been the single largest night of songbird migration ever recorded in southern New Jersey, October 21, 2005. We have also the journal notes of a young naturalist in-the-making, Clay Sutton, age 13, recording a spectacular flight of Whimbrels at Stone Harbor on July 17, 1962.

"Few places on the planet can boast the ornithological history of the Cape May area," the Suttons write. They duck the hard question, however: Can you name any?

Witmer Stone's 1937 classic study, *Bird Studies at Old Cape May,* that did so much to document Cape May as an ornithological wonderland, has been given its sequel here. Stone synopsized all that had been learned about the birds of southern New Jersey in his day and age. The Suttons have updated the state of our knowledge for readers in the 21st century.

In many ways it's a different place than Stone knew, and the Suttons themselves have witnessed transformations in their decades on the scene. Pat recalls the dilapidated Victorian houses of Cape May of the 1970s and the wild, lawless Higbee Beach of her first years. Clay's earliest memories go back to the 1950s when he and his family walked to the enormous ternery at Stone Harbor Point, which soon after disappeared—first squeezed by housing development and then swallowed by beach erosion at Hereford Inlet.

Today, Cape May is a boomtown, fueled by second- and third-home owners, by year-round visitors, and by birding eco-tourists. The hawkwatch platform has been expanded to a double-deck, the predawn parking at Higbee Beach after a cold front can be competitive exercise, and cell phones and laptops link dozens and even hundreds of birders most days of the week spring and fall.

Not all changes have been good for the birds and natural world of southern NJ, of course. Beach fronts and ancient dune forests have disappeared beneath developers' bulldozers, and open space is lost each year, even at Cape May Point, where each green acre represents precious stopover habitat. But, as the Suttons note, we have reason for optimism. The Stone Harbor ternery—"big, bursting, alive, exhilarating"—seems to have resurrected itself in recent years, and is now protected by signs, state law, and volunteers. Other places have been saved or at least have become better protected by diligent, hard-fought conservation efforts: the South Cape May Meadows, the Cape May National Wildlife Refuge, Hidden Valley Ranch, Two Mile Beach, Higbee Beach.

The Suttons are right to celebrate these victories, but are too modest in noting their own invaluable contributions to the efforts. Both of them have been fully engaged in countless conservation efforts over the years and, just as importantly, they have taught thousands of residents and visitors to share their love for this land and its wildlife. Their efforts now also include this book, and I wonder how different Cape May would be had Pat and Clay Sutton not dedicated both their lives to this place and its treasures.

So, romance began the story of this book—Pennsy girl meets Jersey boy—and now thirty years later, love has drawn it together: the authors' love for each other, for the land where they live, for the naturalists and other wanderers who share this corner of the planet, and for the wildlife that blesses Cape May so bountifully.

If you have been a visitor to southern New Jersey or are lucky enough to live here, you will cherish this book. And if you haven't visited yet, what is holding you back? No more excuses please. This delightful volume of ornithological lore and hard-won knowledge gives you all the guidance and inspiration you could possibly require. Come join the migration; come see the magic.

—JACK CONNOR
author of *Season at the Point:*
The Birds and Birders of Cape May
and *The Complete Birder: A Guide*
to Better Birding

Preface

It was in April 1975 that Clay first put binoculars in my hands. We were in Florida on our first vacation together, soon after we met. He showed me how to use them as I studied my first Great Egrets. Each time I asked him to stop for a closer look at an exotic, eye-catching bird, we'd leisurely puzzle through its identification, the teacher and the student. He patiently stopped for five, six, or probably more Great Egrets before I finally caught on and realized we had already studied that one. Clay, as a Cape May boy, had grown up with flocks of Great Egrets but had never seen Caracaras, Sandhill Cranes, Burrowing Owls, Limpkins, or many of the other Florida specialties that were his targets on that trip. Yet the words "It's just another Great Egret" never passed his lips. That experience—the wonder of it all, no matter how common—not only shaped my life and my love of the natural world but also how I teach and how I interact with those eager to learn. After the Florida experience, I was a goner, in love with birds (and Clay), but little did I know that a life of rich natural history encounters awaited me.

I moved to Cape May later that year, lured both by Clay and by a new passion. I thought of myself as a "born-again birder." Visiting friends traipsed through tangled brier thickets at dusk to help search for a suspected Great Horned Owl nest, or else they soon faded away. My new life filled me with a yearning to learn everything there was to know about the outdoors and the natural world. Wanting to do something with that passion, I enrolled in Rowan University. Its environmental studies master's degree program welcomed people from all walks of life, which suited this literature major perfectly. I took electives in journalism, wishing to combine writing and teaching with my new passion. And for the last thirty years I've been privileged to be able to do just that while living and working at one of the greatest natural history meccas in the world, Cape May, New Jersey.

But I clearly remember a very different Cape May in 1975. Back then, I walked the city's streets and couldn't hold back the flow of tears. On street after street, many beautiful Victorian buildings stood silent and empty, unloved, neglected, run down, and boarded up. There were broken windows, porches falling off, and evidence of vandalism and fire. Most of the wooden buildings were painted white, or at least they had been years before; all were in dire need of tender loving care. They were being torn down daily to make room for new cookie-cutter houses and bland motels. Although the entire town of Cape May City and parts of West Cape May had been listed on the federal government's National Register of Historic Places in 1970, it wasn't until October 9, 1977, when Cape May was declared a National Historic Landmark, that a renaissance began. Preservationists started to buy and restore buildings to create income-generating businesses, such as restaurants and bed-and-breakfasts. Today it is hard to imagine how neglected Cape May had been in the 1970s, and I still marvel at the transformation of more than 600 Victorian houses, shops, inns, and B&Bs into the beauty that is Cape May today.

The neglect and disrespect were not limited to the architecture. Protected natural areas to explore and enjoy were scarce in the mid-1970s too. The dune forest Beach Plum bushes at Higbee Beach lured me there each late August. Binoculars around my neck and buckets in tow, I'd walk far through the dunes to Signal Hill, the highest dune overlooking Pond Creek Marsh, to pick Beach Plums for jelly making. Watching migrant warblers, kingbirds, falcons, and whatever the winds delivered was always an added bonus. But the area was so lawless that I was always ready to duck around a bush or tree out of sight. Four-wheelers and dune buggies from all over the state descended on the beach and enjoyed a free-for-all in the ancient dune system. The roots of ancient trees, at least 100 years old, were undermined by the constant traffic on the wide avenues cut through the dunes. One evening I watched a truck roar up Signal Hill only to slide back down. Again and again the trucker played with the dune, roaring up and, just shy of the top, sliding back down, eroding sand from the roots of ancient Red Cedars and wearing down the dune. Each visit saw more trunks and limbs of huge, gnarled Red Cedars, American Hollies, and Wild Black Cherry trees cut for bonfires or just for the fun of it. Destruction seemed to be the favorite pastime at Higbee Beach. In 1978 the state of New Jersey purchased the area and immediately limited access. Barriers were erected, and the dunes were closed except on designated walking paths. Amazingly, by 1990 the dunes had recovered. The wide "highways" had filled in with sand and vegetation and were once again merely pathways. Though softened by more than twenty-five years of protection and shifting sand, signs of the lawless 1970s—sawed off branches and tree trunks—are still evident for those who look. On field trips I am always quick to point out the signs of the bleak 1970s and remind anyone who will listen of this important Cape May lesson—how close we came to losing so much of a priceless heritage.

If it was a time of transition for Cape May and its natural habitats, it was a time of transition for its birders and naturalists too, a time of gains and losses. I was privileged to be taught by and learn from some of the great Cape May naturalists. The old-school naturalists were embodied by the Cape May Geographic Society, and their selfless sharing in many ways enabled the Cape May renaissance in birding and natural history.

After graduating from Rowan University, I began working as the interpretive naturalist at the Cape May Point State Park in 1977. The previous naturalist had just left, I heard about the job opening, applied, and was hired on the spot—timing is everything. But although I knew a little about birds, I didn't know much about anything else. Everyone encouraged me to contact Bill Bailey, the local (self-taught) botanist, naturalist, and historian, and assured me that he'd love to teach me. I did, and sure enough, he did! It turned out that he'd known my father at Curtis Publishing Company in Philadelphia, where they'd both worked, and we bonded. In 1977 Bill Bailey and I walked the state park trails at least one morning each week before my workday began—he as mentor, me as student. I'll never forget my first walk through the park with Bill. We exited the park office, took a few steps, and my world changed forever. That day I moved beyond birds to all that is the world of nature and all that is Cape May. We never even made it to the park trails, but instead crouched down to notice the many weeds and wildflowers growing in an overgrown field (today, a paved parking lot). I had a notepad and pen and wrote as fast as I could as Bill shared rich accounts of every weed I'd previously been oblivious to. With so much beauty underfoot, I was almost afraid to take a step without looking closely first. With Bill's mentoring, and access to the vast library he'd accumulated, I too became a self-taught botanist and naturalist and even a bit of an armchair historian. So much of what I learned from Bill flavored my nature walks at Cape May Point State Park and beyond. I hope that I have in some small way followed in his very large footsteps.

I worked seasonally (spring through fall) at the Cape May Point State Park through 1985. Those golden years, when I had winters off, were key to my growth as a naturalist. Thanks to my lessons from Bill Bailey, particularly his influence as an annotator and record keeper, I used those winter months of freedom to research many questions that had built up over the previous year. I explored for wintering N. Saw-whet, Barn, Short-eared, and Long-eared Owls; prowled the woods for likely stick nests used by nesting Great Horned Owls; and wandered the wilds of the Delaware Bayshore, including many vast farms with absentee owners. I also prowled Cape May County's records room and municipal tax offices, mapping landowner information on important tracts, and shared it with land preservation groups—

only to be told that those lands were not yet in sufficient jeopardy. But of course, they were. In 1976 New Jersey voters approved a referendum that authorized casino gambling in Atlantic City, and the first casino opened in 1978. Because of strong Pinelands protection, development pressure was funneling down into the Cape May peninsula and all that I had grown to love. The prospect of entire cities being built on these lands (for casino-driven growth) became a real threat. Thankfully, much of my research into Delaware Bayshore and (thanks to Anthony Kopke) Great Cedar Swamp landownership, coupled with bird use data, had made its way into the right hands—the U.S. Fish and Wildlife Service—and was a key part of its strategy to create the Cape May National Wildlife Refuge. Miracles do happen.

These were heady times. Much was already gone or on the verge of being lost, and there was a real sense of urgency. One near loss involved the last pair of Bald Eagles nesting in all of New Jersey in 1982. Their nest was deep within Bear Swamp in neighboring Cumberland County. From high atop a distant sand mine mound, Joe Jacobs showed it to us and our mentor, Al Nicholson. The eagles had failed to raise young since 1976, defeated by DDT. Then the female was found dead (shot), and the culprit was never caught. We were so saddened, and the situation seemed hopeless, until the male found a new mate in a matter of a couple months, probably from the Chesapeake Bay area. And with the new mate, for the first time in many years, the last pair of Bald Eagles in New Jersey succeeded in raising young. The killing was a blessing in disguise—the stalwart old female must have been so full of DDT that she never could have laid viable eggs. It was a slow start, but eagle recovery had begun.

At the same time, gains were being made in land protection. There was a deep sense of hope when certain key Cape May tracts were preserved. The Nature Conservancy (TNC) became involved in Cape May in 1981 with its acquisition of South Cape May Meadows, targeting the property because of the diverse concentration of birds that used it during migration. In 1986 TNC purchased Hidden Valley Ranch from the Dickinson family. This was another bright ray of hope and, in retrospect, may have been the turning point that reenergized all parties—private, state, and federal land protection efforts alike—with the hope that Cape May might have a future after all. Yet at the same time, land values were skyrocketing; prices had risen so high that we could not hope to acquire every key property that was still undeveloped. This was when we realized that the birds' future was in our hands; we, as landowners, had to manage our own properties, however large or small, in ways that would preserve or create habitat.

In 1986 I began working full time as a naturalist with the New Jersey Audubon Society's Cape May Bird Observatory (CMBO). Those early years with the New Jersey Audubon Society (NJAS) were formative ones for me. Leading bird walks at Cape May's various hotspots, I couldn't help but notice migrants feasting on seeds, cones, catkins, berries, and fruits of the many native trees, shrubs, and vines. Having grown up in suburbia (Ambler, Pennsylvania), I dreaded seeing it creep into the farmlands and woodlands of Cape May County. I documented bird use of native vegetation and became a fervent promoter of "backyard habitat" and the utilization of native plants. I felt strongly that wildscaping was something that the general public could do to make a difference when so much about the environment seemed out of our control (air pollution, water pollution, habitat loss, and development). And I hoped that this seemingly small step would educate people on the larger issues.

I envisioned bringing local nurseries on board, but I was laughed out the door of a respected and popular local nursery when I stated that Black Cherry was the single most important tree we could plant (fifty-three species of birds feed on the fruits). "It's a weed," the owner firmly stated, "we're not going to waste space on Black Cherry trees." Today, twenty years later, many people still go to this nursery when landscaping their backyard habitats, and it continues to sell unsuspecting property owners Arborvitae rather than the Red Cedar they ask for; although Arborvitae is an evergreen, no birds feed on its fruits, whereas thirty-four species of birds feed on the fruits of Red Cedar. Fortunately, other nurseries have been far more accomodating.

It has been richly rewarding to teach thousands of people in the twenty years I've been with the NJAS, and even more fulfilling is that many of them have gone on to teach others about backyard habitat. In 1997 the NJAS opened the CMBO Center for Research and Education in Goshen, which meant that programs out of the trunk of my car or presentations in borrowed rooms at the Cape May Point State Park, the Cape May Point firehouse, or elsewhere were no longer the only option. The Goshen facility was built with funds donated by NJAS members who felt strongly about the CMBO's work. Rather than build the center on a farm field or clear a forest, the NJAS cleaned up a degraded site and improved it. The Goshen site had been a dump, and the NJAS spent thousands of dollars removing rubble, tires, broken glass, three tumble-down buildings, and discarded tractor trailers full of debris. Part of the twenty-six-acre site was devoted to a model backyard habitat. Friend and colleague Karen Williams was an instrumental force here; the CMBO hired her to create and plant the habitat, which she ably accomplished between 1997 and 2004.

There have been so many memories in the thirty years since Clay drew me to Cape May County. We often try to share some of them during the field trips and programs that we lead and teach. Looking back through my journals, I find brief notes that conjure up priceless visions of migration at Cape May:

October 31, 1983: I reach the Cape May Point State Park at dawn to walk the trails. Last night was perfect for owl migration. Follow the Yellow Trail over the bridge and into the canopy of Wax Myrtles [gone today in 2005]. Large owl flushes, Long-eared? Continue inching forward stealthily till I'm out of the Wax Myrtles. Stand perfectly still, looking into the vegetation beyond. Nothing. Slowly step off the trail for a better angle and all breaks loose, owl shapes flush, others perch.

September 27, 1985: Hurricane Gloria passed 30 miles offshore today, Friday, between 9:00 and 10:00 A.M. with wind gusts to 80 mph. Storm waters washed through the Cape May Point State Park in one big surge, then emptied out. The entire dune was flattened between Cape May and Cape May Point. With news of the approaching storm, CMBO canceled their Cape May Autumn Weekend [scheduled for September 27–29]. A wise move. Streets and beachfront hotels, including The Grand, are flooded.

September 29, 1985: It's just two days after Hurricane Gloria and the day is glorious. Sun shining. Billowy clouds. Northwest winds, and the migration of birds and Monarchs [butterflies] is uninterrupted. Thousands upon thousands of Monarchs pour down the beachfront. Much of their food, Seaside Goldenrod growing in the dunes, has washed away or is covered with sand. Where were they during the storm, just two days ago, and how did they survive it?

November 12, 1986: Migrant's life precarious—on edge of life and death. Watched a jaeger chase a large passerine (probably a flicker) and kill it. Then a group of Great Black-backed Gulls stole it and devoured it.

October 3, 1987: Mayhem. Sky is falling and what's falling is an endless sheet of hawks. Sharp-shins and Cooper's Hawks dashing about eye level, terrifying squealing flickers. High whistling flock of Cedar Waxwings passes through endless stream of Blue Jays. Steady ribbons of Double-crested Cormorants pass over and out across the Delaware Bay. Poison Ivy droops with bundles of berries. I'm nearly decapitated as a sharp-shin races by my nose, loaded down with the headless remains of a flicker, and flies down the very trail I'm walking. Momentarily six flickers alight in the same dead snag, twitching with nerves broken as death cries surround them, telling of multiple sharp-shin vs. flicker confrontations. "Fairy rings" of feathers are scattered along the trail. The low branch of a huge cherry, crossing the trail, is adorned with chunks of red meat and fluffs of feathers. The weak nourish the strong in order that some, the hardiest, survive.

October 9, 1987: 7:30 A.M. State Park. Long-billed Curlew flew over Hawkwatch (first modern-day record), last one was shot in 1898 on Five Mile Beach (today known as Wildwood). It called repeatedly. Came from Cape May down beach, passed over Hawkwatch, and disappeared.

November 5, 1995: 5:30 P.M. South Cape May Meadows. Perfect owl migration night (clear, nearly full moon, gentle NNW wind). 5–6 owls in ½ hour. Short-eared/Long-eared Owl (silhouette hunted and bounded around like Short-eared Owl) over treeline and then hunted near banding station. 2 Short-eared/Long-eared Owls tangle left of path in front of dune; later the same or 2 more hunt in front of banding station. 5:50 P.M. owl passed in front of the moon while focused on it with telescope (high in sky) and many, many passerines. 6:15 P.M. Barn Owl calls while migrating over. Saw-whet calls catlike mew/"phew" twice from near viewing platform.

Such memories energize and renew every time I read them—and always beckon for more adventures outdoors.

As program director of the CMBO, it has been a rich experience to integrate all of natural history—birds, bugs, native trees, and weeds—and the healthy exploration of wild areas into our many programs and have them embraced by a membership and visitors eager to learn about the big picture of our natural world. This book is one more step along that journey to savor and share all that is the magic of Cape May.

—P. S.

I have had the good fortune to live in Cape May County all my life. I was born and raised in Stone Harbor, just about twelve miles north of Cape May Point, at a time when it was still a small town of beach- and bayfront cottages, with few year-round residents. (There were just twelve students in my Stone Harbor Elementary School class of 1963.) Colleagues and friends Karen Williams and her husband Paul Kosten and I often joke that, of the several hundred birders who now live in Cape May, we are the only true natives—the rest being migrants. Actually, we can no longer claim to be the only native naturalists, for there is now a burgeoning group of local teenagers—Karen's sons Dylan and Ian, Tom Reed, Doyle Dowdell, Bradley Smith, and others—who will ably carry the torch and no doubt raise the bar yet again.

I do not mean to imply that having sand in my shoes confers any particular cachet or wisdom, but it does impart some perspective and insight into changes at the Cape and in birding here over time. A recurring theme in Witmer Stone's 1937 landmark book *Bird Studies at Old Cape May* was change—changing habitat, landscapes, and bird life. The idea of change has always dominated ornithology at Cape May. Some changes are natural, some are man-made, and others remain a mystery. Some are subtle, and some have been sudden, dramatic. But in all cases, the perspective of time and history adds a key dimension to understanding and appreciating Cape May's bird life.

Not knowing of my Cape May roots, an acquaintance recently asked what my "hook" was for the Cape May book, and what my credentials were for attempting such a book. It was an innocent yet apt and probing question. Later, when there was a time for quiet introspection, many memories came flooding back—some as indistinct as distant shorebirds in the heat waves of a summer beach, and others with the bold clarity of pale redtails against the crystal blue skies of a November cold front.

As far as I can trace my family tree, my family on my father's side had its roots in South Jersey soil. And we have always been birders of a sort— not the binoculars- or, at the time, spyglass-carrying type, but baymen, hunters, and fishermen. My great-great-grandfather captained a coastal schooner, and my great-grandfather, Captain William Sutton (1838–1910), was one of the first non-Native American people to live on the island that is now Sea Isle City. He went to sea at eight years old as a cabin boy, and by twenty-one he was the master of his own vessel, sailing mainly to southern ports. In later years he was a hunting guide, taking parties out for $2.50 a day. He guided birding parties too, including ornithologist Witmer Stone. He recounted to Stone and his colleagues the earliest references to what would become the famous Stone Harbor Bird Sanctuary. And in Stone's chapter on the Little Blue Heron, Captain Sutton is quoted about egging expeditions to the barrier islands, where heron and egret eggs were collected for food from the thousands of nests present.

My grandfather, Frank Harold Sutton Sr. (1883–1965), from Sea Isle City, followed in his father's footsteps. Licensed to take fishing and hunting parties out at just fourteen years of age, he captained the first head boat, a charter sailboat, out of Sea Isle. Although a house painter in later years, Frank Sutton hunted ducks for the Philadelphia market both near the turn of the century and again during the Great Depression, in order to feed the family. He got fifty cents for a pair of black ducks. Red-breasted Mergansers (shelducks) were also popular among the growing Italian immigrant population of Sea Isle and South Jersey, their fishy flavor lending them to Old World recipes and cuisine. My grandfather "gunned" shorebirds (even my father legally hunted them as a boy) when "robin snipe" (Red Knot) was one of the prizes and "curlew" (Whimbrel) was one of the wariest and hardest to get "to stool" (come to the decoys), as he recalled. My father, Clay Sutton Sr., was never really a bayman but did captain excursion boats for a time, and he and my uncle both guided Wharton Huber from the Philadelphia Academy of Natural Science, among others, on birding and photography trips. I am forever indebted to my uncle, Frank Sutton Jr., who, until his death in 2002, chronicled, through storytelling and on tape, so much of the family history and lore. It was from him and his son Jon that Pat and I learned that our 1820s farmhouse sits on land that was once part of my great-grandfather Crawford Buck's farm (we don't live in his actual farmhouse—that still stands down the street).

Thankfully, I can state that no one in my family was ever involved in the millinery trade, which caused the decimation and extirpation of egrets and terns for the sake of fashion. Nor did they use "punt-guns," the cannons that could wipe out entire flocks. Grandpop used only a time-worn 12-gauge Parker double-barrel, "bored full." Hawks were fair game—not for food or sport, but because they were predators. My grandfather—a church deacon, fire chief, and municipal tax assessor—wasn't a wanton redneck, but he had been taught that hawks were bad with the same fervor that we now teach that raptors are a respected and key part of the ecology and food chain. As a young teenager, I clearly remember my grandfather telling me about the time he "missed the duck hawk" (Peregrine Falcon), the only one he ever shot at, stooping on a flock of teal coming into his decoy spread. "I fired both barrels at it, but never touched it . . . I guess I just didn't lead it enough!" I remember the glint in his eye and his respect for a bird that was so fast. He was a legendary wing shot, but as he told me the story (then in his eighties), I think he was glad he had missed, if only because his grandson was so interested in birds.

Birds were an interest fostered by my family. Afield with my father, first surf fishing and then following our trained English setters in pursuit of quail, woodcock, pheasant, and grouse, he would always point out interesting birds—though not necessarily using their proper names. Royal Terns were "bluefish birds," appearing only in the early fall when the bluefish run began. Shearwaters were "sailor gulls," and Wilson's Storm-Petrels were "Mother Carey's chickens." Black-bellied Plover were "bullheads," and Long-tailed Ducks were "south-southerlys," in reference to their distinctive spring chatter. In time-honored tradition, Green Herons were "shite-pokes," and Pied-billed Grebes were simply "henbills." A favorite annual family event was waiting for and recording the arrival, around March 15, of the first "fish hawk" (Osprey) of the year, and we always celebrated the clamor of the first Laughing Gulls as a sign that spring had finally arrived. And so I grew up in a family that was deeply interested in birds, but one of my first environmental lessons was that none of my childhood classmates either knew or cared about birds.

In addition to the "sporting life" of fishing and hunting, a parallel track was developing. I had grown up with the four-volume *Red, Yellow, Green, and Blue Birds of America* series by Frank G. Ashbrook and soon began to put proper names to birds. For my thirteenth birthday, my grandmother Laura Sutton (née Buck) gave me a copy of Roger Tory Peterson's *Field Guide to the Birds.* I still have the accompanying birthday card, offering the well-known quote from Ecclesiastes, "To every thing there is a season, and a time to every purpose under heaven," perhaps prophetic of coming changes. I still remember paging through the guide and, besides being absolutely amazed that there were so many birds, feeling frustrated because I could not possibly see all those birds in my lifetime.

Surrounded by wetlands (which we called "the meadows"—yet to be dredged and filled), weedy vacant lots, thickets, and virgin dune forest still covering several miles of Avalon and Stone Harbor, I began to find and identify new birds. I already knew Baltimore Orioles, Tree Swallows, and the like, familiar fall migrants in my yard. But the first bird I actually identified with my new Peterson guide (in October 1962) was a Black-and-White Warbler catching insects on the stucco wall of a neighbor's house. I remember thinking, "This actually *does* work. Maybe I *can* see most of these birds someday." My 1962 Peterson still has "Cattle Egret" handwritten in the "Accidentals, Strays, and Others" column of "My Life List"—my first Cape May rarity, seen where they were first found in North America and duly recorded long before they were illustrated in subsequent editions of the guide.

My high school days (1963–1967) are mostly fond memories of being afield with Dad, chasing fish and pheasants. I recall the agony of sitting in class and looking out the windows on crisp, red-leaved, blue-skied autumn afternoons, just aching to be outdoors. I don't remember the exact date, but it was in October, while looking for woodcock in what is now North Cape May and following our English setters through a forgotten and overgrown hedgerow, that I was confronted with a forest of fresh new two-by-fours and plywood. I remember standing open-mouthed, dumbfounded at the beginnings of a new subdivision in what had been, just weeks earlier, fields and dune forest stretching over a mile to Delaware Bay. I recall, too, the resignation in my father's voice as we sought another hunting spot: "We had better enjoy it while we can, because it's all gonna go." It would be the first of many such experiences, but they have not become less painful over time.

College brought biology courses and particularly vertebrate zoology and ecology, both of which had a bird study component, although, to be honest, I was far more interested in herpetology than ornithology. It was finally in Chiapas, Mexico, that this Cape May native became a birder. After graduate school I worked as a research assistant for Dr. John Winkelmann, one of my Gettysburg College professors, studying nectar-feeding bats. After tending bat nets all nights, John always took an early-morning bird walk. I started tagging along, and my interest was piqued by visions such as a Keel-billed Toucan in the mountain mists of the then-vast tropical forest. I clearly remember, however, the moment that ultimately changed the direction of my life: We were enjoying some rest and recreation at the tiny coastal fishing town of Tonala, Chiapas, on a weekend off. I was walking among the vast dunes, which reminded me of my distant home, and a hovering, glowing White-tailed Kite, lit up by a blood-red Pacific sunset, ignited the spark. I was like dry tinder, because as the twilight ebbed and I lowered the binoculars, with still shaking hands, the spark ignited into a bonfire. I ran back to camp in the dark to breathlessly tell John about the wonderful kite.

After six years away, I returned to Cape May as a birder and was astounded to learn that I lived, in essence, at the center of the birding universe. But I hardly recognized my home. Change, the kind of change that Witmer Stone had lamented in the 1930s, had come again, but at an exponential rate. Cape May County, like most seashore communities, was a boom town in the 1970s. The dune forests of Stone Harbor and much of the lower Delaware Bayshore were completely gone, leveled for homes. Wetlands were being filled, and interior forests were falling fast to the chain saws and bulldozers of developers. I became committed to trying to document what was being lost and to save some of what was left. Part of that effort is the book you now hold in your hands.

Change—in the landscape and in bird life—is visited many times in the coming pages. Yet despite the huge changes to Old Cape May, much of it can still be found by those who search. For those who embrace it, Cape May will always be about more than rare birds or even large numbers of birds. It is about rich ornithological history, scenic and varied landscapes, and abundant natural history opportunities. It is also about people and about feeling, passion, and hope.

There is great hope for Cape May. As I see it, the glass is at least half full. The changes, however drastic, have been paralleled by protection. DDT was banned, and birds have recovered. The dredging and filling of the salt marsh were stopped by the Wetlands Act; New Jersey's Freshwater

Wetland's Act, the strongest in the nation, also protects swamps and bottomlands. Brisk building continues, but planning and zoning are at least cognizant of the inherent problems, meaning that most new lots are sizable and wooded and therefore available to migratory birds. The concept of backyard habitat, of planting for birds and wildlife, has been embraced by many. More quantifiable is the vast acreage of protected lands available to visiting birds and birders. Higbee Beach, The Meadows, Cape May National Wildlife Refuge, and state forest, state park, and wildlife management areas have secured a bright future for birds and birding at Cape May. Simply put, there's a lot of green on the Cape May map, and more is being added every day. Although there are still many choices ahead, today we have more than just memories and more than just hope. Cape May has a future.

It is against this historical background of change—of loss but also of recovery—that Pat and I share our beloved Cape May. If we have the privilege of meeting out in the field here, you'll understand why I might behave a bit strangely. If I marvel at an Osprey a little too much, it's only because I know that we almost lost them. If I stare at a big flock of American Oystercatchers a bit too long and say "Wow" out loud, it's because they've come back from the dead. Mostly, though, you'll probably notice how I linger at Davey's Lake at Higbee Beach, enjoying the dune forest of Old Cape May, or see a spring in my step when we reach the wonderful back fields of the Cape May National Wildlife Refuge and stand under the magnificent old pines. I'll try (although I can't promise) not to call out "broadbills!" as a flock of scaup flashes by or inadvertently revert to the name "hairyheads" when the Hooded Mergansers "stool in." But if a Peregrine Falcon sails by and I call out "duck hawk," at least you'll know why. It's what I grew up with, and it's in my blood. Perhaps Cape May is timeless and it hasn't really changed that much at all.

Enjoy your journey through this book and your travels ahead at Cape May. Thank you for sharing your Cape May adventures with Pat and me. I hope our paths will cross.

—C. S.

Introduction

If birds are good judges of excellent climate, Cape May has the finest climate in the United States, for it has the greatest variety of birds.
—Alexander Wilson (1812)

Cape May, New Jersey, is well known in many circles. Cape May City is America's oldest seashore resort, the former playground of society, statesmen, and presidents. The restored town (we have trouble calling it a city) has seen a renaissance of renewal, and today it is a magnificent showcase of Victorian history, heritage, and architecture. It continues to be a playground, one of the best-known resorts on the Atlantic coast, and it has become a year-round destination for those interested in history, architecture, music, film, art, theater, and culture, as well as a crystalline ocean and vast white, sandy beaches.

Yet the Cape May region has so much more to offer. Cape May is world famous for its birds, concentrations of migratory birds in particular. Cape May is one of the top birding destinations in all of North America, attracting many thousands of birders annually. And unlike many other top birding spots, Cape May's status as a premier resort offers visiting birders a wealth of amenities—hotels, motels, bed-and-breakfasts, campgrounds, myriad shops, and fine dining. Both birders and nonbirders love to visit Cape May because there is so much to do—something for everyone.

And, in the interesting way that birds and birding are pervasive at Cape May, it becomes a matrix, with inevitable mixing and feedback. Don't be surprised if your waitress or deli clerk or even a grizzled fisherman asks what birds you've seen or tells you about the Parasitic Jaeger chasing gulls and terns that morning. There aren't many places you can discuss avian taxonomy with your bartender, but Cape May is one of them (OK, not *all* bartenders). We know one Cape May lifeguard who will share with you the fine points of aging Little Gulls or finding Clapper Rail nests.

Cape May attracts naturalists from near and far, drawn by its ambience and infrastructure, its great variety of habitats, its large protected areas open to the public, its key location on the eastern flyway, and its unique peninsular configuration. Once, we apologized to friends for a "slow day" due to bad weather, and their reply was memorable: "A bad day at Cape May would qualify as a great day almost anywhere else." Not to disparage anyone's favorite birding spot, but this is true. Cape May is a birder's paradise in almost any season and almost any weather. It offers spring shorebirds; a wide variety of nesting species; the fabled fall migration of songbirds, hawks, and seabirds; and wintering birds attracted to the mild climate. There are birds in abundance to see year-round—any day, any week, any month. There is always something to see, savor, and enjoy.

There may be certain *best* times to enjoy Cape May birds, but there are no *bad* times to visit. And on those special days, when the peninsula seems to contain most of the birds in the Northeast, the birding can be mythical. Despite having birded Cape May for more than thirty years, a surging warm front in spring or a fast-moving, rollicking cold front in fall brings incalculable excitement and mystery. In an odd natural history paradox, every day is different, yet every day is the same—they are *all* good days.

Migration will always be the focus of Cape May. Beyond being endless, it is completely pervasive. Perhaps more amazing than the spectacle of bird migration at Cape May is the overall, overwhelming pageant of migration in all its forms. The birds are joined by millions of migrating insects: Many thousands of Monarchs heading south in the fall are accompanied by a dozen other species of migratory butterflies, bringing rich accents of color to skies, sand dunes, and gardens. The lepidoptera are joined by the odonates, as migratory dragonflies zero in on Cape May in huge numbers, probably for the same reasons birds do. Autumn cold fronts are often ushered in by vast vortices of dragonflies so thick and endless that their numbers are inestimable. At times, hawks high above are obscured by the kaleidoscope of swirling odonates, the aerial equivalent of zooplankton. Joining birds, butterflies, and dragonflies in Cape May skies are a number of species of migratory bats. Primarily Red Bats are seen, pitching into coastal cedars at first landfall in early morning or lifting off against the glow of twilight. (A few Red Bats are still seen following every early autumn front, but they were once more plentiful. "Flocks" were reported at Cape May in 1902.)

Bottle-nosed Dolphins are an abundant marine mammal in Cape May waters. Delaware Bay is their major calving area on the East Coast, and in the fall, school after school migrate just beyond the surf line. Winter brings the dolphins' cold-water counterpart, Harbor Porpoises (rare but regular visitors) and, much more frequently, Harbor Seals (Harp, Hooded, and Gray Seals have also been recorded). Whales are very uncommon sights from shore, but boaters twelve miles off Cape May at Five Fathom Bank record Humpback and Fin Whales nearly daily in early spring and late fall. These marine mammals, as well as many of our favorite waterbirds, are attracted by the vast schools of migratory fish, from Sand Eels (Launce) to Menhaden to Mullet, which in turn are pursued by predators from Mackerel to Bluefish to Striped Bass (not to mention Parasitic Jaegers). We don't mean to digress from birds, but the key to understanding and fully appreciating Cape May lies in comprehending the magnitude of migration here. Migration in so many forms and at so many levels is a large part of Cape May's mystique.

This book was originally envisioned as a birding guide to Cape May, and we hope that it accomplishes that goal. But the book is much more than that. To paraphrase John Muir (1911), "When one tugs at a single thing in nature, he finds it attached to the rest of the world." As in the science of ecology, the Cape May story is intertwined: You can't talk about fall migration without discussing its huge impact on winter bird populations. You can't understand Red Knots without knowing the Horseshoe Crab connection. And you can't fully enjoy a Cape May Warbler without touching on the pantheon of great ornithologists who have played a role in making Cape May what it is today—Wilson, Audubon, Stone, Peterson, and many more. You can't tug on a Cape May thread without unraveling or revealing a storied past that has created one of the greatest baselines of ornithological information anywhere on the planet.

There is also an ulterior motive in telling the story of the past. As George Santayana said, "Those who cannot remember the past are condemned to repeat it." As you will read, there have been clear patterns of gains and losses at Cape May over time, and although the gains may never outweigh the historical losses, it is up to us to ensure that the ornithological ledger is as balanced as it possibly can be today—that New Cape May resembles Old Cape May in every positive way possible. Only by exploring the Cape May past can we possess the information and perspective needed to both understand the present and make wise decisions for the future. If you are visiting Cape May, or if you already have or plan to someday, you are an ecotourist and a supporter of the nature tourism industry that makes such a compelling economic case to preserve and protect Cape May; you are helping to save it. You too are making ornithological history, for you are part of the unrivaled birding coverage of our shores, woods, and fields. You, collectively, are making our next discoveries, continuing to amass our vast ornithological database, and—more to the point—finding our next good birds. History isn't made every day, but by birding at Cape May, you become part of an ongoing record of discovery and understanding and a rich ornithological tradition. We thank you.

We're glad that you could join us here at the Cape for one day or for many. If you are here in the fall for only a weekend, you will undoubtedly focus most of your attention on the area south of the canal, with perhaps additional stops at Stone Harbor Point or the Avalon Seawatch (see chapter 7 for site guides). If you are here in the spring for only a weekend, much of your birding effort will revolve around the Delaware Bayshore and interior forests, including stellar Belleplain State Forest. But if you have more time to spend, say a week or two, the additional Atlantic coast routes and the two farther afield offerings offer unlimited birding opportunity and potential. Some may wish to sample each and every spot; others may prefer to savor an entire day, or week, at the famous Cape May Hawkwatch at Cape May Point. There are many places and many possibilities—so many birds and so little time. Maybe you will have to visit again and again to enjoy and indulge all that is Cape May. Good luck, and may your winds be always northwest.

PART ONE

THROUGH
THE SEASONS
AT CAPE MAY

THE BIRD SHOW

Driving south on the Garden State Parkway in the November predawn, it soon became apparent that the promise of the previous evening would come true. The headlights revealed wave after wave of birds crossing the road. Nearing the end of the parkway, I began to notice bird carcasses littering the pavement, victims of the thankfully light early morning traffic. Wending my way through Cape May City, so many American Robins were flying west across the road and standing in the street that I was forced to drive only twenty miles per hour, braking constantly for birds.

I turned onto Sunset Boulevard as the coming sunrise painted the eastern sky, the clouds of the fleeing cold front flaring red. As I headed toward Cape May Point, I had the morbid thought that a cartographer could probably plot how close he was to land's end by the increasing density of road-killed birds. Now I had to slow down even more as thousands of robins flowed across the road. I then began to realize that this massive fall flight was a migration of a magnitude I had never witnessed before. If not unprecedented, such drama had never been recorded in the annals of Cape May's ornithological past.

Saturday and Sunday, November 6 and 7, were the dates of the New Jersey Audubon Society's (NJAS's) 54th Annual Cape May Autumn Weekend. This was a deliberate attempt to schedule the event to coincide with the peak of late autumn migration. Now wrapped into THE Bird Show, a three-day birding festival, the event has almost always enjoyed fine views of the spectacle of autumn migration—raptors, seabirds, flickers, and finches. As always, the show's organizers—Cape May Bird Observatory (CMBO) staff—had hoped for a cold front, the meteorological event that can open the floodgates for birds on the coast. Cold fronts, and the high-pressure systems that follow, trigger bird migration. The attendant northwest winds carry birds to the coast, where, reluctant to fly over water, they mass on the Jersey Cape. Yet the festival planners could not have predicted the magnitude of this phenomenon, or that we would witness one of the most amazing Cape May migration events of all time.

Leading up to November 6, we'd been tracking a seemingly inauspicious cold front for several days, waiting and hoping. Yes, the winds would be right; yes, the timing was good; but it didn't appear to be a particularly strong cold front. In retrospect, the amazing flight began about mid-afternoon on Saturday. Michael O'Brien and I were manning THE Bird Show's Leica-sponsored seawatch at Convention Hall on the Cape May

Boardwalk. It had been slow at the seawatch—hazy, unseasonably hot, and humid. The hazy conditions made seawatching difficult, and the few distant birds were fuzzy in our telescopes. Michael was the first to spot first a few, then dozens, and ultimately hundreds of Ring-billed Gulls circling, riding the wind, all pushing south. I distinctly remember him saying, "Where did they come from? It's been dead all afternoon." As we turned to greet a new visitor to the seawatch, the answer hit us. Facing northwest, the wind was in our faces. "That's it," enthused Michael. "Gulls often travel on the leading edge of a front. We just hadn't realized it had passed!" As if to punctuate this remark, a dark Parasitic Jaeger arced by, sailing on the puffy winds as if on a roller coaster, riding the edge of the cold front much like the nearby surfers rode the waves cresting on the Cape May beach.

Late that afternoon, only a few birds were moving as we filed into the hotel for THE Bird Show's evening banquet and program. As we anticipated dinner, drinks, and camaraderie with old friends and new, none of us suspected the spectacle that would soon unfold as night fell. Leaving the beachfront hotel about 10:00 P.M., I had taken only a few steps when the sound of birdcalls began to register—not birdsong, but flight calls made by nocturnal migrant songbirds. The sky seemed to be filled with their calls, but over the sound of the nearby ocean, it was hard to tell which species. Thoughts of sleep forgotten, I walked a block inland away from the surf. Now it was apparent—robins. Not one or even dozens, but hundreds of robins were migrating, traveling on the evening air under a cloudless starry sky. Gazing upward, I could see many visible in the lights of Cape May City. The passage was constant. Some were high, others low—flying down the street and around the buildings. There were, sadly, the expected victims. One was dead on the sidewalk, killed by a wire. Another flew into a hotel window and fell, stunned, at my feet. One, disoriented by the lights, just stood in the street. Thousands of robins passed over, all moving south on the night winds.

I soon realized that I had company on the previously deserted streets. A small knot of fellow birders, likewise attracted by the sounds of migrating birds, stood listening and looking up. We talked in hushed tones, offering perspectives and perplexities. A few American Woodcock punctuated the waves of robins, and a Saw-whet Owl passed low in the glow of the streetlights. With so many trained ears, we began to decipher other birds in the stream overhead: White-throated Sparrows, Hermit Thrushes, Dark-eyed Juncos. Twice we heard the high-pitched calls of flocks of Cedar Waxwings overhead, and we all agreed (portending the enormity of the event) that we had never heard normally diurnal waxwings migrating at night. A car pulled up, and the driver asked what we were looking at. We answered politely that we were listening to migrating birds, and he drove quickly away. We laughed at ourselves, realizing that as we stared skyward, we probably looked like we were watching for UFOs or perhaps members of a strange religious cult awaiting a sign from above. Perhaps we were, paying homage to the glorious pageant in the sky.

The next morning, I headed down Sunset Boulevard toward Cape May Point as the sun crested the horizon, an orange orb in the rearview mirror. Closer to the Point, the flocks of birds were even more concentrated, and I noted other drivers, birders mostly, slowing to keep from hitting flocks of low-flying birds crossing the street. Some birds were just standing in the road. At the former Magnesite Plant site, I pulled over and, looking to the east, realized the magnitude of the movement: it was bigger than anything I had seen in nearly thirty years of birding at Cape May. I tried to do a count and found that it was nearly impossible. Counting by tens, twice I got up to 1,300 robins per minute crossing Sunset Boulevard. Then I realized that I was completely missing a high flight line and estimated that one high flock alone had at least 1,300 *more* robins. At that rate, more than 150,000 American Robins were passing each hour where I stood, and that was only one of many flight lines over the Point.

I contemplated a single robin by the roadside—just one of the multitude—and wondered from where it had come, how far it had journeyed. Did it come from an Arctic tundra willow thicket, or did it nest in an ornamental tree in a suburban yard? Robins have conquered almost every habitat in North America, perhaps the most successful of all native birds. I fondly remembered a day afield with Roger Tory Peterson, when he had stopped to admire the robins on a Cape May lawn. He remarked how successful robins had been and, though not defending Americans' obsession with their lawns, noted that robins had benefited greatly from them. For Roger, the glass was always half full, a major factor in his charm and even his legacy.

I moved to the dune crossover at Stites Avenue in Cape May Point, where huge numbers of Red-winged Blackbirds and American Goldfinches were joining the legions of robins, blanketing the sky above. Bluebirds began to show—heard more than seen as their mournful calls drifted down from the crowded sky. I also heard Red Crossbills, but it was hopeless trying to find them amid all the birds overhead. At the beach, the flight became more dramatic. The winds had sharply increased and were now quite blustery; many flocks, robins and others, struggled against the gale. Birds were at all levels, crisscrossing in the sky. Some flocks struck out over the bay; others tried, faltered, then turned back toward land. Some were low over the water, in real peril. Many exhausted birds would meet their doom, victims of opportunistic and hungry Herring Gulls.

Cape May Point is at the tip of the first major peninsula on the East Coast.

A birder appeared, the first I had seen, and complained that there were no hawks, disappointment showing in his voice. Apparently, he found robins, even in the millions, mundane. This is a curious aspect of birding that I will never understand. I've always felt that if you can't see the birds you love, love the birds you're with. This birder had no sooner turned the corner when hawks started coming, at exactly 7:00 A.M. Sharp-shinned Hawks raced low over the Delaware Bay dunes, bouncing around, visibly buffeted by the gale. These sharp-shins must have been in hawk heaven. Even hawks from the shallow end of the gene pool would have no trouble catching prey that day.

Many of the songbirds appeared bewildered, befuddled, lost. The gale of wind, the specter of land's end, the indecision about continuing, and now the profusion of predators combined to seemingly disorient the birds. Every lawn in Cape May Point was covered with robins; every tree was filled with birds. Five robins tried to drink from a minuscule puddle, the only one around. I briefly considered the whole issue of stopover ecology—the habitat needs of migratory birds, the food and cover needed to sustain them in their arduous voyages. It seemed that all the woods and fields of Cape May County couldn't possibly feed this many birds.

The magic was so great, however, that it banished such troubling thoughts. There were still as many birds as there had been stars in the crystalline sky the night before. I left Stites Avenue and drove toward Cape May Point State Park. With the sun in my eyes, backlit birds crossing the road appeared as glittering gold flashes. The sun shining through their wings gave the impression of an orange light show of glowing, soundless fireworks. It was as if the sky were filled with feathered confetti.

At Cape May Point State Park, I headed to the hawkwatch platform, where a small clot of regulars were gathered, watching in awe. Unlike last night, when we had talked in hushed tones, here we were loud, animated, and excited, all trying to talk at once. We marveled together, compared notes, attempted perspective. We were constantly interrupted by birds: Great Blue Herons high overhead, crabbing (quartering) into the wind; Killdeers calling, heading out; a stratospheric skein of migrating Snow Geese looking like glittery, flickering, brilliant white specks against the deep, clean autumn blue sky.

The passage of birds was easier to assess now. Perhaps the flight was diminishing, or maybe the birds had reoriented, for they now had a singular direction. From the platform, the birds were all heading due west and were finally, mercifully, countable. Surrounded by robins and juncos on the lighthouse lawn, we shared more war stories. Two birders staying at a beachfront hotel couldn't leave that morning until they had rescued two juncos that had flown in an open door. Someone saw a Chipping Sparrow inside the local convenience store. All had the same experience of hardly being able to drive for fear of hitting robins in the road. Naturally, this being Cape May, we discussed rarities too, as regional goodies were called in by cell phone. The Avalon Seawatch reported in with a Franklin's Gull and a Ross's Goose; Higbee Beach had Lapland Longspurs and a White-winged Crossbill; Cumberland County weighed in with a Clay-colored Sparrow and two flocks of Evening Grosbeaks. As we talked, several Cave Swallows dashed by. Before the morning was over, an exceptional hawk flight had developed, including several Northern Goshawks and three Golden Eagles. But mostly we discussed robins. Everybody was smiling, exchanging pleasantries. All were simply happy to have been there, and we knew that we had seen something big, something great, maybe a once-in-a lifetime flight.

By 10:00 A.M., the flight was finally beginning to wind down, visibly diminishing by the minute. We joked that it was no wonder, because there couldn't be any birds left in the Northeast. Then we got serious about trying to estimate the numbers, to put a yardstick on the flight. We were overwhelmed but did our best, comparing point counts, estimates, birds per minute from various locations. Ballpark estimates eventually tallied by Paul Lehman and others were as follows: 1,250,000 American Robins, 300,000 Red-winged Blackbirds, 75,000 American Goldfinches, 5,000 Cedar Waxwings, 4,000 House Finches, 2,500 Eastern Bluebirds, 2,000 Rusty Blackbirds, and simply "thousands" of sparrows, juncos, yellow-rumps, and Pine Siskins. Of considerable note was the comment by veteran observer Bob Barber that farther north on the Delaware Bayshore, "Robin numbers were incalculable, but definitely in the millions." Veracruz, Mexico, might have its incredible "River of Raptors," but on November 6 and 7, 1999, Cape May had its own "River of Robins."

Even many months later, Cape May conversations often returned to the cold front that had rained robins. Pete Dunne, reflecting on the flight, said, "You know, we had a couple thousand participants at THE Bird Show, and many were beginners. For some, it was the first birding they had ever done. I know everyone enjoyed the flight, but I wonder how many went away thinking that that morning is how it *always* is? I told several birders, who looked at me strangely, that they had just experienced the best day's birding they will ever have, no matter how long their birding career. That's how good it was."

The following March, as I wrote this account, I watched spring robins feeding in pastureland. Their hunt-and-peck feeding style reminded me of plovers on a prairie, and I wondered if Linnaeus might have named them "Lawn Plovers" had there been lawns in precolonial America, and had the English not insisted on naming everything after their own beloved birds. But mainly I wondered if these same robins had graced the skies over Cape May on those memorable November days just four months before. I like to think that they did, and I have to smile, remembering the day the heavens filled with birds. Imagine: the annual Cape May Autumn Weekend, when one of America's premier birding events coincided with the flight of many decades. What if they gave a Bird Show and all the birds came? Now we know.

—C. S.

1

MIGRATION AND THE
CAPE MAY PENINSULA

"At night, when a heavy flight is under way, the calls of the arriving migrants may be heard indoors by residents of the village, and the uncertain calling of Night Herons, and flock notes of passerine birds are almost as incessant as the rumble of the surf. These bird sounds, coming with the first cold drafts from the north and northwest, are as stirring as the roll of drums, and eloquent of the whole magnificent pageantry of bird migration."
>   —Roger Tory Peterson and Robert P. Allen
>   "The Hawk Migrations at Cape May Point, NJ"
>   *The Auk*, October 1936

Cape May is synonymous with migration. Even though the Jersey Cape offers substantial winter birding (some of the best in the mid-Atlantic) and a highly significant and varied breeding bird association, Cape May will forever be firmly linked with migration in the minds and hearts of birders. Each and every year, waves of migratory birds funnel through Cape May, washing over the Cape as steadily as the waves of the mighty Atlantic wash its shore. Indeed, one of the very first references to Cape May, in 1633, includes a description of the vast flocks of migratory birds overhead. As long as there has been a cape, and before there was a Cape May, birds have funneled through land's end in their annual passages. And as long as we protect the valuable stopover habitats they need, they will continue to do so.

Although we attempt to delineate and define the specific birding seasons as autumn, winter, spring, and summer, at Cape May, the lines blur. Due to the moderating influence of the Atlantic Ocean and Delaware Bay,

East of the town of Cape May Point, the Cape May Point State Park and TNC's Cape May Migratory Bird Refuge provide over 400 acres of crucial habitat to migratory birds.

the seasons meld and overlap on the Cape May peninsula. With the surrounding warm waters, fall birding can easily stretch into winter, with many lingering birds present. If spring follows a very cold winter, some of the spring migrants might be late; more often, however, a warm winter can mean very early arrivals. Coastal spring migration is generally earlier than in inland regions, but at Cape May, this pattern is magnified. Only insectivores often show a reverse pattern, as a warm spring day inland can still be locally cool on the coast because of sea breezes.

THE NEVER-ENDING SEASON
Migration, in some form or other, occurs all year long at Cape May. There is not a single month, or even week, when some birds aren't migrating past Cape May. As an example, several days of strong northwest winds any month of the year will produce a young Bald Eagle or two soaring over Cape May Point. In January and July you may not know which way they are going, but they are moving. (Actually, with Bald Eagles, we still have a lot to learn. We've seen them cross Delaware Bay heading south in May, and northbound arrivals come in off the bay in September. Apparently, Bald Eagles just like to wander.) Migration is protracted at Cape May. Each year, the first southbound birds are predictably seen in the third week of June—usually a few Greater Yellowlegs that have already been to the Arctic, bred, and are returning south. By the Fourth of July weekend, mudflats again teem with southbound shorebirds. In some years, the last southbound (we can't really call them "fall") migrants arrive on the Cape in February, usually gulls, waterfowl, and attendant Bald Eagles frozen out of northern reservoirs and lakes and forced south. Cape May sometimes sees the arrival of Red-necked

Grebes in February as they are pushed off the Great Lakes by a late final freeze-up, and midwinter incursions of Rough-legged Hawks, Horned Larks, and American Pipits are frequent after heavy snows to the north.

In "spring," waterfowl numbers are already building substantially in February, or sometimes by mid-January during a mild winter. As an example of how the seasons blur, by February, resident (locally breeding) Great Horned Owls and Bald Eagles are already on eggs, and on warm nights, American Woodcock are displaying. The first of our migratory breeding birds arrives soon after. The first Piping Plovers, Osprey, Laughing Gulls, and Tree Swallows are generally seen around the first week of March and sometimes even by late February. In early March, Pine Warblers and Eastern Phoebes are back, and often a few Purple Martin "scouts" too.

Spring migration is protracted. Blackpoll Warblers and Gray-cheeked Thrushes are still regular in early June. The last of the northbound shorebirds, generally Semipalmated Sandpipers, depart by the first week of June, but "spring" migration continues throughout the month with numerous year-old Broad-winged Hawks (in most years) and a few wandering (non-breeding) Mississippi Kites (some probably "overshoots" heading back south—the first southbound migrants of the season). Throughout June, east winds produce a few northbound Sooty Shearwaters off Cape May, as these southern ocean breeders circumnavigate the Atlantic during the Southern Hemisphere winter. Also, northbound Antarctic-breeding Wilson's Storm-Petrels arrive in June, and a few remain to spend much of the summer in Delaware Bay.

With such prolonged migration seasons, southbound and northbound migrants overlap. That first southbound Greater Yellowlegs may pass the last northbound Semipalmated Sandpiper and share Cape May airspace with northbound shearwaters. In late summer, departing Yellow Warblers may actually pass northbound dispersing Royal Terns at daybreak over Delaware Bay. In early spring, a Red-necked Grebe driven south by a solid freeze-up to the north may use the very same pond as a returning, hormone-driven Northern Pintail. In February, southbound low-over-the-water Razorbills need to dodge northbound Red-throated Loons. This protracted, overlapping migration means that there are always migrant birds to look for at Cape May.

An Inescapable Geography

The reasons for migratory bird concentrations on the Cape May peninsula are both simple and varied and complex. Causal factors vary by season and by group of birds, but first and foremost, birds tend to concentrate along the Atlantic coast—mainly in fall, but to a lesser degree in spring too. The so-called Atlantic flyway concept is now debated if not defunct (biologists and banding programs have proved that birds don't follow the finite routes shown on many older migration maps and diagrams), but the immediate Atlantic coast is a definite and major diversion line for most migration. Although the coastline is sometimes referred to as a "leading line," technically, migration leading lines are narrow and lengthy geographic or topographic features that intersect with the axis (direction) of migration. For broad-front migrants, leading lines imply an *attraction* that induces them to change direction and follow the leading line. Mountain ridges with energy-saving updrafts and rivers and riparian corridors with ample food resources are classic examples of leading lines. Diversion lines, by contrast, are features along which

Birders gather in the shadow of the lighthouse at Cape May Point, where many interconnected factors attract migrating birds.

migrants concentrate not because they are attracted to them but because they wish to *avoid* what lies beyond—such as the ocean, lakes, or Delaware Bay. For most birds—the bulk of passerines and many hawks, for example—the Atlantic coastline and Cape May peninsula function as a diversion line. Of interest, the immediate coastline can function as a diversion line for many different birds, from Wilson's Warblers to White-throated Sparrows to Sharp-shinned Hawks, yet act as a leading line for birds such as Sanderlings, Osprey, and loons. In essence, some birds are here because they want to be, and others are here because they have little choice.

Most birds, from hawks to songbirds and even many waterbirds, are averse to flying over water, particularly the vast and foreboding Atlantic, so they follow the coastline south. In general, the Atlantic coast runs northeast to southwest, and southbound migrants heading straight south (most don't) will eventually hit it, concentrating in increasing numbers the farther south they go. (In spring, northbound birds trying to reach New England or eastern Canada are bumping into the Atlantic coastline too.) Think of migrating birds and a diversion line as functioning like windblown leaves swept against a picket fence. They may be carried along it, but rarely through it, and after a while, they are piled high against the barrier.

Although perhaps an oversimplification, the classic theory is that the predominant northwest winds of autumn push migrants to the East Coast, where they turn and follow the coastline south, ultimately reaching Cape May.

Coupled with this, and a major factor in the autumn bird concentrations on the Atlantic coast, is the well-known tendency for North American migrants to move to the southeast in fall. Many or most birds east of the Rocky Mountains (and many from Alaska as well) migrate southeast or even initially due east in fall. Such use of a rectilinear path, whereby birds fly east and then south, is known as a dogleg migration. Waterfowl and waterbirds are imprinted to head to Atlantic coastal and ocean habitats, and many shorebirds from the Canadian Arctic tundra head mostly east in early fall to take advantage of rich coastal feeding grounds. Hudsonian Godwits and American Golden Plovers, perhaps the best known of this group, head for the Atlantic coast in fall; most eventually jump off from New England or the Maritimes and make a nonstop overwater flight to South America.

(Conversely, both are decidedly rare on the East Coast in spring because they take a primarily inland, Texas coast and Great Plains route north.) Many songbirds take a southeasterly route too, especially those wood warblers that winter primarily in the Bahamas or the West Indies, such as the Black-throated Blue Warbler, Northern Parula, Palm Warbler, and Cape May Warbler (which winters exclusively in the West Indies).

Coupled with the northeast-southwest geography of the Atlantic coast, prevailing winds in autumn are from the northwest, especially after cold fronts, when falling temperatures and clear skies, among other factors, trigger and spur migration. For any fall migrant, a wind direction with a northern component is a tailwind, pushing it south and allowing the bird to use less of its precious energy and fuel (fat reserves). It was once believed, somewhat simplistically, that northwest winds (essentially perpendicular to the coastline) pushed migrants to the Atlantic coast in fall. This "wind drift" clearly does happen, but not to the degree once believed. Migratory research has shown that many or even most birds can easily correct for wind drift during migration, at least in the light winds that songbird migrants prefer. (Higher winds produce more marked wind drift.) An emergent and popular theory today (and one that gives fuel to leading-line proponents) is that some migrants actually *prefer* to migrate along the coast—if not necessarily consciously, at least through genetic imprinting (this may be particularly true for falcons, Tree Swallows, and Yellow-rumped Warblers). Typically, coastal areas provide rich feeding opportunities where varied habitat types provide a surfeit of food for hungry migrants. Naturally, wading birds, shorebirds, and waterfowl are likely to find better feeding opportunities in coastal areas, but this may be true for songbirds too because of lush coastal vegetation. And, it would follow that *predators* follow *prey*—again, if not through direct visual choice or strategy, through many generations of genetic natural selection. An example of this would be the comparative abundance of Sharp-shinned Hawks at Cape May; some might be blown here, but mainly, they're here for the abundant passerine food resources. This theory even explains the high percentage of juvenile hawks on the coast: Young, inexperienced hunters need more targets to ensure success, whereas skilled adult sharp-shins don't need the veritable smorgasbord of coastally concentrated songbirds.

The Hourglass Effect

As migrant birds sweep down the eastern seaboard on their autumn journey south, they face two major geographic bottlenecks. The first is the Cape May peninsula, followed by the Cape Charles peninsula. Birds that enter the Cape May peninsula are inexorably funneled to its ultimate tip at Cape May Point. We cannot gainsay the importance of this funneling

A Sharp-shinned Hawk perches on a jetty at Cape May Point.

effect; perhaps more than any other factor, the increasingly narrow funnel concentrates birds at land's end. Once birds get through the bottleneck—think of it as the narrow neck of an hourglass—they spread out again over the geography and landscape (until it happens again at Cape Charles).

Although there are marked exceptions, most migratory land birds avoid flying over water, instead following the diversion lines of lakeshores and coastlines. At Cape May, land runs out, and birds are faced with a dilemma. For many juvenile birds, this might be the first major body of water they have encountered. Birds from much of eastern Canada can arrive at Cape May without having faced a major water crossing. The Saint Lawrence River near Quebec City is less than a mile wide, and even the mighty Hudson River is less than a mile wide at many points. Birds can easily avoid water until they arrive at Cape May Point.

It's interesting to witness the consternation, the birds' visible indecision when they reach the very tip. When watching Sharp-shinned Hawks from a Cape May Point jetty, we have seen juvenile birds follow the beach until they reach land's end at the shore of Delaware Bay. You can actually see them pause, turn and circle, then maybe venture out again, but soon return with their proverbial tails between their legs. We can imagine them thinking, "Gee, Mom never told me about *this.*" Consider that these hawks may be only two months old, migrating on their own. Unexpectedly finding the end of land must be akin to traveling down the interstate only to find that the highway abruptly ends—a dead end with the only alternatives being cross-country travel, a lengthy detour, or doubling back.

Flight Strategies

From Cape May Point, New Jersey, to Cape Henlopen, Delaware, is 9.65 miles of open water at the narrowest point (Cape May Lighthouse to the sandy beach at Cape Henlopen), or 10.5 miles to the dune forest at Cape Henlopen. At its widest point, at the beginning of the peninsula near Dennisville, Delaware Bay is 23 miles wide. By the time the bay narrows to 9.65 miles again, you (or a Sharp-shinned Hawk) are 29 miles northwest of

Cape May (as a sharp-shin would fly over land), just north of Fortescue in Cumberland County.

Different birds avoid water for different reasons. For songbirds, a water crossing is particularly perilous. Tired songbirds, weak from flying all night, face many potential predators over water, not just Merlins and Peregrine Falcons but also gulls—from Laughing Gulls to Great Black-backed Gulls—and jaegers. There is also the very real danger, especially on the strong northwest winds of autumn cold fronts, of being blown out to sea. If a warbler misses Cape Henlopen, the next stop is Bermuda, and many are actually lucky enough to make it there every year. Nevertheless, thousands of songbirds meet their doom at sea on their annual migration.

For our Sharp-shinned Hawk, the dangers are similar. Gulls or peregrines can be a threat, as is the danger of being carried out to sea, although many sharp-shins reach Bermuda each year too. As Roger Tory Peterson aptly put it in his 1948 *Birds Over America*, "The hawks obviously can see Delaware from their point of vantage, but will not attempt the crossing on the northwest wind that has borne them to Cape May. It is a long flight and there is too much danger of being carried out to sea, like a swimmer trying to breach a wide inlet in a strong ebb tide."

Another major concern is energy management. For any migrant bird, fat reserves—the fuel for their journey—are precious and crucial. It is important to keep fuel levels as high as possible. Liken it to your own highway travels. In remote areas, you are always a bit concerned about where the next gas station will be. You'd prefer to keep your tank at least half full, plus you don't want to pay too high a price for gas. Likewise, you'd like to know where the next food stop is—indeed, that there is food available up ahead, not a string of closed restaurants. You need a safe motel too. You guarantee your fuel, food, and rest through the Web, AAA, and guidebooks, but for the sharp-shin on its first trip south, there are no guidebooks. Migration can't burn more fuel than a bird finds along the way. For the sharp-shinned, a lengthy, strenuous flight over water will burn far more energy than that last Yellow-rumped Warbler snack provided and may even leave it too weak to catch the next one. Stopover habitat is a critical aspect of the life cycle of migrating birds.

For birds, migration is all about decision making—when to fly, when to stop, where to fly, where not to fly, where to stop. The decisions a bird makes, based mainly on its fuel status, are key to its survival. The ongoing decision-making process and its result are what is known as a bird's migration strategy. A bird's daily decisions—for instance, whether to cross Delaware Bay or go around it, whether to follow the Appalachians south versus striking out for the coast—are examples of the flight strategies of migrating birds. For our Cape May Sharp-shinned Hawk, there are key

A bird's-eye view of land's end; migrating birds must make a choice when they reach Cape May Point: head out over open water, go around the bay, or put down to feed and rest.

decisions to be made. Good thermals do not form over water, so crossing the bay means using powered, flapping flight—an energetic effort that will burn a lot of precious fuel. A good northeast tailwind can help, but a strong northwest wind spells danger and could carry the bird far out over the ocean. One safe bet is flying around Delaware Bay rather than across it. But Cape May to Cape Henlopen by land, following the tree line and crossing at the Cohansey River on the edge of Salem County, where the bay narrows to just 4 or 5 miles, is about an 80-mile route. This adds a minimum of two or three days to the flight—maybe more, if the weather deteriorates—and suddenly the bird is well behind schedule. For healthy, experienced adult hawks, this may be of little consequence (they likely remember the best food and rest stops), but for an inexperienced juvenile sharpshinned, and maybe one with its "low fuel" light blinking, it can be a decision of monumental proportions with life-or-death consequences. So the next time you see a Sharp-shinned Hawk circling out behind the lighthouse at the water's edge, imagine what is going through its mind, either consciously or by the instincts of evolution, and appreciate that you are witnessing the high drama of migration.

For many thousands of birds, for the short term, the best decision may actually be *indecision*. At Cape May, migratory birds frequently do the easiest thing—land and think about it for a while, refuel, and leave the decisions until tomorrow or next week. This is when the sand gets stuck in the hourglass, when the funnel finally fills the bottle full. Cape May is such a good migrant trap because birds pause at land's end, stop to refuel, and await less windy, less perilous conditions to continue their migration. This is when Cape May fills up with birds and then slowly, for two or three days, empties out again. This is a simplistic explanation of a far more complex happening.

Thus far, we've addressed mainly diurnal migrants—daytime fliers—which include hawks and eagles, most waterfowl, and certain songbirds

(Blue Jays, blackbirds, crows, swallows, and finches). These birds actually see the end of land at Cape May and make their decisions accordingly. Nocturnal migrants, however, are not navigating by geography and are not following the coastline or barrier beaches until they funnel to the tip. Nocturnal songbird migrants are navigating by the stars and are spread out on a broad front. Nocturnal birds are more highly susceptible to wind drift, although along the coast, it is thought that the sounds of the surf and ocean may help reorient them, causing them to head back inland. After a strong cold front, birders at sea—be it 1 mile or 100 miles offshore—will see dozens of tired songbirds flying around their boats; some will be exhausted and land on board, but others will continue on. At first light, songbirds over the sea head for the nearest land, if visible, and even if land is not visible, many reorient toward the northwest or west. This is another important factor in Cape May bird concentrations: The Cape May peninsula is in fact the nearest land for many hundreds of square miles of open ocean and bay. At dawn, birds caught over Delaware Bay or over the Atlantic Ocean head toward the nearest land, which is the Cape May peninsula. We'll never know if the 157.5-foot-tall Cape May Lighthouse, the tallest structure on the Cape, is really a factor, but it can be seen from 24 miles out at sea—even farther for a bird at high altitude—and may help guide some birds to land.

The fact that Cape May is the nearest landfall is a big factor during spring migration too. In spring, many northbound birds do not cross from Cape Henlopen, Delaware, to Cape May but instead follow the shoreline of Delaware as they head to the northwest. Many others, however, do cross the bay in spring, when birds from a broad front converge on Cape May from the south. Cape May Point is the nearest land, and tired or nervous migrants head right for the tip—the nearest safety. This "reverse" concentration convergence is a big causal factor in Cape May's less well known but not insignificant spring hawk and songbird flights.

A Crossroads

Another aspect of the geographic concentration of birds at Cape May, beyond the longitude, is Cape May's latitude. The mid-Atlantic is just that, midway between the far north and the southerly tropical regions. It has often been said that a key element of the biological diversity of the New Jersey Pine Barrens is that it is where north meets south. The Pinelands are the northern limit of many species (Pine Barrens Treefrog and Georgia Satyr, for example) and the southern limit of many others (such as Curly-grass Fern and Hoary Elfin). In Cape May County, Northern Bayberry and Wax Myrtle overlap, with bayberry reaching the southern limit of its range and Wax Myrtle reaching its northern limit. Although somewhat less definitive for birds, New Jersey is where the northern forest meets the southern

The Cape May region offers a surprising variety of habitats, including freshwater swamps such as this one at Fishing Creek.

swamp, where the Magnolia Warbler meets the Prothonotary Warbler, where the Scarlet Tanager overlaps with the Summer Tanager. Southern New Jersey is where northern Whip-poor-wills overlap southern Chuck-will's-widows, where Caspian Terns regularly share the inlets with Royal Terns from the south.

From a birding standpoint, these conjunctions are particularly exciting as they relate to rarities—from the Far North or maybe from the Deep South. Each year Cape May records Glaucous Gull and Razorbill, White Ibis and Swallow-tailed Kite. Added to this overlapping of north and south are the annual western vagrant arrivals, such as the Ash-throated Fly-catcher, Cave Swallow, and Rufous/Allen's Hummingbird, along with a few rare eastern Old World birds such as the Northern Lapwing or White-winged Tern. Cape May becomes a true birder's cornucopia, with vagrants appearing from all points of the compass.

One unique aspect of Cape May birding is the amazing simultaneous conjunctions that sometimes occur, and we locals like to compare notes of our favorite "doubles." One day at the Avalon Seawatch, a visitor told Clay about a Fork-tailed Flycatcher that had been found in West Cape May a few hours earlier (this was in pre–cell-phone days). Clay dashed south and easily found and enjoyed the fork-tail. Hurriedly returning to the seawatch (he was the counter that day), he jumped from the car and immediately spied a passing flock of Harlequin Ducks. This was a good double—harlequins probably from northeastern Canada coupled with a South American Fork-tailed Flycatcher (with not a single raised binocular in between sightings). Meanwhile, back at Cape May, others bested that, combining the Fork-tailed Flycatcher with a Dovekie (breeding in northern Greenland) at the Con-crete Ship, a collision of two birds from a minimum of 5,000 miles apart. Recently, a July Common Eider shared the waters off a Cape May Point jetty with a Brown Booby. And in July 2005, a King Eider and a Brown-headed Nuthatch were on opposite sides of the Cape May Point dune.

Other personal favorite conjunctions are a November Wood Stork and Northern Goshawk a few minutes apart, a January Harlequin Duck and White Ibis just a few miles apart, and a Marbled Godwit feeding a few feet from a juvenile White Ibis one August morning at Cape May Point State Park. Colleague Jim Dowdell's favorite odd juxtapositions include watching a Cave Swallow, Snow Buntings, and a Short-eared Owl simultaneously and a late February Purple Martin and Northern Shrike in his scope at once. If the naturalist needs further proof of Cape May as a crossroads, both Beluga and Manatee have been recorded in Cape May County waters. The point is, Cape May is where the birds of many biomes may meet, and as Witmer Stone wrote, "some straggler from the south or north may come down that great seacoast way farther than any of his kind has come before."

WE'LL ALWAYS HAVE CAPE MAY

In summarizing the attraction of birds to Cape May, it is the hallowed real estate mantra "location, location, location." This key combination includes Cape May's location on the Atlantic coast's migration diversion line in the Atlantic flyway, its location in the mid-Atlantic region (the zone where north meets south in terms of habitat diversity, climate, weather patterns, and the resultant variety of species), and its location at the tip of land's end on the first major peninsula and thus the first major water barrier on the East Coast of the United States. Yet, there are several *other* factors contributing to Cape May's bird and birding fame. When birds arrive at land's end, they tend to linger, a factor related to weather changes (from good to bad, from cold fronts with clear skies and tailwinds to southerly headwinds, rain, or coastal storms), the amount of refueling needed, or the simple fact that birds find Cape May a great place to rest and feed.

Cape May has a variety of quality habitat types: the open waters of oceans and bays, vast salt marshes, brackish marshes, freshwater lakes and ponds, rich swamps, woodlands, and upland fields. These diverse habitat types support a wide variety of bird species. Most importantly, there is a vast amount of quality open space. Many thousands of acres of lush salt marsh are backed by a mainland of forest—both lowland swamp and pine-oak high ground. When birds reach Cape May County, they find good places to rest and feed, to refuel and reorient on their journey. Often, migrants whose needs are amply met are in no hurry to leave. And, importantly, besides being highly attractive to lingering birds, much of the key acreage they rely on is protected land—federal, state, or county owned or protected by nonprofit conservation organizations. Birds today find what they need, and future generations of birds genetically imprinted on the coastal route will find stopover habitat tomorrow. Even in the farthest foreseeable future, there will be a Cape May worthy of birds and birding. Both

A salt marsh with wooded islands meets upland edge habitat along the Delaware Bayshore at Goshen Landing.

birds and places have changed over time, and experiences will inevitably vary, but there will always be places to go and birds to see. Times may change, but we'll always have Cape May.

Last, a prime element of Cape May's reputation as a migrant and vagrant trap is the number of birders afield. Birds drop in to the Cape for many reasons and from many directions, but most are found, enjoyed, and recorded simply because so many people are looking for them. Few areas in North America receive the consistent birding coverage of Cape May. Given the conjunction of all the birders and naturalists at the Cape, dozens of searchers are afield every day year-round. And that's just *local* birders; during peak migratory times and ideal conditions, visitors swell their ranks to hundreds or even thousands. In short, birds are trapped at Cape May by geography and conditions; they linger, and then, due to the scope and quality of birding coverage, they are found. With today's network of cell phones, Listservs, hotlines, rare bird alerts, and phone trees, the word gets out quickly, far and wide. Even first-time visiting birders, if they network at all, will soon learn of any rarities by word of mouth or even through the excellent efforts of the CMBO's education and outreach programs.

Despite so many birders and so much coverage, there is still much magic and mystery surrounding the Cape May migration, with many birds yet to be found. There are always great birding spots that remain uncovered. Even with so much protected and available habitat, birders by nature congregate at what they believe to be the best areas—Higbee Beach, the Meadows, the state park. Although these sites are the best, as the Cape May peninsula fills with migrants, they inevitably spill over and flood the entire Cape. Remember, Witmer Stone considered the whole Delaware Bayshore and the Atlantic coast to be part of his Old Cape May. We've always been amused that, on any given day, 95 percent of the active birders are in 5 percent of the potential area. Some mornings, Higbee Beach may be "crowded" with several hundred birders (it's actually not that noticeable, since it's a big area), but the Beanery may have only one or two birders. And on the same prime fall day, Belleplain State Forest, all 21,000 acres of it, might have *no one* birding it—despite the fact that the mass reverse-direction morning flight of songbirds puts down in the woodlands in the northern part of the county. Birds are more *concentrated* at Higbee Beach, but in terms of *numbers,* many more birds are distributed throughout Belleplain and along the Delaware Bayshore.

Despite the concentration of birders, it is still fairly easy to find peace and solitude at Cape May. The Cape May Hawkwatch may be "shoulder to shoulder" at times, but the nearby state park trails, which also offer good views of the hawk flight (plus many other birds), may be empty. Cape May can be anything you want it to be. You can find camaraderie and fellowship, or privacy and peace. Birding in outlying areas does not mean second-class birding; in fact, many of Cape May's great rarities have been found at out-of-the-way, nontraditional locations. Two of our recent rare birds, the Vermilion Flycatcher and the Sharp-tailed Sandpiper (both first records for the county and state), were found on the short marsh trail behind the Wetland's Institute on Stone Harbor Boulevard, a spot that gets regular but comparatively sparse birding coverage. Friend and record-keeper Keith Seager routinely birds in out-of-the-way places and regularly makes good discoveries. His best find, and one of our rarest birds ever, was the 1990 Lesser Sand Plover (Mongolian Plover), found on an unassuming back street in Wildwood. He found it near a fairly good overlook but far from any mainstream birding spots. The site was probably never birded before Keith's 1990 visit, and we'd wager that it hasn't been birded ten times, by anyone, since then.

When Beach Plum bushes are in bloom, the dunes at Higbee Beach are spectacular.

Given that 95 percent of the birders congregate in a tiny portion of the available habitat, one of the best ways to make Cape May discoveries is to bird the vast majority that is not being covered. A visiting British birder found a mid-September Lark Bunting on a dune walkover in the town of Cape May Point, which was subsequently seen by many. He found it during peak season while hundreds of others were at Higbee Beach and the Cape May Hawkwatch. Someone actually said to him, "Everyone else was at Higbee's, what were you doing at the Point?" His simple reply was educational: Back home in the United Kingdom, he always birded the dunes behind the beach after a good front, and he thought it should work here too. When birding, it's good to follow the rules, but sometimes it's good to shake things up a bit too and find your own way. For all its fame and popularity, Cape May still allows you to either follow others' birds or find your own. It's part of the charm of birding at land's end at Old Cape May.

SUPERLATIVES

With migrant birds from tens of thousands of square miles of Canadian taiga and U.S. eastern forests funneling through Cape May, there is abundant opportunity. But just how good is Cape May, and what can this amazing bottleneck produce? There are actually many barometers by which to measure the Cape May flight. There are scientific benchmarks in the Cape May autumn hawk counts over time; the modern-era CMBO Cape May Hawkwatch averages about 53,000 raptors each year (September 1 to November 30). This flight is easily the largest accipiter and falcon flight in North America, and only the hawkwatches that regularly see huge numbers of Broad-winged Hawks (such as Lake Erie Metropark in Michigan or Hazel Bazemore Park in Texas) consistently score higher than Cape May. The Cape May average is generally less than the esteemed Duluth, Minnesota, total hawk count; about the same as that in Braddock Bay, New York; and usually two to three times higher than the yearly average of Hawk Mountain, Pennsylvania. Kiptopeke, Virginia's hawk flight may rival Cape May's, but counts are usually lower there due to local geography and more broad-front movement.

The Avalon Seawatch project regularly records around 800,000 birds each autumn season (September 22 to December 22) and over a million if preseason and postseason birds are included in the tally. This is the largest reported waterbird migration on the entire Atlantic coast. In its short history, the autumn "Morning Flight" songbird migration count at Higbee Beach has already garnered passerine counts that are unrivaled (or at least unrecorded) elsewhere in the United States. There are clearly superlatives for Cape May based on scientific counting, but admittedly, except for hawks, we don't have good comparison data from other sites by which to measure the amazing Cape May numbers.

The Avalon Seawatch has tallied over a million migrating seabirds in a single autumn season.

Other comparisons are more fanciful and more fun, yet no less impressive. The "Big Sit" is a rather unofficial competition to see (or hear) as many birds as possible in a twenty-four-hour period in one spot—the observers cannot move or change location at all. On September 26, 1988, Clay and Jeff Bouton tallied 118 species from the Cape May Hawkwatch platform, just besting the old record of 117 counted at Elkhorn Slough, Monterey County, California (October 1982). That Big Sit record was in turn buried on October 4, 1996, by Richard Crossley, Michael O'Brien, and Tony Leukering when they counted 128 species from the deck of a private home near St. Mary's by-the-Sea in Cape May Point. This may not be scientific, and it may be silly, but it is still notable that the highest one-spot record in the country has been established at Cape May Point.

Another entertaining competition is the "yard list," the number of species seen or heard in one's own yard over time. Also completely unofficial and unsanctioned (and hard to compare, because nobody has ever defined what constitutes a "yard" in terms of size), it is a fun challenge for birders. Currently, the highest yard list in all of the United States and Canada is from a Cape May yard. In just ten years, Paul Lehman's yard, about one-quarter of an acre, has achieved the "national high" for a private residence yard, which now stands at 314 (as of August 2006). Once again, it is location, location, location. Paul's yard is on Sunset Boulevard, overlooking the South Cape May Meadows (a.k.a. Cape May Migratory Bird Refuge). From his now-famous deck he can view an excellent songbird copse, the entire Meadows, and, with his Questar scope, the ocean, the "rips" at the mouth of Delaware Bay, and the sky over Cape May Point. It is an amazing view and an amazing list—few yard lists anywhere contain such exceptional rarities as the Brown-chested Martin, Fork-tailed Flycatcher, or Black-tailed Gull. This may be frivolous fun, but it is still an amazing testimonial to Cape May.

The May 15, 2004, "Big Sit," on the roof of Paul Lehman's home.

Not all the superlatives for Cape May are from the fall migration period. In recent years, spring has clearly rivaled fall in terms of the excitement level among birders. One major kudo is Cape May's place in the World Series of Birding (WSB), CMBO-NJAS's annual bird-a-thon fund-raiser. The finish line of that event is always at Cape May, and the Cape's birds play a big role in every team's success. They also help New Jersey garner one of the top state big-day totals in the entire country. The record New Jersey one-day total is currently 231 species set on May 10, 2003, by the Nikon/Delaware Valley Ornithological Club team; only Texas has a higher total. (The WSB's highest cumulative total was an astounding 272 species on May 15, 2004; the WSB's cumulative bird list for mid-May from 1984 to 2005 is 320 species.) More importantly, the "Cape May County Only" category of the WSB is now pegged at an amazing 201 species, set on May 10, 1997, by the Leica/CMBO Team, which included Louise Zemaitis, Michael O'Brien, Richard Crossley, and Tony Leukering. Few counties anywhere can boast such a big-day number, and those that can are guaranteed to be far larger than tiny Cape May County. (Monterey County, with California's top big-day total of 207 species, is in Cape May's crosshairs.) The WSB's Cape Island Cup category, established in 1999 and including only the area south of the Cape May Canal, peaked at 173 species seen on May 11, 2002, by the *Wild Bird* team, which included Matt Garvey, Lee Amery, Glen Davis, and Dave Hedeen. Lots of these fun facts are updated annually and posted on New Jersey Audubon's Web site (www.njaudubon.org) under "World Series of Birding."

Cape May's greatest spring acclaim, however, is more serious, quantifiable, and documented. The Delaware Bay's spring shorebird aggregations—gatherings linked to the bounty of horseshoe crab eggs—are the second largest concentration of shorebirds in the New World. Only the gathering in Alaska's Copper River Delta, which also occurs in spring, is believed to be larger (at least in the 1980s). In the modern era, spring shorebirds have indeed vied with the autumn migration movements as Cape May's pièce de résistance.

Superlatives can continue for all seasons at Cape May. Winter raptor numbers recorded for South Jersey river systems and for the Delaware Bayshore are some of the highest reported in the East, and wintering waterfowl numbers for Delaware Bay and the Atlantic bays (from Barnegat Bay south) are also some of the highest in the East for many species. The mouth of Delaware Bay is emerging as one of the top Atlantic coast wintering and spring staging areas for scoters, Long-tailed Ducks, Common Loons, and Red-throated Loons. One well-established yardstick for comparing winter bird-use (and birding) areas is the venerable National Audubon Society Christmas Bird Count (CBC). The Cape May CBC is hands down the top New Jersey CBC; its modern-era average (last eleven years) of 158 species (best total was 167 on December 16, 2001) is unassailable by other counts, and the Belleplain, Cumberland County, and Oceanville CBCs regularly vie for second place. More important, the Cape May CBC total is regularly one of the highest in the East, handily beating *all* counts to the north. Only Cape Charles, Virginia, regularly challenges Cape May for top honors north of Florida. Cape May's CBC totals occur for all the reasons already cited. Fall migrants commonly linger due to the warm air and water temperatures of the Cape, remaining into the winter count period. At Cape May, the CBC truly mirrors the peak possible winter diversity and helps cement Cape May's fame as a place for all seasons. Outstanding fall migration, high numbers of wintering birds, an internationally famous spring shorebird concentration, and even a rich diversity of breeding birds all combine to firmly establish Cape May's place in the pantheon of birding destinations.

As a final yardstick, Cape May has long been regarded in print as one of the top birding destinations in North America and indeed in the world. Popular writers such as Roger Tory Peterson, Edwin Way Teale, Robert Allen, Richard Pough, Jack Connor, Pete Dunne, and others have long extolled the virtues of the Cape, and this will surely continue. Cape May heads many lists of "can't miss" birding spots and places near the top in others. In George Harrison's 1976 book *Roger Tory Peterson's Dozen Birding Hot Spots,* Peterson included Cape May as one of them. The twenty-fifth anniversary edition of *Bird Watchers Digest* named Cape May among the twenty-five must-see birding sites in North America. Also, two of the top U.S. birding magazines recently listed Cape May in their top-ten lists of birding destinations. Although Cape May didn't place first—coming in second to south Texas in one and to southeastern Arizona in the other—if we add the *aggregate* scores, Cape May would have beaten them all. It is also interesting to consider that one relatively tiny place was rated second only to two entire tropical *regions* of North America. If Cape May isn't effectively the center of the birding universe, it comes pretty close.

WEATHER AND BIRD MIGRATION

There is always something to do, something to see, when birding at Cape May. More than most other birding hotspots, Cape May can boast that no matter what the season or weather conditions, there are always birds to be found. In the fall, for example, if there are no migrant hawks, you can always seawatch or go to look at terns or shorebirds. Even a fall nor'easter with heavy rain might be a great time to watch jaegers, lots of them, chasing down terns and gulls and stealing their fish. (And the less hardy can always visit Cape May's fine shops, bookstores, galleries, and museums.) But if you want to maximize your Cape May experience and realize the best returns, you need to pay close attention to the weather.

Weather is not completely responsible for migration. The changing seasons and attendant changing temperature, day length, and food supply stir annual movements. However, it is clear that cold fronts in fall and warm fronts in spring do trigger migration events. At a migratory juncture such as Cape May, weather is a huge causal factor in what you see and when. Cape May birders study weather maps on the Weather Channel and on Web sites every bit as avidly as NFL fans watch ESPN. In autumn, birders await classic cold fronts, large high-pressure cells that sweep across the country bringing cooler temperatures, clear skies, and northwest winds. A front is a boundary between unlike air masses. A cold front advances on a warm front; the wind direction is created by the high pressure flowing toward a low-pressure area and seeking equilibrium. Cold air is denser than warm air. Along the advancing cold front, cold air forces warmer air rapidly upward, cooling it. This results in an intense band of precipitation (cold air holds less moisture than warm, so as the warm air cools, the moisture falls out as rain), but the heavy rain is usually short-lived because the band of convergence is narrow. Warm fronts, in contrast, usually advance from the south or southwest and move much more slowly than cold fronts do. Along a warm front, surging warm air is forced up and over the denser cool air. Because the slope of a warm front is more gradual than that of a cold front, the rain covers a wider area, lasts longer, but is generally lighter than rain triggered by a cold front.

To a Cape May birder, the timing of a front's passage is a crucial determinant of if and when birds will appear. In the fall, the ideal cold front passes midday or later, with rain ending around dusk so that nocturnal migrants have clear skies for navigation. This condition, followed

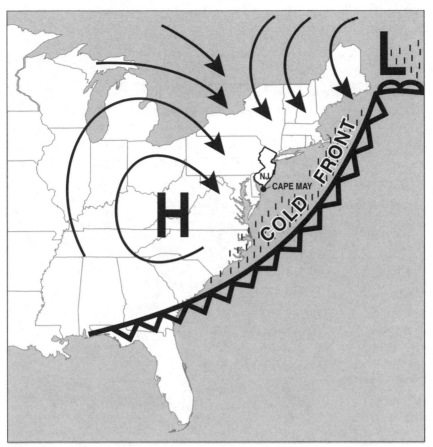

All birders hope for a strong autumn cold front, producing strong winds from the northwest.

by blustery northwest winds the following day, results in a classic Cape May fall flight, with passerines (morning flight) at dawn and hawks all day. Usually the moderating winds on the second night also produce a good songbird flight the following morning. If a front passes too late in the evening, the rain along the frontal boundary may preclude any flight or force passerines to put down before they reach the Cape. The dawn passage of a front is too late to produce a raptor flight, because it takes time for the gradient to form and for winds to pick up. In this case, the following day is likely to be the good flight day.

In spring, warm fronts classically bring migrants riding the warm, surging air masses tracking up from the south or southwest. The

continues on next page

WEATHER AND BIRD MIGRATION *continued*

circulation around the low-pressure area of a warm front is always counterclockwise; migrants ride the eastern side of a warm front, where they
have a tailwind (as opposed to the western side, where they would have
a headwind). These favorable winds behind the tracking low are called
the "warm sector," and this is where migration is occurring. The sector is
warm because of where the air is coming from—the southern and
southwestern states. On the other side of the low, the air mass is coming
south from Canada. But (and this is a big but) low-pressure areas are

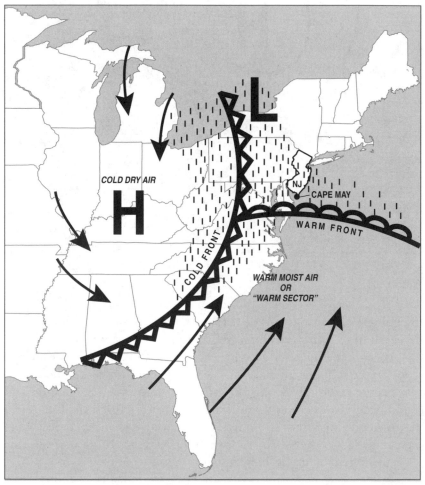

*A warm front such as this produces classic spring migration "fall out" at Cape
May.*

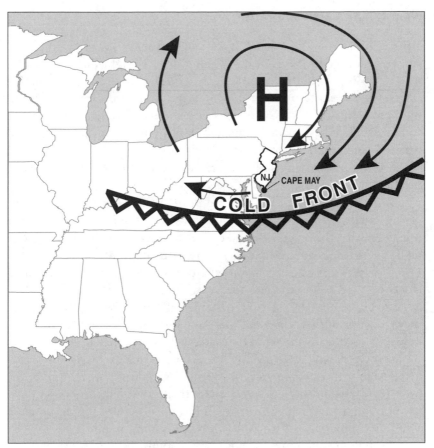

A "back door" cold front, with clockwise winds around the high, produces winds from the northeast at Cape May.

almost always followed by a cold front. Precipitation occurs where the warm front collides with the cold front, and at this collision point, bird fallout occurs. Fallout is exactly what it sounds like. Birds happily migrate in the warm sector, using clear skies and a tailwind to eventually overtake the front. When they encounter fog, rain, or even sleet, and migration becomes perilous, they fall out—put down as soon as possible—often in the middle of the night. Migration is put on hold until conditions improve. No matter where you bird, the passage of a warm front in spring can bring a good fallout, but the heaviest fallout generally occurs in the band of inclement weather that marks the location of the advancing warm front. At Cape May in spring, the timing of

continues on next page

WEATHER AND BIRD MIGRATION *continued*

a front's passage is also crucial. If the warm front is already well past at sunset, you may hear lots of birds going over at night but see few the next morning, because conditions following a front are favorable for migration, and most birds have passed us by. If rain only arrives at dawn, with the front still south of us, most birds will have fallen out south of Cape May. The best spring scenario is a rainy night, meaning that the warm front is right over us, with birds falling out at Cape May and converging on the peninsula from all directions to seek safety, shelter, and food.

Birds travel behind fronts. Cold fronts in fall and warm fronts in spring create classic flights. But Cape May is highly unusual, if not unique, in that the reverse can be true as well. Given Cape May's geography, and given that birds may originate from all points of the compass, spring cold fronts can (surprisingly) create good flights, and fall warm fronts can create strange fallouts. A strong spring cold front can be a great scenario at Cape May. This is especially true for hawks. Whether they've overshot their intended breeding areas or are simply soaring on tailwinds (and resultant wind drift), the best spring hawk flights occur on northwest winds when birds from a wide area are carried back to Cape May Point. Spring Swallow-tailed Kites and Mississippi Kites probably arrive in the region on warm fronts, but cold fronts produce the most sightings, when birds are either purposefully retreating back south or simply pushed to the Point by prevailing winds (kites love to ride the wind). Gentle west winds and the southwest winds of a retreating cold front can also produce good songbird movement in springtime. In both spring and fall, the first or second day after a front is generally the best. Sometimes three or four days of gentle winds and clear skies follow the front—conditions that songbirds love. As expected, the birder sees diminishing returns as waves of migrants pass through and out of the Cape May area, although inclement weather sometimes holds songbirds in the area for a week or so. Usually the pattern is predictable: day one—birds are all over the place, even if in moderate numbers; day two—major pockets form as birds gather in widely dispersed but large feeding flocks; day three—a slow pick, as most birds have migrated on, and the birder must wait for the next front to pass Cape May.

Astute birders never ignore weather patterns elsewhere that could affect Cape May. Although no one expected it at the time (though with the benefit of hindsight, we can try to anticipate it next time), in November 1998 a massive low-pressure area over the Great Lakes eventually moved into Canada (so strong that it produced gale-force winds over a wide area) and greatly disrupted and displaced the migration of Sandhill Cranes and Franklin's Gulls. High winds (west winds on the south side of the low) heavily impacted the route the migrants took, and unprecedented numbers of cranes and gulls were recorded well east of their normal track. At the Avalon Seawatch, more than forty Franklin's Gulls were recorded in a two-day count, which nearly quadrupled the previous record for all of New Jersey. Always pay close attention to potential bird-producing weather patterns. A far-away system may eventually have a profound impact on Cape May.

Finally, despite all our efforts to follow and predict weather and fallouts, some birds show up at the oddest times for absolutely no known meteorological reason. Some rarities have never been linked to any specific weather pattern. Perhaps they arrived on a previous system and were simply overlooked. As CMBO research associate Vince Elia likes to say, "Birds have wings." Their wings can take them to the strangest places at the oddest times. In 2004, we watched an adult male Northern Harrier high over Cape May Lighthouse beating its way due south, crossing the Delaware Bay. The date, though, was early May. In 2005, a flock of seven American White Pelicans was seen over Cape May in the morning, heading north; at 4:00 P.M., seven white pelicans, undoubtedly the same birds, landed on a sandbar at Sandy Hook. They covered the 120 miles in about seven hours. But the amazing thing was the date: December 11. Where were these wrong-way migrants going?

Some birds, either species or individuals, are just itinerant by nature. The great thing is, many of these wanderers eventually end up at Cape May. It was Ernie Choate who said it best: "Given enough time, all the birds in North America are going to show up in Cape May."

2

AUTUMN

From late August until the middle of November there occurs at Cape May Point a series of migratory flights of outstanding interest; especially because of the large numbers of birds concerned both as to species and individuals. The flights are often very spectacular. On a favorable morning the Point woods may be literally alive with migrants. Over the meadows to the north animated clouds of swallows, sometimes in thousands, move gradually towards the tip of the peninsula; or species after species pass overhead, flying very high on a southerly course or northward at a low altitude. Eagles, vultures and buteos circle on soaring wings, gaining altitude. Woodcock spring up on every hand, whirring away in all directions and disappearing into the thickets. One hears the call notes of warblers, sparrows, blackbirds and flickers. Rails sometimes crowd the nearby marshes, and when disturbed add their protesting tones.

—Roger Tory Peterson and Robert P. Allen,
"The Hawk Migrations at Cape May Point, NJ,"
The Auk (October 1936)

Many people, including many new birders, think of fall migration in terms of waves of geese in high chevron flight, making their way south on the blustery cold fronts of October. Although such images are iconic and memorable, much of migration, maybe even most of it, is far more drawn out and certainly more subtle. In fact, it is not even noticeable until it builds to a peak, when it becomes obvious and amazing to all.

Bird migration is often likened to a flowing river. Its sources are far away, seeps and rivulets that gather in tiny streams, which in turn converge into the various forks of a river. The river widens and joins with others until it spills into the sea. At a migratory juncture such as Cape May, though, migration is actually more like the tides. Fall is the ebb tide with birds flowing out, ebbing from the breeding grounds. The various wide bays ebb into tidal creeks; the creeks empty into deeper channels; the channels then taper into narrow inlets, the funnel that leads into Cape May Point. Beyond the narrow inlet, the waters spread out into the vast sea. Spring migration is the reverse, like the returning flood tide, with vast areas channeling into narrow constrictions and then finally refilling the vast sounds or bays. The annual ebb and flood of birds, beyond being the spice of life for birders, is a life-bringing renewal, like the tides nourishing the salt marshes. The returning tide of birds brings life to the landscape and to bird lovers. There is nothing as restorative as the return of bird music in the air over Cape May.

LATE SUMMER SHOREBIRDS

Southbound migration begins early at Cape May. The seasonal lull is a short one; barely three weeks after the last northbound shorebirds have departed, the first southbound arrivals show up. It may be only a trickle, but in late June, birders pushing the season can tease migrants from summer mornings. A few nonbreeding Arctic-nesting shorebirds might summer at Cape May, but the first fall migrants, usually Greater Yellowlegs or perhaps a Short-billed Dowitcher, drop in to the South Cape May Meadows sometime in the third week of June, and fall migration is officially under way. By the Fourth of July, the tidal mudflats again teem with shorebirds feeding heavily on low-tide mudflats and roosting on higher marshes during the height of the shining summer tides. On the Jersey coast, shorebirds' lives are ruled by the tides. The southbound migration of shorebirds ("waders" to the British) along the Atlantic coast and throughout the Delaware estuary region rivals its world-famous spring concentrations. Fall easily bests spring in terms of species diversity and probably numbers too; besides the adults, the populations contain the young of the year (because little fall counting has been done, we don't have a good scientific estimate of fall shorebird numbers). The fall migration is far more protracted and not as locally concentrated as it is on spring beaches. In fall, most shorebird use occurs on the tidal mudflats of the vast bays and sounds.

There are three waves of southbound shorebirds that return to the Cape May mudflats. For most species, the early-arriving birds are mostly adult females (a few may be males from failed nests). Except for a few species, female shorebirds spend little time in the Arctic; they are courted (or, if phalaropes, they display), mate, lay eggs, stage together, and migrate south, arriving in the mid-Atlantic in July. Males stay to sit on the eggs, but because shorebird young are precocial, the males spend relatively little time

Short-billed Dowitchers arrive in the Meadows in late June—and fall migration is under way.

with their broods and soon migrate too, leaving the young behind. Males mostly arrive in August on our shores. We begin to see juvenile shorebirds mixed in the mudflat feeding flocks in mid-August to late August. By late September and October, most remaining shorebirds are youngsters—the young of the year. So although shorebird numbers remain fairly constant, there is a large sex- and age-related turnover.

Of our locally breeding shorebirds, Piping Plovers are mostly gone by mid-September, but American Oystercatcher numbers grow through much of the fall, as more northerly breeders migrate in and form large flocks with our locals. Southern New Jersey is a major fall staging area for American Oystercatchers, and high-tide gatherings at Stone Harbor Point sometimes number 300 to 400 birds. In mild seasons, many remain all winter.

Western Willets come from the Great Plains; a few winter at Cape May.

Locally breeding Willets, the eastern race, are very early migrants; most depart south by early August and go a long way, mostly wintering in South America. Willets seen from late August on are almost all the western race, arriving here from the Great Plains. Western Willets winter on the Atlantic coast, primarily from North Carolina south through Florida and along the Gulf coast. A few usually winter in Cape May County, except during the harshest years.

With a concerted effort, one can often see more than twenty-five species of shorebirds in a day, and in the fall, American Golden Plover, American Avocet, Marbled Godwit, Hudsonian Godwit, White-rumped Sandpiper, Buff-breasted Sandpiper, and Baird's Sandpiper are seen in some numbers. Recent fall shorebird rarities in Cape May and neighboring Cumberland County have included such amazing finds as Pacific Golden Plover, Long-billed Curlew, Little Stint, Red-necked Stint, and Sharp-tailed Sandpiper.

Although Cape May is a prime place to study fall shorebirds, they can be hard to view. If water levels are low (drought related), the South Cape May Meadows and even Cape May Point State Park can be good viewing areas, but in most years, the water is too deep. Forsythe National Wildlife Refuge (Brigantine) is almost always good; there, only heavy rain and resultant high water levels can curtail viewing opportunities. The mudflats behind Stone Harbor Point have recently been one of the best and more consistent shorebird viewing areas in fall and spring. Try to hit half tide (rising is best), because at low tide the birds may be too dispersed, and at high tide many leave to pass the time at distant and inaccessible sandbars and salt marsh roosts. One of the best ways to truly appreciate Cape May's shorebirds is to take a boat trip through the vast back bays and sounds, where in August and September the mudflats can be alive with thousands of shorebirds. To view these areas, birders can rent kayaks or small boats from one of the many summertime boat liveries. (We wouldn't recommend this unless you're a little boat savvy and a lot tide savvy, since you could be stranded for hours by a low tide, although this might not be too unpleasant if you're surrounded by shoals of shorebirds. Kayaks can be difficult against strong tides, so use good advice and judgment when planning.) Better yet, take a guided back-bay boat trip, a "Salt Marsh Safari," into remote regions with a local captain who knows not only the waters and tides but also the birds. This is one way to connect to Old Cape May, to imagine that you are Witmer Stone hiring a local guide to explore ornithologically uncharted lands and waters.

"Wildlife Unlimited" *Skimmer* tours are offered by Captain Bob Carlough and his mate and wife, Linda. They run bird-rich trips from spring through fall, as well as special trips for the CMBO, the Nature Center of Cape May, and the Wetlands Institute. By whatever method, we think that you will agree that watching late-summer waders on their annual southbound passage can be one of the most rewarding of Cape May's plethora of birding possibilities.

FALL SONGBIRDS

In the early stages of autumn migration, not long after those first few Greater Yellowlegs spiral down to the Cape May mudflats from on high, loudly announcing their arrival after a long flight, the first few fall migrant songbirds pass high over the Cape. In the hazy, humid skies of July, the birder, waiting and listening, will witness a few small flocks of Bobolinks (probably, sadly, failed breeders that were mowed out of favored pastures), their *blink-blink* calls filtering down from high over the lighthouse early in the morning. Bobolinks need to get an early start because they are one of our longest-distance migrants; birds from as far north as the Canadian Maritimes and the Great Plains winter in Brazil and Argentina. Thousands of Bobolinks migrate through Cape May, growing from a trickle in July to a flood in late August, and all but a few lingerers are gone by late September.

Songbird migration as a whole is quite drawn out, but different species move at fairly specific and predictable times. Concurrent with the late July and August movement of Bobolinks, Yellow Warblers and Bank Swallows are also migrating in numbers. The Orchard Oriole is a very early migrant; local breeders are gone by early to mid-August, and most of the others have left by about the first of September. Baltimore Orioles aren't far behind. The Lark Sparrow, though never numerous, is a notoriously early arrival from the west. The "Ipswich" Savannah Sparrow also begins early and is numerous by late September. Locally breeding "swamp warblers"— Louisiana Waterthrush, Prothonotary Warblers, and many if not most Hooded and Yellow-throated Warblers (as well as Blue-winged and Prairie Warblers)—have made their exodus by mid-August to late August. The few Golden-winged Warblers and Cerulean Warblers seen are usually tallied in August too. Neotropical migrants pass through Cape May (and the entire mid-Atlantic) quite early, and sometimes even veteran birders are surprised by how early in the season big flights can occur. Neotropical birds, those Canadian and northern U.S. species that winter in the New World tropics—Central and South America and the Caribbean—pull out early, as they have a long way to go. By September 15, about 75 percent of all neotropical songbirds have migrated through Cape May—warblers, thrushes, flycatchers, and Ruby-throated Hummingbirds, for example. In many years, the peak flight (the best numbers and by far the best variety) occurs around Labor Day (still summer, by most reckonings), during peak tourist season and before many visiting birders have arrived. Tuck this tip away: In August, light southwest winds can be particularly good for songbird migration, even without the passage of a cold front.

The Eastern Kingbird migration through Cape May is one of the most obvious and spectacular songbird movements. Beginning in the last half of July and usually peaking in the last ten days of August, recent maxima have been estimated at over 5,000 birds in one day, and 1,000 kingbirds have been counted in one day on a number of occasions. At Higbee Beach, it is sometimes possible to watch 50 or 75 at once, either as flyovers or

A cloud of Tree Swallows forms over the bayberry thickets in the dunes at South Cape May.

festooning Common Mullein stalks in the fallow fields. There are days when they seem to be everywhere. The migration apparently was once even bigger: Witmer Stone estimated over 10,000 Eastern Kingbirds at Cape May on August 30, 1926.

Another equally spectacular phenomenon is the annual Northern Flicker flight through Cape May. As with Eastern Kingbirds, huge waves of flickers move through the Point and Higbee Beach following the passage of cold fronts. The peak time for flicker movement is the month of October, and numbers can be huge—more than 5,000 a day have been recorded several times, and flights of 1,000 to 2,000 are nearly annual. Cooper's Hawks clearly target these concentrations, and frequent life-and-death chases are both heard and seen. Ominous, telltale piles of flicker feathers are a common sight on trails at Higbee Beach and Cape May Point State Park.

Throughout September and most of October, massive gatherings of Tree Swallows have long been a hallmark of the Cape May autumn. Tree Swallow migration in general is decidedly coastal, and the concentrations that build at Cape May can be astonishing. In the early 1880s, Alexander Wilson, in his *American Ornithology,* wrote of an instance when a market gunner near Cape May fired into a cloud of Tree Swallows, killing or maiming 102 birds with a single shotgun blast. The massive gatherings of Tree Swallows at Cape May seems to be more of a staging and feeding phenomenon than a mere migratory bottleneck. Flocks swarm to feed on the fruits of coastal Northern Bayberry and Wax Myrtle. Concentrations estimated around Cape May Point on a number of occasions have exceeded 20,000, but on September 30, 1974, the Tree Swallow population on all of Cape Island (the area south of the Cape May Canal) was estimated at a staggering 500,000. Large roosts form in the freshwater marshes of Pond

Creek, where Tree Swallows use the dense stands of *Phragmites,* a reed grass. Watchers at dusk can enjoy tornadoes of swallows as they descend to their roosts in vast swirling vortices. Scan with binoculars to enjoy this sight, since it occurs when it's too dark to see with the naked eye.

Growing up in Stone Harbor, Clay believed (as did most local residents) that Tree Swallows swarmed around bayberry patches to "wax their wings" on the waxy berries—waterproofing their feathers and lubricating them for the long migration ahead. This is a strange old wives' tale, yet it persists even today among locals. In reality, the Tree Swallow is our only swallow that feeds extensively on berries as well as insects. The enormous flocks of Tree Swallows massing around bayberry bushes in fall cause many local residents and visitors along the affluent barrier islands to complain bitterly about swallows fouling their swimming pools and soiling their precious Porsches and BMWs. Sadly, entire blocks of coastal bayberry patches have been leveled in an effort to eliminate the Tree Swallow "problem." For the birder, though, the swarming clouds and columns of swallows will forever be one of the more memorable and enduring images of fall days afield on the Cape. In 1950, Edwin Way Teale evocatively described Cape May "swallow clouds" in *Autumn Across America* (one of the four volumes of his epic nature odyssey):

> We were heading for the western side of the point—where a concrete ship still lies where it ran aground in World War I and where water-smoothed bits of quartz, "Cape May diamonds," are scattered through the sand—when we came within sight of the first multitude of swallows. Over a wide expanse of open ground they formed a living cloud, acres in extent, continually in motion, continually changing form, swirling this way and that like windblown smoke. The cloud rose and fell. It elongated and contracted. It condensed and grew vaporous. It scudded low across the ground, zoomed as though caught in a violent updraft. Thousands of separate birds were lost in the group movement, lifting, veering, diving, together. There was something hypnotic, something deeply stirring in the sight. Swarm was the word that came instantly to mind.

From early to mid-October through mid-November come the waves of Yellow-rumped Warblers, when it sometimes seems like the world's entire population of yellow-rumps is at Cape May. Here too, numbers can be staggering: 150,000 were estimated to be on Cape Island on October 18, 1995, and 100,000 at Higbee Beach on October 16, 1990. On October 18, 2005, even these numbers were humbled when observers estimated as many as 1 million yellow-rumps migrating through Cape May. On such days, birders can be frustrated that almost every single bird is a "butter-butt," but a few other warblers are usually mixed in. Palm Warblers and Common Yellowthroats are still common in late October and November, and a few Nashville Warblers and Blackpoll Warblers generally linger. Even though blackpolls are the long-distance champion among warblers, flying at least 2,500 miles round-trip to and from South America each year, they can leave late because much of their migration is a single overwater flight from the East Coast to northern South America. (It's an amazing journey for a bird so tiny that two of them could be mailed with a single first-class stamp.) Cape May Warblers can also be found late in the season, lingering through early November; they are often seen at sap seeps—feeding holes drilled by Yellow-bellied Sapsuckers. Often, drab individual Cape May Warblers are easily overlooked among the mobs of Yellow-rumped Warblers. Eastern Phoebe numbers can be impressive too. On October 21, 2002, more than 1,000 phoebes were counted from the raptor banding station just north of Sunset Boulevard.

American Robins are another cornerstone of Cape May migration. Late October to early November is the peak time, but big flights seem to be triggered more by weather and temperature than by a precise calendar date. Severe weather pushes robins to South Jersey throughout December and even into early January. Thousands of robins winter on the Jersey Cape, attracted and supported primarily by American Holly berries. If holly trees are full of fruit, many robins winter; if holly berries are scarce, few robins stay. Peak Eastern Bluebird flights at Cape May occur in conjunction with big robin movements, and daily counts have been as high as 2,500. Sparrows and finches bring up the rear of the autumn songbird push. Sparrows arrive in abundance following cold fronts from mid-October through mid-November, and numbers can be enormous at places such as Higbee Beach and the Beanery, where sparrows sometimes flush at every step a birder takes. Finches (mainly American Goldfinch, House Finch, Purple Finch, and Pine Siskin) also peak in November. Finch "invasions," the irruptive movements of birds such as the Common Redpoll and crossbills, seem to happen far less frequently than in the past but are still actively anticipated and talked about each year by Cape May birders. Some years, finch movements occur very late in the fall, and the Cape May CBC sometimes records crossbill and redpoll migration.

Our largest finch, the Evening Grosbeak, is a total enigma. Witmer Stone listed only three records of Evening Grosbeaks, but by the 1960s and 1970s, they were a common late-autumn migrant and a fairly abundant wintering bird in southern New Jersey (the Cape May CBC maximum is 345 in 1963). In the late 1970s and early 1980s, we always had a winter flock at our backyard feeders in Goshen, as did everyone. Today, as they were in Stone's time, they are again a rarity at Cape May and throughout the mid-Atlantic. Now, Evening Grosbeaks are no longer even annual at Cape May; just one or two are seen every few years as flyovers at Higbee Beach in November. The reason for this change in status and distribution is completely unknown. It may be related to climate change, to the booming prevalence of bird feeding to the north (short-stopping the birds), or possibly to a real population decline in Canadian forests. To put the former abundance of the Evening Grosbeak in perspective, in the late 1960s, Clay's father once accidentally shot an unseen grosbeak while aiming at a quail flying in the other direction. (It was a male, the first Evening Grosbeak Clay Jr. ever saw.) Today, a battalion of hunters couldn't collect an Evening Grosbeak in an entire winter if they tried. The colorful Evening Grosbeaks are sorely missed. They were expensive to keep in feed (some aptly called them "grocerybeaks"), but at least they were dominant at the feeders; it was better to feed grosbeaks than grackles.

For many, Cape May autumn migration is embodied by images such as the crossbow shape of a Peregrine Falcon arrowing high across the heavens or the vast interlocking skeins of determined sea ducks scudding by beyond the crashing surf; for other observers, fall is anchored by smaller, far less obvious, but no less amazing migrants. It's easy to see how a bird as powerful as a Golden Eagle or a jaeger can effortlessly make its way safely south, but the feats of these big birds can pale in comparison to the mighty efforts of tiny warblers, kinglets, and Red-breasted Nuthatches. Sometimes the survival of songbird migrants seems like nothing short of a miracle. For many songbirds, it is a perilous migration, particularly for the young of the year. Although many species "flock," many others do not, or they flock only loosely, keeping in touch with seemingly nervous but probably reassuring call notes at night. They are migrating without parental guidance to a place they've never been, yet, as Pete Dunne has written, they will know and recognize it once they get there. They are doing it purely on instinct, the patterning of a thousand generations. Passerines particularly run a gauntlet of outright predators (hawks and gulls alike), a maze of windows and wires, and barren urban and suburban deserts between welcoming and life-giving stopover habitat oases. On the immediate coast, the problems are exacerbated. The very funnel that is Cape May increases the risks and the density of threats. The northwest winds of autumn, the very winds that spur and carry migrants, can carry many unknowing, unsuspecting songbirds far out to sea at night, and birders frequently witness the compelling sight as they attempt to make it back to land at dawn. It can be one of the most desperate and harrowing acts of the Cape May bird drama—and the most riveting.

Years ago, Clay was surf fishing one October morning, just after sunrise. Standing thigh deep in the surf, he watched many passerines coming ashore after having been carried out to sea by a strong cold front the previous night. He watched one bird for several minutes; it was obviously struggling and weakened from fighting the wind as it attempted to gain the shore. The exhausted Ruby-crowned Kinglet lit on the tip of Clay's eleven-foot surf rod, resting for several minutes before it continued ashore. The fishing rod had been the first perch available, and maybe it even saved the bird's life. Another time, Clay followed a bird not nearly as lucky as it struggled and fought, barely staying aloft just inches over

For a tiny songbird, finding even one acre of intact habitat can mean the difference between life and death.

the water. Its energy exhausted, it finally fell into the surf about twenty feet in front of him. Clay waded out waist deep, reached into the water, and pulled the bird out. He then waded ashore and placed the drenched and panting Golden-crowned Kinglet in a bayberry bush in the dunes. He checked an hour later as he left the beach, and the kinglet was gone, having recovered enough to move farther inland.

Many of the passerines are not so lucky. Once we watched a warbler struggle to shore against a stiff northwest wind, evading gulls and finally gaining the presumed safety of a rock jetty. It lit on the first available perch, an exposed rock, which seconds later was buried in an enormous crashing wave. When the wave receded, the bird was gone. Almost every day in the fall, the alert birder can see gulls picking off exhausted songbirds at sea—Laughing Gulls taking warblers, Herring Gulls teaming up on flickers, robins, and others. As disturbing as it is to watch, it is the stirring, high drama of migration in its fullest.

As birders, we largely forget that what constitutes a great day of birding can be a horrific day for the birds. A spectacular day at High Island, Texas, for example, may mean a disaster for the birds, with countless weaker individuals lost at sea. This can be true at Cape May too. Edwin Way Teale offered these poignant thoughts in his classic *Autumn Across America:*

> On another occasion, when a great wind from the northwest was booming over the boardwalk at Cape May on a September night, I came upon a little kinglet fluttering against a lighted window of the Municipal Pier. I caught it, holding it loosely

in my hand, and felt the violent pounding of its tiny heart. Suddenly it fluttered; the wind tore it from my grasp; it disappeared in an instant, whirled away across the white surf, out over the tumultuous sea, a small, doomed bird in the midst of a night of terror. In that moment I remembered the many times during these autumn expeditions when I had wished for a wind from the northwest to concentrate birds at Cape May. And I regretted every wish. At such times we see only the survivors. We miss the many small migrants that, helpless in the wind and dark, are carried to death at sea.

MORNING FLIGHT

One of the most celebrated aspects of autumn passerine migration through Cape May is the "morning flight." It is easy to see and enjoy the daytime migration of hawks, waterfowl, and many other groups of birds, yet in most locations, it can be frustratingly hard to watch the actual migration of songbirds. Most are nocturnal migrants. Therefore, we often gauge migration simply by what's around the morning after the passage of a cold front. At Cape May, though, in recent years, we have learned that passerine migration is indeed very watchable on early mornings in autumn.

The phenomenon of morning flight has long been known and occurs at many locations throughout North America. Morning flight is, in its most basic sense, the after-sunrise dispersal of migrant songbirds, the final leg of the previous night's nocturnal migratory flight. Morning flight is thought to occur for a number of reasons. In some cases, it consists of local flights—birds moving short distances to favorable roosting or feeding areas (stopover habitat). Another major causal factor is dawn reorientation. At Cape May, many birds, when confronted with sunrise after a long night's flight, find themselves at land's end or often over the ocean or Delaware Bay. Birds reorient on visual landmarks and often fly in a reverse direction (from their southbound flight) in an effort to regain land or suitable habitat. Some morning flight is clearly a compensation for wind drift—birds carried offshore by strong northwest winds the previous night. At dawn, many birds show a clear pattern of flight, arriving on the lower Cape from the east, from over the water. They may head straight inland or follow the coast south to Cape May Point. But at the Point, virtually all nocturnal migrant songbirds reverse their flight, rounding the Point and then following the Delaware Bayshore back north. Some refer to morning flight birds as "redetermined migrants."

Morning flight clearly includes an element of disorientation. Although morning fliers at Higbee Beach are virtually all heading north or northeast (inland), at Cape May Point you often witness birds milling about, circling before finally setting off to the north. Another less quantifiable aspect of morning flight is one of available space—the amount of habitat needed for birds to rest and feed. As someone once oversimplified, but in a logical and succinct way, "On a big flight, the birds simply can't all fit on the Point. They have to go back north to find somewhere to feed." There's probably a lot of truth in that explanation, and it is analogous to how we, at the end of a long day of traveling, when confronted with a crowded fast-food restaurant, readily retrace our steps one or two exits back to a comforting Cracker Barrel and the vacancy sign at the Best Western right next door.

Although morning flight occurs in many places, peninsulas and islands are generally the best places to witness it. In North America, Cape May has by far one of the most visible and dramatic morning flights. In *Bird Studies at Old Cape May,* Witmer Stone referred to the massive northward movement of flickers, kinglets, robins, and other songbirds as one of the most striking ornithological sights of the entire Cape May region. In an article from the *Philadelphia Evening Bulletin* dated October 13, 1939, reporter George Riley got it mostly right: "Birds from far and near get a second wind at Cape May on their long trek. Birds know their weather. If the wind is with them, they take off, a few at a time or in flocks, in graceful flight across the Bay. If there is a capricious wind, or fog, or mist—and there frequently is—it is to them a red light flashing across their migratory highway. They sometimes retrace their course about 15 miles up the Bay for a shorter water hop." We now know that many songbirds go much farther than 15 miles; in fact, some may go all the way around the bay. We also know that the next evening most of the same birds will fly south again, crossing Delaware Bay from Cape May to points south on the Delmarva Peninsula. But as the reporter aptly wrote, "capricious winds," fog, mist, and rain can create some of the most dramatic morning flights and some of the Cape's best birding.

In 1988 and 1989, CMBO director Paul Kerlinger and researcher David Wiedner conducted landmark morning flight studies at Cape May, revealing some interesting and solid facts. Richard Crossley, Paul Holt, and Julian Hough (known affectionately as "the Brits") and David Sibley joined Wiedner as the primary counters. In pioneering counts from the dike at Higbee Beach, they found that a majority (86 percent) of the 24,378 identified neotropical migrants were warblers, and that thrushes rarely made morning flights (accounting for a mere 0.01 percent). A disproportionately large number of migrants was seen on the day of a cold front and the second day after one. Only 23 percent of the migrants flew on days not associated with a cold front, and interestingly, 12 percent flew in rain. Morning flight commenced in late July (or even earlier, but in statistically insignificant numbers), and 72 percent of all neotropical songbirds passed before

September 15. Virtually all morning flight migrants were moving due north at Higbee Beach, and 87 percent of the visible flight occurred within the first two hours after sunrise. The overall peak movement was during the second half-hour interval after sunrise.

In 2003, the CMBO began new morning flight research and counts at Higbee Beach. In a full season, the songbird morning flight numbers were astounding. A total of 375,604 birds were tallied between August 15 and October 31 in counts that lasted for the first four hours after sunrise. (The 2005 total was surprisingly similar at 375,705.) The most amazing days were October 13 and October 19, when more than 67,000 and 77,000 warblers, respectively, were counted in morning flight over Higbee Beach. (This late in the season, the vast majority were Yellow-rumped Warblers: 58,959 and 69,629, respectively.) Other big numbers in 2003 included 1,516 Northern Flickers on October 13; 1,231 Eastern Kingbirds on August 24; 17,615 American Robins on October 31; and 1,473 Palm Warblers on October 13. In subsequent years, the songbird morning flight count has continued to document some amazing flights: 1,939 American Redstarts were tallied on September 1, 2004, and 6,710 Bobolinks were counted on August 30, 2004. In 2005, the peak daily count was 81,432 on October 18 (with 74,337 Yellow-rumped Warblers). Other 2005 highlights included 175 Red-breasted Nuthatches and nearly 200 Baltimore Orioles on September 4; 7 Connecticut Warblers (of 22 total) on September 21; 375 Blackpoll Warblers on September 30. In 2005, American Robins peaked at 37,554, on October 30; Northern Flicker peaked at 1,994, on October 21.

Although we now at least partially understand and have come to expect reverse morning flight migration, several of our biggest passerine movements have involved birds that were all southbound. On the morning of October 18, 2005, a massive movement of Yellow-rumped Warblers occurred, estimated by various observers to be between 200,000 and 1 million birds (a disparity related more to the observers' location than to count technique; the morning flight count at Higbee Dike recorded only part of the flight). Several people pegged the flight as "inestimable." This flight occurred on moderate southwest (not the classic northwest) winds, and virtually all the birds were headed due south or southwest, without hesitation, out across Delaware Bay. The flight included about 2,000 flickers and didn't abate until after 11:00 A.M. The massive Bird Show flight (described at the beginning of this part) also involved mainly southbound birds—at least at daybreak, if not later in the day. There is still a lot to be learned about morning flight migration on the Jersey Cape, and today, studies and wonderment continue unabated.

CMBO-NJAS songbird research goes far beyond identifying and counting the morning flight at Higbee Beach. In conjunction with visible migration counts, the research department monitors songbird migration through the use of radar images and numerous acoustic detection monitoring stations set up around the Cape and across New Jersey (and, through contract work, throughout the Northeast). National Weather Service Doppler radar (NEXRAD) image capability has vastly changed how we study bird migration. Unlike conventional radar, advanced Doppler gives a three-dimensional view of its target—either storms or birds—and clearly shows both the volume and the direction of movement. The radar picture can be immediate, exciting, and gratifying. NEXRAD predictions have been right on the money; promising nighttime radar images of liftoff, tracks, and stopover put-down have been confirmed the following morning by woods and fields full of migrant birds. In contrast, associated acoustic studies can be tedious and time-consuming. Acoustic research involves the use of microphones to record, in real time, the call notes of flyover migrants. Data are recorded, downloaded, and, in a lengthy process, compared with sonograms. In this way, nocturnal songbird migrants are identified and counted. An array of stations can paint a clear picture of both a single night's and ultimately a full season's passerine migration. Such data, especially when augmented by radar studies, can be of inestimable importance in determining key stopover locations and preferences. In turn, such information can be used to guide and focus land protection strategies and efforts.

A key component of acoustical studies is the ability to identify the mystical flight notes that filter down from above. Cape May played a key role in deciphering these secrets when Cape May birder Michael O'Brien and his Ithaca, New York, colleague Bill Evans published, after years of effort, *Flight Calls of Migratory Birds* (2002), a CD-ROM reference guide to the flight calls of 211 species of migratory land birds in eastern North America. It may have been a small CD, but it was a giant step in the study of migration, enabling current acoustical monitoring efforts throughout eastern North America. Much of O'Brien's original sound recording occurred at Cape May, with many recordings done on the venerable Higbee Dike. Similarly, the original pioneering studies at Higbee Beach by Kerlinger, Wiedner, Sibley, Holt, Hough, and Crossley made huge strides in the flight identification of passerines. Many of the flight illustrations in the *Sibley Guide* had their origins on the dike at Higbee Beach, from field sketches drawn as a young David Sibley looked up in wonder and curiosity at the Cape May morning flight.

Today, with the construction of a dedicated observation tower and the seasonal stationing of CMBO interpretive naturalists, morning flight is a wonder and a challenge to be enjoyed by all. For the first-time visitor, it can be mind-numbing. At sunrise, tiny shapes, mostly silhouettes, shoot over

PURPLE MARTIN STAGING

Although the hordes of Tree Swallows are by far the most visible *Hirundinidae* migrants at Cape May, large numbers of Purple Martins also stage in southern New Jersey. Martins are not as obvious to most birders because they feed high in the sky—little specks against the blue—and they also migrate south very early in the season—mainly in August and the first days of September. Purple Martins form large regional premigratory roosts. Recently, many previously unknown roosts have been discovered through the use of NEXRAD, with the martins' predawn departure from the communal roost creating a highly diagnostic and distinctive radar signature—a rapidly expanding ring on the radar screen.

In *Bird Studies at Old Cape May,* Witmer Stone told of a large post-breeding, premigratory staging of martins that occurred each year during the 1920s. Although Purple Martins are common breeders throughout the Cape (there is a booming colony at Cape May Point State Park), and their chortling is heard constantly overhead in June, July, and August, no major staging roosts occur at Cape May today. The major South Jersey roost now occurs on the Maurice River in adjacent Cumberland County, near the scenic bayside village of Mauricetown. Discovered by CMBO director Pete Dunne in the early 1990s nearly in his own backyard (Pete lives in Mauricetown), this premigratory martin roost is easily the largest in New Jersey and possibly one of the largest in the East. The nearest known roost of a similar size is in Presque Isle State Park in Erie, Pennsylvania.

Purple Martins begin gathering on the church steeple in Mauricetown and on wires and vegetation near the Maurice River Causeway Bridge shortly after 6:00 P.M. The real show, though, doesn't begin until much later. About 7:15 P.M., as light dims, it is as if a switch has been thrown. Suddenly, thousands upon thousands of vocalizing Purple Martins and Tree Swallows pour in from all directions and from as far away as the aided eye can see. All are moving low over the Maurice River and the wide marshes bordering it toward the river bend just north of the Maurice River Bridge. Numbers build and build. Masses of martins swirl around over the bend in the river, drop down into the *Phragmites* stands along the tidal riverbank, then flush out to swirl anew in huge flocks. They drop down in a dramatic *whoosh,* get up again, drop down

In some years 100,000 Purple Martins swarm at dusk over the Maurice River roost.

again. Finally, at about 7:55 P.M., at the last bit of light, they disappear for the last time into the *Phragmites,* and a silence settles on the area.

Of interest are the hundreds of Eastern Kingbirds that are some-times seen joining the martin flocks, particularly early in the evening. They seemingly roost with the martins, or at least in the same area. Common Nighthawks are also sometimes seen during the martin watches, although these birds are usually migrating south, not joining the roosts. (For unknown reasons, migrant Common Nighthawks are much more frequently seen along the Delaware Bayshore than at Cape May itself; they seem to avoid the Cape in the fall. Olive-sided Fly-catcher is another fall migrant that is fairly uncommon on the Cape but is increasingly found westward in New Jersey.)

The swarm of Purple Martins can be massive, a vast kaleidoscope of swirling birds. Not always, but often, their final descent to the roost is seen as a vast spinning vortex, a living tornado of birds. Solid counts are almost impossible because of the failing light, milling flocks, flushing and resettling, and late arrivals. Preroost counts (e.g., on the wires) have been as high as 19,000 Purple Martins, but the actual masses over the roost near dark have been reliably estimated at much greater numbers, as many as 80,000 to 100,000 martins in some years. The gathering sometimes includes as many as 25,000 to 30,000 Tree Swallows too.

The numbers are enormous—some would say mind-boggling—and it is a natural history event not to be missed. Visitors can witness what seems to be all the Purple Martins in the Northeast at once. The last fif-teen days of August have been the peak in most years. The numbers vary

continues on next page

PURPLE MARTIN STAGING *continued*

from year to year, but the Maurice River clearly hosts the largest migratory staging roost of Purple Martins in the entire region. It is easy to observe. Simply park in the parking area at the base of the Maurice River Bridge (Route 670, the Mauricetown Causeway) and climb the embankment beside the bridge (on either side of the river). Around 7:15 P.M., begin to seriously scan with binoculars in all directions to pick up martins heading toward the bridge. As it nears 7:45 P.M., focus your attention just north of the bridge at the bend in the Maurice River to see their final descent down into the *Phragmites* marsh alongside the river. Binoculars are essential to fully see and appreciate the martin show, since the peak convergence occurs after the sun has set and it is too dark for the naked eye to pick out the thousands upon thousands of whirling dots. Local conservation groups, including Citizens United to Protect the Maurice River, the Natural Lands Trust, and the NJAS's CMBO, have worked with Maurice River Township and Cumberland County to hold a Purple Martin Festival around the third weekend in August. Recently, we floated in a small boat right beneath the after-sunset peak. Against the retreating, glowing purple light, it seemed that there were more martins in the sky than the number of stars that would soon grace the heavens. The swirling clouds of birds above and reflected in the glassy water below were dizzying, giving us the feeling of floating in a three-dimensional spinning galaxy, a vast nebula of Purple Martins. ■

like bullets, some in flocks and some as singles. Sometimes there are dozens, and sometimes many thousands. Some birds perch briefly, but most keep flying north, disappearing out over the Cape May Canal toward North Cape May. The official counter and regular observers put names to shapes, seemingly with ease. They're going by field marks, "gizz" (general impression, shape, and size), and structure and are often clued by call notes that may sound alike to the untrained ear. When you visit, don't let the morning flight frustrate you. The key to the veterans' skill is that many of them live at Cape May and begin each day from August through November on Higbee Dike. Identifying songbirds in flight can be daunting to the rest of us, but rewarding when it all begins to fall into place. Remember, though, it doesn't really matter whether you can identify every bird going over. The excitement and the enjoyment come from simply witnessing this amazing and magical spectacle of morning flight—when tiny, determined songbirds make their way south in autumn, in a timeless manner, by flying north over Cape May.

And finally, when the morning flight dies down around eight or nine o'clock, be assured that some of these birds will have put down at Higbee Beach and throughout the Cape, to be found and enjoyed the old-fashioned way.

THE HAWK FLIGHT

Each year toward the end of summer, right around Labor Day, changes come to the Jersey Cape. For summer beach and boardwalk goers, the frenzy of their revelry increases as their bonding with the sun nears its inevitable end. For the alert naturalist, nights are cooler, skies clearer, and humidity thankfully lower. The bright orange of Monarch butterflies, the vanguard, punctuates the brighter blue, and vast swarms of migrating dragonflies now populate any westerly winds. For the birder, a shift is occurring too. Terns, including many young of the year, now dance over the glittering swift currents of the inlets, seeking silversides driven to the surface by marauding bluefish, piscatorial predators drawn inshore by the now cooling waters and the bounty of the estuary's summer crop of bait. The high, thin call notes of neotropical migrants now filter down nightly from Cape May evening skies—if you can get away from the sounds of the surf and Labor Day parties. It is an exciting time of year, full of great promise.

Yet it is even more than that. As September dawns, there is something barely perceptible, subliminal yet at the same time palpable, that raises the collective blood pressure of Cape May birders—locals and visitors alike. You can feel it; your pace quickens as you head for Higbee Beach in the morning, and you scan the midday Beanery skies with the hope and the keenness that are the key ingredients in finding new or unusual birds. It's as if the energy level has been elevated almost overnight—a caffeine for the soul—and the birding community has become invigorated, animated. It's a renewal that occurs yearly when it's obvious that something's in the air. There may be no off-season for birding

Migrating dragonflies, such as this Green Darner, fill Cape May's skies in late summer.

The hawkwatch platform at Cape May Point, shown here in 1988, is greatly expanded today.

at Cape May, but many birders do, in part, estivate during the heat, crowds, and traffic of summer. Now there's a new zest and eagerness as Cape May birding goes into high gear. From now on, at Cape May Point State Park, birders will outnumber beachgoers and lighthouse gawkers. And in the evenings, back at home or hotel, birders will crowd around the Weather Channel with the fervor of football fans watching ESPN, waiting and rooting for the next cold front to come through and cheering aloud when it's about to score a hit on Cape May.

A major part of this excitement is the anticipation of the first good hawk flight. It's always been so and always will be. Despite the fact that southbound migration has been under way for two months, and no matter how good the summer's shorebirds or early neotropicals have been, September's first cold front is special because it means the beginning of hawk migration. Once again there is a spot to gather: the hawkwatch platform at Cape May Point State Park, a place to celebrate autumn. It's the *true* fall, as Robert Frost put it, "The fall they named the fall." It's the real deal, the main event. Cape May has turned the corner—it's back to our history and our roots as we collectively turn our eyes northward and anticipate the arrival of raptors of autumn.

There are few experiences more exciting at Cape May than hitting a big hawk flight, when the sky is seemingly filled with hawks. The Cape May Hawkwatch platform at Cape May Point State Park fills, and everyone is scanning and calling out birds: "Peregrine over the lighthouse!" "Coop approaching the close cedars." "Harrier over the back of Bunker Pond." "Redtail over the red building." "Bald Eagle over Cape May City, between two Osprey." "Look up! In the top of the largest puffy cloud, a kettle (a tight flock) of buteos and accipiters . . . look past all the high Monarchs. Two red-shouldereds, a dozen broadwings, another eagle, it's passing under the buteos. Wow! Look at all those sharpies and Coops." "The Turkey Vultures are back, seventy-two this time; they're to the right of the lighthouse, probably over Lily Lake." "Merlin coming, overhead, quick, look up, moving fast, over Saint Mary's, the middle cross, gone!" "Jaeger out over the rips. Heading right toward Saint Mary's. Going left after a tern. Whoa, did you see that?" The excited exchange of observations goes on through much of the day. Some hawks are low on the horizon, others high and lost in the baby blue sky, visible only now and then as they pass in front of a cloud. Toward midday, when temperatures are highest and thermals abundant, the flight can get so high that many visitors miss it all together. But as the afternoon wanes, raptors come back down; many begin hunting and are visible again to all the gathered faithful.

In the mid-1970s, an *American Birds* editor labeled Cape May the raptor capital of North America, a title bestowed because of the large number of hawks being counted. Some believe that this is presumptuous if not patently untrue, but at the time, the autumn counts at Cape May *were* the highest being recorded anywhere in North America. Today, a number of hawkwatches regularly post much higher totals, but in one sense, Cape May still legitimately holds the raptor capital title. With over 100,000 birders visiting Cape May each year, and about 75 percent of those in fall, Cape May has the distinction of claiming the highest number of collective raptor *sightings* of any hawkwatch.

As with shorebirds and neotropical songbirds, the hawk migration also begins early at Cape May. From late July on, a summer cold front (which may lower the humidity but not the temperature) and attendant northwest winds bring the first few American Kestrels south to the Point. Maybe these birds represent local dispersal, but they are more likely failed breeders. Nonetheless, they mark the beginning of the raptor trickle, which will become a regular flow and finally a surging stream of raptors pouring over Cape May. By mid-August, every cold front brings a few hawks—mostly kestrels, a handful of Broad-winged Hawks, and Osprey. Mid-Atlantic Osprey leave early; most of our local breeding adults depart south in August and early September. The few fall kites—Mississippis and the rare Swallow-tailed Kite—are usually seen in mid-August.

One star of the show in late August and early September is the Bald Eagle. We clearly see two separate peaks for Bald Eagles at Cape May. The first eagle spike is composed mostly of southern birds—eagles from Florida and the southeastern states returning south to their nesting grounds and nesting season. In a notable historic discovery from bird banding, Charles Broley learned that many or even most Florida eagles migrate north in spring at the conclusion of their local nesting season. They disperse well to the north, into the northeastern United States and Canada. Perhaps these eagles are seeking better feeding opportunities or resources, maybe they are escaping the summer heat, or maybe they just have wanderlust, but it is an interesting example of migration by southerly nesters. (In spring, southern Bald Eagles create a clear late May–early June spike in sightings as they head north over Cape May.) The second peak lasts from late September through early November and is made up of mostly northern eagles (and mostly juveniles and immatures) migrating south and escaping the coming winter.

September and early October bring Northern Harriers and Osprey, but otherwise, the early-season migration is almost exclusively falcons and accipiters. After the first week of October, the tide begins to turn, and more and more buteos fill the skies and tally sheets. After about the first of November, buteos take center stage—redtails, red-shoulders, and the occasional Rough-legged Hawk appearing from the far north. Interestingly, there is always a fine Thanksgiving flight, a final big buteo push consisting mostly of adults, occurring right around "Turkey Day," at a time when most visiting birders have already left for the season. In many years, flights continue well into December. The first week of December can be particularly good for buteos and eagles, given the right conditions—a belting cold front and snow in upstate New York and New England. Some years, the final trickle of weather-pushed hawks continues into Christmas Bird Count season; more than a few times the CBC has recorded a small but definite hawk flight over Cape May Point. These very late season flights are short in duration, usually lasting from about 11:00 A.M. until 1:00 P.M., the time of warmest temperatures and peak (but weak) thermals.

Accipiters and falcons are predominant in Atlantic coastal flights and, as expected, in Cape May counts. The Sharp-shinned Hawk is the bread-and-butter hawk at Cape May, constituting fully half of the total flight on average. They have become far less numerous since the mid-1990s, however, perhaps related to natural cycles, the loss of neotropical songbird prey, or possibly the growing and booming "industry" of backyard bird feeding. (Every feeder has its Sharp-shinned Hawk, so it figures that the more feeders to the north, the fewer sharpies make it to Cape May.) But we well remember and miss the good old days of the 1970s, with their endless parade of sharpies. We once counted 900 sharp-shins in view at once on the tree line north of the hawkwatch, numbers not even hinted at in recent years.

The oft-discussed ratio of Sharp-shinned Hawks to Cooper's Hawks surprises many visitors to Cape May. The long-term average is about 14:1 at Cape May, but this varies greatly from day to day due to weather conditions. On the first day of a cold front, with strong northwest winds, one might see nearly 100 percent sharpies, with Cooper's hard to find. The second day, with gentler winds and better soaring conditions, the ratio is more likely to be 1:1. And each year there are a few days, or at least a few hours, of excellent soaring conditions when it is hard to find a Sharp-shinned Hawk in the kettles of Coops. The ratio of sharp-shin to Cooper's is clearly changing over time at Cape May, as Cooper's Hawks have recovered regionally and nationally from the ravages of DDT and shooting. (In 2003, for the first time ever, more Cooper's Hawks were banded than Sharp-shinned Hawks; one season later, in 2004, fully twice as many Coops were banded than sharpies.)

To those hawkwatchers accustomed to the predominance of buteos in inland ridge flights, their comparative absence on the coast may be surprising. But in many years, Cape May does see a substantial late October and November flight of redtails and red-shoulders. The magic 1,000 mark for redtails was officially reached just once at Cape May, on November 11, 1994. On that wondrous day, 1,022 "tails" were tallied by raptormeister Jerry Liguori from the hawkwatch. For us, these late-season flights will always be the most interesting: it's a time when the diversity of hawks is at its best and anything is possible. For example, we once saw a kettle containing ten species of raptors. And on a memorable late October day at the Beanery, all five possible buteos were in sight at once: the expected redtails and red-shoulders; a couple of lingering broadwings; a bold, black and white, light-morph juvenile Rough-legged Hawk; and a coal-black, dark-morph Swainson's Hawk (an annual vagrant from the Great Plains). The flight brought high numbers, too; the preceding occurred as part of a 600+ redtail flight, which at one point had a single kettle of 60 redtails and 40 red-shoulders. Few would have argued the title raptor capital that day.

Broad-winged Hawks, the staple of most hawkwatch sites, are surprisingly scarce at Cape May, averaging about 2,800 each fall—a number that doesn't even constitute a good stream or hourly total at some hawkwatch sites. Simply put, Cape May is off the beaten path for broadwings, which are almost exclusively soaring hawks. They probably navigate by landmarks and take a fairly straight shot from New England to the Gulf coast. They are probably the least likely hawk to be impacted, at least on a large scale, by wind drift; they compensate all the while and rarely reach the Atlantic coast in numbers. There is also some evidence that broadwings, known high fliers, avoid the tip of the Cape May peninsula, perhaps realizing that it's a dead end long before other hawk species do. At times, large kettles can be found north of the Point and along the Delaware Bayshore but are never seen by the official watch. Broadwings are also, by far, the hawk least likely to cross Delaware Bay; virtually all broadwings eventually leave the Cape by going around the bay. Either that, or they linger—often too long. It surprises many first-time visitors to Cape May how late in the season broadwings can be found here. They are still daily, in ones and twos, in early to mid-November most years, long after 99.9 percent of the broadwings have vacated the rest of North America. Some years a broadwing is recorded on the CBC, but these lingerers, always juveniles, probably don't survive their first journey south.

About every five to ten years, however, we do have a good broadwing push. It takes a barreling—three- or four-day "killer" cold front occurring right on the magic dates (sometime between September 17 and September 24), when the bulk of the Northeast's broadwings are passing over eastern

Pennsylvania. The strong winds associated with such a front can, apparently, push them off course. Cape May's all-time peak for Broad-winged Hawks was on October 4, 1977, when 9,400 were counted by Pete Dunne, a magical day that also saw 11,096 sharp-shins tallied. There have been several broadwing counts exceeding 5,000 at Cape May, and about 7,000 were counted on September 25, 1981, in a flight that also contained at least 3 Swainson's Hawks. These few big flights have pushed the broadwing long-term yearly average above that of redtails, but in most years, there are more of the latter. Be assured that big broadwing flights at the Cape are rare enough that they are special events indeed. There are just two Cape May records of dark-morph broadwings, and only three or four records of dark-morph Red-tailed Hawks in the long history of hawkwatching here. There

HISTORICAL HAWK COUNTS AT CAPE MAY

	1931	1932	1935	1936	1937
Turkey Vulture	nc	nc	1,678	1,012	1,223
Black Vulture	0	0	0	0	0
Goshawk	0	0	0	0	0
Sharp-shinned Hawk	10,000	5,765	8,206	2,368	4,281
Cooper's Hawk	500	1,222	840	219	373
Red-tailed Hawk	—	177	50	—	43
Red-shouldered Hawk	—	600	12	—	10
Broad-winged Hawk	—	400	367	—	539
Buteo spp.	2,000	—	—	113	—
Rough-legged Hawk	0	0	2	0	0
Swainson's Hawk	0	0	0	0	0
Golden Eagle	0	0	0	0	0
Bald Eagle	40	10	60	59	165
Northern Harrier	100	264	274	223	213
Osprey	Common	102	706	344	504
Peregrine Falcon	20	42	56	80	75
Merlin	1,200	1,707	402	384	372
American Kestrel	200	322	777	197	579
Other	0	0	0	0	0
Unidentified	0	0	22	0	0
Total	14,060	10,611	13,452	5,023	8,377

1931 to 1937 counts carried out by Audubon wardens; 1965 and 1970 counts coordinated by Ernest A. Choate; 1971 to 1975 banding station counts by William S. Clark.

have been two good records of Krider's Red-tailed Hawk, the pale northern Great Plains color morph, at Cape May.

Across the board, for all sixteen species of diurnal raptors (not counting vultures) regularly seen at Cape May in autumn, juveniles (the young of the year) account for the highest percentage of the flight. On average, although it varies by species, 75 percent of Cape May's flight is young birds—a far different composition than that which occurs at traditional inland sites such as Hawk Mountain, which sees roughly an equal mix of young and adult hawks. The reason for this predominance of juveniles is often debated, with no definitive answer. For many species, adults are not nearly as migratory, and it is easy to say that the young, inexperienced hawks are far more susceptible to wind drift and thus more likely to be

1965	1970	1971	1972	1973	1974	1975
152	649	344	303	642	487	396
0	5	0	0	0	0	0
2	5	0	26	101	2	3
909	5,288	6,115	7,910	8,594	7,945	11,014
53	443	152	178	332	441	553
374	800	1,046	997	2,777	1,525	766
117	74	62	29	301	124	96
87	1,831	567	359	661	4,249	730
—	—	—	—	—	—	—
2	4	7	2	2	4	2
0	0	0	0	1	0	1
0	5	1	4	6	7	2
6	5	3	1	3	4	6
192	865	308	279	775	571	638
90	303	219	181	773	268	243
19	110	50	44	116	31	27
66	234	407	525	498	261	431
1,725	30,268	7,132	4,838	6,293	6,849	6,400
0	0	0	1*	0	0	0
157	132	0	0	0	0	0
3,951	41,021	16,416	15,676	21,874	22,762	21,308

*Common (Eurasian) Kestrel trapped and banded in 1972 for second North American record.
nc=not counted.

CAPE MAY FALL HAWK FAST FACTS

Species in each group are shown in order of abundance, and therefore likelihood to be seen (based on long-term average counts) at Cape May, but this can vary greatly by time of season and on any given day. Sizes given are general and in relation only to others in the same grouping.

Falcons
Pointed wings; direct, powered flight; open country—fields, marshes; "speedsters."

American Kestrel: Small
> Pale; strong facial pattern; "dots" on trailing edge of hind wing; male has red tail. Slight; gentle angles; down-curved wings; "banana shape." Hovers; "wanders" (tacking); bounced around by wind.

Merlin: Medium
> Dark; no facial pattern; black and white tail bands; stocky. Bold, swept-back look; hard angles. Fast, low, direct flight; fast, stiff, choppy wingbeat. Feisty—a falcon with an attitude.

Peregrine Falcon: Large
> Juveniles dark; adults have bright white chest; football helmet head pattern (mustache); long wings; long, broad tail; crossbow or anchor shape. Powerful, fluid, whippy, flexible wing beats.

Accipiters
Short, rounded wings; long, rudderlike tail; woodlands (except in migration); adults: gray above, barred below; immatures: brown above, streaked below; "interceptors."

Sharp-shinned Hawk: Small
> Appears small headed ("headless") or mallet shaped; short, rounded wings, pinched at body; curved trailing and leading edge; square tail. Juveniles heavily streaked, "dirty" below; fast, choppy, *flap, flap, flap . . . glide* movement; bowed wings in glide; slight—bounced around by wind.

Cooper's Hawk: Medium
> Large headed; "flying cross" shape; long(er) wings straight cut on both edges; wide, rounded tail. Juveniles thinly streaked, with white

belly contrasting with darker chest and head. More prone to soaring than sharp-shin; slower flap on level wings.

Northern Goshawk: Large (uncommon)

Red-tailed Hawk size with Sharp-shinned Hawk shape; small head and S-shaped trailing edge; stocky, powerful, bold. Adult: pale below, eye patch. Juvenile: more buffy, warmer brown than Cooper's Hawk, with two-tone effect above; "dirty" streaking below.

Buteos

Long, broad, rounded wings; short tail; "soaring hawks" of open country and woodlands.

Broad-winged Hawk: Small

Wings are *not* broad; when soaring, pointed, candle flame–shaped wings that taper on leading and trailing edges; gentle sweep-back in glide, then with straight trailing edge; slightly bowed wings. Adult: black trailing edge, single visible bold white tail band. Juvenile: few useable plumage field marks. Soars extensively; forms large flocks or kettles.

Red-tailed Hawk: Large

Quintessential buteo with which all others are compared. Always pale in East; dark head, belly band, commas, and patagium (leading edge); only adult has red tail (and sometimes lacks belly band). Powerful flier; hovers, kites. Juvenile: pale, square panels in outer wing and noticeably longer tail than adult.

Red-shouldered Hawk: Medium

Wings thrust forward ("hugging"); pale, translucent crescents, or slash at wing tip; longish tail; wings "cupped." Stiff, choppy flap. Adult: rusty red, bold banded tail and wings. Juvenile: streaked below. Doesn't fight the wind.

Rough-legged Hawk: Large (uncommon)

Long wings, dihedral; hovers. Pale tail with dark tip; light and dark morphs. Light: variable by age and sex, but dark belly band and carpel patches usually seen. Dark: appears all dark but with pale flight feathers. Arctic breeder, late fall (and winter).

continues on next page

Northern Harrier: Medium "marsh hawk"
Courses low over fields, meadow, and marshes. Dihedral, "tippy"; white rump; long, rounded wings; very long tail. Juvenile: rusty below. Adult female: streaked and brown below. Adult male: the "gray ghost"—gray above, pure white below, with black wing tips. On migration: the "great fooler"; can look like Cooper's Hawk or Peregrine Falcon, or anything else; steady cadence to flapping when migrating high in the sky.

Osprey: Large "fish hawk"
Usually found near water. White below, with large black wrist patch in wing; gull-like shape, with long, tapered wings but small head; hovers; stiff, choppy flap; M-shaped in glide, both from below and head-on.

Vultures
Gregarious, form large flocks; dark, broad, rounded wings; excellent soarers.

Turkey Vulture: Large
Pronounced dihedral; silvery flight feathers along length of wing; long tail; brown; "tippy"—rocks in flight; slow, ponderous flap.

Black Vulture: Medium
Flat wings or slight dihedral; silvery feathers at wing tip *only;* tail so short bird appears tailless at distance; black. Steady in flight; quick, choppy, "hurry-up" flap.

Eagles
Excellent soarers; dark, big, powerful; Bald and Golden Eagles not closely related.

Bald Eagle: Large
Ponderous, heavy flap mostly above body. Flat, straight-cut wings with parallel edges; large head and bill; short tail. Immatures have white at base of wing, on underwing coverts next to body; variable tail pattern. Juvenile birds are darkest; older immatures have pale belly.

Golden Eagle: Large (much less common than Bald Eagle in East) Lighter (more hawklike) flap. Soars with slight dihedral; small head and bill; long tail; tapered, sculpted wings with bulging trailing edge. Adults appear all dark, unmarked. Immatures have patch of white on outer wing, at base of primaries, and bright white tail with dark tip.

Rarities

Swainson's Hawk: Large (uncommon; average 3 per fall at Cape May; 1 spring record).

Very long, very pointed wings for a buteo; dihedral; in glide, shows M shape (like Osprey) from below. Does not look like a buteo—buoyant flight and shape resemble kite, falcon, or, most often, harrier. Light and dark morphs: light has dark flight feathers contrasted with pale underwing coverts (unlike all other species); dark is all dark with pale undertail coverts.

Mississippi Kite: Medium (rare; average 1 per fall; 10 to 15 in spring). Usually appears all dark. Adult: dark gray with white head. Immature: brownish with banded tail. Changeable shape: gliding—appears falconlike, with bold, angular shape, pointed wings, and long tail; soaring—wing shape similar to Broad-winged Hawk, with tapered wings, but long, splayed tail. Masterful flyer, dynamic glider; feeds on the wing, mostly on dragonflies. Early fall—August and September.

Swallow-tailed Kite: Large (very rare in fall—3 records; 1 to 3 each spring).

Unmistakable, spectacular. Very long, deeply forked black tail and long, tapered, pointed wings; deep, slow flap; white below, with black flight feathers; blue-gray above; graceful, masterful aerialist. Early fall—August.

Gyrfalcon: Large (very rare; only 4 records ever at Cape May—2 fall and 2 winter).

Huge, stocky, powerful falcon. Broad wings and tail; hunch-backed; rapid, direct, low flight; shallow flaps, mostly in outer wing. No head pattern; dark, gray, and white morphs; translucent flight feathers contrast with darker coverts (unlike peregrine). The ultimate raptor—everyone's fantasy hawkwatch bird. ■

carried to the Atlantic coast by autumn's northwest winds. (If they don't know where they're going, they don't know how best to get there.) There is some logic in this. It is well known that raptors navigate by landmarks. A young Red-tailed Hawk that leaves the last ridge of the Kittatinny Mountains to hunt in the Lehigh Valley probably doesn't realize that it's the last ridge—that there are no more energy-efficient updrafts available ahead. From then on, migration requires using less-efficient (for a redtail) soaring (and attendant flapping) flight. To oversimplify, soaring on a northwest wind means that one's next stop is the Atlantic coast, up against the barrier of the ocean. Follow that coast south, and one ends up at Cape May. (Recently, a Cooper's Hawk trapped near Hawk Mountain, Pennsylvania, and fitted with a transmitter was indeed followed to the Jersey coast near Atlantic City, where it stayed for the winter.)

In contrast, an adult or subadult hawk in its second migration probably well remembers what lies ahead of the last Kittatinny Ridge. To anthropomorphize, it probably also remembers being stuck at Cape May and the resultant arduous flight around Delaware Bay. And even if a hawk is successful in this endeavor, it is next faced with the dead end at Cape Charles and the task of flying around Chesapeake Bay. Viewing it this way, it's not hard to figure out why there are so many immatures and so few adults in the Cape May hawk flight. Another valid theory, however, is that young hawks *choose* to be on the coast. Being inexperienced hunters, they need lots of prey items available to increase their chances of a successful kill. For bird-eating hawks in particular, there is far greater opportunity on the coast (and especially at Cape May), where prey—from shorebirds to songbirds— is unnaturally concentrated and abundant. Cape May can be a smorgasbord for hungry hawks. This is also true for Osprey, which have access to a lot more fish on the coast than inland, and for Northern Harriers, which can take advantage of the endless salt marsh on the coast. A corollary is that adult hawks, being far more skilled and successful hunters, can get by on far fewer prey items. They don't need the bounty of the coast, so they remain inland to use the energy-efficient updrafts of the mountain ridges.

Probably a combination of these theories explains the prevalence of juveniles in the Cape May flight, but it is not black and white. Certainly hawks first banded at Cape May as youngsters have been recaptured there as adults, sometimes several times over subsequent years, proving that many birds don't choose to go inland after their juvenile Cape May experience. Conversely, a number of hawks banded at Cape May have been retrapped as adults near Hawk Mountain on the Kittatinny Ridge in subsequent years. There is some evidence that this occurs in songbirds, too, with adults less likely to drift to the coast. It is all wonderful food for thought, fueling endless "postgame" winter discussions in Cape May kitchens and taverns.

There is a clear pattern of juvenile hawks preceding adults in migration. Unlike shorebirds, whose adults always precede juveniles, young hawks generally migrate first. Except for August's failed breeders (adults) and Osprey, virtually all raptor species show a pattern of the young migrating south before adults. For example, almost all of September's Sharp-shinned Hawks are juveniles, but by mid-November, although there are a lot fewer individuals, most sharp-shin migrants are adults. At Cape May there is always added excitement when the blue-backed adult accipiters begin to show up in the daily flights, when "blue jack" adult male Merlins punctuate October afternoons and the long-awaited "gray ghost" adult male Northern Harriers course behind Bunker Pond on brisk November mornings.

High-Pressure Hawks: Cold Fronts and Raptor Migration

Hawks are well known for their soaring and gliding—the flight styles that convert altitude to distance during both daily flight and their annual migrations. Hawks (with the exception of falcons) use powered flight (direct, steady flapping to get from point A to point B) less than any other group of migrant birds; they are not designed for sustained flapping and are therefore dependent on assistance during their lengthy annual migrations. This assistance can take the form of updrafts (winds deflected up and over mountain ridges) or thermals (the rising bubbles of warm air that result from the uneven heating of the earth's surface by the sun). During peak migration season, some movement is occurring every day and on a broad front, regardless of the wind direction or weather conditions (barring heavy precipitation). But at a migratory juncture like Cape May, the bird concentrations due to geography rely heavily on prevailing winds from the northwest to help create them.

Robert P. Allen and Roger T. Peterson were the first to write a paper on the Cape May autumn hawk flights in their seminal "The Hawk Migrations at Cape May Point, NJ," published in *The Auk*, the journal of the American Ornithologists Union (AOU), in 1936. The article detailed their studies at Cape May as National Audubon interns, their discovery (along with Witmer Stone and his colleagues) of the periodicity of Cape May raptor and songbird movement, and big flights' dependence on northwest winds and cold fronts.

> The weather at the place of origin of a movement has an important influence in stimulating migration, but the migrants are affected as they go along by whatever other conditions they meet. For example, they keep on going whether they encounter winds from the north, south, east or west, but the direction of

the wind and its intensity has its *effect* on the birds by *deflecting* their path. They are influenced to a greater or lesser extent by the cyclonic movement of the air bodies. The notes of numerous field observers indicate that the normal lane of migration of the bulk of land birds across the State of New Jersey, passerine birds and hawks, is a diagonal one, which lies north of a line corresponding roughly to the edge of the Newark lowlands and the Piedmont Plateau. This seems to conform to the old coastline and extends from northeast to southwest. . . . The concentrations of a variety of migrants at Cape May seem to be very largely the result of a wind condition—a northwest wind blowing across the lane of travel. The birds lose ground against this wind and gradually slip into the southern New Jersey peninsula. These birds eventually jam into the narrow confines of Cape May Point. A north wind will bring birds, and even a north-northeast wind will bring a few, but a northwest wind almost invariably brings a great many more. The importance of the degree of wind force is illustrated by the observation that clear skies and light northwest winds bring only moderate flights while a northwest wind of fairly strong, or strong force is almost certain to be accompanied by a large influx of migrant hawks besides many smaller land birds.

Today's scientists, armed with radar, satellite tracking, and computer analyses of many decades of data, may dispute the simplicity of Allen and Peterson's findings, yet from a birder's standpoint, if not an ornithologist's, they got it right. The diagrams accompanying their 1936 paper captured the essence of the Cape May migration—the paths that hawks and other birds follow to reach Cape May, and the specifics of what hawks do on arrival at Cape May Point.

Cold fronts create bird migration at Cape May and fuel the autumn hawk migration in particular. Cold fronts create migration virtually year-round, and those from late July through early January produce southbound hawks. The best time is September 1 to November 30, the period of the official CMBO hawk count. We're often asked what constitutes the peak time to be at Cape May. For hawks, that's a fairly easy question. Peak hawk *numbers* almost always occur during the first ten days of October. Usually the strongest cold front in this period produces the biggest sharp-shin flight of the season, although during some Indian summer fall seasons, the peak occurs later. (There is some evidence that the warmer falls caused by climate change and global warming are shifting the flights to later in the season, so twenty or thirty years from now, peak flights may well occur much later.) Peak raptor *diversity,* the greatest variety of species, occurs during the last week of October and first few days of November, when big buteos, Goshawks, and a Golden Eagle or two or three mix in with the standard fare found earlier in the season. (If you're planning a trip, this is the peak time for the Avalon Seawatch too.) There is often an informal quest to see all eighteen "regular" raptor species in one day. It has been done, but not often and not by more than a couple of people. Collectively, it occurs almost every year—when a Rough-legged Hawk is seen at Higbee Beach but not at the hawkwatch, or a goshawk sneaks through the Beanery but isn't seen elsewhere. (The Black Vulture used to be the hard one to glimpse, but not anymore.) It's a fun game and one that can't be played at many places besides Cape May.

During the height of the migration, from around September 15 to November 10, hawks are almost always visible at the Cape May Hawkwatch from dawn to dusk—if not migrants, then local hunting stopover birds. At the true peak of Cape May's fall hawk migration, from the third week of September to about the second week of October, there are always migrating hawks, regardless of the wind direction. In this key period we have on occasion seen flights with more than 1,000 plus hawks on unlikely south or southwest winds, but always on days of gentle winds, since a strong south wind (a strong headwind) shuts down all but Peregrine Falcon migration. Nonetheless, what hawkwatchers always hope for is *the* big flight, a major push created by the passage of a strong cold front.

Cold fronts, the passage of high-pressure cells from west to east, are a major feature of North American weather and climate. Cold fronts occur year-round, but in autumn they spur southbound migration all across the continent. In eastern North America, they induce migration by creating a sharp drop in the temperature and, for songbirds, optimal clear skies in which to navigate during their nocturnal migration. For southbound birds, cold fronts simply create a tailwind and smooth sailing south (or southeast) and are far preferable to having to fight the headwinds associated with low-pressure systems. These warm fronts block most easy fall migration.

At Cape May, the classic cold front that triggers hawk migration is a high-pressure cell passing either right over the Cape or to the south. Because highs always exhibit clockwise winds around the center, these geographic positions create northwest winds for Cape May and the mid-Atlantic, at least for the first couple of days, until the center of the high-pressure cell passes offshore far to the east. (Then, with clockwise rotation, the winds shift southwest and finally south.) The first day of a cold front, with the strongest northwest winds, is usually the best day for numbers—waves of low sharp-shins and kestrels passing the watch in early and midseason. On such days, sharp-shins, kestrels, and harriers are often passing at first light, clear evidence that they begin to move before dawn. Usually by the second day the winds have moderated and soaring hawks take over. The best buteo flights occur the second day of the front and sometimes even on the third day, after many birds have staged to the coast. On rare occasions, with four or more days of northwest winds, we seem to run out of hawks (and songbirds). Then a period of stagnant weather is needed to create a backup of birds, followed by a new front to create the next pulse of migrants—the periodicity of which Stone and Allen and Peterson wrote.

We use words like *usually* for a reason: because it's not always clockwork. There are no magic formulas for big flights. Sometimes a cold front clearly underproduces, and then we all speculate why. The timing of the passage of a cold front can be key for both hawks and passerines. If the cold front actually passes during the night, it is often too late for a songbird flight the next day, but it should be good for hawks. A cold front rolling through in early or midmorning may not even produce hawks, and the next day will probably be *the* day for hawks and songbirds. At times, what seems like a great cold front produces mostly empty skies. Then we all wonder why, until we look at a weather map and learn that most of New York and New England is cloaked in fog, clouds, or rain, in which case Cape May won't have a flight because the "sending district" is socked in and flights are grounded. Hawk-watchers love excuses: the winds are too light, too strong, too north, too west; or there are too many clouds or not enough clouds. We've often joked that we should just number the excuses and expeditiously say instead, "Nope, no good today, 16-A," or "Great day, a classic 9-B!"

"Backdoor" cold fronts are a frequent topic at Cape May and sometimes a source of disappointment. If the high-pressure cell passes well north of New Jersey, say across New York State or southern Canada, the front's clockwise winds create north or northeast winds at Cape May. This generally produces fewer hawks than a classic cold front. If it's a fast-moving backdoor cold front, the rapid shift to east winds generally kills any hope for a flight and means only a few hawks. North or northeast winds create a very different hawk flight than a classic cold front's northwest winds. In strong northwest winds, hawks fight the wind to keep from being driven out to sea. Most birds are low and often point-blank, at least along Light-house Avenue in Cape May Point if not at the hawkwatch platform itself. In contrast, north and particularly northeast winds can be a great tailwind for hawks heading to Delaware and often produce a very high flight, with most birds looking like specks against the clouds. For most birders, this makes for less satisfying views, but there is some good news here. While northwest winds can create a fairly broad front movement over the Cape, winds from due north set up a highway in the sky, with all hawks streaming straight to the Cape May Hawkwatch and the Cape May Point Lighthouse. Under these conditions, those on the hawkwatch platform don't miss anything; they can see every single bird going over. Often, on north or northeast winds, almost all the birds follow the exact same path over the Cape. We call these paths "cloud streets," and you can often see where the best thermals are by the path of cumulus clouds forming over the peninsula—a highway of clouds stretching north and routing hawks right to Cape May Point, with all the hawks on the same flight path. (Cumulus indicates thermal activity. Thermals don't form over the cold waters of the ocean or Delaware Bay—only over the land of the peninsula itself.)

We concede that classic northwest winds are best for big flights, but we've always been partial to north and northeast winds. They are particularly good for eagles (bald and golden) and often produce rarities (from Swainson's Hawk to White Pelican to White Ibis). For us, there are few conditions as exciting as a cloud street right overhead, with Osprey and harriers streaming down it, seemingly beak to tail (both birds often travel in small packs and frequently fly "line astern," one behind the other). This can be Cape May hawkwatching at its best. There's something about a northeast wind, intangible yet perceptible. It seems to energize the flight, to galvanize the hawks. There is a subtle behavioral difference, as if instead of struggling against the wind (as they visibly do in strong northwesters) the hawks are actually enjoying the ride. One thing's for sure: With a brisk northeasterly breeze behind them, hawks can cover some ground. On one occasion, a distinctively plumaged Bald Eagle recorded at Cape May at 1:00 P.M. was seen at Kiptopeke (Cape Charles, Virginia), nearly 150 miles south as the eagle flies, just about the same time the following day. Similarly, in comparisons done by Cape May hawkwatch counter Jerry Liguori and Kiptopeke hawkwatch counter Brian Sullivan, a uniquely plumaged Golden Eagle seen at Cape May at noon was spotted at Kiptopeke early the next afternoon. (Three White Pelicans made the trip even faster; three seen at 9:30 A.M. at Cape May were most assuredly the three seen at Kiptopeke at around 3 P.M.)

Hawkwatching Hotspots

For the best views, and especially for photography, it can be important to vary your position, depending on wind direction. No one would dispute that the hawkwatch platform at Cape May Point State Park is by far the best *overall* place to watch hawks. It's inarguably the best place for the hawkwatch, but it's only the best compromise, taking all conditions into consideration. On north winds, every hawk streams straight over, and on

PEREGRINE FALCONS: CAPE MAY'S HEADLINER

Catching the big peregrine push, the peak peregrine flight, is a coveted goal of many Cape May hawkwatchers, visitors and locals alike. It can be hard to predict. It almost always occurs in the first week of October, but you had better be at the hawkwatch every day to guarantee seeing it. It might start off slow—peregrine flights are mainly a midday to late afternoon phenomenon. Peregrine numbers usually begin to build in late morning, often peaking at about one to three o'clock in the afternoon. A friend once saw forty-four peregrines on his one-hour lunch break from one to two o'clock. We remember seeing seven peregrines soaring together in a midday, single-species kettle.

Of all hawk migration, peregrine flights are the least related to cold fronts. In fact, at Cape May, cold fronts and northwest winds produce very few peregrines, mainly because most are not coming from the north and west. (Those that do may come from as far away as the western Canadian Arctic; peregrines banded as nestlings in the Yukon have been recaptured just south of Cape May at Assateague Island, Maryland. Also, only a few peregrines of the reintroduced eastern population are seen at Cape May each season, verified by trapping ratios at the hawk banding stations.)

Most of Cape May's peregrines come from Greenland. Cape May's migrant peregrines are of the *tundrius* subspecies, the high Arctic breeders that winter largely in Central and South America. Arctic peregrines have been recovered at Tierra del Fuego, at the southern tip of South America, a round-trip journey of 20,000 miles from their Arctic aeries. Although most *tundrius* peregrines probably winter in coastal regions in Florida and throughout Central and South America, many disperse into interior South America. On trips to the vast Llanos of Venezuela, the central savanna region, we saw peregrines daily in some numbers. It is fascinating to think that in a few short weeks they go from sharing Arctic tundra with Golden Plovers and Long-tailed Jaegers (and wolves and Musk Oxen) to sharing the open Llanos with Southern Lapwings and Scarlet Ibis (and Capybaras and Giant Anteaters). In Brazil, peregrines winter along the Amazon and in the Mato Grosso. A peregrine banded at Cape May in September 1987 was found in December 1990 near Recife on the Atlantic coast of Brazil. It was being held in captivity with clipped wings and was transferred to the Brazilian Institute for the Environment, where it was to be rehabilitated and released to the wild.

Greenland peregrines of necessity routinely cross the Davis Strait from Greenland to North America, so water is no barrier to them. At Cape May, peregrines cross Delaware Bay as easily as we step across a puddle. If a peregrine hangs around the Cape, it's because it wants to. Of interest, some juvenile peregrines at Cape May are remarkably tame. Several times we have had young peregrines watch us with seeming fascination from atop a pole as we stand directly below. For just-arrived Greenland fledglings, we may be the first people they have ever seen. Maybe the birds regard us as mighty strange-looking caribou.

Satellite tracking has proved that peregrines can cover many miles a day during migration. A female tundra peregrine, returning to the Arctic in spring, quickened her pace as she neared her summer home. In the final leg of her journey north, she covered over 500 miles in a single day and roosted that night on the ledge of her Arctic aerie. This is a distance we would be hard-pressed to cover in an automobile on the interstate.

There is clear evidence that during fall migration, peregrines are sometimes pelagic travelers. Many are regularly seen at sea from fishing boats and on fall pelagic bird trips—proof that peregrines routinely migrate off the coast, often well beyond the sight of land. They frequently feed (on the wing) by catching exhausted songbirds out over the ocean at dawn. Apparently, adult male peregrines are particularly pelagic; by far, they are the least-seen age and sex at Cape May, and very few are caught by the raptor banding project. Peregrines do nonroutine things on migration. In the early days of radio tracking (before the advent of satellite tracking), a young Arctic peregrine was trapped, banded, and fitted with a transmitter at Assateague, Maryland. It was trapped in the morning, sat on a dune until around two o'clock in the afternoon, then took off and flew straight out to sea. The researchers scrambled into an airplane to follow it, which they did until around two o'clock in the morning, when they had to abandon the chase because they were about to enter Cuban airspace. The peregrine obviously wasn't caught out over the Atlantic but was simply migrating to South America—overnight and many miles at sea.

One of the strangest things we ever saw a peregrine do occurred over Cape May Point late one gray afternoon in a stiff, 25-mile-per-hour

continues on next page

PEREGRINE FALCONS *continued*

southerly wind. The juvenile peregrine appeared to be flapping in place—in effect, hovering in the strong wind. We soon realized that it was climbing, as if on an elevator. We watched it get smaller and smaller until it disappeared from binocular vision—straight up. From 5,000 to 7,000 feet, its subsequent glide probably could have easily taken it across Delaware Bay.

Due to their offshore habits, peregrines are far more likely to be seen on east winds than west winds at Cape May. Strong northeast winds are good, but gentle east and southeast winds seem best to put peregrines on the beach and create the peak flight of the season. This is partly because they are brought in from far offshore, and partly a more local phenomenon. In the absence of a strong east wind, many peregrines head to Delaware from Cold Spring Jetty (the north end of Cape May City) or from the Second Avenue Jetty area—shortcutting the Point, waiting watchers, and the official count. Peregrines are decidedly prefrontal in their flight through Cape May. Big peregrine flights always occur the day *before* a cold front, not after it, when the winds are from the east or even from the south, with attendant warm weather. Maybe they prefer to fly in warmer weather, or perhaps they anticipate the

gentle northwest winds, it's the best place to enjoy kettles of soaring birds. Strong northwest winds, though, create a broad-front movement as birds fight the wind. On strong northwest winds, wind-driven hawks hit the water at Cape May City, then turn into the wind and follow the tree line west. Most are seen from the hawkwatch platform, but many can be quite far to the north. (Once, during a northwest gale, we had over sixty redtails at the Cape May Canal Bridge, whereas the hawkwatch saw only three; most birds were clearly shortcutting the Point.) Often, the end of the Cape May Point State Park tree line, on Lighthouse Avenue, is the best place to watch during brisk northwest winds. You might not see every bird, but you'll enjoy point-blank views of low-flying birds.

The Beanery (a.k.a. the Rea Farm) is a terrific spot to watch hawks in northwest winds. This is particularly true from midday to late in the day, as hawks begin to think about feeding and roosting and the flight begins to shift to the north. The Beanery is also particularly good during northwest winds late in the season, when the flight consists of mostly buteos. Hawks coming cold front and the bounty of songbirds to be blown offshore in the following days. We find that stopover Peregrine Falcons (as well as Merlins) often feed much like the storied Eleonora's Falcon of the Mediterranean, flying to sea early each morning to intercept migrant songbirds caught out over the water at dawn. Tired songbirds are easy pickings for a skilled falcon. At sea, terns and storm-petrels are routinely caught by peregrines too. In the warm waters near the Gulf Stream, peregrines have been seen chasing Flying Fish. Also, we often see peregrines (and Merlins) feeding on prefrontal swarms of migratory dragonflies over Cape May. At dusk and again at dawn, peregrines often try to catch migrating Red Bats. Much like songbirds, Red Bats are commonly seen from both the hawkwatch and the Avalon Seawatch coming in off the ocean at dawn.

The peregrine flight is one of Cape May's true birding hallmarks. The numbers seen annually in fall are rivaled or surpassed only by those seen at Assateague Island, Maryland; at Padre Island, Texas; and in the Florida Keys. Our peak annual total is 1,793 peregrines (1997), and our peak daily flight is 298 (October 5, 2002). We hope that you are here with us on that unseasonably warm early October afternoon when this hallowed daily record is broken. ▪

and eagles that are picked up as distant specks from the hawkwatch are often low and directly overhead at the Beanery.

Another aspect of localized hawk pathways, and a bit of a sour note, is that some hawks seem to completely shortcut Cape Island. Although anecdotal, there is some evidence that, with the continuing development of the Cape and the loss of key farmland to housing, more and more raptors, mostly buteos and eagles, turn near the canal and then head north up the Delaware Bayshore. It's hard to quantify, but it stands to reason that the formerly vast and pristine pastures offered a habitat inducement to migratory hawks—an attractive place to hunt. With that attraction severely depleted, more and more hawks may turn back rather than run the gauntlet of houses. This will always be a discomforting intangible in modern Cape May hawk counts.

Northeast winds can be tough but rewarding. It's best to be at the hawkwatch on north–northeast winds, but if the wind edges farther to the east (true northeast), the flight line will be west of the hawkwatch. Then, the south shore of Lily Lake or Pavilion Circle in the heart of the town of Cape May Point provides a great view of the flight path and good views of birds that are either distant or missed at the hawkwatch. Finally, whereas an east wind often shuts down the flight, sometimes during the rapid wind shift of a fast-moving backdoor cold front, the flight continues on east winds (albeit for only a short time). Then, the Delaware Bay side of the peninsula is the diversion line as birds are pushed to the western boundary of the Cape. In this case, the former Magnesite Plant on Sunset Boulevard or the Sunset Beach–Concrete Ship area provides the closest and best views of the raptor migration.

Partly, the decision about where to be depends on what you want to see. Falcons are always best near the beachfront. American Kestrels, Merlins, and Peregrine Falcons are always best seen from the hawkwatch or the South Cape May Meadows. Timing is important for falcons too. They clearly prefer to feed in the morning and migrate in the afternoon. Some days, the morning hawk flight consists of virtually all accipiters, with nary a falcon; then, around noon, the flight shifts, and a big kestrel push occurs in the afternoon. Cape May is particularly well known for late-afternoon "Merlin madness," when migrating Merlins stop to feed. Sometimes dozens zip around the hawkwatch and the South Cape May Meadows very late in the day. They're hard to count but great fun to watch. Following the passage of a walloping cold front, hawks are already moving at sunrise; Northern Harriers sometimes start at first light. On these days, movement may continue until sunset. We've seen Osprey migrating when there's barely enough light left to see a bird; when in fact, we've lingered to look for owls. Most days, though, the hawk flight proper begins around 8:00 or 9:00 A.M., giving the birder time to enjoy landbirds at Higbee Beach and then move to the hawkwatch as the hawk flight builds. Most days, the hawk flight ends in midafternoon, allowing visitors to go to Stone Harbor, for example, for wetlands and beach birds, or even up to Forsythe National Wildlife Refuge.

Double Counting and Other Issues

"How do you know you haven't counted that hawk before?" is a legendary question at Cape May. It's asked daily and repeatedly during the autumn hawk count—at least as often as the "Where can I buy sunscreen?" or "Where's a really good seafood restaurant?" queries of summer. It's asked so frequently that counters and interns fantasize over the best possible retort. Our favorite is that of veteran counter Jerry Ligouri: "Gee, I never thought of that!" If in a friendly way we make light of the question, it's because it can haunt us. During the first hour of the first day of a raptor workshop we were teaching for the Southeast Arizona Bird Observatory in Bisbee, Arizona, the first question we were asked was, "Say, back at Cape May, how do you know you haven't counted those hawks before?"

It's a really good question, and one we're glad to answer, for it's through the questions of visitors that the best natural history education occurs. It's a question that was given far more consideration in the early years of the CMBO than virtually any other research question. And it's a complex question. At places like Hawk Mountain, Duluth, and Braddock Bay, hawks follow physical features—migratory leading lines or diversion lines that route them to and quickly by the hawkwatch—where they are easily counted. At places like Cape May (and Cape Charles and the Florida Keys), hawks are also following a diversion line, but one that ends abruptly, causing many if not most hawks to pause and reconsider the route—in short, to linger or loiter over the hawkwatch.

Most of the time, this isn't a problem for the official hawk counter. Particularly during strong northwest winds, birds are moving briskly by the platform in a steady procession. You can go virtually anywhere on the peninsula and see that the hawks are not turning around and passing by the hawkwatch again. Farther north, at Stone Harbor and Cape May Court House, hawks are heading south; at Cape May City, they are heading west toward Cape May Point; at the Cape May Hawkwatch in Cape May Point State Park, they are heading west along the tree line; and at Higbee Beach, they are heading due north up the Delaware Bayshore. Similarly, on north and northeast winds, most birds are heading due south and cross the bay. The only lingering (circling or kettling) being done is for the purpose of gaining altitude for the crossing. But as the visitor soon learns, there are many other days when the movement, the direction of the flight, is not clear-cut and is at times downright confusing. This usually occurs the second or third day after a front, when winds are light but thermal activity (and resultant soaring) is high.

Lingering behavior varies from species to species. Except for American Kestrels in strong winds, falcons almost always cross Delaware Bay, as do Osprey and Northern Harriers (harriers are remarkably unafraid of water, commonly migrating well off the beach). Buteos are the least likely hawks to cross Delaware Bay and the most likely to linger. Turkey Vultures virtually never cross; all eventually go around Delaware Bay. Turkey Vultures are the worst loiterers, sometimes remaining overhead for hours (counters often record only the highest Turkey Vulture count of the day—those in sight at one time). Lingering, soaring flights are admittedly hard to count, and it is often a matter of the official counter's best guess. This is an educated guess, though, made by using a combination of clues, such as timing an individual's lingering time, using signpost birds, and noting missing feathers or individual plumage variations on specific birds (which works best on Bald Eagles but can be applied surprisingly often to other birds as well). Careful monitoring of entry and exit points is important and often goes unnoticed by visitors to the watch, but it's a key technique in gauging lingering time. Visitors might be baffled by a confusing and seemingly disorganized mass of hawks circling overhead, but frequently the counter isn't counting those birds at all; he or she is ignoring them and concentrating only on new birds, new arrivals entering the airspace, coming in off the Cape May City skyline well to the east (or possibly birds exiting to the northwest out over the magnesite property).

In the 1970s and 1980s, the CMBO put all its research efforts into quantifying the Cape May flights and testing the veracity of the counts. Efforts included multiple watch sites (entry and exit sites), roving watchers following the flight lines, and investigating the effect of the number of observers on the count. More importantly, it included banding data (focusing on recapture rates), color marking of banded birds (tape on hawks' tails), and radio telemetry. To make an incredibly complex body of work understandable, suffice it to say that there is good evidence that although some hawks that have roosted in the area may be recounted the following day, most birds choosing to go around Delaware Bay are doing so in a direct manner. Studies found that the recount might be as high as 6.7 percent on some days (and varied by species), but these extensive studies also showed that, due to broad-front migration, at least as many birds were never being recorded by the official count at Cape May Point State Park. This was based not only on direct counts and observations but also on known color-marked and telemetry-fitted birds that never went near the count site. One factor balances out the other: Any overcounting is balanced by attendant undercounting.

A related and perhaps larger question, and one that has no clear answer, is the issue of observer bias. In science, it doesn't matter if a count technique is foolproof, as long as it is carried out the same way each time so that each sampling is comparable to the others. At Cape May, every attempt is made to have each year's count conducted in a standardized way, yet human nature means that there will always be some observer bias. Over the years, some official counters have been raptor-counting machines, letting nothing get in the way of the count. Other counters have focused more heavily on education and interaction with the public—an equally important CMBO mission. Certainly, such a differing focus won't make the difference between a record year and an average one, or a poor year (it happens) and an average one, but it definitely has an impact on counts. Some counters are liberal in their count technique, and others are highly conservative. Also, some counters may favor a particular group of hawks, perhaps not missing a single high-flying peregrine but paying comparatively little attention to sharpies sneaking through the treetops. A great example of this type of bias occurred when one counter tallied sixty-two Cooper's Hawks on the same day that banders caught seventy-eight (banding stations normally catch about 6 percent of the total counted flight). The counter was simply focusing elsewhere—maybe on Merlins or the all-important educational mission. The important thing to remember is that this type of bias occurs not

In the 1980s, telemetry studies at the lighthouse and elsewhere gathered hard data about the behavior of migrating raptors.

just at Cape May but at every hawk count worldwide. Our own feelings, based on many years of experience (much of it north of Cape May Point, away from the official hawkwatch, watching both broad-front movement and the substantial flight around Delaware Bay) are that the more liberal counters probably come closer to capturing the true magnitude of the Cape May hawk flight.

Another aspect of the Cape May hawk count technique that bears mentioning is the use of the "unidentified" category. Most hawkwatches use it, and some visitors question why it hasn't been used at Cape May. It's important to clarify that Cape May hawk counters don't egotistically believe that they can identify every speck they see. It's just that due to the nature of Cape May flights—the broad-front movement and the frequent lingering—if a hawk can't be identified, the counter and watchers simply wait for it to come closer. And if it doesn't come closer, it simply isn't counted, because an unidentified bird tells us nothing scientifically. That said, in recent years, "unidentified" has become a more frequently used category, even though most of the past CMBO counts didn't use it.

There has been another curious change in the Cape May count in recent years, as some counters have not counted vultures (and, to a lesser degree, redtails) in any numbers before early October—almost all dismissed as locals. This seems odd, in that, by October, hundreds of thousands of Turkey Vultures have already streamed south over Veracruz, Mexico, and that large numbers of Turkey Vultures can easily be seen daily streaming west up the Delaware Bayshore, going around the bay. Juvenile redtails are dispersing then in good numbers too. This may be additional proof that posted counts are indeed on the conservative side.

In the end, we should remember Pete Dunne's immortal words, offered in fun years ago when someone questioned his count: "It may not be right, but it's official." He wasn't being rude or even pulling rank. It's just that you have to draw the line somewhere, giving it your best effort with the best information available. The Cape May hawk count may not be scientifically ironclad, but over the years, a massive effort has been made to make it as good as it can be. It is relevant, repeatable, and consistent. If not exact, it is still a valid index of the raptor flight through Cape May. It is educational and a lot of fun too. Fall wouldn't be the same at Cape May without the traditional and time-honored hawk count.

Around the Bay

Probably the best proof that overcounting is not a big problem at Cape May comes from raptor studies carried out at East Point in neighboring Cumberland County, about 25 miles up the Delaware Bay "as the hawk flies" (following the bayshore's tree line north up the peninsula and then west to the Maurice River). In 1989 and 1990, Clay Sutton and colleague Jim Dowdell conducted hawk counts at East Point (under the auspices of Citizens United to Protect the Maurice River, and also supported by a small grant from the CMBO). The 1990 count was nearly full time—more than 300 hours were put in over sixty days during the peak season. The 9,042 raptors recorded at East Point were nearly all going due west, following a route *around* Delaware Bay, and represented 35 percent of the Cape May hawk count recorded during those same sixty days. As expected, the percentage varied by species. East Point recorded only 9 percent of Cape May's total for Peregrine Falcons, 12 percent of Osprey, and 21 percent of Merlins. All three of these species were generally headed due south over East Point and out over the waters of Delaware Bay. For most other species, though, almost all East Point birds were headed west, including 26 percent of Cape May's total for American Kestrels, 36 percent of Sharp-shinned Hawks, and 40 percent of Cooper's Hawks. Buteos are the least likely group to cross at Cape May. East Point recorded 91 percent of Cape May's total for Red-tailed Hawks, and 107 percent of Cape May's Turkey Vulture flight was counted at East Point. The biggest surprise was Rough-legged Hawks; 900 percent of the Cape May flight was counted at East Point (twenty-seven, versus three at Cape May), indicating not only a major migratory route up Delaware Bay (many rough-legs winter on bayshore marshes) but that most migrant rough-legs shortcut Cape May. To complete the picture, 18 percent of Cape May's Broad-winged

Hawks were counted at East Point, 23 percent of goshawks, 38 percent of Red-shouldered Hawks, 57 percent of Golden Eagles, 68 percent of Northern Harriers, 90 percent of Bald Eagles, and 166 percent of Black Vultures (for Black Vultures, both counts no doubt included many locals).

East Point, as the name suggests, is a peninsula jutting out into Maurice River Cove at the mouth of the Maurice River. It functions as a mini–Cape May. Raptors following the Delaware Bayshore tree line west are routed south to the lighthouse at the tip of East Point. There they face a simple 2-mile water crossing to the far side of the

At East Point, hawks flying around Delaware Bay are again concentrated.

mouth of the Maurice River. But, just as at Cape May, this barrier is significant enough to reconcentrate the flight line and make the flight readily countable. Birds backtrack upriver, crossing near Heislerville, where the river is only a few hundred yards wide. Later in the day, this bayshore flight becomes a broad-front movement (as thermals allow hawks to fly higher and glide farther). On the few occasions when a second observer was used about 5 miles upriver, 54 percent of the Cape May total was seen when figures from both East Point and the second site were added. If this doesn't necessarily prove that over half of the Cape May hawks eventually go around Delaware Bay, it does show that 35 percent is probably a conservative figure.

This westward flight is still readily visible as far west as Salem County. Near the Cohansey River, where Delaware Bay narrows to about 5 miles wide, some hawks finally work up the courage to cross the bay and continue their journey south (hawks cross there in spring, too). Some go even farther, to near the Delaware Memorial Bridge. (Such backtracking isn't a very energy-efficient migration strategy and can take a considerable amount of time. A sharp-shin hawk banded on September 17, 1990, at Cape May was recaptured by a banding station at Cape Charles on October 15, 1990, nearly four weeks later, although it certainly could have reached there earlier.) At least hawks find plenty of good stopover habitat along the pristine Delaware Bayshore. Then, one or two days later, faced with Chesapeake Bay at land's end at Cape Charles, they have to do it all over again.

THE CAPE MAY
RAPTOR BANDING PROJECT

As would be expected at a major migratory juncture like Cape May, bird banding has long been a part of bird studies. Many first-time visitors are surprised to learn, though, that unlike at most research sites or stations, little passerine banding occurs at Cape May. There was a U.S. Fish and Wildlife Service project run at Cape May in the 1950s, and there have been several small, privately run songbird banding operations over the years, but nothing on a major scale. (Of interest, even with comparatively limited efforts, birds such as Swainson's Warbler and Painted Bunting have been netted at Cape May.) All the CMBO's songbird banding projects have been highly focused, studying primarily stopover habitat selection criteria, as well as weight-gain rates in specific habitats and sites. Such goal- and objective-oriented banding has had far more beneficial impacts than the untargeted banding of large numbers of birds (in many locations, banding projects are largely educational efforts, or even recreational); several of the CMBO's banding studies have played a major role in habitat protection and the purchase of key stopover habitat.

There has, however, been a major hawk banding operation carried out at Cape May for nearly four decades. The Cape May Raptor Banding Project, Inc. (CMRBP) is both the longest-running and the largest hawk banding project in the world. Begun in 1967 by William S. Clark (today one of the world's top raptor banding and identification experts), it has run continuously ever since. Although it once received funding from the CMBO, it is now a fully independent project and run locally today by veteran bander Sam Orr. The CMRBP was created to conduct long-term monitoring of the status and trends of migrating raptors. Up to five individual banding stations are operated each year at various locations south of the Cape May Canal. Birds are attracted mostly by live lure birds (only pigeons, starlings, and House Sparrows can legally be used for this) and then trapped in a variety of different traps, but mainly in bow nets set up around the lures. Birds are measured, weighed, and banded with a U.S. Geological Survey band and then released unharmed, usually within a few minutes of capture.

The number of birds banded by the CMRBP is staggering. Since 1967, more than 121,000 raptors have been banded at Cape May Point. Attesting to the birds' need to feed while on migration (and the need for quality stopover habitat), the CMRBP catches, on average, about 6 percent of the hawks counted at the hawkwatch. The vast majority of birds captured, nearly 95 percent, are juveniles—young of the year—reflective of both the preponderance of juveniles in the Cape May flight and the greater likelihood that healthy, well-fed, and wise adults will avoid the traps. (For many hawk youngsters, hunger overcomes caution.)

A banding demonstration teaches Cape May visitors about the wonders of raptors.

The CMRBP bands an average of more than 4,000 hawks each year and now has band recoveries from more than 2,000 raptors—about 25 percent of these being live recaptures (and re-releases). Some findings have been routine—for example, that many retraps are from Cape Charles—but some discoveries have been quite surprising. Due to the prevalence of western rarities at Cape May each year (Swainson's Hawks are banded nearly annually by the CMRBP, but as yet, there have been no Swainson's returns), it would be tempting to think that many of our hawks come from the northwest—from the Great Lakes and even central Canada. However, banding results have clearly proved that Cape May hawks originate almost exclusively from breeding areas north and east of Cape May—primarily from eastern Canada and New England. A number of hawks, mostly sharp-shins and Cooper's, have been retrapped as adults at Cape May, proving that many birds use the same route each year. One Merlin was recaptured almost exactly three years after it was initially banded—and in the same spot. A few birds have "gone their own way" and bucked this trend. A Sharp-shinned Hawk banded at Cape May in October 1988 was retrapped (caught at a banding station and then released) in May 1991 at Whitefish Point, Michigan. A number of hawks banded at Cape May as juveniles have been retrapped as adults along the Kittatinny Ridge in Pennsylvania.

Returns show that most hawks banded at Cape May winter in the southeastern United States, but recoveries have also come from as far west as Texas and as far east as Bermuda and the Caribbean. A number

continues on next page

RAPTOR BANDING PROJECT *continued*

of recoveries have come from Central and South America. A Merlin banded in Cape May on September 28, 1985, was "caught while hunting" in the Dominican Republic on December 20, 1985, by someone who thought that there was a reward for the band. Another Merlin banded in Cape May on September 21, 1987, was killed in Panama City on March 3, 1988, after it (supposedly) ate seventeen fighting cocks.

We assume, naturally, that most hawks banded in the fall at Cape May are headed south and will end their migration somewhere south of Cape May. But banding has shown that this is not always the case. A Merlin banded at Cape May on September 24, 1985, was recaptured at Democrat Point on Long Island, New York, on September 29, 1985, just five days later. Goshawks banded at Cape May in the fall have also been found well to the north during the winter, suggesting that at least some goshawks are nomadic in their movements.

Several highlights stand out in the work of the CMRBP. An early one was the September 23, 1972, capture of a Common (Eurasian) Kestrel (*Falco tinnunculus*) at Cape May Point by Joseph Harmer and Bob Dittrick. The bird was photographed, banded, and released. At the time, it was only the second record for all of North America (we have had a couple of good sight records at Cape May since then). Grease on the bird's undertail coverts proved that, at some point in its crossing of the Atlantic, it had probably ridden in the rigging of a ship. In 1973, the banders counted an all-time season high of 101 Northern Goshawks from their blinds, documenting a goshawk invasion never seen before or since. On November 7 of that year, artist and raptor aficionado Al Nicholson counted 50 goshawks at Cape May, a number not even hinted at in the modern era of hawkwatching (1973 must have been a difficult year to be a pigeon).

Another highlight occurred when codirector of the CMRBP Chris Schultz (currently a Bureau of Land Management raptor biologist) trapped a juvenile Peregrine Falcon at Cape May on October 16, 1989. The bird wore a fresh, shiny new band, and something about the number seemed familiar to Chris. He reached for his field notebook, looked up the band number, and realized that he himself had banded this peregrine only seventy-eight days previously, on July 30, 1989—at its lonely, windswept Arctic aerie in Greenland. Chris had spent the summer there banding peregrines and Gyrfalcons for the U.S. Fish and Wildlife Service, and at Cape May Point in October, he retrapped his own bird. We can't

CAPE MAY RAPTOR BANDING PROJECT

Raptor Species	Number Banded 1967–2005	Record	Year
Osprey	17	6	1989
Bald Eagle	5	1	
Northern Harrier	3,316	317	1987
Sharp-shinned Hawk	65,899	4,106	1984
Cooper's Hawk	17,463	1,344	2003
Northern Goshawk	351	33	1999
Red-shouldered Hawk	350	27	1985
Broad-winged Hawk	305	113	1981
Swainson's Hawk	18	2	1998
Red-tailed Hawk	6,732	443	1995
Rough-legged Hawk	9	2	1985
Golden Eagle	16	2	1988
American Kestrel	17,516	1,935	1976
Merlin	7,844	407	1985
Peregrine Falcon	1,390	120	1990
Total raptors	121,234	5,653	1976

help but envision a Gary Larson *The Far Side* comic strip, with the peregrine thinking, "I've traveled 3,000 miles, and here's *this guy* again."

Through banding programs, banders have determined migration routes, longevity, breeding and wintering areas, and, most importantly, migratory habitat needs. Even so, we can't help but feel that the greatest contribution of the CMRBP is to environmental education. For many years, the project has conducted weekend banding demonstrations at Cape May Point State Park, where hawks are brought from the trapping stations for the public to see up close while learning about the birds and their migration through Cape May. Immensely popular, these demonstrations have taught many thousands—birders and tourists alike—the basics of raptor biology and hawk identification, the wonders of birds of prey, and the importance of Cape May. The great value of these educational exhibits may well overshadow even the scientific objectives and successes of the CMRBP. ▪

OWL MIGRATION

The autumn migration of birds of prey does not end at sundown but continues anew after dark. Where Northern Harriers have coursed the marshes and fields by day, Long-eared Owls and Barn Owls hunt by night. And where Sharp-shinned Hawks and American Kestrels have bounced low over the dunes and fields in sunshine, Saw-whet Owls silently pass during the safety of darkness. Just as hawks are funneled to the tip of the Cape May peninsula, so too are migrant owls. The Barn Owl migration has long been known. Roger Tory Peterson in *Birds Over America* wrote, "At Cape May, lying on my back among the dunes near the boardwalk, I have squeaked them overhead, while the ghostly forms reflected the light from the street lamps." In his migration paper in *The Auk,* Peterson (and Allen) said in 1936, "The woods area (at Cape May Point) offers natural foods and abundant cover and it is here that the principal concentrations of migrant birds are observed. . . . Barn Owls, occurring in flocks that may number

upwards of one-hundred birds, prefer a grove of half-grown pines in the vicinity." This is sad testimony to the decline of the Barn Owl in the mid-Atlantic and the Northeast, where the loss of farmland has impacted them severely in the manner of so many other grassland birds. Today we are fortunate to find one or two Barn Owls at their daytime roost during an entire fall season.

Interestingly, some researchers claim there is little evidence that Barn Owls actually migrate. They cite band returns that show that in fall, young owls simply disperse equally to all points of the compass. Others believe that Barn Owls do clearly withdraw from the nothern edges of their range, and there is ample evidence of this at Cape May—the regular timetable of Barn Owl movement, the apparent southbound direction of all owls that are seen or heard in fall, and the large numbers of owls

The principal owl species migrating through Cape May today is the Northern Saw-whet Owl.

recorded by Peterson and others in the past. As well, far fewer Barn Owls are found in Delaware Bayshore barns in winter than in summer, although some of these birds may simply relocate to nearby Red Cedar groves. The question, of course, in determining migration versus dispersal, is whether the same birds return north in the spring. Much remains to be learned.

Just as the Cape May Raptor Banding Project traps and bands hawks by day, the Cape May Owl Banding Project (CMOBP) operates a series of mist nets to trap and band owls at night. The CMOBP employs only passive banding—the placement of mist nets in the likely path of owls—although audio lures have been used nightly since 1989. Saw-whet Owl "tooting" calls are used; apparently, saw-whets are curious about others even on migration. If you bird around Cape May Point at night in late October or November, you'll probably hear the taped call being broadcast.

The owl banding project had humble beginnings. Bill Clark banded the first migrant owls (2 Barn Owls) at Cape May in 1969. He and his colleagues continued part-time night banding through 1976 while running hawk-banding stations by day. In 1977, Mary Eloranta ran the Cape May Owl Banding Project full time and banded 184 owls (31 saw-whets, 100 barns, 48 long-eareds, and 5 short-eareds); she ran the project through 1979. Since 1980, the indefatigable Katy Duffy has run the CMOBP, ably assisted by her stalwart husband Patrick Matheny. Katy and Patrick migrate to Cape May each fall from their jobs at Yellowstone National Park in Montana, where Katy is the West District interpretive ranger. They're up all night, every night, checking the nets every half hour or even more frequently if it's a good night. Their CMOBP is a labor of love, as they use all their vacation time to work the migration night shift, unraveling the many mysteries of owl migration.

Owl migration occurs mostly late in the fall. The CMOBP runs from late October through mid-November, although considerable movement is clearly missed both before and after the finite banding project season. The principal species migrating through Cape May today is the Northern Saw-whet Owl, with varying numbers of Long-eared Owls. Both are irruptive, and their numbers can vary greatly from year to year in relation to food availability and production on their northern breeding grounds. In the past twenty-five years (1980 to 2005), Duffy and Matheny have banded 3,684 migrant owls at Cape May, including 2,957 Saw-whet Owls and 474 Long-eared Owls. Through their committed efforts, we've learned the seasonality for each of the migrant owls and, in some cases, where they've come from and where they are going. About 70 percent of Cape May owls are immatures, a lower percentage than that found among banded hawks.

In the early years of the project, between 1973 and 1988, numerous Barn Owls (542) were captured and banded by the CMOBP. The number

Less pastureland in Cape May has led to a drastic decrease in the number of Barn Owl nest sites and the number of migrant Barn Owls recorded.

of Barn Owls banded since the late 1980s has dropped significantly, in part due to a decline in their population, and in part due to changing habitat locally. Thirty years ago, when owl banding began at Cape May, the South Cape May Meadows and Cape May Point State Park included extensive low, grazed pastureland and *Spartina patens* meadows—far more attractive (rodent-rich) to migrant hunting Barn Owls than today's shrubby growth and tall, thick stands of *Phragmites*. (*Phragmites* filled in the *Spartina patens* marshes where Barn Owls had previously hunted.) In 1989, when the CMOBP focused its energies on the Saw-whet Owl migration through the use of audio lures and net placement, the number of Barn Owls banded dropped to less than five per year. Previously banded Barn Owls caught by the CMOBP have come from nest sites in New Haven, Connecticut; Jamaica Bay, New York; northern New Jersey; and Salem County, in south-western New Jersey. Barn Owls are the earliest owl migrant, coming through from mid-September until early November. Saw-whet Owls and Long-eared Owls move through between mid-October and late November.

Since its inception, the CMOBP has banded nearly 700 Long-eared Owls. There have been four recoveries of long-ears that were originally banded at Cape May. Two were recaptured at Cape May (one two years later and the other five years later), still on the same migratory pathway. A third Long-eared Owl was accidentally shot four years later in New Brunswick, Canada, by a Ruffed Grouse hunter who mistook it for a grouse when it flushed in dense cover. A fourth was found dead on Long Island.

The CMOBP has concentrated on Northern Saw-whet Owls since 1989, and more than 3,000 saw-whets have been captured, banded, and quickly released to date. Much has been learned, such as the fact that young are far more likely to migrate than adults, and that females move farther than males. There have been some fascinating saw-whet recoveries at Cape May of previously banded saw-whets from Prince Edward Point in Canada, Wells (Maine), and elsewhere. There have also been 10 live recoveries in Cape May—birds banded here that returned in subsequent years. Sixty-six of Cape May's saw-whets have now been live-trapped at other banding stations, mostly on Assateague Island in Maryland (where an owl-banding operation began in 1991) and on Cape Charles in Virginia. Two reached Cape Charles in less than twenty-four hours. Another saw-whet banded at Cape May was recovered on Assateague Island, nearly 100 miles to the south (including the 10-mile Delaware Bay water crossing) just three and a half hours later. Perhaps the most amazing recaptures were saw-whets caught at Cape May that had been banded during previous migrations in northern Wisconsin (along the shore of Lake Michigan, north of Green Bay) and at

Duluth, Minnesota. (Apparently, saw-whets can come from farther west than most of the hawks banded at Cape May.) There is good evidence that at least some saw-whets are nomadic breeders; one trapped near Boston in fall 2005 had been originally banded in Montana, on the eastern slopes of the Roocky Mountains. In 1994, Project Owlnet formed, networking migrant-owl banding stations; as of 2005, the project included nearly 100 stations across North America that target Northern Saw-whet Owls with protocols of constant-effort mist netting. Cape May has been part of Project Owlnet since its inception.

The CMOBP has caught and banded a few migrant Short-eared Owls over the years (seventeen, to be exact). Short-eareds avoid the net lanes, apparently flying higher or over the ocean during migration. (Short-eareds are seen annually in very small numbers at both the Cape May Hawkwatch and the Avalon Seawatch. They are usually

By day migrant owls like this Long-eared Owl wait for nightfall to continue their migration, sometimes in a well-vegetated Cape May Point backyard.

seen migrating offshore—a mile or two off the beach—much like North-ern Harriers often do. On a very few occasions, short-eareds have been seen kettling with hawks over Cape May Point.) Finally, the project catches a few local resident or dispersing Eastern Screech Owls, Great Horned Owls, and Barred Owls.

The owl project is fascinating work and some of the most original Cape May science. The CMOBP captures not only owls but also the imagi-nation of many visitors to the Cape. Unlike the hawk banders, Duffy and Matheny don't schedule formal owl-banding demonstrations. (Due to their irruptive nature, their dependence on weather conditions, and the fickle timing of their capture—anytime through the night—owls aren't pre-dictable.) But they often hold impromptu demos at 8:00 P.M. in the parking lot of the Cape May Migratory Bird Refuge during the first half of Novem-ber. Sometimes visiting birders wait for hours in the hope that it will turn out to be a good night and that the banders will appear with a saw-whet, which will then be released into the Cape May night to the wonder of all.

Almost all owl captures occur the second and third nights after passage of a cold front, when temperatures are cold, skies are clear, high pressure dominates, and the wind has dropped (either no wind, or gentle from the north or northwest). Higher winds in part deter migration; they also signifi-cantly deter captures because owls can better detect mist nets billowing in blustery winds. Owl movement can occur anytime during the night or all night long. Saw-whets fly low, but long-eareds are often fairly high. On very rare occasions, on quiet moonlit nights, long-eareds can sometimes be seen both hunting and migrating over the South Cape May Meadows and Cape May Point State Park. On one memorable night at the Meadows, after watching owls lift off and head out at dusk, Pat lingered to observe the ris-ing full moon through her scope and saw four more owls cross in front of the moon, along with hundreds of songbirds, several herons, and several American Woodcock. Sometimes owl shapes can be seen as they pass through the revolving beam of the Cape May Lighthouse.

Migrating owls are mostly silent, except for Barn Owls, which are quite vocal. Even though the CMOBP rarely catches and bands Barn Owls today, their distinct screech (schhhhhhhp!) is regularly heard by those listen-ing for them as they migrate over Cape May City, the Meadows, Cape May Point State Park, or the town of Cape May Point. During years with a big Northern Saw-whet Owl movement, they too can be vocal; the call to lis-ten for is thrushlike, a phew, rather than their breeding call, a repetitive toot.

In recent years, it has become popular to watch owl liftoff at dusk, against the red glow of the evening sky. The Meadows is especially good for this; the height of the dune crossover offers a view of the entire horizon. This view takes in the flight path of new owls migrating in and the extensive habitat where migrant owls from the night before may have been hiding all day. The glow from the setting sun helps backlight owls on the move. Cape May Point State Park is another good viewing site, but the glow in the sky is behind the lighthouse rather than out over the park's habitat, where the owls are coming from. Mostly Long-eared Owls are regularly seen lifting out of their secret daytime roosts and circling up into the sky, flapping like huge moths and then heading steadily out over Delaware Bay. One night, a few lucky birders watched seventeen long-ears kettle up together in a circling flock before peeling off to the south toward Delaware. During these twilight vigils, many other nocturnal migrants are seen as well— American Woodcock, Common Nighthawk, Wilson's Snipe, herons and egrets, American Bittern, and bats—as they begin their nocturnal migration. Once, a keen observer at the Second Avenue Jetty in Cape May picked up twenty-one American Bitterns lifting out of the marsh and setting off on their journey across Delaware Bay. Owls can be seen at first light, too. The state park and Lighthouse Avenue are good spots from which to watch the eastern sky as it shows the first hints of dawn.

Targeted and focused searches in the fall can, on rare occasions, lead to the discovery of roosting owls. Every year, on a few special days, birders find a roosting Long-eared Owl or two on state park trails or sometimes in isolated cedars around Cape May Point. Go early, move slowly along the trails, and search the stands of Red Cedars. Search from the trail only. Migrant owls quickly learn that joggers and walkers stay on the trails. One step off the trail will flush an owl. Scan every branch and every trunk from many directions; look ahead and then look back once you are past a tree or stand of trees. Sometimes a well-concealed long-ear might stay all day long if it has found the perfect spot. One year, during THE Bird Show, more than 500 people enjoyed a well-concealed Long-eared Owl along the Red Trail at Cape May Point State Park. It was found during the morning's first bird walk, and for the rest of the day at least one leader remained nearby with a spotting scope in order to offer visitors a view and educate about owls and owling etiquette. Everyone stayed on the trail and the owl sat tight. It was still there at dusk.

On one memorable morning many years ago, following a bountiful nighttime migration, we enjoyed more than thirty owls on the then-primitive, unimproved state park trails—long-ears, barns, a great horned, and even a barred. We missed seeing a saw-whet that day. Despite being the most numerous migrant owl, saw-whets can be maddeningly hard to find in daytime roosts at Cape May. The many birding trails in the area (Cape May Point State Park, Higbee Beach, the Rea Farm, Hidden Valley, and the Meadows) are lined with perfect spots for migrant owls to hide—dense and impenetrable stands of Red Cedar, American Holly, and honeysuckle tangles and thickets. It is a wonder that any are ever found, yet each fall, one or two Saw-whet Owls are discovered at Higbee Beach or the state park. More often than not, they are found by Carolina Chickadees or Carolina Wrens first, whose scolding draws the attention of alert birders.

Beyond the banding operation, one owl project attempted at Cape May in 1982 was the visual study of owl migration through the use of a night-vision scope. It seemed like a good idea to watch nighttime migrants from the hawkwatch and to compare and contrast what was seen there with the results of the owl banding project. But the study was somewhat ill-fated. That year turned out to be a compartively slow one; there was little irruptive movement, and the weather was uncooperative for migration, with very few cold fronts (and the cold fronts that did come through produced very windy nights). As a result, very few owls moved through Cape May, so few were seen, even with the aid of the night-vision scope. Also, the scope, kindly lent by the New Jersey State Police, was an obsolete, first-generation night scope, yielding a terrible image and causing extreme eye fatigue. In spite of all of this, there were a few fascinating sightings: low-hunting Barn Owls, Long-eared Owls kettling together, a few saw-whets skimming the dunes, and, notably, a Great Horned Owl catching and carrying off a feral cat in the state park parking lot. And on two occasions, Northern Harriers were seen, happily migrating past the hawkwatch at midnight and one o'clock in the morning, respectively. Maybe the night-scope project will be tried again in a year with some good cold fronts and state-of-the-art equipment. The Cape May autumn nights still have many secrets.

THE AVALON SEAWATCH

Cape May birding adventures are frequently lighthearted, with constant discussion and banter. But this assembled group was serious—all of them alternating between sweeping the horizon with their spotting scopes and scanning the closer sky with binoculars. It was a businesslike atmosphere back on October 26, 1997, with birders calling out birds like sports announcers calling the play-by-play action.

"Big string of gannets over the bell buoy. Maybe twenty, got 'em?"

"Small group of r.-b. mergs above the gannets."

"Huge wave of scoters coming—over the jetty at twelve o'clock—some teal mixed in. Oh, and three Wood Ducks."

"Hey, giant flock of corms back over the houses—behind us. Maybe 300 or so."

"Yo, get on this pulse of Red-throated Loons—high over the number 6 buoy, maybe forty birds. No, make that fifty, no sixty."

"Look! Jaeger chasing a tern—to the right of the feeding flock of gulls. Wow!"

All comments were punctuated by the constant clicking of the seabird counter keeping count on his bank of tally clickers, with numbers rising by the thousands each hour. And although the atmosphere may have been somewhat intense, there were smiles on everybody's faces, because this was a big day at the Avalon Seawatch— maybe even *the* "big one." Waves of birds were coming on as steadily as the ocean waves broke against the seawall below, and no one wanted to miss a single flock. There was the scientific need to count the flight, but there was more to it than that: This was a spectacular migration, an event not to be missed.

Observers at the Avalon Seawatch have been quietly tallying enormous numbers of migrants over the years.

"Two eiders following this scoter flock," someone excitedly yelled, and all eyes turned. "Yeah, both young males, Common Eiders. No; oh, no— one's a young king!" The two eiders rounded the jetty, disappearing from sight, and the official counter went back to his clickers. Then an even more excited shout went up. "Hey, shearwater, I think, eleven o'clock, over the fishing boat, coming straight in—get on it. Yes—shearwater. Sooty Shearwater!"

At this point, the proceedings were no longer businesslike. As the lone Sooty Shearwater skyrocketed up in its bounding flight and then came right down the inlet, everyone was pointing and hollering. The sooty was an inshore seasonal vagrant, a very good bird. It, along with a Razorbill an hour later, was icing on the cake in a wild day of seawatching at Avalon.

As fall birders at Cape May Point enjoy the passage of thousands of hawks from the multilevel Cape May Hawkwatch platform, there is another major migration event under way. It is just as exciting as the raptor passage, but much less well known and less understood. It occurs at what some parochial south-of-the-canal birders would consider a remote outpost, but in reality, this other migration is best viewed only 14.5 miles north of Cape May Point, at the north end of Avalon, New Jersey. It involves far more birds than are counted at the hawkwatch; more than 1 million birds have been recorded moving past Avalon in a single autumn season. Researchers at the Cape May Bird Observatory may term it "visible diurnal southbound over-ocean waterbird migration," but most birders call it, passionately yet simply, "Seawatch."

Although well known to Witmer Stone, the seabird migration—or, more properly, the migration of waterbirds down the coast—was rediscovered by Cape May hawkwatchers. Even in the hawk count's first year, hawkwatchers realized that huge numbers of Double-crested Cormorants and scoters passed by Cape May Point. The problem was that they were hard to view, showing up as distant strings or even wispy, smokelike waves on the far horizon to the east. There is a reason for this: Many if not most waterbirds—which, of course, are not averse to water crossings—begin to angle offshore well north of Cape May, heading for the now visible Delaware or even Maryland coast. Under many conditions, these birds head due south after they round the Cold Spring Jetty (Cape May Inlet) and move increasingly farther away from the peninsula's shoreline. Thus, they can be many miles from Cape May Point counters.

Local marine biologist and birder Dave Ward was highly intrigued by these waterbird flights. In 1977, he set out to find a place where they could be better viewed and found that spot, not coincidentally, in his hometown of Avalon, New Jersey. Avalon is not a peninsula, point, or promontory (geologic features that in most regions create good seawatching) but a barrier island, one in a long string of barrier islands stretching from Point Pleasant south to Wildwood Crest. Avalon's particular advantage is that it projects one full mile seaward beyond the coastline of Sea Isle City to the north, a quirk of coastal geology and sand deposition. Hence, it acts functionally as a headland, lying directly in the path of birds moving south offshore. Think of a bird maintaining a straight southerly course 1 mile offshore and finding itself suddenly confronted with the town of Avalon. Some birds veer offshore, but many don't, making landfall at Avalon. They then veer to the east and round the Eighth Street Jetty, but in doing so, these nearshore migrants are concentrated and offer lengthy, sometimes very close views. This presents a great opportunity for counting them—far better than at Cape May Point.

Dave Ward conducted part-time counts at Avalon from 1978 to 1992. In 1993, intrigued by his astounding numbers, Dave, Clay, and the late Fred Mears began a full-time count—a full-season effort to learn the true magnitude of the seabird migration down New Jersey's coast. The 1993 count was sponsored by the CMBO, and a count has been conducted every fall since then. (It is now conducted, technically, by New Jersey Audubon's Research Department, as is the hawk count.) The official count now runs from September 22 to December 22 each year, a later season than the Cape May Hawkwatch. In fact, as the hawkwatch is petering out, the seawatch is shifting into overdrive.

As with most Cape May migration, the waterbird movement is protracted. The official count spans the peak times for all key species, but a

The north end of Avalon is positioned almost perfectly to bring nearshore migrant seabirds into view and to make them readily countable. STEVE EISENHAUER

great number of birds are missed by the finite count period. For example, almost all Glossy Ibis, Least Terns, and Black Terns and many Common Terns have passed before the watch begins; also, many Northern Gannets and gulls and more than a few Red-necked Grebes, alcids, and kittiwakes pass after it ends. But one must draw the line somewhere, and at Cape May, one could count migrants every day of the year. In 1995, when waterbirds were tallied by Ward, Sutton, and Mears both well before and well after what is now the official count period, more than 1 million waterbirds migrated past Avalon between late July and early February.

Seawatching, the observation and recording of waterbird migration from land, has long been an honored and popular tradition in Britain and elsewhere in Europe. In the United States, it is far more popular on the Pacific coast than on the Atlantic coast—no doubt because the prevailing currents and deeper water close to shore mean that more true pelagic species pass West Coast than East Coast sites. Despite the incredible opportunities at places such as Cape Ann and Cape Cod in Massachusetts and Cape Hatteras in North Carolina, the seawatch at Avalon is the only full-time watch conducted on the Atlantic coast, making it an important place to monitor the status of and trends in waterbird populations and migration.

The counting is fun, but it's also good science. Nearshore waterbird flights of this magnitude have major implications for coastal ecology and coastal resource management. The concentration of birds from vast areas to the north into a narrow nearshore zone in a relatively short period calls for their protection from the direct and secondary impacts of overharvesting fisheries and potential oil spills in Delaware Bay. (A very high percentage of the birds passing Avalon crosses Delaware Bay a short time later, and many stop to feed in the rich waters at the mouth of the bay. Many ultimately winter there.) Counting at Avalon, even though only a little over a decade old, may already be yielding some good data on the status and trends of waterbird populations. Counts from Avalon have occasioned the U.S. Fish and Wildlife Service to radically reassess its estimates of Red-throated Loon and scoter populations in eastern North America.

The Avalon Seawatch is conducted from dawn to dusk, from official sunrise to official sunset. Usually, the biggest daily pulse occurs in the first few hours after sunrise, with a resurgence in late afternoon. Scoters, however, often peak in the afternoon. The watch is conducted regardless of the weather. Although watching and counting might be difficult, some of the really good flights occur in nasty weather. At the peak of the season, some birds are moving virtually all day long, every day. Wind direction plays a role, but unlike with hawks, it influences not whether birds move but where the flight line is found. Northwest winds spur movement, particularly with cormorants, but often the birds are far at sea, distant from watchers. Northeast winds (the classic wind direction of coastal storms) create a tailwind and a broad-front movement, with birds found almost anywhere; some move over the marshes behind the barrier island of Avalon, others move high overhead, and others move far at sea. The best winds are east, southeast, and, surprisingly, south. Perhaps due to their structure and aerodynamics, many seabirds seem to prefer a headwind for migration. This is understandable for gannets, which often use dynamic soaring for traveling, but it is also true for loons and scoters—perhaps they gain lift by flying into the wind. Southerly winds slow the speed of the flight, making flocks easier to view, but more importantly, they put birds close in, with many flocks going right down the inlet by the watch site. Even after fifteen years of watching, it never ceases to amaze us how, after several fairly slow days, a fresh southeast wind will seemingly open the flood gates, bringing waves of waterbirds in a flight that may last from dawn to dusk.

Peak flights for specific seabirds are not as predictable as they are for hawks and can occur over a wider period. This is because many seabirds, being piscivores (fish eaters), follow baitfish concentrations. The fall pulses of various species of baitfish—mullet early, menhaden midseason, and sand eels (sand launce) late, to oversimplify—migrate south and east to deeper waters in relation to water temperature, not by the calendar. This can vary greatly from year to year. For example, in colder falls, the peak gannet migration may be in early November, while in warmer years it might occur in December. Red-throated Loon peak flights are also clearly related to water temperature but usually occur in mid-November. Scoters, in contrast, seem to move more by the calendar. Being primarily shellfish eaters, they are not as linked to water temperature, because clams and mussels are stationary. The scoter peak almost invariably occurs during the third or

A quickly moving flock of scoters passes the Avalon Eighth Street Jetty. DAVE WARD

perhaps the fourth week of October (on occasion, the first week of November), particularly during a period of moderate south to southeast winds. A number of local birders try to hit the peak day every year, and it's fairly easily done. This is when great "whacks" (an informal Newfound-lander's term for a whole bunch of something) of sea ducks come down the coast and, with frenzied watching, the daily count may exceed 100,000 birds.

Many of the dynamics of the Avalon Seawatch flights are yet to be learned. A frequently asked question is, "How much does the seawatch miss in its count?" We believe that a large percentage of the flight is being counted. Scoters, sea ducks, and loons feed mainly in fairly shallow water; therefore, during migration, they stick to the nearshore zone, where water depths allow them to feed easily. We have made a number of informal counts, keeping track of birds seen on pelagic bird trips and from fishing boats of the numbers seen "beyond the horizon" (more than about 5 miles offshore), and compared them with the seawatch totals for the day. We found that increasingly fewer birds were seen the farther offshore we went, prompting us to believe that for most species, and particularly for loons and scoters, a very high percentage of the total migration passes within view of the Avalon Seawatch. Northern Gannet numbers fluctuate considerably from year to year, and this may be the principal species that often migrates beyond the sight of land. Gannets follow baitfish schools, and if the bait is inshore, that's where the gannets will be. But often (and the pattern is sea-sonal more than daily), if regional fish stocks are thickest offshore—say, 10 to 15 miles off on Five Fathom Bank—that's where most gannets will be found. This can be true for Bonaparte's Gulls too.

Not unlike hawkwatching, there are days when the birds are quite dis-tant. Distant flights, usually occurring on strong northwest winds, can place a premium on the considerable skills of the counter. Then, almost all iden-tifications are based on "gizz" (general impression, shape, and size)—and

Northern Gannets are a staple at the Avalon Seawatch, some close in and others far out to sea.

often on the gizz of the flock rather than of an individual bird. The identification of distant seabirds is not some form of wizardry known only by the counter (though at times it may seem so); such identification skills result from practice, time spent, repetition, and experience. We remember one day with perfect conditions: the lighting (the afternoon light was behind us, not in our eyes), the clarity (high pressure and no haze), the lack of heat waves (air and water temperature similar), and a favorable tide (low tide—the average tidal change is about 4 feet, which in effect placed the counter 4 feet higher). Under these conditions, with our 32-power scopes, we could easily identify adult Northern Gannets going behind the Avalon Shoals buoy, which is 7.3 miles off the beach. These unquestionable gannets were tiny, brilliant white dots of light, arcing up in the sky and then back down, in their characteristic dynamic, soaring flight. To some visitors, this may have seemed like voodoo birding, but the counter was just doing his job, duly counting the passage of distant seabirds.

Northern Gannets, Double-crested Cormorants, the three scoters (black, surf, and white-winged), Common Loons, and Red-throated Loons are the key species monitored by the Avalon Seawatch. They are the big seven, the mid-Atlantic benchmark birds, the primary species passing the watch in the biggest numbers. Each is distinctive. Cormorants move in messy, sloppy V formations, usually low, but sometimes quite high. Scoters pass in fast, long, wavy ribbons low on the horizon. Most days, Red-throated Loons travel low over the water, but they can also move as loose flocks a tier above the scoters and gannets. Gannets sail up and down through the waves low on the horizon, but they often travel in strings too.

In addition to the big seven, the Avalon Seawatch monitors over seventy-five species of waterbirds each season and sometimes fifty species in a day. Waterbirds include all waterfowl, herons, egrets, ibis, loons, grebes, shearwaters, pelicans, jaegers, gulls, terns, and alcids. (Actually, the seawatch counter also logs raptors, shorebirds, and even passing Monarch butterflies.) It is truly surprising how many species migrate over the ocean during the course of the season. Besides scoters, other principal diving ducks include Greater and Lesser Scaup, Common Eider, Long-tailed Duck, Bufflehead, and Red-breasted Merganser. Some find it surprising that many puddle ducks clearly choose to migrate over the ocean. Black ducks, Mallards, Northern Pintails, and American Wigeons are all seen in significant numbers. Green-winged Teal are a common migrant some days, both migrating in pure flocks and mixing in among the strings of scoters. Mixed-species flocks add a definite challenge and spice to the Avalon Seawatch. One of the great surprises is the Wood Duck; they commonly migrate over the ocean, and clearly by choice, perhaps for safety from hawks and hunters. Wood Ducks frequently mix in with other species, and one of the strangest sights (though we're now accustomed to it) is to see several hundred scoters go by with five or ten Wood Ducks happily holding their place in the string.

Except for very early in the season and maybe during frigid December days with gale-force northwest winds, there is rarely a dull moment at the Avalon Seawatch. Late August brings lots of terns. Common Terns migrate early, while Forster's head south much later. Cormorants peak in early October, and scoters peak in late October. Common Loons peak in October, and Red-throated Loons usually peak in mid-November. Late November usually brings the major Northern Gannet and gull flights. There is always something interesting to be seen at the Avalon Seawatch: numerous Bottlenose Dolphins in the inlet, the odd Humpback Whale offshore, migrant songbirds battling their way in off the ocean at dawn, a Short-eared Owl migrating in from offshore, or gannet and gull feeding frenzies. In October and early November, these blitzes of fish and birds are always accompanied by Parasitic Jaegers, the pirates of the sea, boring in to steal fish from hapless gulls and terns.

The Avalon Seawatch is one of the region's newer phenomena, and for many birders, it is one of the most exciting. You never know

Stormy weather sometimes produces excellent flights of seabirds.

CAPE MAY FALL SEABIRD FAST FACTS

Although some seventy-five species of over-ocean migrants are counted during their southbound migration at Avalon, New Jersey, each year, the following species are either the most likely or, in a few cases, the most desirous. Most flight identification is by classic "gizz" (general impression, shape, and size) and by flock behavior. The following "fast facts" hold true for Avalon; relative abundance and timing vary to the north and south along the Atlantic coast.

Loons
Pale below; long, thin pointed wings; long, thin neck; steady, fluid, flexible flap; direct, powered flight; flies low or high.

Red-throated Loon
Abundant in late season. Peaks mid-November; flies all day. Forms very loose (nonformation) but sometimes large (100+) flocks. Droop-necked, hump-backed; light, slim neck; head not much thicker than neck; no obvious feet behind bird; back appears grayish; upturned bill noted if close.

Common Loon
Common. Peaks early November; flies mostly in morning. Very loose and small flocks (5 to 10). Larger, stockier than Red-throated Loon; heavy bodied; thicker neck; larger head with peaked crown and thicker, heavier bill; obvious "rudderlike" paddle feet; frequently flies with bill open.

Northern Gannet
Common in late season. Peaks are variable, dependent on baitfish and water temperature, in November or early December. Very large; very long, thin, pointed wings; long, thick neck; long pointed bill; very long body; pointed tail—the "compass bird," pointed on all four corners. Migrates both singly and in small flocks (25+); flock is usually a string, usually low over water but rarely at medium height. Direct, powered, flapping flight; powerful but stiff flaps with flexing wing tips. Flies "uphill" with head higher than tail. In a strong wind will use shearwater-like bounding or arcing flight (dynamic soaring); sometimes soar. Dramatic dives from high overhead when feeding (plunge diving). Adults are white with black wing tips, juveniles are dark, and subadults are variable.

Cormorants

Large, mostly all dark at any distance; long wings, neck, and body; stiffer flap than loons, but some flex seen; cupped or bowed wings; occasional to frequent glides.

Double-crested Cormorant

Abundant. Peaks in mid–October. Forms very large flocks (100s); wavy, snaking, undulating, sloppy flocks—sometimes in vague V formations, but often just a wavy line abreast; usually low, but sometimes very high. Often soars when over land (flapping frequently to do so), with flock turning in unison. Thin neck and chest give "rear-heavy" look.

Great Cormorant

Uncommon, but usually almost daily. Very small flocks at times (2 to 6), but usually found as singles in Double-crested Cormorant flocks. Noticeably larger than double-crested, with broader wings and heavier chest, neck, and head; therefore appears more balanced. Juveniles show pale belly rather than pale chest of juvenile Double-crested Cormorant.

Geese

Large and chunky; stiff, shallow flap; usually noisy, but not always.

Canada Goose

Common, peaks in October. Usually forms neat, disciplined, tight V-shaped flocks; flies with steady cadence in direct, nonwavering flight; flocks sometimes become sloppy when birds are tired after long flight; usually high overhead, but sometimes low over water.

Snow Goose

Common, October and November. Although white, can appear as dark silhouettes against morning sun to the east. Flocks often form several Vs or Ws; often very high overhead—white flickering against blue. Distinguish from **Tundra Swan** (uncommon) high overhead in late season by quicker flap, shorter neck, and black wing tips.

Brant

Common, mid to late season. Medium-sized, chunky. Stiff, bowed-wing flap. Swept-back wings. Brant move in distinctive irregular, constantly changing, fairly tight flocks; sometimes in strings but

continues on next page

never neat Vs; more of a "bunch" or ball of birds. Short-necked, stern-heavy in shape, yet elegant when close. Fly low and fast.

Scoters

Abundant mid to late season. Peak third to fourth week of October. Under many field conditions, appear all dark. Scoters form very large, fairly tight strings (like wavy ribbons) and vague changing Vs at times; move faster, more purposefully than Double-crested Cormorants; faster, stiffer wing beat; flock shape changes quickly, with knots forming; ripples occur, but not the pronounced undulations of cormorant flocks; usually quite low to the water, but sometimes fairly high.

Black Scoter

Round head; small bill; male shows orange knob on bill if close; female's pale cheek fairly easily discerned, even at a distance.

Surf Scoter

Different profile from Black Scoter: Black shows distinct forehead and bill, but surf shows no forehead, just large triangular bill meeting top of head—a wedge shape visible at some distance. Male's white head patches easily seen; female's head pattern disappears at medium distance (unlike Black Scoter). Surf is slightly thinner bodied, less stocky than black and shows (subtly) more pointed, swept-back wings.

White-winged Scoter

Far less common than surf and black, yet daily in some numbers late in season. Much larger, heavier; white wing patch distinctive and visible, even at great distance.

Jaegers

Closely related to gulls. Predators and pirates; dark, foreboding, powerful fliers; frequently seen energetically chasing gulls and terns; strong, steady, purposeful flight and flap; in chases, uses bursts of speed unmatched by gulls. Look for "wing flash" of white at base of primaries; distinctly down-curved wings are particularly seen in characteristic buoyant glides.

Parasitic Jaeger

Uncommon, but almost daily throughout season. Accounts for 99 percent of jaegers seen from shore at Avalon Seawatch. Laughing

Gull size, but much heavier, more powerful, more efficient flight; usually flies low over water, flapping often interspersed with bow-winged glides; sometimes uses bounding, arcing flight and (rarely) soars; in chases, often evokes small Peregrine Falcon, but wings narrower, more swept back. Acrobatic, maneuverable, piratic behavior is a key feature; often flies straight up to intercept "victims." Small wedge-shaped head with flat crown and pencil-thin bill.

Pomarine Jaeger

Annual in very small numbers. Larger, heavier-bodied, broader-winged than Parasitic Jaeger, at times appearing almost Herring Gull size; flight is direct, steady, and Herring Gull-like, with continuous wingbeats, few glides; piratic flight more direct, less acrobatic than parasitic; often drives subject to the water. Large, rounded head with heavy, thick bill.

Long-tailed Jaeger

True rarity near shore. More pelagic than other jaegers; smaller, slimmer, narrower-winged than parasitic; very ternlike, buoyant flight; rarely pirates; wing flash is minimal or absent; often looks grayish. Small, rounded head; small, stubby bill; short, thick neck; slim belly.

Other Possibilities

With so many species of waterbirds counted each day and season at the Avalon Seawatch, every identification can be a challenge. Expect (or hope for) the following groups and species. Use popular field guides for key identification points, but remember that gizz is more readily used than standard plumage traits to identify distant migrants in flight.

Horned Grebe

Almost daily migrant in small numbers in late season. Look for a small, pale, thin-winged, buzzy bird, low on the water, and flying "uphill"—with the whole body canted at an upward angle.

Red-necked Grebe

Annual in very small numbers; appears similar to Red-throated Loon, but more drooped neck, more humped back, and noticeable paddlelike feet. Look for white wing patches on both grebes.

continues on next page

Brown Pelican

Numerous migrant early to midseason. Look for a huge bird with wide wings, ponderous flap, and long glides; usually low on the water but sometimes high, and often soars.

White Pelican

Annual in fall at Cape May and has been seen on several occasions at Avalon Seawatch.

Great Blue Heron

Frequent migrant, usually early and late in the day. Sometimes in strings, sometimes low on the water, but often quite high. Slow, stiff, heavy flap. All herons and egrets are seen as migrants; big flocks are often noted in evenings on northwest winds following a cold front.

Diving Ducks

A staple of the Avalon and mid-Atlantic seawatches. **Red-breasted Merganser, Bufflehead, Long-tailed Duck,** and **scaup** are the most common, seen in large numbers each year. Red-breasted Merganser may look somewhat like Red-throated Loon, with long, thin neck and bill, but shows distinct pattern and travels in tight flocks and strings. Both **Common Eider** and **King Eider** are seen in small numbers (king much scarcer than common). Most eiders are juveniles and are a much warmer brown than female scoter. Look for big, heavy-bodied, stocky birds with whitish underwings. Slower wing beat than scoter. Common Eider shows wedge-shaped head and drooped head and bill in flight. King is less drooped, lacks wedge-shaped head, and shows straighter bill.

Puddle Ducks

Surprisingly common over-ocean migrants; most usually fly high. **Northern Pintail** are common; use pale coloration and long, thin, attenuated shape to identify. **Green-winged Teal** (small) are numerous; look for tight, irregular, twisting, turning flocks— usually low in the waves; singles and small groups often mixed in with scoter flocks. **Woods Ducks** are also quite frequently seen in scoter flocks (and in small groups); show long tail and raised head.

Gulls and Terns

Counted in large numbers. **Least Terns** are very early migrants, with most gone by late August; look for a small tern with a quick, choppy, deep, energetic flap. **Common Terns** are early season migrants; **Forster's Terns** are late. **Caspian Terns** are early (September–October) and heavier-bodied and wider-winged than royals. **Royal Terns** are common locals until late season. **Bonaparte's Gulls** are a numerous favorite, migrating in tight, dense flocks in late season. **Black-legged Kittiwake** is an uncommon but regular prize from shore in late season; look for a thick-necked, long, thin-winged gull with characteristic buoyant, arcing flight.

Alcids

Sometimes numerous offshore, but rare in the shallow, inshore coastal waters of the mid-Atlantic. All eastern alcids have been recorded at the Avalon Seawatch, but 99 percent are **Razorbills.** Look for a chunky, black and white football shape with short, narrow wings and very rapid wing beats. Sometimes move as singles and sometimes in scoter flocks. Usually low over water. Mostly late season and in winter.

Pelagics

Anything is possible, particularly after hurricanes or coastal nor'easters, but all true pelagics are very rare from land at Avalon (and throughout the mid-Atlantic) in fall. **Sooty Shearwaters** are uncommon but expected in late May and early June, and **Cory's Shearwaters** and **Greater Shearwaters** are sometimes seen from shore in July and August. **Wilson's Storm-Petrel** is frequently seen in small numbers in June and July at Avalon, more often in Delaware Bay. All other pelagics fall into the "how lucky can you get?" category. In autumn, only **Manx Shearwater** is normally expected in nearshore waters, yet is rare within sight of land in the mid-Atlantic region. **Northern Fulmar** has been seen just twice from the Avalon Seawatch in fall and twice at Cape May Point in winter. No albatrosses yet, but they are wished for virtually every day at Avalon and at every seawatch. ◼

what you'll see there—perhaps some storm-tossed waif from far at sea or far away. Avalon's town motto is "Cooler by a Mile," referring to its key geographic location an honest 1 mile farther out to sea than neighboring towns. Seawatchers readily agree with this slogan, as birds coming down the coast hit the beach at the Seventh Street site greeted by the official counter, a bank of tally clickers, and a lineup of scopes and watchers along the seawall.

RARITIES

As we ambled off the Cape May Hawkwatch at Cape May Point State Park with Vince Elia and Bob Barber and headed for our cars on the far side of the parking lot, a young man approached our jovial group. His pace wasn't hurried but was direct, his appearance earnest. As local birders, we are all frequently asked many questions, but his lack of binoculars led us to assume that his question would be of the "Could you tell me how to get to the Concrete Ship?" variety. We stopped in our tracks, though, when the man said simply, "Would you folks like to see a wheatear?" Vince, the grand master of the raised eyebrow, took the lead immediately, replying, "Uh, yeah, we would, but, you know, they don't occur here. Are you sure it's a wheatear?"

The fellow, to his credit, looked exasperated for only a millisecond and then offered quickly and succinctly, "Let me explain. I lived in England for five years and they nested in my pasture. Believe me, there's a Northern Wheatear over by the picnic pavilion." As he pointed, our walk broke into a run, thank you's shouted over our shoulders, and, as we neared the pavilion, a Northern Wheatear flew right by us, bold white tail pattern gleaming. We all shouted at once, the better to alert all the birders within earshot. As heads turned, car doors slammed, and at least one egg salad sandwich hit the ground, the wheatear landed in the grassy field by the lighthouse and began to calmly feed, oblivious of the ensuing eruption around it. Thus began one of the more interesting Cape May rarity events of our memory.

It was a beautiful, sunny, mid-September Sunday at Cape May Point, and the state park was full of people—birders, tourists, fishermen, bathers, and lighthouse lookers. The Northern Wheatear, a handsome juvenile, was cooperative. It stayed all afternoon, feeding on the lawn, long enough for the word to get out far and wide throughout Cape May and even throughout the state. A crowd converged, and soon several hundred people were lined up, all enjoying the wheatear. Clay tried to find David Sibley, who was carrying out stopover ecology research transects at Higbee Beach. Clay wandered around for about an hour, pausing at each survey point to yell, "Daaa-vid, wheeeeeatear." (Remember birding in pre–cell-phone days?) Finally, from deep in the forest, came a soft reply that was typical of David's

focus and commitment: "Yes, I'd like to see it, but I need to finish my transects first." (For the record, he did see it later that afternoon.) As the lined-
up birders looked at the wheatear, they attracted the continuing interest of
nonbirders, beachgoers, and the like, who, to a person, naturally asked,
"What are you looking at?" One tourist turned to his wife and announced,
"They're looking at a weed-eater." Later that day we overheard someone
talking about the rare weed-whacker that the bird-watchers were excited
about.

About midafternoon, a newly arrived group of British birders, fresh
from the airport, drove into the state park for the first time, got out of their
rental car, stretched, and looked around. They immediately saw the group
of wheatear-watchers and headed over. "What have you got, mate?" the first
Brit asked. "A Northern Wheatear on the lawn here," was our proud reply.
"Oh, jolly good," said one Brit, "I guess that's a good bird here, but we saw
about twenty on the tarmac at the airport yesterday in Britain as we got on
the plane. Not really a rarity for us, you know?" he said as he stifled a jet-
lag yawn. The Brits did, however, set up their scopes and look at the bird, if
only so they could add it to their Cape May and North American lists.

A few minutes later, an American birder calmly and without any fanfare noted "Oh, there's a Yellow-rumped Warbler in the cedars. It's the first
one I've seen this year. It's a bit early for them." Someone in the crowd
kindly remembered the Brits at the other end of the assembled crowd and
passed the word down, thinking, correctly, that they might like to see the
warbler. We'll never forget the sight of the U.K. crowd at a dead run down
the park road loudly shouting, "Yellow-rumped Warbler! Yellow-rumped
Warbler!" to a distant compatriot as they raced for the twitch.

What They Are and Where They Come From

There are few better examples of one man's ceiling being another man's
floor than in birding. Due to a bird's given range, rarity is in the eye of the
beholder. Royal Tern is an abundant, everyday bird at Cape May in autumn,
but if you are a birder from Kansas, seeing a flock of Royal Terns on the
beach at South Cape May is a pretty big deal, and rightly so. Conversely, that
Kansas birder likely sees thousands of Lark Buntings in a season at home, but
one in the dunes at Stone Harbor Point makes for a red-letter day for Cape
May birders. Relative rarity is based not only on where a person is from and
the range of various species but also on a birder's experience and the
amount of traveling he or she has done. One of our biggest faux pas as
birding leaders occurred on the final day of a weeklong Cape May workshop, when a participant from California quietly said, "I would have
expected to see Northern Cardinal here." In our quest for godwits, American Avocet, and Swainson's Hawk, we had not once "pished out" one of

Rarities can occur at any seaason; this Fork-tailed Flycatcher in West Cape May was found on December 13, 1994.

our most common birds. Luckily, an eleventh-hour stop that afternoon corrected our oversight. (Visiting western birders frequently ask us about Carolina Wrens, another of our most common birds, which, though not really secretive, can be maddeningly hard to find. Our advice is simple: Make a random stop virtually anywhere in the county and try pishing. Usually one will pop up. But don't even bother trying at Higbee Beach or the Rea Farm. Even though Carolina Wrens are abundant there, they're completely unresponsive. Why? They've heard it all. Each of them has probably been pished at hundreds if not thousands of times. It's much better to find a "virgin" Carolina Wren virtually anywhere else, away from all the birding traffic. The same is true for Carolina Chickadees.)

There are two types of rarities at Cape May. One is the "one man's rags are another man's riches" variety, akin to how great it is for us to see saucy Gambel's Quail at friends' feeders in southeastern Arizona, or how thrilling it is for a birder from Iowa to see a Black Skimmer at Cape May. The other is the true rarity, a bird from far away or far at sea, well out of its normal range. Some call them "hotline" birds—birds to stir the excitement of all— and it's birds of this magnitude, sometimes even "mega-rarities," that help put Cape May firmly on the map of prime birding destinations worldwide.

Rarities are attracted to Cape May for all the same reasons that Cape May is a crossroads of migration. Birds originating from all points of the compass converge on Cape May. The very names of some of Cape May's exciting rarities evoke their exotic origins: Mountain Bluebird (high western meadows), Rock Wren (canyons of the arid West), Atlantic Puffin (far North Atlantic). Even better are Eurasian Kestrel, Eurasian Woodcock, or even Mongolian Plover (an evocative name we prefer over Lesser Sand Plover; Cape May owns the only Atlantic coast record of this Asian shorebird). All our almost semiannual Fork-tailed Flycatchers come from South America (austral migration overshoots). Arguably our rarest bird ever, the Whiskered Tern, hails from the Mediterranean basin. Cape May's 1993 (July 12–15) Whiskered Tern was the first North American record; in 1998 (August 8–12), the same individual (probably) appeared again in Cape May. Thus, Cape May has the only two North American records (although the 1993 bird was subsequently seen across Delaware Bay at Delaware's Little

Creek Wildlife Area and vicinity). Of northern origin, two Black-backed Woodpeckers were seen by 400 observers on October 5 and 6, 1963, during the annual New Jersey Audubon Society autumn weekend event.

We know that our vagrants come from all points of the compass. We know, of course, their general origin from range maps, but rarely do we have the luxury of knowing the exact origin or destination of a rarity. For that reason, a Sandhill Crane that wintered at Cape May from November 14, 1986, to January 20, 1987, was a special bird. Sandhill Cranes are not mega-rarities; they are annual migrants at Cape May—mostly in fall, sometimes in spring—but in very small numbers. (They have become increasingly more frequent in recent years, no doubt a result of the rapid expansion of their breeding range: Sandhill Cranes now breed in Pennsylvania, Maine, and the Canadian Maritimes in small numbers.) Yet to us, cranes are a special rarity. One or a pair of Sandhill Cranes, bugling as they soar high overhead among a kettle of hawks, represent all that is the excitement of birds and birding at Cape May. The Sandhill Crane that arrived in November 1986 was banded and distinctly color-marked. Through research, Dave Ward learned that it had been banded as a juvenile on its wintering grounds, near Gainesville, Florida, in March 1986. The following fall it arrived in Cape May and attempted to winter. However, a freeze-up and snow cover forced it south in January, where it spent February 12 to March 5, 1987, at Kent Island, Maryland (on Chesapeake Bay). August 27 to September 27, 1987, the crane was refound near Massey, Ontario, and October 2–8, 1987, it was in Mackinac County, Michigan. In Ontario and Michigan it rejoined other Sandhill Cranes, back in its traditional breeding and staging areas. These seemingly unusual peregrinations were probably not unusual at all and a good example of how one of Cape May's rarities both got here and where it went afterward. We often assume that a vagrant is doomed, if not a victim of weather and climate, at least permanently removed from the breeding population and the gene pool. Cape May's 1987 Sandhill Crane (frequently and popularly enjoyed at the Meadows, in cornfields at the Beanery, and circling daily over Cape May Point) proved us wrong—a healthy survivor of its long itinerant journey.

Any far-flung rarity traveling the East Coast during fall or spring migration has a good chance of being routed through Cape May by prevailing winds and geography. The funneling effect, the passage of birds through the hourglasslike bottleneck, functions to eventually concentrate any rarities somewhere in the general region of the Cape May peninsula, if not right around Cape May City and Cape May Point. And in most cases, if a rarity is around, it stands a good chance of being found. For a rarity to slip through Cape May, it must pass through a seine of hundreds of searchers, the binocular views of many birders. Certainly one major factor in the number of rarities found is that so many birders cover Cape May, not just at peak seasons but year-round. Cape May has its own version of the Patagonian rest-stop effect, referring to Patagonia, Arizona, where birders searching for the rare and local Rose-throated Becard and Thick-billed Kingbird found numerous other great rarities, such as the Buff-collared Nightjar, Ferruginous Pygmy Owl, Black-capped Gnatcatcher, Yellow Grosbeak, Five-striped Sparrow, and Fan-tailed Warbler at the same roadside rest stop. It implies a snowball effect, where more and more birders find more and more good birds through increased coverage. Commonly, birders searching for one uncommon bird find others, and these sightings are facilitated and disseminated by today's instantaneous information exchange. At Cape May, rarities frequently come in twos and threes—a factor of the sheer convergence of and coverage by birders. As a result, Cape May is one of the best known rarity spots or vagrant traps in North America. In the United States (excluding outposts such as Alaska's Attu and Gambel or whole regions such as southeastern Arizona), Cape May is rivaled only by a few venerable spots such as Point Reyes and Monterey, California; Cape Cod, Massachusetts; or maybe Cape Hatteras, North Carolina, in the frequency, quality, and even dependability of rare birds.

An intangible factor, beyond the amount of coverage, is the *quality* of coverage—the "height of the bar" when it comes to the skill of Cape May birders, both residents and visitors alike. Many local Cape May birders lead tours nationwide and worldwide, and the Cape's visitors include top birders from around the country and globe. Simply put, experience breeds familiarity, and long practice breeds exceptional skill. It bears repeating that several of Cape May's best recent rarities (Rock Wren, Spotted Towhee, and MacGillivray's Warbler) were first found and identified by chip note and then finally pished out and seen for confirmation (and the eventual delight of many). Skill has played a large role in Cape May's large bird list. The local birders are not an insignificant group, and the yearly Cape May guest book includes many of the top birders in North America and beyond.

We also can't ignore the aspect of "standing on the shoulders of giants." So much of today's knowledge is based on the immense ornithological record that came before. Birding skills—know-how and identification points—have grown exponentially in recent years but are nonetheless rooted in the many discoveries of the past. For example, Witmer Stone stated plainly that the "Western" Willet (the western race) was "impossible to distinguish in life." With today's knowledge, this is done routinely by Cape May birders every day. The point is that it took the work of many to reach this place. Certainly the monumental advances in optics have played a key role, allowing us to see more colors and details than were possible as recently as a decade ago. We doubt that any of us could see the paler tone of an adult nonbreeding Western Willet with the binoculars Stone used in the 1920s and 1930s.

Although Cape May is easily best known for its autumn vagrants, rarities can occur in any season. In several recent years, the spring rarity list has surpassed the fall's. And because of the endless migration at Cape May, with birds on the move throughout the entire year, surprises can occur at any time. Two notable examples occurred during the writing of this book, when phone calls beckoned with news of a February Bohemian Waxwing (only the second Cape May County record) at Nummy's Island and a mid-July Brown Booby fishing in The Rips off Cape May Point. For Cape May locals, it can be hard to get any work done. One fall, for five mornings straight, just as Clay was picking up his pen, the phone range with urgent, not to be ignored bird news.

Late Autumn Vagrants

Although rarities can occur virtually any time at Cape May and in almost any weather, there is one key rarity season, late autumn. Just after the sea-watch has peaked in the last few days of October, birders turn their sights away from the numbers and toward the few, maybe the only. This is when the search begins for bigger game. Cape May may be the one place in North America (outside of Alaska) that has actually named and boasts a "rarity season" when, akin to September in the United Kingdom's Scilly Isles, birders gather in anticipation of the expected rarities (although, admittedly, in nowhere near the numbers of the "Scilly twitchers").

For years many, mid-Atlantic birders generally considered November to be an in-between season—good for hawks and eagles on mountain ridges but, from a passerine standpoint, a lull before winter finches arrived. But we were all ignoring at least one key clue—the regular occurrence of Western Kingbirds, often showing up for inexplicable reasons (we thought they must have been blown east earlier in the fall). At Cape May, Western Kingbirds sometimes showed up in numbers; we saw a remarkable eight sitting together on a fence near Higbee Beach on November 24, 1984. But Cape May birders never expected or searched for rare songbirds much after October. The warblers were through, and it was time to hawkwatch or sea-watch. This slowly changed in the late 1980s, partly as a result of the "British invasion." They (and then-resident artist David Sibley) worked nights so that they could bird all day, and they birded all the time, regardless of season or protocol. By 1994, Cave Swallows, of the southwestern race, were seen annually at Cape May in November and in numbers; at the time, Cape May was the only spot in the East to have multiple records. And while many birders were amazed at Cape May's luck (not to mention its birders' skill), others, particularly Paul Lehman, began to think that something else was up. And in

Cape May birders have seen Western Kingbirds in November with surprising frequency.

November 1997, an epiphany of a sort occurred in Cape May birding—one that would soon spread to birders on the entire eastern seaboard. As Lehman wrote in *Birding* in 2003:

> It all began in November 1997 . . . okay, it really didn't "begin" then. A few local birders had known for many years that the late-autumn period was the best time of year in which to look for landbird strays from the west and southwest. But relatively few observers knew of this phenomenon until that fateful year, when an onslaught of rarities and reverse migrants from the west and south at Cape May would forever change the landscape of autumn birding in the East. Now let's fast forward to November 6, 1997. That day a Brown-chested Martin was discovered in Cape May, the second record ever for North America of this austral migrant from South America. In the days that followed, the list of strays and reverse migrants found locally would become the headiest on record: 5 Cave Swallows, Ash-throated Flycatcher, MacGillivray's Warbler, Western Tanager; and late Chimney Swifts, a couple Cliff Swallows, a dozen Barn Swallows, and an amazing 15 or so species of warblers. The late birds were almost all likely not individuals that were finally working their way south. More likely they were birds that followed a southerly wind flow back northwards from well to the south—perhaps from as far away as Florida and the Gulf Coast states! Hundreds of birders from many states descended on Cape May to see the martin, the Cave Swallows, and the other rarities. News spread throughout the East about the "November

rarity season." Following that year, many eastern birders dedicated themselves to search for these waifs between late October and late November, and to carefully keep appraised of the daily and long-term weather forecasts.

For many years, the concept of reverse migration has been well known, if not well understood, and it is thought to be the source of certain vagrant birds. Reverse migration is also called mirror-image migration, where, in theory, migrant birds' innate orientation is 180 degrees off from the direction they should be going. It is maybe akin to inadvertently going the wrong way on a one-way street. (Reverse migration should not be confused with the short-duration morning flight, during which birds reorient. True reverse migration occurs over time—weeks or months.) Reverse migration is not rare. In late autumn, for every reverse-migrant rarity found by birders, probably dozens or hundreds perish, either at sea or with the onset of cold weather wherever they end up. And, of course, it's not just true rarities; as in the list offered by Lehman, numerous individual common species return north at a time when they should be in the far south—for example, the Barn Swallow, which is very uncommon past mid-October at Cape May. One possible facet of reverse migration, rather than an exact 180-degree misorientation, is that birds may simply go with the flow, following an air mass wherever it takes them. This is essentially going in the direction that a tailwind takes them. Such a scenario probably results in many fall vagrants' eventual arrival at Cape May: A warm air mass (warm front) carries them far to the north, then a cold front with northwest winds deposits them back at Cape May Point. This may explain the Cave Swallow phenomenon. It seems that the southern Great Plains population of this species is growing so rapidly that numbers of wandering birds continue to increase in the East, with many carried back to Cape May by northwest winds. As many as 215 Cave Swallows were seen in a single day at Cape May on November 10, 2005, during strong northwest winds.

Since it was first recognized and drew attention in 1997, we now have a fair understanding of the November rarity season at Cape May. The same weather patterns that create good spring migration in the East, and at Cape May, bring us western and southern species in the fall—reverse migrants and go-with-the-flow wanderers. The counterclockwise southwesterly or southerly flow in the warm sector of a low-pressure system (warm front) pumps warm air up from the south, bringing late Indian summer temperatures to Cape May, and often rare birds. Each year, these conditions produce such unlikely birds as Ash-throated Flycatchers, Western Kingbirds, and Cave Swallows at Cape May. It was an unusual variation on this theme—a "perfect storm," as it were—that produced the November 6, 1997, manna

HURRICANE BIRDS

For centuries, Atlantic hurricanes and the potentially equally power-ful winter nor'easters have shaped the lives of Jersey Shore residents and been a powerful force in shaping the landscape as well. Hurricanes have long rearranged beachfronts, inlets, and towns on Cape May County's barrier islands, carnage dating back to our first recorded history. Birders enjoying the seawatch at Seventh Street in Avalon often casually ask, "Why is this Seventh Street? Where are the other six streets?" The answer is sobering: The other six streets are now under-water out in the inlet, taken by successive storms culminating in the storm of 1950. The semi-Victorian home right on the seawall, to the right of the seawatch (the one with the third-story cupola), once sat on Fourth Street but was moved to its current location as water lapped at its foundation. (Clay's parents almost bought that house in 1950 when it was still on Fourth Street. They were always glad they didn't, but Clay some-times laments that decision, since today, in its current location, the third story would be a heck of a spot for seawatching.) Similarly, the town of South Cape May was decimated by the beach erosion of a succession of storms; its destruction was finalized by the 1944 and 1950 storms.

A number of powerful storms have brought varying degrees of destruction to the Jersey Cape, beginning, in our time, with the unnamed storms in 1926 and 1933, the Long Island Express Hurricane of 1938, and arguably the worst-ever hurricane, the Great Atlan-tic Hurricane of 1944. This was followed by the November 1950 storm; Hurricanes Carol, Edna, and Hazel in 1954; Connie and Diane in 1955; Donna in 1960; Agnes in 1972; Belle in 1976; David in 1979; Gloria in 1985; Bob in 1991; Bertha and Fran in 1996; Dennis and Floyd in 1999; and Isabel in 2003. Since the 1870s, eight hurricanes of category 2 through 5 have passed within 65 miles of the New Jersey coast. Glo-ria was the closest, which passed 26

Bad weather can bring great birds, such as this Pomarine Jaeger, close to shore.

miles offshore. It has apparently been more than 100 years since the eye of a hurricane actually made landfall in New Jersey, when an unnamed storm with 75-mile-per-hour (mph) winds came ashore at Ocean City on September 16, 1903. September 3, 1821, was the last time a major hurricane (an unnamed category 3) scored a bull's-eye on the New Jersey coast; it came ashore near Cape May with winds of 130 mph and severed Cape May from the rest of the

Hurricane Donna brought destruction and flooding to Cape May Point in 1960. BILL BAILEY

peninsula, according to sparse press accounts. (The hurricane of 1876 lifted the roof off Congress Hall's dining room.) Most storms that make it this far north tend to remain parallel to the coast, pushed offshore by dominant high pressure and pulled along to the northeast by the Gulf Stream currents of the Atlantic.

The greatest and most devastating storm to strike southern New Jersey, however, was not a hurricane (hurricanes are tropical in origin and occur in late summer and fall). The 1962 Storm, as it will always be known, was a classic three-day nor'easter that occurred March 5–7, 1962. Winter nor'easters often bring heavy snow, wind, flooding, and beach erosion to Cape May County, but the 1962 Storm was different. It was, in essence, the "perfect storm," with meteorological conditions unmatched before or since. It was easily the hundred-year storm, and the Weather Channel has even ranked it as the ninth worst storm of the twentieth century nationwide. This storm was so severe because an intense low-pressure system that moved north out of the Carolinas was in turn blocked by a major high-pressure system coming down from Canada. An intense pressure gradient formed—the counterclockwise circulation around the low abutting the clockwise circulation of the opposing, blocking high—creating storm-force easterly winds. The storm essentially didn't move for three days, fueled by record tides resulting from the spring equinox and a new moon. The storm grew more powerful over five tide cycles, each one bringing higher tides. The result was a massive storm surge to nearly 11 feet, with 20-foot waves

continues on next page

HURRICANE BIRDS *continued*

on the beachfront and sustained 75 mph winds. The ocean met the back bays from Cape May north to Island Beach. The storm claimed thirty lives and destroyed thousands of homes along New Jersey's beachfront.

Clay has graphic memories of the 1962 Storm. For a thirteen-year-old, it was an adventure, but during the storm he remembers worrying about the rising tides (the water outside his house in Stone Harbor was 4 feet deep and lapped over the front steps), the real risk of fire from submerged electrical wires sparking under the floorboards, and the plight of his four grandparents in Sea Isle City. His maternal grandparents watched numerous buildings washed into the sea before they were finally rescued by the National Guard on the fourth low tide in the cycle. Their house survived but was beachfront property after the storm, whereas originally it had been half a block from the ocean. Clay has vivid bird memories from the 1962 storm, too. He found a number of dead gulls after the storm, but more happily, at the height of the storm, he watched a Common Loon swimming down the flooded street—both a lifer and an unexpected new "yard bird" at the time.

It has long been recognized that hurricanes transport seabirds far from their normal range. Witmer Stone wrote of an Audubon's Shearwater that he swam out to inspect off the Cape May bathing beach following the hurricane of 1926. About the influx of storm-petrels in 1933, Stone wrote:

> The memorable hurricane which prevailed at Cape May August 21 to 23, 1933, brought many petrels into the town. On this occasion all of the low grounds and many of the streets and gardens were covered with water and petrels were seen flying like swallows over the inundated Beach Drive and the flooded meadows. All that could be identified were Leach's Petrels. The next day, several were still to be seen in the town and on August 25 I found two on the Bayshore north of Cape May Point which for several hours remained close to the beach beating back and forth and never ranging more than a hundred feet offshore. They flew over the sandy beach as much as over the water. This August hurricane saturated all the gardens and orchards for more than a mile inland with saltwater and killed the foliage as if struck by a heavy frost. Besides bringing these petrels into

Cape May it carried them inland as far as Reading and Lan-
caster in Pennsylvania and to many points in New Jersey.

Based on the date and what we have learned subsequently, it is quite
likely that many or most of these storm-petrels may have been Band-
rumped Storm-Petrels, similar to Leach's in appearance.

Stone also recorded one of Cape May's first storm-related Magnificent Frigatebird occurrences. His enjoyable account follows (and ends
with his typical optimism and wonder):

> This tropical species has occasionally been blown north to
> Cape May by hurricanes. Maynard in his *Birds of Eastern
> North America* states that one was shot on the meadows at
> Cape May Court House in the spring of 1877 but gives no
> details or authority for the record. This was the only
> reported occurrence on the New Jersey coast until the tropi-
> cal storm which swept the West Indies and southern Florida
> on the first days of August, 1926. Immediately following this
> storm, on August 3, a Man-o'–war-bird was seen soaring
> over the boardwalk and bathing beach at Cape May by Mrs.
> Emlen H. Fisher who writes me as follows: "The bird I saw
> had a wing spread of at least three feet, the wings tapering to
> a point, and the tail long and like a king-crab's, only with a
> fork at the tip, possibly made by two long feathers crossing
> when the tail was closed. The bill was long and curved over
> at the tip. The color was slate gray all over, and the neck was
> either drawn in like a heron's or there was a sort of pouch or
> bulge below the base of the bill. The bird hung perfectly
> motionless facing the wind for fifteen or twenty minutes and
> did not move an inch in space nor move a feather except to
> turn his head and look down at the small group of people
> gathered below. He finally flew off to the south and disap-
> peared." Mrs. Fisher later examined a Man-o'–war-bird in a
> museum and at once recognized her Cape May bird. The
> fact that I had been on the beach several times on the day
> that Mrs. Fisher saw her bird and on every other day for a
> week or more shows how easily one may miss these rare
> stragglers to our coast and doubtless many more of this or
> other species go unrecorded.

continues on next page

HURRICANE BIRDS *continued*

In the modern era, Hurricane David on September 7, 1979, was one of the first hurricanes during which birders actively sought storm-blown vagrants, and although the pickings were meager by the standards of several storms since, it was memorable. As a member of Civil Defense (known today as Emergency Management), Clay was hunkered down in a basement bunker, in front of maps and a bank of phones and radios, chaffing at the bit to get outside to look for wayward birds. Finally the wind switched from the northeast to the west, signifying the storm's passage to the east, and he was released from duty. He raced for the beach. At Stone Harbor, cresting what was left of the ravaged dunes, he immediately saw a Sooty Tern struggling to get back to the wild Atlantic. A second sooty and a jaeger fought their way down the beach a bit later. The sooty was not only the first-ever hurricane waif for Clay but also a life bird. Several more sootys were found around Cape May—one in the wrack line was beautiful even in death. The following day, Dave Ward watched a Bridled Tern in the flooded South Cape May Meadows, and the day after that a Brown Noddy flew right over the hawkwatch to the wondering eyes of Pete Dunne and several very lucky observers.

In subsequent years, birders have learned to track and actively anticipate hurricane birds, and all along the coast, a few hardy, stalwart (crazy?) souls attempt to position themselves in the path of a storm. This is often no easy proposition, with flooded roads, mandatory evacuations, and downed trees and power lines. But in recent years, in a science or sport akin to tornado chasing, birders have chased hurricanes. There has been an excellent spinoff: We have learned much about the process of how Atlantic hurricanes impact birds, the origins of birds, and the mechanisms by which storms carry them.

Hurricanes displace and transport seabirds by several methods. Although few birds can survive the hurricane-force winds near the eye wall, some are carried many hundreds of miles while inside the eye; the birds stay in the calm air around which the maelstrom rages. Others become entrained in the winds farther out in the storm. Seabirds can routinely survive 60–plus mph winds by simply going with the flow, flying with the wind until either the storm passes or they are deposited on land. A third method of movement is simple displacement, in which birds move out of the path of a hurricane. Hurricane Hugo in 1992 displaced a Brown Booby to a Cape May Point jetty, even though the severe storm was more than 500 miles away and the winds at Cape May didn't top 25 mph. Hurricane Jeanne in 2004 may have been responsible for the Magnificent Frigatebird seen soaring high above the Second Avenue jetty; even though the storm was over Florida at the time, the outer cloud bands stretched all the way to New Jersey. And in 2005, powerful Hurricane Wilma, passing well off the coast, displaced numerous frigatebirds to Cape May and throughout the Northeast. It is quite likely that seabirds can somehow sense and therefore avoid distant tropical storm systems. The moral here is to look for possible storm birds if *any* hurricane passes within 500 miles to the north or south, and look both before the storm and well after it.

For birding, the "ideal" hurricane, if there is such a thing, is a minimal one, a category 1 or 2. Ideally, the eye of the storm should pass over the bird seeker. The second best alternative is to have the eye track inland, to the west. This is because the northeastern quadrant of a hurricane has the strongest winds and is the most likely place for birds to be entrained and possibly stranded. In the western quadrant, they have a tailwind right back out to sea, decreasing any chance of finding them. After the passage of the storm, errant seabirds might be found anywhere on the beach or back bays, but we have learned that the best place to watch for hurricane birds is from Sunset Beach or its vicinity, at the mouth of Delaware Bay. In any sizable storm, many seabirds are blown inland (birders who can't get to the coast should seek out lakes, reservoirs, or rivers, where birds put down to get out of the wind), but as soon as the storm passes or abates, seabirds try to get back to the ocean. If they are healthy, they may accomplish this immediately on the tailwinds on the back side of the low (counterclockwise winds). If they are exhausted, they may not regain the sea until two or three days later (like the Hurricane David Brown Noddy). Many never make it, either killed outright by the storm, dying from starvation, or "wrecked"—stranded on land where they can't take off (a shearwater can't take off in a forest).

To make a complex picture simpler, in the aftermath of a storm, pelagic birds are reorienting and trying to get back out to sea. Depending on where they ended up, many are following the Delaware River and then Delaware Bay. Disinclined to fly over land, they follow the bayshore diversion line south to Cape May Point, go around the tip and over the rips, and finally reach the open Atlantic. We now know that this is a scenario that works, to varying degrees, after any hurricane that even
continues on next page

HURRICANE BIRDS *continued*

grazes our area. In fact, it works to a degree in any substantial storm. Cape May birders should always consider going to Sunset Beach any time strong easterly winds are followed by winds that switch to the west overnight. Every June, such conditions produce Sooty Shearwaters, and every fall, they produce jaegers. In winter, a coastal storm followed by a cold front may produce Northern Gannets, Black-legged Kittiwakes, and Razorbills. One recent January, a strong east wind switching to west overnight produced a point-blank Northern Fulmar at the Concrete Ship, hugging the shoreline so closely that it veered out to go around the small jetty there. (This was certainly a highlight of our CMBO winter workshop; there have been only about four fulmar sightings from land in New Jersey.) Finally, rain and fog help; birds are more likely to be close to shore when they can't see the beach due to poor visibility. Tide can be a factor too; a flood tide overnight helps carry roosting seabirds miles up Delaware Bay, and they need to come back out in the morning. (This scenario also works in Chesapeake Bay at Cape Charles. There, storm chasers wait at the Bridge Tunnel islands for birds coming out of Chesapeake Bay after hurricanes and coastal storms.)

As crazy as it all sounds, and as infrequently as it occurs, storm chasing has become a big part of Cape May birding. On September 19, 2003, following the passage of Hurricane Isabel to the south and west, about fifty birders gathered at Sunset Beach. Isabel was truly the ideal hurricane—Cape May winds never got above 40 mph, so there was no damage, road closures, or evacuations, and the following morning was warm, bright, and sunny, with only about a 20 mph westerly wind. Lucky birders stationed at the Concrete Ship saw a true smorgasbord of storm-carried seabirds, including close Manx and Audubon's Shearwaters, Band-rumped Storm-Petrels, several Bridled Terns, and an adult Sooty Tern that flew low right over the flagpole on the beach.

Such a classic scenario occurred during two hurricanes in 1996, Bertha and Fran. Hurricane Bertha will probably always be the benchmark for bird bounty. Relatively blown-out and benign by the time it passed west of Cape May up Delaware Bay on July 13, Bertha produced eight Black-capped Petrels and eleven Band-rumped Storm-Petrels, among other goodies, for the fortunate watchers at Sunset Beach. Hurricane Floyd, on September 16, 1999, differed a bit. This powerful storm passed offshore to the east of Cape May; theoretically, we were in the wrong quadrant. But at the height of the storm, about twenty-five of us, sheltered under a porch near St. Mary's by-the-Sea at Cape May Point, enjoyed an unforgettable parade of storm-driven seabirds. As birds came by fast and close, there was an almost festive atmosphere among the huddled birders, despite the horrible weather.

Adventurous birders ride out Hurricane Floyd in September 1999.

Carried inshore that day, on gale-force easterly winds, were as many as thirty Parasitic Jaegers, one Pomarine Jaeger, at least seven Sandwich Terns, two Arctic Terns, ten Bridled Terns, and forty Sooty Terns. The Sooty Terns seen that day nearly equaled all the previous reports for New Jersey. At the height of the storm, just before the winds switched to the west, a single flock of seventeen Sooty Terns passed, fighting their way over the wild Cape May Rips. They passed close in, and their timing was impeccable, for just minutes later the local police forced us to leave—an evacuation order had been posted for Cape May Point. We'll never know what else passed, but what we saw was unforgettable.

Storm chasing is not for everyone and is perhaps truly enjoyed by only a hearty few. If you try it, use extreme caution and a heavy dose of common sense. (And it may now be a thing of the past. In this post-Katrina world, emergency managers have vowed to completely evacuate Cape May County for any hurricane larger than a category 1.) Yet the relatively new avocation of watching for far-off pelagic species in the wake of inevitable coastal storms and hurricanes has been an exciting and profitable genre of birding. Few people other than surfers and birders look forward to hurricanes, but at Cape May, recent coastal storms have yielded unexpected avian treasures and greatly increased both our knowledge of the impact of severe storms on birds and the depth of our understanding of what is possible at Cape May. ■

from heaven fallout at Cape May. In that event, a cold front moving off the southeastern states and causing northwest winds held the warm sector (southeast winds) well off the coast, until birds actually hit the warm front itself coming off the low sitting just off the Delmarva Peninsula. Here, theoretically, the counterclockwise flow pushed birds back to land and dumped them at Cape May. Similar events have occurred in Nova Scotia in the fall. In retrospect, it may have been a similar situation that brought another of our great rarities, a Great Kiskadee, to Cape May Court House in 1960. Found during the Christmas Bird Count on December 26, the kiskadee had likely arrived on an earlier warm front during Cape May's late autumn rarity season. (Great Kiskadees, though not usually migratory, are known to both disperse and wander along the Gulf coast.)

Formerly a quiet time at Cape May (at least before the discovery of the seawatch), November now stirs great expectation and excitement among Cape May birders. Whereas from August through October we look for walloping cold fronts, in November, astute and eager birders hope for a prolonged warm front to pump warm air up from the south and hopefully carry entrained birds along with it. Although vagrants occur throughout the seasons at Cape May, in the annual late autumn rarity season, birders set their sights on southern and western waifs. It still seems odd to longtime veterans to figuratively face south in late autumn rather than toward the chill winds from the north, which presage the coming winter and its bounty of far northern birds.

AUTUMN BECOMES WINTER

Every year, no matter how long we try to prolong it, there comes that realization, often as a surprise, that it's over. Autumn has come to an end. Sure, there were a few late migrant redpolls on the Christmas Count, and several southbound Razorbills from the now empty Avalon Seawatch the day before New Year's, but we've reached the bitter end. Now the fall is only memories, but good memories indeed. Some seasons are better than others. In thirty years, we've seen two almost frontless falls, but generally the memories of fall stoke us for the winter, offering and provoking endless postseason (notice we didn't say off-season) discussions, Power Point and slide shows (favorite photos and mystery quizzes alike), and Monday-morning (usually Thursday night) quarterbacking and statistics reviews for the few (one?) short months before migration begins again in earnest.

At Cape May, where migration is not only protracted and overlapping but also a pervasive influence, one might say that it never ends. If surfers can pursue the "endless summer," Cape May may well represent the "endless migration." Even during a rare winter snowstorm, the birds of seasons past can create a warm glow over an after-work beer in a tavern or at the get-togethers that help us endure until the first crocuses (and phoebes) of spring. For us, the memories can be amazing—and not just those of the rare birds we've seen. Sometimes our favorite recollections are of birds we didn't see, stories that are important because of what they conjure. Favorites include the visiting Brit who, in the predawn hours of his own landfall at Cape May, got his life Common Yellowthroat before even going into the field. He told us, "It was hiding behind the pecan sandy cookies in the local convenience store. Must have flown in the open door, maybe attracted by the lights. I caught it and let it go, but not before I took me some photos!"

A favorite true story concerns Patti Hodgetts, a longtime research associate with the CMBO who, in the 1970s, was working a second job waitressing at a Cape May beachfront restaurant. At the time, she was an apprentice bird bander, and late one night she saw a small black bird flitting around the Victorian Mall and thought that it was injured. She picked it up and realized that it was a bird she had never seen before (few have), but she was pretty sure what it was. She took it to the raptor banders' house in Cape May Point, where one of the banders, Mike Britten, immediately exclaimed, "Oh wow, a Black Rail!" They determined that the bird was not injured and probably just disoriented, so they ceremoniously released it to the peace and quiet of Lighthouse Pond in Cape May Point State Park. Remember, Cape May magic can occur anywhere and at any time.

Memories can involve rarities, individuals, or sometimes numbers of the most common birds. One of our most unforgettable days at Cape May was triggered by an October cold front that hadn't quite cleared the Cape by dawn. The date was October 2, 1994, to be exact, and it was still gray and spitting rain when we arrived early at Cape May Point State Park. We immediately knew that something extraordinary was up—the sky was full of Great Blue Herons, a flock of 30 heading out, 20 milling over the light-house, about 40 in Bunker Pond, dozens perched on snags along the tree line. The resident ranger confronted us, half in fun and a little bit in earnest: "Your damn birds kept me awake all night! I couldn't sleep for all the squawking," referring to a huge nocturnal, and obviously still ongoing, movement of great blues, night herons, and American Bitterns. Flocks continued to both go over and put down all morning. By noon, when it finally ended, the official count from the hawkwatch was 3,200 Great Blue Herons, an astonishing record tally. Untold hundreds, maybe thousands more had passed over in the dark of night, witnessed only by the sleepless ranger and Cape May Point residents. Then, about midday, a migrant young Bald Eagle came in, flapping low down the tree line north of the hawkwatch platform. Startled great blues erupted from the tree line, progressing west in a wave down the wood's edge. As the eagle disappeared out over Delaware Bay, it left in its wake over 500 great blues, all up in the

AMERICAN WOODCOCK

Few birds embody Cape May as much as the American Woodcock. This may surprise many, because poster birds are usually those that are frequently seen. Woodcock, though often abundant, are nocturnal and secretive in the daytime—camouflaged and usually found deep in thickets or in hedgerows and edges. It is easy to pass by a hundred woodcock in a day and never know they are there. But any birder who takes a trained bird dog, a savvy setter, to Higbee Beach the day after the passage of a late October cold front will see a lifetime's supply of woodcock snuggled down in the honeysuckle and Red Maple leaves on the forest floor, sometimes just a few feet from the frozen, raised-tail pose of the trembling setter. The woodcock, if flushed, towers out of dappled, golden clearings on whirring, whistling wings.

Woodcock have long been associated with fall at Cape May. In 1937, Witmer Stone wrote glowingly of the "congested" autumnal flights of woodcock through Old Cape May and lamented the concentrations of gunners who awaited them following cold fronts. Woodcock have been hunted at Cape May for many years. Stone reported that 1,000 were killed in the Cape May vicinity in the great flight of November 17, 1924, and that bags of 300 were routine for the assembled hunters. He noted that woodcock concentrate around the Cape for all the same reasons that both passerines and hawks bottleneck there: Birds that are following coastal diversion lines, and tired after a long migration, are reluctant to strike out over Delaware Bay, particularly during the strong northwesterly winds of a cold front. (Like songbirds, woodcock redistribute throughout Cape May County to rest and feed before continuing their migration.)

The Higbee Beach Wildlife Management Area (WMA) we know today has long been a popular destination for woodcock hunters, first market gunners and later wealthy sportsmen with the finest gun dogs and expensive, sleek 20-gauge double shotguns. Several generations of Clay's family hunted woodcock on the lower Cape, never at Higbee Beach but farther north, at Town Bank, Del Haven, and Villas, in then forgotten farm fields, hedgerows, and honeysuckle tangles. Today, all those old woodcock fields are dense, wall-to-wall communities, with no vestige of woodcock habitat remaining. One November day at Town Bank in the 1940s, Clay's grandfather and uncle took eighty-five woodcock in a morning—shooting so good, with woodcock so abundant, that

The American Woodcock has played a key role in the conservation of the region; this bird is feeding on a bare roadside during a January freeze.

they were back home in Sea Isle City by 10:00 A.M. Appropriately, their big lemon English setter was named "Town Bank," after their inimitable shooting destination. This was wrong; even then, this take was well over the legal bag limit, but at Cape May, over several centuries, the artificial, unique concentrations of migratory birds gave gunners a false impression of abundance. It was easy, knowing little about migration, to assume that woodcock and other birds, be they ducks or hawks, were that abundant everywhere. It is a recurrent theme. Even today, on a good day at Higbee Beach, with birds abundant but unusually concentrated due to not only geography and weather but also the loss of local stopover habitat, we can get a highly false impression of the true plight of bird populations, be they songbirds or woodcock. (For the record, because some readers may wonder, Clay hasn't raised his worn L. C. Smith double at a woodcock since the first time he watched, open-mouthed, their spring ritual courtship dance over the same fields he had so loved to hunt. Also for the record, he sure misses those bygone days, following his dog and his dad, and the fine gamy flavor of the birds. Woodcock were delicious—and probably still are, but as Aldo Leopold wrote in 1949, the woodcock's dawn and dusk sky dances are a "refutation of the theory that the utility of a gamebird is . . . to pose gracefully on a slice of toast.")

Woodcock have long been hunted at Cape May, but perhaps more than any other species, they have also been a driving force behind

continues on next page

AMERICAN WOODCOCK *continued*

conservation on the Cape. Despite all the songbirds and peregrines, it was woodcock that spurred the protection of Higbee Beach WMA in 1978. "Hook-and-bullet" dominated officials moved to save a prime (and their personal favorite) shooting spot and (appropriately) used federal endangered species funds for the purchase. A little-known but early conflict at Higbee Beach WMA occurred when the New Jersey Division of Fish and Wildlife opened it to woodcock hunting soon after the purchase. (Ironically, some animal rights–type environmentalists actually fought the purchase, apparently preferring to see Higbee Beach developed rather than to have any woodcock shot there.) In the end, the sheer numbers of birders actively visiting the site tipped the scales, and Higbee Beach was closed to all early-season hunting. Woodcock would also figure heavily in the protection and creation of the Cape May National Wildlife Refuge in 1989. By the 1980s, woodcock were in strong decline over their entire range, and a major effort was under way by the U.S. Fish and Wildlife Service to protect and manage both woodcock nesting habitat and migratory stopover habitat. The prime cause of woodcock decline is thought to be not habitat loss but forest succession in prime breeding areas. Breeding woodcock clearly select young, wet forests with frequent open areas.

Despite the succession theory, one can only wonder what effect the loss of migratory habitat has had on the American Woodcock. Stopover habitat is hugely important to exhausted and hungry migrants. Anyone who has hunted woodcock with a trained bird dog knows that migrants are *highly* selective in the microhabitats they choose. They select not the deep woods or open fields but damp, tangled edges; hedgerows; and low, wet swales and copses. Woodcock hunters call these areas "spungs" (a spung is a type of wetland, a depression or basin; the name is actually Old English for "pocket"), and they readily know what they look like. And except for Higbee Beach and parts of the Cape May NWR, most of these key woodcock spots are gone from Cape May County, either drained or filled and developed.

For many years, substantial woodcock research has occurred at Cape May. In the 1960s, hunter bag surveys attempted to learn the age and sex ratios of Cape May migrant woodcock (a survey Clay's dad eagerly participated in), and in the late 1960s and 1970s, a major banding project was carried out in Cape May County by the U.S. Fish and Wildlife Service (2,337 woodcock were banded between 1968 and

1973, with 143 band recoveries obtained). It was learned that the vast majority of woodcock passing through the Cape were immature birds, up to 85 percent of the migrants. (All banding for this study was done in November, so adults simply may have been migrating earlier, as is the case with other shorebirds.) Woodcock came from as far away as eastern Ontario and wintered principally on the eastern seaboard as far south as South Carolina. From 1998 to 2002, a series of fascinating telemetry studies were carried out at the Cape May NWR. Monitoring stations were set up at several Cape May County locations, and radiotelemetry recording gear on towers "listened" for passing birds (each of which had individual frequencies). Birds had been banded and fitted with transmitters mainly at Moosehorn National Wildlife Refuge in northeastern Maine; telemetry proved that birds migrated to Cape May in from four to twenty-four days, but most covered the 580 miles in about eight to eighteen days. Virtually all migrated following the passage of a cold front. Most interesting was that in at least one year (1999), nearly 25 percent of the woodcock banded in Maine were recorded migrating through Cape May County. Detection on subsequent nights proved that many woodcock stopped over as well.

Current Cape May NWR woodcock research is attempting to learn the status of nesting woodcock on the Cape. They definitely do nest here; we have seen both a nest and a recently hatched brood (following mom across a road) in Belleplain State Forest. The major question to be answered is what percentage of spring-displaying woodcock is actually breeding here. Beginning on warm nights in very early spring (and sometimes as early as the Christmas Bird Counts), "peenting" and displaying woodcock are frequently heard and seen throughout the Cape wherever there is suitable habitat. Early-succession fields with bare or low-growth patches at Higbee Beach and throughout the Cape May NWR (particularly the Woodcock Lane Trail) are good places to watch. Late February and March are the peak times, but we don't know how many of these displaying birds actually remain to breed. Peenting drops off in April, but perhaps only the promiscuous males move on, leaving silent incubating females behind. This is one of the many mysteries yet to be solved at Cape May.

In mild winters, many woodcock can survive on the Cape. Surrounded by water, Cape May's winter climate is always a bit warmer than elsewhere in New Jersey, and late migrant woodcock take advantage

continues on next page

AMERICAN WOODCOCK *continued*

of this. There is always a weather-related December push of wood-cock into the Cape, as lingerers farther north are frozen out; most of these birds end their migration at Cape May. In mild winters, most survive, but in harsh winters, many if not most perish. In late January 2000, heavy snow, ice, and bitter temperatures persisted for several weeks, and woodcock, unable to feed in their normal low woodland spungs and streams, were pushed to roadsides, parking lots, and plowed areas, where road salt and heated asphalt thawed the road edge. More than 400 dead and weakened woodcock were observed in the immediate Cape May region. Probably very few of the weak and starving birds survived, stark testimony to the dangers of trying to winter at the extreme northern edge of their normal wintering range. Of interest, of thirty-four specimens salvaged in 2000 by Paul Lehman for the Academy of Natural Sciences in Philadelphia, twenty-one were male, and all were adults (unlike the migratory makeup), suggesting, along with banding studies, different wintering areas based on age and sex. Adult males, those wanting to gain an early advantage for the best breeding sites, would be most likely to remain the farthest north. Most years, woodcock winter successfully in good numbers. Quite often, Cape May's CBC records the national high count of woodcock, regularly trading this honor with the Cape Charles CBC. Sometimes after a light winter snow and rising temperatures, dozens of woodcock can be found feeding on Cape May and Cape May Point lawns, offering exceptional opportunities to view and study this unusual bird.

Whether rising over an excited gun dog on a frosty, golden November morning, seen migrating across the face of a rising full moon by birders with trained spotting scopes, busily bobbing and feeding on a warm and thankfully bare Cape May winter lawn, or fueled by hormones and responding to the lengthening days, peent-ing and then towering on twittering wings into the glowing dusk of March, woodcock will always be a hallmark of Cape May. They are representative of a providential past and the need for an attentive future, for a very high percentage of the world's American Wood-cock call Cape May home, if only for a few autumn days and nights during their annual passage south. ▪

air at once, squawking and milling around. Slowly they resettled, all the while squabbling loudly over prime perch sites.

Sometimes, even something as simple as a saved e-mail about a day for the Cape May record books (we're not sure we can ever delete it) prompts the fondest memories and evokes in a few words all that is the fall migration season at Cape May. Paul Lehman wrote:

> Today, Friday, October 21[, 2005], there was truly one of the most impressive fallouts of short-distance migrants seen in a very, very long time in a good part of southern New Jersey. Weather was cloudy overnight, with a few scattered showers, and a light north wind; more persistent rain started mid-morning. The radar images showed a massive late-night flight. The chief component was sparrows, of which the early afternoon estimate is of 50,000 on Cape Island alone! Most are Song, Swamp, and White-throated, but there have also been perhaps 3,500 Chippings and 2,000+ Juncos, with lesser but good numbers of Savannah and Field; plus about 5 Clay-coloreds, 15 Lincoln's, and 9 Vesper Sparrows. Also around 250 White-crowneds, which must be a local record. What is even more amazing than these seething masses of sparrows is that they are truly everywhere, not just in pockets, and the folks 17 miles north at the CMBO Goshen center report hundreds of sparrows in the garden there alone. 2,000 sparrows were reported in just one yard and field near Reeds Beach, and the Suttons counted 119 White-throated Sparrows at their Goshen feeder visible at one time, with many dozens more in surrounding fields, lawns, and hedgerows. And there were gobs and gobs of birds in the pre-dawn gloom even farther northwest at Turkey Point in Cumberland County. So this flight was LARGE-SCALE.
>
> There were also 40,000 Yellow-rumpeds, and almost a thousand Flickers in just one hour at the Higbee Beach dike. Thousands of Robins, lots and lots of kinglets, lots of Phoebes, lawns covered with many, many Palm Warblers, a fair number of Purple Finches, and a few Pine Siskins. A sprinkling of the usual late and lingering warblers, vireos, buntings, orioles, Bobolinks. A late Ruby-throated Hummingbird. A few Dickcissels. One Sedge Wren.
>
> If one wished to extrapolate the sparrow numbers over the good sparrow habitat found in the eastern and western sections

of Cape May and Cumberland Counties, then the total for this event must be FAR in excess of a million birds—but who knows?!!!

It's memories such as these that make Cape May so special—memories that, in themselves, can sharpen and prolong the fall and, in our minds, both sustain and prepare us for the coming, sure to be exciting, Cape May winter.

3

WINTER

The wind blows hard from the north this morning; the water is brown under a choppy surf. The air has turned cold in recent days, with hard frosts on several mornings, and the last warm-weather lingerers— Laughing Gulls, Forster's Terns, Long-billed Dowitchers, Tree Swallows— have departed. The sun has also moved south. In August it rose directly behind the Meadows, coming up over Cape May City. Now it is out over the ocean, rising above the bunker and tracing a lower path through the sky.

—Jack Connor, "Season's End,"
in *Season at the Point* (1991)

Due to the peninsula's buffering by the warmth of surrounding waters, fall conditions may last longer at Cape May than anywhere else in the mid–Atlantic, but try as we might, there comes a point when you can't fight it. The final departure of autumn migrants is as inescapable as the rapidly dwindling daylight. Yet winter at Cape May doesn't mean an end to birding. On the contrary, it's simply a matter of turning the page. One chapter ends and another equally exciting chapter begins. At Cape May, more so than at most other migratory junctures, winter birding is excellent, for a variety of reasons. The exciting diversity of migration may diminish, but this is more than mitigated by the abundance of winter species that make the Cape and the vast coastal and Delaware Bay salt marshes their winter home.

Cape May's excellent winter birding opportunities are rooted in a number of factors. First and foremost is climate. Due to the surrounding ocean and bay, with water temperatures that rarely near the freezing mark, the land is buffered from the bitter temperatures found farther inland. In fact, snow is uncommon at Cape May. Many snow events elsewhere in the region are rain events along the immediate coast. For example, sometimes a major snowstorm in Philadelphia is simply heavy rain at Cape May. The ameliorating influence of the ocean and bay makes the critical difference (really just a matter of a few degrees) between snow and rain. Atlantic City averages about 18.5 inches of snow each winter; Cape May City sees considerably less. But on average, about once each winter Cape May gets hit with a big snowstorm as a large low-pressure center moves up the Atlantic coast. Sometimes these winter nor'easters create blizzard conditions at Cape May. Then, as in most regions, deep snow dictates that the best birding will be at bird feeders and along road edges laid bare by the plows.

Beyond the immediate buffer of warm water, there are several climatological reasons for Cape May's comparatively mild winter temperatures. Even though New Jersey is at the same latitude as Nebraska, it does not experience the same brutal winters of the upper Midwest. The temperatures are buffered to a large degree by the Gulf Stream—the warm river of water that flows from the tropics to the North Atlantic off Europe. Meteorologists and climatologists readily agree that this is a significant reason why Cape May and New Jersey remain warmer than adjacent inland states. Finally, although the jet stream (the flowing high-altitude ribbon of air that crosses North America from west to east) often dips in winter and brings frigid Arctic air to our region, the usual average path of the jet stream differs. More frequently, the dip in the stream (trough) is over the Midwest, and a peak (ridge) of high pressure builds over the Northeast. Then the clockwise flow of air around the high pumps warmer air from the southwest into the mid-Atlantic. Throughout the year, much of Cape May's weather—warm air and moisture alike—comes out of the Gulf states. No single factor keeps the area warm, but the net effect is that the Cape is much warmer than inland regions, an attractant and a boon to birds in the late fall, winter, and early spring. The benefit extends beyond birds. The winter moth diversity on the South Jersey–Delaware Bayshore is reported to be greater than anywhere north of Jacksonville, Florida—which in turn benefits birds that include insects in their winter diets.

Most waters remain open around Cape May in winter. Although freshwater lakes and ponds, such as Bunker Pond and Lily Lake, freeze a few times each winter, it is uncommon for salt water to freeze. In most years, one or two midwinter cold snaps cause the partial icing of saltwater bays, but most deep channels in the back bays and inlets remain open, providing safe refuge for waterfowl.

About once every eight to ten years, a major dip in the jet stream brings a deep freeze to Cape May. Then, most salt water freezes, and bays, channels, and even inlets may be locked in ice, sometimes for several weeks.

In these conditions, there can be considerable waterfowl mortality. Nomadic Snow Geese usually flee to the south, but more sedentary Brant can be particularly hard hit. In the past thirty years, we have seen two significant winter mortalities of Brant on the Jersey coast. About once every five years or so, much of the "cove" of Delaware Bay (the area north and west of Norbury's Landing) freezes, and maybe once a decade the bay freezes solid all the way south to Cape May Point, creating a true arctic landscape. (The shipping channel in the middle of the bay virtually always remains open.) The Atlantic Ocean can freeze during these rare prolonged deep freezes. We've seen the beaches piled with ice and skim ice extending a mile out into the ocean, with the surf muted to a mere gentle rising and falling of the floating ice. It doesn't happen very often, but true winter can come to Cape May.

Ice locks in Reeds Beach in February 2004. Severe winters can have a devastating effect on Cape May waterfowl.

The fields of Higbee Beach lie beneath a layer of ice and snow in 2004—not the Higbee Beach most birders know.

One of the many pluses associated with Cape May's normally mild winter climate is accessibility. It is rare to have any physical impediments to birding. There may be times when you don't want to walk on ice-covered jetties (beware: any saltwater ice is unstable), but usually you can bird all the same hotspots in winter that you frequented in summer or fall, plus places you couldn't access then because of soft, deep mud (we cherish the brief, hard freezes when we can walk across frozen marshes and easily explore wooded swamps). All facilities, such as Cape May Point State Park and Forsythe National Wildlife Refuge, remain open throughout the winter. Some years, the wildlife drive at Forsythe closes for birding one day a week to allow goose hunting, and it also may close for a few days following the rare snowstorm (call ahead for accessibility at Forsythe). One thing to keep in mind is that the temperature can fool you. Due to the ocean and the bay, the Cape often experiences a damp cold—a wind chill far colder than the thermometer suggests. Dress warmly!

One great feature of Cape May in winter is that many motels and restaurants remain open, particularly in Cape May City. The crowds of summer are gone, but bed-and-breakfasts and fine dining are still readily available, often with exceptional off-season rates. In Cape May City, only January and February (up to Presidents' Day weekend) can truly be called off-season. December is festive, with virtually all shops and restaurants open and catering to the holiday crowds in town for Victorian Christmas house tours and many other seasonal events. The Christmas decorations and lighting throughout historic Cape May are not to be missed. Christmas in Cape May is warm, welcoming, and magical.

Along with the mild climate and exceptional accessibility and accommodations, winter birding at Cape May is enhanced by the fact that something is always moving. Some years, even through February, weather-related bird movements occur—birds pushed south by harsh conditions, snow and ice, to the north. Couple these fresh arrivals with lingerers, those hardy and half-hardy individuals trying to make it through the winter at the northern limits of their winter range (the northern limits of possibility), and you have a plethora of winter possibilities.

Cape May's winter fields are populated by a surprising variety of species, but White-throated Sparrows and Dark-eyed Juncos invariably predominate. Northern Cardinals and Blue Jays bring brilliant bursts of color to both feeder and forest. The Cape winter woods can even be noisy at times. Carolina Wrens are common and enliven the landscape by singing heartily even on the coldest and dreariest of winter days; they are permanent residents near the northern limit of their range. Particularly harsh winters, which occur about once every decade, hit Carolinas hard, and it often takes several years for their numbers to rebound. Winter Wrens are secretive yet widespread, usually near dense, brushy tangles. Some winters, vast flocks of American Robins fill the woods. Some find it surprising, but robins winter in large numbers in southern New Jersey if American Holly trees are heavy with berries. As many as 15,000 robins have been tallied on the Cape May CBC. Sometimes evening roost flights of many hundreds are seen at dusk on the upper peninsula. Hermit Thrush also winter in good numbers due to the availability of holly, sumac, and greenbrier fruits.

We've always enjoyed the changeover in winter bird life. Tree Sparrows appear where Chipping Sparrows fed in the fall (although a few chippies do winter). Hermit Thrush replace Wood Thrush. On beaches and bays, summer Laughing Gulls are replaced by abundant Ring-billed Gulls. Bonaparte's Gulls feed where Forster's Terns dove just weeks before (although in warmer winters a very few Forster's Terns may actually overwinter, or at least commute, withdrawing to the south during cold snaps and returning during warm spells). There is redistribution, too. Both Fish Crows and Boat-tailed Grackles, widespread in summer, flock up in winter at specific spots; finding them can be feast or famine. In short, winter rearranges the players at Cape May.

Winter birding at places like East Point can yield memorable results.

Although the Cape's woods and fields are fun in winter, the primary draw is the rich concentration of raptors and waterfowl. Large numbers of hawks and eagles winter in southern New Jersey—not so much around Cape May City, but northward along the Delaware Bayshore and the principal Atlantic coast rivers and estuaries. The mild climate attracts vast flocks of waterfowl—geese, dabblers, and divers—and both Common and Red-throated Loons remain in numbers along the Atlantic beaches and in the bays. Even shorebirds can be found in some numbers. Purple Sandpipers populate jetties and seawalls, and Sanderlings are abundant on winter beaches. Dunlins are common on low-tide mudflats, and a few Black-bellied Plovers remain as well. Amazingly, most seasons a few Red Knots successfully winter as much as 6,000 miles north of their normal winter home in Chile. Significant numbers of American Oystercatchers remain mostly near Hereford Inlet (between Stone Harbor and North Wildwood), except during the most severe winters. Just as in the fall, there is always something to see for birders on the winter Cape.

THE CAPE MAY CHRISTMAS BIRD COUNT

One great barometer by which to measure the Cape's winter birding is the Cape May Christmas Bird Count, part of the National Audubon Society Christmas Bird Count (CBC) network. The first Cape May CBC was carried out in 1903, just three years after the count concept was established by Frank Chapman as an alternative to traditional Christmas hunts. The count was done by William L. Baily, one of the founders and first president of the Delaware Valley Ornithological Club (DVOC). He found thirty-seven species in the Wildwood area, including the then-rare Northern Mockingbird. The next count was done in 1920 by Julian K. Potter, Delos E. Culver, and Conrad K. Roland in the Cape May Point area and recorded thirty-eight species. Potter, with the aid of others, did counts in the Cape May Point area in 1922, 1923, 1924, and 1926 and recorded up to forty-eight species. In 1927, Potter established the current 7.5-mile radius count circle, with Rio Grande as the center, and included Stone Harbor for the first time. The count circle stretches north to Stone Harbor and Reeds Beach and south to Cape May Point. Witmer Stone (and his good friend Otway Brown) participated in the Cape May CBC from 1929 through 1936. In 1930, seventeen observers in six groups found seventy-eight species—the Cape May count was off and running. The count in its current configuration has been run every year since 1927, even during the difficult years of World War II. Potter compiled the Cape May CBCs from 1920 to 1935. From 1936 to 1942, J. Fletcher Street compiled the count and made it a DVOC project. The count was compiled by Dale R. Coman from 1943 to 1951, by Ernest Choate from 1952 to 1972, and by Keith Seager from 1973 to 1993.

It is a grand tradition that continues today. Since 1994, Louise Zemaitis has compiled the count. It is one of the most eagerly anticipated events on the entire Cape May birding calendar and usually has over sixty observers. Based on so much historical precedent and knowledge, and spurred by intense scouting, the count is run like a military exercise, with all nooks and crannies of the count circle scrutinized for their avian treasure. In an attempt to target late migrants and lingerers, the Cape May CBC is always held on the first Sunday of the count period. The modern-era average for the Cape May CBC is 158 species (range, 153 to 167). In 2001, Cape May was the twenty-eighth highest count among the 1,936 CBCs carried out in North America. It was the highest on the East Coast, and beaten only by counts in Texas, California, and one in Louisiana. Most years, unless edged out by Cape Charles, Virginia, Cape May is topped on the East Coast by only a few counts from South Carolina through Florida. Best attesting to the winter possibilities is the cumulative Cape May CBC total: an amazing 260 species, 6 additional forms (races), plus 4 additional count-week birds (Trumpeter Swan, Rock Wren, Lincoln's Sparrow, and Painted Bunting).

The Cape May CBC is exceptional due to varied habitats, late migration, and a mixture of both resident and winter birds, but it is the late lingering species that always create excitement. Recent counts have included such oddballs as Brown Pelican, Least Bittern, Osprey, Broad-winged Hawk, Sandhill Crane, Black Skimmer, Ruby-throated Hummingbird, Blue-headed Vireo, Blue-gray Gnatcatcher, Ovenbird, Wilson's Warbler, Nashville Warbler, and Indigo Bunting. Mix these with good winter species such as Dovekie, Razorbill, Snowy Owl, Red Crossbill, White-winged Crossbill, and Common Redpoll, then add in absolute rarities such as Long-billed Curlew, Rufous Hummingbird, Allen's Hummingbird, Ash-throated Flycatcher, Western Kingbird, Bell's Vireo, Western Tanager, Spotted Towhee, Painted Bunting, and even Cave Swallow and MacGillivray's Warbler, and you have the makings of a truly incredible if not legendary CBC. (The 1997 MacGillivray's Warbler was the first New Jersey record, originally found by Jim Dowdell on November 12 in "rarity season," as are many CBC birds. Sadly, the 2004 Allen's Hummingbird did not survive beyond the CBC, succumbing to an ice storm a few hours after it was tallied. It is remarkable, though, that a bird weighing 3 grams, about the weight of a penny, and 2,000 miles out of range could survive for over a month in the warm climate of a Cape May garden.) To view the Cape May CBC results (and all other CBCs), go to www.audubon.org/bird/cbc/.

The Cape May CBC is complemented by two adjoining counts—the Belleplain CBC and the Cumberland County CBC. Belleplain covers the entire northern part of Cape May County, from Goshen north to the Tuckahoe River and west to the Maurice River. It was begun in 1988 and has been compiled since its inception by Paul Kosten. The Cumberland CBC has been compiled by us for twenty years (1986 to 2005) and extends west up the Delaware Bayshore to the Cohansey River area. Belleplain averages 116 species (range, 93 to 129), and Cumberland's modern-era average (it began in 1950) is 125 species (range, 107 to 136), a tally that is often the second highest in New Jersey. The Cumberland cumulative total is currently 200 species, and Belleplain's is 174. The Oceanville CBC, which includes Forsythe National Wildlife Refuge, is run by the Atlantic Audubon Society. Together, the four South Jersey CBCs are a thorough and fascinating documentation of the area's exceptional early-winter bird life.

WINTERING HAWKS AND EAGLES

The Cape May coastal wetlands, and especially the Delaware Bay marshes, are well known for their exceptional winter raptor populations. For all the same reasons that raptors concentrate at Cape May during migration, many late-season birds terminate their fall migration in southern New Jersey. Many hardy, late-season migrants such as Red-tailed Hawks, Northern Harriers, Bald Eagles, and Rough-legged Hawks remain for the entire winter in the exceptional habitats they find near the Cape. Dispersing north along the Delaware Bayshore and along the major rivers, birds find vast wild areas and food to support them during their winter layover. Long-term studies over the past twenty years by Clay and Jim Dowdell (sponsored by the strong bayshore advocacy group Citizens United to Protect the Maurice River), have proved that winter raptor numbers on the Delaware Bayshore (and particularly on Cumberland County's Maurice and Cohansey Rivers) are exceptional—some of the highest reported in the entire Northeast and mid-Atlantic region. To the north, the Great Egg Harbor River and Mullica River host similar numbers of hawks and eagles in winter. Closer to Cape May, Jakes Landing is a favorite raptor overlook, and winter birders can usually enjoy dozens of harriers, numerous redtails, several eagles, and a rough-leg or two from the parking area or boat ramp there on Dennis Creek.

Northern Harriers and Red-tailed Hawks are abundant in winter in southern New Jersey, with lesser numbers of Sharp-shinned Hawks and Cooper's Hawks present. Many if not most accipters winter near backyard bird feeders. Rough-legged Hawks, an irruptive species, are variable in number, common one winter and scarce the next. They are also prone to midwinter incursions when heavy snow blankets the north. A few Peregrine Falcons winter, mostly the local breeding pairs. Even a handful of Merlins winter along the immediate coast. American Kestrels are rare in winter, present in only a shadow of their former wintering numbers. Conversely, both Black and Turkey Vultures numbers are growing, and both species winter in sizable roosts. Red-shoulders are secretive but present, usually seen perched low on sunlit edges on cold winter mornings. A few Northern Goshawks are found each winter, often right around Cape May Point. Furtive and swift, they usually offer only a glimpse.

Eagles are a prime draw for winter birders in southern New Jersey. A few Bald Eagles are found around Cape May, but their winter stronghold is not Cape Island but along the major rivers—Cumberland County's Maurice River and Cohansey River and Atlantic County's Great Egg Harbor River and Mullica River (near Forsythe NWR). A "good" eagle winter is usually a bitter cold one, when rivers and reservoirs far to the north are frozen over. Then large numbers of Bald Eagles show up on the Delaware Bayshore, and it is not uncommon to see twenty-five, thirty, or even more in a day if you target your observations. On January 12, 1990, during the annual winter Bald Eagle survey, Fred Mears was stationed at a known communal roost at Bear Swamp in Cumberland County. Activity was constant all day long, but over the course of the day, Fred carefully kept track of different plumages and in the end tallied twenty-three different Bald Eagles using the roost. At different times during the day, many of them decorated big, bare trees like animated, oversized Christmas ornaments.

During the day, they hunt the vast marshes bordering the Delaware Bay and river systems. The clamor of thousands of Snow Geese in the air or a large flush of ducks is a dead giveaway that an eagle is hunting the area. Any of the roads out onto the Delaware Bay salt marsh can be good vantage points, from Reeds Beach north through all of Cumberland and Salem Counties.

A few Golden Eagles winter every year. The Great Egg Harbor River and Mullica River regions usually hold a few—maybe six or eight—most winters. These aren't western goldens but mostly birds from the James Bay nesting population, attracted to our region by the abundance of winter waterfowl. Although most Cape May migrants are juveniles, many wintering Golden Eagles are adults. Even though they are present only in small numbers, the South Jersey river system is one of the most reliable places in the East to see Golden Eagles in winter. For best success, look for Golden (and Bald) Eagles at Forsythe NWR on winter days with northwest winds (the windier and colder the better), or better yet, scan from the Leeds Point or Motts Creek area. These goldens disappear to evening roosts mainly way upriver in hidden Pine Barrens bogs, but they ride the gales south to the big "bird feeder" that is Brigantine. Closer to the Cape, goldens are frequently seen at Tuckahoe WMA and the Corbin City impoundments along the Great Egg Harbor River. Some winters, Cumberland County's Maurice River, Bear Swamp, and Delaware Bay marshes attract a wintering Golden Eagle. Winter goldens often make spectacular stoops from on high on waterfowl, and sometimes they hunt cooperatively in pairs. We've seen winter goldens take Snow Geese and Black Ducks and once watched a subadult female Golden Eagle stoop on and kill a Great Blue Heron, a meal she eventually shared with an adult male golden. She spent most of the winter with her companion. We watched stick carrying and even copulation and began to speculate about a possible Pine Barrens nesting, but alas, in late March, they were gone with the advancing spring, probably returning to a James Bay bluff in northern Quebec.

WINTERING OWLS

Little known, hard to find, and often hard to see even if found—a lump in the thickest part of the thickest Red Cedar in the densest woods—wintering owls are an enigmatic yet exciting part of the Cape May and Delaware Bay winter landscape. Just as many late-season diurnal raptors end their fall migration in southern New Jersey, so do their nocturnal counterparts. Good numbers of the three common Cape May migratory owls—Short-eared Owl, Long-eared Owl, and Saw-whet Owl—remain in winter to partake of the bounty of the winter marsh, where meadow voles and rice rats are an abundant food source in most years. "Most years" is the key phrase here, taking into account the vagaries of owl irruption combined with the cyclical nature of local prey items. On the South Jersey marshes, tidal flood frequency and tide heights can greatly impact marsh rodent populations. Thus, there are distinctly good winters and bad winters for owls around Cape May.

The Short-eared Owl, a crepuscular (active in the dim light of dawn and dusk) open-country owl, is by far the easiest owl to see in winter. These owls are often active on overcast days as well. To dependably see short-ears, the Cape May birder needs to journey north to Jakes Landing, where one to eight are regularly seen at dusk in winter. Farther afield, Hansey Creek Road, Turkey Point, Fortescue, and Newport Landing in Cumberland County and Forsythe NWR area, including Leeds Point and Motts Creek, in Atlantic County are prime spots for winter short-ears. The dikes at Tuckahoe WMA (and Corbin City impoundments) are excellent spots to scan for winter short-eareds at sunset.

To enjoy short-ears, pick windless evenings to scan for them; sometimes the wind drops to nothing just at dusk. Short-eared Owls rarely hunt in even moderate winds; common sense explains why: Wind makes it nearly impossible for them to hear their prey in the tall, wind-blown marsh grasses. Some evenings, short-ears don't begin to hunt until it's almost too dark to pick them out with the naked eye. Scanning with binoculars is key to spotting them. The many low-hunting Northern Harriers also catch the eye with their distinctive raised-wing glide. Short-eared Owls hunt very low like harriers but tend to bound around like large moths and glide on bowed wings. They are very feisty and don't hesitate to tangle with harriers. Sometimes their hunting times overlap, and sometimes harriers have gone to roost by the time short-ears become active. Toward spring, and particularly on warm days, short-ears can often be found in mid-afternoon, both hunting and characteristically harassing harriers, rough-legs, or even Bald Eagles.

Short-eared Owls are still a feisty feature of South Jersey winter marshes, even if their numbers have declined drastically. An interesting (and sobering) fact is that *the* monograph on Short-eared Owls was written by Charles Urner from his studies of breeding short-ears on the Hackensack Meadowlands in North Jersey, a marsh that now retains only a remnant of its former size and quality, and where breeding short-ears have been absent for many decades.

Sharing the winter marshes with short-ears on rare occasions are Snowy Owls. Snowy Owls are annual in small numbers in New Jersey. Numbers can vary for this cyclical and irruptive owl, from one or two brief sightings to nearly a dozen individuals. In South Jersey, Snowy Owls are decidedly coastal, almost always appearing on barrier island beaches and dunes or inlet areas with sandbars or jetties. Less frequently, they are found on coastal salt marshes and bays. All these habitats that attract Snowy Owls resemble their open-tundra breeding grounds. They usually first appear in late November or early December but can show up anytime, even as late as the end of March. Around Cape May proper, they are infrequent; most sightings are unexpected, and few seem to stay more than a day or two. Farther north in the Hereford Inlet–Stone Harbor Point–Champagne Island–Nummy's Island complex, Snowy Owls are seen with some frequency, maybe one every two or three years. Recently, two Snowy Owls lingered for several weeks in December along the Avalon and Strathmere beachfront. Snowy Owls occur with more frequency farther north at Brigantine Island, Holgate, Barnegat Light, and Island Beach State Park. There, Snowy Owls can actually be called annual and, in a good year, can be seen almost daily with targeted searches. During the 2001–2002 winter, an amazing three snowys were at Forsythe NWR, and often two were in sight at once on the wildlife drive.

Although Snowy Owls are said to be diurnal, in winter they are not—at least not in South Jersey. To find Snowy Owls, go early and late; they are clearly crepuscular here, most active during predawn hours and particularly at dusk. Hunting on the beaches or marsh at night, they can easily sleep away the day perched on some unseen rooftop or chimney in the barrier island towns. At Cape May, several times we've seen them perched on the roofs of beachfront homes. A snowy wintered in Avalon in 1992. It could not be found during the day but appeared each evening around 5:00 P.M. on top of the Avalon water tower—certainly a commanding view. Most Snowy Owls in New Jersey are juvenile birds, with males much more frequent than the stunning, darker-patterned young females.

The other winter owls (Long-eared Owl, Saw-whet Owl, and Barn Owl) require much more targeted searching than the open-country species. Numerous Saw-whet and Long-eared Owls (and fewer Barn Owls) winter on the Cape, particularly north along the Delaware Bayshore in northern Cape May and Cumberland Counties. By day, they are completely hidden in dense Red Cedar stands, holly forests, or honeysuckle tangles. Finding them requires focused "owling" techniques—crawling on hands and knees into dense tangles and under blowdowns searching for telltale "whitewash" and pellets. It's hard work in South Jersey swamps and brush. Each winter, many owl aficionados "owl" with abandon on Christmas Bird Counts, often leading to impressive totals. Popular with many CBC participants is a combination of nighttime listening and daytime owling efforts; this can lead to amazing totals if the conditions are right, which means a windless night (so owls can be heard) and a cloudy day. We find that a cloudy, gray day is far more conducive to spotting whitewash, pellets, and hidden owls than is a bright day with harsh sunlight and shadows. Of course, a good year with good numbers of irruptive long-ears and saw-whets is always more fruitful.

In addition to the migratory species, resident owls (great horned, barred, and eastern screech) are abundant on the Delaware Bayshore. Peak Cumberland County's CBC totals in the recent past have included Barn

Owl (5), Eastern Screech Owl (161), Great Horned Owl (153), Barred Owl (8), Long-eared Owl (6), Short-eared Owl (28), and Northern Saw-whet Owl (5). Such totals seem unbelievable until you realize that at least five groups of observers begin at midnight, canvassing virtually the entire count circle. The CBC time frame coincides with the peak of Great Horned Owl courtship; being our earliest breeding bird, they are often on eggs by late January. They are also very vocal in late December, leading up to egg laying. On calm, cold December nights, forests reverberate with their deep, resonant calls. If the CBC coincides with a still, windless night, dozens of pairs can be heard, sometimes four or five pairs at once, asserting both their love and their territory. Great Horned Owls are the nighttime counterpart of Red-tailed Hawks, filling the same niche. The peak CBC count for Great Horned Owls in Cumberland County (153) is remarkably similar to the record for Red-tailed Hawks (141); likewise, the Red-shouldered Hawk's peak (10) is similar to that of its wooded swamp counterpart, the Barred Owl (8). Screech owls, though not yet in courtship mode in late December, are both widespread and remarkably responsive to a whistled imitation of their soft tremolo call. Again, a quiet night can lead to significant CBC screech owl totals. Cumberland County has posted the highest national CBC total for Great Horned Owl several times, attesting to the quality and suitability of Delaware Bayshore habitats for this impressive nocturnal predator so aptly called the "winged tiger."

Owls have been responsible for several interesting band recoveries in southern New Jersey. In 2000, a birder found a size 7 band in a Great Horned Owl pellet in northern Cumberland County; the band had been placed on an American Black Duck in Quebec in 1994. At Jakes Landing in February 1996, during one of Pat's "All about Owls" field trips, the group found a Long-eared Owl pellet that contained a band from an Eastern Bluebird banded on November 4, 1995, near Deep River, Connecticut. Finally, one late autumn, Pat found a Great Horned Owl pellet at Cape May Point State Park that contained a Saw-whet Owl skull. It is not surprising that a savvy and skilled resident owl could easily pick off a disoriented migrant unfamiliar with the location of escape routes and safe tangles. We're sure it happens often if not daily around Cape May.

More often heard than seen, owls are a significant and popular feature of the Cape May and coastal winter landscape. Though usually present, they can be maddeningly hard to find, so we often have to be content just knowing that they're there. Yet on that special quiet evening, when short-ears bound over the Jakes Landing marsh against the setting sun and Great Horned Owls boom from the pine forest edge, or when you unexpectedly come upon a sleepy Snowy Owl hunkered down behind a dune on a windswept barrier beach, owls can be a special part of the magic of winter at Cape May.

DABBLING DUCKS AND GEESE

Waterfowl are another key feature and winter birding target in and around Cape May. Because waters normally remain open, vast numbers of ducks and geese terminate their autumn migration in the large bays, coastal marshes, and Delaware Bay wetlands in southern New Jersey. Barnegat Bay has long been famous for winter waterfowl, and (working south) Great Bay, Lakes Bay, and the various sounds of Cape May County host huge concentrations of waterfowl in winter. Southern New Jersey is a particular stronghold for American Black Ducks. Declining in most regions, they remain abundant in winter on the coastal marshes and rivers (and breed here in good numbers too). Mallards are present in smaller numbers, primarily on brackish or freshwater rivers. Northern Pintails don't traditionally winter but are present in large numbers (also in fresh to brackish areas) sometimes as late as early December and as early as February, when they stage here on their journey back north.

No bird is as representative of the Cape May winter wetlands as the Brant. New Jersey is the epicenter of the Brant's winter range (largely Long Island to North Carolina), and many tens of thousands fill the winter bays and sounds along the Atlantic coast, sometimes rising in huge clouds when flushed by a clammer's boat or an eagle. New Jersey hosts about 70 percent of the 140,000 Brant estimated in the Atlantic coast population. They arrive in October and stay late, being one of the last spring migrants to leave (in mid-May to late May). Because they are going to the high Arctic, they need to wait until spring finally touches and defrosts the frozen landscape there. Fueled by a good supply of Sea Lettuce from New Jersey bays, the three-pound Brant flies first to James Bay and then on to its breeding grounds, mostly in the Foxe Basin around northern Hudson Bay and Baffin Island. In fall, they are believed to fly nonstop from their breeding grounds to coastal New York and New Jersey. A Brant found dead on Nummy's Island in May 1999 had been banded on North Spicer Island, Nunavut, in August 1980 and hatched in 1979 or earlier, making it, probably, a twenty-year Jersey winter veteran. Brant may be a common winter bird around Cape May, but they lead a fascinating migratory life.

Look for Brant in Cape May Harbor. Behind the barrier islands, many thousands can be seen and heard in the back bay. Check ball fields on the islands, where they gather to graze on grass and sod. It's fun to watch their feisty antics and listen to their low murmuring, gurgling, and almost henlike fussing. In an interesting example of local distribution, Brant are decidedly rare anywhere along Delaware Bay, probably because of the absence of extensive shallow bays. On the bayshore they are replaced by abundant Snow Geese, a bird that is curiously almost nonexistent on New Jersey's Atlantic coast except on migration and at Forsythe NWR.

Snow Geese are a true hallmark of the Delaware Bayshore in winter. Found in huge numbers from Reeds Beach and the Jakes Landing area north and west to Salem County, they sometimes blanket the marshes, turning the drab brown wetlands landscape white. During the not-infrequent eagle flushes, their clamor can be heard for miles. Numbers are big: The New Jersey Division of the Department of Fish and Wildlife has counted upward of 300,000 Snow Geese in New Jersey in winter. The Cumberland CBC has recorded up to 58,000 in the count circle alone. Wintering Snow Geese are a phenomenon not to be missed. Along much of the bayshore, there is a daily movement inland in the early morning (as geese move to cornfields and croplands to feed) and back to the marsh in the late afternoon. Sometimes dozens of skeins, numbering thousands of birds, cover the sky. Snow Geese also exhibit interesting responses to weather. Their numbers are never static; freeze-ups send them south to Delaware or farther, but after a couple of days of thawing temperatures, they come right back. Some winters, this happens over and over again. It's almost as if they undertake a regular commute to stay ahead of the weather, making them the frequent fliers of the Jersey marsh.

Also, look for the seldom seen but probably always present Ross's Goose hiding in the huge flocks of snows. A few Ross's Geese are found every year, as are tiny Cackling Geese, which fly among flocks of both Snow and Canada Geese. Canada Geese are found along the Delaware Bayshore in big numbers; some of these are wild Canadas, down from Arctic breeding grounds, not just local "golf course" geese. One or two Greater White-fronted Geese are seen most winters, and the vast goose concentration areas always produce a few wintering Sandhill Crane sightings each season.

DIVING DUCKS

The distinctive diving ducks, which are a familiar feature of Cape May winters, were a favorite of Witmer Stone's and remain a popular quest for winter birders today. The healthy bays, channels, and harbors around Cape May and northward up the coast are favorite haunts of winter diving ducks. Cape May Harbor is a great place to enjoy scaup, Bufflehead, Red-breasted Merganser, and, perhaps most spectacular, the dapper Long-tailed Duck. Alexander Wilson wrote fondly of the long-tail: "On the coast of New Jersey they are usually called Old Wives. They are chiefly saltwater ducks, and seldom ramble far from the sea. They inhabit our bays and coasts during the winter only; are rarely found in the marshes, but keep in the channel, diving for small shellfish, which are their principal food. In passing to and from the bays, sometimes in vast flocks, particularly towards evening, their loud and confused noise may be heard in calm weather at the distance of several miles. They fly very swiftly, take short excursions, and are lively, restless birds."

Their name has changed several times. Cape May gunners called them "South-southerlys," reminiscent of their curious call. Then for many years they were "Old-squaws," until that name was no longer politically correct (Long-tailed Duck may be sexist too, since only the male has a long tail). But even though the name has changed, the duck hasn't. They are, as Wilson aptly said, lively, restless birds. This is particularly true as spring approaches, when energetic courtship chases become constant along Atlantic coast beachfronts and in Cape May inlets. Their "south-southerly" calls indeed can, on a quiet day, be heard for over a mile, sometimes long before the birds are seen. We particularly like the feisty long-tails' peculiar and distinctive landing pattern. Whereas most ducks glide in and touch down gently, long-tails seem to "chop the power" about 6 feet up, plummeting steeply to a hard splash—like an F-14 Tomcat dropping to an aircraft carrier deck—so distinctive that you can recognize the landing profile a mile away.

North of Cape May, beachfront waters, inlets, bays, and back-bay lagoons fill with Bufflehead, Red-breasted Merganser, and scaup. Bigger waters have bigger flocks; Great Egg Harbor Bay at the northern border of Cape May County usually has a huge flock of scaup in late winter—up to 7,000 birds some years (mostly Greater Scaup). Bufflehead and Red-breasted Merganser are ubiquitous, enlivening open water wherever it is found. Some of the best winter birding is during partial freeze-ups, when ducks are concentrated in the limited open water. This same condition offers one of the few opportunities to readily see Redhead and Canvasback Ducks in the Cape May region.

If the back bays are good, sometimes the beachfronts are even better for diving ducks, because there you get greater variety. The numerous jetties around Cape May Point and all the way up the New Jersey coast to Sandy Hook perfectly mimic natural rocky coastlines to the north. Each rock pile, or groin, is a full ecosystem of organisms, including invertebrates and attracted baitfish, and all are covered with various seaweeds, barnacles, and Blue Mussels—everything necessary to attract hungry diving ducks. The dozens of rock jetties along the Atlantic beachfront are the best places to find wintering flocks of scoters (primarily Black and Surf Scoters, but sometimes White-winged Scoters too) feeding at high tide and often waiting out low tide in a sleepy raft just a bit offshore. Cape May is near the southern limit of the normal winter range for eiders along the Atlantic coast, but a few are present every winter, and sometimes several dozen can be found in various locations. Most are Common Eiders (and most in juvenile plumage), but King Eiders are annual at both the Avalon Seawatch in fall and somewhere in the South Jersey region in winter. In the winter of 1991–1992, Delaware Bay near Reeds Beach jetty held several thousand scoters, several canvasbacks and redheads, and, for weeks, a spectacular adult male King Eider. Winter flocks can be nomadic; sea ducks can clean out an area of clams or a jetty of mussels, after which they're forced to move on in search of abundant dining fare. Diving duck numbers can vary greatly from year to year in relation to the location of good shellfish beds, which also vary yearly.

One must-see location for the Cape May winter birder, albeit a bit far afield, is Barnegat Light. At the north end of Long Beach Island, next to the famous lighthouse, the mile-long Barnegat Inlet jetties attract some of the best regional numbers of diving ducks. Common Eiders are always present, in some years only a dozen or so, but in winter 2005–2006, nearly 200 were counted. King Eiders are often present, and Red-breasted Mergansers and Long-tailed Ducks can number in the hundreds or even thousands— 7,000 long-tails were there in February 1999. Most importantly, Barnegat also attracts a good-sized flock of Harlequin Ducks from early December through late April. Growing each year, the Harlequin flock numbered as high as 55 in January and February of 2004 and 2005. It's a great winter trek (about two hours from Cape May City), and though it may be cold and require a bit of rock hopping, it's always well worth it, with possibilities such as Snow Bunting, Lapland Longspur, "Ipswich" Savannah Sparrow, Purple Sandpiper, Glaucous and Iceland Gulls, and possibly a Snowy Owl or an alcid or two. Razorbill is the most expected alcid, but from December 3, 2005, through early January 2006, a Black Guillemot was seen feeding almost daily in Barnegat Inlet.

Closer to home, there's often a flock of Common Eiders, a few Harlequins, and maybe a Razorbill or two around the Cold Spring jetties at the mouth of Cape May Harbor, accessible from the Two-Mile Beach Unit of Cape May NWR. It's about a 1-mile walk through soft sand to reach the jetty, but it's well worth it; this is possibly *the* best spot on the Cape for winter gulls and alcids. A color-banded male Harlequin Duck at Cold Spring jetty in February 2004 had been banded on its breeding grounds in Newfoundland.

LATE WINTER STAGING

Although there is excellent winter birding right around Cape May Point, Cape May City, and Cape May Harbor, you may have noted a recurring theme: For winter birding, you usually want to go farther afield. In winter, the focus shifts to areas farther up the coast: along the Delaware Bayshore west through Cumberland County, and north up the Atlantic coast to Forsythe NWR, Absecon Inlet, Longport, and even Barnegat Light. The good news is that due to the size and scope of the southern New Jersey region (it's a small state), distances are fairly reasonable, and the winter birder can easily connect the dots between the various hotspots. Even with the shorter winter days, the birder can easily be back in Cape May City by evening to enjoy a warm restaurant, motel, or bed-and-breakfast.

However, there is one spectacular winter phenomenon that will bring you right back to Cape May Point, with ground zero at Cape May Point State Park or, if the tide is right, at Sunset Beach and the Concrete Ship. This exciting event is the huge, late winter gathering of scoters at the mouth of Delaware Bay. Every winter, usually in February and March, the rich waters in the area of The Rips and extending several miles up Delaware Bay attract untold thousands of scoters (of all three species), creating a living kaleidoscope of swirling waterfowl over the bay. They are attracted to rich shellfish feeding opportunities and congregate in massive rafts. At slack tide, most are at rest, but at strong flood or ebb tide, as birds are being carried by the swift water, they are continually leapfrogging back to favored feeding spots. With many tens of thousands of ducks involved, the spectacle is one of a constantly moving wave of birds over the water, with flocks of many hundreds continually jumping to the head of the line.

No one is sure how many birds are involved, mainly because we don't know the turnover rate—how many come in, how many migrate out, and how long they stay. We *do* know that on March 9, 2004, the best guess was that 186,000 scoters (100,000 Surf, 35,000 Black, 1,500 White-winged, and 50,000 unidentified scoters) were present, a number estimated by veteran seawatch counter Michael O'Brien during an intensive two-and-a-half-hour counting effort. Flocks are predominantly males, which tend to winter farther north than females, but the ratio changes over the course of the season. It is believed that a very high percentage of the Atlantic Ocean Black and Surf Scoter population gathers in Delaware Bay each spring. The numbers vary from year to year and aren't always as high as they were in 2004. Some years the phenomenon is short-lived, but it is almost always an impressive gathering. The exact location varies too. Some years, the rafts of ducks are close to shore and extend all around Cape May Point. Other years, the birds are much farther out in the rips or even in midbay; then, a ride aboard the Cape May–Lewes Ferry may be the best way to view them. The location of the rafts varies in relation to the location of the best shellfish beds—the food that attracted them. This late winter phenomenon is actually an early spring staging of scoter flocks as they begin to slowly work their way back north up the Atlantic coast.

Some years, big flocks of Long-tailed Ducks stage in the same general area. Waters farther out, beyond the rips (out near McCrie's Shoal), seem to be the principal area that attracts Long-tailed Ducks. On several occasions, the impressive long-tail gathering, numbering up to 2,500 birds, was easily viewed during late winter or early spring Cape May pelagic bird-finding trips. Over the years, several U.S. Fish and Wildlife studies have shown that Delaware Bay and the waters surrounding its mouth host some of the highest winter waterfowl populations anywhere in the mid-Atlantic region. The mouth of Chesapeake Bay is similarly rich, as might be expected in areas where nutrient-rich estuary waters mix with the Atlantic Ocean. In addition to sea ducks, the waters at the mouth of the bay and along the New Jersey coast are believed to be one of the principal Common Loon wintering areas. Throughout the winter, Common Loons can easily be seen along the beaches, often just beyond the breakers, as well as in inlets and back bays, feeding on small flounders, sculpins, and crabs. Pelagic trips find even more Common Loons in deeper offshore waters, particularly around fisheries-rich areas such as Five Fathom Bank and Avalon Shoals. In late winter and early spring, Common Loons typically raft in big numbers in offshore shoals, and it is not uncommon to see dozens together. On March 8, 1987, more than 1,000 Common Loons were counted at sea off of Cape May during a pelagic trip. Generally, there is a several-week period in February when Common Loons are flightless as they molt and grow in new flight feathers for use in the coming spring migration—hence the need to congregate in such good fishing areas.

A fascinating feature of the annual gathering of diving ducks around Cape May Point is the constant courtship activity. For diving ducks, February is spring, and as the days lengthen, the pace quickens. In the scoter flocks, besides their feeding movements, courtship chases abound, with small wheeling flocks going every which way, sometimes even right over land and the town of Cape May Point. On quiet mornings, listen for the constant whistling of male scoters; the sound carries a long way over the water. The Black Scoter courtship frenzy is more easily studied, since they are usually closer to shore than Surf Scoters. Each female Black Scoter has already chosen her mate, and much of the constant activity on the water is the result of the females trying to protect their chosen mates and attempting to drive off their eight or ten other suitors. The aerial chases involve mostly males chasing a female.

The scoter staging at the mouth of Delaware Bay is a pageant not to be missed. It varies in number and location from year to year, but at its best, it is one of the avian wonders of Cape May. The calendar may say late February, and if there is a fresh southeast wind off the chilly ocean, it can feel like the Arctic, but to the scoters, Red-breasted Mergansers, and Common

Goldeneyes, it's definitely spring. And, except in the coldest and most prolonged winters, if you scan the waters anywhere from the Second Avenue Jetty to Sunset Beach and the Concrete Ship on a February morning, you will also notice numbers of Red-throated Loons beginning their spring staging at the mouth of Delaware Bay and newly arrived Bonaparte's Gulls feeding in the tidal currents around the Concrete Ship. These handsome, dainty gulls feed by dipping down to the water, alighting, and spinning about (almost like phalaropes) in search of tiny, tasty morsels brought to the surface by the rushing currents. Yes, the calendar may say winter, but to the Cape May birder, winter is fleeting, and it's now fleeing fast.

4

SPRING

The beautiful robing of forest scenery, now bursting into vernal life, was exchanged for the monotony of the dreary ocean and the sad sickness of the sea. As we sailed up the Delaware my eyes were riveted on the landscape with intense admiration. All was new! The life, like that of the season was then full of hope and enthusiasm.
—Thomas Nuttall (April 1808)

Cape May was the first land the famous botanist and naturalist Thomas Nuttall saw in North America, and he was perhaps the first to write about the wonder of Cape May in springtime. In 1808, at age twenty-two, he journeyed from Liverpool to Philadelphia, "come to explore the natural history of the United States." On a late April day, as his dismasted and storm-battered sailing ship, the *Halcyon,* finally gained the protection of Delaware Bay, he penned the above lines, possibly more grateful to see Cape May than any visiting naturalist ever. Although winter doesn't last long at Cape May, nor is it particularly cold or snowy, after surviving March, we too are full of hope as we await the "bursting vernal life" of spring. In many years, March can be monotonous—rainy, windy, cold, and gray. There is no cold at Cape May quite like that of a dreary, gray March day, with the damp wind off the cold Atlantic making the air temperature feel 20 degrees colder than it actually is. But birding comfort aside, even in March there is always something to do and something new to see every day.

The first signs of spring at Cape May actually occur in early winter. On still, starlit December nights, the booming hoots of Great Horned Owls reverberate from Cape May Point to Belleplain, penetrating even into homes buttoned up solidly against the winter chill. Great Horned Owls are the earliest nesting birds throughout eastern North America (late January or early February at Cape May), probably timed so that both brooding adults and those feeding the hungry nestlings can take advantage of winter-stressed prey, and so that newly fledged young can easily catch the fresh hatch of birds, bunnies, and squirrels. Bald Eagles are courting and copulating in the depths of winter too, and the first of the Bald Eagles are brooding on their massive nests before the last of the Great Horned Owls lay their eggs. Most balds are on nests by mid-February to late February in South Jersey.

Following the winter solstice, as the days get longer, the wait for spring can be maddening—the length of a day increases by only a minute every twenty-four hours—but a warm spell in January coupled with longer daylight can bring hints of rebirth to the birder. At about the same time as you hear Spring Peepers, the *onk-a-lee* of overwintering Red-winged Blackbirds greets the dawn. In warmer winters, the drum of Downy and Red-bellied Woodpeckers begins as early as late January, and the cooing of Mourning Doves can be heard as the birds get started on the first of their many broods. In most winters, though, such springtime exuberence is cut short when the cold returns with a vegeance. But the signs are still there—and the first diving Forster's Tern or peenting woodcock can't be far behind.

If it seems anachronistic that the first sign of spring at Cape May, the place where migration never ends, is the onset of breeding season for resident birds, be assured that spring migration is beginning at nearly the same time. Except in the coldest of winters, by late January, waterfowl numbers begin to build, primarily Northern Pintails, Mallards, and black ducks. You might spot a high flock of pintails coming in off Delaware Bay at Cape May Point or a skein of high northbound Snow Geese, but mainly, you just notice that there are many more ducks around than, say, during the CBC season. They may return largely unnoticed, but puddle duck numbers are building. By mid-February, northbound waterfowl begin pouring in, with pintails and Mallards now joined by Gadwall, American Wigeon, Green-winged Teal, and the first Wood Ducks. Ring-necked Ducks and Killdeer are notoriously early migrants too. Cape May ponds and bayshore rivers now fill with ducks, and the peak of spring waterfowl migration always occurs between the last week of February and about March 15 to 20. It varies by species—Green-winged Teal peak in early April, and Blue-winged Teal in mid to late April.

By March, the diving ducks are getting serious about spring. The tight, ice-enforced concentrations of winter are now much more spread out. Divers are very entertaining in their elaborate and noisy courtship rituals—head bobbing, bowing, posturing, and lengthy chases around and around their chosen bit of ocean or bay. At Cape May, the rebirth of spring is rarely as obvious or as dramatic as the lasting impressions of the hormone-driven diving ducks, whether Red-breasted Mergansers in a back-bay lagoon, Common Goldeneyes at Reeds Beach, or the incessantly calling and displaying long-tails in love along the ocean beaches.

Also in March, the spring buildup of Red-throated Loons at the mouth of Delaware Bay reaches its peak. In one of the largest known stagings anywhere, up to 3,000 Red-throated Loons have been estimated off Cape May and Cape May Point. Of interest, very few of these birds show any sign of breeding plumage, even the last to leave in April or May. Conversely, as Common Loon numbers grow in April, many molt into their handsome, bold full breeding plumage. Cape May Point in late March and April is exciting. Standing on a dune walkover, facing south, can be every bit as exciting as waiting for southbound migrants in fall. It's fun to scan the ocean and bay to the south, waiting for northbound flocks to materialize— cormorants, egrets, Glossy Ibis, oystercatchers, waterfowl—all heading north with the spring. And all the while, you're enjoying winter birds—loons, scoters, and growing flocks of Bonaparte's Gulls feeding off the jetties and around the Concrete Ship (places that usually host plenty of Purple Sandpipers too). This is the best time of year to see Little Gulls and Black-headed Gulls around Cape May, often mixed in with the hundreds of milling, feeding, and excitedly calling Bonaparte's.

For all the staging we see in Delaware Bay, the actual observed spring waterbird migration is much less obvious than the one in fall. Northern Gannets are abundant in spring, adults in March and younger birds in April (and often spectacular from Cape May Point and from the Cape May–Lewes Ferry), yet the northward movement along the coast lacks the drama and numbers of the fall. Most gannets apparently move north well offshore. Likewise, the actual spring migration of loons and scoters is largely unseen. It's theorized that scoters head north up Delaware Bay and Delaware River and then head over land to the Great Lakes, that they move at night, or that they move well offshore when they leave Delaware Bay. Probably all three theories are partly true. Only cormorants and Common Loons are particularly conspicuous as migrants in spring; the latter are usually seen high overhead flying due north (rather than following the immediate coastline), a movement that continues into late May.

Birders compete in spring for the prestigious and coveted LAGU Award, given *very* informally by the CMBO to the person who sees the first spring Laughing Gull. In years past, most thought that the first boldly plumaged, black-hooded laugher usually showed up around March 10 to 15, but because of the heated competition for the LAGU Award, now it's usually spotted around March 1 or even late February. The prize is having your name proudly displayed in the sightings log. There are few signs of spring more incarnate or riveting than the first clamor of Laughing Gulls heard high overhead on an early spring morning. Loud and lusty, laughers embody spring renewal on the Cape May beachfront. Herons, egrets, and Glossy Ibis usually show up around March 15 as well. Clay's father and grandfather always said that the first fish hawk of spring showed up right on March 15, but today, with so many birders afield, the first Osprey is usually seen either coming in off the bay at Cape May Point or even sitting on a local nest around March 10. Soon after, the first bold and brilliant breeding-plumaged Ruff is spotted somewhere (rare but regular in South Jersey in spring) among the suddenly abundant yellowlegs. Then the rush is on—spring birding at Cape May is in full swing.

RETURN OF THE SONGBIRDS

The first songbirds to arrive in spring are our breeding birds, pushing the limits of temperature, cover, and food resources as winter retreats north. Amazingly, at Manahawkin we once saw a male Hooded Warbler in a snow squall on the bare branches of a still winterlike swamp in the last few days of March. Pine Warblers are the normal vanguard, arriving in early March or even the last few days of February after a mild winter. By mid-March to late March, Louisiana Waterthrushes and Yellow-throated Warblers are singing loudly on their territories. The Eastern Phoebe is always a welcome sign of spring in Cape May County, brightening dull and dreary March days with their emphatic call. Phoebes overwinter some years in small numbers but don't usually breed around Cape May proper; in Cape May County, a few are found as breeders, but only in the Belleplain area.

By the end of April, spring has spread into every nook and cranny of Cape May County. Birdsong reverberates, creating an exhilarating din. As is true over most of the eastern United States, May is the month for peak songbird migration. Surging spring warm fronts can bring waves of migrant neotropical passerines. The numbers are never as big as they are in the fall, but the spiffy breeding plumage more than makes up for this. Sadly, over much of the country, spring numbers are noticeably smaller than in the past—markedly fewer than even a decade or two ago. In fact, the standards are changing for what constitutes a really good day in spring or fall; whereas once the magic number to be broken was thirty species of warblers, today we're happy with twenty, or even fifteen. It's a sad fact of life for birding over most of North America in the twenty-first century.

Spring songbird migration at Cape May is a bit more of an everyday phenomenon than in fall; birds driven by breeding urgency are always moving and may be a bit less dependent on big weather events (fronts) to drive and carry them. In May, there are always at least a few migrant songbirds to be found, even without substantial weather systems. But a surging warm front with strong southwest winds can produce big pulses of migrants, and if they hit the tracking low-pressure cell, with its associated rainfall, fallout can be spectacular. To be honest, though, these perfect conditions, which produce many hundreds or even thousands of songbirds, happen only once or twice—at best three times—each spring. But often, a good fallout lasts for several days as birds put in to rest and feed and maybe wait for the next tailwind. On a number of occasions, the town of Cape May Point has been full of bright spring warblers—many hundreds of individuals and nearly twenty species—and they lingered for four or five days. Wooded sections of West Cape May can be exceptionally good for songbirds in spring, and the tree-lined streets of Cape May City are often full of birds, with warbler song drifting down from the lush green shade trees surrounding the colorful Victorian homes.

In spring, look for flocks of warblers throughout Cape May County and along Delaware Bay. The upland edge of the bay can be the first landfall for tired songbirds after a long night's flight and the bay crossing. Belleplain State Forest can be exceptional for migrants in May. Look and listen for local flocks of Carolina Chickadees and Tufted Titmice; migrant warblers join the local (veteran) feeding flocks to maximize their feeding opportunities. Also in spring, target areas with big oaks; in early to mid-May, oaks are in full bloom, and their dangling catkins attract lots of insects, which in turn attract voracious migrant warblers. Big oaks grow on many field edges at Higbee Beach WMA; as the rising sun hits the oaks, they fill with hungry songbirds. The upland edge of the Delaware Bayshore harbors extensive oak forests, some of which have been protected as part of Cape May NWR: Wildwood Waterworks, Schellinger Farm, Woodcock Lane, and Kimbles Beach Road. Sections of the Villas and North Cape May also have good stands of oaks and can be great for migrants. In mid-May to late May, blooming Black Cherries are songbird favorites.

Although songbird migration continues up until the first few days of June, the first three weeks of May are clearly the peak. This is by far the time of greatest bird diversity in the region. Combine songbird migrants with a few late lingering waterfowl, the last of the waterbird migration, the peak of shorebird staging and movement, and hosts of resident breeding birds, and you have the makings of some truly memorable big days. Far from coincidentally, this incomparable time of year is when NJAS-CMBO holds its annual World Series of Birding, one of the largest conservation fund-raisers in the nation and the world. Following on the heels of this event, NJAS-CMBO's Cape May Spring Weekend includes field trips to Belleplain State Forest for breeding warblers, vireos, tanagers, flycatchers, and more; to Delaware Bay beaches for the massive gathering of spring shorebirds and breeding horseshoe crabs; to Stone Harbor Point and

Nummy's Island for herons, egrets, ibis, rails, and breeding Piping Plovers, American Oystercatchers, Black Skimmers, and terns; and to Forsythe (Brigantine) NWR for all of the above. Both the World Series and the Spring Weekend are fitting testimonials to the wonders of mid-May at the Cape, a time of maximum possible bird diversity and, as many would agree, maximum birding fun.

SHOREBIRDS AND HORSESHOE CRABS

If we had written this book twenty years ago, or even a decade ago, the annual aggregation of migrating shorebirds and breeding horseshoe crabs probably would have been a centerpiece of the Cape May story. It's still a major event in the Cape May birding year, but sadly, the scope of the phenomenon has declined considerably. Today, the gathering of Delaware Bay shorebirds represents a mere fraction of their abundance in the chillingly recent 1980s. Ironically, the number of nature tourists—birders and nonbirders alike—continues to grow as people come to witness the annual spring shorebird and crab gathering. Ecotourism dollars continue to pour in each year, but at the same time, the Red Knot continues its slide toward oblivion, and we finally may have killed the horseshoe crab that lays the golden eggs.

Alexander Wilson was the first ornithologist to witness and document, however sketchily, the existence of massive shorebird concentrations on Delaware Bay, in 1813 describing numbers of Ruddy Turnstones at Maurice River Cove, below Egg Island. But Wilson would be the last one to see them for over 150 years. It wasn't until around 1978 that the horseshoe crab–shorebird phenomenon was "rediscovered," when bayman and noted bird carver and artist Jim Seibert knocked on the door of New Jersey Audubon Society's fledgling Cape May Bird Observatory and said, "You know, I've got a *lot* of shorebirds on my beach in May." Pete Dunne responded, with a bit of doubt if not healthy skepticism, "How many is a lot?" The rest is history. "A lot" was found to be over 1.5 million, the third largest shorebird gathering in the world, feasting on the eggs of the largest population of horseshoe crabs on the planet. The CMBO carried out the first landmark shorebird counts on foot, by boat, and finally by aircraft, and this phenomenon, as much as the hawks of autumn, put Cape May on the map and made Delaware Bay a definitive destination for birders worldwide. It was a seminal natural history phenomenon that one Red Knot researcher described, aptly, as "sex and gluttony on Delaware Bay."

There is good reason why no one saw shorebirds on Delaware Bay for over 150 years. It is because they weren't there. It has been suggested that Witmer Stone and his compatriots from the Academy of Natural Sciences in Philadelphia and the DVOC simply missed them, that they never

Bayman and carver Jim Seibert helping starving Brant during a harsh winter freeze. He was the first to discover the shorebirds on Delaware Bay.

knew the birds were there. Not so, say others, and in fact, we *know* that they didn't miss much of anything else in the way of regional phenomena. The logical conclusion is that there were no shorebirds. This theory is backed by the lack of a shorebird gunning history for Delaware Bay—no decoys, no lore, no shooting clubs, no journals. There *is,* however, an extensive waterfowl (ducks and geese) decoy record for Delaware Bay and a comparative shorebird record and legacy from the nearby Atlantic coast. Yet there is none for Delaware Bay, even at the height of shorebird gunning and market hunting.

The shorebirds were gone because the horseshoe crabs were gone. Horseshoe crabs may have existed for 350 million years (long before there even was a Delaware Bay or a North American continent, for that matter), but it took less than a century for settlers to nearly extirpate the crabs from Delaware Bay. From the early 1800s to the early 1900s, crabs were harvested for fertilizer and as food for hogs, plus wagonloads of eggs were gathered and carried off to feed chickens. Vast weirs corralled untold millions of horseshoe crabs each season. They were transported to pens where they died and dried; they were then ground up in factories and spread on fields both locally and afar. The harvest of "king crabs" was a major Delaware Bayshore industry, but it was not sustainable. The horseshoe crabs were severely overharvested. Crabs don't breed until they are at least nine years old—a fact learned only in the past decade. Thus, the harvest took all breeders and future breeders right out of the population. As early as 1870, crab populations were reported to be "depressed," and by 1908, there was serious concern about the future of the fertilizer industry. Finally, at some undocumented time in the twentieth century, the crab industry died out because there were no more crabs. (Crabs were still being harvested in

1954, when weirs at Pierce's Point trapped crabs to be processed for pet food. But it was described as a "dying industry" in an Audubon Center report of a field trip to Pierce's Point.)

Although horseshoe crabs never fully disappeared from Delaware Bay, the shorebird connection depends on a superabundance of crab eggs. This is a prime example of an event in nature depending on a surfeit; eggs are in the tide line and available to shorebirds only when they are dug up by the successive nesting of a host of other crabs at high tides throughout May. It takes an excess, many thousands or maybe millions of crabs, to create the egg washup and "slurry" necessary for shorebirds to feed efficiently (eggs have poor nutritional content, so shorebirds need to eat a lot of them to put on weight). So, even if a few crabs still nested successfully, their eggs wouldn't feed the shorebirds. Something that we will never know is what happened to the shorebirds when they disappeared from Delaware Bay. We know that

shorebirds are both opportunistic and long-lived. Did Red Knots disperse elsewhere, or did their populations crash? Sadly, there are virtually no data prior to the CMBO's first surveys in 1981 and 1982. It took the crabs seventy-five years to recover, and when the crabs were rediscovered in 1978, the knots and other shorebirds were already abundant on Delaware Bay beaches. Since then (in less than twenty years, and maybe only two or three generations of Red Knots), the birds have declined by more than 85 percent on Delaware Bay in spring and by 64 percent at their principal wintering grounds near Tierra del Fuego. Delaware Bay Red Knots numbered as many as 100,000 in the early 1980s but plummeted to a paltry 15,000 in 2005. Wintering numbers at Bahia Lomas near Tierra del Fuego fell from 51,000 in 2000 to 18,000 in 2005. Researchers dryly but chillingly state that "demographic modeling

The number of horseshoe crabs that cover bayshore beaches each spring has been in steady decline.

The fate of the Red Knot is directly connected to the status of Delaware Bay horseshoe crab populations.

predicts imminent endangerment and an increased risk of extinction." At the current rate of decline, complete *extinction* of the Atlantic coast population is said to be possible by 2010. At risk is the entire *rufa* race of the Red Knot. To call it an ecological disaster is an understatement.

The reason seems crystal clear: Horseshoe crabs were rediscovered not only by birders and scientists but also by crab harvesters. Horseshoe crabs have now declined 75 percent in just over a decade. In the 1980s, when crabs were still plentiful, researchers (through marking and recapture studies) found that Red Knots were gaining more than 8 grams of weight (migration-sustaining fat reserves) a day. By 2002, they gained only 2 grams per day, assuredly because they couldn't find enough eggs to eat. Predictably, many are no longer able to reach the threshold weight necessary to fly the final leg to the Arctic to breed. Red Knots are disappearing again, along with the vanishing crabs. The Red Knot is a candidate for federal endangered species status (although emergency listing was denied by the Fish and Wildlife Service in 2006). Once again, we have not learned from history. It took only seventy-five years to collectively forget what happened last time.

Despite declining crabs and birds, nature tourism is still important, even growing, on Delaware Bay, valued at an estimated $34 million per year. With such an amazing potential for ecotourism and its huge economic benefits, it should have been a no-brainer to protect the horseshoe crabs that underpinned the entire phenomenon. Sadly, that didn't happen, or at best, it was too little too late. In 2000, the U.S. Fish and Wildlife Service estimated that the entire horseshoe crab harvest industry, from Maine to Florida, was worth a total of $11 million annually. The National Marine Fisheries Service (NMFS) regulates hundreds of species all along the coast, as well as all fisheries harvests. For the NMFS, the simple math on Delaware Bay was not enough; commercial fishermen, like ecotourism interests, claim economic multipliers too. The crabs are harvested today for two purposes: as bait for conch and as bait for eels. The fisheries that use the crabs are valued at $21 million, giving the crab harvest industry a total value of $32 million, which comes close to ecotourism's $34 million. There are some true ironies here, though. Conch, or, more properly, Knobbed Whelk, are sought in the mid-Atlantic because they have been heavily overfished to the south. American eels may not be overfished, but they are either shipped overseas (despite consumption advisories due to the bio-accumulation of chemicals) or used as bait for the burgeoning recreational striped bass fishery. Experiments with alternative eel and conch baits have been promising but inconclusive, perhaps because, as one researcher put it, "Fishermen are addicted to crabs as bait."

As with any addiction, there is money to be made. The industry may be valued at "only" $11 million, but to individual fishermen, crabs are worth big money. In spring 2003, eelers were reportedly paying up to $2 per *individual crab* to procure their precious bait. With values like that, it is no wonder that fishermen continually fight any restrictions on the horse-shoe crab take. It is interesting to compare today's $2 price with those quoted in 1908. Then, for the fertilizer industry, dried crabs ready for grinding were worth $30 per ton, or about 0.015¢ each. Crabs fresh off the beach were worth $8 per 1,000, or about 0.8¢ each. It is sobering to con-template inflation rates on a 350-million-year-old animal, but one thing is certain: Crab eggs may be greenish blue, but for many, crabs have been seen as pure gold.

Whether this natural system has truly crashed is the subject of exten-sive debate and almost frantic research. Larry Niles, chief of New Jersey's Endangered and Nongame Species Program, not only coordinates all the research but also leads the yearly Red Knot banding project on Delaware Bay. At the end of spring migration, he follows the knots to the high Arc-tic, near Nunavut's Southhampton Island, to ascertain breeding success. In winter, like the knots, he migrates south, joining researchers in Chile to conduct key winter censuses. The birds' failure to gain weight while on the shores of Delaware Bay can have repercussions throughout the yearly cycle and throughout the hemisphere. If Red Knots don't gain enough weight to migrate north, they won't breed. Fewer breeders or poor success rates mean fewer fall migrants and wintering birds. It has been a steady downward spiral. An international coalition of researchers has made the plight of the Red Knot a top conservation priority. The decline of the species is the most drastic of any shorebird globally.

Although the outlook remains grim, there have been some key victories. The New Jersey Audubon Society has made horseshoe crab protection its highest conservation priority and has led an all-out effort to guarantee that the crab and bird connection will continue. Partnering with the National Audubon Society, American Bird Conservancy, Defenders of Wildlife, and many others, it has continued to pressure the NMFS. In March 2001, the NMFS established a 1,500-square-mile horseshoe crab sanctuary off the mouth of Delaware Bay, where crab harvesting by any method is prohibited year-round. This sanctuary is a key wintering area for horseshoe crabs and had previously been heavily harvested. In February 2002, New Jersey and Delaware officials announced a decision to close all of Delaware Bay to horseshoe crab harvest between May 1 and June 7 each year, the peak time for spawning crabs and shorebird use. In March 2003, the crab harvest was cut in half. Quotas were set at 150,000 horseshoe crabs, a 50 percent reduction from the 2002 harvest. Finally, in 2006, a two-year complete moratorium was placed on the New Jersey harvest, which conservationists hope will become permanent and coast-wide.

With the reduced quotas, there might be a glimmer of optimism for crabs and shorebirds. Even if the moratorium ends, biologists believe that current quotas may allow for horseshoe crab recovery—that populations will be able to rebound slowly to former levels. Also, a recovery plan for Red Knots has been implemented; current international research efforts on the Red Knot may now be as intensive and in-depth as any ever carried out on any shorebird. On Delaware Bay beaches, stringent regulations and complete beach closures in May (to eliminate disturbance of the birds by people and dogs) have been enacted and enforced since 2003.

Like the mystery of what happened to the Red Knots in the early 1900s, no one really knows what has happened to them currently. Delaware Bay numbers are way down, as are Red Knot numbers on their principal wintering grounds in southern Chile. It is known that shorebirds are long-lived and opportunistic and fairly flexible in response to food availability or the lack thereof (Red Knots, however, are probably much less adaptable than the other principal Delaware Bay shorebirds—Sanderling, Ruddy Turnstone, Dunlin, and Semipalmated Sandpiper—all species that readily feed in a variety of situations and locations). Although all shorebird species are currently down on Delaware Bay, Red Knot numbers have declined the most drastically. Some sightings suggest that many of the birds are feeding elsewhere on the Atlantic coast, but no one is sure. It is hoped that after several seasons of finding limited food on Delaware Bay, Red Knots have simply gone elsewhere in the spring and that the population hasn't truly crashed. (The question remains, however, whether "elsewhere" can sustain the population. Telling is the fact that the percentage of juveniles on the wintering grounds has dropped significantly in the recent past, indicating reduced breeding success in the population as a whole.) "Robin Snipe" survived the decimation of Delaware Bay crabs once before, and at a time when many were still being shot by hunters. It is fervently hoped that they can do so again, but the mostly empty Delaware Bay beaches are gut-wrenching when we remember them so recently full.

For the visiting birder, Delaware Bay in spring is still a must-see destination. All the key species, including Red Knot, are readily seen. If you hit it right, on or near the full or new moon in the middle or end of May, "cobbling crabs"—crabs packed so tightly that they look like cobblestones at

Large flocks of Laughing Gulls also feast on crab eggs in spring.

the water's edge—can still be seen (more so at night than during the day), as can frantically feeding Laughing Gulls and thousands of shorebirds. The spectacle is still just that, but today (in contrast to the 1980s) you need to hit it just right to view the peak—be at the right beach at the right tide at the right time of the season. It wasn't always that way. In what already seem like the good old days, all the beaches were packed with birds virtually all the time. In the early 1980s, at high tide, hundreds of yards of beach would be tinged red with packed Red Knots, Ruddy Turnstones, and breeding-plumaged Sanderlings, and the cobbling crabs were often unbroken in the tide line as far as the eye could see.

On a much brighter note, it is important to remember that the downturn in shorebird numbers is limited to Delaware Bay beaches. The vast mudflats of southern New Jersey's bays and sounds still teem with shorebirds in spring (much like in fall), as northbound migrants put down to

THE BOUNTY OF THE BAY

The horseshoe crab, *Limulus polyphemus,* is an ancient creature, unchanged for over 350 million years. It is not a crab at all but an arthropod, more closely related to spiders than to crabs (making it ironic that they are managed by fisheries commissions). They are found from Maine to Mexico, but by far the largest concentration in the world is in and near Delaware Bay. At nine to twelve years old, horseshoe crabs are mature enough to breed; from that spring forward, they make an annual trek from deeper waters to the beaches of Delaware Bay. Breeding occurs from late April or early May through June, but the peak time is during the full and new moons, when the tides are highest and the crabs can use them to reach the upper beach. In the high-tide line, the larger females are surrounded by males. One lucky male hooks onto a female and is dragged by her to the nest site. She digs a shallow nest (about 8 inches deep) and deposits about 4,000 blue-green eggs, which he fertilizes externally. The crabs make their way back out into the water, and the tidal action covers the nest with sand. Each spring, over the course of several months, each female makes about twenty trips to the beach, laying as many as 80,000 eggs. Each new wave of nesting crabs digs up some of the nests and eggs laid earlier in the spring, resulting in a slurry of eggs in the tide line that attracts hungry shorebirds. Horseshoe crabs do not die after egg laying (they can live from seventeen to twenty years), but many are upended by waves and stranded when the tide recedes, and many die of desiccation.

Horseshoe crabs also play an important yet little understood role in the nearshore ecology and food web of the Delaware estuary. They are bioturbators, aerating the benthic layer, and the crab's larval stages may be a principal food resource for finfish, including Weakfish and Striped Bass.

Horseshoe crabs are also critical to the health care industry; their blood is used in biomedical testing. Lysate, a compound derived from horseshoe crab red blood cells, is currently the only means to test for contaminants in injectable medicines (including smallpox vaccines) and to detect certain diseases, including spinal meningitis. One issue is how far the crab population can slide before the lysate industry cannot obtain enough crabs for testing needs. Four Nobel Prizes have been awarded to scientists whose work focused on horseshoe crabs; one study into the unique physiology of its vision (horseshoe crabs have ten primitive eyes, used to see movement and changes in light, but not clear images) yielded many insights into human sight.

The bounty of horseshoe crab eggs in May attracts thousands of gulls and seasonally supports the largest Laughing Gull breeding population in the world. In the 1980s, the abundance of crab eggs attracted an estimated 1.5 million shorebirds to Delaware Bay beaches. The Delaware Bay shorebird concentrations are the second largest in the New World, second only to spring gatherings on the Copper River Delta in Alaska. Twenty species of shorebirds have been known to take advantage of the crab egg food supply, but the principal species are Red Knot, Ruddy Turnstone, Sanderling, Dunlin, and Semipalmated Sandpiper.

Red Knots truly take a journey to the ends of the earth. Most Red Knots make a 20,000-mile round-trip each year, from the southern tip of Chile and Patagonia to the high Arctic and back again. A color-banded Red Knot sighted in Florida in 2004 had been banded in southern Brazil by Brian Harrington's Manomet Center for Conservation Sciences team in 1984. Banded as an adult, it was at least twenty-one years old in 2004 and had covered almost 400,000 migration miles in its lifetime. By its thirteenth birthday, this 4.5-ounce bird had migrated a distance equal to the moon and back. One can only wonder at this individual Red Knot. How many Peregrine Falcons had it out-flown in its two decades? How many Arctic foxes had it deceived, distracting them with a broken wing display? How many times had it crouched down, frozen on the tundra, as the shadow of a patrolling jaeger passed over? How many dogs had flushed it off beaches? How many birders had viewed it? How many crab harvesters had it flown over unawares?

Red Knots may fly over 4,000 miles nonstop, spending up to sixty hours in the air, from South America to the shores of Delaware Bay. They arrive with no fat reserves, some actually starving, but their arrival is timed to coincide with the peak of horseshoe crab breeding activity. After feeding for two to three weeks, they fly nonstop to their Arctic tundra breeding grounds north of Hudson Bay. Researchers in the 1980s estimated that at least 80 percent of the East Coast race of Red Knot (*Calidris cunutus rufa*) was stopping on Delaware Bay in spring to refuel. The feeding shorebirds, in most cases, need to regain 50 percent of their body weight to make the next leg of their journey and

continues on next page

THE BOUNTY OF THE BAY *continued*

arrive in the Arctic in breeding condition. On Delaware Bay, Red Knots need to gain a minimum of 6.5 grams per day for twelve to fourteen days. This represents approximately 18,000 horseshoe crab eggs per bird per day, or some 13 billion eggs to support current numbers of Red Knots. This requires nearly 1.5 million female crabs to sustain the knot population alone.

There has been a documented tenfold decrease in crab egg density on Delaware Bay beaches since 1990. Red Knots on Delaware Bay declined from a high of over 100,000 in the 1980s to a mere 15,000 in 2005, an 85 percent decrease in just over twenty years. Red Knot numbers continue to drop dramatically, but it is fervently hoped that they are more widely spread out over the Atlantic coast. More than 500,000 horseshoe crabs were harvested from Delaware Bay in 2001. By 2003, quotas were set at 150,000 horseshoe crabs, a level that some biologists believe can lead to crab recovery. In 2006, a two-year moratorium on the New Jersey crab harvest was approved, but many call for a complete moratorium on the take. The lower Delaware estuary was the first site designated for protection by the Western Hemisphere Shorebird Reserve Network, a designation that, unfortunately, has offered little real protection. While federal endangered species status was denied in 2006, the Red Knot remains on the candidate list. The species received the highest degree of protection from the United Nations Convention on Migratory Species; in 2006, it was added to the Appendix I list, which includes animals in need of the strictest protection to avoid extinction. ■

feed. The low-tide flats hold many hundreds of thousands of bright breeding-plumaged shorebirds each April and May: Short-billed Dowitcher, Dunlin, yellowlegs, Black-bellied Plover, Semipalmated Plover, and "peeps." As in fall, they can be somewhat hard to view and are best seen by boat, but Stone Harbor Point (and nearby Nummy's Island) is one outstanding spot to study shorebirds, either at their high-tide roost or feeding on the expanse of sandbars and mudflats at low tide. Forsythe NWR is spectacular for shorebirds in spring, as are the diked tidal impoundments at Thompsons Beach and Bivalve in Cumberland County, just a short drive from Cape May. Maybe the Delaware Bay beaches aren't what they used to be in May, but shorebirds are still a major target for Cape May birders in spring. It is a time when flooding tides can bring hundreds of restless, frenetically feeding birds right to your feet at the edges of the rich mudflats. The flats come alive with the nervous chatter and bright colors of up to twenty species of shorebirds. These spring tides of shorebirds are most memorable and emblematic of Cape May. As has been true for centuries, searching for shorebirds is still one of our finest and treasured traditions.

THE KITE FEST

Spring birding at Cape May is related to both abundance of birds, as with Delaware Bay shorebirds, and to diversity—as evidenced by the high species totals achieved by both World Series teams and even casual birders during the month of May. As expected, the diversity often brings the unusual. While Cape May is better known for its fall rarities, in some years the spring crop is just as plentiful. Most spring rarities have a southern affinity and could be considered as overshoots from breeding populations to the south. Anhinga, White Ibis, White-winged Dove, Swainson's Warbler, and Painted Bunting are found during many if not most springs in the greater Cape May region. Some spring rarities have a more western origin. Scissor-tailed Fly-catcher, Cave Swallow (rapidly expanding its range), and White-faced Ibis have all become annual spring visitors. Curlew Sandpiper, of Eurasian ori-gin, if not quite annual, is expected in spring too.

The World Series of Birding and the NJAS-CMBO Cape May Spring Weekend usually coincide with the beginning of yet another Cape May spring birding phenomenon—the late May appearance of lingering rap-tors. Though just a shadow of the fall hawk migration, there is a substantial spring movement of raptors at Cape May. Beginning in March with north-bound Red-tailed Hawks, Bald Eagles, and Osprey and continuing through early May with returning accipiters and falcons, a few spring hawks can usually be seen, either overhead around the immediate Cape or along nearby Delaware Bay. Hawks appear from both the south, making landfall along the beaches of Cape May and Cape May Point (after departing from Cape Henlopen, Delaware), and the north, arriving on the northwest winds of spring cold fronts. Because a variety of conditions produce hawks, there are usually a few to be found—never huge numbers, but a pretty good variety. In 1980, a part-time spring hawkwatch conducted by Clay found 1,952 raptors in about seventeen days (ninety hours) of observation. Most years, late May brings a fair number of Broad-winged Hawks to Cape May. Sometimes it's just a couple dozen, but in some years, upward of 300 broad-wings have been seen kettling together over Cape May. Virtually all are immature, one-year-old birds. They are thought to be nonbreeders, lingering or loitering on their first journey north with no particular place to go, so they end up at Cape May. Interestingly, at a time when virtually all U.S. spring hawkwatches have folded their chairs, there are still kettles

A few Swallow-tailed Kites make an appearance in Cape May every spring.

over Cape May. Late May, too, always brings some special raptors to Cape May skies.

The excitement of spring hawkwatching comes from the annual appearance of Swallow-tailed and Mississippi Kites in late April and May. Swallow-tailed Kites are seen in very small numbers, usually just one to four every spring, but they keep on a fairly predictable schedule. Almost every year, one or two Swallow-tailed Kites are seen during the last ten days of April; we theorize that they are overshoots from the population heading for Francis Marion National Forest, South Carolina (they arrive there in April; Florida's swallow-tails arrive in late February). These swallow-tails virtually never linger at Cape May; most observations consist of one brief sighting by a single observer or group and can occur anywhere on the peninsula. The second swallow-tail peak, if you can call it that, is the last ten days of May. We theorize that these are birds returning south, having realized that they overshot their prime breeding range. These few birds usually arrive on northwest winds, and most are seen over the Meadows or Cape May Point State Park. These sightings are usually brief, but every few years, a swallow-tail might linger for a couple of days. (An exception was 1972, when a Swallow-tailed Kite lingered for about two weeks in May and could be seen daily feeding over the dragonfly-rich Pond Creek marsh.) But despite small numbers and brief sightings, Cape May is the only place north of Cape Hatteras where Swallow-tailed Kites can be listed as annual.

Whereas swallow-tails are maddeningly hard to see, Mississippi Kites are more numerous and are often seen day after day. The vanguard (one or two) might appear in late April, but late May is the key time. During the last week of May and the first few days of June, targeted watching can produce a Mississippi Kite or two almost every day; on occasion, up to eight or nine have been seen circling together in the spring skies. Look early in the morning, just as raptors begin to get up, or try midafternoon to late afternoon. The Rea Farm and Hidden Valley are two key central locations to watch the sky over the Cape, since both are near Pond Creek, a prime dragonfly-rich feeding area.

Mississippi Kites at Cape May in spring are an enigma. At first, they were true vagrants (Stone saw one in 1923; the next was seen by Al Nicholson in 1976), but they have gradually become more numerous and predictable. Originally dismissed as overshoots, they now come earlier and stay later, and in recent years, a few have clearly summered. Although most are one-year-old birds, a few are full adults (and even most one-year-old kites can and do breed). The recent discovery of kites nesting in suburban Washington, D.C., due west of Cape May, indicates that they can breed at this latitude, and Cape May County certainly has plenty of dragonflies, their preferred prey, in summer. In short, if Mississippi Kites aren't already breeding in southern New Jersey, they probably will be soon. Whether breeders or merely overshoots, Mississippi Kites are one of the joys of spring, gracing the high, billowing cumulus that builds over the Cape on warm, late spring days. To the predictable enjoyment of Mississippi Kites, add the quixotic quest for the Swallow-tailed Kite, and you have the right mix for a classic Cape May springtime adventure. Plus, at land's end, you never know what might turn up. In 1998, Cape May had a three-kite spring: On June 4, two observers searching for Mississippi Kites at Hidden Valley Ranch stunningly photographed Cape May's (and New Jersey's) first confirmed record of a White-tailed Kite. Alas, it was never seen again, gone with the spring.

By the first few days of June, Cape May's spring is fast coming to a close. The last songbirds are moving through, with Mourning Warblers, Blackpoll Warblers, Gray-cheeked Thrushes, and *Empidonax* flycatchers bringing up the rear. The last few holdout Brant and Red Knots are departing daily for the high Arctic. Semipalmated Sandpipers are the last shorebirds to linger on Delaware Bay beaches and back-bay mudflats, but by around June 7, their numbers have dwindled to a handful. As the heat of June builds, spring is over at Cape May. In the scant few weeks between spring and the first returning southbound birds of "fall," it's high time to enjoy summer at the Jersey Shore. For Cape May birders, it's summertime, and the livin' is easy.

5

SUMMER

The first dawn of morn in the Jerseys in the month of June is worthy of a better description than I can furnish, and therefore I shall only say that the moment the sunbeams blazed over the horizon, the loud and mellow notes of the Meadow Lark saluted our ears. On each side of the road were open woods, on the tallest trees of which I observed at intervals the nest of a Fish Hawk, far above which the white-breasted bird slowly winged its way, as it commenced its early journey to the sea, the odor of which filled me with delight. In half an hour more we were in the center of Great Egg Harbor.
— John James Audubon (circa 1829)

It is tempting to say that summer is short at Cape May. The time between the last departing Semipalmated Sandpipers in early June and the first southbound Greater Yellowlegs in late June is in fact agonizingly short for the avid birder who doesn't want to miss anything (and has to do at least some cursory yard work or token home repair). But while summer according to the avian calendar—the time between spring and fall migration—is brief, the actual breeding season is not. The breeding season in the high Arctic is short, but it lengthens as you go south (it's year-round in the tropics). In the Middle Atlantic states, the breeding season is protracted, and at Cape May, it can span over seven months—from the first Great Horned Owl on its nest in late January to the last renesting Black Skimmer fledgling to finally leave the colony in late August. And with the variety of breeders, and the sheer size and scope of the expansive nesting colonies, the breeding season (summer, to some) is certainly more than just a pause between the better known migration seasons. Summer is the season to watch fascinating bird behavior—frenetic singing, courtship, birds busily gathering food and feeding chicks, and, ultimately, fledgling birds making their first tentative, teetering flights. It can be a time of wonder for Cape May birders and, as a bonus, is far more pre-dictable and dependable than the weather-driven migration seasons.

About 112 species breed in Cape May County annually, and another 10 or 12 breed elsewhere in southern New Jersey. This is remarkable diversity for such a

Summer along the Delaware Bay is tran-quil, but birds still abound.

small area—a variety that readily attests to the wide range of habitats pres-ent. The breeding bird abundance also reflects Cape May's mid-Atlantic latitude. As during migration, there is a bit of an overlap between north and south during breeding season. For example, recently we have had both Red Crossbills and Swainson's Warblers on territory in Belleplain State Forest, a fine example of the northern forest meeting the southern swamp. The singing male Swainson's probably didn't find a mate; however, crossbill nesting was confirmed by adults and a youngster at a Dennisville feeder. Also, Ruffed Grouse meet the absolute southern limit of their coastal plain breeding range in Cape May County (they go farther south in the Appalachian Mountains), and the 1993 Black-necked Stilt nest found at Goshen Landing, on Cape May County's Delaware Bayshore, is the north-ernmost modern-day nesting record for this species. Among more com-mon species, both Whip-poor-will and Chuck-will's-widow are common in Cape May County, one of the few places where a conjunction of these northern and southern species can be found in good numbers.

Despite this meeting of north and south, if anything, Cape May's breeding avifauna has a southern flavor. A number of Cape May's forest breeders are near the northern limit of their normal breeding range. Northern Cape May County's extensive forests and swamps have a south-ern affinity, and the breeding birds do too. Prothonotary Warbler, Yellow-throated Warbler, Kentucky Warbler, Hooded Warbler, Worm-eating Warbler, and Louisiana Waterthrush, though not at their absolute northern limits, are all more common in southern swamps than northern forests. Usually hidden but loud and insistent, White-eyed Vireos populate most dense, brushy tangles on the cape, from Higbee Beach to Belleplain and beyond. Summer Tanager, a recent arrival (1970s), is near the northern limit of its range in southern New Jersey (and shares the same forests with the "northern" Scarlet Tanager). Also, Cape May fields and thickets host numerous Blue Grosbeaks, Prairie Warblers, and Yellow-breasted Chats.

Most Cape May breeding songbirds get an early start. The first spring passerine migrants to arrive are our returning breeding species. Pine Warblers normally arrive the first week of March, and Yellow-throated Warblers, Louisiana Waterthrushes, and Blue-Gray Gnatcatchers aren't far behind. Before the classic spring migration for neotropical songbirds even begins, Cape May forests are alive with birdsong—the territorial and courtship singing of characteristic Cape May breeders. In May, we have seen a lustily singing Blackpoll Warbler, still on its way north to its taiga breeding grounds, share the same branch with a local Pine Warbler already carrying food to hungry nestlings.

The vast Cape May salt marshes offer a rich assemblage of breeding birds as well. Seaside Sparrow, Saltmarsh Sharp-tailed Sparrow, and Marsh Wren are common nesters, all somewhat more abundant in the Delaware Bay marshes than those on the Atlantic side. All three are fairly easily seen in spring. Look for them from roads transecting the salt marshes, such as Jakes Landing, Goshen Landing, and Cooks Beach Road. Males like to sing from exposed perches on roadside shrubs or taller vegetation in the marsh. These three are notorious skulkers later in the summer. Prodigious Boat-tailed Grackles are a noisy addition to the lush, green *Spartina* wetlands. Clapper Rail is one of our most abundant breeding species on Cape May

Although hard to see, rails are present in good numbers in southern New Jersey. Sora, the rarest of the breeding rails, is often seen during migration.

marshes, which may seem surprising, given the difficulty of seeing
one. Clappers are, of course, heard
far more often than seen. Sometimes their choruses roll across the
salt marsh like the "wave" in a
football stadium, creating a din of
clapping. To see clappers, you must
be patient. Target either very low
tides, when they frequently pop
out of the grass along the edge of
mudflats or bathe in nearly dry
creek beds, or very high tides,
when they commonly swim across
small creeks. Great looks can be
had by using your car as a blind

*Excellent Black Rail habitat along the
Delaware Bayshore.*

and scanning down a nearly dry low-tide creek bed from the road's shoulder; the creek at the end of Reeds Beach Road has offered up great views
of bathing Clapper Rails to many patient observers. A full-moon tide or a
nor'easter storm tide in fall can produce many sightings, as rails seek high
ground to escape the flooded salt marshes. Then look for them along roadsides—Nummy's Island is usually a sure bet. By far the best way to see
Clapper Rails is to quietly float by canoe or kayak along the marsh edge or
in small creeks.

Virginia Rails breed in South Jersey freshwater marshes at Pond Creek
and the Meadows and along the Delaware Bayshore in the brackish upper
reaches of the salt marsh. Soras have bred just a few times in South Jersey
freshwater marshes. Black Rails once bred in appreciable numbers. Witmer
Stone related that one observer found twenty-four Black Rail nests in
coastal New Jersey, and the legendary Turner McMullen found some eighty
Black Rail nests in South Jersey in the early 1900s. Today, Black Rails are
rare (they are listed as a threatened species), but they are still out there—
confined largely to Delaware Bay marshes and always concentrated in high
marsh areas. Almost impossible to see, they can be hard to hear too. Listen
for them on a quiet night in May or June (and don't forget your mosquito
repellent); they call mostly from about 10:00 P.M. to 2:00 A.M., and usually
only during the low-tide cycle. They virtually never call during the full
moon; perhaps they are more vulnerable to predators then. (These were
some of the findings of the CMBO's targeted Black Rail status and distribution studies in the 1980s.) Remote Cumberland County is best, but
Jakes Landing is still a good spot to try; Black Rails are heard there every
spring, and sometimes into summer.

Willet, another common and conspicuous salt marsh breeder, return in mid-April and remain into August. As Alexander Wilson aptly put it in the 1800s, "This is one of the most noisy and noted birds that inhabit our salt marshes in summer."

ON THE BEACH

Piping Plovers are early arrivals in spring as they return to breed on Cape May barrier island beaches along the Atlantic coast. They usually show up the first week of March, the vanguard of the guild of beach-nesters, and are on nests by late April. Today, between 111 (in 2005) and 144 (in 2003) pairs of Piping Plovers nest in New Jersey at about thirty different sites; of these, usually about 38 to 43 pairs are found at fifteen different sites in Cape May County. They are aptly listed as an endangered species; in 2003, only about 1,676 pairs nested along the entire Atlantic coast. American Oystercatchers winter on the Cape in all but the coldest years, but even if they've pulled out to the south, they will certainly be back on Cape May County beaches and mudflats by early March. Their territorial, piping whistling is a constant backdrop to spring or summer coastal birding. Also a beach nester, Black Skimmers return in April, often staging along Delaware Bay before they move to oceanfront beach-nesting colonies in mid-May. Common Terns and Least Terns arrive relatively late, in early to mid-May for the most part, but their marsh-nesting cousins the Forster's Terns are early arrivals and usually numerous by mid-March to late March.

Signs and ropes protect migrant shorebirds drawn to Horseshoe Crab eggs on Delaware Bay beaches in spring, and also protect beachnesters on Atlantic coast beaches.

The location of beach-nesting bird colonies changes from year to year in response to constantly changing beach configurations (due to erosion and accretion) and to disturbance. The combined Cape May Migratory Bird Refuge and Cape May Point State Park beachfront usually hosts a small Least Tern colony and four or five pairs of Piping Plovers. The Two Mile Beach Unit of Cape May NWR also hosts these birds most years. Farther north, North Wildwood's beachfront near Hereford Inlet has a tern colony and three or four pairs of nesting plovers. Avalon, in the vicinity of the high dunes, often has a small tern colony and five to eight pairs of nesting plovers, and Corson's Inlet State Park usually has a substantial colony of terns, two or three pairs of plovers, and in some years Black Skimmers. Finally, the beach at the center of Ocean City usually has five to eight pairs of nesting plovers; Ocean City's north end near the Ocean City Longport Bridge usually hosts a beach-nesting bird colony and a pair of Piping Plovers.

By far the best and most consistent tern colony, and usually the only Black Skimmer colony in Cape May County, is at Stone Harbor Point. Dating back to Alexander Wilson's time, Stone Harbor Point and nearby islands in Hereford Inlet have long been recorded as prime locations for nesting terns. Witmer Stone noted that the "south end of Seven Mile Beach" (Stone Harbor Point) and "Gull Bar" (today called Champagne Island by locals) were the most reliable breeding locations for terns from the 1870s until the 1930s. Today, Stone Harbor Point and Champagne Island are southern New Jersey's stronghold for beach nesters, usually producing a healthy crop of Least and Common Terns, Black Skimmers, American Oystercatchers, and Piping Plovers.

Nesting success rates at all of these colonies can vary widely from year to year, however. In addition to the changing configuration and profile of beaches due to storms, the height and frequency of high tides can have a major impact on the colonies. For a beach-nesting bird colony, everything needs to be just right. The difference between success and failure can be as simple as the wind direction during a full-moon or new-moon high tide. If the wind is from the west, the colony survives; if the wind is from the east, even if moderate, the colony may be flooded out, necessitating renesting if it's early in the season or ensuring failure if it's late. Despite the dangers of predation, in most years flooding is the major cause of failed Piping Plover nests throughout New Jersey. Because terns and skimmers are relatively long-lived, the population can usually weather a year or two of failure.

Predation rates vary from year to year too. Predators include expected species such as foxes, raccoons, skunks, both feral and outdoor cats, crows, and burgeoning gull populations, as well as unlikely species such as Black-crowned Night-Herons, Peregrine Falcons, American Kestrels, and, amazingly, ghost crabs, which are known to prey on tiny chicks. Human disturbance in many forms (fireworks, kites, ultralight aircraft) also plays a major role in colony failure. Plover and tern nests are extremely vulnerable to vehicular and foot traffic, beach blankets, loose dogs, high tides, and stray volleyballs. Most tourists are oblivious. Volunteers working with New Jersey's Endangered and Nongame Species Program (ENSP) post most beach-nesting bird colonies with fence posts, string, and educational "Area Closed—Endangered Species Nesting" signs to alert beachgoers. In 2005, abandonment was the second highest cause of failed Piping Plover nests (predation was third), and most abandonment is caused by some form of disturbance. For beach-nesting birds, people can be predators.

Beach-nesting birds do not build noticeable nests. Their nests are on the beach and consist of a simple scrape or depression in the sand, often near a collection of shells, beach debris (driftwood), or sparse vegetation to help camouflage them. Their eggs are incredibly well camouflaged and blend in with sand and broken shells. To protect Piping Plovers from predators, the ENSP erects a small exclosure around the nest once it has been established. To see nesting Piping Plovers, simply look for the small circle of dune fence, but heed the signs, look from a safe distance, and do not disturb the birds. The young are precocious, so once they've hatched, you're likely to find them away from the nest foraging in the oceanfront intertidal zone or at the edges of back-dune ponds such as those at Cape May Point State Park and the Meadows.

The longevity of birds plays a large role in the persistence and continuity of tern colonies over time. Local marine biologist Dave Ward has spent considerable time in late summer and early fall focusing on wild birds and reading their band numbers with his powerful Questar spotting scope. The work is tedious, but his findings are fascinating. Of five Black Skimmers roosting on Cape May's beachfront in fall 2004, Dave learned from their band numbers that all were thirteen to twenty years old, and all had been banded in New Jersey from Island Beach, Barnegat Lighthouse, and Holgate south to Stone Harbor. He also learned that the banded Common Terns he observed were three to eighteen years old and had been banded on the St. Lawrence River (New York), Lake Champlain (Vermont), Great Gull Island (New York), and Lake Superior in Minnesota and Wisconsin. In 2005, of twenty-one Common Terns read at Cape May, five had been banded in South America. An adult bird was banded by Great Gull Island researchers on the terns' wintering grounds near Salvador on the central coast of Brazil, and two had been banded by South American banders at Punta Roas, Argentina, near Buenos Aires. A Common Tern seen by Ward in 2004 was banded as a nestling in 1987 near Old Saybrook, Connecticut, by a young bander named David Sibley. Three Caspian Terns seen at Stone

Sandwich Terns join Common Terns and Royal Terns in late summer on Cape May beaches.

Harbor Point in September 2005 had been banded as chicks at Gravelly Island, Michigan, on the south side of the Upper Peninsula, in 1991, 1990, and 1981. The 1981 bird was twenty-four years old.

Royal Terns are heavily banded at colonies south of New Jersey. Amazingly, over 90 percent of the adult Royal Terns that Ward observed at Cape May in fall 2005 were banded. Of the 300 Royal Terns he identified, many birds were at least fifteen years old, and 13 were older than twenty; the oldest was twenty-four. The terns had been banded mostly in Maryland and Virginia, but 12 were from colonies in North Carolina, including one from Kure Beach, a distance of 342 miles. This offers fascinating proof of both the origin of Royal Terns and the mileage they cover. Many Royal Terns travel long distances (and over many seasons) to spend the late summer and fall at Cape May. Most are probably attracted by the excellent feeding opportunities along the beaches and particularly at the fisheries-rich mouth of Delaware Bay. Of interest, two of the Royal Terns that Ward identified at Cape May he later saw again at their (and his) winter home on Sanibel Island, Florida. It's tough and time-consuming research, and Dave Ward is one of the few biologists reading bird bands on wild birds. He has now read over 5,000 bird bands in the past six years. He does this all on his own time, not supported by any project, making it even more impressive— citizen science at its best.

Even though it sometimes seems like a miracle that beach-nesting bird colonies produce any offspring at all, they do. They are resilient, persistent, and determined, and in some years, they are prolific. At Stone Harbor Point in 2003, 926 Black Skimmers produced about 200 young, and 1,500 Common Terns fledged about 464 young. Two pairs of Gull-billed Terns produced 4 young, but most of the 200 Least Tern nests were flooded out by a July new-moon tide. Production was low in 2004, but in 2005, the Black Skimmer colony had the best year in recent memory, with 1,800 adults fledging 550 young. Ten pairs of Piping Plovers fledged 10 young, which is very good, considering that this total equals the number of Piping Plovers fledged at Stone Harbor Point over the last five years combined. In 2005, Least Terns and Common Terns did not fare so well due to flooding, high tides, and predators (mostly Laughing Gulls).

Always of interest at Stone Harbor are the rare terns attracted to the thriving colony. Most years, Roseate, Arctic, and Black Terns are in attendance, sometimes for several weeks. Royal Terns are always seen courting in and over the colony in spring. They have never successfully nested there, but the existence of a thriving Royal Tern colony at Ocean City, Maryland, just 36 miles south of Cape May, means that Stone Harbor Point breeding may well be imminent. Usually by late summer, a few Sandwich Terns and numerous Caspian Terns are about. Mix all these beach birds with both spring and fall shorebirds (Stone Harbor Point is a major regional high-tide and nightly shorebird roost at all seasons), and Stone Harbor Point can be a wondrous destination for the Cape May summertime birder. Be sure to enjoy the lively sounds of the colony up close, at the perimeter fence, where the noise can be almost deafening. The harsh yet musical *keeyer* of the terns, the deep, resonant barking of the Black Skimmers . . . it's all food for the summertime birder's soul.

SUMMER GULLS

Laughing Gulls completely withdraw from Cape May in winter. The last few are usually seen at the end of the seawatch or maybe one or two on the Cape May CBC. They winter in Florida through coastal Texas and south into Mexico. Laughing Gulls aren't gone long, though; the vanguard in mid-March is soon joined by a flood of arrivals. By mid-April, virtually anywhere in the county, the din of clamoring Laughing Gulls can be heard. Behind the barrier islands, the din swells to a crescendo; here, on these vast marshes, is the largest Laughing Gull colony in the world—an almost continuous (broken only by creeks and channels) broad band of nests stretching from Wildwood Crest to Ocean City. The epicenter is behind Stone Harbor, where nearly 30,000 pairs were estimated in the late 1970s.

Such vast numbers of gulls play an unknown but significant role in the nearshore coastal ecology. Laughing Gulls spread out from the coastal colonies to all reaches of southern New Jersey, feeding from far up Delaware Bay to the deep-water canyons 75 miles offshore, from landfills and fast-food parking lots to the boardwalks and beaches. They are a major consumer of horseshoe crab eggs, competing directly with migratory shorebirds for this precious seasonal resource. Indeed, it has been theorized that the former abundance of horseshoe crab eggs may have been an enabling factor in the growth of gull colonies, providing high-protein food at the crucial egg-laying stage. It also seems, anecdotally, that Laughing Gull predation on tern and skimmer eggs and chicks has increased since horseshoe crab egg abundance has declined so drastically. (Laughing Gulls are much more dangerous predators than the "big" gulls, because laughers are faster and more agile—better able to avoid adult terns and skimmers defending their nests and young.)

For better or worse, Laughing Gulls are a part of life at Cape May, for beachgoers, fishermen, farmers, and birders alike. Laughing Gulls are the bird that best embodies summer for many residents and visitors. Skilled robbers at beaches and barbecues, they are either loved or hated, evoking disparate reactions such as Witmer Stone's fondness for his beloved "summer gulls" or remonstrances such as "damned seagulls" from Clay's own mother as they indiscriminately soiled clothes-line laundry, birdbaths, and '65 Chevy convertible. Like them or not, Laughing Gulls are easily the most numerous, visible, and vocal of all of Cape May's summer birds. We like them; they are handsome, alive, full of energy and attitude. They have more than adapted; they have conquered every corner of the Cape, and every niche (except for the deep forests, although even here they frequently fly-catch, foraging for insects above the canopy). The clamor of the vast Laughing Gull nesting colonies on the marshes behind the barrier islands can be an almost deafening din up close, but on otherwise quiet, mid-summer nights, it can be relaxing, constant background music for those who listen.

Laughing Gulls are striking in their displays. A pair faces off, each throwing its head back and calling with its bright red mouth exposed. The call, a *ha, ha, ha, haaaaaa, haaaaaa, haaaaa,* really does sound like someone laughing. In mid-April, if you look closely, you're likely to see a pink blush on their chests—a diet related color visible at the peak of breeding.

A back-bay boat cruise through the salt marshes in mid-summer is a must. By then, there are hundreds of Laughing Gull chicks and many eggs yet to hatch. Newly hatched Clapper Rail chicks are likely, and adult Willet bracket their young. Common Tern, Forster's Tern, and Osprey young have hatched. Laughing Gulls weave their nests around marsh vegetation, so the nest floats up with the rising tide and settles back down with the falling tide, held in place by grasses. Ideally, the tides are never high enough to lift the nest above the grasses and set it loose to drift away from the colony and down a creek, but in some years, storms coincide with a full or new moon's super high tide, and all nests are flooded, float off the marsh, and are lost. If this happens, many marsh nesters begin anew—displaying, pair-bonding, mating, and working on new nests. Some summers, storm tides hit every few weeks or each month, just as young are about to hatch. A series of nest failures may result in a completely unsuccessful nesting season, since it will eventually be too late in the season for adults to renest. Thus, one can't help but admire Laughing Gulls and all the other marsh-nesting birds. It is a precarious nesting strategy—and even more so now with the rising sea level—but the big years make up for the bad ones.

WADING BIRD ROOKERIES
First-time visitors, and sometimes even well-versed birders, are often unprepared for the abundance of wading birds—herons, egrets, and Glossy Ibis—on the Jersey coast. From mid-March through early November, wading birds fill South Jersey marshes, rivers, and ponds. Except if you are birding in the woods and fields, they are always around, always in view. It has been reported that the current colonies of wading birds on the Jersey Shore constitute the largest numbers north of Florida. In most years, Pea Patch Island, in the Delaware River just off Salem County to the west (technically, in Delaware waters), has a huge colony of waders (about 3,000 nesting pairs in 2001, including ten species of herons, egrets, and ibis) and is said to be the largest single colony of herons and egrets north of Florida. (In the 1980s, there were up to 12,000 nesting pairs there.) In late summer and early fall, when local South Jersey breeding waders are augmented by postbreeding dispersal birds from the south, numbers in both the Atlantic and Delaware Bay marshes are huge—Great Egrets and Snowy Egrets everywhere speckling the verdant wetland grasses with brilliant white.

Historically, waders formed large colonies, like the former one at Stone Harbor; today, their colonies are smaller and more spread out. They breed mostly on the overgrown successional spoil islands (created by dredging) scattered throughout the coastal back bays—a strategy that forces them to nest in much lower vegetation than in former colonies in maritime forests, possibly making them more vulnerable to predators. All waders breed on the Atlantic coast; none, except for Green Heron, Great Blue Heron, and Black-crowned Night-Heron, breed on the Delaware Bayshore, other than at Pea Patch Island. This is particularly curious, because thousands of herons and egrets feed on Delaware Bay marshes daily, commuting back and forth from Atlantic coast colonies. (One theory as to why they don't breed on the bayshore is the superabundance of Great Horned Owls there.) Commuting flocks often follow water corridors. The summer skies over the CMBO in Goshen offer a constant parade as wading birds follow Sluice Creek. Waders also commute daily to Delaware to feed. You can stand at Cape May Point in summer and watch their constant comings and goings; the egrets think nothing of crossing the 9.65 miles of water to Delaware and back.

Historically, small numbers of Great Blue Herons nested at the Stone Harbor Bird Sanctuary on occasion, but generally, they form their own

Many heron rookeries are now on shrub-covered dredge spoil islands in the marsh.

single-species colonies. There are no true Great Blue Heron colonies in Cape May County, although the Great Blue Heron is a daily bird in mid-summer in very small numbers; a few pairs probably breed here. The closest big colonies are near Stockton State College (near Forsythe NWR), the upper Maurice River, and west of Stow Creek on the Cumberland County–Salem County border. Great Blue Herons seem to be on the increase; New Jersey great blue rookeries have gone from five in 1973 to about forty today. Tricolored Herons and Yellow-crowned Night-Herons are somewhat near the northern limit of their breeding range in New Jersey and are specifically sought and enjoyed by Cape May birders. Nummy's Island remains one of the best places for both species. Look for Yellow-crowned Night-Herons hidden in high grass, often away from the water, where they feed primarily on fiddler crabs, not fish (and, because they are mostly nocturnal, look for them early and late).

The famous Stone Harbor Bird Sanctuary, 21 acres protected with enlightened and great fanfare in 1947, today stands empty of egrets. It failed for the first time in seventy-five years in 1993, and the birds have never returned. Plausible causes include drastic site alteration by the cutting of Poison Ivy on the perimeter just prior to the nesting season, numerous dead trees resulting from recent ditching and flooding for mosquito control (we'll never learn), the development of a large Fish Crow roost there, predation by Great Horned Owls nesting in the sanctuary, raccoons, the accumulation of guano (bird droppings), and an ever-growing population of feral cats. Also, the Stone Harbor Bird Sanctuary is far more of an "island" today than formerly, when Stone Harbor Point began just beyond the southern end of the sanctuary. The birds from the Stone Harbor Bird Sanctuary have dispersed to numerous smaller colonies on spoil islands in the area, but one of the Cape's most glorious spectacles—the morning exodus and the return of the waders at sunset, spiraling into the canopy by the thousands—is now part of history. It was a sight that Clay grew up with. He'd often ride his bicycle there to watch the nightly pirouette of the herons. Today, it is only a cherished memory from long ago.

Despite both historic and modern-day setbacks, herons and egrets can still be enjoyed daily at Cape May. From mid-April through early summer, rain-flooded farm fields, the pond along Reeds Beach road, and the freshwater impoundments at Beaver Swamp WMA, to name a few sites, attract hundreds of Glossy Ibis. By mid-April, all the egrets and herons have settled into their salt marsh homes and are easily visible from the barrier island causeways (Ocean Drive north of Cape May, North Wildwood Boulevard, Stone Harbor Boulevard, Avalon Boulevard) and the entire length of Nummy's Island. Study all the wading birds, even those you thought you knew intimately, since the breeding plumage transforms them. A Great Egret in breeding plumage with full plumes and bright lime green lores is a show-stopper. Back-bay boat tours offer another excellent window into their world, often cruising by active colonies on otherwise inaccessible spoil islands.

Particularly interesting in late summer are the large feeding aggregations that form on the coastal marshes in early morning, when wading birds find schools of baitfish trapped by the dropping tide in salt marsh pools. Sometimes several hundred egrets, herons, and Glossy Ibis gather, attracting a host of other birds too—yellowlegs, cormorants, gulls, and terns. Migrant Black Terns always show up in these aggregations in July and August, but in far fewer numbers than formerly. If the summer is hot and dry, with little rain, water levels drop in the freshwater ponds at the Meadows and Cape May Point State Park, concentrating the fish. Wading birds appear by the hundreds to feast on fish stranded in pockets of shallow water. A summer rain squall can change the condition overnight, raising the water level and making it harder for the birds to catch fish. Then they disperse until the water level drops again.

Herons, egrets, and ibis are an integral and valued part of Cape May birdlife—common, colorful, and always animated (except, of course, when frozen in place waiting for unsuspecting fish). Their orderly flocks are favorite sights, constantly crisscrossing the peninsula's summer skies in their commute between Atlantic coastal rookeries and the banquet offered by the rich, expansive summer wetlands of Delaware Bay.

EVER-PRESENT FISH HAWKS

Osprey (still "fish hawks" to many locals) are an enjoyable accent in the summer landscapes and skies. Nesting virtually everywhere along the coast, mostly on man-made nest platforms but also on duck blinds, channel markers, transmission poles, and even communications towers, they are always in view, commuting back and forth to the ocean or bay in pursuit of favored Menhaden (bunker) or incessantly whistling from high overhead as a pumped-up male proudly displays a prized catch. Osprey have now recovered from the dark days of the late 1960s and early 1970s, when their population dwindled to a mere 50 largely unproductive nests statewide. Today, they have largely bounced back from the DDT era; nests numbered 366 statewide in 2003, with about 60 nests in Cumberland County's Maurice River region alone. The average 1.54 young produced per active nest in 2005 represents productivity well above the minumum needed to sustain the population. Osprey have once again reclaimed their rightful place and honored, hallmark status in Cape May skies. Osprey numbers continue to grow. Their recovery reflects more than the flushing of DDT from the estuarine system; it also attests to vast improvements in water quality, better fisheries management, and rebounding fish populations.

Banding studies long ago proved that North American Osprey remain on the wintering grounds for their entire first year, making their first return trip to natal nest sites when they are around two years old. In recent years, radiotelemetry—specifically, satellite telemetry—has given us wondrous new insight into the movements of locally nesting Osprey populations. Birds fitted with transmitters from near Stone Harbor and from the Maurice River population have been tracked for a number of seasons. They left the Cape and followed the Atlantic coast south through Florida, then island-hopped through Cuba and the Caribbean to South America. South Jersey Osprey mostly winter in Guyana, Venezuela, northern Brazil, and even along the Amazon River in Brazil. This is an amazing journey and quite a change of scenery for Cape May birds; in just a few weeks, they go from feasting on Delaware Bay bunker and Weakfish to catching piranha and catfish on Llanos ponds and rivers. One adult female Maurice River Osprey originally banded in 1998 was tracked with satellite telemetry for nearly five years and always made an annual autumn journey to Manaus, Brazil. Her satellite signal was lost over the Carribean on her 2002 return flight, which was her final journey north; she never returned to her longtime nest. In her tenure on the Maurice River, she's thought to have raised at least twenty young, an enduring legacy for a remarkable bird.

Bald Eagles have also made an astonishing recovery, from a low of one pair for a decade prior to 1986 to over fifty-seven pairs in New Jersey in 2006. More than forty of these breeding pairs are in southern New Jersey along the Delaware Bayshore. Neighboring Cumberland County hosts more than twenty nests. In Cape May County, at least four nests are present—one in the forest behind East Creek Lake in Belleplain State Forest, one visible from the parking lot in Beaver Swamp WMA, one on the Tuckahoe River, and one on Cedar Swamp Creek—and others are suspected or rumored. Once again, after a long absence, Bald Eagles are a daily sight for Cape May birders. Breeding adults do not migrate but remain year-round in the vicinity of the nest. Birding on the bayshore almost always produces one or more sightings, and most days with northwest winds produce one or two over Cape May Point. This can be true even in summer; these eagles may be locals on an outing, dispersing birds, wanderers, or true migrants. Bald Eagles are good examples of the protracted and overlapping seasons at Cape May. They are one of the earliest nesting birds, second only to the Great Horned Owl, and spend a lot of time in January working on their nests. Some eagles are incubating eggs by early February, and we have seen them refurbishing nests as early as late September, just as fall migration is getting into full swing.

Peregrine Falcons are back too. Today, of about twenty pairs in New Jersey (which fledged 42 young in 2005), four pairs are found in Cape May County—one along the Tuckahoe River, one behind Sea Isle City, one in a nest box erected on an Osprey platform behind Stone Harbor, and one on an abandoned hunting shack in the marsh behind Wildwood Crest. Two others are nearby—one just over the county line near West Creek, and one at Egg Island Point near the mouth of the Maurice River. Look for sturdy platform structures on pilings and the igloolike houses used to create the artificial caves peregrines need. They nest on bridges too; all the major Delaware River bridges host a pair. In Forsythe NWR, one venerable nesting site (which hosted one of the first successful pairs during the early reintroduction program) is the tower readily visible from the wildlife drive.

Another peregrine pair, urban cliff dwellers and skilled hunters of boardwalk pigeons, nest high on a ledge at the Hilton Casino-Hotel in Atlantic City. The female of this pair was one of the first offspring of the original hacked pairs—from an artificial aerie in Barnegat Bay. When she died in 2001 she was sixteen years old, had outlasted several mates, and had raised twenty-five chicks on her clifflike Atlantic City ledge. She was sadly missed by many but was replaced in a few short months by a new bird recruited by the courting tiercel (male). Interestingly, these Atlantic City peregrines seem to like the nightlife; they have been seen hunting over the boardwalk at night, apparently targeting the Laughing Gulls that hawk insects attracted to the bright boardwalk lights. Peregrines are almost a daily sight at any season when birding in southern New Jersey, especially if you are birding near shorebird concentrations. In summer, expect to see clumsy youngsters learning to fly and hunt. Always look for peregrines on barrier island water towers both early and late in the day. They commonly sit and roost on the high towers, where the commanding view offers a perfect vantage point for hunting peregrines. Several times we have seen a peregrine leave a water tower and in a long, shallow, increasingly fast stoop, drop on prey several miles away—prey clearly spotted from the bird's perch on the high, urban water tower. To them, it's just an oddly shaped cliff.

FULL CIRCLE

The end of summer comes subtly at Cape May. Often the first sign of summer drawing to a close and the coming of fall is an absence, rather than any new presence. It may be in the backyard, when you suddenly realize that you haven't heard the chattering of your Orchard Oriole for several days, a bird that has been a constant morning companion for nearly three months. Or when the dawn chorus of robins, a welcome din outside the open window all spring and summer, is suddenly silent. On the wetlands, long before we actually see a southbound flock of Willet, we suddenly realize on a hot August morning that there aren't many Willet around, that their ceaseless piping has subsided, a portent of the changing season. By mid-August, almost all the remaining Glossy Ibis are youngsters. Then, in the waning days of August, you realize that there are no longer any adult Osprey around to respond to the food-begging cries of their fledged young. In a reversal of the classic empty-nest syndrome, the juvenile Osprey wait in vain for the adults to return, but their parents are already winging their way south to the Carolinas, Florida, Cuba, and on to South America.

The end of summer is so subtle that even after more than thirty years of birding at Cape May, it still comes as a bit of a shock. But the seasons go round and round—even while the painted ponies are still going up and down at Cape May arcades and boardwalks, a hint of fall is in the air. It may still be some of the hottest weather of the year, with the late August heat and humidity taking a toll on beachgoers and birders, but autumn has crept up on us. As visitors still enjoy their summer fun in the sun, the blinking of Bobolinks

A summer scene at Jakes Landing: the birding is slower paced, but fall comes quick.

passing high overhead is an almost subliminal sound, barely heard over the waves breaking gently on Cape May beaches. Those who are out and about may notice waves of Eastern Kingbirds, orioles, and neotropical warblers, now muted in plumage and song, passing over the Higbee Beach Dike early each morning. On the coastal marshes, with the din of Laughing Gulls finally done, you can hear the far-off urgent calling of yellowlegs in an unseen flock high above. Cape May's seasons have now come full circle, and will the circle always be unbroken.

PART TWO

A CAPE MAY PRIMER

"GOSH, AN ALBATROSS!"

I turned quickly as my coleader Louise Zemaitis uttered a sharp expletive, mainly into her cell phone, but, with the volume and desperate tone of her voice, also to the parking lot, the nearby woods, and maybe even to the sky above. Her language certainly got the attention of our Cape May Bird Observatory workshop group, bringing all conversation to a standstill. It was only a garden-variety expletive, but the intonation implied so much more. This was not the exasperation of the dog peeing on the carpet, or even the anguish of a broken water pipe. Suffice it to say, she didn't say "gosh."

"That doesn't sound good," I remarked to the gathered birders, for I knew that this expletive—the first I had heard Louise utter in the nearly twelve years I had known her—probably denoted a missed bird—a *really good* missed bird. I also had a pretty good idea of the identity of the missed bird. We were at Brigantine, and the caller was at Reeds Beach, near Cape May, an agonizing hour away. We had been watching multitudes of shore-birds and having a grand time. The caller was Louise's husband Michael O'Brien, and he had just seen the albatross.

An albatross. Not usually a field guide plate much turned to by New Jersey birders. They probably cross the mind of every birder who signs up for a pelagic trip, but seeing an albatross in the North Atlantic can be only a distant, furtive hope, the ultimate wish bird. In my several thousand hours of seawatching over the past twenty-five years, an albatross had always been a background dream, a fervent desire, but, in reality, a faint possibility, akin to winning the lottery. Only once in the storied history of Cape May ornithology had an albatross been seen, when the late, great Harold Axtell watched two Black-browed Albatross together off the South Cape May beach during an easterly gale in October 1974.

The saga of the bird that would become, arguably, the bird of the century for Cape May had begun two days before, on May 21, 2000. Shawneen Finnegan, a Cape May regular of exceptional skill and background and unimpeachable integrity—an important factor, given what she was about to report—was driving north on the Garden State Parkway, about 6 miles north of Cape May City. She was heading for an artists' reception, navigating Sunday-at-the-shore homeward-bound traffic in the left-hand lane, when she saw an albatross gliding just above eye level alongside her car, flying above the grassy median strip. Shawneen would later relate her dive for the right lane, then the shoulder, briefly skidding on the wet grass before coming to a stop and jumping out to watch the bird for maybe a minute longer before it disappeared.

Coincidentally, Pat and I were privileged to have dinner with Shawneen that same evening and relive her story. I'm sure the staff of the nearby lumberyard will be talking for years about the crazy woman who ran into the office, breathless and begging to use the phone, claiming an emergency, then shouting into the phone about an albatross as she attempted to alert the local birding community. Over dinner, Shawneen's excitement was still palpable, infectious, her trademark smile even wider than normal, as she described the sighting. "Then the albatross disappeared behind the trees" is a phrase probably never before spoken in North American birding.

Despite hundreds of hours of searching by dozens of birders later that day and the next (Monday), the wayward overland albatross was not relocated. Shawneen was sure of the identification: an adult Yellow-nosed Albatross. But it looked like it would remain a brief, one-day, single-observer sighting, destined to tease the rest of us forever.

On Tuesday, our workshop group had just finished a tour of the dikes at Brigantine when Louise got the call. "Oh my God, the albatross is back," she revealed to the fifteen riveted birders. "It was first seen over Route 47, then it flew up and down the beach at Reeds Beach. It's still there now!" Louise, Pete Dunne, and I held a brief, hurried leaders' powwow. What to do? Reeds Beach, on New Jersey's Delaware Bay, was at least an hour away. It was after noon, and we hadn't eaten lunch yet. Pete, who eschews bird chasing the way a cat disdains water, lobbied quietly against it, more with a raised eyebrow than with voiced concerns. He had a point. After all, this was a CMBO workshop, not a birding tour; it was intended to foster learning, not the chasing of rarities. An afternoon spent on an albatross odyssey would inevitably bump something else from the busy schedule, either classroom or fieldwork, making it a decision of consequence. We had already "wasted" two hours of precious workshop time in hopeful but fruitless scanning over the Cape May Rips (a likely spot, theoretically, to spot the albatross) on the previous day. What to do now?

Although I held little hope of actually catching up to the albatross, I looked at our dilemma in reverse. What if hundreds of others saw the bird and we hadn't even tried? And, even if we didn't see the bird, what could be worse than *not* trying for the bird of the century? The eager looks on the faces of the workshop participants, even the few beginners, decided the day. We'd go for it! Lunch was forgotten. Smoking down the parkway with the pedal down, two white, fifteen-passenger vans formed a caravan on a wild albatross chase. We drove with one eye on the rearview mirror and the other on the sky (after all, the first sighting had been over the Garden State Parkway).

"Michael called again. It's headed south," yelled Louise, hanging out the van's passenger window like a summertime teenager, as both vans accelerated away from a tollbooth. "Let's head for the Concrete Ship," she shouted. This landmark and excellent seawatch vantage point at the tip of the Cape May peninsula would be the best spot to intercept the bird.

As we pulled into the Concrete Ship's parking lot at the end of Sunset Boulevard exactly one hour later, Louise's cell phone ominously rang again. "The albatross is still north of us—it was just seen at Kimbles Beach—it seems to be working back and forth," related Louise hurriedly. "It's headed toward Reeds Beach again." The workshop participants ate lunch as we leaders desperately scanned the bay and sky to the north, waiting, hoping. Each Northern Gannet drew a second look; a distant speck of a Sooty Shearwater, normally a great bird, got hardly a notice. We were after bigger fish.

Back in the vans, we decided to head north to Reeds Beach. This route meant secondary roads—travel would be slower, and it would take at least twenty-five minutes. Because it was shorebird and horseshoe crab season (not to mention the number of converging albatross seekers), Reeds Beach might be crowded, and parking would be difficult. So a hasty decision was made: we would go to Cooks Beach instead, another landing on Delaware Bay just south of Reeds Beach, but easier to get to.

We turned off Route 47 and raced down the rural gravel road to Cooks. About ten birders were already stationed there, and you could instantly separate the haves from the have-nots. The have-nots scanned furiously, grim looks on their faces. The haves chatted together, animated, with the most self-satisfied smiles imaginable. John Danzenbaker, a New Jersey resident and onetime top American Birding Association world list holder, proved that one never tires of the chase. He had just secured both his ABA area and state Yellow-nosed Albatross, and a bit of history. He said simply, grinning broadly, "For once I was in the right place at the right time."

"It was here just fifteen minutes ago," said friend and colleague, Jim Dowdell. He continued, "I can't believe it. I was looking for the wing pattern. But it was so close, I finally realized—forget the wings, look at the yellow on the top of the bill! It headed south, soaring back over the trees." My heart sank. South? Had we actually passed it en route? Would it return? Did we screw up? We scanned constantly, perhaps a bit desperately, out over the water and back over the trees. Thousands of gulls filled the now lowering skies, making binocular scans a living kaleidoscope. An albatross may be huge, but amidst the spectacle of May on Delaware Bay, finding it could be the proverbial needle in a haystack—one bird out of the tens of thousands that filled the bayshore skies.

After about twenty minutes, albatross enthusiasm began to wane a bit, but there was plenty to do and much to look at. Trying to put the workshop back on track, Pete and Louise continued to teach about horseshoe crabs in the tide line, how to distinguish Sanderling from Semipalmated Sandpiper, and alternative versus basic plumages. Nervous flocks of Red Knot hurried past, brick red and gray against steel water and silver sky.

We don't normally give MVP awards in our workshops, because every participant brings so much—background, perspective, enthusiasm, enjoyment. Nonetheless, we presented John Gluth from Brentwood, New York, with a sculpted albatross (crafted by Louise's son, Bradley) and our heartfelt thanks at our group's farewell dinner.

"I think I have the albatross," John, standing next to me, said quietly yet firmly. I followed his gaze. Size or not, picking the bird out of hundreds of soaring gulls took a few precious moments. The bird was wing-on, going away. Albatross or not? Gannet maybe? I remember a fleeting indecision. Then it turned toward us, offering a full profile from the upper side. The white upper tail coverts gleamed. "Here it is!" I screamed. And there it was, gliding back and forth against the scudding clouds. It was behind us, not over the beach or bay, but unbelievably back over the woodlands.

The albatross rode the sky with the grace of a gull, rock steady in the wind, in full control. It never flapped once, or even circled, but just rode the freshening northeast wind over the marshes and trees, quartering back and forth, a master of dynamic soaring. The albatross seemed to dominate the land every bit as much as it had conquered the sea. I selfishly stole one (OK, two) good views of the banking bird through the scope, then, mindful of our mission and duty, worked to get others up to the scope and on the bird. Louise called out constant directions, instructions. Pete, putting his substantial skills to work, adroitly cycled people through his scope, deftly refinding the bird for each new arrival behind the eyepiece. As it drifted away to the south, still over the trees, I yearningly watched it disappear in my binoculars. The gently down-curved, long-winged shape is indelibly imprinted in my memory.

Then everyone was talking at once—impressions, questions, comparisons, superlatives—savoring a successful chase, the thrill of victory. For beginner and veteran alike, it was a once-in-a-lifetime experience, a life bird for everyone (except Antarctic veteran Pete). Not only was it a wayward bird, at least 4,000 miles out of range, but it was also a bird a full hemisphere away from home. Cape May has seen rarer birds, such as the 1993 Whiskered Tern (a first record for the Western Hemisphere), or maybe even the 1990 Lesser Sand Plover (Mongolian Plover), the first for the East Coast of the United States and even farther out of range (from its Siberian breeding grounds or Australian winter home) than the albatross. Yet I think all who saw the bird will agree that there may never be a bird of greater outright charisma than our Yellow-nosed Albatross. If it isn't the bird of the century, I hope I'm there to see what supplants it.

Much was said and written about the wayward albatross, from the cover story of the *Press of Atlantic City* to the *New York Times* and even to *ABC Nightly News* with Peter Jennings. Excellent photos obtained by several lucky folks graced the covers and pages of *North American Birds, Records of New Jersey Birds,* and many others. What was almost certainly the same bird had been sighted in Buzzards Bay, Massachusetts, on May 9, 2000, and at Fire Island, New York, on May 15. After departing New Jersey on May 23 (it was last seen about an hour after our fortuitous encounter, photographed, unbelievably, sitting on a sandbar near Town Bank), the Yellow-nosed Albatross was subsequently seen in Rhode Island and Nantucket. It is believed that it was visiting land in search of a nesting colony and a mate—extremely unlikely in the North Atlantic. Even though it was winter and the non-breeding season in the Southern Hemisphere at Tristan da Cunha and other islands where the Yellow-nosed Albatross breeds, it is conceivable that years, or perhaps even decades, in the North Atlantic had reset this bird's biological clock. A Black-browed Albatross returned to the same gannetry at Hermaness in the Shetland Islands, United Kingdom, for nearly twenty years, building a nest for a mate that, sadly, never came. It is interesting and curious that such an event as a lost and lonely albatross can be a cause for jubilant celebration for birders.

Yet celebrate we did. The bird was toasted more than a few times. Even two weeks later, whenever two birders met, they talked of the albatross. Has it been refound? Where do you think it will be seen next, Kiptopeke maybe? Cape Hatteras? Do you think it might return next year? For me, there were a couple of interesting footnotes. Cooks Beach, where we finally caught up to the bird, is a place I've known all my life. It's about 3 miles from our home, and Reeds Beach is even closer as the albatross flies. My friend Jerry Liguori (at the time, a New Jersey Fish and Wildlife biologist), was one of the first to spot the albatross Tuesday morning. He followed it up Route 47 into the town of Goshen and watched it fly right over our backyard. Had I been home, I might have had a Yellow-nosed Albatross on my yard list.

Pat and I walk our dog at Cooks Beach about once a week, and we have been visiting Reeds Beach, our local patch, for the past thirty years. I had always thought that someday, among the vast and magnificent spring shorebird concentrations that occur there, someone would find a *really* good bird. Birds such as the Broad-billed Sandpiper, Red-necked Stint, and even

Great Knot crossed my mind. But never in my wildest dreams did I think that I would one day stand at Cooks Beach, surrounded by shoals of shore-birds, and watch a Yellow-nosed Albatross soaring over the woods, or that during a CMBO workshop I would have the privilege to share such a bird with fifteen excited friends and students of bird study. Such is the joy of birding. Few, if any, words can express it. Except maybe "gosh!"

—C. S.

6

WHAT, WHEN, HOW,
AND WHERE

*The proximity of the woodland and upland pastures to the salt
marshes and the beach offers unusual conditions in that it brings into
close association several very different groups of birds, making it
possible to observe a very large number of species in a single day....
The charm of the whole situation, due to these various conditions, is
that one never knows what he may see. There is always the element of
uncertainty. Some straggler from the south or north may come down
that great seacoast way farther than any of his kind has come before;
some waif may be driven in from his true home far out on the ocean;
or we may awake some morning, in autumn, to find that with a
change in the wind, the whole country is deluged with birds, where
but a few individuals had been seen the day before. These are the
things that lure the bird-lover to Cape May and make an intensive
study of its bird life so interesting."*
—Witmer Stone, *Bird Studies at Old Cape May* (1937)

We may not know exactly where that next good bird is hidden—
maybe New Jersey's first White Wagtail or Cape May's overdue Varied
Thrush or Sage Thrasher—but we can tell you where the haystacks are and
the best way to go about looking for the needle. Always remember that
anything is possible, maybe even an albatross.

There is no bad time to bird at Cape May. It is a place where migration never ends, where late fall birds stay to add spice to winter birding, and
where the exciting spring migration brings an abundance of breeding
birds. Cape May is a place for all seasons. There isn't even a bad time of day
to bird at Cape May. First light in spring and fall brings dynamic morning

flight, and the last rays at dusk reveal liftoff for the continued journey. In between, mornings can offer skeins of waterbirds moving by, and afternoons can be filled with shorebirds in spring and hawks and sunset "Merlin madness" in fall. If there are no raptors, you can look for ducks in the state park ponds or scan offshore for gannets and gulls. Many birders continue to bird into the night at Cape May, in fall watching warblers and other songbirds crossing the rising full moon or owls passing through the beam of the lighthouse, and listening for the mysterious chip notes and calls of the host of migrating birds. In spring, some of the best rail choruses occur in the dark of night, and some birds—Yellow-breasted Chats, Ovenbirds, cuckoos, Seaside Sparrows, and nightjars—sing all night long. At the peak of migration at Cape May, it can be hard to find the time to sleep.

There is really no wrong way to bird at Cape May. There is almost always something to find, and it can be found almost anywhere. Remember first and foremost that the Cape May phenomenon is not limited to Cape May Point or Cape Island. In summer and winter, the best action is often farther afield—Belleplain, the Delaware Bayshore, or Stone Harbor—and even during the peak of migration, birds fill the peninsula and spill over the top and sides. For this reason, some of the "better" birds, the vagrants or rarities, are often found at out-of-the-way places or at unusual times of season or day.

We all succumb to the lore and lure of Cape May Point during peak conditions, however. Even New Jersey's most inveterate patch birders, who religiously canvass their prized home turf year-round, will show up at Higbee Beach on that killer cold front. And there is a good reason why they do so, along with hundreds of other birders: There may be no *wrong* way to bird at Cape May, but there is a *best* way. At all seasons there are patterns that veteran Cape May birders use to increase the odds, to increase their chances of finding either lots of birds or the particularly juicy ones. There are peak times, peak conditions, and best places to concentrate your efforts. There are peak weather conditions to be afield and a few to avoid.

Along with telling you what to do at key times and places, we'll tell you what to do when you're dealt a bad hand—what to do if you're at Cape May to watch hawks and the wind is blowing a gale and it's raining (go seawatching, of course). Read on, and we'll tell you the likely places where the birds are hiding at Cape May.

DAILY AND SEASONAL FOCUS
The time of year generally dictates where and on which group of birds Cape May birders focus their efforts. The amount of time you have, how long you will be at Cape May, is a key factor in planning a schedule and route. In fall, the epicenter of birding is Cape May Point—more specifically,

the hawkwatch platform. If you have only a weekend to spend, almost all your birding should be on Cape Island, the landmass south of the Cape May Canal. The scope, the lay of the land, and the distances involved mean that this area could easily be birded by bicycle, if you are so inclined.

Most birders begin an autumn day at Higbee Beach WMA, some starting predawn to listen to the nocturnal flight, or at sunrise to enjoy the morning flight. Sometimes the parking lot is such a good spot that it's hard to leave, but birders normally congregate at the morning flight observation platform next to the Higbee Dike. The morning flight can actually be witnessed and enjoyed virtually anywhere at Higbee Beach. After an hour or two watching the inimitable morning flight, plan to spend another hour or so working the five fields, hedgerows, edges, and woodland trails for "fallout" birds that have put in to rest and feed. By midmorning, many birders gravitate to the hawkwatch platform at Cape May Point State Park (note that whereas Higbee Beach has seasonal portable toilets, the state park has heated bathrooms). At the state park, enjoy the elevated view from the hawkwatch, scan the ocean and freshwater ponds from the beachfront, or hike the various trails (from a half-mile wheelchair-accessible trail to a 2-mile trail through a variety of habitats) for additional passerines, waterbirds, and other vantage points for the hawk flight. The hawkwatch can be good all day, but by noon or 1:00 P.M. the flight may be high and less satisfying. Of note, there is no hint of the midday lull that often occurs at other hawkwatches. The hawks will be higher, because midday thermals are the strongest, but cumulus clouds dotted with the specks of raptors make for the most challenging hawkwatching. Perhaps because of the birds' travel time from the Delaware Bayshore or Mullica River "sending districts," noon to 2:00 P.M. is usually peak eagle time at Cape May.

Afternoon is when many birders visit the Rea Farm, a.k.a. the Beanery, or Hidden Valley in search of warblers, sparrows, and more. Afternoon is good for hawks at the Beanery too, as many put down to hunt. Finally, late afternoon is the time for Merlin madness in season—a time to enjoy low, hunting Merlin in numbers. The state park is a great spot to watch this spectacle, but the Meadows (the Cape May Migratory Bird Refuge) and Sunset Boulevard near the old Magnesite Plant are also a good places to intercept Merlins. The Meadows hosts a variety of birds, but waterfowl, herons and egrets, and shorebirds are the primary targets here. If you have only one or two days to spend at Cape May, this is an iron-clad itinerary—one used by learned locals and savvy visitors alike. Although it may work best in fall, this schedule also works remarkably well in spring and at any season, for that matter.

When asked by potential visitors how much time they should spend at Cape May, we always recommend at least a week, although you can bird the immediate Cape May area in a weekend. In fall, spending a week gives you a far better chance of hitting an exciting, bird-filled, list-building cold front. Cape May autumn weather seems to be, roughly, on a weekly cycle, with cold fronts coming, on average, about once a week. So, if you have a week to spend, you are almost guaranteed to hit a cold front, and the two or three excellent days of birding that follow. Besides, it will take at least a week to sample even some of the fine restaurants in Cape May.

With a week to spend, you will be able to go farther afield and enjoy many of the other great birding spots around Cape May. Although many weekend birders stop at Forsythe National Wildlife Refuge, a.k.a. Brigantine, on their way back north on Sunday, it is often a hurried stop. To bird Brig fully and well can take most of a day, especially when birds are abundant (which is usually the case). The Stone Harbor–Nummy's Island–Hereford Inlet circuit can easily take half a day, and in late October and November, many birders enjoy half a day or even a full day at the Avalon Seawatch. Indeed, if you wish to adequately sample lesser-visited (but not lesser-quality) sites such as Two Mile Beach, the vast Delaware Bay Division of the Cape May National Wildlife Refuge, Bivalve, and the Maurice River, you'll need at least a week.

In winter, the geographic focus of birding shifts to the north. The jetties around Cape May and Cape May Point are exceptional then (at all seasons, actually) and Cape May Harbor can be excellent in winter, but some of the best birding is farther north. Birding on the Delaware Bayshore can be hot during the coldest weather, with the area from Reeds Beach and Jake's Landing north and west along the Maurice River and through Cumberland County producing big numbers of wintering raptors and waterfowl. Beachfront birding can be amazing too, with gulls, sea ducks, and the odd alcid enticing birders. The hundreds of rock jetties from Cape May north to Barnegat Light and beyond attract waterbirds. Back bays and inlets are also important in winter. Forsythe NWR is excellent when not fully frozen, and the big bays and rivers hold large numbers of ducks. Barnegat Light—with its Harlequin Ducks, eiders, Snow Buntings, and much more—is a key winter destination.

Spring brings the birders' focus back to Cape May County. In early spring the axis can be around staging sea ducks and loons at Cape May Point, but by May, most birders begin their day in Belleplain State Forest, enjoying the chorus of a wide variety of breeding birds. This is usually followed by a day at the beach—several hours along the crowded (with shorebirds and horseshoe crabs) Delaware Bay beaches, anywhere from North Cape May up to Reeds Beach, East Point, and Fortescue. Time of day is not critical here, but tide can be. The best (closest) viewing is usually at high tide. Stone Harbor Point and, indeed, all the Cape May fall hotspots are

Back-bay birding can yield great sightings, such as elusive Clapper Rails.

also excellent in spring. If there is a songbird fallout, Higbee Beach, Hidden Valley, the Rea farm, and even the streets of Cape May Point and West Cape May are can't-miss spots. For waterbirds, remember the Concrete Ship at Sunset Beach in spring or at any season.

In spring, if you have only a weekend, spend a half day at Belleplain, a half day on Delaware Bay beaches, and divide the second day between the immediate Cape May area and Stone Harbor Boulevard, Stone Harbor Point, and Nummy's Island. As in fall, you really need a week to visit all the places, see all the birds, and maybe hit a good fallout (you'll probably have to chase a rarity or two as well). We guarantee that you won't get tired or bored of birding Cape May during any week in May.

As spring turns to summer, Belleplain State Forest, South Cape May Meadows, and Cape May Point State Park remain good, but additional summer birding areas include Forsythe NWR and Stone Harbor Point. The tern and skimmer colony at Stone Harbor Point is better in some years than others, but the Point is always a don't-miss location, not only for the abundant expected breeders but also for the unusual birds it attracts. Stone Harbor Point is a major regional shorebird roosting and feeding area. Finally, don't forget the back bays in summer. A back-bay boat trip should yield exceptional views of shorebirds, herons and egrets, nesting terns and gulls, and usually a few Clapper Rail, notorious skulkers.

At any season, an itinerary can revolve around what you want to see. Some prefer to focus on bright, wondrous warblers; others want to concentrate on shoals of shorebirds. In fall, a few birders want to do nothing but watch hawks or may not want to leave the Avalon Seawatch. At Cape May, you can pick and choose or do it all. Weather rarely puts an end to birding at Cape May. In fall, a gray southeast gale may bring hawkwatching to a halt, but this is a great time for seawatching. In spring, a surging warm front can be great for songbirds, but even a "blusterly" northwest wind cold front can bring a hawk flight and maybe a kite or two to Cape May Point. Even rain and fog are well known to produce birds. East winds and rain, although uncomfortable for birders, bring seabirds and migrating shorebirds in close to shore. One memorable May storm brought Red-necked

Phalaropes to Lily Lake and Sooty Shearwaters and an Arctic Tern to Sunset Beach. There is never a dull moment at the Cape for those who venture out. In part, successful bird finding is based on outlook. Despite the conditions, if you fully believe that good birds are out there, you'll work harder to find where they're hidden.

DOS AND DON'TS

Although we're all anxious to get to the Meadows, the Beanery, and all the key spots where Cape May's good birds are found, for first-time visitors, there are a few basic issues to address. There are a lot more dos than don'ts involved in Cape May birding, but there are a few important don'ts.

Birding at Cape May is mostly benign, and there is usually little to think about in terms of comfort or safety—a far cry from, say, the Colima Warbler "death march" in the Chisos Mountains of Texas or the Gray-headed Chickadee (Siberian Tit) trek in Alaska's remote Brooks Range. Mostly, it's literally and figuratively a day at the beach, with little forethought needed. Distances, whether on foot or by car, are mostly short. Trails and roads are usually good, with adequate signage. Temperatures are generally moderate. Expect temperatures in the 70s in May and usually in the 60s in October (at least by midday). We sometimes see 90-degree temperatures in July and August, and sometimes single-digit early mornings in January and February, but temperatures are generally moderated at any season by the influence of the Atlantic Ocean and Delaware Bay. Afternoon sea breezes tend to cool sticky, summer afternoons, and south or southwest winds can warm frigid winter days. Remember, though, that this same Atlantic Ocean can work against you. Cape May in spring can embody Robert Frost's poem "Two Tramps in Mud Time":

> The sun was warm but the wind was chill. You know how it is with an April day when the sun is out and the wind is still, you're one month on in the middle of May. But if you so much as dare to speak, a cloud comes over the sunlit arch, a wind comes off a frozen peak and you're two months back in the middle of March.

A midday change in the wind can drop the temperature 20 degrees in just a few minutes on the Cape May beachfront in spring. Be forewarned, the Atlantic Ocean is still cold in April. The key, of course, is dressing in layers. As Clay's grandfather taught him at an early age, "Whether in a duck blind or surf-fishing, if you have it on, you can always take it off, but if you don't have it with you, you surely can't put it on." The Weather Channel, always good for planning purposes, is Channel 48 on Cape May TV cable, and NOAA Weather Radio (every birder should carry a "weather box," available at any electronics store) broadcasts updated local forecasts, including tides, twenty-four hours a day. Detailed weather forecasts are available on the Internet, too.

We bird most of the year in sneakers but wear warm, waterproof hiking boots in winter. Mornings are often damp, and many wear light boots (wellies) for birding the Meadows, Beanery, or Higbee Beach in the early-morning dew. Cape May receives about 40 to 45 inches of rainfall each year, much of it in early spring, but with the sandy, well-drained soils, mud is rarely an issue (except perhaps on the loop trail through the Meadows), or at worst only a short-lived inconvenience. Usually the only true mud you'll encounter is if you hike the actual salt marshes and tidal mudflats for rail and shorebirds, yet even there, wellies should suffice. One great aspect of Cape May is that amenities are available nearby. If you need a sweatshirt or a raincoat, you have many choices, from boardwalk beachwear stores to commercial fishing suppliers. You can find virtually anything you forgot or anything you need in Cape May. There is a CVS pharmacy at the intersection of Park Boulevard and Mytle Avenue (just north of Sunset Boulevard) in West Cape May. There is an Acme Market food store in Cape May between Lafayette and Washington streets, at the north end of the Washington Street Mall, and a second much larger one just north of the Cape May Canal in North Cape May on Bayshore Road (off Sandman Boulevard—Ferry Road). Both Kmart and Wal-Mart are nearby in Rio Grande should you suddenly need long underwear or whatever. There are a number of banks near the Cape May Acme too. Convenience stores abound; in southern New Jersey virtually every town has a Wawa convenience store or two, offering a variety of sandwiches, soups, other food, and hot and cold beverages. Many are open twenty-four hours a day, and all have ATMs (look for the flying goose logo). Someone once determined that the average distance between Wawas in South Jersey is less than 5 miles. Only Super Wawas have gas pumps and public bathrooms, however. There are several well-stocked liquor stores for either celebrating your sighting of the Northern Wheatear, or drowning your sorrows over the missed Fork-tailed Flycatcher. Many of Cape May's restaurants do not have liquor licenses and encourage you to bring your own bottles of wine or beer. (Those that *do* have liquor licenses definitely frown on you bringing your own, so always call ahead and ask.) Dress is casual almost anywhere, and no one will mind if you dine in your field clothes. Be sure to wear your binoculars proudly—show business owners and locals that you value open space and that, as a nature tourist, you are doing your part to support the local economy. Many first-time visitors who are not used to classy beachfront resorts may find Cape May rather pricey. But be assured, there are accommodations and restaurants in most price ranges.

Dialing 911 will summon emergency services anywhere in Cape May County, and there are very few dead zones where cell phones don't work—

perhaps only the most remote areas of Belleplain or the Delaware Bayshore. The closest hospital and emergency room, Burdette Tomlin Memorial Hospital, is on Stone Harbor Boulevard in Cape May Court House, just west of the Garden State Parkway at Exit 10.

There are a few things to watch out for. Never exceed the speed limit in coastal towns and barrier island communities (Cape May, the Wildwoods, Stone Harbor, Avalon, and on north). Twenty-five miles per hour means

Many birders begin an autumn day at Highbee Beach WMA.

25 mph, not 35 mph, and numerous speed traps catch teenagers, tourists, and birders indiscriminately. In particular, note that the roughly 2-mile stretch of Sunset Boulevard between Cape May City and Cape May Point has varying speed limits that change by season. Many a wide-eyed birder has become even more wide-eyed after a Sunset Boulevard encounter with local law enforcement. Also, Cape May is well known for its aggressive enforcement of parking regulations. Be sure to have plenty of quarters with you to feed the meters (25 cents gets you twenty minutes), or else you'll be the recipient of a $32 parking ticket. When parking on a road shoulder (especially in Cape May Point), always park with traffic, not against it, to avoid a ticket. Heed all No Parking signs, especially those on New England Road near the entrance to Higbee Beach WMA and Hidden Valley.

In most Atlantic coast seaside communities, beach tags are required from Memorial Day to Labor Day for beach use, including birding, wherever and whenever lifeguards are on duty (usually from 10:00 A.M. to 5:00 P.M.). Beaches without lifeguards, such as South Cape May and Cape May Point State Park, do not require beach tags, and birders away from the surf at Stone Harbor Point are usually OK, although it's best to bird early and late. Swimming at unprotected beaches (those without lifeguards) is not advised; due to coastal erosion, many hidden hazards lie under the water. Cape May is notorious for steep dropoffs and rip currents, particularly around jetties. Even strong swimmers should use caution, particularly during and after coastal storms. Also, remember that beachfront jetties can be slippery to walk on, since they are covered by marine algae. We have seen more than one birder blithely walk out a jetty only to creep back on all fours (jetty fishermen wear spikes on their boots for a reason). We've also heard many tales of scopes and tripods lost to the ocean when a gust of wind toppled the equipment or a big wave caught the birder unaware.

Birders should be aware of tides. Besides being important to quality shorebirding, there is a safety aspect to understanding tides. The tidal range, from mean low water to high, is usually about 4 to 5 feet (more during storms), and there are two high tides and two low tides in each twenty-four-hour day. For example, if low tide occurs at 6:00 A.M., high tide will be about six hours later, around noon, and the following low tide will be about six hours after that, at 6:00 P.M. Each day the tides are about fifty minutes later than the day before, and high tide in the back bays is about an hour later than that on the beachfront. The incoming tide is known as the flood tide, and the outgoing as the ebb tide. Parts of most of the barrier islands are low lying and can flood during coastal storms and even during spring tides. Be aware of tide cycles and use common sense when parking and leaving your car for extended periods. This generally applies only to Delaware Bayshore dead-end roads or low-lying, barrier island back-bay areas. We have, however, seen birders stranded at both East Point and Reeds Beach by rapidly rising storm tides. During nor'easters and hurricanes, we have seen ocean waves crashing over Cape May's seawall, leaving deep water trapped on Beach Avenue. Although it's generally not dangerous to drive through a few inches of water, remember that salt water can cause major corrosion damage to automobiles. In any Southern New Jersey coastal area, ponded water can easily be salt water. The Weather Channel and NOAA Weather Radio give tidal forecasts and broadcast warnings about tidal flooding. Most marinas carry free local tide charts, and tides are published in the local newspapers. Tidal problems are rare and almost never impact your birding—simply be aware and cautious.

There are few public-safety issues to worry about when birding Cape May. Virtually all areas are safe, even for those birding alone. However, use common sense when birding. Periodically over the years there have been car break-ins at both Higbee Beach and Hidden Valley. Don't leave valuables (cameras, scopes, purses) exposed; lock them in the trunk or, better yet, leave them in your room if you don't expect to use them. Naturally, if you're birding some of the more urban sections of the region, use a greater measure of caution, and always carry your cell phone with you.

For a long time, Higbee Beach was one of the most popular nude beaches in the entire mid-Atlantic region, with hundreds of nude sun worshippers on the beach on weekends. This, in turn, attracted some unsavory elements, and prostitution and drug deals were once a chronic problem in Higbee Beach parking lots. Nudity is now illegal, and regulations are strongly enforced by both the local police and state conservation officers. Despite this policing, don't be totally surprised if in summer you encounter a nudist in the remote dune areas of Higbee Beach. Simply be aware of its past history and use common sense to avoid any odd encounters. Should you ever feel uncomfortable at Higbee Beach, or anywhere else, simply dial 911.

Late autumn and winter birders in Southern New Jersey need to be cognizant of hunting seasons. Many of the wildlife management areas (WMAs) highlighted herein are stocked with pheasants in November and December, and there is a good amount of hunting pressure on Saturdays. Late fall is a good time of year *not* to bird WMAs. In New Jersey there is no hunting at all allowed on Sundays (except on private game farms, which are found along Delaware Bayshore and in the vicinity of Woodbine). Waterfowl hunting remains quite popular in both coastal and Delaware Bay marshes. The various (and complex) waterfowl seasons are mostly from late October to February, but duck and goose hunting, done mostly in remote blinds in far coves and bays, should have virtually no impact on birding. Goose and duck hunting is permitted at Forsythe NWR, but here too, hunters should have no impact on birding. Some years, though, on one day a week in October (usually Wednesday or Thursday), the Brigantine wild-life drive is closed to birders to allow special Snow Goose hunting in the impoundments. This has a *very* direct impact on birders. Visiting birders are *not* allowed access during the goose hunts, and we've found that the refuge is devoid of all birds for a few days after each hunt, driven off by the shooting. If possible, bird the day before the closure, not after. (Closures are posted on the Web site: www.fws.gov/northeast/forsythe. Take note or call ahead: 609-652-1665.)

In an effort to control exploding white-tailed deer populations, there are many different deer hunting seasons in southern New Jersey. Bow hunting season runs from October through November and again in January. Bow hunting is a solitary endeavor, and it would be rare to encounter a bow hunter unless you are deep in the woods at dawn or dusk. Between the last few days of November and the end of the first week in January, various firearm deer seasons occur, both shotgun and muzzle-loader (other than black powder, hunting with rifles is illegal in New Jersey). These seasons are more of an issue for birders. This is when hundreds of hunters are in the woods and fields, and we strongly recommend that you don't bird in the woods at these times (but if you do, wear blaze orange). There is very little hunting on Cape Island, none on the barrier islands, and no hunting is permitted anywhere on Sundays.

An interesting aspect of the rural nature of southern New Jersey, particularly the Delaware Bayshore and Barnegat Bay regions, is the reliance on fishing, hunting, and muskrat trapping by a fairly large percentage of the residents. It has been a way of life for hundreds of years, supported even today by the vast expanses and wildlife resources of the region. City attitudes and value judgments are out of place in rural New Jersey, where hunting and fishing have been major pastimes for many generations, and fish and game are still a major source of food on the table for many rural families today. Deer hunting in particular should be supported. It is beneficial to birds (and birders) as a means of controlling major damage to the forest understory from the overbrowsing of the burgeoning deer populations.

A couple years ago, we would have said that there were no bears in southern New Jersey, but there have been several recent sightings of black bears in Belleplain State Forest and in remote areas of Cumberland County. Black bears have finally reappeared after a nearly 100-year absence, finally making their way south through the Pine Barrens from their stronghold in the Kittatinny Mountains of northwestern New Jersey. Nonetheless, they are rare—probably as rare as frigatebirds over Cape May. Eastern coyotes are fairly common but completely harmless, even though they may be somewhat bold around Higbee Beach. Timber Rattlesnakes, an endangered species in New Jersey, are very rare and secretive and, in southern New Jersey, are found only in the Pine Barrens. It has been more than 50 years since one was seen in Belleplain State Forest, and today they are found only in remote areas of Ocean and Burlington counties. Although many locals claim that Eastern Cottonmouths (water moccasins) are found here, they are not and never have been. Cottonmouths reach the northern limit of their range in Virginia. In New Jersey, "moccasin" reports always turn out to be the common and similar-looking (and totally harmless but aggressive) Northern Water Snake.

There may be nothing large to be afraid of out there, but there are some very small things to worry about. Perhaps the only downside of birding at Cape May is the bugs. Friend and colleague Dr. Dale Schweitzer, an internationally known entomologist, once said (half in fun but all in earnest) that he has traveled all over the world studying insects, and nowhere has he encountered bugs as bad as they are on the Delaware Bayshore (fortunately, they aren't nearly as bad around Cape May itself). We have often joked that there is good reason that the bayshore is pristine, rural, and undeveloped. Probably more than a few developers have visited in winter and thought, "Here's a great place for waterfront condos." But upon returning in July, they probably got only a few yards from their cars before running back, swatting and screaming—all dreams of development heartily dashed by the bayshore's dependable insects.

Spring brings abundant tiny, biting gnats, or no-see-ums, on any windless day, and by the first of June, expect biting flies—deerflies, strawberry flies, and the dreaded kamikaze greenhead flies. They are mostly absent around Cape May City, but along the bayshore and coastal marshes, these flies can be so bad on windless summer days that you need a head net. Many a birder has happily birded from the car, windows rolled up,

rather than face the swarms of greenheads at Brigantine. Salt marsh greenhead flies first show up in early June, peak in July, and are encountered into
September. Chiggers are sometimes a problem on grassy trails and when
walking through fields in late summer and fall.

Wet weather brings mosquitoes in all seasons and throughout the
region, since many species lay their eggs in pooled water. Mosquitoes have
long been a concern at Cape May. In 1893 George Spencer Morris, colleague and friend of Witmer Stone, added a bit of humor when describing
an expedition to the Jersey salt marshes: Mosquitoes "were also numerous
upon the meadows the next day. Stone shot one that he mistook for a mud-
hen [Clapper Rail], but of course the mistake was a natural one." Mosquitoes can be particularly bad around Cape May Point at times, but mainly
they are a problem only near sunset. Of all the insects, mosquitoes are the
only real public health concern, as West Nile virus is found annually in
southern New Jersey, and eastern equine encephalitis is reported every few
years. Don't be deterred, but be forewarned and bring insect repellent. By
fall, the problem has subsided, but it's always a good idea to have bug spray
or a long-sleeved shirt, just in case.

A bigger problem is ticks. Lyme disease, carried primarily by deer
ticks, is a major problem throughout New Jersey, and ticks are very abundant in most areas and habitat types. Be aware of the high potential for
encountering them. Wear long pants with your socks pulled up over the
pant legs, and tuck your shirt in; light-colored clothing is best for spotting
ticks. The larval stage of the deer tick is the size of a pinpoint. The nymph
stage is about the size of the period at the end of this sentence, and their
bites can be mistaken as chigger bites. Spray heavily with state-of-the-art
insect repellent, and avoid walking through tall grass. Grassy stretches of
trails can harbor nests of "seed" ticks, or nymphs. If you walk through such
a concentration of seed ticks, you'll know almost instantly by itching
ankles and dozens or even hundreds of tiny ticks charging up your leg. Also
avoid brushing against shrubs. The American Lyme Disease Foundation
(www.aldf.com) shares the following information: "Deer Ticks cannot
jump or fly and do not drop from above onto a passing animal. Potential
hosts (which include all wild birds and mammals, domestic animals, and
humans) acquire ticks only by direct contact with them. Once a tick latches
onto human skin it generally climbs upward until it reaches a protected or
creased area, often the back of the knee, groin, navel, armpit, ears, or nape
of the neck. It then begins the process of inserting its mouthparts into the
skin until it reaches the blood supply." Despite daily tick checks, we've
missed ticks that were attached to an earlobe, between toes, or in the scalp.

Once a tick attaches to your skin, it sucks your blood and begins to
swell up. The blood meal is needed for the tick to pass into its next life

stage. According to the American Lyme Disease Foundation, "Not all ticks are infected, and studies of infected Deer Ticks have shown that they begin transmitting Lyme disease an average of thirty-six to forty-eight hours after attachment. Therefore, your chances of contracting Lyme disease are greatly reduced if you remove a tick within the first twenty-four hours. Remember, too, that the majority of early Lyme disease cases are easily treated and cured." You should be perfectly safe as long as you take your nightly tick check seriously. Ticks are so much a part of the environment that all field birders should do a tick check every evening, whether they have been out in the field or not. Ticks from one day's outing may still be wandering around in the car or on a jacket a day or two later.

There's no need to panic if you find an attached tick. The American Lyme Disease Foundation suggests: "without jerking, pull firmly and steadily directly outward. Do not twist the tick out or apply petroleum jelly, a hot match, alcohol or any other irritant to the tick in an attempt to get it to back out. These methods can backfire and even increase the chances of the tick transmitting the disease." Along these same lines, don't try to crush the tick to kill it. Simply drop the removed tick into a jar of rubbing alcohol to kill it (or burn it with a match). Flushing it down the toilet won't necessarily get rid of it. They've been known to crawl back out. If you find yourself covered with seed ticks, a 3- or 4-inch piece of duct tape or wide masking tape works wonders. Press the tape onto your ticky skin and then peel the ticks off with the tape.

We've each had Lyme disease. In fact, almost everyone we know who spends considerable time in the field has had it, and it's no fun. A tick bite is no reason to run screaming for home and medical treatment, but if you find a tick bloated with blood and believe that it could have been attached to you for longer than 12 hours, watch yourself for symptoms and ask your doctor for advice and recommendations. Ticks can be active every month of the year in South Jersey, so take precautions even in winter if the day is mild. Ticks are unavoidable in South Jersey, but knowledge and precautions will certainly lessen your chances of being bitten or contracting Lyme disease. There are few or no ticks around beaches or barrier islands and few around birding spots on Cape Island. There are dog ticks at Higbee Beach (which reportedly don't transmit Lyme disease), but supposedly no deer ticks there, although white-tailed deer are present.

Another word of caution: Poison Ivy is abundant everywhere in South Jersey, which is actually good because its berries are an excellent food source for many migratory birds. Poison Ivy thrives in sandy soil and salt spray, and Poison Ivy "trees" line the trails at Cape May Point State Park. There are actually few places on the Cape where you won't find it. Always remember that the shrubs you step into while trying to get a look at that skulking Connecticut Warbler may be Poison Ivy.

Finally, expect abundant ragweed when birding fields and edges in late summer and early fall. Hay-fever sufferers are forewarned.

CAPE MAY ETHICS

Good birding behavior is important everywhere and all the time, but it can be crucial in an area where so many birders concentrate. At Cape May, you might be sharing the playing field with hundreds of other birders on weekends during peak season.

Birding is a highly recognized activity around Cape May. Certainly the residents of Cape May Point, Cape May City, and, to a lesser extent, West Cape May have come to expect birding activity. This expectation diminishes the farther away you get from Cape Island, such as the more remote areas of Cumberland County. Even near the epicenter of birding at Cape May Point, the average tourist may not know that he or she is in the birding Mecca. Remember, in warm months you'll be sharing the beaches and roads with hundreds or even thousands of nonbirders and tourists focused on historic Cape May. Please don't stop your car suddenly or indiscriminately for a bird; use your turn signals and pull well off onto the shoulder. Just be safe and be careful.

Birders frequently bird on foot in the streets of Cape May Point, Cape May City, and West Cape May. Tree-lined streets offer some of the best songbirding, particularly in spring. Your birding here shouldn't cause residents any alarm or concern, but use common sense. Occupants of a Cape May Point cottage might be first-time renters who have never encountered birders before. Bird in small groups, and keep your voices down at all times, but especially in the early morning. Enjoy birds in yards and tree-tops, but refrain from scanning bushes in front of windows. Discretion and respect are key.

At peak seasons and at peak times, birding groups frequently encounter one another. It is certainly not bad etiquette, to use a golfing term, to "play through." Pass by another group discreetly and as quickly as possible so as not to disrupt their birding. If you are a group leader, urge your group to stay together on one side of a trail or footpath so that others can easily pass behind you. This sort of courtesy allows many groups to enjoy a place like Higbee Beach in relative peace and harmony. Because so many people share the same turf around Cape May, we discourage the use of tapes to attract birds; in fact, the use of tapes is illegal at Higbee Beach and on NWR lands. There are simply too many birders about, and the use of broadcast CDs or recorded tapes would be too disruptive to other birders and overly intrusive to the birds. Discreet pishing is perfectly acceptable and expected.

As at most popular birding destinations, there is a friendly climate of sharing at Cape May. If you see a good bird, such as a Vesper Sparrow in

Spreading the news about a good sighting allows other birders to share the fun. Here a crowd gathers to see the Northern Lapwing spotted in Goshen on the first day of 1997.

the last hedgerow, pass it on so that others might have the experience. Also, accept shared information graciously. There is nothing so disturbing as offering information only to be rebuffed with a condescending attitude. There is no room for ego or one-upmanship at Cape May. Remember that there are many levels of ability and experience among the birders of Cape May. Understand and respect such diversity. Visiting birders come from all over the world, and something that we consider common, such as a Northern Cardinal, may be a dazzling sight and a brand new bird for them.

If you find a *really* good bird at Cape May, make an effort to alert others. Such reporting is quite simple—a quick cell phone call or a stop at the CMBO's Northwood Center in Cape May Point or its Center for Research and Education in Goshen, or even a phone call (with details) to the answering machine from the road on your way back home. If you are not sure of a bird's status—whether it's rare or not—consult the checklist at the end of this book or ask another birder. Don't be embarrassed, we're *all* new to an area the first time we visit.

GETTING THERE

Traveling to Cape May is far easier than getting to many of North America's popular birding spots. Cape May is centrally located in terms of the mid-Atlantic's major population centers. The Cape is about four hours by car from New York City, two hours from Philadelphia, three hours from Baltimore, and under four hours from Washington, D.C. Bus service is available from Philadelphia, New York, and Atlantic City; Atlantic City is also served by rail. Car rentals are available at Atlantic City International Airport and also locally in Cape May Court House (Exit 10 off the Garden State Parkway) and Rio Grande (Exit 5). Cape May is just a one-hour drive from Atlantic City International Airport (on the mainland, not the barrier island), although airline service there is somewhat limited. A number of air carriers provide a few flights, but only Spirit Airlines flies a full schedule to and from Atlantic City International. Philadelphia International Airport is served by many carriers and is a major hub for US Airways, which flies from Philadelphia to virtually all major cities and many international destinations.

The route to Cape May is easy and direct. From New York and points north, simply follow the Garden State Parkway (GSP) south to its end, Mile Marker 0, or "Exit 0" as it is frequently called. From Atlantic City International Airport, follow signs to the Atlantic City Expressway. Take the expressway east to Exit 7, to reach the GSP southbound.

Once on the GSP, it is 38 miles to Cape May. The GSP is a scenic drive, and your first birds will no doubt be seen in the salt marsh vistas—maybe a perched and patient roadside Red-tailed Hawk or perhaps a hungry Great Egret or Great Blue Heron in repose at a wetlands creek crossing. On a crisp autumn morning, your first bird may be a Sharp-shinned Hawk blasting across the road at sunrise, buffeted by the "blustery" northwest gale.

From Philadelphia International Airport, take Route 95 north to the Walt Whitman Bridge (Route 76). Take the Walt Whitman Bridge across the Delaware River to New Jersey. Route 76 becomes Route 42. Follow Route 42 south until the Atlantic City Expressway angles off to the left. Follow the expressway east to the GSP and continue south on the parkway to Cape May. An alternative route, preferred by some, is to exit from Route 42 onto Route 55 south. Route 55 is an excellent four-lane freeway for the first 40 miles, but at Exit 20 it flows into Route 47 (two lane) at Port Elizabeth. Route 47 then flows into Route 347, which eventually flows back into Route 47. (The Route 55 freeway was never completed due to a combination of budget issues and environmental constraints. We hope that it is never completed, as it would cut through several designated wild and scenic rivers, The Nature Conservancy's premier Manumuskin River Preserve, Belleplain State Forest, several wildlife management areas, and the Cape May National Wildlife Refuge. Politicians like to refer to these as "minor environmental concerns.") Expect traffic backups at the juncture of Routes 55 and 47 (and all along Route 47 in the vicinity of traffic lights) on Friday afternoons in summer. On Sunday afternoons in summer, northbound tie-ups occur along Route 47 at traffic lights, but the congestion finally eases at Route 55 when the two lanes become four lanes. On peak summer weekends, the Garden State Parkway–Atlantic City Expressway is the better route—although at peak hours, it's not much better. (If you are visiting before Memorial Day or after Labor Day, this should be less of a problem.) The advantage of taking Route 55 to Route 47 is that it places you much closer to Delaware Bayshore birding sites. Another alternative route from the Philadelphia airport is to take Route 95 south to the Commodore Barry Bridge. Take the bridge east to Route 322 (a two-lane road that also gets backed up at traffic lights at rush hour and on summer weekends), which connects with Route 55 near Glassboro.

RECOMMENDED READING

For all your Cape May and New Jersey travel, we highly recommend the *New Jersey Atlas and Gazetteer*, published by DeLorme, which includes large-scale route and topographic maps for the entire state and is a bargain at around $20. This book is sold at all bookstores and many convenience stores, as well as at the Cape May Bird Observatory's two centers. This book will guide you to all the sites covered herein as well as to sites shared on the Voice of New Jersey Audubon, New Jersey's rare bird alert, where the directions often include the DeLorme page number and quad. Essentially, you can't actively bird New Jersey without this book.

Other items you shouldn't be without are the many useful maps and brochures published (and updated regularly) by the Cape May Bird Observatory (CMBO), including its bird checklist, a two-sided birding map to Cape Island–Cape May and Cape May County, and a two-sided birding map to the Delaware Bayshore. (These maps work for butterflies too, and a butterfly checklist is also available.) Also be sure to pick up the **Kestrel Express** (the CMBO's seasonally published program schedule), the "Cape May Birding Workshop" brochure, and the "Places to Eat, Shop, Stay, & Play" brochure (a guide to the CMBO's business supporters, including hotels, motels, campgrounds, restaurants, and other businesses). By supporting these businesses, you support those who support conservation at Cape May; some of them offer discounts to CMBO members. These maps and brochures are available for free at either CMBO center and are included in the CMBO's "Cape May Birding Packs," which are available for free during any CMBO program or walk. You can also request an information packet from the CMBO by phone before a scheduled visit; this includes membership information, the program schedule, and the "Places" brochure. Many items are also available on the New Jersey Audubon Society (NJAS) Web site: www.njaudubon.org.

Be sure to check the CMBO's **Cape May Birding Hotline** updated weekly (usually on Thursday evening), and online at the NJAS's Web site by clicking on "Quick Links"; or you can call 609-884-2626 (birds). The **Voice of New Jersey Audubon** covers bird sighting for all of New Jersey and can also be read online.

At either CMBO center, always check the logbooks for bird sightings and nature sightings, updated daily by visiting and resident birders and used to create each week's hotlines. There are also logs at the Cape May Migratory Bird Refuge (the Meadows) kiosk and at Cape May Point State Park, but these may not be current. At Forsythe NWR, always check the log in the small building next to where you pay your fee. This is updated daily by visiting birders.

While in cyberspace, visit **www.CapeMayTimes.com**, *the* online guide to anything and everything in Cape May, including accommodations, dining, theater, other cultural and historic events, weather, tides, and lots more. The Web site also hosts a number of interactive forums (covering Cape May birding, nature, gardening, fishing, boating, and vacation tips), as well as fishing, nature, and birding columns, including one written by your authors.

For the serious student of Cape May, a few books (in addition to this one) are important for a total understanding of Cape May birds and birding. **The Birds of Cape May**, by David Sibley, is an annotated, species-by-species account of Cape May's birds, including rarities. It was published in 1997 by the CMBO and is available for sale at each center. The excellent seasonal bar graphs for each species, found in the back of the book, are based on over twenty years of records (sighting sheets kept by the CMBO). The NJAS's quarterly journal of bird sightings, **New Jersey Birds** (formerly *Records of New Jersey Birds*) is an excellent ongoing information source. It is edited by Paul Lehman and is available through membership in the NJAS.

Also important to visitors and residents is **Birds of New Jersey** by Joan Walsh, Vince Elia, Rich Kane, and Thomas Halliwell. Published by the NJAS in 1999 (available at all NJAS centers), this tome is the result of the intensive five-year New Jersey Breeding Bird Atlas project, but it also includes full seasonal accountings of New Jersey's migrants and wintering birds. This book is a necessary tool for anyone who plans to spend much time birding in New Jersey. Finally, if you are birding north of the geographic area covered by this book, you will need **A Guide to Bird Finding in New Jersey**, by Bill Boyle (published in 2002 by Rutgers University Press). This revised and expanded edition is a key tool for New Jersey birders. For in-depth coverage of Cumberland County (the adjacent county north and west of Cape May), **Birding Cumberland: A Birder's Guide to Cumberland County** (2003) by Clay Sutton, with illustrations by Louise Zemaitis, is a key resource.

continues on next page

RECOMMENDED READING *continued*

Finally, we urge you to read, at your leisure, Witmer Stone's timeless classic, ***Bird Studies at Old Cape May: An Ornithology of Coastal New Jersey***. It may have been published in 1937, but it is guaranteed to enhance and enrich your Cape May experience. Highly readable and still available (reprinted by Stackpole Books in 2000), it is lively and fun and offers a rich perspective of times gone by. Some of these experiences and events we can only dream of, but much of Old Cape May can still be found by those who search. ▪

From Washington, Baltimore, or other points south, take Route 95 north to Route 295, which flows into the Delaware Memorial Bridge and across the Delaware River to New Jersey. Follow signs for Route 40, which angles off near where the New Jersey Turnpike begins. Follow Route 40 east (through some very rural and scenic farmland) to Route 55 south. A pleasant alternative route, after crossing the Delaware Memorial Bridge, is to immediately exit onto Route 49 south. Route 49 follows the Delaware River and Bay south and crosses Mannington Marsh and the Salem River at the historic town of Salem, New Jersey. Route 49 is a two-lane road but offers birding possibilities for its entire length. Route 49 eventually connects with Route 47, then Route 55, or eventually Route 50—which in turn connects to the GSP.

A fun route to Cape May from the south is to take the Cape May–Lewes Ferry, which runs from Lewes, Delaware, to the Cape May Canal (right across from Higbee Beach). From the ferry terminal, Sandman Boulevard (a.k.a. Ferry Road or Route 9; Route 9 becomes Route 109) connects to the terminus of the GSP at Mile Marker 0. The ferry crossing takes about one and a half hours. Reservations are accepted and recommended in summer and on weekends. You can actually drive around Delaware Bay to Cape May in about the same amount of time that it takes to cross by ferry (if you include the crossing time and the wait for the boat—it's a good idea to arrive at least an hour ahead of time in summer). This may be appealing to those who find the ferry fee too expensive. Be sure to have a photo ID for ferry access, and be sure that both your driver's license and car registration are current (cars have been impounded here for out-of-date registrations). The Cape May–Lewes Ferry ride is scenic and offers excellent birding possibilities at all seasons.

7

SITE GUIDES

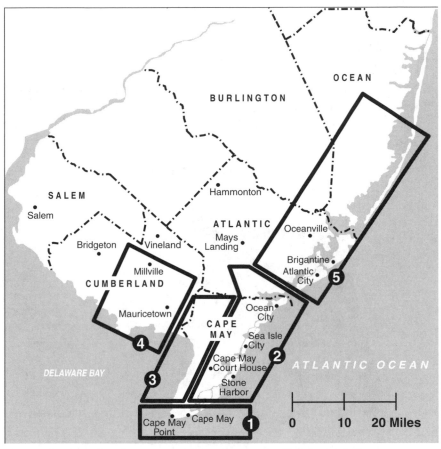

1. *South of the Canal*
2. *The Atlantic Coast and Barrier Islands*
3. *Delaware Bayshore and Interior Forests*
4. *Cumberland County*
5. *Atlantic County and Beyond*

Directions to each site start from the previous site, although at times shortcuts are suggested as alternatives. Mileage figures are individual segment distances, not cumulative odometer readings, unless otherwise noted. Associated smaller sites are bold-faced within the text.

SOUTH OF THE CANAL

Many of Cape May County's most renowned birding sites are concentrated in the region south of the Cape May Canal, which stretches from Cape May Harbor just northeast of Cape May City to the Delaware Bay, separating the very tip of the Cape May peninsula from the rest of New Jersey. Within these dozen or so square miles is something very much like a birder's paradise.

CAPE MAY POINT STATE PARK

If the key to Cape May's ornithological fame is its location, then Cape May Point State Park is the epicenter. The park is the very tip of the funnel, where the constriction can't get any tighter. It is land's end, where many

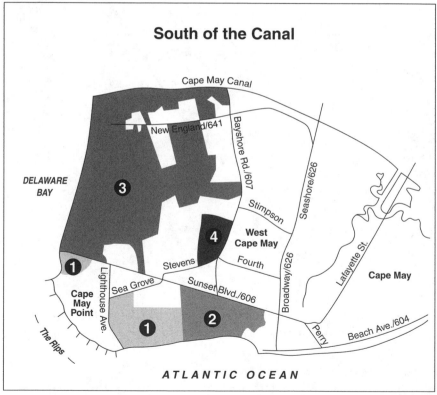

South of the Canal

1. *Cape May Point State Park*
2. *Cape May Migratory Bird Refuge*
3. *Higbee Beach WMA*
4. *Rea Farm*

(and, at times, on magical fall days where seemingly *most*) of the region's birds end up. It is some of the most important migratory bird habitat on earth. Cape May Point State Park comprises 235 acres of freshwater ponds and marsh, bayberry and wax myrtle thickets, Red Cedar groves, Mockernut Hickory and pine-oak woodlands, beachfront, man-made dunes, and ponds behind the dunes (created during the most recent beachfill project in 2004–2005). Extensive freshwater ponds and marsh right next to the Atlantic Ocean attract many birds in all seasons. Habitat diversity is considerable. An aggressive effort to remove nonnative plants (Porcelainberry or Asiatic Ampelopsis, Yam-leaved Clematis, and other invasive vines and shrubs) along the trails began in 2005 and will hopefully transform the once vine-smothered area into a site where native trees and shrubs have a chance. As recently as twenty-five years ago, the park's marshes contained considerable Salt-meadow Grass *(Spartina patens)* and both Broad-leaved and Narrow-leaved Cattail, but a long string of dry years and drainage by mosquito control ditches helped the spread of the invasive Common Reed Grass *(Phragmites australis)*, which choked out all else in the park's wetlands. Before it became a park, most of the area was wet pastureland, the grazing land of a local dairy farm. In 2005, as part of the U.S. Army Corps of Engineers' "Ecosystem Restoration Project," Phragmites was ground-sprayed with herbicide. By late 2005, visitors could see ponds that for years had been hidden by a sea of *Phragmites*. Time will tell if these efforts are long lasting.

Cape May Point State Park is a day-use park, open from dawn to dusk. Admittance is free. If you choose to climb the historic lighthouse, the Mid-Atlantic Center for the Arts (MAC) charges a fee from their post at the base. The park's environmental education center (the building closest to the ocean) has a small but interesting museum and a classroom that can be reserved for lectures (for a fee) by educators or birding groups. The building on the right houses the park's office and heated public restrooms (at the right end). The park has a full-time naturalist on staff. Be sure to stop by the office to learn of current walks and programs and to pick up a copy of the "Cape May Point State Park Wildflower, Tree, and Shrub" brochure (written by Pat in 1984 when she was the park naturalist), a guide to the vegetation of Cape Island. There are three picnic shelters in the park, but there are no trash or recycling receptacles, since all New Jersey state parks have a carry-in, carry-out policy. The park's entrance gate is opened at sunrise and closed at sunset, but there is a small parking lot outside the main gate for those who wish to walk in early or stay late.

Most of the park, some 153 acres, is a state natural area known as the Cape May Point Natural Area. It contains an excellent hiking trail system with three trails (red, yellow, and blue), all beginning at the far end of the

Some of the region's most productive bird-ing can be done within sight of the Cape May Lighthouse in Cape May Point.

parking lot left of the East Shelter, which is just left of the Wildlife Viewing Platform (used as the Cape May Hawkwatch from September through November).

The dominant feature of Cape May Point State Park is the Cape May Lighthouse. The historically correct, light-beige tower (it was painted white until 1994) soars to 157 ½ feet high and can be seen by mariners 24 miles at sea (and by high-flying migratory birds even farther). It was completed in 1859. The engineer in charge of the construction was none other than Major George Gordon Meade (who would soon be a commanding Union general during the Civil War, playing a prominent role in the Battle of Gettysburg). It is the third lighthouse built at Cape May Point. The first U.S.–built lighthouse at Cape May Point was a 65-foot structure erected in 1823 of bricks imported from Philadelphia. Its location has been a bit of a mystery, since erosion and storms long ago washed it away; but an old corduroy road exposed by a storm in 1931 was believed to once have led to the structure. The road led toward Prissy Wick Shoal. In 1847, the second lighthouse was built but never completed because when the Fresnel lens arrived from Paris it was too big. Work began anew in 1859 on a third lighthouse, this time one-third of a mile farther inland than the 1847 lighthouse and the encroaching sea. Over the ensuing years, the 1847 lighthouse was dismantled, except for its base, which was used for storage. In 1966, the old base broke in two and stood for many years on the beach east of the park's Environmental Education Center. By 1980, only remnants of it could be found; after the winter of 1982, all signs of it were gone.

The Cape May Lighthouse is owned by Cape May Point State Park. Under a lease arrangement with the state of New Jersey, it has been restored and is maintained by MAC, a dominant force in Cape May culture and history. The active light itself is maintained by the coast guard. A small welcome center and gift shop is open to the public and housed in the old oil shed, a separate building near the base of the lighthouse. For a migratory bird's view of the cape, be sure to climb the lighthouse's 199 steps. One memorable day from the top of the Cape May Lighthouse we watched several peregrines arrow by, below eye level.

Remnants of the base of the 1847 lighthouse were visible until the 1970s.

The land that is the state park today was an Army base and a naval and coast guard station during World War II. A prominent feature of the park is the Bunker, a gun emplacement and magazine that sits on the beach near the hawkwatch platform. Completed in 1942, its purpose was to protect Delaware Bay shipping from enemy submarines. There is a sister gun emplacement at Cape Henlopen State Park in Delaware—together, their 155mm guns could cover the entire 10-mile-wide entrance to the bay. The guns were never fired in anger. The gun mounts are situated to each side of the ammunition bunker itself but are currently covered by sand. A number of associated "spotting towers," or fire control towers, were constructed nearby as well. One built in 1941 (the 71-foot-tall "Fire Control Tower No. 23" that is soon to be restored by MAC) is located next to Sunset Boulevard on the way to the Concrete Ship. The Grand Hotel on the Cape May beachfront was built around another; the top of the tower is visible if you're looking for it.

When first built, the Bunker was almost a half-mile inland and camouflaged, covered with sand and vegetation. By 1980, constant and severe erosion had swept the land away from around and under the Bunker, leaving it perched precariously on its foundation pilings with waves washing under it. Peregrines, goshawks, and Cooper's Hawks used it as an artificial cliff perch and actively hunted the pigeons that nested and roosted inside. One fall, a skilled young Arctic peregrine, "Buffy the Pigeon Slayer," scored daily to the wonder of gathered hawkwatchers. A massive Army Corps of Engineers beachfill project in 2004 and 2005 has the Bunker again surrounded by sand, but perhaps by the time you read this or visit, the coastal

Until recently, beach erosion undermined the Bunker. Beachfill projects have once again surrounded it with sand.

erosion will again have made the Bunker a concrete island at sea.

From April to August, there is a bustling Purple Martin colony next to the park office. Long-time naturalist Fred Mears played a major role in the success of this colony. Today, CMBO volunteer Dave Thomas maintains it in Fred's honor. In 2005, thirty-two pairs, using every compartment in two state-of-the-art Purple Martin Houses and gourds, successfully fledged over 100 young. The Wildlife Viewing Platform, commonly referred to as the Hawkwatch, is another key feature of the park, dominating the skyline at the far end of the parking lot. It is expansive and fully wheelchair accessible. It is the third platform to have been built on the site since the inception of the CMBO-conducted hawkwatch in 1976. It offers a terrific view of Bunker Pond, an extensive freshwater pond and marsh, and the tree line to the north, the direction from which the hawks of autumn come. A kiosk at the foot of the platform displays the hawk count to date in season. The official CMBO hawk counter is present from sunrise to near sunset, September 1 to November 30, except on very rainy days. He or she is likely to be friendly and maybe even talkative on slow days, but friendly and focused on the flight (i.e., busy) on big flight days. CMBO staffs the hawkwatch with seasonal interpretive naturalists from September 1 to October 31. The naturalists field questions, help visitors understand the hawk flight, and offer mini hawk ID workshops each Friday, Saturday, and Sunday. Their talent, skill, passion, and spirit are a real part of what makes Cape May so special. Hawk banding "demos" are given at ten in the morning on Saturdays and Sundays, from mid-September through October, by volunteers from the Cape May Raptor Banding Project. The demos are conducted next to the East Shelter, which is also used for Monarch tagging demos five days a week, from mid-September to mid-October, usually at 2:00 P.M.

If you are a first-time visitor to Cape May or new at hawkwatching, we recommend the following approach. Upon arriving at the hawkwatch, begin by scanning the horizon straight out toward Cape May City and to the left above the tree line, taking notice of landmarks. Try your hand at picking up raptor shapes on the distant horizon and watching them come closer until they're right overhead, kettling and breaking apart, kettling again, eying the wide Delaware Bay. Often a hawk flight follows a certain path across the sky, and different weather conditions will trigger different flight paths. At times, most of the hawks fly straight down the tree line from Cape May City to the lighthouse and out over the bay. Other times, the flight is high overhead. And at other times, the flight is out over the dune line. Sometimes it's all of the above at the same time. During a big flight, it can be hard to know which bird folks are talking about when they call out.

The hawkwatch, shown here in 1997, is still the epicenter of Cape May hawkwatching.

At times when the flight is high the best way to fully enjoy it is to lie down on your back and scan the skies from a prone position (otherwise the neck rebels). The park's large grassy lawn is perfect for this and often right under the flight. Bring a blanket and a pillow and enjoy the show. If you prefer a seat, there are scattered benches around the perimeter of this lawn. Early season you may need sunscreen at the hawkwatch more than warm clothes. But by late October and November many big flights are often associated with cold winds from the northwest, so be prepared with long underwear, mittens, a warm hat, and lots of winter layers. As the day warms up,

Don't just look up—this pair of Dickcissels was spotted on the ground near the hawkwatch.

you can always peel off a layer or two. The hawkwatch is exposed; the last thing you want is to be too cold to experience a great November flight.

The South Shelter, at the base of the dune near the park buildings, was once as popular as the hawkwatch, especially since it offered shade from the sun and cover from rain and wind. And until 2004, this was one of the best spots to observe migrating seabirds and schools of Bottle-nosed Dolphin in the surf. The beachfill project created a vast dune that today blocks much

The dune crossovers at Cape May Point State Park are great vantage points for hawkwatching, seawatching, and enjoying waterbirds in the park's freshwater ponds.

of the view. There is hope that this pavilion would either be raised or moved closer to the water, but this now seems unlikely. More likely, in a few short years the relentless erosion will again mean the water is close by. There is a wide and lengthy wheelchair accessible dune walkover leading from the pavilion to the beach that functions, in essence, as a raised observation deck. This "deck" offers a good view of the ocean, but no cover during foul weather.

From the beach or dune walkover, on a clear day, you can easily see Cape Henlopen and the Delaware coast to the south and west. To the right of the pavilion, as you look seaward, is the other dominant structure visible from the hawkwatch, Saint Mary's-by-the-Sea. This beautiful old building, white with a red roof adorned with many crosses, was built in 1890 as the Shoreham Hotel. It was sold in 1909 to the Sister's of St. Joseph of Chestnut Hill, Philadelphia, who have used it ever since as a summer retreat. It too was once in danger of being washed into the sea. Today, it is protected by a seawall and a wide beach. Look for falcons perched on the crosses on the roof—kestrel, Merlin, even peregrines.

With its varied habitats and opportunities, Cape May Point State Park is good at any season or any time of day. Even in midwinter or midsummer the park hosts lots of birds, and scanning the ponds and ocean is profitable at all times of the year. It is your best window for autumn hawks and can offer good views of the turmoil of The Rips. While most birders in the fall begin their day at Higbee Beach, on a morning following the passage of a major cold front, the park too can offer a stirring and exhilarating view of the pageant of migration, with morning-flight songbirds, ducks, skeins of geese, cormorants, shorebirds, and clouds of swallows all converging and crisscrossing in the sky. The park is a great way to begin

your Cape May birding adventure—or to end your day, as evening falls and
the night shift of migrants takes over the Cape May twilight.

Birding the Site

From the Garden State Parkway (GSP), travel through Cape May City
before traveling on to Cape May Point: The GSP ends at Mile Marker 0.0,
at a traffic signal. Go straight where the road feeds into Route 109 (entering from the right). Go through the second light and over the Canal
Bridge. You are now on Cape Island. You will pass several gas stations in
this stretch and see, on the left, the gigantic sign for the Lobster House
Restaurant and Seafood Market. You are traversing bustling Cape May
Harbor and will pass the whale-watching boats on your right. Travel over
the second small bridge; you are now in Cape May City. (The very first left
takes you to Pittsburgh Avenue and directly to the beaches.) Proceed
straight on Lafayette Street (the strictly enforced speed limit is 25 mph) for

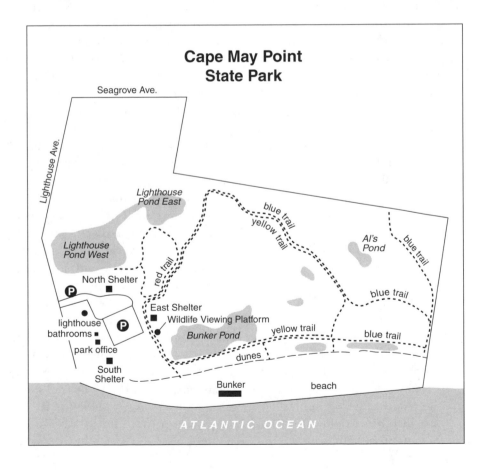

1.3 miles until you reach a T at Jackson Street (at Colliers Liquor Store). Go right on Jackson, which becomes W. Perry Street. About 0.4 mile from the T, you will reach the traffic signal at Broadway. Here W. Perry Street becomes Sunset Boulevard (Route 606). Go straight through the light (a left would take you to the beaches) and continue west on 606. Again, watch the (changing) speed limit on Sunset Boulevard. In early September, you're sure to notice and smell blooming Yam-leaved Clematis (or Virgin's Bower, a carpet of tiny white flowers draped over shrubs and trees) along this route; this nonnative, invasive vine has become a huge problem in the area. After 1.7 miles (from Broadway) you will reach Route 629, Lighthouse Avenue. Turn left, and in 0.7 mile you will reach the entrance to Cape May Point State Park on your left. Proceed into the park. (If the park gate is closed, park in the overflow lot to the left and walk in.) The road bends right, then left, then right, into a large parking lot. The park office, museum, environmental education center, and heated restrooms are to your right. The hawkwatch platform and trailheads are to your left. Straight ahead is the beach, where the Delaware Bay meets the Atlantic Ocean, and where land meets the sea at the very tip of the Cape May peninsula.

The trails begin left of the East Shelter, which is on the left of the Wildlife Viewing Platform as you approach it from the parking lot. The Red Trail, ½-mile long and wheelchair accessible, has overlooks at both Lighthouse Pond West (with a blind) and Lighthouse Pond East (with a platform and benches)—good for waterfowl in almost any season. If the hawk flight is hopping and the hawkwatch is overflowing, Lighthouse Pond East puts you right under the action, and you often have it to yourself. Lighthouse Pond is excellent for secretive American Bittern, Sora Rails if muddy edges are exposed, feeding herons, egrets, Osprey, Kingfisher, and, by October, waterfowl hidden in the edges. High ground along the Red Trail wanders under sizable Pitch Pines and Sour Gums, also known as Black Gum or Black Tupelo. Very attractive, they are the first tree to turn color, bright reds and purples, in the early fall. Stands of Southern Arrowwood, a native viburnum, line sections of the Red Trail. The final stretch (also the beginning of the Yellow-Blue Trail) winds under one of the densest stands of Red Cedars in the park. These cedars were planted naturally by the birds after the military moved off the site after the 1962 storm, so you can easily discern just how old these trees are. This stand of cedars and others like it provide excellent cover for migrating owls in late October and November. The Yellow Trail is 1.3 miles long and runs concurrently with the Blue Trail for half its length. The beginning of the trail wanders through the dense Red Cedars, then bears right off the Red Trail. It soon crosses a bridge over one of the old ditches dug to drain the freshwater ponds and marsh in the days when draining was thought to be the way to control mosquitoes. The trail then wanders through an upland pine-oak forest. Many large oaks can be found here: Spanish Oak (*Quercus falcate,* with sweeping lobes that resemble falcon wings), Willow Oak (with willowlike leaves), White Oak, and others. The trail soon crosses a field once planted in Japanese Black Pines in the early 1980s that today is a dark forest and an owly stretch in late October and November. It then meanders through the pine-oak forest again (where sunlit edges are often excellent for land birding), crosses the freshwater marsh behind Bunker Pond via the old salt hay dikes (where you have a sweeping view back to the hawk-watch platform and the lighthouse), enters an island of Persimmon and Mockernut Hickory trees with an overlook at Al's Pond (with a platform and bench), and crosses another section of freshwater marsh before exiting out to the beach. From there, you

The park's extensive boardwalk trail system leads to a variety of habitats and overlooks.

can return to the parking lot by doubling back on the Yellow Trail or by following the beach or the trail behind the dune back toward the Bunker.

The Blue Trail and the Yellow Trail are one trail until the final leg of the Yellow Trail. From here, the Blue Trail bears left and continues through a bayberry and wax myrtle thicket, crosses a freshwater marsh via an old salt hay dike, and enters an upland forest of pines and oaks. This final portion of the Blue Trail goes through some of the best woodlands in the park and can be excellent for songbirds in spring and fall, particularly at the dead-end spur, a left-hand turn that follows an old road. Returning from this dead-end spur, continue out to the beach. Either follow the beach or the path behind the dune back to the parking lot. The Blue Trail is 2 miles round trip. (In fall, park trails may be closed for a few days for *Phragmites*

Seaside Goldenrod attracts Monarchs and other migrating butterflies in the fall.

control, the regular spraying that is part of ongoing restoration efforts. The Cape May Migratory Bird Refuge may close too at these times; unfortunately, this peak time for bird migration and birders is said to be the best time for spraying success).

Birding is excellent anywhere in Cape May Point State Park. Be sure to walk the trails, but also bird right around the edge of the parking lot and perimeter road and along the paths behind the dune, which give you the best views of Bunker Pond ("Shallow Pond West" on the park brochure). The trail behind the man-made sand dune or berm is particularly productive, offering views of Bunker Pond and other small pools. Check the entire pond edge and all nooks and crannies for Least Bittern, American Bittern, Sora Rail, Common Moorhen, and Pied-billed Grebe. Bunker Pond is an excellent place to enjoy swallows feeding low over the water during light rain or in windy conditions. Large numbers of terns often loiter at Bunker Pond. Check flocks of Forster's and Common Terns for Roseate and Sandwich Terns. Common Terns are more abundant from May to September, and Forster's Terns are more abundant in October and November. Roseate Terns are most likely in May and June, Sandwich Terns from July through September. From mid-fall through spring expect a good-sized flock of American Wigeon (and often a Eurasian Wigeon) along with Gadwall, Northern Pintail, and others. The two shallow ponds behind the dunes (the "Plover Ponds") near the ends of both the Yellow and Blue Trails were created during the 2004–2005 beachfill project and have proven to be excellent for shorebirds: Piping Plover and their young during the breeding season and Buff-breasted Sandpiper, Baird's Sandpiper, and American Golden Plover in September. In fall, enjoy countless Monarchs and Common Buckeyes nectaring on the abundant Seaside Goldenrod growing on the dunes and behind them.

The wooded portions of the park trail system are also very good for frogs, toads, snakes, and turtles. Southern Gray Treefrogs (endangered in New Jersey) frequently perch on the railings of the hawkwatch platform and have been a highlight of many a visitor's day. With the warm micro-climate caused by all the surrounding waters, sunning snakes (black rat, black racer, water, garter, and ribbon) and turtles may surprise you almost any month of the year. Even if you don't hike all the trails, be sure to check all the ponds in the park. And check them daily during your visit—new birds are always coming and going.

How much the major and ongoing *Phragmites* control and marsh restoration efforts will affect birds and birders at Cape May Point State Park is unknown. (These efforts are part of the larger U.S. Army Corps of Engineers' beachfill and shore protection project at Cape May.) While *Phragmites* removal is good and will no doubt

More than just birds—a migratory Red Bat roosts in the woods on the point.

be beneficial to most birds in the long term (not all birds however; massive flocks of Tree Swallows roost in *Phrag* at both the park and in Pond Creek), it remains to be seen just what Cape May Point State Park will look like in ten or even five years from now. The park's invasive plant eradication effort along the park trails has already greatly opened up large areas of the park that were formerly dense and impenetrable tangles. Some birds, such as migrant sparrows, should benefit; others, such as migrant owls, may experience detrimental impacts. As with so many Cape May changes over time, some birds will prosper and others will not.

CAPE MAY POINT: LAKE LILY, CMBO, AND PAVILION CIRCLE

Before we route you to classic locations such as Higbee Beach, there is plenty more to see and do in Cape May Point. The point, although changing, is still pretty much a sleepy little seashore resort. (European visitors find that Cape May Point reminds them greatly of Falsterbo, Sweden, as does much of the Cape May migration and birding experience.) Founded in 1875 and originally named Sea Grove, the town was once a Presbyterian summer resort. Many original structures still stand, including the Wanamaker

Purple Sandpipers, Ruddy Turnstones, and Sanderlings feed on the jetties at Cape May Point.

Cottage, home of one of the original members of the Sea Grove Association, John Wanamaker. A classic "gingerbread church," Saint Peter's by-the-Sea on Ocean Avenue near the beach, is an Episcopal Church built in 1880. It has been moved three times, each time further back from the encroaching sea. In 2005, this famous little church celebrated its 125th anniversary service. The pines and cedars around the church often hold migrant birds in season.

All of Cape May Point's beachfront jetties are excellent in any season. Purple Sandpipers are a staple in winter. Scoter are present from fall until spring, and most years a few scoter summer here, too. Various gulls are present all year along with lots of terns in the warmer months. The various jetties and elevated dune walkovers also offer exceptional views of the avian repast of the rips (the rough waters where the Atlantic Ocean meets the Delaware Bay). The point's vegetated paths hold passerines in spring and fall.

All of Cape May Point's dune crossovers and jetties are worth exploring.

In late September and early October, an almost daily and mesmerizing spectacle is the thousands upon thousands of sparkling Tree Swallows dropping into the dunes to feast on bayberries. Bird the dunes from the quiet streets that run along them or from the walkovers (it is illegal to walk on the dunes themselves). Also, be aware that these shrubby dunes contain lots of vigorous Poison Ivy.

Another key spot in Cape May Point is Lily Lake. This 40-acre freshwater lake attracts birds in any season. Even in the harshest winters, a spring (and the volume of waterfowl) generally keep a portion of the lake icefree, attracting a variety of ducks, including Ruddy Duck, Canvasback, and Redhead. In summer, herons and egrets drop in, and if water levels are low, shorebirds—primarily Solitary, Spotted, and Least Sandpipers— feed around the edges. Every year a couple of good rarities are found at

Lily Lake is worth a stop in any season, particularly in winter for waterfowl.

Lily Lake. Red-necked Phalarope, White Pelican, and Fulvous Whistling-Duck are a few recent favorites. The lake is also an excellent fall hawk-watching spot, especially when northeast winds are blowing. The benches at the south end offer a good view to the north. Dredging in 2004 was designed to improve flood control, flow, and water quality by removing a century's accumulation of waterfowl waste (mostly from tame ducks and geese). It appears that this deepening may have benefited waterfowl, or at least was not detrimental, as Lake Lily continues to be a top waterfowl spot.

The Cape May Bird Observatory (CMBO) Northwood Center, one of New Jersey Audubon Society's ten centers in the state, overlooks the north end of Lily Lake. It's at 701 East Lake Drive on a nearly one-acre wildscape. The building is nestled in a dune forest of Beach Plum bushes, Dwarf Hackberry, Wild Black Cherry, Persimmon, American Holly, Sassafras, and oaks. This small copse of woods around the observatory can be surprisingly good for songbirds during migration. Fifteen-species warbler days occur here most years, and both Golden-winged and Cerulean Warblers are found here almost annually. Spring fallout can be particularly exceptional, sometimes lasting for days. Barred Owl has been seen behind the building on occasion. An array of bird feeders stocked year-round, small ponds, and a mister-drip system are good at any season. A small hummingbird and butterfly garden is found here, too. This is a particularly good place to see Fox Sparrow in late fall and winter, and Dickcissel has wintered at these feeders. Consider this your birding headquarters for books, gifts, and optics—and for the latest information on what birds are around. At the observatory, you can read a printout of recent Cape May Birding Hotlines and check the daily sighting sheets. Share your own sightings while you're at it. You can also get a birding map, bird checklist, and the *Kestrel Express,*

Pavilion Circle is maintained as a wildlife garden in the center of the Cape May Point community.

CMBO's seasonal program schedule of walks, workshops, and special programs.

Pavilion Circle is another important stop in Cape May Point. The name refers to the Sea Grove Pavilion, built in 1875 in the center of the circle and used as a place of worship but gone since the 1880s, when the Sea Grove Association sold its holdings. Today in its place a circular borough park attracts residents, visiting birders, and butterfly watchers. In 1993, the Cape May Point Taxpayers Association, with support from residents and a tree grant, transformed the circle—an area of sand and Prickly Pear Cactus—into grassy lawns, tree and shrub plantings for wildlife, gardens for butterflies, scattered benches, and two playing fields. The circle's pathway of brick pavers recognizes donors: "Bed Fellows" adopt and maintain gardens in the circle, so each year brings new surprises, while "Bed Warmers" help fund plantings and maintenance. The trees of Pavilion Circle attract songbirds in spring and fall, and the place bustles with migrants on good migration days; it's particularly good for Red-breasted Nuthatch and Yellow-bellied Sapsucker late in the autumn, along with a Cape May Warbler or two attracted to fresh sapsucker seeps. The circle is another good hawkwatching spot, both in late spring (for high-flying Mississippi Kites) and in fall, sometimes offering better views than the hawkwatch platform, especially when northeast winds are blowing. Pavilion Circle is also home to a general store, a longtime Cape May Point staple, good for breakfast, lunch, sandwiches, and supplies in season. It's the only deli in Cape May Point and is birder-friendly.

The Saint Agnus Church at the corner of Cape Avenue and Pavilion Circle is landscaped for wildlife with gardens and Butterfly Bushes. The community of Cape May Point embraces migrating Monarchs and birds, and it really shows. There are probably more butterfly gardens packed into this community than anywhere else in the nation. Many yards in Cape May Point, and elsewhere in the lower cape, display a Cape May Stopover Protection Project sign, which states that the property "has been designated a wildlife sanctuary for migrating birds, butterflies, and other wildlife by providing plants for food and cover." In 1990, Cape May Point passed a

Landscape Ordinance after much hard work by the environmental commission, with chairperson Sally Sachs at the helm. This ordinance limits the clearing of a property for development: Sixty percent, regardless of the size of the property, must remain vegetated. Buildings can take up no more than 30 percent of the property, leaving 10 percent for permeable paths and driveway. The ordinance also requires mitigation of a 2:1 ratio if trees greater than 3 inches in diameter are cut within a footprint covering the building foundation and 6 feet beyond. It directs homeowners to CMBO's backyard habitat publications to select native trees most beneficial to birds. Cape May Point's Landscape Ordinance was inspired by CMBO's efforts to educate about the importance of backyard habitat, especially at migration crossroads, and is a role model for communities around the country. The point's naturally vegetated appearance has been protected by this ordinance, but the battle is ongoing. Some continue to do as they please, clearing entire lots of sprawling trees and shrubs to build their mansions, seeing the $500 fine as a mere inconvenience. But residents that care are working hard to strengthen the ordinance and win this latest battle.

Cape May Point yards and undeveloped lots are well vegetated with huge Spanish, Willow, and White Oaks, Wild Black Cherries, Red Cedars, and American Hollies. In this sandy, windswept, bayfront community many of these trees are over a hundred years old. Birders can't go wrong walking the sleepy streets of the point, which offer a heartwarming glimpse of the Old Cape May experience and seashore days largely gone by at most resorts.

Birding the Site

Leaving Cape May Point State Park, go across Lighthouse Avenue and jog slightly left, past St. Mary's. Favorite dune crossovers are at Ocean Avenue (by the gingerbread church), at Cape Avenue, along Pearl Avenue, at Stites Avenue, and the end of Alexander Avenue (which offers an excellent view of the Concrete Ship area to the north). The diligent birder should check all nine of the rock piles. Scan the rocks the length of each jetty and the surrounding waters. It's fun to walk Cape May Point's entire beachfront, birding as you go (you can leave your car at the state park and start from there). During both spring and fall migration, many songbirds can be found in the dunes. Alternately, to reach Lily Lake and CMBO, when you leave Cape May Point State Park, make a right onto Lighthouse Drive. Go 0.5 mile to East Lake Drive and make a left. The **CMBO Northwood Center** is on your right. Parking is permitted on one side of the road shoulder only and may be difficult in peak season; you may need to walk a block or so. Do not park facing traffic—the local constables frown on people parking against the grain.

THE RIPS

The Rips is an odd name for a local landmark, especially if you aren't a mariner and are hearing it for the first time. Although virtually all fishermen, and even most locals, know The Rips well, a birder new to the area may wonder where it is and what it is all about. For veteran Cape May birders, The Rips is one of the best birding spots on the entire East Coast. The Rips is at land's end, at the tip of New Jersey and the Cape May peninsula. It is where the land meets the sea, where the Delaware Bay meets the Atlantic Ocean. The Delaware Estuary is big, and a lot of water moves in and out of the bay on the twice-a-day tides. Shoals, or sandbars, characterize The Rips—sand deposited by the enormous tidal forces scouring the beaches and bay. The Rips is a series of powerful tidal currents. On a calm day, from the Cape May–Lewes Ferry or even from land at Cape May Point State Park, you can see the tide lines, the energized moving water meeting with less powerful, calmer eddies and backwaters.

Even on the calmest days, if the wind is against the tide, high standing waves form where deep water hits the shallows, as the current dumps water first up the slope and then down into the deep holes behind the shoals. Local fishermen joke that they're not fishing "close enough" to the shoals if they're not bumping bottom once in a while, as the water can go from 20 to 2 feet deep in the length of a small boat. It is a rippled sea bottom, with an extensive series of holes and sandbars where Striped Bass are sometimes packed like cordwood. Once in a while, fishermen get too close, and a high breaking wave fills the boat. Every season, more than one boat "turns turtle" in The Rips, sometimes with disastrous results.

Fishermen love The Rips. It is a world-famous fishing spot nearly year-round where strong currents sweep baitfish into the turmoil. Baitfish, in turn, attract game fish—stripers, Bluefish, Weakfish (sea trout), and more. Spring through fall, Bottle-nosed Dolphin feed daily in The Rips, and every year a few Humpback Whales feed there, too, spotted by whale-watching boats and even sometimes from shore.

The Rips is as famous for birding as it is for fishing. On almost any given day throughout the seasons, there are birds feeding in The Rips ("bird-play," in the parlance of fishermen), actively diving and chasing bait either driven to the surface by game fish or tumbling in the turmoil of the waves. In winter, The Rips attracts mainly large gulls but also Bonaparte's Gulls and the odd kittiwake. Spring is exciting, with Roseate and Black Terns seen sometimes daily among the abundant

Laughing Gulls. Brown Pelicans and even Wilson's Storm-Petrels frequent The Rips in summer. Late summer and early fall are best, with a true cornucopia of gulls, terns, and the ever-attendant jaegers. Pirates of the bird world, Parasitic Jaegers are seen daily over The Rips in fall, boldly chasing down hapless gulls and terns to steal their catch. Northern Gannets are daily visitors in midfall to late fall (and again in spring), sometimes numbering in the hundreds, and often quite close to shore.

The Rips is often at its best during a storm—a hotspot in what most would consider the worst birding conditions: strong east winds and rain. Some of the Cape's best birds, the true pelagic species, show up in these conditions. Possibly they are storm-driven, but maybe, with the rain and fog, they just don't see the land at Cape May Point until they are right on it. Birders have learned that the bigger the storm, the better the birds.

You never know what will turn up in The Rips, or when. Midwinter has produced Razorbills and even Northern Fulmar. In several recent summers, Sooty, Cory's, and Greater Shearwaters were seen daily for weeks. Manx and Audubon's Shearwaters were tallied too. Wayward Brown Boobies have been seen at least three times in recent years. One of our rarest birds ever—the first North American Whiskered Tern (from the Mediterranean)—was found after it came flying in from The Rips to rest on the beach on July 12, 1993. Way back in the 1960s, the legendary Harold Axtell saw *two* Black-browed Albatross over the storm-tossed autumn Rips. Besides being one of Cape May's best birding spots, The Rips is one of the easiest to bird. Simply set up your spotting scope on the beach at Cape May Point State Park and look south. The Rips is the boiling waters right in front of you, sometimes close, sometimes (depending on the wind and tide) a ways out. On calm summer days, it can look benign, but on windy days the explosive, towering, crashing waves on the outer Rips are sometimes mistaken for breaching whales by first-time observers. Moving tides are needed for bird activity, but slack tides last only about an hour or less around the tide changes. A midmorning falling tide seems to be the best, but this can vary.

The dune crossovers and beaches anywhere in Cape May Point north to Second Avenue Jetty in Cape May City are all excellent vantage points. Also consider watching from the decks of local whale-watch boats, which daily pursue dolphins (and birds) in the area of The Rips. Look for local birders huddled over their scopes looking seaward in the early morning (often the best time, but not always), particularly in foul weather, and you'll know you are at the right spot.

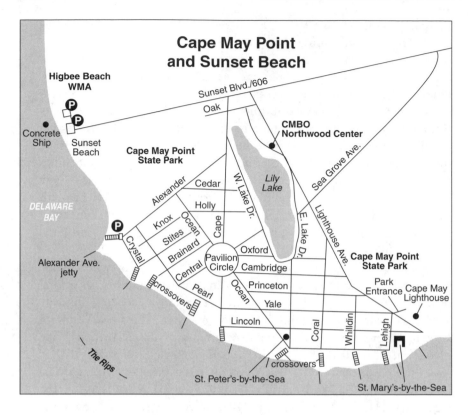

Continue on around Lily Lake (on your left) either by car or on foot. Go left on Oak Avenue, then left on Cape Avenue. Cape Avenue will take you directly to Pavilion Circle, or, after one short block, make a left onto Lake Avenue to continue your tour around Lily Lake. Following Central Avenue away from Lily Lake will also take you to Pavilion Circle. (It's a small town, so you can't really get too lost. And if you do, enjoy it!) There are front yard and backyard butterfly and bird-friendly gardens throughout Cape May Point that attract big numbers of Monarchs in fall. To return to Sunset Boulevard, follow either Cape Avenue or Lighthouse Avenue until they dead-end back at Sunset Boulevard.

SUNSET BEACH: THE CONCRETE SHIP AND THE MAGNESITE PLANT

Cape Island, as the area south of the Cape May Canal has long been known, is actually one of the few spots in the United States where the sun both rises and sets over the water. A favorite spot to view Cape May sunsets is the appropriately named Sunset Beach, at the end of Sunset Boulevard. From Memorial Day through September, hundreds gather for the evening flag-lowering ceremony to honor those who have served the country and to enjoy the sunset and hope for the elusive "green flash" as the sun passes below the horizon. (Because of the ever-present humidity and haze, we've seen it just three times over the years.) Sunset Beach is also one of the very few places on the coastline where in bad weather you can "seawatch" in comfort from your warm, dry car. This favorite Cape May pastime finds many birders gathered here in rainy, windy, murky conditions hoping for that waif from far at sea. In better weather, spring through fall, the deck of the birder-friendly outdoor Sunset Beach Grill snack bar is a fun place to enjoy breakfast or lunch while scanning the bay.

Sunset Beach is famous among tourists as *the* place to search for "Cape May diamonds," wave-tossed quartz pebbles of all sizes and colors (the clear ones appear most like diamonds). These pebbles have broken free from quartz deposits along the upper Delaware River and tumbled downriver onto Delaware Bay beaches all the way to Cape May Point, a 200-mile journey said to take thousands of years to complete. Apparently, the Lenni Lenape were the first to search for these stones. When faceted and polished, they indeed look like real diamonds. Enjoy these gems in the Sunset Beach Gifts shop to your right, or search for them on your own. (Sunset Beach itself is highly picked over. Good Cape May diamonds are much more abundant and easily found a quarter or a half mile to the north, or even farther north, at sites such as Town Bank.)

The other draw of Sunset Beach, for tourists and birders alike, is the famous Concrete Ship, the SS *Atlantus*. The unlikely construction technique, using 5-inch-thick reinforced concrete, was a response to the shortage of steel during World War I. The *Atlantus* was one of twelve concrete ships built—a freighter 250 feet long and weighing about 3,000 tons. Launched in November 1918 in Brunswick, Georgia, a month after the war ended, the ship crossed the Atlantic several times, bringing troops back from Europe. Later, the ship hauled coal in New England. In 1926, the *Atlantus* was towed to Cape May. Three such ships were to be run ashore at the end of Sunset Boulevard to create a Y-shaped ferry dock, but a storm in 1926 broke the *Atlantus* from its moorings, and it ran aground on a shoal and has been there ever since, immovable because of its great weight. In the 1950s, the ship began to break up. Today, it hardly resembles a ship at all, looking more like rubble jutting out of the bay several hundred yards off the beach. Locals say that the *Atlantus* is the world's slowest sinking ship.

For birders, the Concrete Ship is a unique attraction. When the fast-moving bay currents encounter the remnant ship, huge eddies and upwellings occur, attracting gulls, terns, loons, and sea ducks in season. In early spring, sometimes hundreds of Bonaparte's Gulls gather here, often joined by a Black-headed Gull and a Little Gull or two (up to eight have

The concrete Atlantus *transported troops after World War I. Brought here to be placed with two others as part of a ferry dock, it broke loose in a storm and sank at its present location. This is how it appeared in 1926.*

been seen here at once). This is the best spot to see Red-throated Loons in February and March; dozens are often present. The Concrete Ship is a reliable high-tide roost for Purple Sandpipers and Ruddy Turnstones (when local jetties are covered by water) and a predictable spot to find perched Great Cormorants fall through spring. You never know what might turn up in the waters around the Concrete Ship. Northern Gannets are numerous and Parasitic Jaegers are regular in fall and spring. Sooty Shearwaters are always possible in June. Brown Pelicans are daily in summer and Wilson's Storm-Petrel nearly so. Red-necked Phalarope, Black-legged Kittiwake, Arctic Tern, and even Northern Fulmar have occurred there. Perhaps the strangest bird to ever appear at the Concrete Ship was not rare, just way out of habitat. One morning, Fred Mears scanned the hulk for Purple Sandpipers and was rewarded with a hen Ring-necked Pheasant sitting on top of the ship, the only one seen south of the canal in many years.

The land along Sunset Boulevard that you pass on your way to Sunset Beach was once the Witmer Stone Bird Sanctuary. Roadside birding can be good here, and accipiters skim low over the cedars and dunes in fall. Today, lands to the south of Sunset Boulevard are part of Cape May Point State Park and include the soon-to-be restored (by MAC) 71-foot-high tower built in 1941 known as "Fire Control Tower No. 23." (Barn Owls have nested in this structure). Lands to the north of Sunset Boulevard include an undeveloped section of Higbee Beach Wildlife Management Area. This barren, grassy area (currently being revegetated) is the site of the former Magnesite Plant, and birders still refer to it as such, even though the water tower is all that remains of the once-massive factory. Check the tower at any season for roosting Peregrine Falcons, and remember that this area is a good hawkwatching spot, often better than the state park when east-northeast winds are blowing.

The Magnesite Plant was built in 1941 by Dresser Industries to extract magnesite from seawater salt. It was infamous in the area. The alkaline particulates in the smokestack emissions were responsible for stunting and killing the acid-loving Red Cedars and pines nearby and throughout Cape May Point. The stunted forest is still recovering today. Until 1983, the factory smokestack plume of smoke was an excellent windsock, used by hawkwatchers to determine the wind direction and raptor flight path. The factory was demolished in 1989; and in 1999, the 153-acre property straddling Sunset Boulevard was purchased by the state for $1.7 million. Some of the former site on the north side of the road (now part of Higbee Beach WMA) is still fenced off, but parking and trails are planned once restoration and recovery is completed. Because of the very poor soil conditions, nutrient-rich dredge spoils are being used as fertilizer. Grassland habitat is being created out of this former barren area.

From Sunset Beach, you can walk south along the beach to Alexander Avenue Jetty in Cape May Point or north up the beach into Higbee Beach WMA proper, where Signal Hill and Davey's Lake are found. From Sunset Boulevard, you are closer to both of these spots than you are when you're in the main Higbee Beach parking lot on New England Road. Signal Hill, the highest dune at Higbee Beach, and all of the Delaware Bayshore, is just north of Davey's Lake. Historically, it was a vantage point used to signal ships in the bay. Davey's Lake is more than 300 yards long, 90 yards wide, and 12-feet deep in spots. The freshwater lake was commercially dug in 1910 by the Cape May Sand Company for sand. Davey's often holds interesting waterfowl—sometimes Canvasback and Redhead in winter. Recent rarities there have included Red-necked Grebe, Northern Shrike, and a Trumpeter Swan (which probably originated from the Great Lakes reintroduction program).

Alkaline particulates in the smokestack emissions from the controversial Magnesite Plant along Sunset Boulevard stunted acres of pine and Red Cedar. The Plant was demolished in 1989.

Birding the Site

From Cape May Point State Park, return on Lighthouse Avenue until you reach Sunset Boulevard (Route 606). Turn left onto Sunset and proceed 0.5 mile to the parking lot at the end of the road, on Delaware Bay. The Concrete Ship is right in front of you. In inclement weather, get there early to be assured a beachfront parking spot so that you can bird from your car. The former Magnesite Plant area is always a good stop on your birding itinerary. In early fall, numerous Eastern Kingbirds (sometimes a Western) and American Kestrel perch on the fence. Merlin frequently hunt the open spaces here, particularly late in the day. Later in the fall the grassy areas are good for grassland sparrows—the somewhat unique habitat here is one of the best places in Cape May to find Lark, Clay-colored, and Vesper Sparrows. Short-eared Owl and even Rough-legged Hawk have been seen hunting this grassland in winter, and a Swainson's Hawk recently spent several days here one fall. Recent rarities have also included Scissor-tailed Flycatcher, Say's Phoebe, Loggerhead Shrike, and Northern Shrike.

The high ground behind the former factory site offers a good overview of Pond Creek Marsh. It's mostly *Phragmites* today, highly degraded from its former status as a healthy freshwater wetland. But Pond Creek Marsh is still scenic and interesting, and the expansive view from the magnesite grassland edges can offer good views of the raptor flight—and insight into the possibilities should planned restoration efforts ever come to fruition. A major federal, state, and local *Phragmites* control project is imminent for Pond Creek Marsh. Plans call for flooding the area with salt water and returning it to tidal flow to force out the invasive plants, a controversial plan because of the possible effect on local wells, the cattail–water lily freshwater upper reaches, and the vital Hidden Valley upland edge. (Even though construction of the sluices and channels has not yet begun, the project is under way. Hurricane Fran washed out the existing sluice in 1996, and the lower reaches of Pond Creek have been flooded daily by tides since.) If the project goes as planned, there should be great benefits to birds (excepting Tree Swallows, which use the vast *Phragmites* stands for roosting) as the badly degraded marsh is restored, but there is deep concern that the crucial berms, designed and slated to protect the sensitive freshwater areas, have not survived project budget cuts. Without the berms, salt water could cause extensive damage to the Higbee Beach and Hidden Valley upland edges. For many, the jury is still out—and will remain so for years.

To bird the Magnesite Plant section of Higbee Beach WMA, you can park in the Concrete Ship parking lot, although this lot is sometimes crowded with tourists. Better yet, turn right into the parking lot just before the Sunset Beach Gifts shop. Proceed past the gift shop parking spaces and the Sunset Beach Fishing Club parking area into the marked state WMA parking area. Park and walk to the beach. Here you can walk north (right) to the Pond Creek sluice/outfall. There are good views of Delaware Bay, and this is a good Cape May diamond area. A bridge across the sluice is planned; crossing the shallow water flow now means getting your feet wet (OK in summer, but ill advised in winter). Higbee Beach WMA proper is beyond this outfall but not usually accessed from here.

Bonaparte's Gulls feed at the Pond Creek outfall in winter and early spring. Behind the dunes, emergent salt marsh attracts shorebirds in season. Retrace your steps to the parking lot. Then walk back toward Sunset Boulevard and go around the end of the old chain-link fence. Turn back to the north and walk toward the large water tower. You will soon reach a path that will route you toward Higbee Beach. This is the section of former factory wasteland that is being restored into grassland. Look for sparrows here during migration. Migrating hawks hunt here in autumn. Proceed a few hundred yards and you will cross the Pond Creek channel, which is really just a ditch (when Pond Creek restoration is complete, this bridge may be gone, replaced by one out near the beach; formal trails and signage are also planned). Work the grasslands here. To your right is the vast Pond Creek Marsh. Tidal inundation here has already killed extensive *Phragmites*. Look for shorebirds on the emergent mudflats and scan for hunting harriers. Eagles sometimes perch on distant Sassafras Island. Merlin and peregrine routinely hunt here in late afternoon in autumn. Expect abundant Sharp-shinned Hawks on northwest winds in September and October.

Follow the admittedly obscure road/path, and in a few hundred yards you come to vegetated dunes. Through the shrubbery, you can see Davey's Lake. A path will route you around the lake: The right hand (east) side is easily traversable; the left (west) side is densely vegetated in places. Beyond Davey's Lake, you can enter the classic dune forest of Higbee Beach. The dunes are ancient, vegetated with windswept Beach Plum and bayberry bushes, Dwarf Hackberry, Wild Black Cherry, American Holly, and Red Cedar trees. Beyond Davey's Lake, Signal Hill is the highest point on Higbee Beach. By climbing the bare, high sand dune, you have an exquisite view of Pond Creek Marsh, a vista that includes the distant Beanery/Rea Farm, Hidden Valley, and Higbee Beach. In autumn, fallout occurs throughout the dunes and the Davey's Lake area, and the morning flight can be watched anywhere. It is a long early morning walk, but there may be nowhere as exciting to watch the morning flight as from atop Signal Hill.

CAPE MAY MIGRATORY BIRD REFUGE
(THE SOUTH CAPE MAY MEADOWS)

One of Cape May's classic birding areas is the Cape May Migratory Bird Refuge. It is still evocatively called the Meadows by local birders, even though succession has inexorably changed the storied pastureland of yore to shrub habitat. Owned and managed by The Nature Conservancy as one of their premier New Jersey preserves, it was the very first TNC acquisition in New Jersey, purchased in 1981. Abutting the state park to the west, this 250-acre site (plus or minus: plus following ongoing beach-fill projects, minus following erosion from coastal storms) is a wondrous expanse of open meadow, bayberry-covered dunes, open beach, and extensive fresh-water ponds and marsh. There are large areas of Red Cedar, Wax Myrtle, Groundsel-tree, and Winged Sumac along the paths.

The town of South Cape May—fifty or sixty cottages—once stood on this beachfront. It was accessed by a trolley line that ran along the beach from Sewell's Point in Cape May City to Cape May Point and by two roads that today serve as the Meadows' center and east paths. Established in 1884, South Cape May was continually battered by storms; by 1955, scattered chimneys and pilings were all that stood. The pink Victorian cottage on the corner of Sunset Boulevard and Bayshore Road is actually the top floor of a house that originally stood on the beachfront. For many years, it has been appropriately named Seaworthy Angel. A large gray house several doors down to the west was also moved from South Cape May. It, too, is actually the salvaged top floor of the original house.

The Meadows offers exceptional birding in any season. In both spring and fall, migrants fill the site: waterfowl (good numbers and variety), shorebirds in the ponds, songbirds along the paths. It is an exceptional spot for Least Bittern, American Bittern, Sora, and Virginia Rail. Big flocks of gulls and terns loiter on the beach in spring and fall; it's one of the most consistent spots to see Sandwich Tern at Cape May. In fall, the dune crossovers are great spots to enjoy hawks skimming the dunes—sharp-shins, kestrel, and Merlin—and to scan the ocean and rips offshore. Don't forget to look up. A parade of hawks heading to the point might be right overhead or visible to the north. Expect breathtaking clouds of glittering Tree Swallows in late September and early October, swirling overhead, racing along the dunes, dipping into the ponds for a drink, or feeding on bayberries along the loop trail. At times, in autumn, Monarchs cover Seaside Goldenrod growing in the dunes and are counted in the thousands on peak days.

The Meadows can be good at any time of day and is particularly popular for watching the evening departure (the "lift off") of migratory herons, bitterns, and even owls in fall. On days with northeast or east winds, which put birds on shore that may otherwise be migrating off the coast, birders often have a steady progression of shorebirds dropping in on their way south. Often these migrant shorebirds don't linger and sometimes only circle overhead, but we remember days when diligent watchers recorded twenty species here, including Upland Sandpiper, Buff-breasted Sandpiper, Ruff, and American Avocet.

The Meadows can be at its best in summer, when both Piping Plover and Least Terns breed on the beach (up to five pairs of Piping Plover and sometimes up to seventy-five pairs of Least Terns). Even though this colony is patrolled by a seasonal warden and protected by fencing, productivity is rarely high due to predators and beach foot traffic, which keeps the young from feeding at the water's edge. Ponds created behind the dunes in 2005, as part of the Army Corps of Engineers beach-restoration project, were heavily used by foraging plovers and led to greater success than in many years. To find Piping Plovers, look for the exclosures, fencing and netting placed around nests to keep predators out.

Wader-watching in July and August is a favorite at the Meadows. Large flocks of herons, egrets, and ibis feast on fish concentrated by low water levels (if there has been a lot of or recent rain, the high water level means fewer birds). Fall shorebirds begin arriving in July. They too concentrate here if there has been little rain, the water level is low, and muddy edges are exposed. In summer, the ponds host a few uncommon breeders such as Gadwall, Blue-winged Teal, Least Bittern, and Common Moorhen. Amazingly, in the 1990s, Black Rail bred in the Meadows for at least one season, probably two. Marsh Wrens sing from the dense vegetation around ponds; in summer, Willow Flycatcher breeds here. Also in summer, scan the waters offshore for feeding Wilson's Storm-Petrel. In winter, scan the beach and dunes for Snow Bunting and "Ipswich" Savannah Sparrow. In spring, look for courting American Woodcock against the last light of sunset.

The Meadows is open dawn to dusk. It's a place where you can spend an hour or two, or, when conditions are right, a day or two watching the always-changing kaleidoscope of migration. A 1-mile loop trail begins and ends at the parking lot. It follows two old roads through the Meadows (the center path and the east path, each running north-south) and includes two dune crossovers with soft sand and a stretch of open beach connecting the two paths. Large buses or motor coaches are not permitted in the Meadows' small parking lot. Visitation guidelines are posted at the parking lot.

Birding the Site

From Lighthouse Avenue in Cape May Point, turn right onto Sunset Boulevard (Route 606), and proceed east back toward Cape May City. Go

Patient birders in the Meadows might be rewarded with a glimpse of a Least Bittern.

0.9 mile and turn right into a clamshell parking lot. As you face away from Sunset, the trailhead and kiosks are in the right corner of the lot. Follow the loop trail down the center path and out to the ocean. An observation platform midway down the path on your left has lost some of its view due to successional growth—the transition from grazed meadow to young forest. The small pond to the right of the trail and visible from the platform is good for Virginia and Sora Rail and Orange-crowned Warbler in fall and winter. Continue south along the center path. Stands of Purple Gerardia host Common Buckeye caterpillars, sometimes lots of them in September. Enjoy the various freshwater pond overlooks.

Spotting scopes are useful here. The trail may be muddy or under water after rain. The large pond left of the center path stretches across to the east path. In the early morning, the sun will be in your face as you look into the pond. Late afternoon or early evening offers better viewing. The center path crests the high, wide dune and goes out onto the beach. Head left (east) to continue the loop. In spring and summer, rope or string fencing will route you around the tern and plover nesting area if it's active. Alternately, you can easily walk west to Cape May Point State Park—about 1 mile—or east to Second Avenue Jetty in Cape May City—also about 1 mile. A short walk east along the beach brings you to the next dune crossover and the east path (there is no west path). Ponds east of the east path are good for Pied-billed Grebe, Common Moorhen, and Least and American Bittern. Leasts breed in small numbers here; American Bitterns are seen in spring and mainly fall, most often by those who tirelessly scan the water's edge with binoculars and a scope. Eventually, a bittern will step into view, but sometimes it can take hours. In late afternoon and evening, the sun is at your back as you look into these ponds. Early-morning and late-afternoon bitterns are sometimes seen in flight. Check the many different views into the ponds along the east path. The path turns west at Sunset Boulevard and parallels the road back to the parking lot. The grassland meadow along this stretch can be good for Bobolink, Eastern Meadowlark, and sparrows. The entire loop trail is 1 mile long.

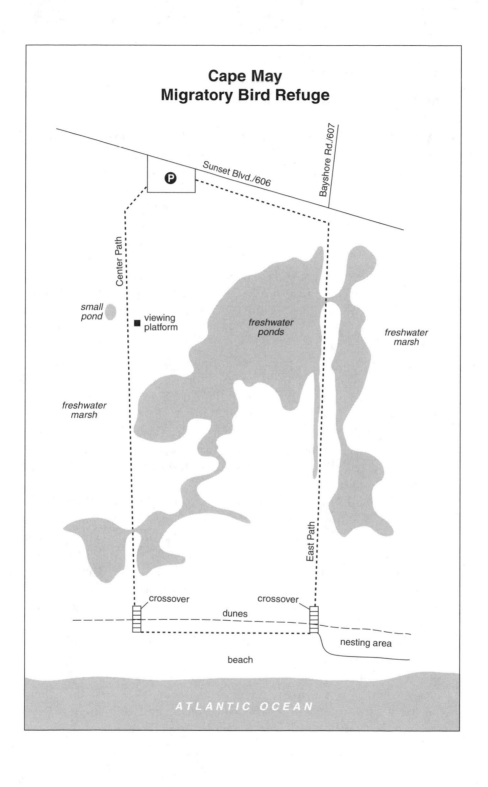

THE TIMELESS MEADOWS
ON AN AUGUST DAY

The Meadows is at its peak in August, and the Meadows at its peak is about as good as it gets. The heat, drought, and lack of rain have taken their toll, but in this case, the benefits outweigh the costs. In the Meadows, lack of rain means low water levels, and in August, low water means mudflats, and mudflats mean shorebirds—lots of them. We're at the peak of southbound shorebird migration now, and Cape May's wetlands and mudflats are filling fast with these long-distance Arctic refugees.

Although there are in fact tens of thousands of shorebirds on the coastal mudflats now, they can be hard to see—way out in inaccessible areas, they look like distant dots shimmering in heat waves. At the Meadows, they are up-close, point-blank, and often at your feet as they work the grassy edges of the ponds.

A walk through the Meadows in August is a study in shorebirds—yellowlegs, dowitchers, Stilt Sandpipers, "peeps," and plovers. You might see fifteen species in a one-hour walk. Add in lots of roosting terns, dozens of egrets and ibis, families of Mallards and Gadwall, a couple of Blue-winged Teal, and the excited burbling of Marsh Wrens, and you get the picture. The Meadows of today recalls the Meadows of yesterday (yesteryear, actually), when it was always full of birds. Indeed, a walk through the Meadows has a timeless quality.

What is not timeless about the Meadows is the name. Some know the area as South Cape May or the South Cape May Meadows. Many newcomers know the area as the Refuge or, more properly, the Cape May Migratory Bird Refuge. Most properly, the full title is the William D. and Jane C. Blair Jr. Cape May Migratory Bird Refuge, owned and managed by The Nature Conservancy—hence the references to the TNC Property. A few old-timers still refer to it as the "cow pasture," as Witmer Stone did in the 1930s.

These different names reflect the history of the place. South Cape May was actually a town, now eroded away; the last few houses were lost forever in the 1950 hurricane. The cow pasture refers to the many years when it was actually used for that purpose—first for a herd of dairy cattle (the Rutherford dairy farm), and later for Les Rea's herd of beef cattle (Les Rea is the birder-friendly owner of the Bean-cry). There was a time when you couldn't bird the Meadows because of one very mean bull. More than one birder learned to climb, or vault, a fence much more quickly than he or she imagined possible. The final names, reflecting The Nature Conservancy's ownership, also reflect one of the greatest conservation victories on the Jersey Cape, when TNC bought the Meadows in 1981 at the eleventh hour to prevent a proposed campground for the site.

In 1982, the Meadows was pasture-land and attracted many more shore-birds than it does today.

But the Meadows is timeless, even if the name has not been. Of course, the area has changed over the years. When it was a wet cattle pasture, the area was wide open, with none of the dense cedars and shrubs of today. Shorebirds were abundant then, including regular Upland Sandpiper and Buff-breasted Sandpiper, rarities there today. With cattle no longer grazing there, the Meadows grew up (seeded by migrant birds) and the vistas suffered, along with shorebird use. Water is the real problem, or, more specifically, water levels. Too much water (rainfall), and the area attracts only waterfowl; too little water, and no birds are attracted at all—the Meadows can completely dry up. It seems that one birder or another is always complaining about the water level at the place—too much, too little, or whatever.

Others complain that the Meadows isn't what it used to be, isn't nearly as good for birds as it once was. Writer Peter Benchley once said, "Nothing is more responsible for the good old days than a bad memory." Perhaps "the good old days" at the Meadows weren't quite so good at the time, or maybe some only remember the good times, not the bad. There were indeed some bad times for the Meadows. Not long ago, the area was private property, and no one could bird there. We've mentioned the bull, but the cows too caused problems. Many remember water so foul and

continues on next page

polluted that there was little aquatic life or so stagnant that the Meadows had to be sprayed daily for mosquitoes.

Times change. Where pasture stood in the mid-1980s, dense Red Cedars are found today—cedars that fill with migratory songbirds in spring and fall. One birder glowingly shared how he had found a Long-eared Owl hidden in the cedars, then immediately described how he hated that the Meadows had grown up! Another time, as we stood in the Meadows and listened to a litany of complaints about the water levels, Sedge Wrens and Black Rails were calling in the background. Yes, the Meadows has changed, but it is still one of the best places to bird, at Cape May or anywhere.

Right now, scanning across the Meadows, all problems fade. The water level is just right. Shorebirds flock in every day—an American Avocet and a Hudsonian Godwit last week, Wilson's Phalarope a couple of days ago. A Black-necked Stilt tomorrow? Two days ago, a White Ibis graced a flock of glossys. In short, the Meadows is great, superb, and at its peak. Bobolinks call from the grasses, Least Terns plunge for tiny

The Cape May Migratory Bird Refuge, like the state park, is slated for habitat restoration and *Phragmites* control. Water-control structures are planned to restore natural water flow and allow for control of water levels, and for flood control. *Phrag* removal should allow native freshwater wetland plants to flourish. Work began in 2006, and when completed, the site should look more like the Meadows of yesteryear, and the benefits to birds should be great. In the meantime, expect flux here, and temporary closures.

The Cape May Migratory Bird Refuge is but one of many Nature Conservancy properties in southern New Jersey. An important South-of-the-Canal property is TNC's Cape Island Creek Preserve situated along a salt marsh creek that cuts behind Cape May City. It is an exceptional area, former agricultural fields that today have become hugely important to migratory birds, primarily sparrows. Unfortunately for birders, TNC allows access to Cape Island Creek only through prior permission of the organization, which mostly limits birding to TNC staff-conducted field trips. This restriction is unavoidable, however: the spot can be reached only by crossing an active railroad right-of-way. Contact TNC directly for more information, and take solace in the fact that birds have no problem using Cape Island Creek.

fish. A sea of blooming wild hibiscus (Crimson-eyed Rose-Mallow) greets viewers from the observation platform, and Marsh Pinks line the path. Common Buckeyes lay their eggs on Purple Gerardia. The first Mistflower or Blue Boneset is out, and Salt-marsh Fleabane is blooming. The first Monarchs of the fall, the vanguard, drift by on the gentle hot summer breeze.

Yes, there are problems with the Meadows. The planned water-control structures are needed. The meadows will inevitably change again. But on this steamy summer morn, none of that seems to matter. Today, the Meadows seems timeless. As shorebirds tilt and dapple the sparkling shallow pools, an older man in a straw hat sits on a bench in the background, far away across the pond. Indistinct in the morning mist and backed by Cape May's Victorian skyline, it's not hard to imagine that the gentleman is Witmer Stone himself, smiling and enjoying the cow pasture, one of his favorite haunts in Old Cape May.

Only the Meadows can lead both the eye and the mind to such visions. Alive with birds and color, the Meadows, by any name, is timeless. ■

THE REA FARM (THE BEANERY)

We try hard to refer to it by its proper title, the Rea Farm, in honor and recognition of its birder-friendly owner, Les Rea, but somehow, during urgent bird discussions, we say, "Did you hear about the Townsend's Warbler at the Beanery this morning?" It just comes out like that; tradition takes subconscious precedence, and we revert back to its former, once-descriptive name. The Beanery was for many years a lima bean farm, part of a vast acreage in southern Cape May County where limas were grown for an out-of-state buyer—one of the big food conglomerates. For many years, the Rea Farm was where most of the region's lima beans were shucked before shipping. In the 1960s and 1970s, a formidable row of the huge lima-shelling machines dominated the Bayshore Road site. In the 1980s, smaller, more efficient machines replaced the giant ones (remnants of these machines still stand south of the Rea Farm parking lot on Bayshore Road). By the early 1990s, South Jersey's lima bean market dried up. Following this severe setback, the Rea Farm reemerged, a phoenix rising from what could have been the ashes of development. Buoyed by farmland preservation status, the farm was reinvented as a truck farm, a flower-growing operation, and a farm stand. Birders too are a cash crop; since 1999, Les and Diane Rea have leased

The Beanery, shown here in the 1970s, derived its name from the lima bean shucking machines, now long gone.

the birding rights to New Jersey Audubon Society's Cape May Bird Observatory in a unique arrangement that benefits all. (The Migratory Bird Conservancy is a cosponsor of this forward-thinking and worthy agreement.) If you encounter Les Rea while birding the Beanery, thank him for all he's done to keep his farm from being developed. Better yet, stop at the Rea Farm Market around the corner on Stevens Street and purchase some "Jersey Fresh" fruits and vegetables.

Sadly, the Rea Farm is one of the last working farms on the lower Cape. Farming disappeared as the fields were consumed by development; houses grew in the fields where crops had once flourished. Today, a walk at the Beanery is in part a walk through time, a glimpse of Old Cape May. And as the last of the rusted machines attest, it is also a walk through the long and difficult history of the small farmer in New Jersey.

The Beanery has long been one of the Cape's most popular birding destinations. Even in the 1960s and 1970s, Les and his father greeted birders with a hearty wave and a smile. Today, the Rea Farm comprises 82 acres. It is a mix of farm fields (some active, some fallow, some planted with wildlife food crops), weedy edges, ponds, and wet woods. The northern edge of the fields meets Pond Creek Marsh. Hidden Valley is beyond. It is mostly a place that time forgot. And on the lower Cape, that is a good thing for birds and for birding.

The Rea Farm concentrates migrants because of its diverse habitats and location, squarely in the center of the very tip of the Cape May peninsula. On some days, the weedy edges support thousands of birds. The farm is a good birding destination at any season, but certainly best known in fall; it shouldn't be overlooked in spring either. Expect breeding Great Horned Owls in February and Prothonotary Warblers in May and June (in wet years, the Beanery supports several pairs). A few pairs of Blue Grosbeak should be present, too, as well as lots of Indigo Buntings, and often Yellow-breasted Chat. Also expect breeding Ruby-throated Hummingbird, Yellow-billed Cuckoo, Green Heron, Belted Kingfisher, and Wood Duck, to name just a few. Willow Flycatcher might be found around the wet edge of Pond Creek Marsh to the north.

Check the Beanery daily in winter. It's one of the best sites for lingerers. Every year a few "half-hardies" try to winter here, surviving until the mid-December Christmas Bird Count and beyond. Baltimore Oriole, Blue-gray Gnatcatcher, White-eyed Vireo, Nashville Warbler, and Dickcissel are a few recent examples; some of the rarer winter lingerers have included MacGillivray's Warbler and Ash-throated Flycatcher. In winter, especially in the early morning, check the sunny edges shielded from the wind. Red-shouldered Hawk is always present, and most winters a goshawk sets up residence here. Even on the coldest winter days, Carolina Wrens are vocal, and bare fields often hold American Pipit.

In spring, the Rea Farm is one of the best spots to witness a songbird fallout. From finches and sparrows in late March and April, to warblers, thrushes, and flycatchers in May, working the Beanery's fields, hedgerows, and edges almost always produces a good list, and sometimes a few surprises. The place is the epicenter for kite-watching in late spring. Because it is in the center of the peninsula and because of the open fields, the Beanery offers a good view in every direction—you can look south toward the point or northwest toward Higbee Beach. Spring Mississippi Kites often roost at or near the farm. In the early morning (eight or nine at the latest) be there to see kites "getting up," beginning to soar and hunt over the cape. These birds range far. By midmorning to late morning they may be quite high or far and wide, away from the point, though they may return in late afternoon. Scan constantly. Mississippi and Swallow-tailed Kites are attracted to the Beanery area because of its proximity to the vast Pond Creek Marsh wetlands, which hold copious dragonflies, the kites' favorite food.

In fall, the Rea Farm should be worked into every itinerary: from early fall (early August actually) for warblers to late fall for sparrows and finches. Although the farm does not experience the huge morning flights that occur at Higbee (its central location is off both the diversion line and the redetermined migration path), it does draw in birds later in the morning and sometimes all day long. These birds are often migrants in search of habitat and food. Most birders visit the

The Rea Farm trails explore field and pond edges and wet woods.

Beanery after their early-morning hike through Higbee Beach, but there is nothing sacrosanct about this schedule. Those "birding against the flow" make some key finds at the Rea Farm.

The Beanery is an excellent place to watch raptors in fall. Because of its central location, kettles and streams of hawks eventually pass overhead. It's particularly excellent for raptors later in the season (mid-October through November), in the afternoon, and in strong northwest winds, when many hawks (mainly buteos) shortcut Cape May Point and stream over Pond Creek and the Beanery. Later in the day, hawks are lower, with many coming down to hunt or roost. The place, even the parking area itself, is known for its stunning views of hawks and eagles in the afternoon. You may not see as many hawks as at the hawkwatch, but many will be point-blank, low, and lit up by the late-season afternoon sun. The Rea Farm can be a photographer's dream.

It's also great for dragonflies and damselflies. On some fall days in August through October hundreds of Common Green Darners and Swamp Darners hunt and roost here, coursing back and forth along sheltered sunlit field edges. Blue-faced Meadowhawks (September and October) and Autumn Meadowhawks (until early December) can be observed here too, as well as late-season butterflies.

Finally, the Rea Farm seems to excel in rarity season, even more so than Higbee Beach. Every year, some good late-season rarities are spotted, some annually—Western Kingbird and Ash-throated Flycatcher. As fall turns to winter, in spite of the calender, insect activity persists along the warm, sunny edges of the Beanery's fields, attracting lingering birds.

Birding the Site

The Beanery is located virtually in the center of Cape Island. It is accessed via a parking area on Bayshore Road. To bird here, you must either be a NJAS or CMBO member. Nonmembers can purchase a day pass at the CMBO Northwood Center for $15 per person, or a group pass for four or more people at $50 a day ($100 for the duration of a visit). A colored decal allows access for members and is available at the CMBO Northwood Center, too. Please respect and support this lease program, which benefits the farmer and keeps the land open for birds and birders. There are no restroom facilities at the Rea Farm, but you are only a few minutes from Cape May Point State Park. Do not walk on freshly plowed or planted fields. All trails follow field edges. Do not trespass on the adjacent vineyard beyond the Rea Farm's fields.

To reach the Rea Farm parking area, turn right as you leave the parking lot at the Cape May Migratory Bird Refuge. Drive 0.2 mile to

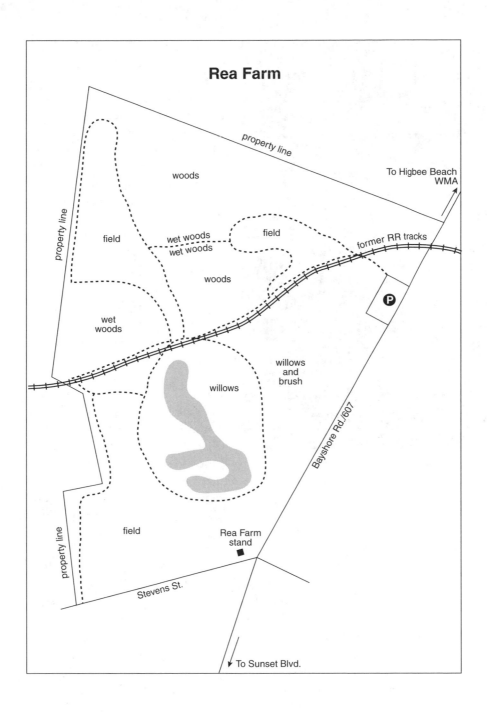

Rea Farm

property line

To Higbee Beach
WMA

woods

property line

wet woods
wet woods

field

field

former RR tracks

woods

P

wet
woods

willows
and
brush

willows

Bayshore Rd./607

field

Rea Farm
stand

property line

Stevens St.

To Sunset Blvd.

Nesting Prothonotary Warblers are found each May in the wet woods at the Rea Farm.

Bayshore Road (Route 607). Turn left and proceed north. In 0.3 mile you will reach the intersection of Route 635 (Stevens Street to the left and Fourth Avenue to the right). To reach the Rea Farm Market, turn left onto Stevens Street and immediately pull off on the right. Support them in season. To reach the birding area, continue north on Bayshore Road for 0.3 mile and turn left into the Rea Farm parking area, just beyond a loading ramp and remnant machinery. The trailhead begins to the right, just behind a small kiosk. The trails at the Rea Farm are informal. There is no signage. A Rea Farm trail map is posted at the kiosk, and is also available at CMBO. A counterclockwise walking loop will take you around the various fields and edges and back to the parking lot. Follow the right edge of the first field, backed by wet woods. This is frequently one of the best areas. Where the path enters the wet woods with its canopy overhead is one of the best spots for breeding Prothonotary Warblers.

Continue into the second field, where you can either go right or left to reach abandoned railroad tracks. Turning right, follow the right edge of the second field. The path turns left and follows the edge of Pond Creek Marsh (at the north end of this field), continues past oak woodlands, turns left again, and follows the edge of a private vineyard (where migrant kestrel, Eastern Phoebes, and Eastern Kingbirds perch on grape arbors and hunt), turns left again, and circles around a deciduous wet woods and pond. It then reaches the tracks that go west into a wet woods. These abandoned tracks once offered the best birding access to the area, continuing all the way to the Magnesite Plant. Today, they are both heavily overgrown and traverse private property. No birding is allowed beyond the Rea Farm.

Where the tracks enter the wet woods, look for Prothonotary Warbler in season, then loop left out into a field. Here, and elsewhere on the trails where big areas of sky come into view, look for migrating and hunting raptors. Continue along the left edge of the field. Upon reaching the willow-lined farm pond, bird around it in either direction. There are several routes back to the parking lot. Some of the better birds have been found nearer the house and farm stand, amid the willows and farm equipment.

Usually the Beanery trails are dry, but recent rain or heavy morning dew can leave them muddy and wet. Many birders wear wellies here in early morning. It normally takes about two hours to bird the site well—more if it's really good. You might find yourself spending most of a morning scanning for kites in spring or an afternoon watching hawks in fall. The Rea Farm at any season is a great place to get away from the crowds and leisurely poke around to see what you can find.

The Beanery can be good for the common or the unusual. We remember times when the "common"—Yellow-rumped Warblers and White-throated Sparrows—were counted in the thousands here. And the "uncommon" was one of our all-time favorite Cape May finds: a female Common (Eurasian) Kestrel coming down the tracks until it was in point-blank range. Sadly, we failed to document this ultimate vagrant with photographs. Our camera, 50 feet away with the lunch bag, was forgotten in the excitement until too late. It was a stunning bird and a stirring migration moment that neither we nor Al Nicholson will ever forget. The date was October 14, 1979, one of the Beanery's best "good old days" indeed.

HIGBEE BEACH

Cape May ably competes with such must-see birding destinations as Point Pelee in Ontario, High Island in Texas, and Ramsey Canyon in southeastern Arizona. And Higbee Beach can ably compete with renowned specific sites such as Galveston's Bolivar Flats, Bentsen–Rio Grande Valley State Park, and Bolinas Lagoon near Point Reyes. Internationally known Higbee Beach can be an electrifying location for birders, not only on the perfect morning but on *many* mornings in both spring and fall. It is a place where migration is given form, both overhead in blizzards of seasonally and weather-driven birds, and in the woods and fields as hungry songbirds make the place a definitive example of a migratory stopover habitat.

The beach, or, more properly, Higbee Beach Wildlife Management Area managed by the New Jersey Division of Fish and Wildlife, is a 1,069-acre site protected largely as migratory bird habitat. Birding is the major use, although hunting is permitted here in late fall and winter, beginning the third Monday after Thanksgiving. Higbee Beach WMA consists of mixed oak forest wrapped around five sizable fields, each with bird-producing edges, wide hedgerows, and shrub islands throughout. The largest stand of old-growth deciduous forest south of the canal is in Cordez' Woods, the woods south and east of the fifth field. This stand adds considerably to the site's inimitable charm.

A key feature of Higbee is its majestic dune forest, the last natural dune forest along New Jersey's Delaware Bayshore (except for scattered beach-front lots in Lower Township that are even now being consumed by bull-dozers for trophy homes). Extensive dune forests once stretched north along the Delaware Bayshore nearly to Reeds Beach, and so today Higbee Beach protects more than migratory birds—it protects our irreplaceable natural heritage, too. Its wide, rolling dunes are forested with sprawling Beach Plum bushes and windblown Northern Bayberry, Common Wax Myrtle, Scrub Oak, Dwarf Hackberry, American Holly, Sassafras, Wild Black Cherry, Red Cedar, and vigorous Poison Ivy. The dune forest, wood-lands, and fields at Higbee Beach are one of our best and most pleasant reminders of Old Cape May. Walking the verdant paths you can experience the wooded Cape May that Witmer Stone knew and loved in the early part of the twentieth century.

Higbee Beach has a fascinating history. Cape Island's steamboat landing was once located there, just north of New England Creek (today the mouth of the Cape May Canal). Owners of the area kept a tavern at the landing from about 1807 to 1823. Joseph Higbee, a Delaware River pilot, purchased the property in 1823 and ran a hotel there called the Hermitage, which stood until about 1940. Parts of an old foundation can still be found just left of the dune trail that begins in the main parking lot, perhaps a remnant of the hotel. The Higbee Beach landing was first used by sailing vessels, then steamboats until 1852, when a new wharf was built at the end of Cape Island Turnpike (today's Sunset Boulevard). Steamboats came to Cape Island from Philadelphia several times a week during the "bathing season," stopping en route at Wilmington or New Castle to take on addi-tional passengers from Baltimore and Washington. Passengers and their lug-gage went ashore via whaleboats, often staying at the Hermitage overnight before resuming their journey to the city by wagon or stagecoach the fol-lowing day.

During World War II, a munitions factory was located at Higbee Beach. Among other items, it manufactured .45 ACP cartridges used by both Thompson submachine guns and Model 1911 automatic pistols, used by officers and pilots. Today, all remnants of the munitions factory are gone, yet .45 cartridges can sometimes still be found in the dunes or along the beach.

This bird's-eye view, looking south from the Cape May Canal, shows the extensive dune forest on the right, the dike on the left, and fields, forest, and Pond Creek Marsh in the distance. STEVE EISENHAUER

After the war, parts of Higbee Beach were farmed and parts were largely forgotten until the mid-1970s, when it was discovered by dune buggies and offroad trucks (whose owners saw these dunes as their private playground), nudists, and, finally, birders. Protection of Higbee Beach by the New Jersey Division of Fish and Wildlife (DFW) in 1978, which happened in part with federal endangered species funds, remains one of the true miracles of modern conservation. It happened in the nick of time, when a private campground, favored by the locals, was planned for this somewhat-lawless area. (Although the survey marker has long since disappeared, a 6-foot-high pile of sand can still be seen beyond "catbird corner" in the northwest corner of the fifth field. This is where the campground developer and his consultant did their test borings so they could claim to meet the legally required 6-feet-to-groundwater stipulation required for a campground's septic system.)

While Higbee Beach WMA is a worthwhile stop at any season, its fame will forever be linked to fall migration, particularly to the wealth of songbirds found here. It is the place to watch the well-studied, yet still-mysterious morning flight, the daybreak movement of nocturnal-migrant songbirds back up the Cape. As well, hundreds of hawks can be seen heading north up the peninsula at Higbee Beach on fall days with blustery northwest winds—hawks zipping low over the fields and dunes as they battle the headwind. Higbee Beach is a great spot to watch hunting hawks, both early and later in the day.

It's also the most reliable place to see a fallout. On good days, the forests and edges twitch with songbird activity, from treetop warblers to understory thrushes, and even on a bad day there are still at least a few migrants to be found. The fields of Higbee Beach are undoubtedly the best spot on the entire cape to find sparrows; late in the fall, waves of sparrows sometimes flush ahead of visitors as they walk the paths around the fields. On peak days, sparrows have numbered in the tens of thousands at Higbee Beach. While most birding is done on the field-edge paths, don't neglect the woodland trails. The few paths here (some marked and some not) can be excellent. Remember: most thrushes are found deep in the woods, not on the edges.

While Higbee Beach has comparatively little to offer in winter, it is still worth a visit. Because migration is perpetual at Cape May, December mornings can sometimes produce such goodies as crossbills and redpolls. On at least one occasion, Pine Grosbeaks have been found at Higbee Beach in December. Because of its lingerers, half-hardy species—Blue-headed Vireo, Blue-gray Gnatcatcher, Baltimore Oriole—pushing the limits of their winter range, Higbee Beach is one of the best territories on the Cape May Christmas Bird Count. The site is a regular stop for veteran "month-listers," too. In recent years, Nashville Warbler, Prairie Warbler, Yellow-breasted Chat, and even White-eyed Vireo have successfully overwintered in the dense, food-filled thickets of Higbee. In late February, the first signs of spring are generally found at Higbee Beach—the first Eastern Phoebe or Pine Warbler. By early March (or even mid-February in warm winters), displaying male American Woodcock *peent* at dusk then shoot skyward and sing and dance over the fields, performing for potential mates.

With spring's resurgence, Higbee Beach is one of the best places to watch songbird migration, from sparrows in early spring to waves of warblers in mid-May to late May. It's good for numbers, variety, and rarities, too. The birding is usually best in early morning—activity can shut down by 8:30 or 9:00 A.M. But during big fallouts, good birding can continue into the afternoon, particularly on rainy or cloudy days. A bonus in spring is that many migrants give away their presence with hearty song. There is also on occasion a noticeable morning flight movement at Higbee Beach in spring. On some May days, particularly when a warm front is overtaken by a cold front, movement begins soon after dawn, when hundreds of warblers, dozens of orioles, and possibly several hundred Eastern Kingbirds move about and disperse inland. And almost annually, the waves of kingbirds sweep a Scissor-tailed Flycatcher or two along with them.

Part of the spring variety at Higbee Beach is because of the overlap of migrants and breeding birds. The site, together with adjacent Hidden Valley, is sizable enough to support a substantial population of breeding birds: Yellow-breasted Chat, Prairie Warbler, Yellow Warbler, White-eyed Vireo, Blue Grosbeak, Indigo Bunting, Carolina Wren, and Ruby-throated Hummingbird in spring and summer. All in all, there is no bad time to bird

Higbee Beach, except perhaps on summer weekend afternoons, when its beaches fill with sun-worshippers.

There is no one way to bird Higbee Beach, but on chilly, fall mornings you should target sunny areas. As the rising sun hits the woods along field edges, insects are activated, and warblers and other insect-eating birds congregate. Mourning Warblers and Connecticut Warblers, when found, are often low in the weedy edges of fields, unless that is also where the birders are congregated. If so, try the shady weedy edges instead. In spring, when oaks are leafing out and festooned with catkins, focus on the huge Willow, Spanish, and White Oaks, watching for songbirds attracted to insects that have been attracted to the trees. When you find a hotspot alive with birds, you might sit back and get comfortable and enjoy wave after wave of hungry migrants as they move through. On the other hand, some birders search out a pocket of bird activity and then follow the constantly moving group of feeding birds around field edges as the throng swells with newcomers. The field edges and hedgerows at Higbee Beach are full of berry-producing trees, shrubs, and vines—Winged Sumac, Wax Myrtle, bayberry, Sassafras, Wild Black Cherry, Dwarf Hackberry, walnut, Persimmon, oaks, Virginia Creeper, Poison Ivy, and Greenbriar—most of them planted by the birds.

The five fields at Higbee Beach are managed for migrants. They are rotated through different stages of succession. The fields of ragweed and Lamb's Quarters are in early succession; those full of goldenrods and asters are in later succession. Shrub islands of Winged Sumac in the fields are part of the management plan. Good birders need to be part botanist to recognize and seek out feeding opportunities for birds.

Birding the Site

Higbee Beach WMA is located on the absolute northwest corner of Cape Island. It lies at the western end of New England Road, on the edge of the Delaware Bay, and is directly across the Cape May Canal from the Cape May–Lewes Ferry Terminal. From the Rea Farm, proceed north on Route 607 (make a left out of the parking area) 1.1 miles to the first stop sign, at the intersection of Bayshore Road and New England Road (Route 641). Turn left on New England Road toward Higbee Beach (a right would take you to Seashore Road/Route 626 and the canal bridge). The mansions near the intersection occupy former hayfields that were until recently the best place on the cape to see Bobolink, Eastern Meadowlark, Upland Sandpiper, and Buff-breasted Sandpiper. The loss of these pasturelands in 2003 was tragic, one of the worst heartbreaks we've suffered in the ongoing war against the complete development of the cape. Fork-tailed Flycatcher was seen here twice; one was Roger Tory Peterson's lifer, seen during the World Series of Birding.

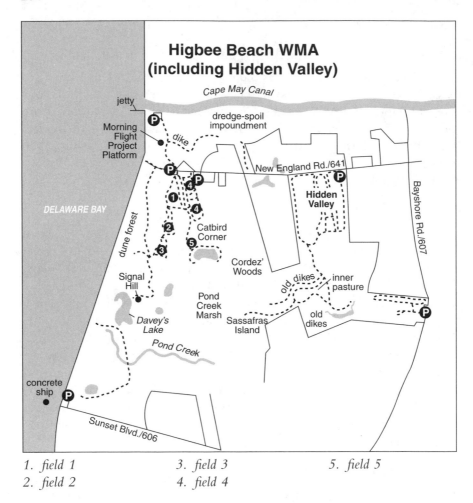

**Higbee Beach WMA
(including Hidden Valley)**

Cape May Canal

jetty

Morning
Flight
Project
Platform

dredge-spoil
impoundment

dike

New England Rd./641

DELAWARE BAY

dune forest

Hidden
Valley

Bayshore Rd./607

Catbird
Corner

Cordez'
Woods

old dikes   inner
                 pasture

Signal
Hill

Davey's
Lake

Pond
Creek
Marsh

Sassafras
Island

old
dikes

concrete
ship

Pond Creek

Sunset Blvd./606

1. field 1   3. field 3   5. field 5
2. field 2   4. field 4

Follow New England Road west 2.2 miles to the Higbee Beach overflow parking lot on your left; 0.1 mile farther will take you to the main
parking lot, where the trailheads begin. There are portable toilets in these
parking lots May through November. (By the way, along New England
Road, you will pass the privately owned Cold Spring Campground on
your right. This bird- and birder-friendly campground is highly popular
with visiting naturalists. It offers a great chance to camp in the thick of
migration and migrants. Birders often report having trouble leaving the
campground because the birding is so good there. If camping is your thing,
this campground is for you.)

Parking at Higbee Beach is limited; during peak birding seasons (May,
September, and October), get there early—particularly on weekends—or
get there late, after about 10 or 11 A.M., when the parking lots begin to
empty. You have several choices. The main lot fills first. If there are no obvi-

ous spaces (the lot is small—don't even *try* it in even the smallest camper or motor home), backtrack 0.1 mile on New England Road to the overflow lot and park there. If the overflow lot is filled, there is a third lot available that rarely fills. This is the jetty parking lot by the Cape May Canal. To reach it, make a right onto the unpaved road just before the entrance to the main lot at Higbee Beach. Wind through the woods about 0.2 mile until you dead-end at the canal. Drive slowly and carefully here; this road is excellent for fallout and frequented by birders on foot during peak hours. You may compete with fishermen for parking spots at the jetty lot. Be courteous—at this and all Higbee Beach lots, park carefully and tight. Once beyond the woods, you can also park along the road next to the dike or the morning flight observation tower. One last parking lot that will work for those who don't mind an energizing walk is at Hidden Valley. It's a small clamshell lot 0.8 mile back on the south side of New England Road.

If all three Higbee Beach parking lots are full, you simply must wait until someone leaves. Do not park along New England Road. It's tempting, but the no parking rule is strictly enforced by the local constabulary. This seems unfortunate, but is an example of the geography and demographics of Cape May birding territory. Higbee Beach WMA is located in Lower Township, not in Cape May City. A few township residents managed to get the road legally posted so they wouldn't be bothered by birders, and local officials seemed happy to oblige. Why? Perhaps because Lower Township receives little of the ecotourism money birding brings in. Cape May City, which contains very few birding sites, receives probably 95 percent of these dollars. Officials at West Cape May (which includes the Rea Farm) and Cape May Point, with few or no businesses, listen first to residents. It's a prime example of parochial thinking, but also of why birders must be on their very best behavior in and around Cape May County.

Of course, adding more parking options at Higbee Beach would impact or eliminate key bird habitat. A great way to avoid any parking problems is to arrive at Higbee Beach by bicycle. It's just a short ride from Cape May City on lightly traveled, low-speed roads, and there are bike racks available at the Higbee parking lot. Consider biking to Higbee Beach as well as to the Rea Farm, Hidden Valley, the Meadows, and Cape May city sites. It offers an excellent way to explore the wonders of Cape Island since the hot spots are all relatively near one another. Once at the sites, you can proceed by foot.

Along the unpaved road that leads to the jetty parking lot, you pass through a deciduous and holly forest offering excellent roadside birding. When the road exits the woods, it reaches the morning flight observation tower on the left. The tower is the best place to watch the postdaybreak dispersal of autumn migrant passerines. At the tower, CMBO provides an interpretive naturalist to explain the complexities of the flight and help with ID each morning in September and October from sunrise until about 10:00 A.M. The tower offers an excellent view of the wood's edge, where many migrants drop in. Across from the tower is the famous Higbee Beach Dike, a berm or levee that surrounds an Army Corps of Engineers dredge-spoil impoundment, where the spoils from the constantly shoaling Cape May Canal are placed.

CMBO's Cape May Morning Flight Project is conducted from the top of this dike. Because many birds are identified by flight call, the official morning flight count of songbird migrants is separate from the interpretive site on the tower. The peak time to witness the morning flight is usually the first two hours after sunrise. A trail at the base of the dike heads east along the tree line. There are plans to connect this trail with additional acreage, a 2006 land acquisition. At times, the dike impoundment is excellent for shorebirds, especially after rain or pumping activity. Numbers may be modest but diversity is frequently high. White-rumped Sandpipers are at times expected, and recent rarities have included Red-necked Phalarope, Red Phalarope, Black-necked Stilt, Hudsonian Godwit, Ruff, and Cape May's first record of Little Stint, a bird enjoyed by hundreds of visitors. White-faced Ibis, White Ibis, and Black-headed Gull have been seen here too. The climb up to the top of the dike is difficult, on a trail that's not much more than a narrow, slippery, sometimes muddy path up a very steep slope. It's not for everyone.

An often-overlooked aspect of this section of Higbee Beach is the excellent opportunity it offers to "baywatch" from the beach near the base of the Cape May Canal jetty for seabirds coming out of Delaware Bay. Most waterbird vigils are done at the Concrete Ship, but the beachfront at Higbee Beach rivals the ship as an observation point. There is a regular southbound movement of Parasitic Jaegers along the bayshore at Higbee Beach in late September and October.

Higbee Beach proper, including trails around the five fields and through forest, is all south of the main parking lot. A kiosk with trail maps is found in the near corner of the fourth field, to your left as you enter the main lot. Trails are minimally marked with colored posts. All yellow trail markers lead to the beach. The orange trail leads south from the main parking lot through fields one, two, and three and is 1.1 miles long round-trip. The white trail leads south from the main parking lot through fields four and five and is 1.2 miles long round-trip. There are connecting trails between the white and the orange trail. There is no right or wrong way to bird Higbee Beach. You can go in any direction and walk the trails or mowed paths around the edges of virtually all the fields. Wildlife food crops (millet,

Sorghum, and sunflower) are sometimes planted on field edges and are key areas for sparrows. Sunny edges, where fields meet forest, or wooded hedgerows are best for warblers, particularly on cool mornings. Search the western edges of all five fields. It takes several hours to bird Higbee Beach— and that's on an average day. On a good day, you might want to stay much longer. It can take a long time to bird all the edges of all five fields, especially as new birds drop in. Such are the hardships of Higbee Beach!

The five fields of Higbee Beach offer excellent opportunities for sparrow spotting.

One of the best spots at Higbee Beach in fall is the main parking lot, and immediately south of the lot, along the close, or northwest, edge of the first field. On big days, you might not get out of the Higbee parking lot. Keep an eye on the sunny side of the huge Red Cedar here. Many birds land in it, work the cedar needles and branches for insects, and then fly on. (This tree is probably at least a hundred years old, and maybe several hundred. All the trees in and near the dunes at Higbee have grown old very very slowly in the inhospitable environment of sandy soil and day after day of salt spray.) The north-facing tree line at the base of the dike is another fallout hotspot, as migrants pause before they strike out across the Cape May Canal, which on some days involves running a gauntlet of accipiters.

The western end of New England Road can be excellent for birding too. Walk the road shoulder, enjoying migrants passing over and dropping into treetops. Do not in any way block vehicle traffic however; not all cars are filled with understanding visitors. If you backtrack on New England Road nearly to the Cold Spring Campground you'll reach a 4-acre field on the north marked with Fish and Wildlife "restricted area" signs. This property is open to foot traffic, although there is absolutely no parking allowed.

Often ignored, perhaps due to time and distance, are the far fields at Higbee Beach. The fifth field, past "catbird corner," has a large freshwater pond in the center and can frequently be excellent. Cordez' Woods, an old-growth forest, is beyond the pond. Any small side path into the woods at Higbee can be rewarding. Thrushes and waterthrush are prevalent in the forest interior.

A young Great Horned Owl on its nest in Cordez' Woods, one of the lesser-explored spots in Higbee Beach.

Sometimes the best way to see birds is to just sit quietly in the forest interior and wait. If a big hawk flight is under way, songbirds are present but not readily active; they may stay below the canopy in denser brush rather than make themselves conspicuous. American Woodcock are decidedly best seen when flushed by those who follow side paths into edges and cover. Take side trails, even faint ones, but do not bushwhack into undisturbed areas. There are too many birders at Higbee Beach for each one to blaze his or her own trail. Be mindful of ticks and Poison Ivy when taking side trails. Remember, too, that the use of tape recorders is not permitted at Higbee Beach. Discrete pishing is acceptable, however, and should be adequate.

Be sure to experience the dune forest at Higbee Beach. To get there from the main lot, take the yellow trail straight ahead (at the far end of the lot, as if you were continuing straight on New England Road). This trail of soft sand continues west through the dunes and onto the beach along the bay. Huge, ancient Dwarf Hackberry trees grow along this trail just past the parking area. Masses of sprawling Beach Plum bushes cover the rolling dunes. In late April and early May, they are covered in small white flowers that turn the dunes virgin white. In early September, they are heavy with marble-sized purple plums. Insects attracted to the flowers in the spring and the fruits in the fall in turn attract warblers. A second trail from the southwest corner of the third field accesses the dune forest. A spur off to the right of this trail offers an awesome view of the dunes and the bay. The main trail eventually reaches Signal Hill and Davey's Lake. The views from this area are spectacular as well—wild dunes, the Delaware Bay, and Pond Creek Marsh behind you.

The Davey's Lake section of dunes at Higbee Beach can also be accessed from the WMA parking lot at Sunset Beach behind the Sunset Beach Gifts shop. Although the dunes don't offer the best birding opportunities, they are magnificent and well worth seeing.

HIDDEN VALLEY

Hidden Valley is a wonderful collection of wet deciduous woods, fallow fields, horse pastures, and the freshwater wetlands of the vast Pond Creek Marsh. The site is another conservation triumph at Cape May. The long-time former owners, the Dickinson family, refused multimillion dollar offers from developers for their land and sold the property to The Nature Conservancy in 1986. TNC then deeded the 192-acre family farm to the state to become part of Higbee Beach WMA. Today, the entire 1,069-acre Higbee Beach WMA (including Hidden Valley) is managed as one large area by the New Jersey Division of Fish and Wildlife. Think of Hidden Valley as a unit of Higbee Beach WMA.

Hidden Valley offers many of the same stellar birding opportunities as Higbee Beach. The autumn morning flight is evident, although not nearly as concentrated as at Higbee because it's closer to the center of Cape Island. For this same reason, however, fall raptors are often better at Hidden Valley than at Higbee Beach, particularly on days with good soaring conditions, when raptors are attracted to the fields and edges and the vast open wetlands of Pond Creek Marsh. The Hidden Valley trails offer one of the longest and best walks on Cape Island. From the parking lot and trail head on New England Road, the trails (occasionally marked with red-topped posts) cover several miles and traverse a number of habitats—from fallow fields and wooded swamp to inner pasture and old dikes overlooking Pond Creek Marsh. During wet periods, the wooded swamp trail usually requires boots. One can easily spend a few hours or even a half day at Hidden Valley. One of our favorite activities is simply to watch the skies over the fields, pastures, and marsh for Mississippi Kites in May and June or a bold Golden Eagle in a late October or November gale.

Like Higbee Beach, Hidden Valley is a place for all seasons. In early fall, August and September, neotropical songbirds fill the forest and feed along edges. In late fall, Hidden Valley fields and edges are excellent for sparrows. Many remain in winter, and Hidden Valley is another spot where lingerers are consistently found. Throughout autumn, hawks are numerous both hunting along edges and high overhead. The wooded wetlands and ponds hold waterbirds at all seasons as well as breeding Virginia Rail and Least Bittern. Purple Gallinule and White Ibis have both been seen in Pond

Late fall in Hidden Valley is great for sparrows, including the Vesper Sparrow.

Creek Marsh from the inner pasture area. Hidden Valley's healthy swamp forest is home to Barred Owl, and a few Red-shouldered Hawks are always present fall through spring.

Spring is exceptional at Hidden Valley. Breeding birds—Eastern Bluebird, Blue Grosbeak, Indigo Bunting, and Yellow-breasted Chat—arrive early, set up territories, and are soon joined by migrants such as Bobolink, orioles, and warblers in bright breeding plumage. As at the Beanery, a few pairs of Prothonotary Warblers breed in the wet swamp forest. With its extensive trail system, Hidden Valley is one of the best places for those who enjoy dappled woodlands, unexpected edges, and solitude as components of their birding adventure.

Part of Hidden Valley is still leased as a horse-riding facility and stable. Following active farming, this was for many years the use of the land. The Dickinson's Hidden Valley Horse Ranch was one of the Cape's most popular riding facilities. When the conservation-minded Dickinsons sold the land to the state, a leaseback agreement allowed the riding operation to continue. The "Hidden Valley Ranch" driveway on Bayshore Road offers access for horse-riding lessons and boarding horses. Birders should NOT use this road or access. Birding access is via the parking lot on New England Road, where the walking trails begin. Birding and horse-riding operations coexist fairly well at Hidden Valley, and birders will only encounter riders if they walk the full length of the red trail into the inner pasture. Hunting is prohibited throughout Hidden Valley.

Birding the Site

From the main parking lot at Higbee Beach WMA, head east on New England Road for 0.8 mile. Hidden Valley's small clamshell parking lot will be on your right and is somewhat hidden. There is a portable toilet in this lot (May through November). The lot sometimes fills on peak weekends, and some use it as yet another overflow lot for Higbee Beach when all others are full. Although Hidden Valley and Higbee Beach are contiguous and managed together, no trails connect the two units, probably because in wetter months such a trail would require a lengthy boardwalk through swamp forest.

The Hidden Valley trail is long, and you may want to carry water. If the birding is good, the complete route can take easily from three to five hours. The trail is marked with occasional red markers and begins at the parking lot. The trail begins by partly circling three fallow fields that stretch from New England Road back to a sizable wet deciduous woods. Follow the mowed paths looking for bird activity in the fields, field edges, or the hedgerows between the fields. These wide hedgerows are natural supermarkets for hungry migrants—full of native trees (sizable Wild Black Cherry, Sassafras, and Dwarf Hackberry), shrubs, and vines. The sun's first light activates insects, which attract hungry migrant warblers, flycatchers, and others. For this reason, the west side of each field (or the right side as you face the fields from the parking area) may be better in early morning and the east side better later in the day. The first field was seeded with wildflowers and grasses in 1995. Scan the birdhouses for nesting Eastern Bluebirds and Tree Swallows in season, and listen for the chatter of Yellow-breasted Chats and the *chink* of Blue Grosbeaks. These fields can be excellent for migrating Bobolinks in spring and early fall if the fields have recently been cut. The second field is used by hawk banders some falls; when banding is going on, much of this field is posted or fenced off and not part of the trail system. Do *not* take the road leading into the woods at the back of the second field; this leads to the horse compound and is off limits to birders. Between the second and third fields a farm pond on the right sometimes holds Green Heron, Belted Kingfisher, and Solitary Sandpiper.

Midway along the back of the third field the trail enters the woods and passes through a sizable swamp forest of American Holly, Sweet Gum, Sweetbay Magnolia, oaks, and Red Maple. These woods are excellent for warblers in fall and spring, particularly when insects are feeding on catkins and blossoms. Barred Owls are found here too. Parts of this trail can be wet following rains. Plan to wear wellies or expect to get your sneakers wet and muddy. After a few hundred yards, the trail passes between freshwater ponds. Look for Wood Duck, Green Heron, Glossy Ibis, or even bitterns in season. Prothonotary Warblers, the one eastern warbler that is a hole-nester, breed here or near here in spring and early summer. Look for a small tree cavity in the wet woods and you just may find the nest site. Ahead, the trail reaches a gate wide enough for a person (but not a horse).

Look for rails, bitterns, and moorhens in Pond Creek Marsh from Hidden Valley's trails.

After the gate, the trail leaves the woods and comes out onto Hidden Valley's inner pasture. The area on the left, which includes ranch headquarters, stables, and riding rings, is off limits to birders. Horses are also often pastured in the large, open pasture in the birding area. Use common sense if they are, and do not disturb them in any way. If they approach, walk away. During major competition riding events, stay clear of this activity.

Hidden Valley's inner pasture is on a peninsula of high ground that extends into the heart of Pond Creek Marsh and is surrounded by old dikes, edged by deep channels, and cattail (or *Phragmites*) marsh beyond. The channels were created when soil was dug out to create the dikes, which were built so that the marsh could be filled with dredge spoils, which thankfully never happened. Today, the channels of fresh water are covered with native, wild Fragrant Water-lilies and lined with cattail marsh. The dikes are cool and shady and topped by no-longer-used horse trails under large trees. Be cautious of fallen trees and muskrat burrow holes on these trails. The dikes offer a good view of Pond Creek Marsh. The channels are usually filled with turtles. Wood Ducks, Common Moorhen, Virginia Rail, Sora Rail, Least Bittern, and American Bittern are seen and heard here on occasion. Sadly, *Phragmites* is obscuring some of the vistas. From the western dikes, you can see Cordez' Woods on the back side of the fifth field at Higbee Beach. From the southern dikes, you can look across the marsh at the large trees on the north side of the Rea Farm fields.

An easy way to bird this area is to simply circle the inner pasture, which is generally barren (overgrazed or mowed); although we've seen American Pipits and Horned Larks here on occasion. But the tall trees around this field are excellent for warblers, flycatchers, vireos—just about anything! This is also a great spot to scan for soaring raptors, particularly Mississippi Kites in late spring. (New Jersey's only White-tailed Kite was photographed here on June 4, 1998—a one-day, two-observer wonder.) Or you can explore the many dikes surrounding the inner pasture and the forested areas beyond, including several sizable stands of American Hollies. A woodland road off the southwest corner of the pasture is a walk through yesteryear, lined with huge trees. This road ends at Pond Creek Marsh and the former dike that once led to Sassafras Island, a large wooded island in the center of the marsh.

To return to the New England Road parking lot, retrace your steps. The walk back should be enjoyable since by now you will have fond memories. We bet you'll find something new on the return trip, too. Scenic Hidden Valley rarely fails to please.

Near Hidden Valley, additional access to Higbee Beach WMA is found on Bayshore Road/Route 607. Here, two deep fields (separated by a private house and yard) stretch from Bayshore Road west to Hidden Valley. The deep waters of the marsh and wooded swamp block access to Hidden Valley itself. Park in the designated parking area on the west side of Bayshore Road, 0.4 mile north of the Rea Farm and marked with state WMA signage. Parking along Bayshore Road is limited to a car-length-deep, mowed, grassy area on either side of the trail head, marked with a pink-topped trail post. A 0.25-mile trail begins here, passing through a field of dense Red Cedars and Winged Sumac and dead-ending at a wet Red Maple, Willow, and Sweetbay Magnolia swamp edged with large Sweet Gums. The state's habitat management plan for this field includes keeping it in shrub-scrub, so every now and then it will be cut back so the vegetation will be much lower. A right-hand spur off this dead-end trail leads north into a second field, being maintained in early succession as a weedy field. A loop trail circles it. Turn left (west) to follow the edge trail along a wet woods. Expect breeding Prothonotary Warblers along this edge.

Continue around the field; the far side (the north side) follows a hedgerow. A horse pasture lies beyond. A mowed trail crosses the center of the field to return to the scrub-shrub field trail and back (go left) to the parking area. Or you can follow the entire field edge of the second field out to Bayshore Road, around the private home and yard, and back to the connecting trail (go left into the scrub-shrub field) and another left to return to the parking area. In total, this trail is about one mile long.

These fields are particularly good for hawks in the northwest winds of October and November and sparrows in late fall. Along the woods edge and hedgerows, look for songbirds on sunny edges. These trails are little used, so there are discoveries to be made.

CAPE MAY CITY

Cape May City itself offers a number of birding opportunities, from open beachfront and back bays to dense forest at Sewell Point. While Cape May beaches and boardwalk can be crowded during the peak tourist season, and even on spring and fall weekends; for much of the bird-migration season, these places will be sparsely populated, if not deserted. This is especially true on weekdays and in the early-morning hours, usually the peak times for birders to be afield. Indeed, birding in Cape May City offers the special charm of watching birds among the town's ornate, gingerbread-clad, and many-colored Victorian buildings.

Cape May is steeped in history. It is America's oldest seashore resort. Wood-burning, side-wheeler steamships began bringing passengers from Philadelphia to the Cape as early as 1816. Cape May was a resort enjoyed by statesmen and presidents. Abraham Lincoln visited as a congressman in 1849, and the United States Hotel was the summer White House for President Ulysses S. Grant in 1869. The completion of the first rail line from Philadelphia in 1863 allowed Cape May to flourish, but major fires in 1869 and 1878 were staggering setbacks—the second consumed thirty-five acres of the city's hotel district. The Chalfonte, built in 1874, survived the fire and today is the oldest hotel in Cape May.

The rebuilding of Cape May during the Victorian era created the classic architecture so lovingly preserved and protected today. The Physick Estate and Congress Hall were both built in 1879. Widely enjoyed today, both of these structures, and much of historic Cape May, were nearly lost in the 1960s to an odd combination of decay and building—an explosion of development that nearly replaced the creaky old with garish modern.

An enlightened grassroots preservation effort in the late 1960s and 1970s turned the tide. Cape May City was listed on the National Register of Historic Places in 1970, and the Cape May renaissance began. The Physick Estate was saved from demolition in 1970 and spectacularly restored by the Mid-Atlantic Center for the Arts. Congress Hall closed in disrepair in 1994, but reopened to great fanfare and acclaim following a multimillion-dollar renovation in 2002.

The historic Chalfonte welcomes birders and beachgoers.

One sad loss was the huge and stately Hotel Cape May, built in 1908. It was a navy facility during World War II, and later a religious retreat known as the Christian Admiral Hotel. This Pittsburgh Avenue landmark fell on hard times and disrepair. It closed in 1991 and was demolished in 1996, although funds from the sale of this valuable beachfront property funded the repair of Congress Hall, which was owned by the same investors. For many years, New Jersey Audubon Society held its Annual Cape May Autumn Weekend birding event at the Christian Admiral. We'll always remember our first two autumn weekends we attended, the last ever at this monumental 12-story brick hotel. We remember well the climb up the Admiral's massive marble staircase, and the breathless excitement of meeting the country's preeminent naturalists. We remember, too, how fall peregrines hunted pigeons around the Christian Admiral, endlessly riding the afternoon updrafts off the face of the building and then stooping down to engage in lengthy tail-chases of their quarry around the stately structure. Sadly, the historic Hotel Cape May is but a pleasant memory today. We wonder if any aging adult peregrines that still pass Cape May today look for the Christian Admiral and wonder where the out-of-place "cliff" has gone.

In Cape May City, the entire beachfront can be good for birds. Because you never know just where that resting flock of gulls and terns might be found, where the Brown Pelicans are feeding, or which jetty may hold a small flock of eider, it is important, time permitting, to bird the whole beach. Beach Avenue runs the entire length of the beachfront. You can drive it, stopping often to pop over the dune to see what's about, but parking is all metered spring through fall. A better way is to walk or bicycle the promenade, birding as you go. If you are with a friend or group and have a second vehicle, park one car at the far end of Beach Avenue and start at the other end.

Perhaps the best place to start is the Second Avenue Jetty. This is the southernmost (and westernmost) jetty in town and usually offers the best birding. At Second Avenue, you are adjacent to TNC's Cape May Migratory Bird Refuge, which begins just to the west. There is a wonderful viewscape here—a panorama stretching all the way to the Cape May Lighthouse, Cape May Point, and beyond. There is a superb view of the Atlantic Ocean and the famous Rips off to the west. It's a great place for seawatching, rivaling Cape May Point State Park and the Concrete Ship in many wind conditions. In fact, Second Avenue may be the best seabird site in spring. Gannets, terns, cormorant, and scoter (and a few shearwaters) moving north across the mouth of the Delaware Bay often hit land more or less around Second Avenue instead of Cape May Point to the west. In late May or early June, it's a perfect place to intercept Roseate Terns, Black

The Second Avenue Jetty offers a view of Cape May Point and the lighthouse, and is a great vantage point for seawatching.

Terns, and Sooty Shearwaters. Parasitic Jaegers are regular here in spring and fall, sometimes close in, chasing gulls and terns, but usually fairly far offshore; plan to use your spotting scope.

Sizable flocks of gulls and terns often gather on the beach just east, or left, of the Second Avenue Jetty. For the past decade, the beach here has also attracted a large flock of postbreeding Black Skimmers in September and October. Skimmers are largely nocturnal; they use the beach as their daytime roost site before eventually moving on to the south. Roosting flocks of gulls, terns, and skimmers occur anywhere along Cape May's beachfront, and sometimes you need to search them out.

One popular game plan is to walk from Second Avenue west to Cape May Point. It's 2.7 miles round-trip, but the ocean and beach provide good birding opportunities the length of the walk. On Cape Island, this is your best bet for beach-feeding shorebirds (Sanderling, Dunlin, others) and sizable flocks of gulls and terns. This is a particularly good stretch of beach to find Sandwich Terns in late summer and early fall, when one, two, or more may join the Royal Terns that gather in their postbreeding dispersal north from their southern breeding grounds. In most summers, a sizable Least Tern breeding colony forms on the beach between Second Avenue and the Meadows. A few pairs of Piping Plover always nest in this stretch of beach as well. You can access the Cape May Migratory Bird Refuge trails at two dune crossovers along this stretch or, beyond, the Cape May Point State Park's blue and yellow trails before reaching the park's parking lot, headquarters, restrooms, and the Cape May Lighthouse.

Besides seawatching and beach birds, Second Avenue can be a good place to watch hawks in early autumn. Southbound Osprey and falcons often "jump off" from here, heading directly to Delaware instead of due west to Cape May Point. In fact, on days with strong west winds you can sometimes see more peregrines and Merlin at Second Avenue than at the point. Beachfront erosion has created a cove between the city and the point, in effect creating twin capes here, and at times altering the flight path of migratory birds. Second Avenue rivals St. Mary's in Cape May Point as the southernmost point in New Jersey. It's a changing designation that depends on erosion or accretion. (The friendly competition for the title is currently a dead heat.)

The north (or easternmost) end of Cape May's beachfront is known as Poverty Beach because it was once the workers' beach, where Victorian-era servants and laborers bathed. The birding here can rival Second Avenue. There is a good view offshore. This deep-water area is in part a cove formed by the Cape May Harbor jetties to the north. It's a good spot for diving ducks in winter; Common Eider is expected, and Harlequin is annual here. It's one of the most reliable spots for Razorbill, probably because of the deeper nearshore waters here.

There is a good view from the beachfront walkover; and from here one can walk about 0.75 mile farther along the beach to the boundary of the U.S. Coast Guard property. (Do not go beyond the clearly signed boundary. You will be stopped and possibly even detained if you do.) Birds are usually distant so bring a spotting scope. From October to May, the pilings ahead usually hold a few Great Cormorants. In autumn and spring, the greats are joined by many Double-crested Cormorants. This is a good spot for Lesser Black-backed Gull. A Brown Booby was once seen sitting on these pilings, and a recent late-summer Magnificent Frigatebird rode the winds high over Cold Spring Inlet.

From Poverty Beach, travel west and then north on Pittsburgh Avenue toward the Cape May Harbor area. East of Pittsburgh Avenue is the Sewell Point tract, part of the former dredge-spoil area that Witmer Stone knew

as "The Fill." Most of this land has been built up, first by the coast guard and then by developers, but an area of about 110 acres remains natural. In Stone's day, it was bare mud. Today, it's a lush, scrubby, shrubby, dense coastal forest. This will be the next Cape May birding area to come online. Cape May City, in concert with state Green Acres funds and other private environmental funding, is acquiring the Sewell Point tract to both preserve open space and prevent development. About 80 acres are slated for protection. By the

A flock of skimmers fills the beach in front of Congress Hall.

time you read this, the first birding trails may be open through the Sewell Point tract, but, as of 2006, the complex acquisition has not yet been completed.

Sewell Point is excellent for migratory songbirds. In 1988, transect studies were conducted here by Clay Sutton and Jim Dowdell for the Environmental Response Network (ERN) as the first step in the lengthy protection and acquisition process. The studies found birds to be as numerous at Sewell Point in fall as at Higbee Beach (when compared with CMBO transect studies carried out at Higbee Beach by David Sibley). Interestingly, the species composition at Sewell Point was found to differ from that at Higbee Beach, with thrushes far more numerous at Sewell Point. Thrushes clearly do not perform a morning flight dispersal on migration but pitch into the first available habitat at the first hint of daybreak. Sewell Point seems to act as an oasis for many songbirds—thrushes and others—as they make their way down the barrier islands or in from over the ocean. The Sewell Point tract is as important to birds as any habitat on the lower Cape, and due to the foresight of ERN and Cape May City, will soon be available to birders, too.

Cape May Harbor is a vast bay bounded by beaches, a military facility, private homes, fisheries, docks, marinas, and salt marsh. It is a deep water harbor of refuge, home to the the U.S. Coast Guard Recruit Training Center, where recruits nationwide receive basic training. First opened in 1917 as a navy base, it became a coast guard facility in 1925.

The Port of Cape May receives, in most years, the second highest tonnage of fisheries landings on the entire East Coast—second only to New Bedford, Massachusetts. In 2004, it was the nation's fifth largest fisheries port, with seafood landings valued at $68 million. Cape May is a major sport-fishing center too, with fishing boats always coming and going.

Cape May Harbor is good at all seasons for waterbirds. There are good overviews along Delaware Avenue, where Cape May recently purchased 18 acres of beach, salt marsh, and uplands to protect them from development. New Jersey Audubon's Nature Center of Cape May (NCCM), a multifaceted environmental education facility, is located on Delaware Avenue. In contrast to CMBO, NCCM specializes in marine education and programs for schools, children, and families. It offers a wealth of programming for children of all ages and is a favorite with local birders who have kids. Stop in and support the education and conservation efforts. A gift shop, seasonal exhibits, bookstore, and bathrooms are available. The new purpose-built environmental center has a porch/observation deck and tower that offer exceptional views of Cape May Harbor. Scan for birds here at any season. The site also contains wildlife gardens and a short nature trail. The harbor can also be seen well from the street end beyond the landmark Lobster

House Restaurant. From fall through spring, the harbor is the best spot on Cape Island for Brant, diving ducks (primarily Bufflehead, Red-breasted Merganser, and Long-tailed Duck), and a good gathering of gulls. On bitter winter days, much of the Cape May Harbor area can be birded from your car.

Finally, birding can at times be excellent right in Cape May City. During migration, songbirds sometimes take shelter in the many large shade trees that line the streets of many of the older sections of town. These streets were one of Witmer Stone's favorite birding spots, but they are largely ignored today as birders head for greener pastures. During fallouts, particularly in spring, when rainy weather grounds birds sometimes for several days, warblers often seek the taller trees along the city streets. Once while enjoying wine and cheese on a Victorian porch as guests at an inn on Washington Street, we heard seven species of warblers singing from the old trees above. And our best-ever day for Blackburnian Warblers was when we saw or heard at least twenty-three Blackburnians as we walked the tree-lined streets of West Cape May in May.

The streets of Cape May may not be your primary birding destination, but by all means don't ignore them. A couple of the best spots are the Cape May Kiwanis Community Park on Madison Avenue, where the small pond sometimes attracts wild ducks among the domestic (Eurasian Wigeon has wintered here). Peregrines often perch on the nearby water tower, and dine there, too, as a pile of Bonaparte's Gull wings below the tower once indicated. Up the street from this park, the grounds of the Emlen Physick Estate, on Washington Street, are excellent for migrants at times. The Physick Estate is a large compound with many plantings and large trees, both on the grounds and nearby. (Otway Brown, the naturalist who catalogued the plants of Cape May County between 1893 and 1931, was the groundskeeper at the Physick Estate and was probably responsible for many of these plantings.) It is a great spot for watching warblers in a fine Victorian setting (be sure to wear your straw hat and bow tie or hoop skirt). The immaculately restored and furnished mansion is managed by MAC and open to the public for tours, a great idea for rained-out birders.

Birding the Site

There are innumerable ways to reach the beach in Cape May City, including a well-marked route as soon as you enter town on Lafayette Street/Route 633. But to follow the loop tour of the town as outlined, return to Sunset Boulevard/Route 606 and follow it east toward Cape May City. At the traffic light at the intersection of Broadway and Sunset Boulevard, turn right onto Route 626 and travel 0.4 mile to Beach Avenue/Route 604. Turn right onto Beach Avenue, go 0.2 mile until the road ends, and park.

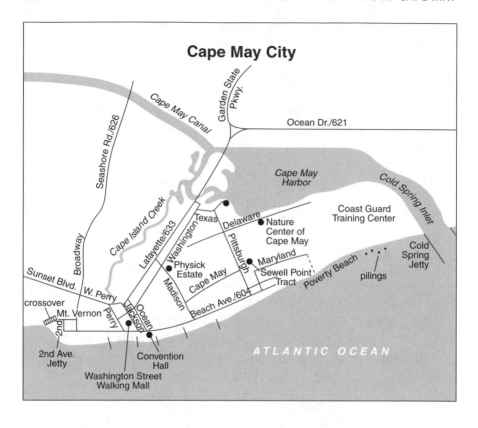

This is the extreme western end of Cape May City, and the expansive beach and walking route to Cape May Point begins just beyond the **Second Avenue Jetty**. The walking promenade also begins here and extends east (or northeast) 1.4 miles to Philadelphia Avenue. There are public restrooms on the promenade (at Broadway, Grant Street, in the Convention Center at Stockton Place, and at Philadelphia Avenue, Trenton Avenue, and Wilmington Avenue), although they are closed during the colder months. Several others in the vicinity of the Washington Street Walking Mall are year-round. From the Second Avenue Jetty, or anywhere along the beachfront, scan in every direction for gulls and terns, and check offshore for "bird play," the frantic action of feeding seabirds that can be a magnet for marauding jaegers.

The pavilion on the promenade at Second Avenue is drafty, but it offers some protection from the wind and rain if you need it. In both spring and fall, this is a great place to wait for migrating seabirds. Avoid this pavilion area on sunny weekend afternoons however; not only is it a major tourist stop, it is a popular seashore wedding location. For an alternate view, go east on Beach Avenue 1 block to Second Avenue. Turn left, go 1 block to

Mt. Vernon Avenue, turn left again, and park in the designated spaces near the end of the road. Walk the gravel path at the street end; it soon becomes a boardwalk dune crossing, which is wheelchair accessible. At its highest point, this dune walkover provides a great view of the beach and the ocean, and a panorama stretching to Cape May Point. Check the small pond to the right (north) of the walkover for ducks, herons, egrets, and shorebirds in season.

Return to Beach Avenue. Proceed east or northeast for 2.2 miles to reach **Poverty Beach,** checking the beach and ocean a few times as you go—especially near the jetties at Grant Street, Jackson Street, Stockton Place, Queen Street, and Philadelphia Avenue. It is hard to predict where the best duck or gull concentrations may be. It varies from week to week, day to day, even from tide to tide. Recent beach replenishment may nearly cover the jetties with sand and make them unproductive.

As you follow Beach Avenue, be alert: Frigatebirds have been seen high overhead here on several occasions—the first in 1926, as described by Witmer Stone, and more recently to the delight of participants in New Jersey Audubon's 2004 Bird Show. You will see hawks overhead here in the fall. In winter, Snowy Owls have been found along Beach Avenue, perched on either the beach or nearby rooftops. Park at the end of Beach Avenue or turn left and park on Wilmington Avenue, where there is a restroom and a wheelchair accessible boardwalk dune crossing. Poverty Beach stretches to the northeast toward the Coast Guard Base and Cold Spring Jetty, which marks the entrance to Cape May Harbor. A scope is necessary here to check the pilings in the surf to the northeast. Search for waterfowl—antici-

pate Common Eider and Harlequin Duck in winter, and, with time and luck, Razorbill, or even Black-legged Kittiwake.

As you leave Poverty Beach, drive 1 block north to New Jersey Avenue and turn left. Follow New Jersey Avenue for 3 blocks until you reach Pittsburgh Avenue/ Route 622. Make a right onto Pittsburgh Avenue. Go 8 blocks (about 0.6 mile) and turn right onto Delaware Avenue/Route 640. The area bounded by New Jersey, Pittsburgh, and Pennsylvania Avenues (the street south of Delaware) is the **Sewell Point** tract,

Many businesses in Cape May are well aware of the value of catering to birders, and of protecting bird habitat.

soon to be acquired as open space. When acquisition is complete, formal trails are planned. (There is an undeveloped small loop trail that begins on Pittsburgh Avenue, opposite Cape May Avenue and marked by a section of split-rail fence at the trail entrance. This short walking trail hints at the eventual possibilities of Sewell Point.) Roadside birding here can be very productive in fall. Your best bet might be the edge of the Sewell Point tract from the bike path on Pennsylvania Avenue. It's a place where discoveries can be made—Gray-cheeked Thrush, Dickcissel, Lark Sparrow, and Clay-colored Sparrow all have been found here recently.

Cape May Harbor is along the left side of Delaware Avenue. Stop anywhere to scan the harbor, which should be productive September through May. Shorebirds feed on horseshoe crab eggs here in May. In winter, Brant are numerous and surprisingly tame at times. Look for loons and diving ducks. This stretch can be a surprisingly good spot to watch hawks in strong northwest winds. Watch for gull flushes as a sign of an incoming eagle. As you head east on Delaware Avenue, New Jersey Audubon's **Nature Center of Cape May** is on your right. A gift shop, seasonal exhibits, bookstore, and restrooms are available here, along with a wealth of learning opportunities for children and families. The center's observation deck and tower offer an exceptional view of Cape May Harbor. Their annual Harbor Fair, held on Columbus Day weekend, is a family event featuring nature tours and programs, food, music, and presentations by the Coast Guard and other groups.

For another view of the harbor, backtrack on Delaware to Pittsburgh Avenue. Turn right onto Pittsburgh Avenue and after 0.25 mile, turn right onto Texas Avenue. **Harborview Park**, which is wheelchair accessible, is at the end of this road and offers a good view of the upper harbor, including the Lobster House Restaurant and Seafood Market complex, fish docks, and Cape May's commercial fishing fleet. Check the gulls around the boats and buildings. Follow Texas Avenue back to Pittsburgh Avenue and turn right. Just ahead you will reach a T at Washington Street. Turn right (your only choice, since Washington is one-way here). If you want to go north to the Lobster House or the Garden State Parkway, stay in the right-hand lane. If you want to go south and visit a few more Cape May spots, get into the left-hand lane.

If you go north, turn right onto Lafayette. Just ahead, on the right, look for a huge sign and the road to the Lobster House. Turn right here. Park in the Lobster House lot and walk to the street-end for another good view of the harbor, gulls, and waterfowl. (Another way to explore the harbor and back-bay areas is aboard *The Skimmer,* docked at the Miss Chris Marina, across Lafayette from the Lobster House sign. Captain Bob Carlough and

Cape May Harbor as seen from Delaware Avenue by the Nature Center of Cape May.

first mate Linda Carlough offer many special excursions with CMBO, NCCM, and the Wetlands Institute.)

Return to Lafayette Street and turn right (north). Just over the large canal bridge, about 0.5 mile ahead, is the entrance to the Garden State Parkway (straight ahead) and Ocean Drive/Route 621 (bear right) toward the Two Mile Beach Unit of the Cape May NWR. Wildwood is beyond.

If you go south from Washington Street, turn left onto Lafayette and proceed 0.7 mile to Madison Avenue (at the first traffic light). Watch your speed here; this is a known speed-trap zone. Make a left onto Madison Avenue and cross Washington Street. The Cape May Kiwanis Park is on your left. Park and bird around the pond. Be particularly watchful for tree-top warblers in spring. Continuing three more blocks on Madison Avenue brings you to the Cape May City Water Conservation Garden on your left, at Cape May Avenue. This garden is usually good for butterflies in fall. A good way to bird the **Emlen Physick Estate** is to walk up the drive next to the Kiwanis Community Park pond into the property. (Or, of course, drive back and park in the Physick Estate parking lot.) Check the trees here, and virtually anywhere in the more heavily shaded sections of Cape May City, for spring fallout, and less predictably, birds that put down in fall. Listen for birdsong. From the Physick Estate and Washington Street, go 1 block west to Lafayette. Make a left onto Lafayette and continue back south 0.6 mile to a stop sign facing Collier's Liquor Store. Turn right onto Perry Street, which flows into West Perry Street and then Sunset Boulevard/Route 606. Your tour of Cape May City is now complete.

If the birding south of the canal is good, as it most often is in spring and fall, all the routes we cover may take you several days to complete—maybe even a week in peak season, since you'll want to visit places such as Higbee Beach again and again.

THE ATLANTIC COAST AND BARRIER ISLANDS

Although birders tend to make a distinction between south of the canal and areas north, migratory birds usually don't. Admittedly, the land lying south of the Cape May Canal is the epicenter of birding and hard to beat on most days. The birder with one weekend to spend at the Cape will probably not venture off Cape Island. Indeed, many veterans rarely venture beyond. A few longtime birders pursue a "south of the canal list" in addition to Cape May County and New Jersey lists. The World Series of Birding has a "south of the canal category." But, the canal is a barrier only to birders—certainly not to birds.

Birders with more than one weekend at their disposal, particularly those visiting in winter and spring, will want to venture north of the canal to savor more of the area's avian treasures. "North of the canal" is a bit of a bland title for an area that encompasses many exciting birding sites, yet is apt. The Cape May Canal was dug in 1942 to connect Cape May Harbor and the Delaware Bay so coastal shipping could avoid the dangerous waters off Cape May Point. Before it was built, ships had to bypass the shallow rips by traveling in deeper waters, which, during the war, were often patrolled by German U-boats. The canal offered safe passage along the coast via the Delaware Bay and on to the Chesapeake & Delaware Canal.

The Cape May Canal was a conservation tool of sorts for many years—a barrier or buffer preventing the dense development of North Cape May and the Villas from spilling onto the lower Cape. The canal no doubt helped Higbee Beach and Hidden Valley to survive long enough to be conserved. (The Garden State Parkway, first opened in 1955, had a similar unintended conservation bonus. It cut off developers' access to the all-important upland edge of the Atlantic Coastal wetlands.)

TWO MILE BEACH AND SUNSET LAKE

Two Mile Beach is the southernmost unit of the Cape May National Wildlife Refuge and the refuge's only coastal tract on the Atlantic Ocean side of the Cape May peninsula. It is a wonderful amalgam of salt marsh, ponds, coastal scrub and maritime forest, and open barrier beach. It is on the north side of Cape May (or Cold Spring) Inlet, across from Poverty Beach and the U.S. Coast Guard Recruit Training Center. The Two Mile Beach Unit was once controlled by the coast guard. For many years, it was a LORAN navigation station, broadcasting radio navigational signals along the East Coast. After LORAN was replaced by the Global Positioning

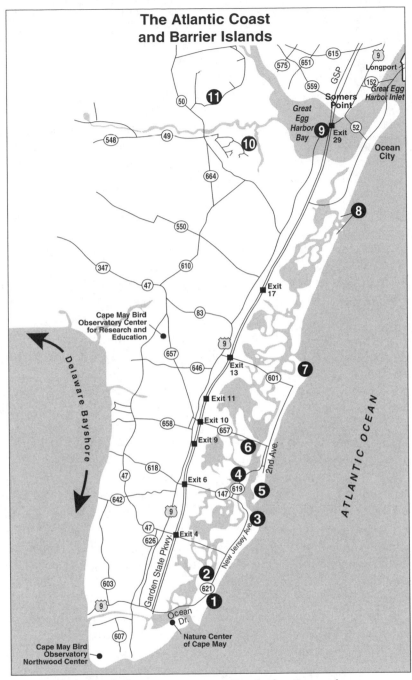

The Atlantic Coast and Barrier Islands

1. Two Mile Beach
2. Sunset Lake
3. Hereford Inlet
4. Nummy's Island
5. Stone Harbor Point
6. The Wetlands Institute
7. Avalon Seawatch
8. Corson's Inlet State Park
9. Great Egg Harbor Bay
10. Tuckahoe WMA
11. Corbin City Impoundments

System, with its satellite navigational signals, most of the station was transferred to the U.S. Fish and Wildlife Service to become part of of the Cape
May NWR. Soon, most of the buildings were demolished, which allowed
the area to revegetate with native plants. Two Mile Beach now contains
507 acres of exceptional coastal habitat.

The coast guard did retain a portion of the site—the part that contains
the tall, guy-wired LORAN tower. Sadly, this 675-foot-tall tower is one of
the top bird-killers in the country. Because of its location, untold numbers
of nocturnal (and even daytime) migrants are killed annually. In the 1980s,
CMBO did studies of bird kills at this site and discovered many bird carcasses under the wires daily. Accurate mortality numbers were hard to
assess, however, due to the density of vegetation underneath and because so
many predators were habituated to the reliable food source. At one time,
LORAN was considered nearly obsolete, largely replaced by satellite-based
GPS. But today, LORAN is being resurrected and integrated with GPS for
homeland security purposes. A target date to phase out the LORAN base
here has yet to be finalized, and the tower is unlikely to be dismantled anytime soon, dooming untold numbers of Cape May migrants.

The dense, scrubby-shrubby forest at Two Mile Beach is excellent for
migratory passerines. The Cape May NWR ponds along Ocean Drive
generally hold excellent numbers and diversity of waterfowl in spring, fall,
and winter. These are tidal salt ponds, and at low tide, they can be great for
shorebirds. Tides here can be hard to predict, however. Projected highs and
lows occur several hours after beachfront or inlet predicted times and can
vary with wind direction and strength.

The beachfront is always good at Two Mile Beach. The walk to the
northernmost of the two Cold Spring jetties at the mouth of Cold Spring
Inlet is a long one, but usually productive. The refuge beach is the 0.6-mile
northernmost stretch, and the coast guard section is to the south and
immediately adjacent to the jetty. In fall and winter, the ocean, and particularly the inlet, can be great—look for gannets, loons, diving ducks, even
alcids. Harlequin Ducks are regular here in small numbers, usually very
close to the jetty. Look for gulls, both roosting on the rock jetties and feeding in the inlet. The inlet is a likely spot in winter and spring for Little,
Black-headed, Iceland, and Glaucous Gulls. Late fall through spring, expect
Ruddy Turnstones and Purple Sandpipers on the rock jetty and Great Cormorant on the navigation towers at the end of each jetty. One memorable
late-fall day, a coal-dark juvenile Pomarine Jaeger stood nonchalantly on
the rocks here! Snowy Owls have been seen on a number of occasions, too,
either sitting in the dunes, along the beach, or on the jetty. Expect Bottle-
nosed Dolphin April to October. Seals are frequent here in winter. One

early May day, we were treated to both dolphins and a Harbor Seal in our binocular fields at the same time.

During migration, the beaches at Two Mile fill with both roosting and feeding shorebirds. In summer, several pair of Piping Plover nest here. Least and Common Terns sometimes nest here, too. To protect beach-nesting birds, the refuge beach is closed to public access, including birding, during nesting season—from April 1 through September 30. While you can walk the entire beach from October 1 through March 31, in spring and summer, you must observe the beachfront only from two viewing platforms. Each one offers a fair view by spotting scope. Even when the refuge beach is closed, the Dune Trail through the maritime forest is open year-round. It skirts behind the dunes and leads out onto the coast guard beach, which remains open to foot traffic.

From here, you can walk the beach south to the foot of the Cold Spring jetty and inlet. Tern flocks feeding on Bluefish-driven baitfish are frequent at the mouth of the inlet in summer and fall. Most years, someone sees one or a few Sooty Shearwaters rounding the tip of the jetty on their way north in May or early June. Two Mile Beach is good in any season.

Just north of Two Mile Beach, in Wildwood Crest, a large saltwater bay known (oddly enough) as Sunset Lake is your next birding stop. Here, sedate sidewalk and park-bench viewing provides one of the easier and best looks at this major tidal bay. Sunset Lake is best known for its fall-through-spring birds: lots of Buffleheads, Red-breasted Mergansers, Common Goldeneye, Ruddy Ducks, and often a good raft of both Greater and Lesser Scaup. The bay is also known for grebes. Horned Grebe is frequently numerous here, and it is one of the most reliable places for Red-necked Grebe. Common Loons are usually numerous. Finally, Sunset Lake is known for spring lingerers, attracting many World Series of Birding teams. Willet, oystercatcher, and Osprey are expected in summer. Check the distant spoil islands, overgrown with Red Cedars, for heron and egret rookeries in summer. At sunset here, you will face the lowering sun, so viewing opportunities are best in morning.

Birding the Site

From Cape May City, follow Lafayette or Washington Street north out of town. Go over the first small bridge and continue past the Lobster House on your right. Lafayette soon becomes Route 109. Cross the large Cape May Canal bridge, and in 0.2 mile, Route 109 joins Ocean Drive/Route 621 at a traffic light. Make a right at the light onto **Ocean Drive/Route 621.** Continue past pristine salt marsh. This is a well-traveled road—when stopping to bird, be sure to pull well off onto the shoulder. This section can

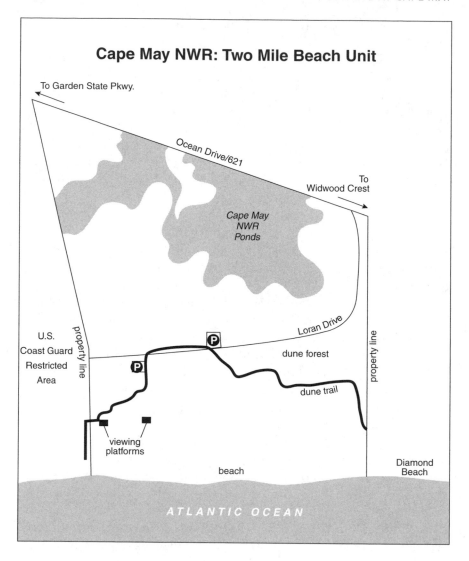

Cape May NWR: Two Mile Beach Unit

To Garden State Pkwy.

Ocean Drive/621

To Widwood Crest

Cape May NWR Ponds

Loran Drive

U.S. Coast Guard Restricted Area

property line

property line

dune forest

dune trail

viewing platforms

beach

Diamond Beach

ATLANTIC OCEAN

be good for shorebirds in spring and fall, and numerous Black Ducks and Brant in winter. The marsh on the right (just beyond the Canyon Club, and just before Breezy-Lee Marina) is a particularly good area to find breeding Saltmarsh Sharp-tailed and Seaside Sparrows and migrant and wintering Saltmarsh and Nelson's Sharp-tailed Sparrows. One of Cape May's few Gyrfalcons was seen from here, on February 28, 1987.

In 1.6 mile you come to the fish-packing plants and an active commercial fishing anchorage. Cross the toll bridge over Middle Thorofare. On the far side of the bridge, stop and park beyond the no-parking signs. Scan the ever-present gull flocks around the packing plant, boats, and beaches, and on the water. Birders call this area the **Shellpile,** and it is the most reliable spot around Cape May for the rarer gulls: "white-wings" and lesser black-backed and black-headed alike. The best place to watch Shellpile gulls is from the beach on the north side of the bridge; you can even stand under the bridge in foul weather. Most gulls will eventually come out to sit in Middle Thorofare to give you a good view.

Proceed east on Ocean Drive. Two Mile Beach Unit is now on your right. Stop to scan the **Cape May NWR Ponds** (for years known as the "Coast Guard Ponds" but now part of the refuge) on your right for all waterbirds. These salt ponds are tidal; expect waterfowl at all tides, but shorebirds only at low tide. Viewing is best here in the afternoon because of the sun's angle. Fish Dock Road, on your left across from the ponds and marked with the huge sign for Two Mile Landing, offers a view of Jarvis Sound. Bird the marsh from this 0.3-mile-long road or from the clam-shell parking lot to the right of the Two Mile Inn (a good seafood restaurant in season). Marbled Godwit is often seen from here on Jarvis Sound's mudflats in fall. This is also a good place to try for salt sparrows near the scrubby vegetation in the marsh. Return to Ocean Drive and continue a short distance to Loran Drive on your right (just before the sea of condominiums). This is the entrance to the **Cape May NWR Two Mile Beach Unit.** It's co-signed as a coast guard base. The gate is open sunrise to sunset. A 0.5-mile road through the gate leads to the first parking lot, on your right, and second lot, on your left, not far beyond. Birding is good anywhere along Loran Road. Walk the road and open areas and work the edges. An observation blind is planned for the back side of the ponds. Do not go beyond the coast guard signs, which demarcate the refuge boundary; this area is frequently patrolled. A refuge visitor center and outreach facility is located here, although it is not always open. Outdoor signage explains the site and orients visitors.

The 0.9-mile Dune Trail traverses the refuge's maritime forest. The trail begins on the beach at the north boundary of the refuge (known as Diamond Beach), weaves through the dune forest, comes out on Loran Drive across from the first parking lot, and continues along the road to the second parking lot and then out toward the beach. It then turns right just before a wheelchair-accessible boardwalk begins (leading to the first of two beachfront viewing platforms) and weaves through dune forest to the beach at the south boundary of the refuge. A second beachfront viewing platform is located here. The property south of here is owned by the coast guard, and walking access is permitted only on the beach, which leads to the **Cold Spring Jetty** and inlet. Observe all seasonal signs to guide your access. Upon reaching the jetty, climb up to scan the inlet. Be careful: walking on jetties is an option only for the hearty. Rocks are slippery and placed far apart. More than one spotting scope has been lost to the sea on this jetty because of falls, rogue waves, and strong winds. Use common sense. When the refuge beach is open (October 1 to March 31), walking the entire length of the beach can be productive. Despite its name, Two Mile Beach is about 1.25 miles from Diamond Beach to the Cold Spring Jetty.

To reach **Sunset Lake,** return to Ocean Drive/Route 621 and turn right, or north. Ocean Drive soon becomes Pacific Avenue in Wildwood Crest. After 8 blocks, turn left on Jefferson, go 1 block, and turn right on New Jersey Avenue (also signed as Park Boulevard, which flows into New Jersey). After 0.6 mile, Sunset Lake is on your left. Park and scan the bay and shoreline. Birds could be anywhere, so several stops along the lakeshore are usually in order. When Park Boulevard angles to the left, follow it to continue along the shore of Sunset Lake. Any street-ends here are good spots for back-bay birding in the winter.

You can now retrace your steps to Cape May or continue north on Park Boulevard, which becomes Lake Road (and finally Susquehanna Avenue). At Rio Grande Boulevard (a major intersection), a left will take you to Wildwood Boulevard/Route 47, which will take you to the Garden State Parkway. Go south on the parkway for about 4.5 miles to reach Cape May. To continue on to the Hereford Inlet area of North Wildwood, follow New Jersey Avenue north through the Wildwoods for 3.6 miles until it dead-ends at Spruce Avenue. In summer, this route is congested, but in the dead of winter, the Wildwoods can feel like a ghost town.

HEREFORD INLET

Hereford Inlet, named no doubt because of the colonial practice of pasturing cattle on the wild barrier islands in summer, is one of five major inlets flooding and draining Cape May County's vast Atlantic Coastal salt marshes and back bays. Hereford Inlet is the waterway between North Wildwood and Stone Harbor. While the south side of the inlet is highly developed—with the hotels, motels, and honky-tonk taverns of North Wildwood—the inlet itself is a vast collection of sandbars, tidal mudflats, salt marsh, and deep channels. The main sandbar is a semipermanent island in the center of the wide inlet affectionately known to Witmer Stone as Gull Bar. Today, it's popularly called Champagne Island.

Birding possibilities are many here. Like the inlet itself, Champagne Island ebbs and flows, gaining and losing sand, and size, because of sand deposition and erosion caused by coastal hurricanes and winter storms. When the sand has had a chance to accumulate and gain height, Champagne Island usually hosts a sizable tern and skimmer breeding colony, as well as roosting gulls, terns, cormorants, and shorebirds by the thousands. The island is a major Brown Pelican roost in summer and fall, attracting birds from far and wide. Pelican counts of over one hundred are made here often.

Hereford Inlet is good in any season. American Oystercatcher should be easily found year-round. Winter is excellent for gulls, Brant, diving ducks, and loons. Snowy Owls have been found there on a number of occasions; one snowy clearly wintered on and around Champagne Island. Spring brings returning terns as well as shorebirds. Look for courting Royal Terns in late May, overshoots from colonies to the south. (If tern and skimmer colonies don't form on Champagne Island, they are probably on Stone Harbor Point. Only rarely will colonies form at both sites.) In fall, seawatching is excellent from the North Wildwood seawall and beach. North Wildwood rivals Avalon as a great place to enjoy the autumn passage of waterbirds, although because of the vast sandbar complex, birds are usually farther away than at Avalon.

The Hereford Inlet Lighthouse is a destination in its own right. Built in 1874, it holds a light 57 feet above sea level and has been totally and authentically restored by the City of North Wildwood, a project that began in 1982. The lighthouse features a museum and is open to the public. In 1986, work began to transform a bare beach-sand yard around the lighthouse into gardens. Steve Murray, superintendent of parks for the City of North Wildwood, designed, planted, and maintains a beautiful and award-winning, bird-friendly English Cottage-style garden that now complements

the lighthouse wonderfully. Songbird and butterfly fallout is frequent in the gardens, which are an oasis in spring and fall. A short path leads to the Hereford Inlet seawall, which usually offers one of the best views of the inlet. Depending on sand deposition, the beach here or off Spruce Avenue can be a major high-tide shorebird roost, when refugees from flooding tides on the mudflats and sandbars seek higher ground. Check the nearby planted pines for birds (and roosting migrant Monarchs). At times, many of the paths to the beach in North Wildwood,

The gardens surrounding the Hereford Inlet Lighthouse can be great for songbird fallout.

especially east and south of the lighthouse, can be good. A few of these walkways pass through dense Bayberry thickets, which are great spots for fallout. Dense clouds of Tree Swallows feed on the bayberries in fall.

Birding the Site

From Sunset Lake in Wildwood Crest, take Ocean Drive/Route 621 north about 4 miles. This route will be more commonly signed as New Jersey Avenue. Expect unbearable traffic in the summer tourist season. Pass through three different communities: Wildwood Crest, Wildwood, and then North Wildwood.

Alternately, you can reach North Wildwood via North Wildwood Boulevard/Route 147. From the north, go south on the Garden State Parkway to Exit 6N, a southbound exit only, and turn right toward North Wildwood. From the south, go north on Route 9 through Rio Grande. At the intersection of Route 9 and North Wildwood Boulevard/Route 147, turn right, or east, toward North Wildwood.

When New Jersey Avenue reaches Second Avenue, make a right and go east for 5 blocks to John F. Kennedy Boulevard. Park here. There are several dune and seawall walkovers along John F. Kennedy Boulevard, offering good views of the beach, inlet, and ocean. The one at the end of Second Avenue offers the best autumn seawatching, since birds will be the closest. Proceed south down John F. Kennedy and try any paths to the beach that seem to be well vegetated. These produce migrant songbirds in season.

To continue your tour, retrace your steps to Second Avenue. At Atlantic Avenue, make a right. Go 1 block to First Avenue and make a left. At Central Avenue, make a right; the **Hereford Inlet Lighthouse** will be on your right, opposite Chestnut Avenue. Park in the lighthouse parking lot to bird the grounds. Restrooms are available at the lighthouse. Paths lead through the small gardens, offering many sheltered spots attractive to tired and hungry migrants.

Continue through the gardens to the seawall and benches. Walk the seawall in either direction for good views of the inlet and beach. The vista can vary; sands move here, often drastically over the course of just one winter. If we haven't visited this area for six months or so, we never know what to expect as we crest the seawall. Explore the beachfront for deep inlet waters and sandy, buffering beaches. In North Wildwood (as at Avalon), construction of a bigger seawall will bring even greater change to all viewing opportunities.

Leaving the lighthouse, turn right and follow Central Avenue north where it flows into Spruce Avenue at the curve. On your right, opposite New Jersey Avenue, an observation deck offers an alternate look at either a deep inlet or a big beach. Immediately past the deck, Spruce crosses New

York Avenue. Turn right onto New York Avenue and wind along the sea-wall until the road dead-ends. This is the spot known by fishermen as "the Greek church." It offers one of the best views of deep water and, perhaps, winter loons and ducks. It's also a good overlook of Champagne Island to the north.

To continue the tour, retrace your steps to the junction of New York Avenue and Spruce Avenue. Go west and north on Spruce Avenue/Route 621 until you reach the traffic light at Anglesea Drive. Turn right. Past the condominiums to your left, there are additional places to crest the dune/seawall. Park and look for these informal crossovers, being careful not to walk on dune vegetation. Here you will have your best spotting-scope views of Champagne Island. Beyond the sandbars is Stone Harbor Point.

NUMMY'S ISLAND

Nummy's Island is named for Chief Nummy, or "King Nummy," of the Lenni Lenape native American tribe. Folklore holds that his people sum-mered on this salt marsh island south of Stone Harbor and that King Nummy may be buried there. Nummy's Island today is a birding destina-tion requiring little effort and offering great reward. The island is only about 1.25 miles in length, and mostly less than that in width, but it offers probably the best and no doubt the easiest salt marsh birding on the Atlantic side of Cape May County. Nummy's Island is roadside birding, but the charm (at least before Memorial Day and after Labor Day) is that Nummy's has less traffic than any of the major boulevards or causeways crossing the marsh. There is much to see and hear. From near the bridges at either end of Nummy's, you have excellent views of the two major tribu-taries to Hereford Inlet, Grassy Sound Channel and Great Channel—the large waterways that flow from behind Stone Harbor past Stone Harbor Point. The salt marsh here is graced with numerous shallow ponds, known as pans, that attract birds at all seasons except when they are frozen.

The lure here is marsh birds—lots of them—offering excellent looks. Clapper Rails are abundant spring through fall, mostly heard yet often seen. They are best seen on the highest tides: moon tides when much of the marsh is covered with water. During moon tides, they are frequently seen swimming through the marsh grass, often right at your feet, as they seek high ground along the road edge. Low tide can be good for rail watching, too. Scan nearly dry creek beds, looking for sneaky rails that slip out to drink and bathe in the exposed trickle of water. If they do, they can be in full view. Marsh Wrens and Seaside Sparrow are common, Saltmarsh Sharp-tailed Sparrow less so. Herons, egrets, and Glossy Ibis are abundant in season. Nummy's is reliably the best place anywhere in the Cape May

region to see Yellow-crowned Night-Heron, Little Blue Heron, and Tricolored Heron. May through October, if you put your time in, they are
almost guaranteed. Brant are abundant in winter, and the ponds fill with
dabblers and the creeks and bays with divers in winter. Common Loon,
Red-throated Loon, and Horned Grebe are almost always present in both
Great Channel and Grassy Sound Channel. In winter, look for Great Cormorants perched on channel markers or on the pilings at Dad's Place
marina, south of the toll bridge. In late April, the birds' breeding plumage
is evident, and fun to compare with breeding Double-crested Cormorants
perched nearby.

Shorebirds are a major draw at Nummy's. Oystercatcher and Willet are
abundant breeders, and they are joined in late April through early June and
in July through October by many migrant shorebirds. The high marsh on
Nummy's is a major high-tide roost site for shorebirds virtually year-round.
Many thousands are sometimes present, tens of thousands counting those
on adjacent Stone Harbor Point. Yellowlegs, Short-billed Dowitcher, Dunlin, and Black-bellied Plover may be the most obvious, but at least fifteen
other species are usually present. The stately flocks of bold, breeding-
plumaged Black-bellied Plover, Dunlins, Ruddy Turnstones, and Red Knots
in May are a stunning illustration of the region's wonderful and productive
salt marshes. The huge shorebird concentrations inevitably attract hunting
peregrines and Merlins. Be alert whenever shorebirds flush en masse.

*Nummy's Island is best for shorebirds at high tide, when they gather to roost in or
around the salt marsh ponds.*

The Nummy's Island area seems to attract rare and less-common shorebirds regularly. Marbled Godwit is annual in numbers, and Cape May County's only record of Bar-tailed Godwit was at Nummy's. Long-billed Curlew has been seen here twice in fall (and one wintered nearby along North Wildwood Boulevard—probably all the same individual). Two Curlew Sandpipers at Nummy's were present for the 2005 World Series of Birding and seen by hundreds of observers. Nummy's and

Birders line the roadside at Nummys Island to enjoy a Long-billed Curlew discovered in October 2002.

nearby Shellbay Landing (on the mainland, east of the Garden State Parkway at exit 9) are the best locations to see Whimbrel in Cape May County without a boat. The white-rumped Eurasian race of Whimbrel has been seen in this area twice. One fall, a Great White Heron, the Florida morph of Great Blue Heron, was repeatedly seen at Nummy's.

From the northern end of Nummy's Island look for a high sand-mound rising out of the marsh to the west. Looking like an unexcavated Mayan temple, it is really just a dredge-spoil mound (they dot the coastal wetlands along the intercoastal waterway). In spring and summer, this mound is host to a large breeding colony of Herring and Great Black-backed Gulls. With a scope, you can observe fluffy chicks in July. Gull colony or not, this spoil mound is slated for removal, the material to be used as beachfill. Some Laughing Gulls breed on Nummy's, but the epi-center of their huge, continuous, coastal colony is Ring Island, the salt marsh island north of this spoil mound and behind Stone Harbor. The din coming from the colony is synonymous with summer for many of us. Watch for gull pairs displaying for one another. As they give their long laughing call, their bright red bills and mouths are fully displayed. In late April, look for a subtle pink wash on the bellies and chests of some Laughing Gulls, a short-lived result of their spring diet.

Finally, the dense stand of Red Cedars at the north end of Nummy's Island (on the north side of the road) is both a year-round roost and, in some years, a summer breeding rookery for herons and egrets. Black-crowned Night-Heron and Great Egret are the most likely, but Glossy Ibis, Green Heron, Yellow-crowned Night-Heron, and others have nested here. Watch from the roadside. *Do not* enter the rookery (not that you'd want to; dense Poison Ivy carpets the area below the cedars). The cedars here are, at times, good for songbird fallout. A Bohemian Waxwing spent part of one recent winter here, dining on abundant Red Cedar and Poison Ivy berries. Look for sparrows along the roadside at Nummy's. Tree Sparrow is possible in winter, and Lapland Longspur has been seen at Nummy's. High storm-tides can push salt sparrows (and rails) to the roadside throughout the year.

Nummy's is good in any season. One year, two young Osprey fledged in August from one of the active Osprey nest platforms. By September, the same platform was used daily by passing peregrines as a perch and roost site. Finally, in late November, a Snowy Owl took up residence on it for a few days, before moving on to both Champagne Island and Stone Harbor Point. A bird list at Nummy's can be big. You can see the ocean, bay, inlet, sandbars, mudflats, and salt marsh. Add on songbirds using the cedar grove and raptors overhead and you can expect a full dance card.

Nummy's is yet another spot to anticipate the unlikely. On January 28, 1980, a cold, gray winter day, Clay was driving across Nummy's Island and found an equally gray Gyrfalcon perched at point-blank range on a road-side post. The bird flushed quickly to chase Brant over the marsh and bay for the next fifteen minutes. Panicked waterfowl filled the somber sky, but the gyr was more playing than hunting.

Birding the Site

Nummy's Island can be reached from the north by following Stone Harbor Boulevard/Route 657 into Stone Harbor and turning right (south) at the first light onto Third Avenue (becomes Ocean Drive). Alternately, to reach Nummy's Island from North Wildwood, follow Ocean Drive/Route 621 north, which becomes North Wildwood Boulevard/Route 147. This road offers good salt marsh birding, with abundant herons, egrets, Willets, and Osprey (many on artificial nest platforms) in spring and summer. Brant abound in winter. Go about 0.6 mile to the traffic light at Ocean Drive/Route 619. Turn right (north) onto Ocean Drive. The quarter-mile stretch of salt marsh before the toll bridge ahead is called Grassy Sound Meadow and is particularly reliable for Yellow-crowned Night-Heron. A Northern Wheatear once entertained dozens of birders here during a Cape May Autumn Weekend. Cross the toll bridge (there's no toll in the winter) over Grassy Sound Channel. The salt marsh island in front of you is Nummy's Island. Half of it, all land north or west of Ocean Drive, is private property and half is state owned, the land south or east of the road. No sign on this rich salt marsh island declares it as Nummy's Island, but maps show it as such, and birders have used the name forever. All birding at Nummy's Island is roadside birding.

Traffic can be high speed and oblivious of birders. When stopping, pull well off onto the road shoulder or grassy edge next to the marsh. Excellent

An Allen's Hummingbird visits a North Cape May garden. DOYLE DOWDELL

Calliope Hummingbird, another garden visitor, in October. D. D.

Le Conte's Sparrow at Higbee Beach in October.
KEVIN KARLSON

Buff-breasted Sandpiper, a prize find during a narrow window in the fall. D.D.

American Bitterns are present but hard to spot at Cape May Point State Park and the Meadows. D.D.

Sooty Tern at Cape May Point in September 2003 after Hurricane Isabel. JERRY & SHERRY LIGUORI

Fork-tailed Flycatcher, West Cape May. K. K.

Lark Bunting at Stone Harbor Point in September. K. K.

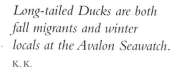

Thousands of Surf Scoters migrate past the Avalon Seawatch in late fall. K. K.

Long-tailed Ducks are both fall migrants and winter locals at the Avalon Seawatch. K. K.

Waves of Northern Flickers wash over Cape May in October. K. K.

Whiskered Tern at Cape May, July 1993, first record for North America. K.K.

Ash-throated Flycatcher at the Rea Farm, an annual rarity at Cape May. K.K.

Some fall days dozens of Osprey hunt Bunker Pond right in front of the Cape May Hawkwatch. KIM STEININGER

The robin flight of November 7, 1999.

A feeding frenzy of Northern Gannets in The Rips.

Bohemian Waxwing on Nummy's Island in February. D. D.

Cooper's Hawks commonly visit backyard feeders in winter. D. D.

A few Virginia Rails winter in brackish and freshwater marshes. D. D.

Sanderling is an iconic bird of the Cape May winter beach. D.D.

Snowy Owls (opposite) are attracted to tundralike habitat, such as Stone Harbor Point. K.K.

Barnegat Light in late fall and winter is the place to see Harlequin Duck. D.D.

Look for Long-tailed Ducks feeding in the surf along the beachfront from Cape May north. K.S.

Short-eared Owls hunt the Jakes Land-ing marshes at dusk and on overcast days during the winter.
MARC LOMBARDI

Not staged at all, this Saw-whet Owl roosted on a Christmas wreath in Cumberland County.
DOT LASCARIDES

Townsend's Solitaire at East Point in January 1999. K.K.

The massive scoter numbers at Cape May Point.

A Red-throated Loon near the Concrete Ship in February.

Brant, one of the hallmark species of the back bay marshes in winter.

Black-headed Gull near Norbury's Landing in April. D. D.

Purple Gallinule at the Wetlands Institute garden in April 2004. D. D.

Bonaparte's Gulls often feed near the ferry terminal in late winter and early spring. D. D.

*American Black Duck
pitches into a coastal
marsh pond.* J. L., S. L.

*"Gosh an Albatross!"
A Yellow-nosed Albatross
near Reeds Beach,
May 23, 2000.* J. L., S. L.

Red Knot, the most studied shorebird in the world at present (note colored flags on legs). K.K.

Arriving in spring, Yellow Warblers are common summer breeders on the Cape.
BILL GARWOOD

Yellow-crowned Night-Herons nest on marsh islands in the back bays. K.K.

Osprey commonly breed on the salt marsh and back bays. K.K.

Least Bitterns breed in the freshwater marsh at the Meadows. K. K.

Ruby-throated Hummingbird on its nest at the CMBO Center in Goshen.
PAM HIGGINBOTHAM

Blue Grosbeak, an expected sight at Hidden Valley or Higbee Beach in spring and summer. K. K.

Seaside Sparrows are abundant breeders on South Jersey salt marshes. K. K.

The South Cape May Meadows of yesteryear, a pasture with grazing cattle.

habitat, salt marsh and salt ponds, is found on both sides of the road. Use the sun to your advantage and enjoy the side with the well-lit birds. If you cross the road, do so with great care. Keep tripod legs and limbs out of traffic lanes, and try to keep birding groups together on the same side of the road.

Scan the waterways in either direction (Grassy Sound Channel to the west, Hereford Inlet to the east). Champagne Island is the sandy island in the distance out in Hereford Inlet. This is a great spot for waterbirds— Long-tailed Ducks and Common Loons in winter and spring. At low tide, a mudflat is exposed south and west of the bridge. Check it for godwits and other more expected shorebirds. It's almost impossible to miss American Oystercatcher here except in the dead of the coldest winters.

Proceed north across Nummy's Island. There are good salt ponds the length of the island. Check each one, although the ones at the far, or north, end are usually the best. Look for Brant and ducks in winter, wading birds in summer, and shorebirds on migration (or all of the above as seasons overlap). In spring and summer, enjoy close looks at hunting terns— Forster's by April, Least and Common by May. Nummy's is best for shorebirds at high tide, when they gather to roost in or around salt marsh ponds. Some will be feeding here, but most feeding occurs on distant mud-flats at low tide. Whimbrel, if present, will usually be up on the top of the marsh in the grass, grazing on mud snails and fiddler crabs. Sometimes all you can see is the top of a Whimbrel's head and its long, downcurved bill until you scan and spot another, and soon an entire flock. Scan every nook and cranny. Night-herons and Tricolored Heron hide in the high grass. Constant scanning, with a bit of patience and luck, should reward you with a Clapper Rail or two, maybe an American Bittern. Listen for Seaside Spar-rows, Fish Crows, and Boat-tailed Grackles on the marsh in summer. Every Osprey platform here is active March through August. Listen for the Osprey's whistled calls as they court, defend their nests, or hover over the channels while fishing.

The north end of Nummy's Island, just before the free bridge over Great Channel to Stone Harbor, is another good stop. Here, you may glimpse some of the secretive herons in the heron roost/rookery in the roadside Red Cedars. Walk in either direction along the bank of Great Channel (although it can be muddy). There is a boat-launching ramp on the north side of the road, so be careful when parking so you don't block access to it. (This is a great place to launch a kayak, by far the best way to get close to these vast shallow-water mudflats. Tides are strong here though, so use good judgment.) The road shoulder near the base of the free bridge often offers the best views of the mudflats behind Stone Harbor to the north and behind Stone Harbor Point to the south. This is the best afternoon viewing spot, since the sun will be behind you. Low tide will be more birdy. Vast shorebird roosts form behind Stone Harbor Point, and because of the large size of the mudflats, viewing is frequently just as good from Nummy's Island as it is from Stone Harbor Point. American Oyster-catchers are fairly common here, wheeling and chasing each other throughout the nesting season. And this is the most predictable spot in the Cape May region for Marbled Godwit—up to thirty have been seen here. August to December is best, but a few have wintered in milder years. Lots of terns and Black Skimmers are expected in season. Eared Grebe has been found here on several occasions, and one recent May, an adult Sabine's Gull fed by the free bridge for several days.

Continue north on Ocean Drive, across the free bridge toward Stone Harbor. Immediately after the bridge, park on the right side of the road. This marsh area south of the road is highly dependable for Yellow-crowned Night-Heron, among other waders, and offers another good view, maybe the best, of the mudflats behind Stone Harbor Point. Late in the afternoon glare can be terrible here, the birds mere silhouettes, but because low tide is crucial for shorebirds here, you may not have the luxury of choosing between morning and afternoon. In winter, Brant are numerous and close.

STONE HARBOR POINT

Stone Harbor Point sounds so rock-solid that one imagines a sturdy, granite promontory into the steely Atlantic, but Stone Harbor Point is really just a sand spit, a peninsula jutting south into Hereford Inlet. It is, however, enduring. Once a tiny spit, now a several-mile-long beach, it has been there forever, or at least long before Witmer Stone's time. It is found on the area's earliest maps. Once, numerous other inlets broke up the many barrier islands; they would come and go with hurricanes. Today, most have been filled and built over, but Hereford Inlet and Stone Harbor Point have prevailed.

Even though it is only a sandbar, it's a good one. In fact, Stone Harbor Point is widely regarded as one of Cape May's top birding spots, unmatched for many bird phenomena. Stone Harbor Point offers a window on all the avian wonders of Hereford Inlet, from the first Piping Plover of spring to the last lingering Christmas-count Willet. The point is easily the best beach walk in the Cape May area. The once-expansive high dunes of Clay's youth are gone—victims of development and then erosion—but it is still a vast, wide-open, inviting beach.

The ocean and offshore bars make for great seawatching in autumn and even winter as scoter flocks linger around the inlet. If the jetties are exposed, it's even better, usually with a few eider present, but beachfill has recently buried the two jetties at Stone Harbor Point and others in Stone Harbor to the north. Seawatching at the north end of the point is sometimes as good as at Avalon. Some birds go offshore here around the outer bars; others head right into Hereford Inlet. In October, we've seen a dozen Parasitic Jaegers chasing gulls and terns over the inlet. Gannet-watching is good here. Sometimes in late fall, November and December, clouds of diving gannets can be seen offshore, out around the Hereford bell buoy, mostly over schools of herring and

The high dunes that once graced Stone Harbor Point, seen in this 1977 photo, are now lost to development and erosion.

menhaden pushed to the surface by Bluefish and Striped Bass. It is good again late winter through April.

Beach birds abound at the point, roosts of gulls and terns and myriads of Sanderlings scurrying after each receding wave. From the southern tip of Stone Harbor Point, where it drops into Hereford Inlet, you have an excellent spotting-scope-view of Champagne Island to the south. Look for Brown Pelicans May through October, distant, maybe, but distinct. At low tide, vast sandbars and mudflats on the back side of the point stretch into the distance as you look across Great Channel to Nummy's Island. These flats are a phenomenal shorebird spot, one of the Cape's best and most consistent. Flocks of terns and gulls gather here, but the main attraction is shorebirds. The flats teem with them for much of the year. Shorebirds feed on the flats at low tide, and are sometimes distant, but at high tide they roost on higher ground, where the mud meets the sandy beach. At this stage, many can be point-blank close. An amazing twenty-four species have been seen here in a single day by observers who, like the birds, followed the entire tide cycle. Up to thirty Marbled Godwit have been found here in October. American Golden-Plover and Buff-breasted Sandpiper are found annually, and rarities such as Curlew Sandpiper, Ruff, and Little Stint have been seen here recently. The white-rumped Eurasian race of Whimbrel has been seen here several times, too. In fall, the American Oystercatcher flock builds to upward of three hundred birds. After the fall, even in winter, Dunlin and a few hardy

The mudflats on the backside of Stone Harbor Point provide a banquet for scores of shorebirds.

Western Sandpipers frequent these flats, while Sanderling are busy in the tide line on the nearby ocean beach.

Stone Harbor Point is good year-round. In winter, enjoy Long-tailed Ducks feeding in the ocean waves and loons beyond. Expect Brant, ducks, loons, Horned Grebes, and usually a few oystercatchers in the back-bay waters behind the point. Snow Bunting, Lapland Longspur, Horned Lark, and "Ipswich" Savannah Sparrow are annual in winter here. Spring brings a flood of seabirds, and shorebirds surge north. Spring shorebird roosts hold tens of thousands of birds. Over twenty thousand Red Knots have been counted roosting here in recent years in late May. Their favored mudflat roost sites are then roped off to prevent disturbance. Most Delaware Bay shorebirds fly to the Atlantic coast marshes and mudflats to roost nightly on higher and safer spots than those found along the bay. The shorebirds are scarcely gone a month before their return, and big fall roosts assemble. Then they are joined by huge numbers of dispersing terns, herons, and egrets from both the south and north.

Overlapping all of this in spring through early fall, are active beach-nesting bird colonies—Piping Plover, American Oystercatcher, Common and Least Terns (with a few other goodies, such as Gull-billed Tern, often mixed in), and Black Skimmers. In 2005, 10 pairs of Piping Plover were present; over 1,000 Common Terns and some 2,750 Black Skimmers were counted here in late August. (Nine hundred pairs of skimmers fledged 550 young, the best year in recent memory).

When it's good, Stone Harbor Point is as good as it gets, with the best beach-nesting bird colonies in New Jersey south of Brigantine Island and Holgate. Success varies from year to year, however, affected by coastal storms and flooding. Chronic beach erosion and rising sea levels don't help much either. In 2002, Black Skimmers nested at twelve coastal sites in New

Jersey; six of these failed due to flooding, one because of nesting gulls. In 2004, Stone Harbor Point was the *only* nesting colony in all of New Jersey. Remember that the booming colonies don't occur every year, but it's the good years that buoy the bad.

An evening walk at Stone Harbor Point is particularly pleasant. Birds are returning to roost, and nocturnal Black Skimmers are heading out to feed. If the walk coincides with high tide, expect a blizzard of restless shorebirds coming to roost on the safe high ground at the point, maybe even small groups of Whimbrel heading out to points unknown, their staccato whistles lingering long after the wind birds have been absorbed by the purple twilight to the southeast.

Birding the Site

From Nummy's Island, take Ocean Drive/Route 619 north across the free bridge. You are now in Stone Harbor (watch your speed, posted at 25 mph). Continue 0.3 mile. When the road bends left, turn right onto 117th Street. Go 1 block, skirting the south side of the Stone Harbor Bird Sanctuary, to Second Avenue. Note the historic coast guard lifesaving station built in 1895 on your left. Make a right, and go 5 blocks to the dead end. Make a left into the parking lot. In summer and early fall, portable toilets are available here. (Year-round heated restrooms are available at the Municipal Water Works, across from Borough Hall, on Second Avenue, between 95th and 96th Streets.) Walk over the ramp and onto the beach. Seawatching is good here, and sometimes in the off-season when the beach is not wall-to-wall tourists, beach birds are good here too. In summer, it's only beach balls (or maybe they don't allow them anymore; do read the many beach rules posted in the parking lot). Walk south, to the right and—most years—it's about a mile to the tip, where the sand bends back around to the west. Beach tags are required between 10 A.M. and 5 P.M., Memorial Day through Labor Day. You can buy tags from the onsite inspector or at Stone Harbor Borough Hall, at 95th Street and Second Avenue. A spotting scope is a must at Stone Harbor Point. You can enjoy a beach walk here without it—and a jaeger may be right over the surf—but shorebirds can be distant, and a scope-filling Black Skimmer chick is hard to beat.

Along the way, scan the ocean, beach, and inlet. Observe all signage. Small exclosures of dune fencing protect Piping Plover nests and are used to keep predators, and people, away from the eggs. Larger areas cordoned off with ropes and signs protect the tern and Black Skimmer colony and roosting shorebirds. When you reach the tip of Stone Harbor Point, begin to work the mudflats on the backside as you head north to the parking lot. In the nonnesting season, you can work the mudflats all the way back, but in the nesting season, a large part of this area will be cordoned off. Some of the best mudflats will be half-way back to the parking lot. Walk west until you get your feet wet (in warmer months, we prefer sandals or sneakers to wellies or knee-high rubber boots).

As you return to the parking lot, you might want to follow the crushed-shell road just behind the beach. In the bayberry thickets along this road and around the parking lot, fallout frequently occurs. Look for warblers, sparrows, and swallows. One fall, a cooperative Lark Bunting spent several days here. Glossy Ibis and a few other waders have nested in the shrub and tree-covered areas deeper in.

Upon exiting the parking lot, take the first left onto 121st Street and then the first right onto Third Avenue. The lush, vegetated area on your left, which extends to Ocean Drive, is a well-known Monarch roost in fall. Check the Red Cedars late in the day or just after sunrise as the sun first hits them. We have seen hundreds or, on a few occasions, thousands of Monarchs festooning these trees, covered in early-morning dew.

At the stop sign, continue straight (north) to Third Avenue and drive through Stone Harbor. At 117th Street you come to the 21-acre **Stone Harbor Bird Sanctuary.** This designated National Landmark was abandoned by nesting herons and egrets in 1992. But it is still a worthwhile stop during migration, particularly following fall cold fronts. Park in the small sanctuary parking lot opposite 114th Street and walk around the perimeter of the sanctuary, birding the edge. This forested area is the way much of Stone Harbor (and for that matter all the barrier islands) looked before roads were built. Songbirds can be very good here at times. The sanctuary may be devoid of herons now, but it is still an oasis for passerines—a haven of berry- and seed-producing native trees, shrubs, and vines in a desert of stone lawns and ornamental shrubs. There are ambitious plans to restore the sanctuary in hopes that nesting waders will reoccupy it, but it remains to be seen if the herons will ever find the place attractive again, given the number of buildings that now surround it. Herons, egrets, and Glossy Ibis have moved to more rural settings on remote, vegetated, dredge-spoil islands in the back-bay marshes behind the Wildwoods, Stone Harbor, and Avalon.

Opposite the sanctuary parking lot and kiosk, walk west down 114th Street about a quarter block to the street-end at the back bay. This is a great overlook for Brant, loons, and diving ducks in winter. Some summers, herons and egrets nest in the low shrubs on Sedge Island, the small salt marsh island just across the channel. Northern Harriers and even Short-eared Owls patrol Sedge Island on late fall and winter days around sunset. Any of the streets in Stone Harbor (and Avalon) that dead-end at the back bays are good November through March for rafts of diving ducks, Common Loons, and often a few Great Cormorants. Check each and every overlook and you will be rewarded, particularly when frozen waterways concentrate birds in pockets of open water. The parking lot at the **Stone Harbor Municipal Marina,** on the back bay between 81st and 80th Streets), offers a particularly good winter view, often with close rafts of Brant, Bufflehead, and Red-breasted Merganser. There is a gazebo at 81st Street here that offers a rainy-day way to view the bay. This is a good spot in summer, too, to savor the clamor of nesting Laughing Gulls at sunset.

On the beachfront, there are covered pavilions at 101st and 88th Streets that offer excellent possibilities for all-weather seawatching. Both pavilions are handicapped-accessible, as is an elaborate dune walkover and overlook at 95th Street. These pavilions may offer

This Osprey nest on Cedar Island grows larger and larger as the birds add to it year after year.

the best rainy day seawatching opportunities in all of Cape May County. Be sure to check the ballfield at 81st Street, between First and Second Avenues, for Brant in winter and roosting shorebirds during nor'easters, when high tides force them here, the only open high ground around. Hundreds of Dunlin, Sanderling, and Black-bellied Plover can often be found at the peak of the storm high tides.

If you plan to visit the Avalon Seawatch, continue north on Third Avenue (Ocean Drive/Route 619). Stone Harbor ends and Avalon begins at 80th Street. Avalon's **Marion P. Armacost Community Park,** between 74th and 71st Streets, was used as a rookery by herons and egrets for a few years in the late 1990s. It is currently deserted, although prospecting birds are still seen here each spring, and the rookery could someday be reoccupied. Like Stone Harbor Bird Sanctuary, it is an oasis for songbirds. Park and walk the perimeter in fall. Then continue north on Ocean Drive (Third Avenue). Good back-bay overlooks are at the **Municipal Boat Ramp and Marina** between 53rd and 56th Streets, and at 38th Street, 24th Street, and 21st Street (or follow 21st Street west to its terminus, an overview of Ingram's Thorofare). The Osprey nests on Cedar Island (a

BACK-BAY BONANZA ON A "FOWL-WEATHER" JANUARY DAY

The term "back bays" is somewhat imprecise. It does explain that the bays are behind the extensive barrier island system that stretches from Cape May Harbor to Ocean City and northward to Barnegat Bay. But, it doesn't really tell you much about what the bays are, their variety, or how they are configured. It is also a dry term, and certainly doesn't hint at the bays' amazing birding potential.

First a bit about the variety. Cape May's back bays are numerous and vast—expansive, open bays that are an integral part of the coastal estuary system. Mostly shallow, they show extensive mudflats at low tide. There are also deep, dredged channels, most of which are part of the lengthy Intracoastal Waterway route from Maine to Florida. And they offer sheltered coves that are part of the barrier island communities, all created by the once-common but now illegal dredging and filling of wetlands. Locals here grew up calling these man-made coves "basins," and many today refer to them as "lagoons." Surrounded by houses and private property, the coves don't exactly jump to mind as we enumerate our favorite birding sites. But in the dead of winter, on dull, cold, leaden days when you just may want to bird from your car, the basins and back bays can be red-hot for waterfowl watching.

During an "old-fashioned" winter with below-average temperatures, January ice clogs much of the bays and lagoons. And while the cold and ice drives some birds farther south, most of our waterfowl are hardy, and it almost seems as if they relish the cold. Frozen waterways and lagoons can make birding easier, because birds concentrate in the swifter-moving, icefree stretches. The worse the weather, the more ice; the more ice, the more concentrated the ducks.

A recent January outing started at the northern fringes of Cape May, at Strathmere. In the back bay at Corson's Inlet State Park, Long-tailed Ducks cavorted as if it were balmy, even though the temperature was barely in the teens. At Townsend's Inlet, there was little ice, but the 8th Street jetty held a huge flock of all three species of scoters, Horned Grebes, Red-breasted Mergansers, and more long-tails. These saucy ducks dove right next to the car at 7th Street. Purple Sandpipers rooted around on the lower rocks of the jetty, and a few Bonaparte's Gulls bounded over the outer bar.

The neat thing about back-bay birding, at least in very cold weather, is that you don't have to search for birds, you just need to look for open water. Cruise Ocean Drive and the backstreets until you find an icefree channel or basin. The back-bay waters and basins don't freeze uniformly; currents and wind always keep *some* water open and free from ice, but this changes daily. Access can be a bit of a problem, but you can almost always find public street-ends or municipal piers that offer a view. Twenty-first Street in Avalon is an example; simply go west at the stoplight, heading for the bay.

On this day this spot offered great views of scaup, Ruddy Ducks, Red-breasted Mergansers, and hundreds of handsome Hooded Mergansers. Oblivious of the cold and wind, many were displaying, a pleasant reminder that spring would eventually come.

Back-bay birding always provides a surprise or two. Some years, it's numerous Red-necked Grebes. One year a Razorbill in the bay behind Stone Harbor was nearly picked off by a stooping peregrine. The flying alcid made a last-millisecond flying dive into the bay, soaking the falcon with its splash. Today's surprise was a young goshawk, perched on a No Wake Zone sign, hungrily eyeing a group of mergansers. The look was a fleeting and tantalizing glimpse of a back-bay ghost.

Another fun part of back-bay birding is watching ballfield Brant. Check all municipal parks and soccer fields for herds of grazing Brant; It's common in winter for Brant to leave the frozen bays to feed on the green grass of ballfields, offering exceptional views. Often, at high tide, a few Dunlin and Black-bellied Plover join them, too, awaiting the low-tide flats to reappear. And always check the numerous municipal water towers—all are favored peregrine perches and roosts in winter and on very rare occasions have hosted a Snowy Owl.

The best bonanza of this particular back-bay day was in Stone Harbor, where an icefree pocket at 104th Street held four or five hundred Scaup (both Lesser and Greater, offering a great chance for comparison), and over a hundred Hooded Mergansers. But the real prize was a stunning drake Redhead—almost a hotline rarity any more in New Jersey. And best of all, we enjoyed point-blank looks from the warmth of our car at a street-end overlook. Often it's best *not* to get out and risk flushing the always-wary ducks. The next day, the very same route produced Canvasback, a number of Common Goldeneye, a couple of Common Merganser (*uncommon* in the back bays), and an amazing thirteen Redheads!

The final stop was Hereford Inlet, viewed from the North Wildwood side. Here there are a number of back-bay and inlet overlooks. A

continues on next page

BACK-BAY BONANZA *continued*

---

number of Great Cormorants sat on the inlet sandbars, and lingering American Oystercatchers fed determinedly despite the cold (although they didn't look too happy about it). Gazing out over the vast sandbars and channels of Hereford Inlet, we were struck by the wildness of the scene, despite the condos, motels, restaurants, and taverns behind our backs. It may not be wilderness, but Hereford Inlet is a big, wide, wondrous natural area. We couldn't identify all the distant birds on the low-tide flats, but that was OK. It was important to know they were there and to ponder the rare or unusual birds Hereford Inlet would not give up on this winter day. ■

---

lovely remnant of old Red Cedars between 18th and 7th Streets) to the north are sometimes used by nesting Great Horned Owls in March. The eastern end of 6th, 7th, and 8th Streets in Avalon all end at the seawall next to Townsend's Inlet. These overviews are good in all seasons, offering close views of the inlet and ocean. In fall, they are an excellent window on the spectacle of the fall waterbird migration down the Atlantic coastline.

THE WETLANDS INSTITUTE

"Boulevard birding," bird-watching along the numerous causeways leading out to the developed barrier islands—roads that cross the vast salt marshes that separate the mainland from the barrier islands—has long been popular in the Cape May region, especially in the 1950s and 1960s. It is less pursued today, probably because increased summer traffic detracts from the quality of the experience, but there is a place where the tradition of boulevard birding survives. The venerable Wetlands Institute, a rustic-looking but modern facility just outside of Stone Harbor on the causeway connecting Stone Harbor to the mainland (Exit 10 on the Garden State Parkway), is at the center of salt marsh birding today. The institute was founded in 1969 owing to the enlightened conservation and education vision of Herbert Mills, a national conservation titan and executive director of the World Wildlife Fund. Established when wetlands were still being destroyed, dredged, and filled for seashore housing, the Wetlands Institute has over the years educated many thousands of visitors about the importance and wonders of our coastal habitat. The institute promotes appreciation of the vital role of wetlands and coastal ecosystems and encourages stewardship of these habitats both locally and worldwide through education and the sponsorship of research.

Originally established as a field station of Lehigh University, the Wetlands Institute has hosted hundreds of scientists and students, all performing research that in many cases has become a part of the cornerstone of wetlands-protection legislation and efforts. Today, the

Birders gathered on the marsh at the Wetlands Institute to search for a Sharp-tailed Sandpiper in October 2002.

institute is in part affiliated with Richard Stockton College of New Jersey, which features a strong environmental philosophy, curriculum, and commitment. One of the institute's most important accomplishments was to help conserve the Diamondback Terrapin, a threatened saltwater turtle.

The Wetlands Institute's annual "Wings 'n Water Festival," always held the third weekend in September, is one of the nation's major wildlife arts festivals and celebrations of the coast. Begun in 1982, this popular festival features paintings, sculpture, photography, crafts, and wildlife carving, including sales, demos, classes, and exhibits by internationally known decoy carvers. Bird walks and boat tours are always a key component. Also popular at the Wetlands Institute is the educational George Clark Lecture Series, named for a gentleman who was one of our most avid conservationists (and a president of the Cape May Geographic Society in the 1960s and 1970s).

For the birder, the Wetlands Institute is a key stop. The observation deck of the main building offers one of the best overall views of the coastal wetlands and many creeks and ponds, with their attendant waterbirds. In season, a remote video camera puts you virtually in a nearby Osprey nest. A bookstore and restrooms are on site. There is an entrance fee to visit the exhibits and displays, but birding the grounds and trail is free and can be enjoyed dawn to dusk. The short walking trail to Scotch Bonnet Creek (sometimes called Anchorage Drive and closed to vehicular traffic except for research-related boat launches) offers good views of several salt ponds, Osprey nests, and the creek. This overlook is good for waterfowl, mainly Bufflehead, in winter. The first pond, just off the parking lot, is a good

A Purple Gallinule was a surprise visitor to the Wetlands Institute grounds in May 2004.

high-tide shorebird roost almost year-round unless frozen. Expect Black-bellied Plover, yellowlegs, and dowitchers. White Ibis and Black-necked Stilt have been seen here, too. The ponds across Scotch Bonnet Creek are also very good for shorebirds, but a scope is absolutely necessary. Watch for feeding aggregations of herons, egrets, and terns. Expect anything along the walking trail—Vermillion Flycatcher in spring and Sharp-tailed Sandpiper in the fall have been found here, both Cape May County firsts. The gardens, although small, can be good for migrants in spring and fall. A recent surprise here was a Purple Gallinule that spent the month of May feeding in wetlands ponds, the gardens, and the parking lot!

Birding the Site

To reach the Wetlands Institute from the mainland, take Exit 10 on the Garden State Parkway and head east 2.8 miles on Stone Harbor Boulevard/Route 657 to the entrance on the right. From Stone Harbor, take 96th Street west. Cross the Great Channel Bridge and go 0.4 mile west on Stone Harbor Boulevard/Route 657 to the entrance on your left. Always check the schedule for the lecture series, birding trips, and family events. The Wetlands Institute hosts back-bay "salt marsh safari" excursions in summer, always an excellent way to view the wetlands and its denizens.

One popular stop nearby is **Shellbay Landing** at the eastern tip of Shellbay Avenue in Middle Township. It offers an exceptional overlook of Jenkins Sound. Viewing is from the road end and a small park and pier. Shellbay is well known as a consistent spot to see numbers of Whimbrel, in both April and May and July and August. At times, large flocks numbering several hundred birds gather here. Tides move Whimbrel around, however, so if you visit and see no Whimbrel, be sure to go back at a different stage of the tide. At high tide, Jenkins Sound is a sizable bay, but at extreme low water, you will be scanning mudflats. The sound is good for waterfowl, Brant and diving ducks, from fall through early spring. From Stone Harbor Boulevard, turn left (south) onto the parkway. Go 1.5 miles to the traffic light at Shellbay Avenue (Exit 9). Make a left, and go about 0.5 mile to the parking lot at the end of the road. Scan the marsh from the park and pier for Willets and Whimbrel and the bay for waterbirds at any season. Nummy's Island can be seen in the distance to the southeast.

THE AVALON SEAWATCH

Rivaling the Cape May Hawkwatch in pageant and excitement, and far surpassing it in seasonal span and sheer numbers of migrants, the Avalon Seawatch remains, if not less known, far less visited. On peak days, the hawkwatch may see a thousand visitors, while the seawatch will probably host less than a hundred. This is, however, gradually changing as more and more people manage to hit a good day and discover that the rewards of seawatching can be numerous. Since 1993, the Cape May Bird Observatory has conducted a full-time waterbird migration monitoring project at the north end of Avalon. The official count period is September 22 to December 22, but be assured that some seabirds move in numbers both a month

and a half before this period and sometimes a month and a half after. Accordingly, the seawatch can offer quality birding July through January.

The CMBO Avalon Seawatch is located on Townsend's Inlet, the coastal inlet north of Hereford Inlet. Townsend's differs considerably from Hereford, lacking the extensive sandbars, mudflats, and shoal areas. This deep–water inlet is characterized by a lengthy outer barrier bar; Avalon itself juts out to sea a full mile beyond Sea Isle City's coastline to the north. This official count is conducted at

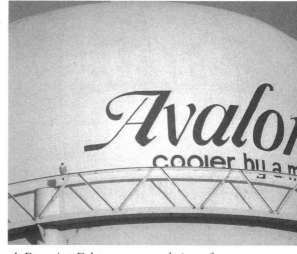

A Peregrine Falcon gets a good view of passing waterbirds.

7th Street, although on several occasions seawall construction activities have necessitated moving the count location to the beachfront at 8th Street.

Townsend's Inlet and Avalon are good windows for watching waterbirds at any season. In summer "local" gulls and terns ply the inlet constantly, joined daily by Brown Pelicans, Black Skimmers, and the like. Cory's Shearwaters and Wilson's Storm-Petrel are sometimes recorded in summer, although they are usually distant, "outside the bar." In winter, Avalon's four inlet jetties are consistent hotspots, offering the expected Purple Sandpipers, diving ducks, and loons, but also frequent eider and sometimes Harlequin Ducks. Spring migration is fair here, but not nearly as concentrated or as close in as in the fall. Fall migration has put Avalon on the map. From the trickle of Least Terns and Black Terns in July, to the steady flow of Common Terns, Glossy Ibis, and Double-crested Cormorants in August and early September, to the flood of birds in October, there is almost always something to be seen. (In early season, almost all movement is very early in the day, in the first couple of hours after sunrise; the same is true very late in the season.) Only in peak season, mid-October to late November, do flights last all day. Unfortunately, lighting is bad in early morning, since you are often looking toward the rising sun. By mid-October, though, it's a dream—waterbird movement continues unabated all day, and afternoon migrants are well lit with the sun at your back.

There are two key requirements to bird the Avalon Seawatch. One is a good spotting scope. Yes, there are days when the birds are close—scoters, loons, and even gannets going right down the inlet—but there are many days when birds are far, passing beyond the bar, and you need your scope to enjoy that distant jaeger. The second requirement is patience. As with hawkwatching, you wait for the birds to come to you. Seabirds pass in flocks, but in pulses too. A slow hour can be followed by a great hour or two or three at peak season, sometimes precipitated by just a subtle wind shift. Mid-October to late November is peak season, when bird movement is usually steady through the day. Some would say a third requirement for the seawatch is a good bladder. For many, the waiting game, coupled with late-season cold weather, means warm beverages to help ward off the chill. And there are no facilities at the Avalon Seawatch. The nearest are at the tennis courts one block south and one and a half blocks west, between Dune Drive and Ocean Drive on 8th Street; and at the baseball field south of the tennis courts on Dune Drive opposite 9th Street. These locations are good in summer and early fall, but by peak seawatch season they are usually locked, except maybe on weekends. If so, your nearest bets are the local restaurants on Dune Drive (several are open for breakfast) or the Avalon

Municipal Building at 30th Street and Dune Drive. Use the Police Department entrance on weekends and outside of regular business hours.

Birding the Site

To reach Avalon from the mainland, take Exit 13 on the parkway and head east on Avalon Boulevard/Route 601. Birding can be exceptional along this route. Just before the first small bridge, look to the left for a good view of Stites Sound. Expect shorebirds and wading birds in spring, summer, and fall; clouds of Brant in winter. The next and larger bridge crosses Ingram's Thorofare, good for back-bay ducks in winter. Peregrines often perch on the transmission towers right next to this bridge, as well as on Avalon's two water towers.

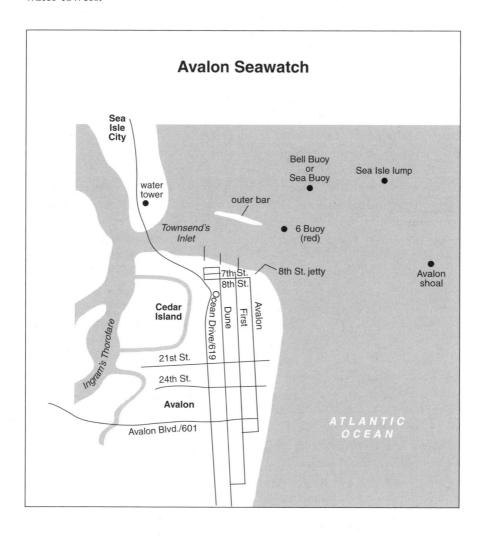

To reach Avalon from Stone Harbor, head north on Ocean Drive (enjoying back-bay birding as you go) or, alternately, on Second Avenue, which becomes Dune Drive at 80th Street where Avalon begins. Along Ocean Drive at 37th Street, public access to the marsh and back bay via a short boardwalk offers excellent winter waterfowl watching. Look for night-herons year-round roosting deep in the dense cedar islands in the marsh. Along Dune Drive, any street end to the right, or east, offers good access to the beach and ocean. Snow Buntings, American Pipits, and "Ipswich" Savannah Sparrows are found here most winters, and, rarely, Snowy Owls. This is usually a good zone for sea ducks and loons in winter. At 58th Street, the summer "mansions in the dunes" begin. Public dune walkovers here offer great fallout birding in fall and, potentially, in spring. The dunes are brief, mostly remnant, but the beach vegetation can be fairly extensive, and birdy. The tallest dune in New Jersey, the magnificent Sugar Bowl, once stood at 58th Street. As the name implies, it was a giant bowl of white beach sand and a popular place for kids to play. Clay remembers sledding in winter and playing king of the mountain in summer. The dune held on until the late 1960s, but when Clay returned home from college, it was gone, leveled for one of the very first trophy mansions. We'd bet the worth of the home sitting there today (if we had that kind of money) that the owners have never heard of the Sugar Bowl. Soon no one will have.

In summer, Piping Plover and sometimes terns nest somewhere between 58th and 44th Streets. At the 44th street dune crossover, you can often find roosting Black and Yellow-crowned Night-Herons. The dune walkover at 40th Street and First Avenue is a particularly good one—the planted Japanese Black Pines frequently hold warblers, kinglets, and Red-breasted Nuthatches on autumn mornings. At 32nd Street and the beach, the Avalon Fishing Pier pilings can attract winter seaducks. The Avalon boardwalk, a brief but pleasant walk, begins at 32nd Street and stretches north for about a dozen blocks. At 21st Street and the beach, a covered pavilion offers an all-weather seawatching alternative, although you are not nearly as close to the water as at 7th Street. The view from this pavilion was once far better for seawatching, but a beach-replenishment project a few years ago effectively placed the pavilion far from the surf. Since all of the area's beachfronts are constantly rearranged, this could soon change again.

Follow First Avenue north to 7th Street. Pull into the small parking lot along the seawall. (First Avenue is 1 block east of Dune Drive and 2 blocks east of Ocean Drive.) Expect the CMBO seabird counter to be present from sunrise to sunset from September 22 to December 22, no matter how bad the weather (the best flights are sometimes in the worst weather). CMBO seasonal interpretive naturalists will be there to educate and assist

Dunlins crowd the beach at Avalon.

with identification on weekends in October. Note the various landmarks to the north; these will be helpful when approaching seabirds are called out. On most days, you can readily see the casinos in Atlantic City, about 25 miles away on the northeast horizon. The close town to the northwest is Sea Isle City, with Strathmere beyond. Straight out is the red 6 Buoy and beyond that the distant red Bell Buoy, also called the Sea Buoy. All are reference points as birds are excitedly called out.

The 8th Street jetty, one block to your right (east), is particularly good for photographers and close looks at waterbirds. It was built as a wide promenade for easy and safe walking, and the boardwalk dune crossing to reach it is wheelchair accessible. Use common sense here if a gale is blowing or waves are crashing over the jetty, which happens during storms. NEVER step away from your scope or take your hand off your tripod; a simple gust of wind, and it could be gone. The end of the nearly quarter-mile-long jetty puts you closest to the birds; many ducks, loons, and gannets literally round the tip of the jetty as they head south. Frequently, a small flock of Common Eider can be found here in fall and winter among the many scoter. King Eider and Harlequin Duck have both wintered here, and Razorbill is annual too.

Even when few waterbirds are migrating, Townsend's Inlet is usually good. Check the 8th Street jetty and others in the area for diving ducks, Ruddy Turnstones, Dunlin, and Purple Sandpipers in fall and winter. Look for smaller Western Sandpipers among the Dunlin. Red-throated and Common Loons are easily seen in the inlet in late fall and winter, sometimes Horned Grebe. The 8th Street jetty is a great spot for Long-tailed Duck; listen for their "south-southerly" courtship calls in February and March, sometimes earlier in warm winters.

Follow Dune Drive north to 6th Street, where Dune Drive ends at a seawall. This is another good vantage point of Townsend's Inlet. As you meander in your car from road end to road end, don't forget to check the ballfield at the intersection of Ocean Drive and 8th Street for Brant in winter and roosting shorebirds during the very high tides of nor'easter coastal storms. Sometimes hundreds of Dunlin, Sanderling, and Black-bellied Plover flock here to escape the highest tides. When you reach Ocean Drive/Route 619, turn right and head toward the bridge. Park safely on the road shoulder before the bridge and view Townsend's Inlet to your right. Scan the rock pile across the inlet in Sea Isle for sea ducks. Look inland at the channel, banks, and mudflat. The close cove to your left is usually great—oystercatcher are nearly year-round here, and it can be a good feeding area and high-tide roost for shorebirds. Up to a thousand Dunlin and hundreds of Black-bellied Plover sometimes use this area from October through spring. Expect abundant Brant in winter, numerous terns in summer, and gulls in good numbers, especially in fall and winter. Royal Terns and Caspian Terns are daily in early fall. Glaucous Gull has been seen here several times in late fall and winter.

To reach the next hotspot, continue north on Ocean Drive across the toll bridge over Townsend's Inlet to Sea Isle. Follow Landis Avenue/Route 619 north through Sea Isle to Strathmere and Corson's Inlet.

CORSON'S INLET STATE PARK

Corson's Inlet is the next tidal inlet to the north of Townsend's Inlet, draining and filling a vast estuarine area, including Ludlam's Bay, behind Sea Isle City. Corson's Inlet State Park is another Cape May County gem, offering one of the better and more lengthy beach walks and a healthy remnant scrubby-shrubby dune system. Established in 1969, it protects about 340 acres in total. Corson's Inlet State Park occurs as two units. The first, smaller section is at the north end of the small town of Strathmere, on the south side of Corson's Inlet, and is reached from Sea Isle City. The second, larger parcel is across the inlet, accessed from the south end of Ocean City. Because of their relative remoteness, Strathmere and the Corson's Inlet area receive little birding attention, despite having many of the same avian offerings as Townsend's Inlet and Hereford Inlet to the south.

Birding is good year-round at Corson's Inlet State Park. In summer, large concentrations of terns feed in the inlet and roost on the beach; in fall, the dramatic sea bird migration passes by. In summer, depending on beach erosion or accretion, a sizable Common Tern and Black Skimmer colony can form, sometimes on the south side of the inlet, but more often on the north side. Piping Plover always nest, or attempt to nest, on the north side of the inlet, and one or two Roseate Terns sometimes hang around the Corson's Inlet colony in summer. Because there are no huge jetties here, Corson's Inlet is at the mercy of the elements, both winter storms and hurricanes.

Winter bird-watching is exceptional here. You can bird most of the day and often not see another person on the beach. The inlet holds many Common Loons and a Great Cormorant or two; scoter and other sea ducks are usually found in good numbers. From Ocean Drive where it crosses the inlet and marsh between the two units of the park, Bald Eagle and Rough-legged Hawk are possible. Northern Harrier are expected. The beaches, particularly the sand spit that often forms on the Strathmere side, hold roosting gulls at all seasons. White-winged gulls are possible in winter. Along Ocean Drive, south of Strathmere, the empty beaches can hold shorebirds at almost any season but, in particular, they host several thousand Sanderling, Dunlin, and Black-bellied Plover in fall and winter. Surprisingly, a few Red Knot usually winter here, too.

This section south of Strathmere is known as Whale Beach, so named for the several dead whales that washed up there early in the twentieth century. Whale Beach, Strathmere, and Corson's Inlet State Park are extremely underbirded and with more coverage could probably produce many more good birds. Clay's first memory of a Snowy Owl was one his father told him about, a snowy his dad had seen repeatedly one winter at Whale Beach, from the window of the train which he rode daily to high school in Ocean City in the 1920s, when Sea Isle was connected to Ocean City and Avalon only by train trestles. Clay has yet to see a Snowy Owl at Whale Beach, but, remembering his father's story, looks for one every time he is there in winter. In recent years, Snowy Owls have been spotted several times on the beach at Corson's Inlet State Park.

Birding the Site

From Avalon, follow Ocean Drive/Route 619 north across the Townsend's Inlet toll bridge. On the far side of the bridge there is a parking lot and a small park on the left, at the foot of the bridge. It can hold songbird migrants in fall and offers beach- and bay-walking access. Try street-end dune walkovers anywhere in the town of Townsend's Inlet. This area (just across the inlet from the seawatch) always holds good roosting flocks of gulls, and the bight, or cove, formed here by the long Townsend's Inlet sandbar is a regular spot for rafts of scoter and other ducks in fall and winter. To continue your tour, head north through Sea Isle City on Landis Avenue/Route 619 (also known as Ocean Drive). There are numerous jetties on the Sea Isle beachfront; they are virtually never birded yet hold good duck numbers some winters. About 3.8 miles north of the

Townsend's Inlet Bridge, around 22nd Street in Sea Isle, the houses begin to thin out (many were victims of the 1962 storm). This deserted stretch of beach holds good flocks of shorebirds, except in summer. In another 1.1 miles, at 2nd Street, **Whale Beach** and Upper Township begin. Go 1 block farther and park near Taylor Avenue, which will be on your left and take the dune walkover. This is a good spot to begin a beach walk either north or south. The Taylor Avenue jetty is particularly good for sea ducks in winter, with Common Eider frequently seen. Recently a "Black Brant" fed with "regular" Brant on this jetty at low tide in November. Beach shorebirds are usually abundant here.

To continue, proceed north on Ocean Drive/Route 619 (signed as Commonwealth Avenue in Whale Beach and Strathmere). In 1.3 miles, at Willard Avenue, Ocean Drive will bend sharply to the left. Instead, go straight on Commonwealth Avenue/Route 636 until it dead-ends. The Corson's Inlet State Park trail head (really just a simple path) begins here. Autumn songbird fallout often happens here, particularly in the cedars and pines. Night-herons often roost in these cedars, too, in beach house backyards. Walk through the dunes a few hundred yards to the beach on the backside of a sand spit that extends into Corson's Inlet. The deep water here is good for ducks, loons, and even eider; the sand spit itself may hold gulls and terns. In fall, the shoals of the inlet attract Northern Gannet and sometimes Parasitic Jaeger. Frigatebird has been reported from here, and a Brown Booby was once seen here on the Marmora Christmas Bird Count! A word of caution: Although the extensive low-tide sandbars and mudflats that can form here can be extremely inviting, don't venture too far. More than a few fishermen have been forced to swim back to the beach when the flooding tides return with a vengeance, and rivulets become deep channels in minutes.

You can hike out and then retrace your steps, but the best way to bird this small unit of Corson's Inlet State Park is to work clockwise around the point of Strathmere, birding the beach and (meager) dunes. They should be good for beach birds, and usually a few oystercatchers. In fall, oystercatcher and Black Skimmer usually flock up here before departing south. Osprey, peregrine, and Merlin are daily in fall. Take any of the dune walkovers; they lead to Neptune Avenue, or, farther south, to roads that connect to Commonwealth. Portable toilets are available in the warmer months at the south end of Neptune. Bird your way back to your car.

Return to Ocean Drive at Willard. Make a right turn and immediately go over the toll bridge that spans Corson's Inlet. On the far side, scan the mudflats and sod banks along Ocean Drive. This is a good spot for salt marsh birding. In about 1 mile you will reach a second bridge, the Middle Thorofare Bridge. Immediately after crossing it, make a right turn into the parking lot and boat ramp for the north unit of Corson's Inlet State Park. Park and walk the bay beach heading southeast. Soon, you will round the tip onto the open beachfront. Look for beach birds and for migrants along the edge of the dense bayberry thickets of the dunes in spring and fall. Walk as far as you like. From the parking lot it is about a 3-mile round trip to the remnant fishing pier, where the pilings sometimes hold ducks in winter. There is also access to Corson's Inlet State Park, and the old pier, from 59th Street in Ocean City.

Alternately, a trailhead in the parking lot leads through the dunes. Dense bayberry thickets should yield migrant songbirds in spring and fall. This trail also leads to the 59th Street Pier parking area in Ocean City. Most birders make a loop, taking the dune trail one way and the beach walk the other. In some years, a sizable Least Tern colony forms on the beach at the south end of Ocean City, and it can be one of the largest in New Jersey. A small salt-water pond at the north end of the bridge parking lot is good for herons and egrets in summer and ducks in winter. Boat-tailed Grackles should be conspicuous spring through fall. Clouds of Tree Swallows occur here in autumn. Look for "Ipswich" Savannah Sparrows and Snow Buntings on the upper beach in winter.

You can also bird this section from the south end of Ocean City. Follow Ocean Drive north until you enter Ocean City on 53rd street. Go 3 blocks east to Central Avenue and turn right. Drive 4 blocks south and park anywhere in the beachfront parking area. The Corson's Inlet State Park entrance path is just ahead. About 50 yards down this sand road, the marked hiking trail begins (the same trail that connects to the foot of the Ocean Drive Middle Thorofare bridge). The trail goes off to the right through the dunes. Restrooms are located between 58th and 59th Streets but are only open in summer between 8:00 A.M. and 5:30 P.M. Dune walkovers lead to the beach and the remnant 59th street pier. Walk south, to your right, to Corson's Inlet. The beach is closed to vehicles May 15 to September 15, but in fall, you will no doubt encounter a number of surf fishermen in their "beach buggies," as they like to refer to their four-wheel-drive vehicles. Vehicle access is by permit only.

With maritime forest, open beaches, and the sparkling inlet, Corson's Inlet State Park can offer a pleasant walk and good birding at any season. You may well find The A. R. Ammons 1965 poem, "Corson's Inlet," to be apropos: "the walk liberating, I was released from forms, from the perpendiculars, straight lines, blocks, boxes, binds of thought into the hues, shadings, rises, flowing bends and blends of sight." To return to the Garden State Parkway, retrace your route to Sea Isle City. Turn right onto John F. Kennedy Boulevard/41st Street and follow it west out of town. This road becomes Sea Isle Boulevard/Route 625. An active artificial peregrine eyrie can be seen in the distance to the north of the boulevard. Access the parkway at exit 17, a north-bound entrance only. To go south, you must go north on the parkway 1 mile to the service plaza, where you can pull in and turn around. Alternately, you can return to the parkway by heading north through Ocean City to 34th Street. Go left (west) on 34th, which flows into Roosevelt Boulevard/Route 623. Continue west to the parkway at exit 25—there are both north-bound and south-bound entrances here.

GREAT EGG HARBOR BAY

Alexander Wilson both collected and painted at Great Egg Harbor, and his fondness for the area was clear in Robert Cantwell's 1961 biography of the great naturalist: "On the winding northern shore of Great Egg Harbor, on the edge of narrow passages of blue sea water, bordered by rushes or silver white sand, there was an old tavern, Beasley's Tavern, still in existence a century and a half later, and it became one of his refuges. . . . Wilson was surely a happy individual when he wrote of Great Egg Harbor, something that could confidently be said of him at few times in his life."

As its name implies, Great Egg Harbor played a major role in the history of the southern New Jersey region; its vast colonies of birds provided the fresh eggs for the first explorers and, later, the first European settlers. It also played a role in our ornithological history, as the setting for a number of John James Audubon's paintings and a delightful chapter in his journals. Despite such history, today Great Egg Harbor Bay and Inlet are underbirded, but for no good reason. Great Egg Harbor provides exceptional opportunities for the intrepid Cape May County birder. Perhaps the major reason for Great Egg's relative obscurity is its very size. Great Egg is indeed great—it's a big area and hard to bird by car or on foot. In fact, the vast bay is best seen by boat. Many sections of the Great Egg Harbor River and Tuckahoe River, its major tributaries, can *only* be birded well by boat.

The driving dike at the Corbin City impoundments traverses freshwater ponds to the west and salt marsh to the east.
STEVE EISENHAUER

The Great Egg Harbor River watershed forms a full quarter of the official Pinelands Protection Area. The lower river and bay are wide, up to 6 miles at the widest point—so wide that in autumn, on strong northwest winds, most raptors fly around the basin rather than cross it. The north side of the Great Egg Harbor River functions as a diversion line, and hawks follow the upland edge, the forested tree line, west for many miles before they cross, usually near Gibson's Landing, where the river and marsh edge narrows to only a mile. On autumn days with strong northwest winds, hundreds of hawks can be seen working west up the north shore of the Great Egg Harbor River.

The Beesley's Point power plant marks the western horizon of the Great Egg Harbor Bay's south side.

Great Egg Harbor Bay is the largest bay in Cape May County (Atlantic County begins midbay) and one of the largest on the Jersey coast. If you came south on the Garden State Parkway, you crossed it just south of exit 29. No doubt you noticed the Beesley's Point coal- and oil-fired power plant (often mistaken for a nuclear power plant) off to the west on the south side of the huge bay. Great Egg Harbor Bay is a combination of deep channels, shallow waters, and vast mudflats at low tide. It is the estuary fed by the Great Egg Harbor and Tuckahoe Rivers—where the waters of these two rivers mix before emptying into the Atlantic Ocean through Great Egg Harbor Inlet, which passes between Longport to the north and Ocean City to the south. Great Egg Harbor Bay is one of the largest and most pristine wetlands complexes in New Jersey. As it has in the past, it still holds great avian treasures today.

There are several phenomena unique to the Great Egg region. In winter, the vast bay holds a huge raft of scaup, numbering over 8,000 birds in some years. Most are Greater Scaup, but Lesser Scaup are also present. One year, a Tufted Duck wintered near Longport in Atlantic County, but it never wandered south into Cape May County waters. There are also huge numbers of other diving ducks present—many Red-breasted Mergansers and hundreds of Bufflehead. The 1,168 Bufflehead that Clay and colleague

Jim Dowdell counted on the bay and inlet on February 1, 2004, are an all-time high for New Jersey. Great Egg Harbor Bay and Inlet are reliable spots for Common Goldeneye in the region, and possibly the most consistent for Red-necked Grebe. In most winters, Longport Jetty, on the north side of the inlet, is the best bet for Harlequin Duck south of Barnegat Light. Many thousands of Brant grace the vast bay in winter too, some of the bigger numbers in the region.

Shorebird numbers, although largely untallied, are big on the bay's low-tide mudflats in spring and fall. This is where the breadth of the site works against you. You can often see mudflats teeming with sandpipers that are too far away to identify. This area needs boat work. It lends itself well to kayaking, although it is big, rough in any wind, and would require experience to paddle. As yet, there have been few back-bay safari boat tours of this area. Even though the birds of Great Egg Harbor have been studied for nearly two hundred years by such luminaries as Wilson and Audubon, there are still major ornithological discoveries to be made here.

Birding the Site

From the north unit of Corson's Inlet State Park continue north on Bay Avenue/Route 619 (also known as Ocean Drive). In Ocean City, Route 619 is signed as Central Avenue. This is the street that runs along the beach. At 28th Street, go right 1 block and turn left onto Wesley Avenue, which becomes the best through route. Wesley Avenue flows into "Gardens Parkway" (only about 5 blocks long), and this routes you onto the Ocean City–Longport Bridge, a toll bridge over the Great Egg Harbor Inlet.

Alternately, from the Garden State Parkway at exit 25, you can enter Ocean City by going east on Roosevelt Boulevard/Route 623 to Central Avenue, then turning left (north) onto Central Avenue, right on 28th Street, and left onto Wesley Avenue.

A third route, and actually the best one for birding, is to follow the parkway north over the Great Egg Harbor Bay. At the north end of the bridge take exit 29 onto Route 9. At the first traffic light, turn right onto Route 559 (Somers Point–Mays Landing Road). In 0.7 mile, just before you reach a traffic circle, make a very hard right onto Broadway, a residential street. In a few hundred yards, the road ends at a parking lot and **Kennedy Park,** a small municipal park that provides one of the best views of Great Egg Harbor Bay. Scan the bay at any season. In winter, Brant may be at your feet, but many birds will be distant. Look for abundant Bufflehead and the huge raft of scaup, usually visible from here but sometimes out of sight behind one of the many marsh islands. Osprey nest on Drag Island, the marsh island under the parkway bridge (to your right), and peregrines often perch on one of the structures of the looming Beesley's Point power plant beyond the bridge. Check the trees in the park for passerine fallout, particularly in spring.

To continue your tour, exit the Kennedy Park and turn right onto Route 559. Just ahead is one of the state's infamous traffic circles. Stay in the right lane and take the first right off the circle onto Route 52 (often called the 9th Street Causeway to Ocean City). This causeway provides another excellent view of the channels and bay. Be careful—this is a busy road and there are no pull-offs along much of it, but there are several wide cinder pull-offs on the north shoulder, just before the small bridges. These are excellent spots from which to scan. There is a heron and egret rookery on the south side of the road, to your right, just before you enter Ocean City, but it is hard to view.

Follow Route 52/9th Street into Ocean City. At Wesley Avenue/Route 619 turn left. Wesley Avenue will route you to Ocean Drive and the Ocean City–Longport Bridge. Don't cross it; just before the bridge, pull into the small municipal parking area to your right. A short path over the dunes takes you to the water's edge and a fantastic view of Great Egg Harbor Inlet. Walk to the right.

Snow Buntings and "Ipswich" Savannah Sparrows are often seen here in winter and Piping Plover in spring. Scan the offshore bars for waterbirds. Walk south to the first jetty and look for sea ducks and Purple Sandpipers fall through spring. When you're finished, return to your car and cross the Ocean City–Longport Bridge. Immediately on the far side, turn left into a small parking lot. Many fishermen use this lot to access the fishing pier. Scan to the west. The channels hold Brant, mergansers, and loons; mudflats have oystercatcher and other shorebirds. The pilings to the left often have a few Great Cormorant among the many double-crested, and seals are frequent here in winter.

The far island may have hunting harriers or a perched, waiting peregrine, daily here in winter (check Osprey platforms for peregrines in winter). Be advised that a white Gyrfalcon spent the entire winter in this area, from November 1982 to April 1983, but because of its huge winter range was seen by very few birders. To view down bay, either go out on the fishing pier and look under the bridge or, better yet, walk to the east side of Ocean Drive to the embankment. This offers a great view of the lower bay, the Longport Sod Banks to the left (look for shorebirds on the beach), and in the distance, the Longport Jetty on the north side of the inlet. This is a great spot in winter. Rafts of scoter are usually present, and over four hundred Long-tailed Ducks have been counted here. Look for Common Loons, Red-throated Loons, Horned Grebes, and seals.

Continue the tour on Ocean Drive. The next 1.5 miles, toward Longport, is good salt marsh birding or, by parking and walking, good mudflat and bay birding. This is technically the Malibu Beach Wildlife Management Area, but birders will forever know it as the **Longport Sod Banks,** perhaps best known for the Bar-tailed Godwit that spent late April to late May here from 1972 to 1982, the most dependable bar-tailed ever seen anywhere in the eastern United States! Sadly, this beach has become a popular place for people to run their dogs, but this will perhaps diminish through state management and enforcement. The beach here offers an excellent view of lower Great Egg Harbor Bay.

Continue into Longport and bird the bayside street-ends for more ducks or the oceanfront to the south until you reach the **Longport Jetty** at the very southern tip of town. The streets are confusing here and parking can be a nightmare. Plan to walk a distance, but the jetty can be well worth the effort, with Brown Pelicans regular in summer and Harlequin Ducks sometimes reported in winter. The jetty area yields a great view of the inlet and ocean and promises good birding at any season. As a birding diversion, Lucy the Elephant is just 1 mile north, at 9200 Atlantic Avenue and Decatur Avenue in Margate. This 65-foot-high elephant-shaped edifice was built in 1881, as, you guessed it, a tourist attraction. Lucy still stands, now beautifully restored and open to the public. She was not, in fact, the only South Jersey pachyderm. A sister elephant, "The Light of Asia," was built in South Cape May in 1884. Also a tourism promotion, here a 10-cent admission would offer a view from the "howdah" overlook, 60 feet high on the elephant's back. Constructed of wood and some 13,000 square feet of tin, The Light of Asia deteriorated rapidly and was demolished in 1900.

Alternately, as you leave the Ocean City–Longport Bridge, go 0.6 mile north to the traffic light. Turn left onto Route 152 (Ocean Drive goes to the right). In 0.6 mile, cross a high bridge. At the foot of the bridge, turn left into a small municipal park, offering a view of Broad Thorofare, which you previously viewed from the bridge parking area. To continue, proceed 1.3 miles west on Route 152 to Somers Point. At the second traffic light, turn left onto Shore Road/Route 585. Go 0.7 mile to the traffic circle. On your right, facing the circle, is the Somers Mansion, built in 1725. It is rumored that John James Audubon stayed here during his excursion to Great Egg Harbor. This historic building is open to the public. For information, stop at the Atlantic County Historical Society Museum, on Shore Road.

Enter the traffic circle carefully. Take the second right onto Route 559. At the first traffic light, turn left onto Route 9, which flows into the parkway south and back to Cape May. Alternately, to go north on the parkway from Somers Point, turn right onto Route 9 and continue about 0.5 mile to Route 52. At the light, turn left onto West Laurel Drive/Route 52 and go 0.7 mile to the parkway entrance at exit 30 North.

TUCKAHOE WILDLIFE MANAGEMENT AREA
AND CORBIN CITY IMPOUNDMENTS

Just as the Great Egg estuary is where the waters of the Great Egg Harbor and Tuckahoe Rivers meet and mix with the salty bounty from the Atlantic Ocean, so too is this where the coastal route of our birding tour of the Cape meets up with the vast interior forests of southern New Jersey. If you are following these sites in order, this is where you will first enter a mix of Pine Barrens–type uplands and riparian lowland forests and swamps. Now, as we enter the "heartland," we come to a place of exceptional breeding and wintering bird populations.

The Great Egg Harbor River's headwater origins are far off, in Atlantic County and beyond, but for our purposes this river begins at the dam at Lake Lenape in Mays Landing. The Tuckahoe River, a second major tributary to Great Egg Harbor Bay, has origins in Atlantic County; Cumberland County, in Peaslee Wildlife Management Area; and in Cape May County, in Belleplain State Forest. The Tuckahoe River is lined with many abandoned cranberry bogs along its upper reaches. The mostly lowland forests in the area are healthy and largely unharvested and undeveloped. Atlantic City–related housing is beginning to encroach on the north side of the Great Egg Harbor River, but, fortunately, vast public lands are protected in the region, including the stellar Atlantic County system of parks and the wonderful Tuckahoe Wildlife Management Area. Wetlands breeding birds of this region are mostly similar to those found on the coastal strip, but the more brackish sections along the rivers hold both Virginia Rail and King Rail. Black Rail was once found on the higher marsh sections of the rivers, but have become much more difficult to find because of ongoing mosquito-control activities. Several pairs of Northern Harrier nest in the vast marshes of the middle sections of the rivers.

The woodlands hold a good mix of breeding species. Breeding songbird diversity is similar to nearby Belleplain State Forest, although it may be a little lower because of the relative lack of cedar swamp habitat. There is far less coverage here than at Belleplain, however, and so there are many discoveries to be made, each season and collectively, in the Tuckahoe/Corbin City region. This area is good for migrants, too, spring and fall, but again, there is little coverage in these seasons. Waterfowl and shorebirds are good at both the Tuckahoe and Corbin City impoundments, and passerines may fall out anywhere. While migrants are far less concentrated here than farther south on the peninsula, you can usually find some good pockets of birds, both early-season warblers and sparrows late in the fall.

Key highlights of the Tuckahoe/Corbin City area are the wintering birds, both raptors and waterfowl. Tidal rivers usually remain open, with

Because tidal rivers usually remain unfrozen, winter brings good raptor and water-fowl opportunities to Tuckahoe WMA.

swift-running, unfrozen stretches in even the coldest winters. Dabbling ducks, primarily Black Ducks and Mallards, joined in late February by returning Pintail and Green-winged Teal, concentrate in big numbers along the rivers. Common and Hooded Merganser can be found on the river itself and the impoundments when they are not frozen. Numbers of Tundra Swans join the ever-present Mute Swans in winter and spring. Prey attracts predators, and ducks attract eagles in winter. The Tuckahoe River is the best place in Cape May County to see numbers of Bald Eagles, and the dozen or more Bald Eagles present in winter are always joined by a Golden Eagle or two. The Tuckahoe/Corbin complex rivals the Mullica River as the most dependable place in all of New Jersey, possibly the entire Mid-Atlantic region, to enjoy Golden Eagles in winter. There are always two or three present on the Tuckahoe and three or four present in the vast Mullica wetlands complex. They are mostly adult Golden Eagles, probably the same individuals returning year after year.

Tuckahoe/Corbin is also one of the best spots for Rough-legged Hawk and Short-eared Owl in winter. The area rivals Jakes Landing in reliability and always bests the bayshore in numbers. Numerous rough-legs (pale ones and coal-black ones alike) can be found on these marshes in winter, usually along with many Short-eared Owls. Harriers abound, with dozens present. (Clay and colleague Jim Dowdell carefully counted, in studies conducted for the Great Egg Harbor Watershed Association, as many as forty-seven Northern Harriers in a day here, and highs of ten Rough-leggeds, fifty-eight Red-tailed, eighteen Bald Eagles, and two Golden Eagles.)

The Tuckahoe WMA includes 14,446 acres. It is one of the oldest wildlife management areas in New Jersey; the first acquisition was in 1933. Duck hunting, deer hunting, and upland game hunting (rabbit, squirrel, woodcock, and stocked quail and pheasants) are all popular here. It has two units, the Tuckahoe Area on the south side of the Tuckahoe River and the Corbin City Area on the north side of the river.

Birding the Site

From Cape May, take the Garden State Parkway north to exit 20 (northbound exit only). Exit onto Route 50. In about 0.5 mile you reach Route 9. Services are available here, and also your last restrooms for a while. Cross the intersection and take Route 50 north for 6.4 miles into the small town of Tuckahoe.

Alternately, from northern Cape May County, take the parkway south to exit 25 (Marmora–Ocean City). Exit and head west toward Marmora. At the traffic light, continue straight across Route 9. At the Tuckahoe Road/Route 631, turn left. Continue to Route 50, about 5.2 miles ahead into the small town of Tuckahoe. This scenic route crosses the pristine Cedar Swamp Creek.

In Tuckahoe continue north on Route 50. The next landmark is a traffic light where Route 49 goes off to the left; stay straight on Route 50 for another 0.2 mile to Mosquito Landing Road—on your right just before the small bridge over the Tuckahoe River. Be alert: the road is poorly marked. Turn right onto Mosquito Landing Road. Wend your way past the busy Yanks Boat Works. As the road enters the forest, the first left will take you to a small boat landing and municipal park. For a better view, continue past the park and take the next left to reach a parking lot, boat ramp, and outstanding overlook. This is an excellent canoe, kayak, or small boat launch site, yielding access to the entire Tuckahoe River. Be aware, though, that a special Division of Fish and Wildlife permit is required to launch here. You are now in Tuckahoe WMA. This spot is your first window on the huge tidal wetland complex. Here, and from now on, Bald Eagle is likely at any season, and Golden Eagle, Rough-legged Hawk, and Short-eared Owl are possible late fall through early spring. Clapper Rails, Marsh Wrens, Seaside Sparrows, and egrets are constant in spring and summer.

To continue, return to the gravel road. In 0.6 mile, a small road branches off to the left. You now have two options: Continue straight for an inland woodland route or take the left to explore an area of freshwater impoundments and extensive tidal marshes via a gravel driving dike.

If you go straight, the next 1.5 miles offer excellent woodland birding in breeding season and on migration. Wild Turkey are common, and Ruffed Grouse were once found here in numbers, although today they are scarce. Near the WMA headquarters buildings, the wooded wetlands may produce Wood Ducks. A left here will take you to Tuckahoe Lake. Bald Eagles once nested here, but now nest farther up the Tuckahoe River. Expect Hooded Mergansers and Ring-necked Ducks here in spring, among other ducks. When the gravel road reaches the paved road, turn right to return to Route 50 in about 0.5 mile.

If you go left, you'll soon be greeted by salt marsh vistas that extend all the way to the Beesley's Point power plant. Look in both directions to cover the area fully. The first impoundment is the slowest, and the second generally holds the most waterfowl, fall through spring, unless it's frozen. The third impoundment generally has the lowest water levels and most of the shorebirds. There are no established overlooks here, but openings at the various sluices usually offer the best views. When you reach the third impoundment, a road on the left leads to a dead end. It is best to park and walk before taking this left since it may be difficult to turn around at the end (or you could encounter another car and need to back all the way out). Expect teal, Northern Pintail, and Common and Hooded Mergansers in numbers in late winter and spring. (All ducks are far less common here during the fall because of duck-hunting season.) Check for Tundra Swans among the abundant Mute Swans in winter and spring. Three individual Common Teal (Eurasian Green-winged Teal) have been seen here on two different occasions. They are annual here, although it takes dedicated searching by scope to find one mixed in with the abundant Green-winged Teal. Eurasian Wigeon have been seen here too, and Black-necked Stilt have been seen several times in spring. Perhaps the coolest record for Tuckahoe is the flock of seventeen Fulvous Whistling-Ducks found here in early May 1974 (undoubtedly the same flock that turned up at Brigantine NWR the next day). Scan the open water, tree line, and sky for raptors.

Continue on the main road and reenter the forest. The road winds around but soon comes to fields planted in wildlife food crops. Avoid this area in fall and winter (except on Sundays) since it is heavily hunted for small game, deer, and pheasants. When you reach the T at a major gravel road, turn left. (If you were to turn right here, the road would route you back into the WMA, past the headquarters and Tuckahoe Lake, and eventually back to Mosquito Landing Road, which leads back to Route 50.) Continue until you reach the stop sign at Route 631. Turn right onto Route 631. Route 50 is just ahead.

Turn right onto Route 50 and continue through Tuckahoe and over the Tuckahoe River (soon after the Route 49 traffic light). In 1.4 miles from the Tuckahoe River bridge, turn right onto Griscom Mill Road next to the small Corbin City city hall. Continue past the few houses. You are now entering the **Corbin City Area of the Tuckahoe WMA.** The paved road becomes a gravel road, and the forest becomes wet lowland. American Redstart, Yellow-throated Warbler, Worm-eating Warbler, Hooded Warbler, and Prothonotary Warbler all breed here, along with abundant Ovenbirds and Wood Thrush. Wild Turkey is common, and

Ruffed Grouse is still possible. At 0.7 mile, the road takes a hard right. (A path goes straight here—good for walking, but not for driving. The path eventually leads deep into the swamp forest. Boots are a must.) Make the right and continue past small roadside ponds. Note: following heavy rain or snow and snow melt this section of the road can become difficult. The target impoundments ahead can also be reached from farther north on Route 50 (via the Gibson Creek Road entrance 3.4 miles north of the Griscom Mill Road entrance).

Ahead, a small power line right-of-way crosses the road. Scan it for perched raptors, Red-tailed Hawks on tops of poles and Red-shouldered Hawks perched low, in a sunlit spot and out of the wind on cold winter mornings. Barred Owls are found here too. On a number of occasions, we have seen Pileated Woodpecker here, one of the few places they breed in all of southern New Jersey. A hike north up the right-of-way is not for the faint of heart; hip boots are a must because of the deep water. Continuing down the road a short distance beyond the right-of-way the southernmost of three impoundments comes into view on your left. The tidal salt marshes to the right stretch all the way to the Beesley's Point power plant, visible far to the east. Like the Tuckahoe impoundments, the Corbin City impoundments are backed by forest. Also like Tuckahoe, the first of the impoundments usually has the fewest birds, although the first section of marsh on the right is often good for Short-eared Owls in late fall through midspring, especially on windless evenings. Begin scanning for the owls about an hour before sunset. On warmer spring days, short-ears may be hunting and harassing harriers (or vice versa) as early as two o'clock in the afternoon.

There is an observation tower at the far end of the first impoundment. It is ideally placed, overlooking the entire Great Egg/Tuckahoe wetlands here. It is without a doubt one of the best spots in southern New Jersey to see Golden Eagle in winter. The area is big, and Golden Eagles range over many miles, but with patience you can find a Golden Eagle here almost daily December through early February, weather permitting. The best weather is blustery northwest winds, when the eagles hunt and when they are carried downriver from their hidden inland bog roosts. Midday seems best, the time when they head back upriver and inland after the morning's hunt, although we have also seen them flapping inland to roost almost at sundown. Bald Eagles are seen here daily in numbers—winter is best, but several pairs nest near here, too. Rough-legged Hawk is *almost* guaranteed here December through mid-March. The colder and snowier the winter, the better; these conditions force Rough-legged Hawks out of their northern haunts.

After leaving the tower, continue driving north on the dike. The second impoundment is the largest and requires several stops to check all its nooks and crannies for ducks. Tree Sparrows are likely on the dikes in winter, and Northern Shrikes have wintered here on several occasions. Migratory fallout can occur here in spring and fall. We've seen good numbers and variety of sparrows in early November. Look for River Otter too. The final impoundment is usually the best for ducks. In early spring, Hooded and Common Merganser can be common, along with Northern Pintails and teal (green-winged earlier and blue-winged in late spring). Look for Common Teal here, too, in March. As the dike jogs left, there is a small parking lot and gravel launching ramp to your right known as Gibson Landing. This is good boat access and is also a good spot to scan up the Great Egg Harbor River. Bald Eagles are expected (a pair nests near here) and Osprey are numerous spring through fall, sometimes nesting on the transmission towers. To continue, leave the parking lot and travel up the road across the final section of dike. In early spring, listen for Spring Peepers and Leopard Frogs along the road here before it reenters the forest.

The power line right-of-way you cross here is the same one you saw earlier. It provides higher and drier access here than it did at the other end. This is now Gibson Creek Road. The woods here are also drier, with less-swampy lowlands than at the other end of the impoundments. Pine Warblers, Eastern Towhees, and Chipping Sparrows abound in summer. The fields on the left are planted in wildlife food crops and are hunted in season. From Gibson's Landing, it is 1.6 miles back to Route 50.

Upon exiting the Tuckahoe WMA on Gibson Creek Road, turn right onto Route 50 to go north to Mays Landing. The **Atlantic County Estell Manor Park** is 4 miles ahead. This 1,700-acre county park is rich in history and contains healthy woodlands and great trails. It is a great spot for woodland birding at any season. Barred Owls are here, and Whip-poor-will are numerous in spring and summer. Pileated Woodpeckers are occasionally seen here too, part of the same small population we have encountered in the woods behind the Corbin City impoundments. Stop in at the Warren E. Fox Nature Center for maps. The extensive trail map is also available on their Web site.

Alternately, upon exiting the Tuckahoe WMA on Gibson Creek Road, a left turn onto Route 50 will route you south and back to the parkway. This route passes near some overviews of, and access points for, the **Cape May NWR's Great Cedar Swamp Division,** one of the largest and wildest units of the refuge. Since 1989, when the Cape May NWR was created, 6,600 acres of the proposed 10,200 acres have been acquired in the Great Cedar Swamp Division. This, NWR continues to grow as funding and properties become available. Follow Route 50 from Gibson Creek Road south 8 miles through Tuckahoe and three traffic lights to Upper Bridge Road. Bear left onto Upper Bridge Road and immediately cross the railroad. Continue 0.2 mile and park near the end of the paved road. Do not block driveways. Continue on Upper Bridge Road on foot to Cedar Swamp Creek. This might be a spot to listen for King Rail. Return to Route 50 and turn left. In 0.5 mile Route 50 crosses Cedar Swamp Creek. The small bridge over the creek and marsh is a good spot to stop and scan (pull as far off the road as possible, next to the guardrail, and be extremely careful of high-speed traffic). Up river or north, to your left, is the vast Great Egg wetlands complex. The plume from the Beesley's Point power plant tower is visible. Downriver to your right is Great Cedar Swamp, where the Cape May Canal was originally planned but thankfully not built. King Rail has been heard here. This is an excellent spot to put in a kayak or canoe and explore south into Great Cedar Swamp via Cedar Swamp Creek, though be sure to play the tides.

Breeding Barred Owls are common in the Great Cedar Swamp.

Continue on Route 50 for 1.5 miles to Tyler Road/Route 616, a sharp left. Take Route 616 and continue 1.6 miles to a small parking lot on the right marked with NWR boundary signs. Park and explore a series of fields, backed by wet woods, and the 1-mile-long "Cedar Swamp Trail" through a pine-oak forest with an understory of American Holly. Barred Owls are found here; the Great Cedar Swamp Division is a stronghold for breeding Barred Owls. Return to Route 616 and continue 0.3 mile north to a small bridge and great overlook of Cedar Swamp Creek and surrounding marsh. This is an excellent spot to listen for Clapper and King Rails, far better than on heavily traveled Route 50. Make a safe U-turn and return south on Route 616 to Route 50.

Turn left onto Route 50 and continue 0.6 mile to Peach Orchard Road, on the right. Turn right onto Peach Orchard Road and follow it for 1.1 miles (it begins as a paved road, becomes dirt, then becomes paved again) to where it intersects with Somers Avenue. Park along Somers Avenue. Walk the continuation of Peach Orchard Road beyond the gate to explore another portion of the Cape May NWR Great Cedar Swamp Division. This road passes through a pine-oak woods (Pine Warblers and Yellow-throated Warblers breed here) and eventually drops down into Mountain Laurel thickets and a narrow Atlantic White-cedar water crossing. Both Hooded and Prothonotary Warblers breed here, far from the madding crowd.

A pleasant alternate way of viewing the vast **Great Egg Harbor River** basin is from the north (or east) side of the Great Egg Harbor River. From the parkway, take exit 29. Follow Route 9 to the traffic light at Route 559/Somers Point–Mays Landing Road. Turn left (west) onto Route 559. In about 2.5 miles, turn left onto Jeffers Landing Road/Route 651. Jeffers Landing Road become Jobs Point Road; both provide wonderful views of the lower Great Egg Harbor River and tidal wetlands. You are now about 5 miles across the river and marsh from the Tuckahoe WMA impoundments. As we said, it's a big area. Numerous active Osprey nests on platforms are visible here. Turn around at the small gated bayside community and return to Route 559. Turn left onto Route 559 and continue for 2 miles. Turn left onto Wharf Road (hard to spot, it's directly across from English Creek Road). Proceed 1 mile down Wharf Road for more great views of the Great Egg basin and the Corbin City Area of Tuckahoe WMA beyond. This is another great spot for nesting Osprey and Northern Harriers, Rough-legged Hawks, Bald Eagles, and Golden Eagles in winter. As you traverse the banks of this historic river, remember that you are following in the footsteps of Alexander Wilson and John James Audubon.

DELAWARE BAYSHORE AND INTERIOR FORESTS

It is now time to work our way up Delaware Bay, the third act of our Cape May birding play. And just as the third act of a play usually ties it all together, the vast and pristine Delaware Bayshore is what ties all of Cape May together. Not only do Delaware Bay and the bayshore tie New Jersey to the Delmarva Peninsula (both physically and for migrant birds), through the vast forest of Belleplain and Great Cedar Swamp, they also connect the Cape to the Atlantic Coast—a greenbelt routing birds north in the spring and south in the fall. Delaware Bay connects us in time too. To bird the bayshore is to step into the past, far from the frenetic pace of the Jersey Shore and even Cape May, to enjoy a life that is far less harried, less complicated, and less urban than the modern Cape. Finally, the bayshore connects us to the future—tying up the opportunities ahead for birds and

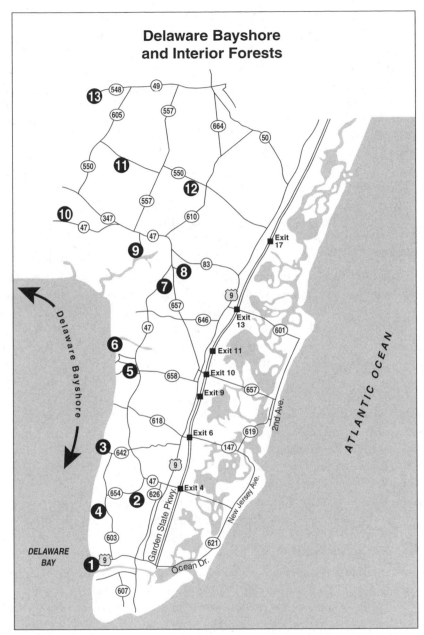

Delaware Bayshore and Interior Forests

1. North of the Cape May Canal
2. Cape May County Airport
3. Norbury's Landing
4. Villas WMA
5. Cape May NWR headquarters
6. Reeds Beach
7. CMBO Gardens in Goshen

8. Beaver Swamp WMA
9. Jakes Landing
10. The Nature Conservancy's Eldora Nature Preserve
11. Belleplain State Forest
12. Woodbine Airport
13. Weatherby Road

birders. The Delaware Bayshore, with its tens of thousands of acres of protected land—public and private open space—offers hope that the Cape
May phenomenon and the Cape May bird experience can be guaranteed
for many generations to come.

Although the lower portion of New Jersey's Delaware Bayshore—the
portion in southern Cape May County—is fairly highly developed, the
remainder is largely rural, undisturbed, and, in many places, breathtakingly
scenic. From Norburys Landing north and west through Cumberland
County and into much of Salem County the bayshore contains vast salt
and brackish marshes and tidal rivers. In northern Cape May County and
into Cumberland County, these waters are bounded by extensive forests of
hardwood, riparian swamps, and coastal holly hammocks. On the higher
ground, pine-oak forests resemble those of the Pine Barrens. In western
Cumberland County and into Salem County, the forests give way to open
areas and some of the most extensive agricultural areas in the state.

The Delaware Bay Estuary contains some 405,000 acres of wetlands.
And even though 25 percent of those are altered or degraded, the remainder is prime habitat for myriad fish, birds, and other wildlife. In fact, the
estuary has been classified as a "wetland of international importance" by
the Ramsar Convention, a global environmental body, and a vital component of the Western Hemisphere Shorebird Reserve Network. Most tidal
wetlands are under public ownership, managed for wildlife, and easily
enjoyed by birders.

The Delaware Bayshore plays a major role in Cape May birding. While
many autumn migrants are routed down the Atlantic coast, the famous
morning flight routes them back up the bay to rich and varied habitats and
feeding opportunities. It's where many fallouts end up and where many of
the hawks enjoyed overhead at Cape May spend the night or a week or
maybe even the winter. Due to the forested interior greenbelt, the bayshore
is in fact the sending district for Cape May migrants, routing them both to
and from Cape May Point. The bayshore is where many of the Atlantic
side's herons, egrets, gulls, and terns feed before returning to nightly
Atlantic coastal rookeries. So too, many Delaware Bayshore shorebirds
roost nightly on Atlantic barrier beaches such as Stone Harbor Point.

There is an interconnectedness between the coast and the bayshore. It
is a matrix of ecological dependence—you couldn't have one without the
other—and Cape May wouldn't be what it is without such key backup
areas. Although several parts of the matrix are strained, constrained, and
impacted by growth and development, the Delaware Bay piece is intact—a
key and wonderful part of the foundation on which Cape May is based. It
was true in Witmer Stone's day—he readily considered the bayshore part of
Old Cape May—and it remains so today. If there will always be a Cape

May, it is because we have managed to conserve and protect so much of the incomparable Delaware Bayshore.

JUST NORTH OF THE CAPE MAY CANAL

Beyond the Cape May Canal, in the area that lies just across the deep channel from Higbee Beach, are several areas of interest to birders. These include the small Lower Township David Douglass Park, the Delaware Bay beaches and remnant dunes in North Cape May, Bennett Bogs, and Cold Spring Village. Among these Cape May outliers, David Douglass Park, sometimes called Canal Park, is the one that receives the most coverage by birders.

David C. Douglass Memorial Rotary Park is located next to the Cape May–Lewes Ferry terminal and includes the north jetty at the western entrance to the canal. The main attraction here is the ferries themselves. The constant docking churns up a lot of water, and the big propellers of the boats create constant upwellings of mud, benthic organisms, and small fish. Gulls and terns are always attracted to this churning water. It is almost always here that the first Laughing Gull of the season is seen in early March; likely as not, the last lingering Laughing Gull is also found here, possibly on the Cape May Christmas Bird Count. More importantly, Black-headed and Little Gulls are annual here in winter and early spring, usually found with Bonaparte's Gulls and sometimes remaining for a week or two. Roseate Tern has been found among the many Forster's Terns here in spring.

The beach and jetty here are good spots to watch for pelagic birds coming out of Delaware Bay after storms—both coastal nor'easters and hurricanes. Several Black-capped Petrels and Band-rumped Storm-Petrels were seen here in the immediate wake of Hurricane Bertha in 1996 (they were also viewed from Sunset Beach, at the Concrete Ship). The beach can be good for shorebirds at low tide and the jetty at high tide if there are no fishermen. Piping Plovers are sometimes seen here in early spring, and the small dunes can fill with sparrows in fall. Look for the morning flight overhead on early fall mornings. Also work the sandy, scrubby areas along the road that leads to the park. Finally, the beaches and small jetties to the north, in North Cape May, should be checked. Although never as good for birds as those farther north (Miami, Norburys), they sometimes hold sea ducks and Purple Sandpipers in winter, gull roosts year-round, and terns in summer. We remember a tame Upland Sandpiper here sitting on a picnic bench at a dune walkover one April. You're still close to Cape May Point, so anything is possible.

The second area just north of the canal is Bennett Bogs. Bennett Bogs Preserve is primarily of interest to botanists. It is New Jersey Audubon's oldest sanctuary (now managed jointly with TNC), established in 1950 to protect the vernal bogs and the numerous rare plants they support, such as Rattlesnake Master, Pine Barrens Gentian, Muhly's Dropseed, Small's Yellow-eyed Grass, and Snowy Orchid (sadly, gone since 1988, probably due to encroaching development and resultant change in water quality and level). Bennett Bogs is of interest to birders for the excellent songbird fall-out that can occur there. In fall, it is a recipient of some of the morning flight leaving Higbee Beach. In spring, the rich old oaks, black willows, and Red Maples attract good numbers of bright songsters. Mississippi Kites have been known to roost here in late spring and early summer too. Bennett Bogs is not a primary Cape May spot, but it provides a good change of pace and scenery.

A final stop just north of the canal might be Historic Cold Spring Village, which is owned and operated by a non-profit educational organization. It is a historic village with arts, crafts, food, exhibits, displays, and events. Numerous historically themed festivals are held here among the mostly original buildings (most have been moved to the site and painstakingly restored). The draw for birders are the big old shade trees and the migrants they attract in spring and fall. A self-guided nature trail follows Bradner's Run through a swamp forest on the village's southern edge. A trail brochure is available at the admission gatehouse. The County Cold Spring Bike Path runs past the property, and you can follow this north or south for pleasant migration birding in spring and fall. Sometimes, when Cape May Point is dead, fallout has occurred farther up the Cape. Small pockets of migrants can occur anywhere in the county in spring and fall.

Birding the Site

From Cape May, cross the Cape May Canal on Seashore Road/Route 626, and proceed to the traffic light on Sandman Boulevard/Route 9 (also signed as Ferry Road). Turn left, following signs to the Cape May–Lewes Ferry. The field immediately on your left is preserved open space but leased for farming, so not open to walking access. Mississippi Kites often hunt over this field, high among the gulls, in late spring and early summer. If fallow, the field edges can be good for sparrows. If freshly plowed, the field can hold shorebirds in spring particularly after rain, principally Black-bellied and Semipalmated Plovers. To best view this field, take the next left which is Shunpike Road/Route 644, and park on the roadside and scan.

Proceed west on Sandman Boulevard. Two miles west from the intersection of Route 626 and Sandman Boulevard, the entrance to the Cape May–Lewes Ferry terminal bends off to the left. This is where you would enter if you wanted to take the "poor man's" pelagic boat trip across Delaware Bay in the hope of seeing seabirds. (Note: Obey the speed limit all along Sandman Boulevard.) A photo ID is required for a ferry ticket, and your vehicle registration must be up-to-date. Proceed past the ferry entrance road and follow Lincoln Boulevard 0.2 mile to the dead end on Delaware Bay. You can park here and walk south on the beach to the canal and **David Douglass Park.** Or, take a left turn onto Beach Drive and drive south to the parking lot next to the ferry terminal. There is a small deck overlooking the water and there are portable toilets here year-round. Walk right to the jetty and beach. You are directly across from Higbee Beach here. Check for gulls roosting on the ferry lawn (Common Black-headed and Franklin's Gulls have been seen here) and for birds feeding in the turmoil of the ferry props. Ferries arrive or depart about once an hour in winter and much more frequently in summer, but idling ferries churn water too. Check to see what birds are following the newly arriving ferries at the canal entrance; gannets, jaegers, and even Black-legged Kittiwakes are possible. If looking for storm-driven birds in the wind and rain, you can park in the western-most parking spaces to bird from your car. There is a fair view of the bay, but not as good a view as at Sunset Beach.

Leaving David Douglass Park, you can bird your way north up the bayshore along Beach Drive, checking jetties as you go. This is the area where the first settlement in Cape May County was located, the whaling village of Town Bank. To reach **Bennett Bogs,** return on Sandman Boulevard to the third traffic light, which is Shunpike Road/Route 644. Make a left onto Shunpike. Travel 1.5 miles north, crossing Town Bank Road/Route 648 and Fishing Creek Road/Route 639, to the small parking lot on your right. If you reach Tabernacle Road/Route 647, you've gone about 0.1 mile too far. Walk the vague trail along the edges of the bog to bird for passerines on migration. Enjoy the plants and butterflies here too. Boots are a necessity here at any season, except in drought years. High grass is possible, so be alert for ticks.

To proceed to **Historic Cold Spring Village,** continue north on Shunpike 0.1 mile to Tabernacle Road/Route 647. Make a right and go 0.7 mile to Seashore Road/Route 626. Make a right onto Seashore Road. In 0.2 mile turn left at Bennetts Crossing Road to reach Route 9. At Route 9 turn right. In 0.5 mile the entrance to Historic Cold Spring Village will be on your right. Pull in and park. The bike path and walking path are near this entrance. Walk the edge of the parking area to look and listen for migrants. Pay the entrance fee, pick up a copy of the Bradner's Run Nature Trail brochure, and walk among the wonderful old buildings and along the nature trail in search of additional migrants. (A second public entrance is on Seashore Road/Route 626.) To reach our next location, the Cape May County Airport, head back north on Route 9 0.5 mile. Turn left at Bennetts Crossing to reach Seashore Road/Route 626. At Seashore Road turn right. Continue 1.2 mile to the traffic light at Breakwater Road/Route 613. Turn left onto Breakwater Road and follow the signs to the airport, 0.4 mile ahead. Or return to Shunpike and make a right. Follow it until it ends at Breakwater. The airport entrance road is across the intersection.

CAPE MAY COUNTY AIRPORT

The County Airport, as many call it (others still call it Wildwood Airport), represents a unique habitat type for the southern Jersey Cape—a vast grassland, meadow, dry-field area. As with most airports, it is an artificially created and maintained short-grass prairie, but as such, it provides a habitat type that is rare in the region, shared only by the Woodbine, Millville, and Atlantic City airports. The County Airport is sizable, and despite a long history of cargo and commuter service, it is now used only by private aircraft. There is an office and industrial park and a large aircraft renovation facility. The airfield currently hosts an aviation museum that commemorates the U.S. Naval Air Station Wildwood, established early in World War II to train naval aviators. The museum and the aircraft are located in the original hangar, and it is worth a stop for anyone interested in aviation or World War II. A restaurant and restrooms are adjacent to the museum in the old airport control tower building.

For birders, the County Airport offers rare grassland birding possibilities. Access is very limited—you must bird from behind the parking area fence—but here and Woodbine Airport are the only places in Cape May County where you can still find breeding Horned Larks (they once bred on bare dune areas on the barrier islands even into the mid-1970s). Apparently, there is still a pair of American Kestrels that breed here—possibly the only pair left in all of Cape May County. A few pairs of Eastern Meadowlarks may still breed too and are usually present during migration.

Scissor-tailed Flycatcher has been found at the Cape May County Airport.

Grasshopper Sparrows are reported but probably don't breed there because the grass is mowed too short to support them. Expect American Pipits in migration and possibly in winter. Lapland Longspurs and Snow Buntings are possible in late fall and winter.

A number of rare birds have been found at the County Airport. Say's Phoebe, Scissor-tailed Flycatcher, and Western Kingbird have all been seen along the runways and fences. Anhinga and Swainson's Hawk have been seen soaring high overhead. This is significant because the County Airport is rarely birded. The airport is also worth checking during the high tides of coastal storms and hurricanes, when shorebirds are forced to seek high ground away from flooded beaches and meadows. American Golden Plover, Hudsonian Godwit, Whimbrel, and others have been seen in these conditions, along with hundreds of Black-bellied Plovers. Search for Upland Sandpipers during migration in April and primarily in July and August. Buffbreasted Sandpipers are possible in late August or early September, but again, the area is big and access is limited; a scope and luck are required here. Just north of the airport there is an opportunity for swamp forest birding off Fulling Mill Road in a section of Cape May County Park South.

Birding the Site

Follow the directions given earlier for access from Historic Cold Spring Village, or follow Seashore Road/Route 626 from Cape May to Breakwater Road. Breakwater is 2.4 miles north of the intersection of Sandman Boulevard/Route 9 and Route 626. Make a left on Breakwater, following Airport and NAS Wildwood Aviation Museum signs. Go 0.4 mile to the airport entrance. Follow signs to the museum and proceed to the administration building and restaurant beyond. Park in the smal lot by the restaurant and bird from behind the chain-link fence. Do not go beyond the fence for any reason. If security stops you, explain that you are birding. Scan runways and grassy verges; in particular, check runway light fixtures, towers, and windsocks for perched Horned Larks, American Kestrels, and Upland Sandpipers. In spring, listen for the high, tinkling notes of the aerial courtship of larks overhead. When you leave the parking lot, there are a few more views of the airfield from the road that leads west, but soon after you reach the woods, this road is posted. Check areas around industrial buildings too. The airport is large—a big patch of green on the Cape May map.

Swamp forest birding off **Fulling Mill Road** is excellent. Fulling Mill Road/Route 654 runs from Route 47 west of Rio Grande to the Villas and follows the north side of the airport property. It passes through a dense, deep, wet swamp—part of the headwaters of Fishing Creek. The airport property on the south side of the road is fenced and completely off-limits but the north side of Fulling Mill Road is part of Cape May County Park South and open for walking access (although there are few trails). You will likely see orange private property warning signs with the words "private property" and "trespassing for any purpose" crossed out and the words "hunting, fishing, trapping is strictly forbidden" left. The spot is indeed open for birding. Many of the southern swamp-forest breeders nest in the wet woods here: Prothonotary and Kentucky Warblers and Northern Parulas. Broad-winged Hawks nest here, too. Barred Owl are numerous, and it may be the last place in Cape May County where Red-shouldered Hawks still breed (many World Series of Birding teams include Fulling Mill Road on their route). Although rarely birded in the fall, it should be excellent then, too. The best area along the road begins 1 mile west of Route 47 and continues for another mile beyond that. The dawn chorus in May and June is wonderful.

There is a small and easily overlooked parking lot at this site; it's on the north side of the road quite close to the airport runway (1.5 miles east of Bayshore Road in the Villas, 0.9 mile west of Route 47 near Rio Grande). Signage in the lot directs visitors to a set of nature trails (mostly old fire breaks). If you don't use the lot, be sure to park well off the road; the shoulders are narrow and the traffic can be heavy.

Fulling Mill Stream crosses Fulling Mill Road and flows north into the vast Fishing Creek marsh complex, now largely protected as part of Cape May County Park South. A few interpid adventurers bird the creek by kayak, launching from Bayshore Road/Route 603 where it crosses Fishing Creek, about 1 mile north of Fulling Mill Road. Pied-billed Grebe, Common Moorhen, and Least Bittern all bred here in the past and perhaps still do. On the water, heading upstream, a *Phragmites*-choked section opens up into a healthy freshwater marsh, eventually becoming a Red Maple-dominated swamp forest. This is truly a rarely birded Cape May spot. Who knows what might be here.

BAYSHORE BEACHES AND NORBURYS LANDING

The beaches of Delaware Bay differ considerably from those on the Atlantic side. Not nearly as wide, and with much coarser sand, they are backed by bulkheads and houses south of Norburys Landing and salt marshes farther north. The beaches themselves may be a bit steeper in profile, but beyond the meager surf, the water remains very shallow for a good distance—many hundreds of yards in some places. These shallows allow for vast mudflats at low tides; sometimes the water is half a mile or more from the beach. The water itself usually lacks the crystal-clear quality of the Atlantic side. Phytoplankton, zooplankton, and mud—not pollution—produce the brownish, seemingly dirty color. In strong northwest winds, a steep chop develops and turns the water a thick brown.

These shallows and the wealth of plankton, clams, oysters, and fish make the bayshore beaches highly popular with shorebirds, wading birds,

Shallow water along the coast of the Delaware Bay creates vast mudflats during low tide.

gulls, and terns. Yet surprisingly, the bounty of the bay beaches has yet to become particularly popular with birders. The bay beaches remain an underbirded part of the Cape May scene. They are visited fairly frequently in May for the shorebirds and horseshoe crabs, but rarely by anybody else for the rest of the year. These beaches are almost deserted, except in summer, making them likely places for discoveries to be made.

It's more than 10 miles from the ferry terminal and David Douglass Park area north to Kimbles Beach (south of Reeds Beach), the next spot that gets regular coverage. Except for stretches north of Pierce's Point, access is good—mostly street-end birding. The best way to bird these areas is to park and walk—a good sunrise or sunset walk in summer and an invigorating hike on cold winter days. Large roosting groups of gulls, terns, and skimmers feed on these vast flats, and herons and egrets frequently feed in the shallow pools left by the receding tides. A few Bald Eagles feed on these flats daily from fall through spring, and peregrines visit them every day in fall. Look for Brown Pelicans in summer, either roosting on the flats or cruising offshore. Dozens of Osprey fish offshore here in spring and summer, carrying their catches back to Atlantic-side nests. Shorebirds are the major attraction. May is certainly best, but they can be found year-round. Expect Black-bellied and Semipalmated Plovers throughout the fall; many Dunlins and Sanderlings remain in winter. A few oystercatchers breed north of Norburys, and Willet are abundant April through August. Look for Little Gulls and Black-headed Gulls among the Bonaparte's in late winter and early spring. North of Norburys, Seaside and Saltmarsh Sharp-tailed Sparrows are in the marshes behind the dunes. Marsh Wrens are numerous in the summer, and a very few remain in winter. Clapper Rails abound in spring, summer, and fall; a few "mud hens" winter too.

Birding the Site

There is no one best spot, nor even a wrong one here. Beaches are good for shorebirds from around the Cox Hall Creek outfall in Villas north beyond Norburys Landing. The Miami Beach section of the Villas is one of the best areas (north and south of Miami Avenue), and Norburys Landing is easily the location most visited by birders. Flocks of shorebirds are spotty and move around a lot in response to tides (and people and dogs), so you need to search them out.

From Fulling Mill Road/Route 654, drive east until you reach Route 47, just north and west of Rio Grande. Turn left (north) onto Route 47 and drive 1.7 miles to the Green Creek traffic light. (If you are leaving from Cape May, take Route 109 and Route 9 north to Route 47; you can also reach Route 47 via the GSP at Exit 4. Turn left onto Route 47 and go 2.9 miles north to the second traffic light.) Turn left at the Green Creek light onto Bayshore Road/Route 642, formerly known as Norburys Landing Road. In 1 mile, at a blinking light, the road jogs hard left and becomes Bayshore Road (Route 603). Go straight at this blinking light on Millman Boulevard for 0.9 mile to dead-end at **Norburys Landing**, overlooking the Delaware Bay. Park and enjoy the viewing area, with benches and seasonal shorebird signage. All the beaches on the Delaware Bay are roped off and closed to public access from the middle of May through the first week in June to protect feeding shorebirds from disturbance. Road ends and observation areas like Norburys Landing offer excellent viewing opportunities from behind the ropes. Outside of this period, you can walk left and enjoy the beach and Delaware Bay at high tide and the extensive flats at low tide. Walk the beach to the right (north) beyond the house (private property begins at the high-tide line) to enter a tract of the Cape May NWR.

Returning to the blinking light at Bayshore Road, go right. You will soon cross Fishing Creek Marsh, an area that historically held breeding Common Moorhen, Pied-billed Grebe, and Least Bittern. They may still be there, but *Phragmites* now blocks virtually all view of this extensive marsh area. After 1 mile from the blinking light, turn right onto **Miami Avenue** and again go to the edge of the bay to find street-end parking. This is a particularly good stretch. A storm-water outfall here attracts Bonaparte's and sometimes Little Gull and Black-headed Gull in early spring; Franklin's Gull has been found here too. Sometimes it's a waiting game— waiting for time and tide and for birds to fly by. If you see bird concentrations to the south, seek them out on foot or by car.

Return to Bayshore Road and turn right (south). Follow Bayshore Road through the Villas for 2.1 miles. This route will take you through three traffic lights (Fulling Mill Road, East Greenwood Avenue, and Village

Road). Go 0.2 mile past the third light (at the Lower Branch of the Cape May County Library) and turn right onto Shawmount Avenue. Follow Shawmount 0.1 mile to a large brick entrance gate, the entrance to the new 239-acre **Villas WMA,** purchased in 2006. Proceed through the gate and follow signs for parking.

Asphalt paths wind through former golf-course fairways, now maintained as grasslands and savannahs, wooded copses, and a beautiful swamp forest along Cox Hall Creek. Barred Owls, Red-shouldered Hawks, Bald Eagles, and considerable songbird fallout have been seen here over the years by birders who golf. A Pileated Woodpecker was seen here one spring. Strategically situated in the autumn songbird morning flight corridor, this site is a welcome addition to an otherwise densely populated part of Cape May County.

One nearby stop in the Villas is **Lake Champlain,** a small freshwater lake of just a few acres that is usually full of ducks fall through late winter. All of the common puddle ducks have been seen here, as have most of the diving ducks. The lake offers safety for the birds (since hunting is not permitted in residential neighborhoods) and open water during freeze-ups. The birds' activity is generally enough to always keep a part of the water ice-free. Once during a midwinter incursion, eleven Red-necked Grebes were found here. It's good for gulls during freeze-ups, too; Iceland, Glaucous, and Black-headed Gulls have all been seen here. To reach Lake Champlain from the Villas WMA, return to Bayshore Road and turn left (north). Take either the first or second left. Proceed to Fourth Avenue and turn left. Follow this to Shadeland Avenue and turn right. Follow Shadeland to Bay Drive and turn left. Go 2 blocks to Champlain Drive and turn left. The lake is 0.1 ahead mile on the left. View it from the road, looking over the chain-link safety fence.

Return to Bayshore Road, turn left, and follow it north to Route 47. Or you might wander north along the Delaware Bay by taking almost any road to the left and parking at street-ends. Along the journey north through the Villas (or south through North Cape May) enjoy the many huge old oaks in yards, some dating back more than a hundred years, when this entire area was a rich oak forest along the bay. The tree-lined streets are known for excellent songbird fallout in spring and fall.

When you reach Route 47, turn left and head north. At 1.8 mile you will reach **High's Beach Road.** Turn left and go 0.8 mile; the road dead ends at the bay. There are extensive mudflats here during low tide. Except when the beaches are closed during May, a pleasant walk is to the left (south). You will soon pass the Rutgers University Oyster Research Laboratory (a sattelite facility of the large lab in Bivalve in Cumberland County). It's about 1 mile south to the mouth of Green Creek, a sluice.

Bird the mudflats, beach, and behind the beach as you walk. We almost guarantee you won't see another birder here.

Return to 47 and turn left. In just 0.2 mile you'll reach Pierce's Point Road. Go left for about a mile to the tiny community of **Pierce's Point.** Turn right along the beach to the last house and park. A walk north beyond the bulkhead offers a wonderful view of the beach, looking north to where Dias Creek empties into the bay. Like High's Beach, Pierce's Point can be excellent for shorebirds in the spring.

CAPE MAY NATIONAL WILDLIFE REFUGE

Unlike many national wildlife refuges that exist as one large property or unit, the Cape May NWR is an amalgam of separate sites. In time, most of the lands will be linked and, along with state wildlife lands and nongovernmental organization conservation holdings, will form a greenbelt stretching from Rio Grande north to the Great Egg Harbor River and beyond. Currently, the Cape May NWR consists of three distinct units: Two Mile Beach, Delaware Bayshore, and Great Cedar Swamp.

The Cape May NWR was established in 1989 with a targeted acquisition goal of 21,200 acres. Currently, the refuge is about half completed, with 11,500 acres purchased to date. Fortunately, the acquisition area has been enlarged several times to accommodate important properties as they became available. (Cape May NWR does not use eminent domain. All additions to the refuge are from willing sellers, and fair market value is negotiated and paid.) Acquisitions continue as funding becomes available, adding more land for Cape May birds and birders.

The Delaware Bay Division of Cape May NWR consists of a variety of habitats, almost a cross section of the county itself: Delaware Bay beaches to backing salt marshes to lowland forest and finally high and dry fields and pine-oak forests in the center of the peninsula. Such diverse habitats protect a variety of wildlife, including shorebirds, horseshoe crabs, Clapper Rails, muskrats, Great Horned Owls, American Woodcock, American Kestrel, migrant songbirds, and river otters. There are perhaps three major "themes" of the refuge's intent, design, and management: spring migrant shorebirds, American Woodcock, and the neotropical songbirds of spring and fall. Cape May NWR is the area from which many of Cape May Point's migrants stage on their way south in autumn, and it is the receiving area for Cape May morning flight migrants as they disperse to find quality feeding habitat. In spring, many northbound passerines overshoot Cape May proper and fall out in the rich woodlands in the heartland of Cape May County—acreage now protected by Cape May NWR. We cannot overemphasize the importance of this godsend area to the future of Cape May birds and birding.

The Cape May NWR boundary signs can be intimidating: "National Wildlife Refuge, Unauthorized Entry Prohibited." All NWRs use the same signs. The responsibility lies with the visitor to learn what activities are allowed and what is prohibited. In the case of Cape May NWR, walking access is permitted on all refuge lands except in a few spots where Area Closed signs are posted. Consider the boundary signs invitations to explore. Wildlife observation, nature study, hunting, and pets on leashes are permitted. Driving, bicycling, horseback riding, camping, campfires, feeding wildlife, and entering closed ares are prohibited. Most trails are mowed paths that follow old trails or dirt roads. Formal signed trails are minimal (but increasing). The refuge is open daily dawn to dusk. Seasonal hunting—September through February—for deer and migratory gamebirds is allowed in designated areas; if you visit during these months, call or stop in at the refuge headquarters on Kimbles Beach Road to find out what is being hunted where and what precautions you should take. Remember that no hunting is allowed on Sundays anywhere in New Jersey. At the headquarters you can also learn about new refuge acquisitions.

Birding the Site

You will encounter Cape May NWR signs at many places on the Cape, particularly as you cross the spine of Cape May County—on Indian Trail/ Route 618, Dias Creek Road/Route 612, Hand Avenue/Route 658, and along the Cape May Court House–Goshen Road/Route 615. Many parts of the refuge offer no formal birding access except roadside birding. (Information about access into the Great Cedar Swamp Division is covered in the Tuckahoe WMA site entry. Information about access to the Two Mile Beach Unit is covered in the Two Mile Beach entry.)

For access to the Delaware Bay Division, from the junction of Routes 9 and 47 in Rio Grande, go north on Route 47/Delsea Drive for 1.7 miles. Just north of Menz's Restaurant the NWR boundary signs on the right mark the **Wildwood Waterworks Tract,** a 312-acre acquisition made in 2005. Some fields here are still leased for farming—don't walk on crops if the fields are planted; follow field edges and woodland trails. The pumping station pond next to Route 47 is part of the tract and holds much potential. Osprey fish here in spring and fall.

Continue north on Route 47 for 1.1 miles to the Green Creek traffic light. Turn left onto Bayshore Road/Route 642. In 0.2 mile, just past the Green Creek Volunteer Fire Company, turn right into a small mowed parking lot to access the **Bayshore Tract.** A mowed trail crosses the field ahead and follows the edge of a wooded copse to the back corner of the field, where it enters a beautiful woodland and follows a dike into Green Creek Marsh. The fields can be great in summer for Yellow-breasted Chats,

Blue Grosbeaks, and Indigo Buntings and are exceptional in fall for sparrows and fallout warblers at the wood edges. Both Yellow-billed and Black-billed Cuckoos are found in the tract as breeders.

The dike across a corner of Green Creek Marsh offers excellent views ahead and to the right of an extensive area of dead trees (a result of Mosquito Commission flood-type management) where Red-headed Woodpeckers can be expected year-round. The view to the left of the dike takes in Green Creek Marsh and the Delaware Bay beaches and bay beyond. Migrant raptors use the dead trees as perches. Look for River Otter slides down the sides of the dike and otter scat, which is gray and contains many fish scales and tiny bones.

From the Bayshore Tract parking lot turn left and return to the traffic light at Route 47. Go straight across Route 47 onto Burleigh Avenue (it's actually a slight jog left and then straight). Continue 0.2 mile to the NWR boundary sign delineating the **Burleigh Tract** on the left. Park safely off the road on the field edge. Walk the mowed trail to the back of the first field, past an old farm pond, into a "hidden" field, and finally a short distance into wet woodlands. Expect good birding throughout the tract. Blue Grosbeaks and orioles breed here. Yellow-breasted Chats breed here and have been found here on the Christmas Bird Count. Migrant Bobolinks are found spring and fall. Good spring fallout can occur here. Sparrows are great on fall migration, and woodcock are seen here in fall and winter. The fields are excellent for butterflies in summer.

Return to Route 47 and turn right. Go 2.2 miles to the first traffic light. Turn right onto **Indian Trail Road**/Route 618, so named because it was once a Native American route from the Delaware Bay to the Atlantic marshes and beach. Proceed 1.2 miles and park on the shoulder just shy of the guardrail on the right side (south) of the road. The wet woodlands bounded by this guardrail are *the* place in Cape May County to hear (if not see) Kentucky Warblers in spring and early summer. There is an overgrown woodland road marked with The Nature Conservancy signage off to the right. Walk a short distance to get away from traffic noise (it's wise to go very early in the day, when it's usually quieter). Kentucky Warblers may be in the wet woodlands on either side of Indian Trail, although they are usually on the south side. Be patient and listen for the bird's song. You might even be rewarded with a view of this notorious skulker—at least *somebody* sees a Kentucky here every spring. These woodlands are also a key tract for many lowland swamp-forest breeders, including Ruffed Grouse (possibly now gone), Barred Owls, and Prothonotary Warblers. In your car, continue 0.5 mile on Route 618 to the power line right-of-way just past the guardrail. Park on the shoulder and walk south along the power line for additional birding. Return to Route 47 to continue to explore Cape May NWR, or follow Indian Trail Road to Route 9 to return South to Cape May. Just beyond Route 9 there is a northbound entrance onto the Garden State Parkway (but not a southbound one).

By far, one of the best hikes in the Cape May NWR's Delaware Bayshore Division is **Woodcock Trail** off Route 47 near Dias Creek. Here a parking area, kiosk, and well-planned trail beckon and offer a good overview of the various heartland habitats that the refuge so diligently protects. From the traffic light at the intersection of Route 47 and Indian Trail/Route 618, turn right onto Route 47 and go 1.4 miles. Look for Woodcock Lane, a residential street on the left (just after Dias Creek Road/Route 612, on the right and Bobwhite Lane on the left). Turn left onto Woodcock Lane and go 0.2 mile to the dead-end cul-de-sac. Park at the trailhead. Woodcock Trail begins here; it's a 1.5-mile trail, including spurs.

The trail first goes through lovely old-field habitat, now a rare habitat type on the Jersey Cape. Eastern Bluebirds nest in the boxes placed for them and winter here as well. Expect Song Sparrow, Field Sparrow, Carolina Wren, Northern Cardinal, Prairie Warbler, Blue Grosbeak, Indigo Bunting, and Yellow-breasted Chat in spring and summer. Look for American Kestrel on migration and abundant sparrows. Northern Shrike has wintered in these fields. Anywhere on the loop is a good spot to watch and listen for courting American Woodcock in late February through March. Watch for their towering display flights against the last glow of sunset. Expect Chuck-will's-widows here in the spring and summer; May and June is when they are most vocal. The booming of Great Horned Owls reverberates through these woodlands in December and January. Long-eared and Saw-whet Owls have both been found wintering in the woods around this field. Partway down the left side of the field, a 0.4-mile spur enters the forest and parallels the field, passing through dark hollies. This spur turns left at the back corner of the field and follows an old woodland road through a wonderful mixed forest with abundant holly, sassafras, and dogwood, as well as some magnificent old-growth Loblolly Pines towering above. Autumn and spring fallout can be excellent here. Expect Orchard and Baltimore Orioles, Scarlet Tanagers, and Yellow-billed and easily missed Black-billed Cuckoos in migration. In summer, expect Wood Thrushes, replaced in winter by Hermit Thrushes.

Follow the woodland trail (no longer a loop—now a spur) through the holly forest until you reach the salt marsh. Scan the edges for raptors at any season, and expect Clapper Rail and Marsh Wren in spring through fall. This is a high, dry marsh, and if you don't mind getting your feet wet, you can walk out into it for a view to the south and west toward Delaware Bay. This is a remote, quiet, tranquil place—far from the normal hustle and bustle of the Jersey Shore. Almost better than anywhere else, Woodcock Trail captures the feeling of Old Cape May—the relatively undisturbed forests that Witmer Stone so loved early in the twentieth century. It may not be the "birdiest" spot on the Cape, but it shouldn't be missed.

Return to the field. The mowed trail completely circles it, taking you back to the parking area. Return to Route 47. Go left and head north. In 0.5 mile, make a left onto Kimbles Beach Road. The Nature Conservancy's **Hands Landing Preserve Trail** begins at a mowed parking area on the left 0.1 mile ahead. This trail meanders through lovely woods paralleling the road and eventually reaches the Delaware Bay beachfront.

The headquarters of the Cape May NWR is on your left 0.1 mile further down Kimbles Beach Road. Stop by to obtain maps and information and to support the refuge. This length of lightly traveled **Kimbles Beach Road** is a good walk itself, passing through late succession fields and forests. Pay particular attention to the wires along the road. Expect Eastern Bluebirds and American Kestrels on migration, and Eastern Kingbirds in spring through fall. Scissor-tailed Flycatcher in spring and Say's Phoebe in fall have been seen sitting on the wires and in the fields here.

From headquarters, take **Songbird Trail,** a 0.6-mile loop that offers good open-field and woodland birding in any season. Behind headquarters, the trail connects to TNC's Hands Landing Preserve Trail. In front of the

Ruddy Ducks are winter regulars at Kimbles Beach.

headquarters, follow Songbird Trail across Kimbles Beach Road into a field on the north side. The trail crosses the field, passes through a hedgerow into a second large field, wanders west, meets up with a hard trail that's wheelchair accessible, crosses Kimbles Beach Road again into another field, and connects with the TNC trail. (The wheelchair-accessible trail can be accessed directly from Kimbles Beach Road by proceeding 0.1 mile beyond headquarters to a cinder parking lot on the right.)

From headquarters continue 0.9 mile to the road-end at the Delaware Bay. Park to the side of the road and avoid blocking private property. Walk in either direction to enjoy bayfront birding. This is a good spot for Brown Pelican in summer and Ruddy Duck in winter, among other divers. Check the marsh for Seaside Sparrows and Clapper Rails. Kimbles Beach can be as good as Reeds Beach for shorebirds and horseshoe crabs in spring. From the middle of May through the first week in June all Delaware Bay beaches are closed to public access, but enjoy good views from behind the signs and rope.

Return to Route 47. Go north for 0.5 mile and make a left onto **Cooks Beach Road** (just beyond the Cape May County Mosquito Commission complex). Drive about 1 mile until you dead-end at the beach. Here again, you can walk in both directions. Cooks Beach is another excellent spring shorebird beach. It is usually posted in May but offers good scope viewing. This is a good spot to get an up-close view of a horse-shoe crab—a few are usually trapped in the rubble of the old boat launch at the end of the road. Seaside Sparrows are abundant here, and both Salt-marsh and Nelson's Sharp-tailed Sparrows can be found on migration. Check the marsh area behind the beach and the meager dunes. Hint: The very high tides of autumn storms will push the birds out of the marsh and right to the edge of the dune, allowing exceptional views of these normal skulkers. Essentially, the tides flush the birds to you. We've seen Le Conte's Sparrow here under these flooded conditions.

Remember that at Kimbles and Cooks Beaches and from here north along the bay, expect the unexpected. Mississippi and Swallow-tailed Kites and American White Pelicans have been seen here following the leading line of the Delaware Bayshore either north or south. Anything is possible at these remore bay beaches, even a Yellow-nosed Albatross.

REEDS BEACH

In the past twenty-five years, Reeds Beach has changed in cachet, if not in physical appearance. It is still a sleepy little fishing village on the banks of Delaware Bay, the way the shore used to be. In the 1970s, birders rarely if ever visited Reeds Beach, except maybe for the Christmas Bird Count. But in the early 1980s, Reeds Beach changed dramatically in the eyes of birders when the May shorebirds were discovered by the earliest CMBO foot, boat, and aerial surveys.

Today, Reeds Beach is the epicenter of spring shorebirding. Delaware Bay horseshoe crabs and shorebirds are widespread—found from the Villas north beyond Fortescue in Cumberland County (and all along the Delaware shore, too), wherever sandy beaches are found. But Reeds Beach is still the prime destination for naturalists, because it is where the birds are most consistent and often the most abundant.

The Reeds Beach area is more than beaches and shorebirds, however. The rich salt marshes of Bidwell Creek (or Bidwell's Ditch, as the locals call it—the creek was dredged and channelized to allow turn-of-the-century shipbuilding) lie behind Reeds Beach, supporting an abundance of herons, egrets, ibis, and Clapper Rails, and vast clouds of Snow Geese in winter. Goshen Landing, north of Reeds, is quality salt marsh offering good birding at any season. Willet, Marsh Wrens, and Seaside Sparrows abound in summer, and winter proffers American Black Ducks, Snow Geese, abundant Northern Harriers and Red-tailed Hawks, daily Bald Eagles, and the occasional Golden Eagle. We once watched a successful stoop by a Golden Eagle on Snow Geese here in late February. Of note is that at Reeds Beach and Goshen Landing, you can enjoy vast bayshore panoramas—sweeping views of the scenic bayshore marshes, wooded islands, and peninsulas and the bold bayshore skies, ranging from the stark drama of winter snow squalls to the brilliant light shows of summer lightning storms out over the luminous Delaware Bay. When you bird on the bayshore, the backdrop is unequaled anywhere in New Jersey for its expanse, wildness, and unsullied landscapes. From Reeds Beach north and west through Salem County, you will be seeing and enjoying the real New Jersey, where Old Cape May and New Cape May are still, miraculously, one and the same.

Birding the Site

From Cooks Beach Road, go north on Route 47 for 0.3 mile and make a left onto Reeds Beach Road/Route 655. In 0.6 mile, just as the road bends to the right, there is a small, wooded freshwater pond on your right. Pull to the side of the road to view the pond through several openings in the vegetation. (This is private property, so do not leave the roadside. Also, don't park on the far side of the road in residents' front yards.) This small pond has been astounding over the years, and large flocks of Green-winged Teal are here in fall through early spring (best), as long as it remains unfrozen. In spring and fall there is usually a night-heron roost in the trees to the left, and many herons and egrets feed here. Belted Kingfishers often rattle across the pond, seemingly never happy with your presence. The real draw is the Glossy Ibis—in spring, many dozens both feed and loiter here. White-faced Ibis have also been found here in May on at least three occasions. In 2005 two White-faced Ibis were present—an adult and an immature. This unnamed pond is always worth a stop.

Continue along the road, which soon crosses the salt marsh. Bird the creeks and ponds along the way. At 0.3 mile from the pond, the road crosses a small creek. Pull off on the left roadshoulder (south side of the road) and use your car as a blind. At low tide this creek is an excellent spot to watch for bathing and feeding Clapper Rails, especially in spring before the marsh grasses have grown tall enough to hide the creek. Just ahead (0.1 mile) is the Delaware Bay. Wind to the right onto Beach Avenue (unmarked), which parallels the bay. Drive slowly and be alert for Dia-mondback Terrapins hatchlings and adult females seeking sandy areas to lay their eggs. Keep terrapins in mind as you travel all the beachfront roads along the Delaware Bay. In summer, winter, and fall, you can stop any-where to view the beach and bay, but from mid-May through the first week in June, the New Jersey Division of Fish and Wildlife posts and ropes off these areas—not only to prevent entry onto the beach, but also to keep you from stopping your car. (Currently, high tide laps at the road, so cars left there would flush shorebirds.)

Don't despair—a viewing plat-form is found (only in May) about 0.5 mile farther north, just before you dead-end at Bidwell Creek and the jetty.

There is limited parking at the end of the road (enough for bird-ers in fall or winter), but in May, we recommend that you park in the marina parking lot to your right. This is Smoky's Marina, and there is a $1 charge for parking (honor system) for as long as you like. We support this small fee; it is an example of ecotourism help-ing the local economy. Since this parking arrangement with Smoky's Marina was worked out by state ENSP biologists in the 1990s,

The viewing platform at Reeds Beach provides spectacular spring shorebird opportunities.

Reeds Beach residents have been far more tolerant of birders than they were when birders blocked the length of Beach Avenue.

It's a short walk to the viewing platform at the edge of the dunes overlooking the bay beach. From May 15 to June 1, expect abundant Red Knot, Sanderling (many in bright breeding colors), Dunlin, Ruddy Turnstone, and Semipalmated Sandpiper. Although it's easy to become lost in the pageant, be sure to look for oddities too. Curlew Sandpiper, Ruff, and Red-necked Phalarope have been found here recently, and a probable "Siberian" Red Knot—the bright Asian race. Also look through the sometimes thousands of gulls. Lesser Black-backed Gull (annual in spring in numbers on the bay, mostly in first summer plumage or heavy molt), Iceland Gull, and Franklin's Gull have been seen here and nearby on the bayshore in late spring. Enjoy the frenetic feeding by flocks of noisy Laughing Gulls. Noisy Boat-tailed Grackles breed at Reeds Beach, and search the tideline for horseshoe crab eggs. A Western Grebe was found here in the Delaware Bay waters off Reeds Beach in May 2006.

The jetty offers an alternative view of the beach and bay. The beach is closed from mid-May through the first week in June to protect feeding shorebirds from disturbance. At other seasons you can walk the beach southward. Scan north of the jetty in May and at any season. Search (by scope) the mudflats and sand spits stretching north toward Dennis Creek. These are very good in May for shorebirds and in fall and winter for ducks and Snow Geese. In winter, scope the bay for rafts of waterfowl—mostly scaup, but also Common Goldeneye, Ruddy Duck, Red-breasted Merganser, Bufflehead, and even Canvasback. In some winters rafts of scoters are found here. Check the marsh for Northern Harriers, the odd Rough-legged Hawk, Bald Eagles, or Short-eared Owls (at dusk and on overcast days). Snowy Owl has been seen here too. Snow Buntings are scarce but possible in the grassy area next to the jetty.

Viewing opportunities are also available at the south end of Reeds Beach; simply follow the sandy road south past the houses until you reach a dead-end turnaround. (High tides sometimes flood this turnaround; if flooded, back up and return to the paved road.) Walk south along the beach (except in spring) to the small creek entrance. The grassy, weedy zone behind the beach on the edge of the salt marsh is particularly good here for "salt sparrows" at high tide.

From late April through June, horseshoe crabs come ashore in scores to mate and lay eggs. They use the highest nighttime tides, which fall on the full or new moons, to help carry them onto the upper beach. Refer to a calendar and a tide chart and plan to visit the beachfront by the Reeds Beach jetty or at the south end (or on the edge of Cape May Harbor in front of the Nature Center of Cape May). Bring a flashlight and be mesmerized by the site of this ancient ritual.

Retrace your steps to Route 47. Make a left onto 47 and drive north 2.6 miles to **Goshen Landing Road** on your left. It is just beyond the post office, and opposite where Route 615 goes off to your right. Drive west on Goshen Landing Road. Scan the pastures to your right for Bobolink, Eastern Meadowlark, Eastern Bluebird, and sparrows in season. Amazingly, both Black-headed Grosbeak and Rose-breasted Grosbeak have successfully wintered (in separate years) at a feeder near here. About 1 mile from Route 47, the paved road becomes gravel. We recommend that you park here and walk the rest of the way. (Pull well off to the right, and don't block the driveway here.) Road conditions can vary from here on. If recently graded, it's easily driven, but most often it's very rutted, and it's frequently flooded by high tides. Boots are almost a necessity here at any season. Walk a short way to clear the woods and scan the salt marsh. A fairly close Osprey nest platform on the left is usually active in season. One year Great Horned Owls raised young in this nest, January through April. Willet, Clapper Rails, and Marsh Wrens are abundant here in summer (as are greenhead flies). Salt marsh ponds often attract feeding herons, egrets, and shorebirds. Look for raptors on and over the tree lines in both directions. The red cedar grove can hold migrants in spring and fall. It's private property, so bird from the gravel road.

Walk to the end of the road where it dead-ends at Goshen Creek. At low tide, the extensive dock pilings sticking out of the bank attest to the area's shipbuilding heritage. In summer, seek Seaside Sparrows and maybe Saltmarsh Sharp-tailed Sparrows. In fall and early winter, this spot has produced Sedge Wrens on a number of occasions—perhaps the best site in Cape May County for this bird. Marsh Wrens, common in summer, winter here in small numbers. Expect puddle ducks in winter, mainly Mallards and black ducks, and either thousands of Snow Geese or none—flocks are somewhat nomadic on the bayshore winter marshes, and it can be feast or famine. Across Goshen Creek is where Black-necked Stilts nested in 1993 but not subsequently. Black Rails nested here into the 1990s but are apparently gone today. They and the Black-necked Stilts were probably victims of Mosquito Commission marsh management flooding. Goshen Landing is still a good spot to listen for rails in spring and summer. Expect choruses of Clapper Rails and Virginia Rails from the upland edges. Black Rails are still possible during spring migration (migrants vocalize in spring), as are Soras. Once, during the World Series of Birding (WSB), we had Yellow Rails here. During another WSB, a singing Sedge Wren entertained us at our midnight starting gate at the always productive Goshen Landing Road.

THE CMBO'S CENTER
FOR RESEARCH AND EDUCATION

New Jersey Audubon's Cape May Bird Observatory Center for Research and Education (CRE) has a title as lengthy as its mission is big. In fact, the goals and mission became so large and urgent that the CMBO outgrew its small facility at the Northwood Center in Cape May Point, where it had been headquartered since 1976. Following a lengthy fund-raising effort, the CMBO opened the doors to its modern center by the bay, the CRE. The Northwood Center remains an integral part of the CMBO, operating as a bookstore, gift shop, and "birding central"—with a key role in the rapid dissemination of birding information. The CRE is where the all-important research arm of the NJAS is headquartered and where both NJAS's and CMBO's educational efforts are based. Today, a staff of thirteen (swelling with seasonal researchers, counters, and interpretive naturalists in season) is working from Goshen to spread knowledge throughout New Jersey and even beyond.

For the birder, the CRE offers a wealth of information, an up-to-date and well-stocked bookstore, an amazing array of optics (and knowledgeable people to talk about them), and bathrooms which are scarce along the Delaware Bayshore. More to the point, the 26-acre CRE has a number of excellent birding possibilities. The property has salt marsh, pine-oak forest, and a meadow managed for wildlife. The meadow has nesting bluebirds, Tree Swallows, and House Wrens; in some years there is a small Purple Martin colony (but not every year, despite yeoman efforts to establish them). Indigo Bunting and Blue Grosbeak nest in the wooded edge. The meadow area may be the most reliable spot we know for Orchard Orioles; they're found in the pines or around the building virtually constantly from May through July.

The backyard habitat gardens are second to none. Established as a teaching and learning tool, they abound in native plants, nectar sources, and host plants for butterflies. A healthy dragonfly pond attracts scores of frogs too. More than sixty-five species of butterflies have now been seen in the CRE gardens and meadow. A plethora of bird feeders are in operation year-round, attracting Rose-breasted Grosbeak and Indigo Bunting in spring and sparrows in fall through spring. The extensive hummingbird feeders (backed by the attractant gardens) are amazing. Hummingbirds are seen daily from mid-April through early

October, but from late June through early September, they can be astounding. Up to thirty-five Ruby-throated Hummingbirds have been seen at once here—numbers usually more indicative of Texas coast feeders. Both Allen's and Calliope Hummingbirds have been seen here in fall, and Rufous/Allen's types are almost annual in fall.

The best bird ever found at the CRE, a Northern Lapwing, was a flyover at the champagne breakfast kick-off event the day the center opened on January 1, 1997. It dropped into farm fields to the south of the CRE and was seen by hundreds of birders over the next four days. This lapwing was the first record for Cape May County and only the second for New Jersey of this dramatic Eurasian plover. Clay will never forget standing next to Michael O'Brien, who was the first to sight the incoming bird. Excitement, incomprehension, and certainty were evident as he quietly said, "I think this is a lapwing." The stated missions of the CRE may be research, education, and conservation, but pure fun can be a component too.

Birding the Site:

From Route 47 in Goshen (where both Goshen Landing Road and Route 657 intersect with Route 47), drive north on Route 47 for 2 miles. The entrance for the CRE is on the right as the road curves right. The CRE can also be reached by driving south on Route 47 for 1 mile from the traffic light at the intersection of Routes 47 and 657 (Court House-South Dennis Road). The entrance is on the left, just past Sluice Creek. Park in the stone parking lot and bird (and butterfly) the property.

Large native trees on either side of the parking lot often hold orioles, Blue Grosbeaks, and Cedar Waxwings in spring and summer. A wheelchair acccessible paved walkway, beginning on the left side of the building, winds past the feeding station, through butterfly and hummingbird garden beds, to a pergola overlooking the meadow, past the dragonfly pond, and to a circle-of-friends garden at the end of the walkway. Arbors and the pergola (covered in wildlife plantings like Coral Honeysuckle, Trumpet Creeper, and Virginia Creeper) offer shade, seating, and close looks at Ruby-throated Hummingbirds in season.

Mowed trails off the paved walkway explore the wildflower and grass meadow. They pass by brush piles, overlook the marsh, pass under

continues on next page

large pines (where a Yellow-bellied Sapsucker often winters—look for its ring of drilled holes around the huge Sweet Gum trunk on the marsh edge), and follow the forested edge of the property, rich in native trees, shrubs, and vines. Ruby-throated Hummingbirds nest in the pine stand and elsewhere on the property. Ticks and chiggers are prevalent, so it is wise to remain on the mowed paths.

The building's back deck offers an excellent view up Sluice Creek (a tributary to Dennis Creek) east toward Beaver Swamp WMA. The skies over Sluice Creek are a regularly used flyway. Raptors, including the resident pair of Bald Eagles from Beaver Swamp, are daily. In summer, flocks of herons, egrets, and ibis criss-cross the sky on their way to and from the bounteous bayshore marshes. Mississippi Kites have been seen here in spring and Golden Eagles in fall. Many Red-tailed Hawks and both Black and Turkey Vultures are daily overhead. ■

BEAVER SWAMP WILDLIFE MANAGEMENT AREA

Beaver Swamp WMA, created in 1964, is a state-owned and managed 2,922-acre wooded and wetlands swamp complex east of the CMBO Center for Reasearch and Education at the headwaters of Sluice Creek. This large area, along with Cape May NWR, serves as a crucial greenbelt that allows migrants to travel across the peninsula and into and out of the Cape May area more easily. Beaver Swamp is big, bounded on the west by Court House–South Dennis Road/Route 657, on the east by Route 9, and on the north by Route 83. Its uplands are pine-oak, holly, Sassafras, and American Beech; the extensive woodland swamps comprise dense Red Maple, Sour Gum, and Sweetbay Magnolia.

Access is limited (although ATVs and dirt bikes frequently find a way in), and there are no established trails. Nonetheless, birding is good along Beaver Dam Road and from the walking dike at the end of Beaver Dam Road. The impounded area of freshwater on the east side of the dike is an active beaver pond; a beaver lodge is located in the pond's southern corner. This pond, known by many as Clint's Millpond, is sizable and provides good birding at any season. In winter (if unfrozen) and spring, look for Ring-necked Ducks and Hooded and Common Mergansers. Migrant Pied-billed Grebes drop in to the pond and Wilson's Snipe to the wet edges. Wood Ducks are frequent in spring and fall and breed here. Belted Kingfishers have nested here—one of few places in Cape May where they breed. In summer, the pond holds wading birds and sometimes a few shorebirds—yellowlegs and Spotted and Solitary Sandpipers. This pond is probably the most reliable spot in Cape May County for Gull-billed Terns in summer. Forster's Terns are numerous. Bald Eagles occur here year-round and a Sandhill Crane has recently been resident here.

A sizable Bald Cypress can be seen if you look down Sluice Creek toward the Delaware Bay from the walking dike. This tree and a few others in the area have caused controversy—it is hotly debated whether they are native or were planted (across the bay in Delaware are native Bald Cypresses; these are generally assumed to be at the northern limit of their range).

Birding the Site

From the CMBO's CRE (be careful pulling out; there's a curve, and traffic can fly here), turn right and head north on Route 47 for 1 mile. At the first traffic light, turn right onto Court House–South Dennis Road/Route 657. In 0.2 mile, make a left onto Gravel Hole Road and immediately turn right onto Beaver Dam Road. Drive slowly through this residential area. When the paved road becomes gravel, you are in the WMA. You can park here and walk to enjoy forest birding (the first wet area on your right holds Prothonotary Warblers), or you can drive about 0.5 mile to the small parking area at the road end.

Walk around the guardrail and out onto the walking dike for a view of the freshwater pond on the left and the upper reaches of Sluice Creek and tidal salt marsh on the right. If the tide is low, look for Clapper Rails on the muddy banks of the creek. River Otters feed in the creek; look for their mud slides on the banks and distinctive gray and fish-bone-filled scat on the dike. Scan the pond for waterfowl, including breeding Wood Ducks. In late April through mid-August, Gull-billed Terns hunt the back of the pond almost every day, picking insects and frogs from the lily pads. Look for perched terns on logs, posts, duck blinds, and duck boxes. Forster's Terns, too, occur here in good numbers.

Look for a huge Bald Eagle nest in a dead tree on the right side of the back edge of the pond (in line with a distant radio tower). This nest was completed in 2004, and the eagles have been year-round residents of Beaver Swamp ever since. It is one of three or four active Bald Eagle nests in Cape May County and the only one visible from a public viewing area. Nest-building (actually, nest-sprucing-up) begins in December or January; incubation occurs through February or March. The young hatch late

Sluice Creek offers tidal salt marsh opportunities, including Clapper Rail.

March or April, becoming quite sizable and visible in the nest in May. They fledge in June or July. The adult eagles on this nest fledged two chicks in 2005, but none in 2006. This pond is an excellent place to canoe and kayak, but the back portion is closed from February 1 to July 31 to boat access because of the active eagle nest. Immature Bald Eagles from other areas are attracted to the pond and can sometimes be found roosting here. Osprey fish the pond regularly.

Yellow-throated Warblers nest in the pines along Beaver Dam Road. Pronthonotary Warblers nest in holes in the smaller dead trees around the pond, including those next to the parking lot. Ovenbirds, Wood Thrushes, Yellow Warblers, Great-crested Flycatchers, and Common Yellowthroats are common along the road; Pine Warblers are abudant.Check the pond for hunting Purple Martins, swallows, and Chimney Swifts. At the far end of the dike, an ancient corduroy road made of logs laid side by side enters the wet forest but is soon lost to deep water. The patch of woods here is excellent for breeding songbirds. A Pileated Woodpecker has been seen here, too.

In late April and May, huge numbers of Glossy Ibis gather to feed in the pond, often hidden in the emergent vegetation. Search among the Glossy Ibis for White-faced Ibis—two adults were seen here in 2006. Sluice Creek serves as a flyway all summer long, so expect commuting herons, egrets, and ibis overhead daily. Spring and summer bring native wildflowers to the pond: Fragant Water-lilies can cover much of the water's surface, offering excellent perches for dragonflies, damselflies, and frogs, including uncommon Carpenter Frogs (listen for their distinct hammering calls).

Along the water's edge, Pickerelweed attracts numerous butterflies. Rare Skippers can be seen here in July on blooming Pickerelweed along the walking dike.

Additional access to Beaver Swamp WMA is possible from a power-line right of way that crosses Route 646. To reach it, follow Beaver Dam Road back to Gravel Hole Road and turn left. Turn left immediately onto Route 657. Continue 2.8 miles to the intersection of Routes 657 and 646. Turn left onto Goshen-Swainton Road/Route 646. Drive 0.9 mile to the power line. Park and walk north. This access point is often used by hunters and illegal ATVs. The walk—a lengthy one—may produce Red-headed Woodpeckers; one or two pairs still breed in this area, perhaps refugees from the now-defunct colony in Cape May County Park. A Pileated Woodpecker was recently seen here.

Backtrack west on Route 646 to the intersection with Route 657. The extensive old fields south of the intersection are part of the **Lizard Tail Swamp Preserve,** an 850-acre site managed by The Nature Conservancy and co-owned by the New Jersey Department of Environmental Protection. These field are excellent for grassland birds in any season, but particulary sparrows and Eastern Meadowlarks in the fall. Wild Turkeys are common here. Look for American Kestrels in April and in September and October; they're often perched on roadside telephone wires. To walk the fields, park on the road shoulder. Or, to reach the preserve's entrance, turn left on Route 657 toward Cape May Court House and go 0.4 mile. Forest trails begin here. You can return to Cape May Court House and the GSP by turning left (south) on Route 657. Turn right (north) on Route 657 to reach Route 47 at the first traffic light. To continue north and west up the expansive Delaware Bayshore turn right here onto Route 47. To return to the CMBO CRE, turn left and continue one mile.

JAKES LANDING

We don't know who Jake was, but Jakes Landing was historically both a fisheries landing and a component of the extensive shipbuilding economy of historic Dennisville. Ships were constructed of the then-abundant Atlantic White-cedar; sizable coastal schooners were built here and floated to the bay on full-moon high tides.

Today, Jakes Landing is still a landing, an excellent boat ramp and kayak and canoe launching area. (Be aware that tides are swift in Dennis Creek. Also, a special launching permit is required both here and at the Tuckahoe River launch.) From Jakes Landing, it is about 1 mile by water back to Route 47 on both Dennis Creek and Sluice Creek (taking you past the CMBO CRE). Sluice Creek is the major fork to the right as you head upriver (to the east) on Dennis Creek. It is about 3 miles by water down Dennis Creek to the mouth of Delaware Bay.

Jakes Landing Road off Route 47, west of Dennisville, leads through a wooded section of Belleplain State Forest and then onto salt marshes that are part of Dennis Creek Wildlife Management Area. Birding is good year-round, from the first Pine Warbler and Yellow-throated Warbler in early March (the earliest for New Jersey are almost always found here), to the chorusing rails in summer, to the autumn fallout and the clouds of Snow Geese and resolute hunting harriers of winter. Yet these birds are not Jakes Landing's only draw—maybe not even its greatest attraction. That would be the beauty of its landscapes—sometimes pastoral in the muted haze of early summer, and sometimes stark during the snow squalls and dramatic sunsets of winter. Jakes Landing offers one of the most remote and beautiful vistas in all of New Jersey, a panorama of meadows, marsh, and distant tree lines that better recall the landscapes of Stone's days, or even Wilson's, than those of the twenty-first century. For the nearly forty years of Clay's memory of the site, the only vestige of humans (besides the road and parking lot itself) was the church steeple in Dennisville, miles to the east. (Sadly, this changed somewhat a few years ago when several cell towers spoiled the skyline.)

No matter how good the birds and birding are, many remember Jakes for its scenic beauty. Recently we led a field trip there that included a few first-time visitors. As we boarded the van to leave, a young couple lingered outside, and we asked if everything was OK. They answered, "Yes, we're OK. It's just so amazing, so wonderful here. Frankly, when we planned our trip here, we knew that Cape May would be old and pretty, but we pretty much figured that elsewhere we would be birding around refineries, factories, maybe landfills. We weren't prepared for this. This is spectacular." We could only add that this was just the beginning. We said that the next 50 miles of Delaware Bayshore to the west and north looked very much the same—verdant and largely unsullied open space—rich habitats filled with birds. This is the other New Jersey, where Old Cape May still exists.

Jakes shouldn't be missed at any season. The forests are best known for the breeding songbirds, but fallout occurs here in spring and fall. In fall, you can sometimes actually witness morning-flight northbound songbirds crossing the marsh toward you and then quickly dropping down and ducking into the forest at the upland edge—their migration done for the day. It's a good spot for lingerers too. Several Baltimore Orioles recently wintered successfully near the small field halfway out the road. Sedge Wrens have wintered on the marsh here too. The tidal marshes are exceptional in

Summer sunrise birding at Jakes Landing offers timeless views of an unsullied landscape.

any season, filled with herons, ibis, and egrets in summer and alive with Snow Geese, ducks, and hawks in winter. At times, several dozen harriers are present here—some near, some far—and many redtails dot the tree line and sky overhead. It's a key place for Bald Eagles—sometimes with as many as six or eight about—and Golden Eagles are seen in fall and occasionally winter. Jakes Landing is a reliable spot to see winter rough-legs (second only to Tuckahoe WMA), with at least one or two present even in off winters.

One key draw of Jakes Landing in winter is the Short-eared Owl. From November through March, a few are present every year. Some are far off to the west, out by the bay, but others hunt the salt hay farm right across the creek from the boat launch parking area. The privately owned salt hay farm is a key area for birds. It is one of the last of the many salt hay farms that were once found all along the bayshore. It offers higher ground (high marsh) habitat diversity and attracts short-ears, rough-legs, and harriers in winter and supports nesting Eastern Meadowlark, Saltmarsh Sharp-tailed Sparrow, Virginia Rails, and Black Rails in summer. A couple of pairs of Northern Harriers nest here too, and Willet are abundant.

Jakes is amazing for rails. In May, nighttime rail choruses can be deafening. It can be quiet one minute (or maybe even for an hour), but then one clapper sounds off and leads to a cacophony that rolls across the marsh in a domino effect that may take ten minutes to die down. Hundreds of clappers nest here and are seen along low-tide mudflats at the edge of the creek and swimming across creeks and ditches at high tide. King Rail and Sora have been heard here on migration, and the Virginia Rail nests. Black

Rails were more prevalent here before marsh management, but they can still be heard calling from the salt hay farm every spring. (If you're kayaking, don't land on the far side of the creek. It's private property, and the salt hay farm owner will prosecute trespassers.) Except for the salt hay farm, virtually everything else in view is public land, beckoning for exploration and enjoyment.

Birding the Site

From Beaver Swamp WMA and the intersection of Routes 657 and 47, go north on Route 47 past Dennisville. Just beyond Dennisville, Johnson Pond and then Ludlam's Pond, about a mile farther on your right, can be good for ducks in late winter and spring. Look for Ring-necked Duck, Hooded Merganser, Common Merganser, and Common Goldeneye. Osprey frequently fish here in early spring particularly during bad weather when salt water bays are rough and, as a result, murky. Both ponds are posted No Stopping and Standing, but fishermen commonly park off the pavement against the woods on the side opposite the ponds. Pull well off the road, and don't park along the guardrail. Jakes Landing is 0.4 mile beyond Ludlam's Pond on your left. Look for the state boat launch sign. Jakes Landing Road is 3.2 miles from the intersection of Routes 657 and 47.

As soon as you turn left onto Jakes Landing Road, you enter Belleplain State Forest. The first section is cut over but good for Prairie Warbler and Blue-winged Warbler in summer. The slight bend to the left is a good place to park and walk along the little-traveled dirt road blocked off by a metal guardrail. Continue on the paved road. Yellow-throated Warblers are numerous between here and the marsh edge, mostly around the planted White Pines. These pine plantations date back to the Civilian Conservation Corps (CCC) projects of the 1930s. One or two Long-eared Owls roost in these trees most winters, and once in a while a Barn Owl. They are usually confirmed by pellets only; they can be impossible to see in the high, dense pines. Also, wintering Saw-whet Owls have been seen and heard along Jakes Landing Road a number of times over the years. Expect White-eyed Vireo, Scarlet Tanager, Pine Warbler, Common Yellowthroat, Great-crested Flycatchers, and more in May and June. In 2003 a Swainson's Warbler was on territory here for most of May—probably never attracting a mate—and was heard by hundreds but seen by many fewer (they skulk deep in heavy, dense understory). Both Whip-poor-wills and Chuck-will's-widows nest throughout this area. Yellow-breasted Chats and Blue Grosbeaks nest in the partially overgrown field on the left side, midway down Jakes Landing Road. This field is also a good place to watch American Woodcock perform their amazing aerial courtship display on warm, still evenings in February and March.

You can continue to walk, or return to your car and drive to the end of the road. The parking lot on the creek is about 1.5 miles from Route 47. As you enter the marsh, scan the many dead snags to your right and left for perched raptors. The snags are a remnant of the once-dominant Atlantic White-cedar forest here. Redtails and Bald Eagles commonly sit in these snags, and Great Horned Owls are often seen flying out to perch there at dusk by those with the patience (and warm clothes) to wait for them on winter evenings. Great Horned Owls have nested on the Osprey platforms here. Check them in February and March for mom sitting on eggs or brooding young. Several pairs of Osprey nest here in summer.

At the parking lot, scan in all directions. A wonderful observation tower once stood here, but vandals burned it down. There are plans for a new, fireproof metal tower, but the timetable remains unknown. Listen for Seaside Sparrows and Eastern Meadowlark in May and June. Seaside and Sharp-tailed Sparrow winter here and can sometimes be pished up. Marsh Wrens breed abundantly, and a few winter. Sedge Wrens are rarely but regularly found on migration and in winter. A final joy here is the rare possibility of witnessing the sky dancing of Northern Harriers in February or March. Just a few nest here, but if you are fortunate enough to see their exuberant, somersaulting sky dance, you will never forget it—particularly if you view it in the wide open spaces of Jakes Landing.

River Otters are regulars at Jakes Landing and Beaver Swamp WMA.

TNC'S ELDORA PRESERVE

Just before scenic West Creek, at the western border of Cape May County, is The Nature Conservancy's Eldora Preserve, the headquarters for TNC's protection efforts in southern New Jersey. The office here coordinates all outreach and acquisition efforts for the region and particularly targets the preservation of key Delaware Bay habitats. The office is housed in the former home of noted entomologist C. Brook Worth, which TNC admirably restored. The Eldora Preserve is the first TNC project dedicated to protecting rare lepidoptera (*catocala* or underwing moths, to be particular). The preserve honors and continues Worth's landmark studies carried out on the property in the 1960s and 1970s.

TNC's Eldora Preserve offers much to birders. A trail goes from field to forest, with Blue Grosbeak, Indigo Bunting, Yellow-breasted Chat, and Black-billed Cuckoo present in spring and summer. Kentucky Warbler has been found on territory here too. The Eldora office offers a small gift shop and bookstore and friendly advice from scientists and naturalists. More importantly, Eldora can provide information on all TNC's protected properties. Some preserves are small, and some are huge. For example, in Cumberland County, the Manumuskin

Retrace your steps back toward Route 47. Right before you reach Route 47, a gravel road goes off to the left. This is **Old Robbins Trail**, a 2-mile, little-traveled Belleplain State Forest road that is exceptional for hiking or biking. There is good diversity here. First, planted pines attract nesting Yellow-throated Warblers; then, wet woodlands sometimes have Hooded Warblers. Successional areas have Prairie and Blue-winged Warblers, and finally an extensive white cedar swamp (Robbins Branch) has Acadian Flycatchers, Prothonotary Warblers (sometimes), and Barred Owls.

You can return to Route 47 or follow Old Robbins Trail, which joins 47 as well. Drive slowly; this is a key area for butterflies "puddling" in spring, with Mourning Cloak, Question Mark, Eastern Comma, Brown Elfin, Henry's Elfin, and pine elfins (and several of the azure complex) readily seen here in March and April. At Route 47, go left. In 2.5 miles, look for **Stipson's Island Road** on your left. Follow it through some private land and some state land to a dead end at a parking area on West Creek. Be alert along the road; Loggerhead Shrike and Scissor-tailed Flycatcher have been

Preserve protects over 3,600 acres of key Pine Barrens, cedar forest low-lands, and freshwater marsh and river (the Manumuskin is a major tributary to the Maurice River), including myriad rare plant and animal species that depend on these habitats. Visit Eldora to obtain information about and maps to the growing number of protected sites and to learn of birding opportunities, projects, and the excellent natural history pro-grams, tours, and nature walks. Be sure to support TNC's important efforts to protect key Cape May and Delaware Bay habitats.

From Stipson's Island drive west on Route 47 for 0.9 mile to the entrance to the preserve on your right. Before and after hours, kiosks can guide you to the trails. Walk the road shoulder 0.1 mile west to the bridge over Route 47. Don't stand on the bridge—this is a high-speed road—but there is a good view down West Creek and over the pristine salt marsh to the west from the boat launching area to the left (south) of the bridge. (This is a good canoe or kayak launch site.) Expect Marsh Wren, Seaside Sparrow, Clapper Rail, Northern Harrier, and Osprey in season, and Bald Eagle and Red-tailed Hawk throughout.

Return south on Route 47 to the Cape May area, or continue north on 47 to enter Cumberland County and the many exciting bird-ing locations there or to check out some of the fascinating TNC pre-serves you have just learned about. ▪

found here. At the parking area and small boat launch (yet another good kayak spot), scan in all directions for more Jakes Landing–type experiences. Here, at West Creek, is the Cape May County line (anything across the creek is in Cumberland County). There are sometimes tens of thousands of Snow Geese here in winter. In summer, Black Rail might be heard, and the Yellow Rail has been heard here on migration in May. Retrace your steps to Route 47. Go straight across Route 47 and make an immediate left onto Paper Mill Road/Spur 550. You now traverse a sod farm that often holds Killdeer, and Black-bellied and Semipalmated Plovers when heavy rains and high tides coincide in spring and fall. Look for American Golden Plovers (rare) among the black-bellies. Wild Turkeys are frequently seen here. Do not pull off the road here; the edges are soft, and sod is planted right up to the roadside. Continue past the sod farm to **Pickle Factory Pond** (also called Paper Mill Pond) on your right. Park in the small parking area on your right, just before the pond. This area is part of Belleplain State Forest and offers a kayak/canoe launch site. Scan the lake for ring-necks in early spring and Bald Eagles anytime. Wood Ducks can be seen down West Creek (to your left), and Prothonotary Warblers nest here. The fields beyond the lake often have Eastern Bluebirds and Wild Turkeys. Retrace your steps to Route 47. To return to Cape May turn left, or to continue on to TNC's Eldora Nature Preserve turn right.

Jakes Landing remains one of our favorite areas. It's an area we return to again and again. Admittedly, it's almost in our backyard, part of our patch, but the real joy of Jakes is how changeable it can be from season to season and even from day to day, as birds ebb and flow. You may not always see a lot of birds, but what you see is always interesting, particularly because it is backed by the incomparable bayshore landscape. We think of these Jakes encounters as "visions"—maybe of a rough-leg high overhead, maybe of the din of Wood Frogs on a warm February day, maybe of a family of river otters playing in the creek (they are frequently seen here). One vision that we missed was seen by a friend—a Snowy Owl floating down Dennis Creek on an "iceberg" as the creek and bay broke up after a hard winter's freeze. Every vision is different at Jakes, yet in a way, they are all the same—amazing snapshots that complete the picture album of a special and beautiful place.

BELLEPLAIN STATE FOREST

Belleplain Sate Forest, established in 1928, is one of the treasures of the Cape May region and can even be called one of the great forests of the East. It readily compares with such amazing areas as Allegheny State Forest in western Pennsylvania and Francis Marion National Forest in South Carolina for breeding bird use, and it probably bests them for migratory bird use. At 23,000 acres today (and growing), Belleplain may still seem small compared with great places such as the Highlands of northern New Jersey or the Great Dismal Swamp of Virginia, but when one considers Belleplain in conjunction with other protected lands here, the comparison becomes valid.

Belleplain State Forest is a key part of the vast greenbelt that stretches from near Rio Grande (with the Cape May NWR), through Beaver Swamp WMA, then north and west through Belleplain State Forest, and north through Great Cedar Swamp and the Great Egg Harbor region. Belleplain adjoins Peaslee WMA in Cumberland County, which then joins Millville WMA (a.k.a. Bevan WMA) west of the Maurice River. Add in Bear Swamp and the vast conservation holdings of public and private organizations along the Delaware Bayshore, and you have a vast, protected natural area easily rivaling the Pine Barrens and the Worthington State Forest area in northwestern New Jersey. When you look at the aggregate acreage and the exceptional avian ecovalues (to use a technical term), it is not a leap to compare the Belleplain region with any of the famous forests of the East.

The forest is a wonderful mix of pin-oak, lowland swamp, Atlantic White-cedar, and associated streams, lakes, and old-field areas. At places such as Jakes Landing, the forest meets brackish marshes and tidal salt marshes. It is mostly a contiguous forest, but as active acquisition efforts continue, many outliers in both Cape May and Cumberland County are now part of the forest. Belleplain is one of New Jersey's oldest state forests, and in the 1930s it benefited from Civilian Conservation Corps reforestation efforts. Historically, Belleplain timber was cut for shipbuilding, housing, and firewood, and today it is far more forested than at the turn of the twentieth century or even into the 1950s, as agricultural areas were lost and reclaimed by successional growth. Some legal state-sponsored firewood cutting still occurs in Belleplain. This is highly controversial due to its impact on interior forest species such as Ovenbird, Wood Thrush, and Barred Owl (not to mention that most neotropical migrants can better use older growth than scrubby successional forest).

Belleplain is a place for all seasons. It is very sparsely birded in fall, when most folks focus their efforts around the immediate Cape May area, but on some days it holds huge numbers of migratory songbirds. Belleplain is a place where many morning flight migrants end up for a day or more. It always surprises us when birds we thought were long gone for the season turn up. For example, none of the Cape May regulars would think of targeting breeders in the fall, but on a number of occasions, visiting British birders in September and October obsessed with our warblers have opened our eyes. "Oh yeah, had Hooded, Worm-eating, and Yellow-throated Warblers in Belleplain yesterday, right where you said they breed."

Belleplain in winter is bare but not barren. Large numbers of White-throated Sparrows, Dark-eyed Juncos, American Goldfinches, and (in most years) Pine Siskins and Purple Finches winter, Redpolls, Common and Red Crossbills are reported at least once most winters. White-winged Crossbills are less common, but in some years, small numbers of this irruptive species winter in Belleplain. A few American Tree Sparrows are usually found on the Belleplain Christmas Bird Count, and in most years, Eastern Phoebes, Baltimore Orioles, Pine Warblers, and Common Yellowthroats linger here. Hermit Thrushes are abundant, Wild turkey are thick, and Ruffed Grouse are still possible here as well.

Belleplain is at its best in spring and early summer, when the morning forest reverberates with the lusty dawn chorus of breeding birds. Belleplain in spring is a can't-miss spot and is a regular component of Cape May

An American Woodcock on its nest in Belleplain State Forest.

spring birding. Sixteen species of warblers regularly breed in the varied habitats of Belleplain. Add in Cerulean Warbler, which has bred occasionally, and Swainson's Warbler, which has been found on territory there, and you have an exceptional list of breeders—equaled in few areas of New Jersey or beyond. Throw in even just a fair number of spring migrants, and a twenty-five-warbler day is often possible in Belleplain State Forest.

The forest has a southern flavor to it, with a number of southern swamp forest breeders present: Barred Owl (fairly common), Red-shouldered Hawk (rare), Northern Parula, Worm-eating Warbler, Prothonotary Warbler, Louisiana Waterthrush, Kentucky Warbler and Hooded Warbler. Yellow-breasted Chat and Blue Grosbeak are numerous around old-field areas, and Summer Tanager is common in pine-oak sections and along edges. Yellow-throated Vireo is uncommon but always present along edges of the drier mixed forests. Check dense, early-successional areas for Blue-winged and Prairie Warblers. In May and early June, some singing occurs virtually all day long, but by mid-June the forest quiets down, except at dawn, as the nesting season progresses and parents are busy feeding hungry young.

Belleplain is a stronghold for Whip-poor-wills. They breed there in large numbers, and each spring evening shortly after 8:00 P.M. their insistent calling can be heard throughout the forest. Numbers appear healthy, and southern New Jersey and the Pine Barrens remain key areas for them in New Jersey and the mid-Atlantic. Encroaching, colonizing Chuck-will's-widows are found on the periphery of the forest, primarily near wetland edges in places such as Jakes Landing and Stipson's Island Road. Common Nighthawk, formerly much more common, is still reported once in a while in the Belleplain region in summer, but its breeding status is unknown.

Belleplain is big, and you get the feeling that there are always discoveries to be made. Red-breasted Nuthatch has bred on occasion, as have Brown Creeper and Red Crossbill. Saw-whet Owl is heard in the region every early spring, and Hermit Thrush has bred not too far away in the Jersey Pinelands. As yet, Black-throated Green Warbler, an uncommon breeder in the central Pine Barrens, has not been found breeding along Belleplain's white cedar streams, but would not be unexpected. Two other possibilities may be Rose-breasted Grosbeak and Warbling Vireo. Both breed not too far to the north and west but are curiously absent from South Jersey (Warbling Vireo is expanding its range). We won't say that anything is possible in Belleplain, but if you go there with a spirit of expectation and wonder and with the attitude that discoveries can be made, perhaps you will find New Jersey's first breeding Mississippi Kites. Wondrous Belleplain State Forest can stimulate endless possibilities in the minds of attuned birders.

Birding the Site

There is really no wrong way to bird Belleplain State Forest, but there is a recognized classic way. A tour via Pine Swamp Road, Sunset Road and Sunset Road Bridge, and then back to Franks Road and on to the State Forest Office should encompass most if not all of the regular breeders in fairly short order—if it is done in early morning and in May. Later in the day and later in the season require more time and patience, so plan accordingly. (World Series of Birding [WSB] teams can get all the target species in less than an hour at 6:00 A.M., but at 5:00 P.M. it will take several hours, and there will probably be a few blanks on the list.)

Belleplain is mostly back roads and begs to be explored by bicycle. Otherwise, plan to park and walk some or many of the gated-off (by guardrail) trails and roads. There are plenty of drive-up sites for the hurried or the handicapped, but the essence of Belleplain is poking around to see what you can find. Birding by bicycle allows for birding by ear. You can still cover a distance without missing the less common breeders—maybe Parula or a calling Broad-winged Hawk. Most Belleplain roads are paved—even the blocked-off ones. There are a number of hiking trails too for even greater access, but they are tick infested except in the dead of winter.

The **Belleplain State Forest Office** is a good starting point and quite birdy. From the intersection of Route 47 and Jakes Landing Road, go left (north) on Route 47 for 0.35 mile and turn right onto Route 557/Washington Avenue toward Woodbine. Go 3.2 miles to the blinking light at Route 550/Webster Street (which soon becomes Woodbine Avenue).

Turn left onto Route 550 and go 1.4 mile to Henkensifkin Road and the entrance to Belleplain State Forest. Turn left and immediately right into the State Forest Office parking lot for information, bathrooms, and camping registration. The state forest campground is very popular with birders, in excellent habitat, and open all year, unlike all other campgrounds in Cape May County. Ask for copies of both the state forest map and the trail map. You'll find that nearly every road in Belleplain State Forest is known by at least two names, depending on which map you are using, plus a number of roads change names mid-way at intersections. Belleplain State Forest is a Carry In–Carry Out forest (in other words do not expect to find trash cans).

Bird around the headquarters. Phoebes often nest here under the eaves and on top of one of the building lights. Yellow-throated Warblers nest in the large pines around the parking lot. Ruby-throated Hummingbirds frequent the feeder. Acadian Flycatchers call from behind the office. Watch the sky for Black Vultures overhead, and Mississippi Kite has been seen here on several occasions. Enjoy the cattail pond and its dragonflies and frogs.

Turn right out of the parking lot and continue south 0.4 mile to **Meisle Road**. Park and bird this intersection, one of the best spots to hear and see Acadian Flycatchers. Goosekill Trail, on the right just before this intersection, explores the white cedar forest behind Lake Nummy. Dirt trails like this and any dirt roads in the forest are excellent for spring butterflies and dragonflies which frequently perch on the warm road surface or congregate around wet puddle edges or horse manure. Turn right onto Meisle Road to enter the **campground and Lake Nummy Recreation Area** (entrance fees are charged Memorial Day to Labor Day). E. Phoebes often nest at one of the campground buildings, including the entrance booth ahead. Follow the road around Lake Nummy, turning onto Champion Road, to reach the Picnic Area entrance and parking lot. Bathrooms (open 24 hours) are just beyond the playground equipment. Birding can be very good throughout this area (except in swimming season), as is the case for any of the forest roads and trails.

Return on Meisle Road to the campground entrance. At the stop sign turn right (south) on Franks Road (known as Henkensifkin Road north of this intersection). Continue 0.9 mile to the stop sign on Sunset Road. (The continuation of Franks Road south of this intersection is known as Pine Swamp Road, excellent for birding and a spot we'll return to.) To add to the confusion of these multi-named roads, road signs are absent throughout much of the forest. The **Sunset and Pine Swamp Roads intersection** is a consistent spot for Summer Tanager and Yellow-throated Vireo and Blue-winged Warblers north of the intersection. Again, park and walk in all directions. Turn right onto Sunset Road. There are a number of private

inholdings with houses and the
assorted paraphernalia of developed areas along this road (and
along Pine Swamp Road), but
soon you're back in the forest
again. Be courteous; there is no
need to bird private front yards.
Proceed through the forest, keenly
listening for spring song. Stop
anywhere that "sounds" good.
Proceed 1.2 mile to "the triangle,"
where a fork in the road creates an
island-like intersection. Park by
the roadside and walk straight
ahead to the Atlantic White-cedar
swamp and **Sunset Road Bridge**
across Savages Run. Sunset Road
Bridge (a.k.a. The Bridge) is
nearly as famous in Cape May lex-

*A birding group enjoys Sunset Road
Bridge in Belleplain State Forest.*

icon as Higbee Beach or The Meadows, for here some of the finest spring
birding can be found. Within a quarter mile of this bridge you can usually
hear (and hopefully see) almost all of the breeding species. The best
method is to listen and quietly wait. Pishing is verboten here because it is
such an epicenter of activity. Plus, it won't work; these birds have heard it
all. So, simply wait, enjoy the singing, and be alert for movement. Birds
cover sizable territories. A Hooded Warbler that's singing way back in the
swamp will probably soon be singing right beside the road. It's just a waiting game at The Bridge.

Sunset Road is a through road and, although still lightly traveled, there
can be more traffic here than elsewhere in Belleplain State Forest. When
cars come through, try to keep your group on the same side of the road
and stand off to the side of the road. Eastern Phoebes often nest under the
bridge. Actually phoebes are fairly uncommon breeders this far south in
New Jersey. Belleplain State Forest is one of the few reliable sites in Cape
May County. The Bridge is a great spot for Prothonotary Warbler and Aca-
dian Flycatcher. Know their songs and wait for them to make their rounds.
Prothonotary Warblers nest in holes in trees (or nest boxes placed in wet
habitat) and have occasionally nested in the metal guardrail pipes at The
Bridge. Yellow-throated Warblers call from the tall pines. Worm-eating
Warblers breed in the wet woods along Savages Run. Louisiana
Waterthrush can be a tough one. They arrive very early in the spring (early
April) and by mid-May they aren't singing very much, except at sunrise. If

they aren't singing, scan the muddy banks of Savages Run for movement. Be patient.

Return to the triangle and take the right hand fork (as you or your car are facing the bridge) north. This is Dean's Branch Road, though there is no sign. Follow it 0.5 mile to a second bridge over Savages Run, the length of which closely follows Savages Run and the swamp forest (to your left) and high and dry forest to your right. Listen and look for swamp forest breeders to your left and Blue-winged and Prairie Warblers and others of dry habitats to your right. The road bends sharply left and becomes **New Bridge Road** (where Dean's Branch Road continues straight and is gated off) and crosses Savages Run again. Park and bird the roadside; scan the creek edge for Louisiana Waterthrush and other species you may have missed at The Bridge. Northern Parula and American Redstart are always found here in spring and both occasionally nest. Yellow-throated Warblers abound in the stands of White Pines along New Bridge Road. Black-and-white Warbler is expected.

From the second bridge, continue 0.5 mile to a T-intersection at **Cedar Bridge Road** (no road sign). Summer Tanagers call from the woods to the right and Hooded Warblers from directly ahead, across Cedar Bridge Road. Park and bird this intersection in all directions. Turn left on Cedar Bridge Road and continue 0.1 mile. Park and walk the dirt road on the right to a cut over area surrounded by electric fencing. This area and others like it in Belleplain are likely to attract nesting orioles, Blue-winged Warblers, Yellow-breasted Chats, and Blue Grosbeaks. Remember though that this is a case of here today, gone tomorrow. In a few short years open areas quickly grow up in dense saplings; within ten years there is dense forest again—forest succession at its best!

Return to Sunset Road and turn right. Cross Sunset Road Bridge and in 0.1 mile turn left onto Tom Field Road (Narrows Road on some maps), a dirt road. **Tom Field Road** is 1.3 mile long and ends at Route 347 (the major Route 47 bypass). Walk or drive this road, the length of which passes through excellent habitat bordering Savages Run. Listen for Worm-eating Warbler, White-breasted Nuthatch, Yellow-billed Cuckoo, and the tremulous song and *tickety-tuck* call of Summer Tanagers. In 0.3 mile a dirt walking path begins on the left. Park and walk this 0.4 mile long path (an old woods road), which eventually loops back to Tom Field Road. In 0.1 mile take the left spur to reach a beaver dam, where the wet white cedar forest along Savages Run meets the back of East Creek Lake. Look for active beaver workings and expect to hear (and hopefully see) Louisiana Waterthrush, Prothonotary Warbler, Worm-eating Warbler, and Wood Ducks. Return to the path and continue 0.2 mile further to a second spur on the left. This spur overlooks a bog on the back of East Creek Lake. Bald

Eagles nest near here and are often seen fishing the lake. If it's not frozen, this lake is great for ducks in winter and in early spring. Expect Wood Ducks, Green Herons, and Belted Kingfishers in season. Return to the path and continue 0.1 mile, where it loops back to Tom Field Road. Turn left on Tom Field Road and bird the wet woods just ahead, where Prothonotary Warblers can easily be seen some years. Return to your car by walking right on Tom Field Road 0.3 mile. Continue driving south on Tom Field Road 0.8 mile to Route 347, where you can expect major traffic on this Route 47 bypass. Turn left on Route 347. In 0.4 mile turn left into a small dirt parking lot and boat launch area next to East Creek Lake, that begs for you to explore the lake by canoe or kayak.

Return to Sunset Road via Tom Field Road. Turn right on Sunset Road and follow it 1.3 mile to Pine Swamp Road on your right and Franks Road on your left. Turn right on **Pine Swamp Road**. Like all the other roads, the length of this road passes through excellent bird habitat. In 0.8 mile park on the roadshoulder before the sharp left-hand turn. Walk in either direction to listen for breeders attracted to these wet woods. Acadian Flycatcher, Hooded Warbler, Yellow-throated Warbler, and Worm-eating Warbler should all be here, along with loud, abundant Ovenbirds and many others. To get to this spot on Pine Swamp Road immediately from the intersection of Route 47 and Jakes Landing Road, go left (north) on Route 47 for 0.35 mile and turn right onto Route 557/Washington Avenue toward Woodbine. In 0.5 mile Pine Swamp Road will be the first left. In about 1.6 miles you will reach the sharp right-hand bend on Pine Swamp Road.

These routes outline the key areas of Belleplain State Forest, but you've barely scratched the surface. Return north on Pine Swamp Road (which becomes Franks Road and then Henkensifkin Road) to the Belleplain State Forest Office and Route 550 just beyond. Turn right on Route 550; follow it 1.4 mile to the blinking light at Route 557 in Woodbine. Go left onto Route 557/Washington Avenue until Route 550 again goes off to your right. Turn right onto Route 550 and follow it through Woodbine. Turn right in 1.8 mile to reach the **Woodbine Airport**, which has a few nesting Horned Larks and once in a while a Grasshopper Sparrow (but these are usually mowed out). Twenty-five years ago Upland Sandpipers nested here, but they are now long gone (as they are in most of New Jersey), although they are still possible here during migration in July and August. Continue east on Route 550 to Route 610/Dennisville-Petersburg Road. If you continue straight on Route 550, you will soon cross the Great Cedar Swamp Division of the Cape May NWR. No trails are established here, but several old logging roads (now just paths) can route the brave into the swamp. All the same species that nest in Belleplain State Forest can be found here, and breeding American Redstarts and Prothonotary Warblers are particularly common in this section. Continue following Route 550 east to Route 9. A left will take you north to Route 50. Go right on Route 50 to the Garden State Parkway (southbound entrance only) to return to Cape May.

To continue exploring the Belleplain region, from the State Forest Office go left on Route 550. Go 2 miles until you reach Spur 550. A left will take you to Route 347. This section is good for Ring-necked Pheasant, Bobwhite, and even Chuker, but they are all game-farm birds from private hunting preserves. A right at this intersection puts you on Route 605/ Tuckahoe-Belleplain Road. Go 3.4 miles until you reach Route 548. Turn left onto Route 548 (signed as Route 632), also widely known to birders as **Weatherby Road**. This is a key area. Weatherby Road stretches some 8.4 miles west to Port Elizabeth (and Route 47, just below where it joins Route 55 north). For about the first two-thirds of your route, Belleplain State Forest will be on your left, and the vast state-owned Peaslee Wildlife Management Area will be on your right. To fully explore the nearly 25,000-acre Peaslee WMA, use *A Birder's Guide to Cumberland County* by Clay Sutton.

After taking a left onto Weatherby Road, go 0.6 mile to **Tarkiln Lake** on your right. Park beyond the lake and walk back along the guardrail. This freshwater lake (look for the beaver lodge) and Tarkiln Bog behind it should hold Wood Duck, Green Heron and other herons, possibly American Bittern during migration, kingfisher, and many swallows in season. Pied-billed Grebes have nested here in the recent past. Below Tarkiln Lake's outfall, the swamp behind you (as you face the lake) is an exceptional spot. There is no real access here except to bird from the guardrail and walk the gravel road to the north from where you parked, but for birding by ear, this is enough. In this wet lowland forest (and adjacent fields), several WSB teams have found all the breeding warblers here in May, including the tough Louisiana Waterthrush and Northern Parula. The Cerulean Warbler has bred here on several occasions—the only spot in Cape May County where it has been confirmed as a breeder. Know the cerulean's song, and keep it in mind here. Finally, Mississippi and Swallow-tailed Kites have both been seen over this area; this is the heartland where they hide when they are not at Cape May Point (and the itinerant kites can easily cover the distance to the Point and back again in the same day).

Proceed west on Weatherby Road. This becomes higher, drier, pine-oak Pine Barrens affinity forest here. Wild Turkey, Summer Tanager, and Yellow-throated Vireo can be found anywhere along Weatherby. This once was a stronghold for Red-headed Woodpecker, but forest succession (recovery from Gypsy Moth damage) has meant many fewer Red-headed Woodpeckers, although they are still found in small numbers. Wetter areas hold Barred Owl and swamp-type warblers. Saw-whet Owl has been found here in breeeding season, although never confirmed as a successful breeder. Eastern Towhee, Ovenbird, and Wood Thrush are abundant here in summer (although *abundant* doesn't do justice to the density of towhees in New Jersey's pinelands regions).

Return on Route 548/Weatherby Road to the junction of Route 605. Just before you reach 605 is a small road that goes off to your left, called **Head of River Road**. Go left, and when you reach the wet area, park and walk. Prothonotary Warbler virtually can't be missed here from late April to early June, with several pairs normally present. Continue on Head of River Road about 0.25 mile to reach Route 49.

A left will eventually take you to Route 55 and Millville. At about 2.5 miles from Head of River Road, scenic **Hunter's Mill Bog** is on your right, a key destination for birders, botanists and for butterfly and dragonfly enthusiasts. A dirt road to the right follows the upland edge along the bog. King Rail has been heard at Hunter's Mill during migration, and Sora is possible at this rarely birded spot. From Head of River Road, a right on Route 49 will take you east to Route 50 at Tuckahoe. Turning right on Route 50 will get you back to Route 9 and the Garden State Parkway at Interchange 20 (southbound entrance only, but you can get into the northbound lane via the the service plaza just 1.9 miles south of the interchange).

CUMBERLAND COUNTY

Even when you have exhaustively birded places such as Reeds Beach, Jakes Landing, and Stipson's Island Road, you have barely dented the ornithological or the scenic possibilities of the vast bayside marshes and rivers. Birders spending more than a few days at Cape May may want to venture farther afield, into the western reaches of what Witmer Stone considered to be Old Cape May. This can be particularly alluring during slow periods at Cape May, when stagnant weather means little migration. It can be crucial in the spring, when horseshoe crab numbers farther up the bay can lure many or even most shorebirds to areas north and west of Reeds Beach (shorebirds move around a lot in relation to crab egg abundance, and sometimes you need to follow them). For breeding songbirds, the expansive forests of Cumberland County can rival Belleplain State Forest.

The Cumberland County and Salem County bayshore region is particularly beckoning in winter, when tens of thousands or even a few hundred thousand Snow Geese and Canada Geese descend on the region. It's a

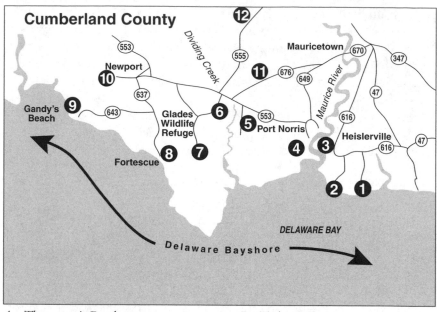

1. *Thompson's Beach*
2. *East Point*
3. *Heislerville WMA*
4. *Bivalve and Shellpile*
5. *Hansey Creek Road*
6. *Maple Street Impoundments*
7. *Turkey Point*
8. *Fortescue*
9. *Gandy's Beach Preserve*
10. *Newport Landing*
11. *Bear Swamp Natural Area*
12. *Millville WMA*

major spectacle in its own right, but these huge numbers always include a few Ross's Geese and Cackling Geese, a Greater White-fronted Goose or two, or possibly even the always controversial Barnacle Goose. A few Sandhill Cranes are always found around these vast goose concentrations too. Raptors abound on the winter bayshore. Regional numbers of hawks and eagles represent not only the highest numbers in New Jersey but also some of the highest concentrations documented anywhere in the mid-Atlantic region. A few other birds entice here too—White-crowned Sparrows are always far more common in Salem County than anywhere in Cape May or even Cumberland County, and Yellow-headed Blackbirds are annual, sometimes in numbers, on the upper bayshore. Brewer's Blackbirds are sometimes reported in these agricultural areas and pasturelands too.

If you are at Cape May for an extended stay, consider working your way up the bay. It's a day trip from Cape May, doable even during the short days of December. It's a rural area, much of it empty, open space, and parts of it remain if not pristine then at least wild and relatively untouched. The birding too can be wild in these western territories.

THOMPSON'S BEACH

Like at Cape May, the Delaware Bayshore has long been shaped by storms, erosion, and, in more recent times, the rise in sea level due to climate change. All along the bay, once thriving communities and ports have succumbed to the relentless march of the bay as shorelines continue to shift inland. In the 1970s Moore's Beach was not only a beachfront town but also a birding hotspot; today, only a few pilings commemorate the town's existence. So too has Thompson's Beach disappeared through erosion, flooding, and finally buyout and condemnation. Only pilings remain, occupied by gulls, cormorants, and the occasional Brown Pelican and Bald Eagle. Yet Thompson's Beach is still a key destination. You can't reach the beach anymore, but a paved road leads to an excellent canoe and kayak launch and a wonderful observation deck.

Thompson's Beach is owned and managed by Public Service Electric and Gas (PSE&G), one of New Jersey's major utilities. This 1,400-acre property and those you will encounter at Stipson's Island, Bivalve, and along the Cohansey River collectively constitute what is supposedly the world's largest salt marsh restoration project—over 20,000 acres. These are largely diked salt hay farms that have been reopened to tidal flow, carried out to mitigate the environmental impacts (mainly fish kills) at the cooling intakes for the Salem nuclear power plant. The flooding has created healthy tidal *Spartina alterniflora* salt marsh and the attendant food chain—from invertebrates such as grass shrimp and crabs to forage fish and game fish to a wealth of birds.

Thompson's is an excellent window into the spring shorebird phenomenon. You can't get to the beach (at least not without boots and a long walk), but tidal mudflats attract thousands of Dunlin, Short-billed Dowitchers, and Semipalmated Sandpipers in spring. (They're here in fall too—July through September—but in fewer numbers.) Herons, egrets, and ibis abound, and boisterous Willet entertain. Clapper Rails are constantly heard and often seen from the observation platform—sometimes right underneath you. Osprey and Bald Eagle nest here. Look for rarities, Curlew Sandpiper, Black-necked Stilt, Ruff, Marbled Godwit, White Ibis, White Pelican, Mississippi Kite, Northern Shrike, and Northern Wheatear (all of which have been seen here recently). The distant box on pilings to the east is an active peregrine aerie. Snow Geese clamor in winter as attendant eagles keep them agitated and frequently in the air.

Birding the Site

From Route 47 at West Creek (at TNC's bayshore office and the Cape May County line), take Route 47 north. At 3.25 miles, turn left onto Route 616

The concentration of breeding Horseshoe Crabs at Thompson's Beach attracts great numbers of shorebirds.

Low tide mudflats at Thompson's Beach fill with shorebirds in spring.

(Glade Road), following signs to East Point Lighthouse. At the bridge over the small tidal creek (Riggins Ditch—a great spot for Hooded Mergansers in winter), look to your right (north) and try to spot the huge but somewhat hidden active Bald Eagle nest to the right of the creek. Continue on to Thompson's Beach Road on your left (1.5 miles from the Route 47 intersection). Bird the road at any season—for sparrows in fall and winter and for Blue Grosbeak and Indigo Bunting in summer. The vast meadow on your left is the last place Henslow's Sparrow ever bred on the bayshore—a salt hay farm and pasture where they persisted until about 1970. Today, Chuck-will's-widow and Willow Flycatcher both nest in this general area.

The road bends right, and you'll soon come to a small parking area and observation tower. Do not block the two boat ramps. If you launch a kayak here be extremely aware of tides; this is an area of extensive mudflats and dry creek beds at low tide, and you can be stranded. Launch on a flooding tide and return *early* in the ebb. Scan marshes and mudflats. A flooding tide is best, pushing shorebirds close to the platform. At high tide, sometimes hundreds of shorebirds sit right on the boat ramp or even in the parking lot. One cautionary note: Although Thompson's Beach is currently a great site, the mudflats are rapidly filling with marsh grass. If this progression continues (PSE&G is managing it for fish, not shorebirds), the value of the site for birds and birders may be substantially reduced. Thompson's could go the way of Moore's Beach, where tidal flooding and increasing vegetation eventually rendered the site unavailable to shorebirds; it is now used mainly by Clapper Rails, Black Ducks, and tons of Snow Geese in winter. Always expect change in these protean, transitional bayfront areas.

EAST POINT AND HEISLERVILLE WILDLIFE MANAGEMENT AREA

East Point offers one of the best vistas on Delaware Bay and is a fun stop even if there are no birds about. The historic and photogenic East Point Lighthouse was built in 1849 and predates even the Cape May Lighthouse. It served continuously, marking the mouth of the Maurice River, until it was extinguished in 1941 as part of the total coastal blackout of World War II. Damaged by fire in 1971, it was rebuilt by the Maurice River Historical Society and relit in 1980. Today it is opened to visitors a few times a year. Cumberland County hosts many other lighthouses too. Ship John Shoal Light, off the Cohansey River, was commissioned in 1877, using the iron superstructure from the lighthouse exhibit at the 1876 International Centennial Exhibition in Philadelphia. Miah Maull, Fourteen Foot Bank, and Brandywine Shoal (west of Cape May and visible from the Concrete Ship) are all historic Victorian-era lights. Both the Bayshore Discovery Project and Cape May whale-watching boats take occasional tours to these scenic Delaware Bay lighthouses.

East Point is at its best during fall migration, when it functions as a mini–Cape May by concentrating birds near the tip of the wooded peninsula as they migrate south (or west) along the upland edge of the marsh. Watch the hawk flight from the small gravel turnout west of the road, just before a small bridge north of the East Point Lighthouse, or watch from the lighthouse parking lot itself. Some of the best hawkwatching can be from the small roadside berms north of the lighthouse. Search the sky overhead and the tree line to the north. Mornings are best, but afternoons produce Merlins here daily from mid–September to late October. Some 2,000 Broad-winged Hawks were counted here on September 22, 1988. (Sometimes, by midday, the flight shifts inland, making the Heislerville dikes the optimal spot.) Not only hawks are concentrated at East Point; songbirds can also be abundant here on migration. Daily counts of 1,000-plus Blue Jays, 4,500 Yellow-rumped Warblers, over 2,000 sparrows, thousands of robins, and hundreds of bluebirds and Cedar Waxwings have been obtained here, even with little birding coverage. Monarch butterflies gather in big numbers too. As elsewhere on the coast, birding here is best following the passage of a cold front. East Point is a hotspot in fall but is good at any season. It is currently underbirded and has tremendous potential for numbers and rarities. Swainson's Hawk has been seen here twice in fall, and Barrow's

The tip of East Point concentrates migrating birds in the fall, much as Cape May Point does. STEVE EISENHAUER

Goldeneye in late winter. From December 1998 to April 1999, a Townsend's Solitaire wintered at East Point. It was one of the few Townsend's Solitaires ever recorded in all of New Jersey and was seen by hundreds of birders during the three months it was present.

The 6,900-acre Heislerville WMA is a well-known area of Cumberland County and is almost always good for a variety of water-birds. Here Matt's Landing Road affords excellent views of the Heislerville impoundments. The gravel dikes can be driven and lead south, back to East Point Road. A bike path leads north to Leesburg. The impoundments are excellent—one of the best places in Cumberland for a good variety of waterfowl in winter and early spring. Bufflehead and Red-breasted Merganser predominate, but Ruddy Duck and Hooded Merganser are often present, and good birds such as Red-necked Grebe and Eurasian Wigeon have been seen here. A sizable flock of Canvasback regularly win-ters here. Scan for raptors—Turkey and Black Vultures, Red-tailed Hawk, and Northern Harrier. Bald Eagles are seen here daily in winter, sometimes in large numbers. At low tide, the mudflats south of the south dike can be spectacular for shorebirds and waterfowl. In recent Mays, as a shorebird management technique, the southernmost impoundment has been drawn down. In May 2006, 12,000 shorebirds were counted in the shallow impoundment (at high tide, when water levels push birds off surrounding tidal flats). Dowitcher, yellowlegs, and Dunlin abound, and rarities such as Ruff, Black-necked Stilt, and Spotted Redshank have been found here. An amazing 2 Curlew Sandpipers were together here on May 11, 2006. Sea-sonally, Black Skimmers, terns, herons, egrets, and Glossy Ibis fill these flats and impoundments as well. Mornings are best for viewing the flats, because in the afternoon you'll be looking into the sun, but tides are the most important factor; low is best, or flooding, when the rising tide pushes birds toward the Heislerville dikes.

Birding the Site

From Thompson's Beach, go west on Glade Road (Route 616). In about 0.2 mile, Route 616 takes a hard right in the town of Heislerville, but proceed straight, following signs to East Point. After you leave the houses behind, this entire road is good for migrants. Bird the various paths and wildlife food crop patches. Be aware that hunting for stocked pheasants is heavy here in November and December. Near the end of the road, make a right and park at the historic East Point Lighthouse to scan the bay, or continue straight ahead to the seawall. Walk east on the gravel road; you can scan both marsh and tree line and the beaches for shorebirds in spring. Do not walk on the beaches—this will disrupt or flush shorebirds—and respect private property here.

Watch the marshes for Northern Harrier, Rough-legged Hawk, and Short-eared Owl in winter. Scan the Delaware Bay and Maurice River Cove for gulls, terns, and waterfowl. Diving ducks are abundant here some winters, and it is the only place in Cumberland County where Northern Gannet (spring and fall) and Wilson's Storm-Petrel and Brown Pelican (summer) can be reasonably expected from shore.

Returning to Route 616/Main Street, turn left onto it at Heislerville and proceed 0.7 mile, making another left onto Route 736/Matt's Landing Road. The woods here hold breeding and migratory songbirds. Leaving the forest, you will come to the tidal impoundments. Make a left onto a gravel road marked "Wildlife Drive" to drive around the southern end of the impoundments. At low tide, the mudflats to the south of this dike are excellent, so allow plenty of time here. The southernmost impoundment is drawn down in May to attract shorebirds. Following this gravel dike will take you to a third impoundment, and then through some good woods and

WMA fields—particularly good on migration (but avoid this area in hunting season). This gravel road eventually reaches East Point Road. Retrace your steps by either route, and take the gravel road to the right off Matt's Landing Road to view the northern impoundment. At the culvert, this road is blocked; it becomes a bike/walking path. The impoundments can be readily viewed from the Matt's Landing Road itself if you encounter rain, mud, or snow on the dikes.

Scan the Maurice River, woods' edge, impoundment, and

The restored 1849 lighthouse offers a scenic backdrop to East Point birding.

The Maurice River, a major tributary to the Delaware Bay, offers good birding all year.

marsh. Matt's Landing's marinas have luncheonettes that are open in summer, and rental boats are available if you wish to tour the scenic Maurice River by boat. Retracing your steps, follow Route 616 north through the historic shipbuilding towns of Leesburg and Dorchester. Where the road passes close to the Maurice River, scan for raptors— Osprey in summer, Bald Eagle year-round. Across the river, the unbroken tree line is the vast Garren's Neck Swamp. The area is now protected by the Natural Lands Trust, Inc., as the Mauricetown Preserve.

Follow Route 616 north until it reaches Route 47. Go north (left) on 47 for 0.4 mile to the intersection of Routes 47, 347, and 670, the Mauricetown Causeway, which will lead you on to Bivalve or Turkey Point.

BIVALVE AND SHELLPILE

The Delaware Estuary has long been known for its fisheries. Shad and sturgeon were major industries during much of the nineteenth century, and oysters drove much of the Delaware Bay economy. Hundreds of oyster schooners sailing from the Maurice River harvested oysters under sail well into the twentieth century, but the industry was devastated by MSX, a parasite that claims oysters long before they reach marketable size. Today, the industry is but a shadow of its former glory, yet a few schooners, now powered by diesel engines, still ply the bay each season. At the small fishing villages of Bivalve and Shellpile are found some of the same packing houses and wharves from which the great fleet set sail. (One is now the Maritime Traditions of the Delaware Bay Museum, maintained by the Delaware Bay Discovery Project and well worth a visit.)

Today Bivalve and Shellpile have become major destinations for birders. In a few short years since the efforts of the Public Service Electric and Gas Estuary Enhancement Project (EEP) have come to fruition, this rural and mostly forgotten region has become known as one of New Jersey's best birding sites. It may be second only to Forsythe NWR in consistent numbers of waders, waterfowl, and shorebirds. The best and most extensive of the EEP sites, from a birding perspective, is the Commercial Township wetlands restoration site, more commonly referred to as Bivalve by birders. Located just south of and adjacent to Port Norris, near the mouth of the Maurice River, the Bivalve site comprises 4,200 acres of wetlands, forested upland edge, and open, fallow fields. Public-use enhancements installed by PSE&G include an observation platform, two lengthy boardwalks, over 2 miles of nature trails, and a car top boat launch. All are served by excellent parking areas. Birding success can vary by season, weather, tide, and even day to day, but when Bivalve is hot, it's about as good as it gets.

Fall offers a good window on migration, with fields and edges filling with passerines, primarily sparrows. Waterfowl are numerous, but flats and pools are often empty due to duck and goose hunting, which is legal here. Winter birding is excellent unless the wetlands are completely frozen (rare). There is always a sizable flock of Snow Geese present, and Dunlin winter in big numbers (up to 10,000). Spring is stellar at Bivalve. Early spring (March) brings thousands of ducks—pintails, blacks, shovelers, wigeon, and teal. Late spring (May) is when Bivalve is truly a shorebird mecca, with tens of thousands of Semipalmated Sandpipers present. Look for the vast, wheeling, restless flocks. The last of the northbound, Arctic-breeding shorebirds leave in the first week of June, but don't despair, the first southbound returnees show up by the last week of June. Late summer birding may be even better than spring. July and August are when 30,000 Semipalmated Sandpipers have been counted at Bivalve, along with an estimated 3,000 Short-billed Dowitchers. Up to 6,000 (postbreeding) Snowy Egrets and 1,500 Great Egrets have been estimated in August, along with 1,000 Forster's Terns and 50 Caspian Terns. In short, Bivalve mudflats are highly significant regionally and represent major waterbird and shorebird concentration and staging areas. Bivalve offers arguably the best birding on the New Jersey bayshore.

Although the numbers of birds are breathtaking, Bivalve offers unusual birds too, including regional rarities. Marbled Godwit, Hudsonian Godwit, American Avocet, and Black-necked Stilt are nearly annual here, along with numbers of White-rumped and Western Sandpipers. Ruff, Red-necked Phalarope, and Wilson's Phalarope have been found at Bivalve, as well as White Ibis, White-faced Ibis, Wood Stork, and White Pelican. Bald Eagle is daily here (perhaps a dozen in winter), and Peregrine Falcons can be seen hunting shorebirds most days (there is a local breeding pair on a tower near Egg Island Point). Osprey are abundant in season (mid-March through September); a number of pairs nest here on platforms provided by PSE&G. Over sixty pairs nest along the length of the Maurice River.

Tide can be a crucial element when birding here. At high tide, very few shorebirds will be seen; they are out of sight at distant high-tide roosts. Low tide is when mudflats teem with birds, and an incoming tide may be best of all, when rising water levels push shorebirds toward the higher edges—often right at your feet. Tides are hard to predict here, however. NOAA Weather Radio and newspapers usually give tides for nearby East Point, but tides on the Bivalve mudflats are generally an hour or more later. On top of that, wind direction can have a major effect. South winds "push" the tide, flooding the area faster. North or northeast winds tend to drain the flats more quickly. If tides are too high, simply go land birding until the tide falls. There's always something to do at Bivalve. Surrounded by birds, be they swirling shorebirds or clamoring Snow Geese flushed by an eagle high overhead, every visit will be different but memorable.

Birding the Site

From the intersection of Routes 47 and 347, take the Mauricetown Bypass (a.k.a. Mauricetown Causeway, or Route 670) west. Convenience stores and gas stations are located at this intersection (and provide the last bathrooms for a while). As you cross the bridge, set the odometer. Go straight through the blinking light. At 2.5 miles you'll come to a T. Turn left toward Port Norris on North Avenue. Go another 2.5 miles to a second T. You have reached Route 553, a.k.a. Main Street in Port Norris. Here you can turn left and follow signs to Shellpile, or turn right to go to Bivalve; basically, you end up in the same place no matter which way you go. At Shellpile, scan across the Maurice River from riverside parking lots (you are looking across at Heislerville WMA), or work the roadsides for sparrows. Wilson's Snipe are often seen in flooded fields here.

If you turned right onto Main Street, go 0.4 mile and then make a left onto Route 631/High Street. You will soon exit the town of Port Norris and emerge into salt marsh. You are now entering Bivalve. Soon you'll see the Rutgers University Oyster Research Lab on your left, as well as the masts of New Jersey's official Tall Ship, the 1928 oyster schooner *A. J. Meerwald* (restored by the Bayshore Discovery Project) if it is in port. Go 1.3 miles (from the Route 553 intersection) and dead-end at an old, abandoned, white concrete building on your right. Don't be deterred by the bumpy clamshell road or the often bustling activity at the shellfish packing facility on your left. (Do try to steer clear of puddles; the run-off from the shell piles is smelly and will linger on mufflers and wheelwells.) Park behind the white concrete building by the signs that indicate the trailhead. Here, both a walking trail and a bicycle route begin. Walk left to the clearly visible PSE&G observation tower. This tower gives an exceptional view of the scenic Maurice River and the distant Delaware Bay, as well as the wetlands restoration site.

Walking to the right yields great ongoing views of the mudflats. Here you have a choice—you can either bird the entire site on foot (recommended if you want to see everything) or continue your driving tour, rec-ommended if you want to avoid greenhead flies in summer and the wind chill of winter. Return by car the way you came for 0.4 mile, and then turn left onto an unnamed street directly across from the **Bayshore Discovery Project** office and museum. Stop in for details on its important Delaware Bay education and conservation efforts and for information about the occa-sional birding trips on Delaware Bay aboard the *A. J. Meerwald*. Go 0.1 mile and park in the marked lot on your right. Here you again meet the walking and bike trail (dike), as well as a long boardwalk that extends into the wet-lands. The small islands visible may contain a Black-crowned Night-Heron roost in late summer to winter, or even a Brown Pelican roost in summer. Although the best birding is on the mudflats and tidal creeks, work the edges of the dike for sparrows at any season, but particularly during migra-tion. "Ipswich" Savannah Sparrow and Palm Warbler can be thick here in fall. Also, be sure to scan the Maurice River itself (best viewed from the bank or dike near the concrete block building) for terns in late summer and diving ducks, including Canvasback, and sometimes Long-tailed Duck in winter. Check the clamshell parking lots and clamshell piles for gulls— Iceland, Glaucous, and Lesser Black-backed Gulls are seen here some win-ters. Bonaparte's Gulls are sometimes over the river or on the mudflats, and Black-headed Gulls have been found here.

Return to Route 553, turn left and go 0.6 mile. Turn left onto Route 680/Strawberry Avenue. Drive south 0.5 mile to a parking lot on your right. You cross the hiking and bike trail again, but go straight to yet another excellent boardwalk observation deck. This can often be the best of the three observation sites; shorebirds pack in here during migration, and it's great for ducks in winter. Both Eurasian Wigeon and Common (Eurasian Green-winged) Teal have been spotted here in recent winters or in early spring. A few Blue-winged Teal can usually be found among the abundant Green-winged Teal. Try to avoid late afternoon, when you'll be looking into the sun's glare. Note the amazing Atlantic White-cedar stump near the base of the boardwalk. It attests to the ecological history of the site. Precolonial cedar swamps were magnificent; this stump is far larger than any living white cedar in New Jersey today.

Once again, work the field edges around the parking lot for sparrows in season. Clay-colored Sparrow and Lincoln's Sparrow have been found here and are probably annual. Keep in mind that the tree line can be great for passerines in migration. These trees are the last stop for migrants before Delaware Bay in fall and their first stop after crossing the bay in spring. Timing is everything for songbirds; check after warm fronts in spring and cold fronts in fall. This is a good spot to hear Bobwhite in spring and see displaying woodcock at dusk in early spring (March). Chuck-will's-widow can be heard from this parking lot in late spring and early summer. Yellow Warblers are abundant breeders here.

Return to Route 553. The fields north of here are worth a scan, but they are private property, so bird from the roadside. In fall, Eastern Meadowlarks and Eastern Bluebirds should be easily seen here, and American Kestrels perch on electric lines overhead. Check rain-flooded farm fields for shorebirds in season, particularly when high tides force them off the marsh and mudflats. Go left (north) on Route 553 for 0.8 mile. Make a left onto Robbinstown Road. This will take you to a car top boat (canoe or kayak) ramp on your left, which is another good viewpoint. Robbinstown loops onto Berrytown Road, which will return you to Route 553. Note that there are still numerous PSE&G trails and dikes to be explored here, but there are no additional developed overlooks or boardwalks in this section. The adventurous, however, will find many trails, pockets, and hidden overlooks. Who knows where those American Avocets or Black-necked Stilts are going to be hiding? Remember, this area is vast and changeable due to tides, so it may take you all day to bird it completely. A second swing through the whole site may yield many birds not seen the first time around. Give Bivalve plenty of time, and you will rarely be disappointed.

TURKEY POINT TO FORTESCUE

Few places in South Jersey offer such scenic backdrops for birding as the Turkey Point–Dividing Creek area. Near the historic town of Dividing Creek and the bayside fishing village of Fortescue, inviting panoramas of pristine salt marsh unfold, unequaled in scope anywhere in the state. Birding is excellent year-round. In summer, herons, egrets, Glossy Ibis, Willet, and Marsh Wrens bring color and sound to the marsh. Clapper Rails are abundant, and the secretive Black Rail nests here. Fall brings lots of waterfowl to the creeks and impoundments, and winter hosts the largest concentration of Snow Geese seen anywhere in New Jersey. Excellent winter raptor numbers include Rough-legged Hawk and the occasional Golden Eagle. Spring promises ducks and shorebirds, and during the month of May, Fortescue provides an excellent window to the famous shorebird gatherings on Delaware Bay beaches.

Aside from the vast open areas and the pristine, undiked, and unditched salt marshes, much of the draw of this area is that virtually all of it is protected public open space. Fortescue Wildlife Management Area and Egg Island Wildlife Management Area provide over 10,000 acres of quality wetlands to birds and birders. In addition, the Glades Wildlife Area Refuge, owned by the Natural Lands Trust Inc. (NLT), protects another 7,500 acres of wetlands and uplands. Also, the adjacent state-owned Bear Swamp

Natural Area and Millville Wildlife Management Area (known as
Bevan WMA) provide well over
15,000 acres of protected habitat.
All these sites create one of the
largest contiguous protected open-
space areas in New Jersey.

Dallas Lore Sharp, in his 1908
book *Lay of the Land,* said that
"Bear Swamp is the least-trod area
of primeval swamp in southern
New Jersey." He called it a "land
of tree giants: huge tulip poplar
and swamp white oak." His words
are still true today. Among the
wildest areas of New Jersey, Bear
Swamp is the only sizable remnant
of old-growth hardwood, lowland
swamp forest on the entire coastal
plain of New Jersey. Totalling
more than 3,500 acres of wet forest with islands of higher oak-pine
forest, Bear Swamp lies north of
Dividing Creek and east of Newport. Some active and overgrown
fields are present on the periphery,

A Willet welcomes visitors to Fortescue.

and two large sand-mining com-
pany properties are active within the historical boundaries of the swamp.
These create a number of large, deep lakes adjacent to the bottomlands.
Some of these lakes are recent and sterile; others provide remote high-
quality wildlife habitat. Three tidal creeks touch the area as well, further
increasing both botanical and avian diversity.

Approximately 500 acres of the forest are virtually uncut—unlogged
climax forest—and contain at least three record New Jersey trees (Pond
Pine, Basket Oak, and Sweetbay Magnolia), as well as near-record specimens of Tulip Tree, Red Maple, Sweet Gum, Black Gum, Beech, and
American Holly. Some trees are estimated to be more than 500 years old,
and some experts have called Bear Swamp the oldest hardwood forest in
the northeastern United States. Trees escaped the loggers' axes only because
so many of them are hollow and much of Bear Swamp is so wet, making
tree removal difficult. While the Tulip Trees are the biggest and grandest—
some measure over 15 feet in circumference—they are not the oldest. The

Black and Sweet Gums are older—some may have been standing when Columbus first saw America.

Bear Swamp hosts the biggest winter Bald Eagle roost in the Delaware Bay region, with as many as 25 eagles present some years. Approximately 119 species of birds have been found to breed in Bear Swamp, an unusually rich breeding bird diversity for New Jersey. As in Belleplain State Forest, Bear Swamp's association of southern breeding birds is significant, and the swamp has a southern flavor more commonly associated with the southeastern states. Although virtually all species are known to breed elsewhere in New Jersey, the density of certain southern forest dwellers is highest in Bear Swamp. Wood Duck, Barred Owl, Blue-gray Gnatcatcher, and Summer Tanager are common. Red-eyed, White-eyed, and Yellow-throated Vireos are all common. Prothonotary, Yellow-throated, Hooded, and Kentucky Warblers are all found in good numbers, and Bear Swamp is one of the most important breeding areas for Prothonotary and Yellow-throated Warblers in the northern portion of their breeding range. Northern Parula, once extirpated as a breeder in southern New Jersey swamps, has now recolonized in some numbers. Worm-eating Warbler and Acadian Flycatcher are common. One or two pairs of Pileated Woodpeckers have recolonized as well—one of the few places they can be found in southern New Jersey. Bear Swamp contains an amazing diversity and abundance of breeding birds directly related to its range of habitats, both natural and man-made, and to its great size. Managed as a natural area, the site doesn't have trails and boardwalks. Nonetheless, birding can be excellent from rural roadsides and railroad rights-of-way.

North of Bear Swamp and on higher ground, Millville WMA (a.k.a. Bevan WMA) offers a seemingly endless assemblage of upland fields, hedgerows, and pine-oak forest for naturalists to explore. Bevan has a rich diversity of breeding birds: Pine, Prairie, and Yellow Warblers; Eastern Bluebirds; Indigo Buntings; and Blue Grosbeaks. Eastern Meadowlarks are uncommon as breeders but abundant in winter. Yellow-throated Vireos and Worm-eating Warblers are present in small numbers; Ovenbirds and Wood Thrushes are abundant. Whip-poor-wills are common and are easily heard between dusk and dawn. Both Yellow-billed and Black-billed Cuckoos breed here, and the Red-breasted Nuthatch has nested (rarely). Buckshutem Creek, a tributary of the Maurice River, adds habitat diversity to Millville WMA, and the forested wetlands along the creek support Barred Owl, Wood Thrush, Hooded Warbler, and Prothonotary Warbler. Summer Tanagers are surprisingly common here, and it is not unusual to see or hear Summer and Scarlet Tanagers side by side. Think of Bear Swamp and Millville WMA as the place where the Deep South meets the northern forest. Millville WMA also offers excellent birding during migration and in winter. A winter list includes flocks of juncos and Field Sparrows, but also a few Chipping Sparrows, Fox Sparrows, both nuthatches, and Brown Creepers. Hermit Thrush and Golden-crowned Kinglet are common in winter. Cooper's Hawks are found at all seasons. Red Crossbill has been recorded here recently, in small numbers, in both winter *and* summer; a few pairs probably breed, but this is one discovery waiting to be made.

Birding the Site

From Bivalve, go west on Route 553 for about 3.25 miles. Take a hard left turn onto **Hansey Creek Road**, which leads to some of the vast Egg Island WMA lands. Bird the woods in spring for migrants and in summer for breeding Brown Thrashers, Great crested Flycatchers, and others. Great Horned Owl and Screech Owl are common here; listen at dusk or before dawn. This is also a great place to observe woodcock courtship flights in March. Both Whip-poor-will and Chuck-will's-widow are here—the whips in the woodlands and the chucks near the fields and marsh. Tree Sparrows are usually found here in winter. To be frank, this is one of South Jersey's *worst* areas for biting bugs, so you'll probably want to avoid these fields in June and July unless there is a strong wind to keep the flies away.

When the road dead-ends, you are surrounded by salt marsh. Northern Harriers nest here in summer and share winter skies with Short-eared Owls. King Rail has been reliably reported in summer, among the abundant Clapper and Virginia Rails. The Virginia Rail is found in the more brackish areas near the upland edge. Seaside and Saltmarsh Sharp-tailed Sparrows both nest in this entire area. Marsh Wrens are abundant in summer, and Sedge Wren has been found recently in winter. The road ends at a creek, which is an excellent canoe or kayak launching spot. Remember, though, that these are tidal creeks, and returning against the tide could be difficult. Note the town of Fortescue on the horizon to the southwest.

Retrace your steps to Route 553, go north for 0.7 mile to the town of Dividing Creek, and turn left onto Maple Street. The town quickly gives way to fields and wetlands. The **Maple Street Impoundments** soon appear on both sides of the road. They are excellent for shorebirds during migration (these are tidal impoundments, so low tide is imperative for shorebirds here) and for a good variety of waterfowl in winter and spring. Tundra Swans are sometimes found among the throng of Mute Swans. Bufflehead, mergansers, Gadwall, and teal are abundant in season, and Common Goldeneyes and Canvasbacks are often present.

The woods you enter next are sometimes great for migratory songbird fallout in both spring and fall. You are now in the Natural Lands Trust's 7,500-acre **Glades Wildlife Refuge.** Feel free to walk any trails you see in areas marked with NLT signs. The trails take you through extensive

The walking bridge at Turkey Point is an excellent vantage point.

fields, edges, woodlots and lead to salt marsh overlooks. Boots are usually required here, even for what appear to be upland trails. Ticks are abundant.

Continue on Maple Street until Turkey Point Road/Route 664 comes in from the right. NLT's Maple Street Trail begins here on the left. Continue straight. You are now on **Turkey Point Road;** the vast Glades Wildlife Refuge is on either side of the road, which makes a sharp left turn and enters a salt marsh. NLT's Bald Eagle Trail is on the right, just beyond the sharp left. This trail is of historical interest; it leads to where Bald Eagles were "hacked" in the state's vigorous and successful reintroduction program from 1982 to 1990.

Next, the road crosses two small bridges across tidal creeks—both are excellent vantage points. Look for Glossy Ibis, yellowlegs, and Dowitchers in ponds, and all three species of merganser in the creeks in winter. The road dead-ends at the second bridge. Park to enjoy the excellent views from the observation tower and footbridge. Often there is a Red-tailed Hawk (or Great Horned Owl) nest visible from the tower. Mainly enjoy the vista. Healthy tidal salt marsh stretches to infinity here, or at least a full 5 miles to Egg Island Point. This is one of the wildest views in New Jersey and is especially pleasant at sunset.

Walk across the footbridge to enjoy a short trail, to the left, in the Egg Island WMA. Throughout the area, scan for Snow Geese, raptors, shore-birds, and waders in season. This is a great spot for winter Rough-legged Hawks—there are usually one or two even in nonflight years. Short-eared Owls are present, in varying numbers, every winter. Ruby-crowned Kinglet should be here in fall and winter, and a few Marsh Wrens always winter (and breed in good numbers). Sedge Wren has wintered here. Common Moorhen, Least Bittern, Black Rail, and Gadwall all nest in this area, as do a few pairs of Northern Harriers. Boat-tailed Grackle can be common here.

Retrace your steps and take the first left onto Route 664/Turkey Point Road to return to Route 553. NLT boundary signs line the left (west) side of Turkey Point Road and NLT's Warfle Farm Trail begins on the left, directly across from Hickman Avenue. Remember to scan freshwater ponds for waterfowl and perched raptors. Yellow-breasted Chat, Orchard Oriole, Blue Grosbeak, and Indigo Bunting all nest along this road in summer. Also in summer, consider renting a boat from one of the boat liveries in the Dividing Creek area for unparalleled access to the salt marshes and tidal creeks (but be prepared for greenhead flies—wear long sleeves and pants).

At Route 553, turn left and proceed north (Bear Swamp is now on your right). Proceed 2.6 miles toward Newport and make a left on Route 656. Go 0.9 mile, and make a left onto Route 637/Fortescue Road. Beyond the town of Newport and farmland, Fortescue WMA is on your right and the Glades Wildlife Refuge is on your left. On Route 637 go 1.1 mile until the road forks. Take the left fork, remaining on Route 637. Continue 0.9 mile to the entrance on the left for the National Park Service office (New Jersey Coastal Heritage Trail Route Pinelands Interpretation) at NLT's Bromley Camp. Stop in for brochures and maps to the Coastal Heritage Trail. Some of the sites are detailed in this book but there are many other sites too, all of them interesting. On Route 637 proceed 0.4 mile to a small parking area on the left (at the end of a short road). This is the trail-head for NLT's Russell Farm Trail, an extensive trail system. If the gate is chained across the road and parking area, park safely on the roadshoulder and walk in. On Route 637 proceed 0.3 mile to a gravel road on the left. If this road is chained, again park safely on the roadshoulder, otherwise follow the road to a parking area. From here explore the fields and woods around the parking area and follow a nature trail through upland and lowland woods (par-

ticularly good during migration). Long-eared Owls have been found roosting in Red Cedar and holly along this trail in winter. The trail eventually reaches the salt marsh where a narrow, elevated boardwalk continues across the marsh. An observation tower at the end of the trail offers one of the most remarkable views in South Jersey and one which ably demonstrates the vastness of the Fortescue marshes. In winter, check the creeks for diving ducks, Pied-billed Grebe, and river otter. Raptor numbers are good here. The ponds to the north of this boardwalk trail are always worthwhile;

Birders gather at the Glades observation tower during a November CMBO "Birding Cumberland" event.

up to 7,000 Dunlin, 100 Canvasbacks, and 1,000 Green-winged Teal have been counted here in season.

Continue on Route 637 1.4 mile to the bayside fishing village of **Fortescue**. Cross the bridge over Fortescue Creek and continue on the main road until it curves to the right and then dead-ends at the bay. Here, turn left onto New Jersey Avenue and drive southeast along the Delaware Bay. Scan the bay, beach, and marsh along the way. The road will dead-end in 1 mile just beyond a small bridge over a tidal creek. You are now over-looking Fortescue WMA. From November to March, this is an excellent spot to scan for Short-eared Owls. Snow Geese numbers can be spectacular here in winter. Scan the bay for diving ducks and loons in winter; Common Goldeneyes are often numerous here. Brown Pelicans and even Wilson's Storm-Petrel are sometimes seen in summer. In May and early June, these beaches host vast numbers of shorebirds: Red Knot, Ruddy Turnstone, Dunlin, Sanderling, and Semipalmated Sandpiper. Look for the uncommon White-rumped Sandpiper and scan gull concentrations for Lesser Black-backed Gulls. Observe signage so as not to disrupt shorebird feeding. These beaches are the best area in Cumberland to view the spring shorebird and horseshoe crab aggregations. The best viewing site is NLT's Raybin's Beach just before the small bridge; look for signage directing you to the observation area.

Retracing your route, take Route 637/Fortescue Road north. Take the first left off Fortescue Road onto Route 734/Schoolhouse Road. After 0.7 mile, turn left onto Route 643/Newport Neck Road (usually unmarked). Here too, vast unspoiled marshes can be viewed. Northern Harriers nest here, and Short-eared Owls and Rough-legged Hawk are common some winters. The road leads to the little towns of Gandy's Beach and Money Island. Gandy's Beach provides another Delaware Bay overlook. At the far end (to the right) is The Nature Conservancy's **Gandy's Beach Preserve**, protecting 2,580 acres of beach, salt marsh, and forest. This is another great spot to observe shorebirds in spring. The distant navigation tower has nesting Double-crested Cormorants, the only place in South Jersey where they are known to breed. Return to Route 637, but before continuing to Route 533, make a left onto Route 656/Newport Landing Road when 637 ends. This road dead-ends at **Newport Landing** on Newport Creek and provides another excellent vantage point. A restaurant, boat ramp, and boat rentals are available here. One reward here is the resident pair of Bald Eagles. Over the years, they've built huge nests on each of the two wooded islands in the marsh and most recently in the treeline to the right. Eagles should be present in any season, as the adults use the nests as roost sites year-round.

As an alternative route, to focus on **Bear Swamp Natural Area** and Millville WMA, begin at the junction of Routes 47 and 347. Take

Route 670/Mauricetown Causeway west, over the bridge. Go straight at the blinking light onto Route 649 (follow signs for Port Norris). At the next intersection, make a right onto Route 676/Highland Avenue or Haleyville-Mauricetown Road. Proceed 3.3 miles until you reach a small bridge, just before a sharp bend. Park here, off to the side. Scan the lake for Wood Ducks, Belted Kingfisher, and Great Blue Herons. In spring, listen for Louisiana Waterthrush downstream. Wood Thrush and Prothonotary Warbler are found here, and Pileated Woodpecker has been heard (rarely) as well. The left-hand turn here, Toms Bridge Road (0.5 mile long), is a pleasant mix of habitats ending at a tidal creek and is fun at any season.

From here, travel west on Route 676/Haleyville Road. This road, moderately traveled, passes along the southern boundary of Bear Swamp. Bird along the road, listening for Blue Grosbeak and breeding warblers. It's hard not to hear or see Wild Turkeys here. Route 676 dead-ends onto Route 553 in the town of Dividing Creek. Turn right; proceed north 0.3 mile to Route 555 and turn right again.

This road goes north through the center of Bear Swamp, with Bear Swamp Natural Area still on your right. Scan the man-made lakes here and throughout the area for Common Loon in spring and fall and Common Merganser, Common Goldeneye, and Ruddy Duck in winter. Check gull flocks if present. Bald Eagles perch around these lakes at all seasons. The first pond on the left, 0.2 mile north of Route 553 and just beyond the Dividing Creek Fire Company, is particularly good. Park off the road (not in front of the firehouse) and bird near the picnic tables and spillway. Belted Kingfishers are almost always present here. Expect Hooded Merganser in winter and spring. Bald Eagle is daily here. Remarkably, Osprey has been found here on the Christmas Bird Count.

Proceed north, birding along Route 555. One of the best areas is near the culvert on the sharp curve 1.6 miles north of Dividing Creek. Although this is not a heavily traveled road, pull well off to the side, particularly at this curve. Listen for Acadian Flycatcher, Yellow-throated Warbler, Prothonotary Warbler, Hooded Warbler, Worm-eating Warbler, and the rarer Kentucky Warbler. Brown creeper has nested here. There are woodland roads and trails off Route 555, but they are only for the adventuresome; they are not marked and are often overgrown and tick infested. If you go in here, take a compass; Bear Swamp is large.

Proceed north 0.9 mile to the railroad tracks and park in the pull-off to your right. Walk to your right (east) on the dirt road, paralleling the tracks. Bear Swamp, with its lowland breeding species, is on your right, and Millville WMA is now on your left. On the higher, drier slopes here, look and listen for Yellow-throated Vireo, Summer Tanager, Hairy Woodpecker, and Eastern Bluebird. Red-breasted Nuthatch has nested in this area twice. White-breasted Nuthatch should be common at any season.

While much of Bear Swamp Natural Area is largely inaccessible (compared to most other places highlighted herein), the Natural Lands Trust is developing some overlooks and access to its major recent acquisition of over 1,500 acres in the western section of Bear Swamp. Probably the best way to experience Bear Swamp is by supporting the great conservation efforts of the Natural Lands Trust—and by contacting them for the dates of their irregular but annual guided expeditions into the wondrous world of Bear Swamp where you can still witness "the largest, least-trod area of primeval swamp in southern New Jersey" of which Dallas Lore Sharp spoke in 1908. It remarkably remains so today, and is where the haunting notes of Barred Owls still punctuate the pre-dawn in deep and dark primordial woods.

As you again proceed north on Route 555 you are now passing through the vast **Millville Wildlife Management Area**. At 1.4 miles north of the railroad tracks, take Ackley Road/Route 718 in either direction. To the left (west) this dirt road will pass through pine-oak woods and fields. Look for Chipping and Field Sparrows in summer, many others in winter. Bobwhite, Ruffed Grouse and Wild Turkey are all found here. Hooded and Worm-eating Warblers are in low-lying areas, Blue-winged Warblers in successional tangles. Prairie Warbler is abundant and Summer Tanager common. At 0.7 mile farther north on Route 555, an unmarked gravel road on the left offers extensive access to Millville WMA. This road is generally closed to vehicles from March 15 to September 1, but foot and bicycle travel is encouraged. Because of its huge size, off-road bicycles are an excellent way to traverse Millville WMA. Explore any and all side roads and trails; be sure to take plenty of water. Most roads are hard-packed gravel and easily ridden. Any could lead to discoveries.

ATLANTIC COUNTY AND BEYOND

New Jersey barrier islands and the vast salt marshes that separate them from the mainland stretch many miles north, to the northern tip of Barnegat Bay. As you can imagine, birding opportunities do not end at the Cape May County line. We've already explored parts of Atlantic County—Great Egg Harbor Bay and the Great Egg Harbor River at the Corbin City impoundments—but once again we've only scratched the surface of possibilities beyond Cape May's borders.

Foremost on our list of must-see places to the north, and foremost on every New Jersey birder's list—residents and visitors alike—is Forsythe NWR, forever to be known as Brigantine Refuge. In fact, Cape May has claimed Brigantine as its own. Few birders who visit Cape May can resist

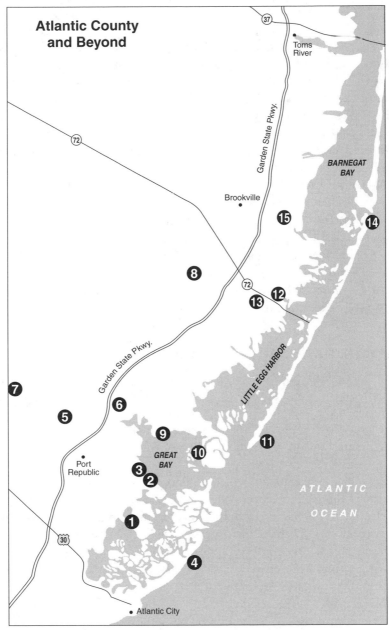

Atlantic County and Beyond

1. Forsythe NWR (Brigantine)
2. Leeds Point
3. Mott's Creek
4. Brigantine Island
5. Mullica River
6. Amassas Landing
7. Wharton State Forest
8. Stafford Forge WMA (pygmy forest)
9. Graveling Point
10. Great Bay Boulevard
11. Holgate
12. Manahawkin WMA
13. Cedar Run Dock Road
14. Barnegat Light
15. Barnegat Impoundment

the urge to visit Forsythe at least once during their stay—no matter what the season. Most stop by Brigantine on their way to or from the Cape— Friday or Sunday afternoon for quick weekend visitors. For those spending more time, the visits often come when the winds are wrong for classic migration at Cape May Point.

Beyond Brigantine (geographically), there are many other possibilities within an easy day's drive from Cape May proper. The fabled Pine Barrens lie just northwest of Forsythe, beyond the mighty Mullica River that feeds Great Bay to the north and east of the refuge dikes. Finally, the causeway to popular Long Beach Island leads to two of New Jersey's best birding desti-nations—Holgate on the southern tip of the island and Barnegat Light at the northern tip. Although it takes a full day to bird these remote Cape May outposts, for birders spending a week or two at any season, they are places that always beckon. They are both birdy (at all times of the year) and scenic, offering vast, pleasant beachfront and ocean vistas. They are good bets for any extended Cape May itinerary (particularly so in winter), and these great northern places rarely fail to please.

FORSYTHE NATIONAL WILDLIFE REFUGE (BRIGANTINE)

Edwin B. Forsythe NWR, one of more than 525 in the National Wildlife Refuge System, is one of the oldest, originally established in 1939. In the eastern United States, it is also one of the biggest and finest, a true gem that is visited by more than 250,000 people each year. This visitorship has been estimated to add 9.4 million dollars to the local economy, an amazing nature tourism success story.

Today totaling some 46,000 acres, Forsythe NWR was once primarily a waterfowl refuge, protecting American Black Duck and Brant (and it still does). But Forsythe has evolved into much more, and the refuge now man-ages vast and varied habitats that support a wide variety of both migratory and nesting birds. Over 300 species of birds have been found at the inimi-table Brigantine. Even more impressive than the number of species is the sheer numbers of birds present—waterfowl can total upward of 100,000, and shorebirds can near this number too. The spectacle of birds at Brig, from thundering rises of waterfowl to immense flocks of wheeling shore-birds, is a beautiful and heartening sight enjoyed at few other places in east-ern North America. When Forsythe is good, it is the best of birding.

Forsythe exists primarily in two divisions—the original core Brigantine Division, and the newer, ever-growing Barnegat Division, first established in 1967. More than 80 percent of these combined divisions are composed of tidal salt marshes and shallow bays, but Forsythe also protects wooded uplands, fresh and brackish marshes, barrier islands, dunes, and oceanfront.

Forsythe is known primarily for the Brigantine Division that lent its former name and its stellar wildlife drive. Here, diking has created nearly 1,500 acres of impounded fresh and brackish marsh habitat—a magnet for birds in an otherwise saltwater environment. The famous Brig impoundments are managed primarily for waterfowl in fall and winter and for shorebirds in spring and summer. The Wildlife Drive, a leisurely 8-mile, one-way loop, offers spectacular views of the various impoundments and of tidal salt marsh on the "other side" as you traverse the well-maintained gravel road.

Over 6,000 acres of Forsythe NWR is designated as a wilderness area, including Holgate and Little Beach Island. Holgate is at the south end of Long Beach Island, a 2.5-mile-long sand spit with dunes, vegetation, and mudflats on the bay side. Little Beach (on some maps called Pullen Island) is a roughly 3-mile-long barrier island lying between Holgate Inlet to the north and Brigantine Inlet (and Brigantine Island) to the south. It is the only undeveloped barrier island on the entire New Jersey coast and, sadly but wisely, is closed to all public access. It is an oasis and stronghold for colonial nesters—terns and skimmers, and herons and egrets. Piping Plovers also nest there in numbers. The south end of Holgate and the tip of Great Bay Boulevard, as well as the north end of Brigantine Island, offer good views across to Little Beach, although not close enough for birding, except for the distant Brown Pelicans on the beach or Snowy Owl atop the dunes.

Forsythe NWR is a joy to bird (except maybe in greenhead fly season). It offers a great variety of habitats, birds, and experiences. When you combine the Brigantine and Barnegat Divisions, they are a major destination in their own right, and you could easily spend a week birding all the nooks and crannies of this vast refuge. The Brigantine impoundments are heavily birded daily, but most of the rest of the refuge rarely is—partly because of inaccessibility, partly because of closures, and partly because of the long walks involved. One of the best ways to see the refuge is by boat, but the rough-water bays, Great Bay and Barnegat Bay, do not lend themselves well to kayaks (probably only experienced ocean kayakers should attempt to tackle these large bays and swift-moving inlets).

In the end, we like the inaccessibility of much of Forsythe. Major discoveries of rare birds are made frequently, yet the sheer size and scope of the refuge make us feel that there are still great avian discoveries to be made. It is in part this mystery that lures us back again and again to this keystone area.

Birding the Site

To bird Forsythe well, even just the Brigantine Division, it's best to set aside an entire day. You can make a quick hit on your way north, maybe even finding the staked-out rarities, but changing tides bring constantly changing conditions, so a day of exploring is most productive. High tide is best as shorebirds, Brant, and others are forced off the tidal wetlands and into the impoundments to find fresh water and mudflats for roosting. Veterans will drive around the loop two or three times before they feel they've done it justice. The "north dike" is best in the early morning, the "south dike" is best in the afternoons because of the angle of the sun.

Forsythe is about an hour-and-a-half drive from Cape May. To reach Forsythe's Brigantine Division, the offices and headquarters, and the wildlife drive, take the Garden State Parkway north from Cape May to mile marker 41. Exit into the service area (gas and restaurants), and exit the service area between the northbound and southbound lanes, following signs for Jimmy Leeds Road. At the traffic signal, go right onto Jimmy Leeds Road, and in 0.4 mile bear left at a fork onto Great Creek Road. Proceed for 3.1 miles to a traffic signal at Route 9. Go straight across. Lily Lake on your right sometimes holds Ring-necked Ducks and others. In about 1 mile you enter the NWR. From the north, it is easier to take Exit 48 and head south on Route 9 for 6 miles to reach the entrance road (on your left) in Oceanville.

Just beyond the entrance sign, at a small bridge, search the freshwater ponds for Wood Duck, Pied-billed Grebe, coot, and, rarely, Sora and Virginia Rail. Proceed to the refuge headquarters area and the small parking area to your left. The Brigantine Division of Forsythe charges an entrance fee, payable on the honor system at the kiosk by the bathrooms, just beyond the parking area. Daily passes are available, and Duck Stamps and Golden Eagle Passports are honored. Use the restroom facilities here, because they are the only ones available until you complete the 8-mile loop. Be sure to check the sightings log in the small building by the kiosks; this log is updated regularly by birders—sometimes hourly. Sightings are logged using a grid system, so check the grid map here. Also, brochures, bird checklists, and the self-guiding wildlife drive brochure are available here; the wildlife drive brochure contains the grid map. The headquarters and visitor center, with a number of wildlife displays, are across the entrance road. In summer, a lively Purple Martin colony can be seen in the field just beyond the facilities area.

Enter the wildlife drive. It is two-way to Gull Pond, about 1 mile, but when you make the left off the dead-end Gull Pond Road onto the main loop, it becomes one-way traffic only. You are free to stop anywhere, but be sure to pull off to the side so that other cars can easily pass. Leap-frogging of other cars is readily acceptable here, as few groups bird at the same pace.

The observation tower at the end of Gull Pond Road is a key stop for both shorebirds and waterfowl. Also, you are close to the woods' edge here, the upland edge of the marsh, which is one of the best spots in the refuge

Vast stretches of good habitat at Forsythe NWR can easily provide a full day of birding.

for raptors in fall and winter. It's a key area for both Least and American Bitterns too. Return on the two-way road. You can either go back to the headquarters area or turn left onto the main wildlife drive. From now on, tidal salt marshes, mudflats, and bays are to your right, and impounded fresh and brackish waters are to your left as you drive east on the south dike.

The stretch from here to the cross dike is usually one of the best areas for ducks in fall, winter, and early spring and for shorebirds from April to November. Look for Clapper Rail where the marsh grass meets the mud-flat to your right. Wait long enough, and one usually pokes its head out. Look for Saltmarsh Sharp-tailed Sparrow and Seaside Sparrow here too. At the observation tower, scan to the north for ducks and shorebirds at any season. This is West Pool, where you can expect anything—Garganey, Cinnamon Teal, Black-bellied Whistling Duck, and Fulvous Whistling Duck have all been seen here. Check for the resident peregrines perched on the artificial aerie on the cross dike. The original pair at this hack tower were one of the first successful breeding pairs in the early days of peregrine reintroduction. Check the bay for Double-crested Cormorants and diving ducks. There is usually a sizable raft of Canvasbacks here in late winter and a few Common Goldeneyes. Eared Grebe has been found here on several occasions. Check mudflat banks to the south for Brant, oystercatcher, and Black-bellied Plover.

Osprey are over Reeds Bay here from March through October, and they nest on numerous platforms on the salt marsh. Look for diamond-backed terrapins, a true saltwater turtle, laying eggs on the dike in June or swimming in the bay during the warmer months. The Atlantic City sky-line is about 7 miles to the southeast. The largest building is the Borgata Casino at 40 stories and 480 feet, the fifth tallest building in New Jersey (the first four are all in Jersey City). Also on the horizon here you can see

South Jersey's first "wind farm," five windmills that went online in 2005 to power the Atlantic County Utilities Authority sewage treatment and recycling facilities. They are being closely monitored for any impact on bird populations. If powering residential development, these five 380' tall turbines would power about 2,400 homes.

A scope is a necessity at Brigantine, where shorebirds are often distant. Plan to spend considerable time searching through flocks of thousands of shorebirds and thousands of ducks. Numbers can be massive here. Also massive are the numbers of greenhead flies in summer. If possible, bird on windy days, and wear long sleeves and pants. There are some days when you can't even get out of the car because of the kamikaze greenhead attacks. Brigantine can be great in the rain, however. On the wildlife drive you can do a lot of birding from the car. Window mounts for scopes are popular here.

Continue down the south dike. Past the cross dike, East Pool is now on your left. East Pool never holds the numbers of birds that West Pool does, but it can still be very good. Large flocks of Greater Yellowlegs in fall often harbor late-lingering Hudsonian Godwits, sometimes surprisingly camouflaged among the yellowlegs. Wilson's Phalaropes are regular here, and Red-necked Phalaropes are possible. Where the dike turns sharply to the left, at the corner onto East Dike, look for egrets, ibis, and roosting nightherons. This is a particularly good stop at any season. Once, in the summer of 1971, all the world's godwits were seen in a single flock here—a Blacktailed Godwit and a Bar-tailed Godwit joining a small mixed flock of Marbled and Hudsonian Godwits—probably the only time this has happened anywhere in the world. This was before our time, but our fondest memory of "the corner" is of two Snowy Owls chasing each other one December day—two of the three that were present at the refuge at the time.

At the northeast corner of the dike, check Broad Creek and Perch Cove. At the bend, you begin heading back west toward the upland on the north dike. The dogleg, where the cross dike meets the north, is another important stop. This is usually a mudflat teeming with shorebirds in spring and fall. This grassy verge is the best spot in the NWR for American Golden Plover, Upland Sandpiper, and Buff-breasted and White-rumped Sandpipers in fall (late August and early September is the key time for buff-breasts). Check here too for American Avocet (annual), which is likely to be seen swimming in deeper water. Cackling Goose and Ross's Goose are found here (or hereabouts) annually by those willing to sift through the thousands of Canadas and tens of thousands of snows. Check among the numerous Mute Swans for American White Pelican, which can blend in surprisingly well. White Pelican is annual here, and recently, one was virtually resident. Tundra Swans can be abundant here in late fall and winter (when the impoundments aren't frozen).

Prolonged winter freezes can empty the refuge when all waters are frozen, including, at times, even Reeds Bay. Normally, though, Brigantine remains excellent throughout the winter, with Rough-legged Hawks, Short-eared Owls, and many harriers present. Bald Eagles patrol in numbers and herd flocks of geese, looking for the unhealthy or the unwary. On the northwest gales of December, Golden Eagles are expected over the impoundments. The north dike is the best area to

The East Pool in fall is usually good for both Greater and Lesser Yellowlegs.

look for raptors. Scan the tree line to the west and to the north toward Leeds Point and Great Bay.

Proceed west along the north dike. This offers the best view of West Pool, except in late afternoon, when the glare of the sun can be a problem. Look for Caspian and Gull-billed Terns in late summer; a few gull-bills breed here. This final stretch can be exceptional. Brigantine holds the state record for Stilt Sandpiper (475 seen from the west dike on August 5, 2004). Finally, the dike enters the uplands. The fields are good for Indigo Bunting and Blue Grosbeak in summer, and sparrows in fall and winter. Bluebirds nest here, and Bobwhite hold on here, too. The white cedar swamp and the pine-oak woodlands are good for migrant songbirds in spring and fall. The bridge over Doughty Creek offers more views of a freshwater marsh and pond, a great place for Hooded Merganser in winter. After the bridge, you cross a treadle to return to Great Creek Road. Exit the refuge, or return to the bathrooms and kiosk area. Be sure to log your sightings for fellow birders.

There are several underbirded areas in the Brigantine Division. The Leeds Eco-trail is a half-mile-loop footpath along the edge of the marsh, with boardwalks over wet areas; the initial section is wheelchair accessible. This is good for Clapper Rail, Seaside Sparrow, Common Yellowthroat, Yellow Warbler, and Marsh Wren. Sedge Wren has been found here several times on migration. The Leeds Eco-trail begins to the right of the wildlife drive, just beyond the headquarters area. Even better can be the Akers Woodland Trail, which honors Jim Akers, an important conservationist in the 1970s. The Akers Trail, a quarter-mile loop through wooded uplands beginning near the bathrooms, can be an amazingly good spot for songbird fallout in spring and fall. Because it largely follows the immediate upland edge of the marsh, a lot of birds drop in here. Some of the fallouts are legendary here: One mid-May, a series of NJAS field trips collectively found thirty species of warblers in a single day. Another time birders enjoying myriad treetop warblers looked up through a break in the canopy to see a Swallow-tailed Kite floating overhead at treetop level. Any and all are possible at Forsythe NWR.

There are several other key areas of the Brigantine Division that lie outside the immediate area of the wildlife drive but should be visited if possible. Just north of the wildlife drive, **Leeds Point and Mott's Creek** offer excellent vistas of the vast Great Bay marshes at the mouth of the Mullica River. Leeds Point and Mott's Creek are particularly good for raptors from November through March, offering a good shot at Bald and Golden Eagles, Rough-legged Hawks, Short-eared Owls, Peregrine Falcons, and more. To reach Leeds Point from the refuge, return to Route 9 and make a right to head north. In 0.2 mile, bear right onto County Road 618/Leeds Point Road. At 1.9 miles, turn right onto Alternate Route 561/Oyster Creek Road, which soon bends hard left and goes about 1 mile before it dead-ends at Oyster Creek. Scan from the roadside, paying particular attention to the marsh islands and tree line to the west. Most raptors will be soaring.

Morning is best for rough-legs and eagles; late afternoon is best for hunting Short-eared Owls. Do not block the private commercial crabbing docks here. Returning on Route 561, turn left onto Scott's Landing Road to reach **Scott's Landing Boat Launch**, part of the refuge, which offers another good view of this vast region. All along 561 the Red Cedars can be good for fallout. Northern Shrikes have wintered here several times. Return to Route 9 via 561. At the Smithville traffic light, go right (north) on Route 9, and at 1.1 miles make a hard right onto Route 657/Mott's Creek Road. You will soon be on refuge property. The creeks to your right are excellent for Hooded Merganser in winter and spring, and raptors can be anywhere overhead or over the tree line. Leaving the woods, scan to the north toward the Mullica River and south toward Leeds Point. Look for refuge signage, and avoid the numerous homes and private property. At the end of this dead-end road, scan from the bulkhead next to the currently closed bar-restaurant. The area across the creek is particularly good for rough-legs and short-ears. Return to Route 9.

Another important birding area in Forsythe NWR is **Brigantine Island,** the barrier island north of Atlantic City. Brigantine is a highly developed seashore town, but at the south end, extensive mudflats along Absecon Inlet provide exceptional shorebirding in fall and even winter. Here, up to 400 Black Skimmers, 150 American Oystercatchers, and 200 "Western Willet" have been tallied, along with hundreds of Black-bellied

Plovers and other shorebirds. This is a key fall staging area and, a remarkably good winter roost as well. It is the best spot to see Marbled Godwit in New Jersey—200 were once counted here by a shorebird researcher, and as many as 37 have been known to winter here. In addition, gulls and terns abound here in season.

To reach the Absecon mudflats area from Forsythe NWR (Great Creek Road), go south on Route 9 for 3.7 miles until you reach Route 30. Go left onto Route 30, heading east toward Atlantic City. Travel about 6 miles until you reach the outskirts of Atlantic City. Follow signs to Route 87, Brigantine Boulevard (you will be following signs to Harrah's Hotel/Casino and Trump Marina Hotel Casino), but don't exit—remain on Brigantine Boulevard. Cross the high bridge over Absecon Inlet. Here Route 87 becomes Route 638. In 1.2 miles, take Harbor Beach Boulevard to your right. This will route you back south toward the inlet. Go one block to Lagoon Drive; turn right on Lagoon and follow it until it ends at a sandy road, which is the entrance to the beach.

Park at the entrance to the municipal park, and walk south to the beach and inlet. Shorebirds may be roosting to your right in the marsh or sometimes to your left, out toward the jetty. Remember that this is a high-tide spot; as the tide drops, most shorebirds disperse to feed on distant mudflats. Check the casino buildings for perched peregrines and the inlet waters at any season for waterbirds.

To your left is the Absecon Lighthouse, somewhat of a twin to Cape May's. More than 170 feet high, it was also built by George G. Meade. It was first lit in 1857. Shorebirds can sometimes be seen on the west side of Atlantic City–Brigantine Drive. To check, go down one or both of the two dead-end streets that go west off Route 87 before Lagoon Drive. These will offer views to the west. A couple hours before or after high tide are always the best times here. On low tides birds disperse widely to feed.

To reach our final destination, retrace your steps to Brigantine Boulevard. Turn right, heading north. In about 0.5 mile, Route 638 turns north, becoming Brigantine Avenue. Go about 1.7 miles through the town of Brigantine, north to the last possible left. Make a left onto Fourteenth Street north. Go 1 block to the end. Make a right onto East Beach Avenue and follow this to the gravel parking lot. Walk to the north. You are at the entrance to one of the most underbirded but wonderful areas in southern New Jersey—the **North Brigantine Natural Area** (NBNA). This is possibly one of the very best of our barrier island beachfront areas. It is underbirded in part because you have to go through part of Atlantic City to get there, but also because of its expanse. The undeveloped barrier beach stretches over 2 miles north to Brigantine Inlet, and a 4-mile round-trip walk in soft sand can be daunting.

The main shorebird roost area at NBNA is near the north tip, about 2 miles from the parking lot—a long walk, but well worth it. Counts of over 5,000 Sanderlings, 1,000 Semipalmated Plovers, 960 Black-bellied Plovers, and thousands of Dunlin have been obtained here. August counts of nearly 1,200 Red Knots have been tallied here. Curlew Sandpiper and Marbled Godwit have also been seen here. It is a major Piping Plover breeding area (eight to ten pairs usually nest here) and fall staging spot—up to 48 Piping Plovers have been counted here in August, one of the best concentrations in the state. In season, the beach is quite wisely closed to all vehicular traffic to protect them. Terns are here in numbers, as are Black Skimmers in some years. Brown Pelicans roost here daily.

Finally, attesting to the fact that NBNA can be good at any season, one dedicated observer once watched a gray Gyrfalcon repeatedly stoop to harass a Snowy Owl sitting on the deserted beach on a snowy January day that mirrored the muted colors of the birds. On that day, these ultimate Arctic visitors boldly embodied the wilderness values of the North Brigantine Natural Area.

MULLICA RIVER AND THE PINE BARRENS

For those with an interest in botany and herpetology as well as an interest in birding, the New Jersey Pine Barrens require little introduction. This wonderful ecosystem is unique among the great natural areas of the East. On the surface a vast, seemingly endless stretch of stunted pine forests, a closer look reveals the Pines to be so much more than that—from a complex and varied landscape to a fascinating characteristic ecosystem formed by high water tables, sandy soils, and frequent fires.

As Cape May field trip and tour leaders, it is surprising how often we are asked, even among hard-core birding groups, whether we are going to visit the Pine Barrens. Although a pinelands visit may not fit into a Cape May weekend or even a week, those who are staying longer and returning visitors may want to take a look at this fascinating area.

Actually, if you're following the itinerary of this book, you already have visited parts of the Pine Barrens. The protected area stretches south to Cape May and Cumberland counties, and we have visited the Pine Barrens at places such as Belleplain State Forest, Millville WMA in Cumberland County, Corbin City WMA in Atlantic and Cape May counties, and particularly along Weatherby Road. Just west of Route 9 on Great Creek Road, Forsythe NWR protects Oceanville Bog—both a representative pinelands bog and one known for a number of extremely rare plant species.

At first glance, the Pine Barrens seem to have little to offer birders beyond its abundance of Eastern Towhees, Pine Warblers, and Prairie Warblers. But although much of the area is mostly an avian monoculture, a closer look reveals some surprises. The first is the small population of breeding Black-throated Green Warblers found along white cedar streams in the central pines. Some believe that these birds may represent the southern race of this species, not the far more numerous race found in the mountains of northern New Jersey and beyond. Research on song dialect is clearly needed to establish the subspecies found in the Pine Barrens. Other interesting outlying populations are the small number of Hermit Thrush and Veerys that breed in the central pinelands, far removed from their highlands brethren. Also in this outlier category is Northern Goshawk; the New Jersey Atlas Project confirmed two pairs of Goshawks nesting in the pines, far from their normal range in the mountains of northwestern New Jersey.

Red Crossbill is a very rare but confirmed breeder in the Pine Barrens. Although it is certainly not present every year, successful local breeding has occurred a number of times following major winter incursions. A recent confirmed breeding record was near Dennisville, and they have been found in recent summers in Millville and Peaslee WMAs. Fascinating but unfathomable is a record of a juvenile Pine Grosbeak at Chatsworth in July. Also in this strange but true category are the numerous summer (July-August) banding records of Yellow-headed Blackbirds (including hatching-year birds) around Barnegat Bay in the 1970s, which might indicate that a small outlying population of this species bred in New Jersey for a time. Finally, rumors persist that a few Painted Buntings breed somewhere in the pinelands region but kept quiet by locals in order to protect the birds.

Stranger things have happened, such as Virginia's breeding Scissor-tailed Flycatchers.

More down to earth, a few pairs of Sandhill Cranes now breed in the Pine Barrens region—confirmed in Atlantic County in 2005 and probable near the Ocean County–Monmouth County border for several years. These birds supplement, or perhaps are the progeny of, the Cumberland County crane flock, with up to fifteen cranes reported there throughout the seasons. Members of this group, including a (probably) escaped Eurasian Common

Canoeing is a popular way for naturalists to experience the Pine Barrens.

Crane, several pure Sandhill Cranes, and numerous hybrid youngsters, have successfully bred on numerous occasion in northern Cumberland and Salem Counties and may be expanding into the Pine Barrens. It is well known that sandhills are expanding and recolonizing in the East. They now nest in New York, Pennsylvania, and northern New England.

Another avian wonder of the Pine Barrens is the waterfowl that winter along the numerous pristine rivers, including big numbers of Tundra Swans. Tundras are attracted to pinelands cranberry bogs when unfrozen (where they are considered a nuisance by farmers), and they gravitate to the wider, moving water during cold spells. Up to 1,150 have been recorded on the Wading River in December, and up to 1,000 at Forsythe NWR (they trade back and forth up and down the Mullica River).

The Pine Barrens birder in late fall, winter, and early spring should focus his or her efforts along the expansive Mullica River, New Jersey's largest coastal river and tributary to the Great Bay estuary. A Mullica tour is an easy extension during a Forsythe NWR visit. The Mullica is a lengthy tidal river; the tidal portions stretch about 14 miles from Batsto east to Great Bay. The upper river region has vast cedar swamps, bogs, and fresh to brackish wetlands, and the lower portion contains vast, healthy tidal salt marsh. Although such species as King Rail, Least Bittern, and Northern Harrier breed on these marshes, the real draw is winter waterfowl and raptors. Thousands of American Black Ducks, Mallards, Northern Pintails, and Canada Geese, as well as Tundra Swans, winter in the moving, open waters of the upper river; Brant, Common and Red-breasted Mergansers, scaup, and Bufflehead populate the lower. In good winters, up to twenty-five Bald Eagles can be tallied in a day, and this is a consistent stronghold for Golden Eagles, with three to four reliably present most years. We have seen as many as twenty-one rough-legs in a day hunting the vast and empty marshes of the great Mullica River.

Birding the Site

These directions are divided into two parts: a specific tour of the Mullica River area, and a more general reference to some classic Pine Barrens scenic sites. To enjoy the Mullica River from Forsythe NWR north and west to Batsto, go north on Route 9 for 5.4 miles until Route 9 flows into the Garden State Parkway. Cross the Mullica River on the high bridge. Peregrines are often seen here, both hunting pigeons and perched on towers. The wondrous expanse of marsh here lasts almost 2 miles, offering a great view of Great Bay to the east. Take the first exit after the bridge, Exit 50, for Route 9 and New Gretna. Immediately as you come off the exit ramp, an unmarked hard left heads off to the east—in essence, an exit off the exit. Take that left onto **Amassas Landing** Road. Go 0.4 mile on this bumpy road to a gravel parking area next to an abandoned building on your right. You are looking at Bass River, flowing south out of Bass River State Forest. This area is good at any season, but in winter, expect Bald Eagle, Golden Eagle, multiple harriers, and Rough-legged Hawk. This vies with Manahawkin as the most consistent spot to see rough-legs in New Jersey. In bad years, there's one or two present; in good years, we have seen as many as twelve at once. It's also quite good for Short-eared Owls. Virtually everything in view here, as far as you can see, is protected, part of Forsythe NWR or the hundred-year-old, 26,800-acre **Bass River State Forest**.

Retrace your steps, and at Exit 50 go north on Route 9. In New Gretna, about 0.8 mile ahead, take Route 542 west (this is a hard left on a curve; follow signs to Batsto). Go west and north for 2.5 miles. At a sharp bend to the left, pull off to the right at the Wading River Bridge. This spot offers a great view up and down the **Wading River**, a major tributary of the Mullica. Bird from the walkway on the north side of the bridge. Look for Bald Eagles, both perched and in flight, or the odd Golden Eagle in winter. Expect Common Mergansers and Tundra Swans from December through March. Continue west on Route 542 for 2.5 miles, and take Route 652 to Lower Bank.

At the **Lower Bank** Bridge there are more good vistas up and down the scenic Mullica River. Return to Route 542 and go left (west) for 1.8 miles to Route 563, which takes you south to **Green Bank** and yet another good view of the river and brackish marshes. Beyond the bridge, Route 563 leads you to white cedar swamps that may hold Black-throated Green Warbler in summer (as does Route 652/ Lower Bank Road).

Return to Route 542 and continue west for 3.6 miles to historic **Batsto Village**. This restored and re-created late 1700s mining town (bog iron) is a major Pine Barrens destination for historians, botanists, and naturalists. Enjoy the historical buildings and exhibits. Bathrooms are available here, as well as information regarding the vast **Wharton State Forest**—at 114,800 acres, it's New Jersey's largest. Birders should look for

A juvenile Red-headed Woodpecker forages on a dead tree near Batsto Village.

eagles and waterfowl on Batsto Lake and Red-headed Woodpeckers in the picnic area behind the administration building. Several pairs breed here and often winter as well. Listen for Black-throated Green Warblers along white cedar streams on the many hiking trails available here. Northern Saw-whet Owls, though secretive, breed here. Listen for them tooting in late winter, before the din of Spring Peepers drowns them out.

For a classic Pine Barrens experience, **Brendon T. Byrne State Forest** (formerly Lebanon State Forest; renamed for the governor who authored the preservation legislation) is another good place to visit. Found on Route 72, east of Route 70, the forest offers extensive hiking trails and camping. Byrne State Forest is another classic spot for Red-headed Woodpecker, although here forest succession has diminished its numbers. Summer Tanagers are common at Byrne, and it's a great spot for Whip-poor-wills. Unlike the Cape May region, Common Nighthawks still breed in the pinelands in some numbers. Black-throated Green Warblers also breed here, as do Hermit Thrushes and, rarely, Brown Creepers.

Another Pine Barrens destination is the New Jersey Conservation Foundation's **Franklin Parker Preserve,** covering 9,400 acres and over 14 square miles. This wondrous preserve in the heart of the Pine Barrens offers extensive hiking trails. It is a fine cross section of the Pine Barrens—pine-oak forest, over 150 acres of lakes and freshwater wetlands, and 80 acres of former cranberry bogs that are being actively restored to natural native wetlands. Because it was only recently protected (2004), comparatively little is known about this area, although Bald Eagles nest here and it is apparently a

Breeding Common Nighthawks, gone from Cape May, can still be found in the Pine Barrens.

breeding stronghold for American Kestrels. It is a known Golden Eagle roost area in winter. Wood Ducks, Hooded and Common Mergansers, Ring-necked Ducks, and Tundra Swans are common in season. It is a classic Pine Barrens area, with all the indicators—from Pine Barrens Tree Frogs and pine snakes to Pine Barrens Gentian. Its preservation story is lengthy and a modern-day miracle, the largest not-for-profit acquisition ever in New Jersey. It honors Franklin Parker, a pinelands conservation

Atlantic White-cedar streams are found throughout the Pine Barrens.

legend and one of its saviors. The Franklin Parker Preserve sits astride Routes 563 and 532 east of Wharton State Forest and south of Byrne State Forest.

A final Pine Barrens stop might be a visit to the famous **Pygmy Forest** region, where sandy soil (with few nutrients) and frequent forest fires have combined to create a pine plains area of severely stunted trees—both Pitch Pines and oaks. Think of it as a vast bonsai forest, with fire, the wind, and poor soil sculpting the trees. The amazing part of the pygmy pines story is that many of these trees are over 300 years old yet stand only about 5 feet high. You can actually see for miles over this stunted forest—one of the many wonders of the Pine Barrens. To enjoy the classic Pygmy Forest from Exit 58 on the GSP, go west on Route 539. The 7-mile stretch between the GSP and the small town of Warren Grove is mostly classic dwarf forest, particularly in higher areas. This area is all part of the vast **Stafford Forge WMA**, so it is public property. The open heath areas here, the "Pine Plains," are where Heath Hens were once found.

The New Jersey Pine Barrens are certainly not best known for their bird life, and birds will always be eclipsed here by botany, history, herpetology, and much more. At certain times and places, however, the ornithology of the area is interesting and different. We remember a brisk January hike in Wharton State Forest where we covered many miles of the sandy, forested trails. At dusk, we counted our minuscule bird list—a whopping total of seven species. But the day was memorable. The list contained Ruffed Grouse, Long-eared Owl, Tundra Swan, and a glorious young Golden Eagle soaring over a frozen, hidden bog in the middle of nowhere. The white wing patches and tail were glowing, lit up by the snow below. (The other three species were Blue Jay, Carolina Chickadee, and Dark-eyed

Junco.) Some days, and in some places, you don't judge your day by the length of the list. The still mysterious Pine Barrens is one of those areas.

GREAT BAY BOULEVARD AND HOLGATE

The Mullica estuary has much more to offer, from the aptly named Great Bay to Little Egg Inlet, which carries the bounty of the bay to the sea (and vice versa, as the Atlantic brings life to the bay on the twice-daily flooding tides). The estuary is the 110,000-acre Jacques Cousteau National Estaurine Research Reserve, so designated because of its pristine character and unmatched research potential. If the Pine Barrens can be a bit . . . well, barren of birds, the lower Mullica offers a surfeit of avian riches at any season, as well as wide open spaces equaled only on the Delaware Bayshore. Although the area is big, there is some terrific access to Great Bay and adjoining Little Egg Harbor Bay. Most of this area is still part of the huge Forsythe NWR or part of the state-owned Great Bay Boulevard WMA.

A key birding area in this region is Holgate, the undeveloped barrier island beach and dunes that form the southern end of Long Beach Island. Holgate is owned and managed by Forsythe NWR and is excellent for birds year-round. However, Holgate is not good for birders year-round, as it is completely closed to all public access from (usually) April 1 though August 31 to protect the endangered Piping Plover, as well as other beach nesters such as skimmers and terns. Holgate is a major national stronghold for Piping Plover populations. Because of this yearly closure, winter is the season when Great Bay and Holgate are birded most. It is also the time when the bay and inlet fill with waterfowl. Despite the draw, if you bird either Great Bay Boulevard or Holgate on a weekday, you will almost surely be the only birder there. For many, this solitude and remoteness are what they like about Holgate—an opportunity to share the empty beach with only Sanderling and Dunlin and maybe a Snowy Owl.

Birding the Site

Depending on specific interests and available time, there are a number of stops to be made on the way to Holgate. You had a limited view of Great Bay from Leeds Point, north of the Forsythe dikes, but there are much better views from Graveling Point and Great Bay Boulevard south of Tuckerton, where the "boulevard to nowhere" offers exceptional birding anytime. From the GSP bridge over the Mullica, take Exit 50 onto Route 9 north at New Gretna. Remain on Route 9 for about 6 miles until you reach Tuckerton. In Tuckerton (where many services are available), make a right onto Great Bay Boulevard and head south. In 0.3 mile, make a right onto Radio Road, which winds through the vast Mystic Islands complex, an area dredged and filled prior to the Wetlands Act of 1970. After about 5 miles, Radio Road dead-ends at **Graveling Point** and a small parking area that overlooks Great Bay. This can be fun at any season—for terns and egrets in summer, and migrants in spring and fall. The small grove of cedars here can host some fallout in spring or fall, as it is the first landfall for birds crossing the open water of Great Bay. Orange-crowned Warbler has wintered in these cedars with yellow-rumps.

This site is best from late fall through spring, when vast rafts of waterfowl populate the bay, taking advantage of the shallow water and myriad food sources. Canada Geese may predominate, but a sizable flock of Snow Geese is usually here too. Brant abound, distant skeins crisscrossing the bay. Diving ducks are a major draw, with abundant Red-breasted Merganser, Bufflehead, Greater Scaup, and Common Goldeneye. Look for eagles, both bald and golden, hazing waterfowl over Forsythe NWR in the distance.

Return to Tuckerton via Radio Road. When you again reach Great Bay Boulevard, make a right. This will route you back south to Great Bay, but about 4 miles east of Graveling Point. The birding zone begins in about 1.3 miles. Great Bay Boulevard, commonly known to birders as Seven Bridges Road, is a real gem. About 6 miles long and little traveled, 5 miles of it traverses pristine salt marsh. The "bridges" cross both creeks and channels, and salt ponds abound. All this area is **Great Bay Boulevard WMA**. At the end of the road, a scenic former U.S. Coast Guard station is now a research laboratory, the Rutgers University Marine Field Station. The crumbling factory in the distance to the west is the remains of the 1930s Fish Products Co. of New Jersey, a fish processing facility where Menhaden (bunker) were ground into oil for chicken and livestock feed. A combination of declining fish stocks and the plant's incompatibility with the "modern" seashore (odors were intense—putrid and pervasive) forced the facility to close around 1975. (Clay as a boy remembers the "Bunker Factory" on Wildwood Boulevard. It produced such foul odors that you sometimes had to close the windows on summer evenings in Stone Harbor.) Today, the factory on Great Bay is used by only seals, gulls, a pair of Barn Owls, and peregrines that nest in a nest box on the water tower.

Great Bay Boulevard is good in all seasons. In summer, herons, egrets, Willet, oystercatchers, and salt sparrows abound. During migration, anything is possible, and American Avocet, Black-necked Stilt, White Ibis, White-faced Ibis, and others have been found here. In fall, Seven Bridges Road is known as one of the best places to find and compare Saltmarsh and Nelson's Sharp-tailed Sparrows. The Red Cedars along the road and at the tip are good for migrants in spring and fall.

Bird each of the creeks from the base of the bridges and, if there is no traffic, from the bridges themselves. (Two of them are narrow, with one-way traffic controlled by lights.) Bird the length of the road. Muskrat and river otter are found here, and even mink have been seen here. At the tip, park by the informational signs and walk about 100 yards to the beach. Scan the bay to your right and the inlet to your left. The area directly across the bay is Little Beach Island—the sole undeveloped barrier island on the New Jersey coast. The lengthy sand spit in the distance to your left is Holgate. Scan the bay for diving ducks in fall, winter, and spring. Harbor seals are common here, with up to a dozen or so possible in winter. In early morning or late afternoon, check Holgate for a Snowy Owl. When seen from here they are distant but easily identified, as they characteristically perch atop a dune for their own view of the beach and bay.

Return to Route 9. To reach another good overlook, make a right and proceed into the center of Tuckerton. In 0.3 mile, turn right onto South Green Street/Country Road 603. Head south for about 2 miles to reach the small muncipal **South Green Street Park**. Picnic tables are found here, but no bathroom facilities, so be sure to stop in Tuckerton if need be. A small building in the park features a raised observation deck that makes a great windbreak during cold winter birding. The park offers a great view of Little Egg Harbor Bay. (The north end of the bay adjoins Barnegat Bay, but is technically separated by Manahawkin Bay.) From the overlook in the park you can see several of the bridges of Great Bay Boulevard. Boat-tailed Grackles are common here, except in winter.

Return to downtown Tuckertown via South Green Street. Check out **Gifford Mill Lake**, just north of Route 9, almost in the center of town. It's opposite Great Bay Boulevard, diagonally to your left as you reach Route 9 from the south. The Tip Seaman Municipal Park offers an excellent view. Waterfowl are always present; many are domestic, but the tame birds attract wild ducks fall through spring. Wood Ducks are usually present in the boggy white cedar areas across the lake. Ring-necked Ducks are often present in spring. Osprey fish here frequently.

In Tuckertown, you are well positioned to visit the Pine Barrens at Bass River State Forest. Look for the signs or follow Stage Road to the west. Route 539 meets Route 9 in Tuckerton. Follow Route 539 north to reach the Pygmy Pines region south of Warren Grove.

For those heading directly to Long Beach Island and Holgate from Cape May, take Exit 63 and head east on Route 72. From Tuckerton and Great Bay Boulevard, head north on Route 9 for about 8 miles until you reach Route 72. Travel the 5-mile causeway east onto Long Beach Island. Make a right onto County Road 607 (Long Beach Boulevard) and head south toward Beach Haven. Long Beach Island is a long island, with only the Route 72 access. It is 9.3 miles to the southern tip and the parking area for

Holgate. Watch for posted speed limit signs here. Along this route, almost any bayside street-end or dune walkover can offer birding opportunities, but your main destination is Holgate itself—a unit of Forsythe NWR. Park in the parking area by the kiosks and head south. It's a long walk—about 2 to 2.5 miles to the tip (depending on erosion)—but a rewarding one.

After September 1, the normal beach-reopening date, expect lingering terns and skimmers, and gulls in late fall and winter. In March, prior to closure, look for Piping Plovers and oystercatchers, among other shorebirds. The oceanfront here is excellent for seabirds—cormorants, gannets, loons, and scoters in fall, and jaegers hunting close in at times. The inlet has lots of diving ducks from fall through spring, as well as Horned Grebe and possibly Red-necked Grebe. Sandy areas at the base of the dunes should have Horned Larks, Snow Buntings, and the rare Lapland Longspur in winter. Expect "Ipswich" Savannah Sparrow. A key draw at Holgate in winter is Snowy Owl; it is virtually annual here. On nonflight years, there is usually a report or two in early December, and in good years, one or two are usually seen throughout the winter. Go early or late—the owls tend to hide down in the dunes during midday. Gyrfalcon has also been seen here several times in winter, adding real spice to the many possibilities of Holgate.

BARNEGAT LIGHT AND MANAHAWKIN

The final stop on our tour of the great north is one that many birders would consider the best. Barnegat Light, or, more properly, Barnegat Bay, inlet, and ocean, offers numbers and varieties of waterbirds rarely found farther south at other inlets. Barnegat is good at all seasons, but it is in winter—late November through March—that Barnegat Light shines the brightest. Then, it is not only one of the best spots in southern New Jersey but also one of the best anywhere in the mid-Atlantic states. Barnegat (not to be confused with the town on the mainland side of Barnegat Bay) is best for ducks. Specifically, it is the best place for Harlequin Ducks anywhere in New Jersey and is certainly the best place anywhere on the coast south of Montauk Point. Each winter, a small yet consistent and reliable flock forms there, and it is growing every year; more than 55 were seen together in one recent year. But harlequins are not the only draw at Barnegat. Common Eiders winter in considerable numbers, usually the highest in the state (in January 2006, nearly 200 were counted here). King Eider is annual here. Rafts of scoters (all three species) sit off the mouth of the inlet, and the numbers of Red-breasted Mergansers and Long-tailed Ducks can be amazing. The state maximum of Long-tailed Duck was recorded at Barnegat Inlet, with 3,000 counted on February 15, 1997.

In winter, search through the flocks of gulls at Barnegat and you might spot an Iceland Gull (at center) in their midst.

Both Red-throated and Common Loons are abundant here, often point-blank from the rocks. Gulls are abundant, from Bonaparte's and sometimes kittiwakes off the jetties to Glaucous and Iceland Gulls on the beach and rocks. Barnegat is one of the best places in south Jersey for white-winged gulls in winter. The same is true for alcids. Razorbill is almost expected, if not daily, at Barnegat Light most winters, and other alcids are seen here too. This is yet another spot to expect the unexpected. Brown Booby and White-tailed Tropicbird have been seen here—the tropicbird on the odd date of November 23, 1985. Parasitic Jaegers are regular off the mouth of the inlet in fall, and Brown Pelican is expected summer through fall. (Brown Pelicans have built "starter nests" on Barnegat Bay islands and may nest here someday.)

Finally, don't ignore the beach and dunes. Snow Bunting is regular here in winter in sizable flocks, and Lapland Longspur is annual. Expect Horned Lark and "Ipswich" Savannah Sparrow. The cedar thickets around the lighthouse hold migrant songbirds in spring and (mainly) fall. Always scan for Snowy Owl on the beach or perhaps perched on a beachside roof top. Snowys are probably most frequently seen sitting across the inlet on the jetty or dunes of Island Beach State Park—distant, but still a fair view by scope. In March, the Barnegat Lighthouse State Park holds their annual "Harbor Seals and Harlequins" event, with birding tours, interpretive programs, and talks.

Birding the Site

There are a number of ways to do this part of the tour. For geographic purposes, we have divided the routes into south of Route 72, Great Bay Boulevard and Holgate, and north of Route 72, which includes Barnegat Light and Manahawkin. Great Bay Boulevard and Holgate offer views of Great Bay and Little Egg Harbor Bay; Manahawkin and Barnegat Light overlook the waters of Barnegat Bay. Barnegat Light and Holgate are on opposite ends of 22-mile-long Long Beach Island and it can take almost an hour to get from one to the other.

Usually, Barnegat Light provides enough birds for a full day's worth of exploring, but in winter, few birders can resist the Rough-legged Hawks and Short-eared Owls at Manahawkin, which is actually a combination of Forsythe NWR's Barnegat Division and the state-owned Manahawkin WMA. (You will be birding at the WMA, but most of the vast area you see is part of Forsythe.) Manahawkin is highly regarded as one of the best, most consistent, and most reliable spots in New Jersey for both Short-eared Owl and Rough-legged Hawk in late fall, winter, and early spring. In fact, they are hard to miss here. The draw is an expanse of high marsh. Much of this area was once salt hay farms. Although the farms are gone, much of the high marsh habitat still exists. Perhaps because the land is federally owned, there has been less of the pervasive ditching and flooding found almost everywhere else. As a result, birds such as short-ears, rough-legs, and harriers abound here (a few harriers nest). Sedge Wren and Black Rail are found here on migration, and Black Rail probably still breeds here. Manahawkin is an exceptional place—not to be missed on your Barnegat Bay day.

From the GSP at Exit 63, head east to Route 9. At this intersection, Manahawkin Lake holds Hooded Merganser, Common Merganser, and Ring-necked Ducks in winter. Go north on Route 9 for 0.9 mile to Hilliard Boulevard. Go east on Hilliard 0.9 mile to Stafford Avenue. Make a left onto Stafford, which soon becomes a gravel road (bumpy and rutted, but passable). You are now in **Manahawkin WMA**. The woods here can be good, and Barred Owls are found in this section, known as Manahawkin Swamp. In about a mile you come to impounded ponds on your left that can hold a variety of ducks and shorebirds in spring (Cinnamon Teal has been seen here), and the weedy edges can be great for sparrows in late fall. Keep going until the road dead-ends at a bridge—the "bridge to nowhere" (actually, it once led to the salt hay fields, now abandoned). Scan from the bridge for rough-legs and short-ears. Rough-legs can be seen any time of day, either perched or hovering, but midafternoon to late afternoon is best for short-ears. The vast array of towers to the north is the former AT&T transatlantic cable facility. Nobody's quite sure why it's still here in the satellite age, and the guy wires must kill a lot of birds. Check the poles for perched rough-legs, redtails, and peregrines. You can see an artificial peregrine aerie here—the box on pilings beyond the towers. In good winters, expect eight to ten short-ears and many rough-legs if you are patient. Scan low and even high overhead for both rough-legs and short-ears. Harriers should also be numerous in winter, and a few pairs still nest in the Barnegat Bay region.

There are several other spots nearby that are worth visiting. South of Route 72, and off Route 9 to the east, **Cedar Run Dock Road, Bay Avenue,** and **Dock Road** are all little-traveled roads that lead to Barnegat Bay. All offer good views of bay waterfowl and can provide good sightings of rough-legs and short-ears. In some years, these sites are as productive as Manahawkin. Cedar Run Dock Road is about 1 mile south of Route 72; Bay Avenue is about 4 miles farther south, and Dock Road is 0.5 mile beyond Bay Avenue. North of Route 72 and east of Route 9 near the town of Barnegat, Forsythe NWR maintains the 600-acre **Barnegat Impoundment**. On Bayshore Drive/Route 609, between Ridgeway and Edison Avenues, an observation deck provides good views of this underbirded section of the Barnegat Bay region.

Return to Route 72 and drive east to Long Beach Island. Once on the island, take County Road 607 (Long Beach Boulevard) north. Watch speed limits. If you are coming from Holgate, simply stay on 607 as you pass Route 72. It is 8.4 miles to the town of Barnegat Light, where you bear left, following signs for Barnegat Lighthouse State Park. When in doubt, just look for the tall lighthouse and head for it. Scan from the bulkhead opposite the park entrance (often quite good), then pull into the state park parking lot. At the entrance, note the park closure times; in winter, they close the gate early. (If you think you'll be later, park outside the lot by the bulkhead.) In the winter, bathrooms are in the small maintenance building by the entrance. In spring through fall, they are in the interpretive center on the path to the lighthouse. Bird around the edge of the parking lot and along the vegetated path for migrants in season. Check with the resident naturalist for recent sightings.

Barnegat Light (affectionately known as "Old Barney"), like the Cape May and Absecon lighthouses, was built by Lieutenant George Meade. It

Bundle up and hit the Barnegat Light jetty in winter for wonderful duck and seabird opportunities.

was completed in 1859 and stands some 170 feet high. It once stood much farther from the inlet than it does today. Walk to the lighthouse and follow the concrete walkway along the inlet. You are right over the rocks of the jetty, but it is surrounded by sturdy railings (and is wheelchair accessible). Scan Barnegat Inlet. Tides are intense here (all of Barnegat Bay empties through this inlet, and the rushing water is often rough near the mouth). The twin jetties stretch

Harlequin Ducks seem quite at home in Barnegat's rough winter waters.

nearly a mile to sea, attempting to tame what is notoriously one of the toughest inlets on the East Coast for mariners. Despite the rushing tide, diving ducks abound, handling the swift currents with remarkable insouciance and grace. Seals are daily in winter, Bottle-Nosed Dolphin in summer.

Walk east toward the ocean. When the concrete path ends, either return to the lighthouse to gain the beach or climb through the railing and down the rocks to the beach (fairly easy for most). The good news is that the Harlequin Ducks are virtually always here in winter (they love rough water); the bad news is that they are usually out near the end of the jetty. The rocks are somewhat hard to walk, so most birders pop up onto the jetty every few hundred yards to scan. You can be fooled here—you may be scanning far ahead and miss the perky harlequins right at your feet. They're fairly tame, but too close an approach will push them off. Often if you sit and wait quietly, they'll swim right up to you.

Look for Great Cormorants on the navigation towers and for Ruddy Turnstones and Purple Sandpipers on the rocks. Eiders can be anywhere—near the base of the jetty or off the tip. Scan gull flocks, both those perched on the rocks and any feeding off the jetty. Returning commercial fishing boats often have clouds of gulls following them, and a few times we've seen Black-legged Kittiwakes follow them right up the inlet. Jaegers follow the gulls in fall. Terns are good here in summer and fall, and Bonaparte's Gulls are usually present in winter and especially in spring. Keep Little Gull and Black-headed Gull in mind. A Black Guillemot recently wintered here.

The very end of the jetty is often the best, but the footing gets worse near the tip. Most birders view the end of the jetty from the adjacent beach. A second, mostly buried jetty angles in from the south, and this area can be good for a variety of birds—from Brant to shorebirds to gulls and terns. Once in a while the harlequins are found around this jetty (and once in a great while along the north jetty, across the inlet). Bird the sandy beach and dune verge for "Ipswich" Savannah Sparrows. Snow Buntings are usually here, but to find them you may need to be patient until the flock flushes;

they can be well camouflaged, even in bare sand. A Snowy Owl might be here, or perhaps on the dunes on the far side of the inlet. A Gyrfalcon was once seen here for several days at the peak of a severe winter, when all of Barnegat Bay was frozen and thousands of Brant and ducks were forced to the open water of the inlet. To the gray, strafing Gyrfalcon, it was just a big bird feeder, a cornucopia of birds for the taking. It's usually that for the birder, too.

Retrace your route. As you work back south, follow the bayside. The various lagoons and harbors can be good if they're not frozen. Diving ducks are often right next to the bulkheads, and Red-breasted Mergansers, Bufflehead, Common Goldeneye, and scaup are numerous. Canvasbacks and Redheads are possible too. All the way back to Route 72, any bayside street-end can be good for ducks, as well as any dune crossover on the ocean side. There's a lot of habitat on the Long Beach Island beach and bay that rarely if ever gets birded, as most people focus on Barnegat Light.

Though worth a visit at any season, winter at Barnegat Light is exceptional. It can be cold—brutally cold, in fact. If possible, try to pick a fairly warm day, or one with no wind. Out near the tip of the jetty, you are really exposed to the elements. Dress as warmly as you can, and then add another layer. If you hit a rare, windless, fairly balmy late winter day, Barnegat Light can be a glorious experience. If you are there on a day with single-digit temperatures and a 30-knot northwest wind, you'll be sorry you bought this book.

Play the weather, and enjoy Barnegat Light to the fullest. As a winter birding experience, it is unequaled in the Cape May region or elsewhere. Sitting on the rocks, surrounded by diving loons, loud and lusty long-tails, a curious Harbor Seal, and a flotilla of saucy harlequins, you'll likely agree that a winter day in the shadow of "Old Barney" is an experience that's hard to beat.

PART THREE

AN ORNITHOLOGICAL HISTORY

June 7, 1910, was a memorable day for me. I learned . . . that one of the two remaining Laughing Gull colonies in New Jersey was located at Stone Harbor. Captain Ludlam of West Cape May was the warden protecting the colony. He no doubt would be pleased to take me to see the birds.

I journeyed from Camden, NJ, by train on June 6 and stayed at the captain's home in West Cape May that night. Early the next morning we boarded a train for Wildwood Junction and there changed to the old jerkwater going to Sea Isle City. We got off at Grassy Sound where my guide hired a row boat. After about an hour and half of steady and sometimes hard pulling we came in sight of the gulls. We estimated that there about 1,500 Laughing Gulls in the colony and it was said to be the larger of the two colonies on the New Jersey coast.

Those who are familiar with bird life as it is today in June about Stone Harbor can hardly imagine that there could be such a great scarcity of water birds as there was in 1910. In that row boat we did not see a single tern or skimmer, only one species of heron and not a single late shore bird. It was about 1910 that the birds of the salt marshes and beaches were at an all-time low in New Jersey.

The Laughing Gulls had survived in some numbers but the market gunners for the feather trade had made severe inroads on these formerly very numerous birds.

Times have changed, the birds, given a fair chance, have come back, but now are threatened with new and fearful dangers.

> —Julian K. Potter, excerpts from
> "A Guided Trip, 1910" in
> *Naturalist's Digest,* Audubon
> Center of New Jersey (1954)

TIME TRAVEL

Certain events punctuated each of my childhood summers and are still memorable even today. There were the exciting nights with my sister and cousins on the Sea Isle City boardwalk, sugar cones at Springer's Ice Cream, and 35-cent Wednesday matinees at the Harbor Theater. There were boat rides, fishing and crabbing trips, and even the dreaded back-to-school shopping trip, made bearable only by the neat new pencil box. Even more enjoyable were the Sunday drives with my grandparents, sometimes all the way to Belleplain State Forest to see the loblolly pines (which I called "lollipop pines"). Summer vacation also included an annual pilgrimage to the Concrete Ship. Checking the ship might be a daily activity for Cape May birders today, but back then it was a once-a-summer treat, a long car ride and a pretty big deal for a kid growing up in Stone Harbor, New Jersey, in the early 1950s.

But of all the summer sacraments, the trip to the Point was the best. It wasn't a long journey by any standard, but our ritual summertime trip to Stone Harbor Point to see the tern and skimmer colony was the highlight of this young boy's summer vacation. It required planning—an early rise, sneakers for the hot sand, suntan lotion, and a picnic basket packed with sandwiches and drinks. The drive wasn't far from our house on 98th Street to the end of town, but it was much farther than I was allowed to ride my bike at the time. The Coast Guard station on 117th street (still there today) was on the last street in town then, before bulldozers and trophy homes leveled the irreplaceable dune forest (my playground) for many blocks beyond.

To a six-year-old, the anticipation may have been keen, but the walk took forever. The heat was unbearable, the sand scratchy and hot. Yet the discomfort was worth it when, exhausted, we finally reached the tern colony. Baseball cap in place to keep from being pecked on top of my crew-cut head, I'd walk among the nesting birds, being careful not to step on eggs. We'd marvel at the fuzzy tern chicks and the awkward, roly-poly Black Skimmer babies. Maybe we'd even pick up one or two of the cute cottonball-like chicks. I still have (somewhere) the souvenir black-and-white photos I took one year with my Brownie box camera. I became as adept at dodging the aerial bombardment from the adult terns as today's kids are at dodging incoming video-game weaponry.

I now realize that this was poor form, horrible behavior, terrible birding etiquette. One would never venture into a nesting colony today, not even consider it. Doing so would risk arrest by a conservation officer, not to mention being ostracized by fellow birders. But back then, when Eisen-hower was in the White House, back before the building boom, when the main intersection at 96th Street in Stone Harbor had a single flashing yel-low light, my parents and I had never heard of birding ethics, or even of birding. We weren't bird-watchers; they were the geeky people who lined up on Stone Harbor Boulevard one or two weekends each fall. We were just a local family taking our ritual summer walk to the Point to look for hidden eggs, try to keep from being pecked, and enjoy the nesting birds. And it was pure fun, a simple pleasure that makes me wonder why Jet Skis, boutique shopping, and palatial seashore mansions came to be so singularly synonymous with summer fun in the sun. On that 1950s deserted barrier beach, terns and Black Skimmers were abundant, not yet troubled by thou-sands of summer-at-the-shore vacationers usurping their space, dogs and cats and exploding gull populations robbing their chicks, and rock jetties stealing the very sand out from under them. There were certainly no tern colony fences, signs, or wardens. Usually we didn't even see any other people on the beach. We had never heard the word *endangered*.

I don't remember many exact details about those walks, just the antici-pation, the fun, the excitement of our summer jaunt to the Point. I recall the clamor of the colony; the raucous, grating, scolding of terns overhead; and the hot white sand hurting your feet and eyes alike. I also remember knowing that we *had* to go, although I didn't know why. I don't know if Mom or Dad consciously meant it as such, but these trips became more than just pleasant memories. They became a key influence. They provided a spark that would grow into a flame and eventually a bonfire of love for the outdoors, natural history, beaches, and birds.

A number of years later, maybe during the seventh or eighth grade, I started attending the Witmer Stone Bird Club meetings held in the Stone Harbor Public School on Friday evenings. It was there that I learned that the birds of Stone Harbor Point were Common Terns and Least Terns and that there were Piping Plovers nesting there too. It would be a number of meetings before I learned who Witmer Stone was and of his 1937 land-mark *Bird Studies at Old Cape May*. But it would be many years, when I returned home after graduate school, before I would understand what Old Cape May actually was, and I would learn it only because Old Cape May was gone.

By the late 1970s Black Skimmers and Least Terns were endangered species, Piping Plovers were in danger of extinction, and the few remain-ing Common Terns nested only on remote spoil islands. The dunes were gone, replaced by seasonal summer homes—second homes with barren stone "lawns." Stone Harbor Point was gone too, eroded into Hereford Inlet. The tern colony of my youth was under 20 feet of water a mile out in the inlet. Old Cape May, and happy boyhood sojourns to view nesting bird colonies, seemed like ancient history. Over time, the memories became melancholy and indistinct, elusive, as hazy as humid summer days themselves.

Stone Harbor Point is much easier to get to today. You park in the tidy parking lot at the end of town (bathrooms are to the right, RVs to the left) and simply walk south. Beyond the last jetty, which is mostly buried under sand, simply look to the right. In the 1950s there was no such thing as the Beach-nester Program (or even a Department of Environmental Protection, for that matter), but today, a rope fence and prominent signage are in place to protect the terns and skimmers from errant joggers and beachcombers. You will probably find the "warden" there, often a friendly young woman who teaches more than guards and happily educates more than enforces. Her engaging smile may belie her fierce commitment to the birds' protection and nesting success.

Today the colony is well marked and well patrolled. You can no longer walk in the colony like I did as a kid (thank God), but you can get a great view from outside the perimeter at a safe distance. Terns and skimmers are abundant: many hundreds of Black Skimmers, Common Terns, Least Terns, and even a pair or two of Gull-billed Terns. Hundreds of fat, fluffy chicks—terns and skimmers alike—beg for food. Four or so pairs of Piping Plovers are there. In mid-July their tiny chicks look like cotton puffs with legs. A single Royal Tern and a Roseate Tern tease—are they nesting too? American Oystercatchers are plentiful, each keeping a wary eye on you all the while. The colony is big, bursting, alive, exhilarating. It has come back.

That the colony not only has returned but is thriving seems, to one who saw it go, to be nothing short of a miracle. That Stone Harbor Point exists again may be claimed as a testament to shore protection, but it's probably more related to the vagaries of coastal erosion, sand deposition, littoral drift, and the constantly moving, changing coastline. That the birds have come back from the brink of extirpation is more easily understood—it represents the hard work, dedication, and dogged determination of many hundreds of employees and volunteers of the New Jersey Division of Fish and Wildlife's Endangered and Nongame Species Program. Buoyed by thousands of supporters, they persevered. They knew that it could be done, and they did it.

I admit I had my doubts. To say that beach-nester recovery represents blood, sweat, and tears is not to exaggerate, for I've seen wildlife workers' hands raw from stringing protective fencing, or with splinters buried to the bone from putting up wooden snow fencing. And I've seen the anguished, sand-encrusted tears when a warden arrives at dawn to find a Least Tern colony empty, all the chicks vanished, and the telltale tracks of a rampaging dog—Rover off the leash—revealing the sad and stinging truth. But it was such red-eyed pain that brought such deep resolve, and success.

For one who hiked these beaches in the 1950s and watched it all disappear, birds and sand alike, the beach-nester comeback represents more than wildlife management or even the amazing resilience of the birds themselves. It is more of a rebirth, the ability to step back in time. Going to Stone Harbor Point today is to travel back in time, to revisit Old Cape May, to see what Witmer Stone or even those before him saw, and to relive the joy of a healthy, thriving tern colony through the eyes of a child of the 1950s.

As Pat and I enjoyed the colony through our spotting scopes, two figures appeared far up the beach, hand in hand, one reaching down, the other up. One was a tall man, a father, the other a tiny boy, young enough that this was probably his first visit to the beach, at least under his own power. It wasn't an idle visit—the backpack, water bottles, binoculars, and camera indicated a purpose to their beach walk. They approached and quietly asked questions about the skimmers. The man was friendly, inquisitive, and appreciative. The boy was apprehensive, almost wary of us, but he looked up to his dad with what approached awe. He hung on his dad's every word as resolutely as he clung to his hand. The smile never left the boy's face as he gazed at the booming bird colony beyond the rope. As I looked at the father and son, I saw the spark pass. They may have been unaware, and it might take years to ignite, but the spark was there. Fueled by memories and visions of beaches filled with birds, the fire would grow. I recognized it from experience. I'd been there.

I *was* there, the fifty intervening years gone. For me, the time travel was complete. Stone Harbor Point seemed many, many miles long; the tern colony stretched to infinity. The sky was an infinite blue, the sand white and hot. I pounced on a prized skate egg case. I was too small to look through the telescope and wanted to know why I couldn't pick up the fuzzy tern chicks. I wanted to take the broken eggshells home, whined for my dad to carry me on his shoulders, wanted my sandwich, wanted to swim in the sparkling sea. The summer sky was filled with brilliant white birds.

As Pat and I began the walk back, even though we were hundreds of yards from the perimeter rope, two Common Terns dive-bombed me repeatedly, missing my hat by inches, and only because I deftly ducked, a behavior somehow summoned from many years before. Scolding bitterly, the bold terns showed no interest in Pat, only me. Through a handed-down spark of their own, I think that maybe they remembered me too.

—C. S.

8

A DISTINGUISHED TRADITION

Few areas in the New World have been documented as consistently as Cape May . . . perhaps only Concord, Massachusetts and the New York City region can claim as complete a record. . . . Nearly thirty years have passed since Witmer Stone put the finishing touches on his intensive study of the birds at Cape May. During that interval many changes have taken place. To me the fascinating part . . . is this evidence of flux, the ebb and flow of populations, the disappearance of species, the invasion by others . . . debit birds are balanced by credit species.

—Roger Tory Peterson, 1964
Introduction to the Dover Edition
of *Bird Studies at Old Cape May*

As Winston Churchill aptly wrote, "The farther back you can look, the farther forward you are likely to see." It is the discoveries of the past, and their record, on which advances in learning are predicated and on which predictions for the future are based. This is particularly true in ornithology, and Cape May birding is where it is today, and where it will be going, because of those who have gone before. Cape May today is synonymous with bird migration; it is a place more famous for its birds than virtually anywhere else in North America because, to paraphrase Sir Isaac Newton, if we have seen farther than others, it is because we have stood on the shoulders of giants.

Few places on the planet can boast the ornithological history of the Cape May area. A list of those who have studied birds here reads much like a Who's Who of North American ornithological history. The ornithological record at Cape May may indeed be unequaled anywhere, and this baseline of ornithological data—besides being important in itself—is a classic and sometimes tragic case study in environmental change and the crucial need for habitat protection.

EARLY HISTORY

It is notable that the first "record" of the bird concentrations at Cape May comes from prehistory. Cape May County's first inhabitants were the Lenni Lenape ("original people"), a branch of the Algonquins to the north. Many place names remain from these Native American roots—Tuckahoe, Muskee, and Manumuskin (originally "Minnemuska"), to name a few. Nummy's Island, which is birded daily today, is named for King Nummy, a leader of the Kechemeche subtribe of the Lenape, and some early accounts claim that he was buried there. Indian Trail (Route 618), a popular birding location in Middle Township (notable for Kentucky Warblers, among others), was originally just that—a major Native American route from Delaware Bay to the Atlantic coast marshes. Although fish and shellfish probably attracted Native Americans to the Cape, it is clear they had an avian interest too, for birds were a staple in their diet. We know this because of the numerous small, very finely made arrowheads found in southern New Jersey. Known as "bird points," they were clearly used for hunting birds and other small game. Such points are still commonly found today, mostly along the eroding beaches of Delaware Bay. (With the loss of active farm fields to housing developments, locals can no longer search fresh-plowed furrows for artifacts.) It is known that our Native Americans made seasonal movements, probably occupying interior forests and rivers in winter and bays and barrier islands in summer and fall—movements linked to fish and wildlife migration. There is evidence even today of the Lenape. Some of the small Red Cedar islands of the salt marsh are on shell middens, the oyster shells providing the high ground on which Red Cedars grow.

The first European to view Cape May was none other than Henry Hudson, who in August 1609 entered Delaware Bay and landed (probably near Town Bank) to obtain fresh water. It was in 1620, the same year the Pilgrims landed at Plymouth Rock, Massachusetts, that Dutchman Cornelius Jacobsen Mey, in his ship *Glad Tidings,* surveyed Delaware Bay and named the cape. Soon after, we have our first written record of the birds of Cape May. In 1631 Dutch settler David Pietersen De Vries established a colony across Delaware Bay, near Cape Henlopen in what is now Delaware, but it was soon wiped out by Native Americans. In 1633 De Vries visited Cape May for the first time and wrote of how "an immense flock of wild pigeons in April obscured the sky," a clear and poignant reference to migrating Passenger Pigeons.

Around the same time, King Charles I of England commissioned Captain James Young "to occupy and exploit America" (an ominous charge). Sailing with Young was his nephew, Robert Evelyn, as his master or lieutenant. Evelyn spent four years exploring the Delaware Bay region. Returning to England, he wrote an "advertisement" entitled "Direction for Adventurers and Description of New Albion." It was a write-up that would make today's chamber of commerce proud. He glowingly wrote of a land of plenty, of magnificent forests, cedar swamps with lumber for the masts of ships, good soils, wild animals, and trees laden with fruit. He continued with our bird record: "I saw there an infinite quantity of bustards, swans, geese and fowls, covering the shores as within a like multitude of pigeons and stores of turkeys, of which I tried one to weigh 46 pounds" (evidence that even our first fishermen and hunters told tall tales). Proving the theme of exploitation, the last Passenger Pigeon in New Jersey would be recorded in 1896, and the last one on the planet in 1914. Swedish settlers on the Maurice River in neighboring Cumberland County recorded killing great quantities of geese for their feathers; having more food than they could eat, they left the carcasses. These were probably Snow Geese, today found in the hundreds of thousands on the Delaware Bayshore in winter.

Evidence of the early settlers' interest in and reliance on birds can easily be seen—in place names such as Egg Island Point, Little Egg Harbor, Great Egg Harbor, and Great Egg Harbor River. Much like the Native Americans had done, early settlers gathered bird eggs in season for food—the eggs of gulls, terns, herons, and egrets primarily. As early as 1616 a map calls the area just north of Cape May County "Eyerhaven," or harbor of eggs, and the name stuck. Today, Egg Harbor is both a township and a city in neighboring Atlantic County, and the large bay that forms the northern boundary of Cape May County is Great Egg Harbor Bay (it is still an exceptional place for birds and birding).

In 1633, De Vries had "caught seven whales; we would have done more if we had good harpoons" (fishermen have been making excuses for at least four centuries), and by 1685 Cape May's first real town was settled—a whaling village on 25-foot-high banks and dunes from which the residents

Oyster schooners once plied the Delaware Bay in great numbers.

could scan for whales (and no doubt watch for birds as a clue to where whales were feeding). The settlement was originally named Portsmouth Town and later became known as Town Bank. The town's original site has since eroded into Delaware Bay, but it was about a half mile northwest of today's Cape May–Lewes ferry terminal. Pilot whales, Humpbacked Whales, and Right Whales, among others, were the principal targets. By the early 1700s, indiscriminate killing of cow whales and their young had thinned the whale numbers considerably, the first example of overfishing or overharvesting our coastal resources. (No doubt, those commercial fishermen would have said, "There's plenty of whales.") The final historical record of local whaling was in 1775.

With whales gone, early residents turned to farming, cattle raising, trapping, and shipbuilding. Hunting was a way of life too, and early subsistence hunting gave rise by the mid-1800s to late 1800s to market gunning for waterfowl. Birds and a variety of game were still plentiful. Clay's family lore holds that Captain William Sutton killed two timber wolves on Wolf Pit Hill Road (today Route 83), perhaps the last ever recorded in Cape May County, and Clay's grandmother had a panther follow her home from Sunday school near South Seaville in about 1875. Clay's father remembers seeing Bobcats and the tracks of Black Bears as a kid, in about 1915. Cape May County never had the intensive market hunting that occurred in both Chesapeake Bay and Barnegat Bay to the north, but significant numbers of ducks and geese were shipped from Cape May County to Philadelphia during the 1800s and early 1900s. Gunning for ducks to send to Philadelphia and Atlantic City continued during the Great Depression of the 1930s.

THE DECOY RECORD

The duck decoy record is a significant part of the ornithological history of Cape May. Although Cape May County never had the distinctive style of either Barnegat Bay or the Delaware River, it did host several generations of one of the most famous American carving families—the Shourds family. Harry Vinuckson Shourds (1861–1920), from Tuckerton in Ocean County, is widely acknowledged as one of the master decoy carvers of all time. His son, Harry M. Shourds (1890–1943) of Ocean City, was equally skilled, and his decoys are highly prized and collectible today. His son, Harry Shourds III, carries on the tradition today in Linwood, in Atlantic County. Harry is an incredible link to a remarkable history, and we have fond memories of studying under him when we took several decoy carving classes he taught in the early 1990s. We'll never forget his classic tongue-in-cheek admonition the first night of class: "The secret to carving is to take a piece of wood and then remove anything that doesn't look like the bird." Today Cape

Duck decoys, such as this Black Duck and "broad bill" (scaup), once disposable tools for Cape May hunters, are now valuable collectibles.

May hosts a number of well-known contemporary carvers, including Jim and Joan Seibert of South Dennis, Tony Hillman of Cape May Court House, and Jamie Hand of Goshen, who still carry on this time-honored tradition. Decoys were once hung in burlap sacks in sheds during the off-season; today they grace mantels and tabletops and are widely regarded as one of the finest examples of true American folk art.

That these decoys would come to be highly prized as valuable works of art would have been imponderable to those who originally created them. It was during World War II that Clay's grandfather, Frank Sutton, gave up duck hunting. The duck bag limit had been drastically reduced to a mere twenty-five. He lamented, "It just wasn't worth it anymore if you couldn't bring home fifty or sixty ducks." (This is perhaps an eyebrow-raising statement today, but an amazing testament to the former bounty and abundance of waterfowl.) He sold his own hand-carved decoys, three burlap bags of "stools"—black ducks, mergansers, and shorebirds—"to a young couple who wanted to start a collection or something like that" for $5 per bag. Clay's father, stationed in England at the time, came home after the war to find them gone and was pretty upset. He hadn't necessarily planned to use them, but he sensed that something was amiss, that a part of his family history was gone forever. Most likely the decoys were sold to William Mackey, who went on to publish *American Bird Decoys,* an early bible of the growing decoy collecting hobby. Several of Frank Sutton's decoys ended up in Mackey's famous collection and are illustrated in the book. But the lesson wasn't learned. Clay's uncle sold his own decoys for $5 apiece in a yard sale in the 1970s. To turn-of-the-century carvers, these faux birds were nothing but a tool, akin to a hammer or a shovel. When they were no longer needed, many were sold, discarded, or used as firewood. Clay's grandfather would not have believed that "fence-post pheasants" (historical slang for ducks carved from old cedar fence posts) could become cherished "bookcase broadbills," as Pete Dunne fondly described them.

The decoy record offers interesting insight into our ornithological history. The prevalence of Redhead, Canvasback, and Ruddy Ducks among turn-of-the-century New Jersey decoys hints at their former abundance compared with their scarcity today. We have a canvasback decoy that was summarily repainted as a Canada Goose, stark evidence of both fewer canvasbacks because of the loss of eelgrass from the bays (their preferred food) and the growing goose population. The paucity of Snow Goose decoys corroborates that they were much less common then. Shorebirds were avidly gunned too, and the existence of godwit and Long-billed Curlew decoys is tangible proof that these birds once occurred in the mid-Atlantic region in some numbers. (The Marbled Godwit was called the "Marlin," and the Hudsonian Godwit was the "Ring-tailed Marlin," a name that compared the bird's long bill to that of the fish known as marlin.) The widespread existence of historic Golden Plover decoys hints of a much greater abundance historically. Even Eskimo Curlew decoys were made along the eastern seaboard and in New Jersey, a poignant reminder of the loss of this almost certainly extinct shorebird. The Federal Migratory Bird Treaty, passed in 1913 in response to rapidly disappearing bird populations, put major legal restrictions on duck limits (quotas) and effectively ended all shorebird hunting except for Wilson's Snipe and American Woodcock, two upland species not heavily impacted at the time.

Today, the rich history of "Down Jersey" waterfowling is all but forgotten, save for a few old photographs, gunners' journals, and the surviving wooden decoys. The decoys today attract only collectors and admirers, yet they summon memories of when legions of wildfowl paused in their migration, turned and set their wings, and stooled in to lavish wooden counterparts bobbing on the bays of Cape May. Over cold, dark waters against rain-flecked leaden skies, the gunners would rise in their sneakboxes, their classic Jersey duck boats, and play a little regarded yet major role in our birding history and heritage.

THE GREAT MASTERS

Although many places can claim a rich avian heritage, few birding locales can claim that many of the greatest ornithologists of all time studied there and contributed to the vast wealth of knowledge that is the baseline for all we know today.

Cape May City is aptly billed as America's oldest seashore resort. Its seaside location was an attractant to the educated and wealthy, and a rich Victorian tradition evolved here. As early as 1801, advertisements were touting Cape May as a summer vacation destination. A journey from Philadelphia to "Cape Island" by stagecoach took the better part of two days. Around 1820 it became popular to make the journey by water—first by sail and later by steamboat. If the weather was good and the tide and wind were right, the trip by boat could be made in one day. Although most came for sun, surf, and seafood, both the Cape Island area and the Pine Barrens soon became popular with early naturalists, in part because of their accessibility. Philadelphia was the hub of scientific discovery in the New World, and naturalists there soon discovered the wonders to be seen at the "nearby" Jersey shore.

Alexander Wilson (1766–1813) is generally regarded as the father of American ornithology. His *American Ornithology* was the first comprehensive book on American birds. From his base in Philadelphia, Wilson made six recorded trips to the coastal areas of southern New Jersey. Three visits were in May, June, and December, all prior to 1811. The other three were with his close friend and benefactor (and later biographer), ornithologist George Ord (1781–1866), in July 1811, November 1812, and a four-week visit in May and June 1813 (there is some question as to how many trips Ord made with Wilson). They traveled either by boat from Philadelphia to Higbee's Landing, near Higbee Beach, or by stage from Camden, across the vast Pine Barrens, and on to Great Egg Harbor by boat. Wilson wrote fondly of the region, referring to all of his South Jersey haunts as "the Cape May Country." At Great Egg Harbor, Wilson often stayed at Beasley's Tavern, where the front porch faced the inlet and the sea. A prize specimen from his first trip, in 1810, was a Snowy Owl. Not unlike today's birders, Wilson and other early American ornithologists were most interested in collecting, recording, and describing species of birds new to them. At this time, many species that were new to Wilson were also unknown to science. Wilson's influence on Cape May birding was lasting. Thomas Beasley, the local with whom Wilson often stayed, would later note that "the interest awakened there by Wilson in the study of ornithology has never ceased." The Thomas Beesley house, built in 1803, still stands today in Beesley's Point, in Upper Township, but it has never been proven that this was in fact the Beasley Tavern (note the spelling discrepency, a not-uncommon problem in history and geneology). It therefore remains unknown if this is indeed where Wilson stayed.

In 1812 George Ord collected a small bird in a Red Maple swamp in northern Cape May County near Tuckahoe and presented it to his friend. Wilson "wrote it up," describing the bird for science. He named it the Cape May Warbler (one of only four birds in North America named for cities) in accordance with his usual procedure of naming birds for the first place he found them. The popular name has remained, but interestingly, Wilson's

The Cape May Warbler, so named because it was first collected near Tuckahoe, is only a visitor to the region.

scientific name did not. *Dendroica tigrinum* was the technical name that English naturalist George Edwards had given to a specimen that had landed on a sailing vessel near Jamaica prior to Wilson's description; the Cape May Warbler therefore remains *Dendroica tigrinum* today. Cape May Warblers do not breed in Cape May and are found only as uncommon migrants in spring and as fairly common migrants in fall, passing the Cape during their annual commute between their northern U.S. and Canadian breeding grounds and their winter home in the West Indies.

On May 13, 1813, on the shores of Cape Island, probably at or near South Cape May Meadows, Wilson shot three birds that were new to him, two males and a female, but he died before he could write the scientific description. Ord, who had accompanied Wilson, subsequently did the write-up and, in honor of his late friend, named the species Wilson's Plover (*Charadrius wilsonia*). (Ord also eventually completed and published the final volume of Wilson's *American Ornithology.*) The Wilson's Plover, according to Ord, was "pretty common" at the time, and a breeding bird in New Jersey. However, Wilson's Plover was one of the species extirpated by gunners in the 1800s, along with the American Avocet and Black-necked Stilt. Wilson's Plover reappeared as a rare breeder from about 1940 to 1963, but today it has again withdrawn to the south. There have been about sixteen records for New Jersey in the past forty years, most in the southern part of the state. Despite being discovered and described on Cape Island and proudly recorded in volume 9 of Wilson's *American Ornithology,* this handsome plover remains a rare and coveted find for Cape May birders today.

South Jersey played a role in one of Wilson's most controversial finds, the infamous "Small-headed Flycatcher." Wilson said that he had shot the bird "near Philadelphia" in April 1811 but had also seen the bird in the swamps of South Jersey. This bird figured prominently in the famous rivalry and frequent charges of plagiarism between Wilson and Audobon. It is a complex story, and whether Wilson copied Audubon has never been resolved. The species may have been a figment of Audubon's healthy imagination or even a "ringer"—for the purpose of catching the plagiarist. The

bird was probably a wood warbler and possibly a hybrid (to us,
it looks a lot like a confusing fall
warbler). The existence of the
small-headed flycatcher has never
been proved, nor has the bird ever
been seen again. It exists only in
Wilson's and Audubon's plates—
our only records of an enigmatic
species that may have gone extinct
due to the heavy cutting of white
cedar swamps.

Wilson's successor and champion George Ord, who was to
become Audubon's greatest critic
and detractor, tangled with Audubon over the Cape May Warbler,
too. Apparently, Ord at one point
deliberately changed the date (in
his writings about his and Wilson's

*The Wilson's Plover is named for
ornithologist Alexander Wilson, who
made six trips to the coast of southern
New Jersey in the early 1800s.*

Cape May trip) from 1812 to 1811 so that their Cape May Warbler would
predate one that Audubon drew and published in 1835 which included an
annotation that it had been taken in May 1811. Given the times, it's a wonder that Ord and Audubon never dueled with flintlock pistols over their
frequent and bitter disputes and grievances.

Beyond his paintings and journals, some of Wilson's finds are preserved. Originally, most of the birds Wilson collected went to Peale's
Museum, later called the Philadelphia Museum. Because of the crude taxi-
dermy of the day, very few of Wilson's extensive collection of skins are still
extant, although a number can still be found in Philadelphia. Two of Wilson's skins, a Broad-winged Hawk and a Mississippi Kite, are preserved
at the Academy of Natural Sciences in Philadelphia as the "type specimens"
of the species—the first ever described to science—among its world-
renowned bird collection.

The academy also has in its collection the shotgun that Wilson used on
many of his storied collection trips. In 1997 we presented a program there,
and Bob Ridgely, then head of the academy's Ornithology Department,
showed the group both Wilson's shotgun and several of the specimens he
no doubt collected with that fowling piece. Bob almost nonchalantly
handed the antique gun to Clay to inspect, and Clay later recalled that
moment in a presentation (recorded in the CMBO's journal the *Peregrine
Observer*):

A 1940s view from the Cape May Lighthouse, looking east at the still-extant town of South Cape May. FROM THE COLLECTION OF BILL BAILEY

I was awe-stricken. Completely unannounced and unscripted—here I was holding Alexander Wilson's shotgun. It was a fine precision shotgun, about 32 gauge, French built, the one which he probably used to shoot a bird on the beach at South Cape May in 1813, a bird which George Ord would describe as new to science and name the Wilson's Plover in Alexander's honor. It is a species now extirpated from New Jersey, I might add. To hold that shotgun was to hold ornithological history. I pointed it towards the ceiling, tracked and led an imaginary Passenger Pigeon. At that moment, I felt an overwhelming connection to the past. But it was a connection which led not only to the past, but to the future as well, a connection to those who continue to work so hard today to perpetuate the ornithological history of Cape May."

This small event remains a giant and cherished memory of Clay's ornithological career.

If Cape May contributed to Wilson's life and work, some say that it contributed to his death as well. Wilson made his final trip to Cape May in the summer of 1813, remaining about a month, although accounts vary. Ord's account of Wilson's death, which may have been embellished, or possibly a blend of stories that took liberties with the time line, was that Wilson had spotted a bird he had long wanted and was forced to swim a river to shoot it. He then "took cold from exposure," which brought on dysentery; Wilson supposedly lived only ten days after that. This sounds like a variation on one of Wilson's own stories, wherein he shot and winged an oystercatcher and plunged into an inlet to retrieve the struggling bird. Wilson went in over his head and reached the shore exhausted, lucky to survive the "deep and rapid inlet"—possibly the Great Egg Inlet. Whatever the exact circumstances, Wilson died shortly after his final trip to Cape May.

Ornithologists Spencer F. Baird (1823–1887) and his brother William M. Baird (1803–1872) were also part of the Philadelphia scientific scene in the middle nineteenth century. Spencer Baird was the first secretary of the Smithsonian Institution. William Baird's attraction to Cape May was not exclusively birds; he married a woman from Cape May Court House, and the noted pioneer ornithologist John K. Townsend married her sister (the Holmes sisters).

In a certain sense, these were the golden years of natural history discovery in southern New Jersey. It was John Bartram and his son William, both naturalists and botanists who had studied extensively in South Jersey, who originally steered Alexander Wilson to Cape May as the focal point for birds in America. Also among Wilson's acquaintances and colleagues were Rubens Peale and Titian Peale (the sons of artist and curator Charles Wilson Peale), who for twenty years journeyed to Cape May to procure specimens for their father's museum—the country's first natural history museum housed on the second floor of Independence Hall in Philadelphia. Among other birds, Titian Peale collected a Hudsonian Godwit at Cape May for the museum.

John James Audubon (1785–1851) also studied and painted at Cape May, at least if we define "Cape May" as Cape May County rather than the Cape May City area alone. Known to be great rivals, it is not inconceivable that Wilson's great success at Cape May spurred Audubon to visit the Jersey Shore himself. It has been said that Wilson was an ornithologist who used the paintbrush as a tool to record the plumages of birds, and that Audubon was an artist and adventurer who also enjoyed birds. Audubon's lively journals and rich, evocative plates, such as those from his journey to Great Egg Harbor, seem to bear this out.

Upon returning to the United States from England in 1829, where he had been working on his *Birds of America,* Audubon spent some time in Camden, New Jersey, where he continued to paint. Among many other birds, he secured and painted a Fork-tailed Flycatcher at Camden in June 1832 (perhaps South Jersey's first megararity). In June 1829 he set out for Great Egg Harbor, on the Jersey coast. He lived with a bayman (his guide) and his family "only a few hundred yards from the shore," supposedly occupying the same "cabin" that Wilson had once stayed in. It has been reported that Audubon was a guest at the Somers Mansion in Somers Point, but confirmation remains elusive. The Somers Mansion was built around 1725 and today is the oldest house extant in Atlantic County. (This historical building is in the care of the Atlantic County Historical Society and open to the public.) Because the owner-builder Richard Somers had ten children, it is quite possible that Audubon stayed with another member of the Somers family.

Audubon remained at Great Egg Harbor from June 13 to July 4 and recounts his adventures there in his journals (*Ornithological Biography,* Volume 3, 1835), where he states in an early and glowing testimonial, "To such naturalists as are qualified to observe many different objects at the same time, Great Egg Harbor would probably offer as ample a field as any part of our coast excepting the Florida Keys. Birds of many kinds are abundant, as are fishes and testaceous animals. The forests shelter many beautiful plants, and even on the driest sandbar, you may see insects of the most brilliant tints." At Great Egg Harbor, one of Audubon's "principal objects was to procure certain birds known there by the name of lawyers"—known today as Black-necked Stilts—and he "collected enough to satisfy us." By the late 1800s, Black-necked Stilts had been extirpated by hunters.

Plate 81 in *Birds of America,* the Osprey, was painted at Great Egg Harbor. A faint notation reads that the painting was "begun Friday at 11 o'clock, finished Sunday evening." The Osprey is depicted carrying a weakfish (sea trout), a great choice then (and today) to represent the fish in the Cape May area. Today, birders like to try to identify what species of fish an Osprey is carrying. Some visitors may be surprised when local birders call out, "Menhaden going over," as an Osprey, with fish in talons, flies by. It is fun to read in Audubon's journal how a similar joke was played on him. He wrote: "I inquired if the fish hawks were plentiful near Great Egg Harbor, and was answered by an elderly man who with a laugh asked if I had ever seen the weakfish along the coast *without* the bird in question. Not knowing the animal he had named, I confessed my ignorance, when the whole party burst into a loud laugh, in which, there being nothing better for it, I joined." Some Cape May traditions haven't changed much over time.

BIRD STUDIES AT OLD CAPE MAY

Following the Civil War, the New Jersey Pine Barrens and Jersey Shore again became important destinations for Philadelphia-based naturalists and scientists. As train service brought the coast closer to the city, and as the barrier islands began to develop and become more accessible, more and more ornithologists began to visit and, in the custom of the times, carefully document the area's changing bird life in their extensive field notes, many of which still exist today. Back then, ornithologists such as the eminent George Spencer Morris were true men of letters, extensively documenting and circulating their findings and adventures. What today is disseminated in mere moments by cell phone or Listservs was then laboriously elaborated in pen and ink under the glow of gas lanterns. But the record was permanent, perhaps more so than many of today's hurried cyberspace reports. Many of these ornithological records of the nineteenth and early twentieth centuries are preserved today at the Academy of Natural Sciences in Philadelphia.

Beyond what exists in repositories, there is a summary of ornithological records so complete that few disciplines can rival it. Witmer Stone's *Bird Studies at Old Cape May* is a true bible of Cape May bird life from the first historical records until the time of its publication in 1937. Although it summarizes and references older records, the focus of *Bird Studies at Old Cape May* is the nearly fifty-year period from about 1888 to 1937. Stone spent about twenty summers at his beloved Old Cape May and often visited at other times of the year as well. His skilled and careful observations, and those of his colleagues, are the basis of the book, yet it is still highly engaging and enjoyable to read today.

Witmer Stone (1866–1939) was a titan in the ornithology of the Americas. He was the son of a historian, and his scholarly background and training served him well in ornithological record keeping. In 1888 he began a lifelong association with the Academy of Natural Sciences of Philadelphia, eventually serving as both its director and vice president. He

was a president of the American Ornithologists' Union (AOU) and chairman of its Committee on Protection of North American Birds (bird protection is an enduring theme in *Bird Studies at Old Cape May*). He was editor of *The Auk*, the journal of the AOU. In 1908 Stone wrote *The Birds of New Jersey: Their Nests and Eggs (A Report of the New Jersey State Museum)*, which contained many references to southern New Jersey. It was published just before one of the first field guides for the area, *A Guide to the Birds of New Jersey* (1911), by Stone's contemporaries Beecher S. Bowdish and Chester A. Reed (published under the auspices of the New Jersey Audubon Society, which was founded in 1897).

In 1890 Stone and five other renowned ornithologists (George Spencer Morris, Samuel N. Rhoads, William Baily, Charles A. Voelker, and J. Harris Reed) formed the Delaware Valley Ornithological

Witmer Stone's writings ensured that Cape May would long be known for its amazing variety of bird life.

Club (DVOC). One of the United States' oldest bird clubs, it is still hugely popular and active today. The Delaware Valley region includes the entire Delaware Bay shore and, of course, Cape May. The DVOC's journal *Cassinia* was named after John Cassin (1813–1869), the long-serving curator of ornithology at the Academy of Natural Sciences in Philadelphia, who named 193 species of birds worldwide and was the first native-born American to gain an international reputation in ornithology. For more than 100 years *Cassinia* has been an important repository for Cape May bird lore, particularly in the period between 1937 and 1976 (when the Cape May Bird Observatory partially assumed that role). To list all of Stone's titles, affiliations, writings, contributions, and ornithological awards would leave room for little else. He was equally proficient and famous as a botanist and penned the landmark *The Plants of Southern New Jersey: With Especial Reference to the Flora of the Pine Barrens* (published in 1911 as part of the *Report of the New Jersey State Museum 1910*). Like *Bird Studies at Old Cape May,* it is timeless and still highly applicable today.

Stone was the consummate scientist, but like all ornithologists of his day, he was an avid bird "collector," procuring myriad specimens for the Academy of Natural Sciences, most of which are still there. He was dedicated, determined, and even surreptitious in his collecting, as the writings of his friend and colleague, George Spencer Morris, attested:

> I have a double-barrel twelve-bore; Stone has a curious little contrivance which he calls a gun; in reality, it's kind of a cross between a pea shooter and a slingshot, but when handled by an expert like the owner, it becomes a deadly weapon and carries havoc into the ranks of swallows and seasides. It has many good points (this is a tribute to Stone's marksmanship) and goes up the sleeve nicely; it is well-suited to suburban collecting; its gentle crack is doubtless not an unfamiliar sound in the wild back yards of Germantown, and for ought I know, it may have made the welkin ring [made a very loud noise] in the trackless wastes of Logan Square [the urban location of the Academy of Natural Sciences].

There is some evidence that Stone had largely abandoned his collecting habits by the time of his visits to Cape May. Yet, in earlier years, that was how a birding expedition was carried out. In the same story as quoted above, "A Day in the Salt Marshes Near Atlantic City" (a paper presented to a DVOC meeting in 1893), Morris goes on to offer proof that after all the days of millinery shooting, Common Terns had finally returned to breed on the Jersey marshes, which he confirmed by shooting a number and collecting the only eggs and chicks he found. These specimens are still in the collection of the Academy of Natural Sciences. Interestingly, although he was also collecting Least Sandpipers for scientific purposes, Morris repeatedly mentions how he was looking forward to the bird pie that would be cooked that night in the boat's galley.

Stone was a giant among scientists, and his major ornithological legacy, *Bird Studies at Old Cape May*, is the cornerstone of our avian heritage at Cape May. It is an in-depth primer on bird life along the Jersey Shore. It focuses primarily on Cape May but includes the coast north to the Barnegat Bay area and west along the Delaware Bay to Hancock's Bridge near Salem. The tome includes wonderful illustrations by Stone's cronies Earl Poole, Conrad Roland, Richard Bishop, J. Fletcher Street, and Herbert Brown. Many of the observations are Stone's, but he summarizes the large contributions of his contemporary friends and colleagues Otway Brown, Walker Hand, Frank Dickinson, and Julian K. Potter, all of whom lived at least seasonally at Cape May, and other greats who visited him at Cape May, such as Alexander Wetmore, Ludlow Griscom, and the redoubtable Arthur Cleveland Bent. Julian Potter of Collingswood, New Jersey, had a home in Goshen, Cape May County (not far from the CMBO's Center for Research and Education), where he spent considerable time. As we write, we can see his former home and yard from our home-office window, a fun connection to history. Somewhere in or near that yard, Potter and the great Philadelphia nature writer and columnist Dale Rex Coman found a Eurasian Woodcock on January 2, 1956, one of only a few North American records (actually, their bird dog found it first). We've always wondered, fancifully, if that woodcock ever entered our yard—a fantasy "historic" addition to our yard list.

Bird Studies at Old Cape May is an ornithological classic. The original printing by the DVOC consisted of only 1,400 copies. Today the original two-volume edition is highly prized, commanding high prices at used book sales and auctions. In 1965 it was reprinted by Dover Publications, and in 2000 it was reprinted by Stackpole Books. Few books in any field or discipline have enjoyed such "staying power." Despite its original 1937 publication date, it is still assigned as required reading in modern ornithology classes. Stone's insights and analyses of status and trends, the dynamics of migration, the effects of weather, and conservation offer much to today's students of birds. We recommend it as a primer for any serious birder visiting Cape May. Besides being educational, it's fun to read and a way to experience the magic of days gone by at Old Cape May.

In a memorial published in *The Auk* in 1941, Stone's friend and colleague James A. G. Rehn warmly wrote:

> Witmer Stone was born a naturalist, nurtured a naturalist and a
> naturalist he lived until the end of his days. Most of the many

activities that filled his busy life flowed from his profound interest in nature. Scientist, man of letters, biographer of science and
scientists, and protector of wildlife, he combined with these
attainments what another old friend, Dr. Cornelius Weygandt,
has most aptly called "a genius for friendship." To a buoyant spirit
he added an enthusiasm which he kept through life, a keen sense
of humor, a touch of whimsey, a sympathetic understanding, a
love of good literature and the instincts of the historian and bib-
liophile, attributes all of which broadened his outlook upon the
world and drew him closely to his fellow men.

We can only add that this enthusiasm and genius have endured over
time, and even today, reading *Bird Studies at Old Cape May* makes us feel
that Witmer Stone is an old friend.

KEEPERS OF THE FLAME

It can easily be said that Witmer Stone's death, shortly after the publication
of *Bird Studies at Old Cape May,* marked the end of an era. Many of his colleagues were passing on too—as Pete Dunne once said, "now getting dor-
sal views, rather than ventral, of migrants over the Cape." But as one era
ended, another began. Bird study at Cape May was now driven by a sense
of urgency. Market hunting had decimated shorebirds, and plume hunters
were ruthlessly eliminating terns, herons, and egrets. Hawks were targets
too, and the hawk slaughter at Cape May was not only for sport (as at
Hawk Mountain, Pennsylvania) but also for food, as many gunners shot
them for the dinner table. Beginning in 1931 the National Audubon Society (NAS), as part of its growing and yeoman effort to protect birds,
began to send observers—wardens, of a sort—to Cape May Point to monitor and control the shooting. In 1935 the Witmer Stone Wildlife Sanctuary
was established by the NAS on what is today Cape May Point State Park
and Higbee Beach WMA. By "controlling the field," the NAS effectively
ended most of the shooting. These wardens conducted hawk counts too,
and the list of the first group of hawkwatchers reads much like an honor
roll of American ornithology.

The first hawk count was conducted in 1931 by George B. Saunders of
the NAS. The 1932 count was made by Robert Porter Allen, a noted
researcher and writer. In 1935 the first "full-time" count was conducted for
eighty-four days by William J. Rusling (who went on to do similar, pioneering counts at Cape Charles, Virginia) and none other than the young
Roger Tory Peterson. This was just a few months after the publication of the
first edition of Peterson's monumental *A Field Guide to the Birds.* The count
effort in 1936 was undertaken by James T. Tanner and in 1937 by Richard G.

Kuerzi of the NAS. The year following his Cape May count, Tanner began his monumental study and monograph on the Ivory-billed Woodpecker (published in 1942) at the Singer Tract in Louisiana. At Cape May, Tanner and Peterson saw, among the hawks, a Common Raven high over the Point on October 25, 1936, a last remnant of the soon-to-be-gone breeding population in the South Jersey white cedar swamps. Forty-eight years passed before another raven was seen over Cape May, when we and hawk counter Frank Nicoletti thrilled to one riding 50-knot gale-force northeast winds on the backside of a hurricane that passed well offshore on October 13, 1984. There have been a handful of records since—possibly birds dispersing from the few returning nesting pairs in northwestern New Jersey.

Roger Tory Peterson (1908–1996) first visited Cape May as a teenaged art student, when he and two birding buddies hitchhiked to the Cape from New York. On his first trip he saw his "life" Louisiana Heron (now known as Tricolored Heron), a true rarity then. Peterson returned to Cape May many times as a bird artist, as a warden, and finally as an authority and a celebrity. He was a frequent speaker at New Jersey Audubon's annual autumn weekends and further immortalized Cape May in his popular book *Birds Over America* (1948). Later, in George H. Harrison's *Roger Tory Peterson's Dozen Birding Hot Spots* (1976), Peterson chose Cape May as one of his twelve favorite places in all of North America: the chapter was titled "Cape May: The Morning of Birding Madness." On May 18, 1984, while participating in New Jersey Audubon's *World Series of Birding* on a team with Pete Dunne, David Sibley, Bill Boyle, and Pete Bacinski, Peterson saw a Fork-tailed Flycatcher, his 698th North American bird. In his later years, Peterson was an avid nature photographer and made numerous trips to Cape May. We had the extreme privilege and pleasure of accompanying Roger several times as his "local guides" on excursions to photograph spring shorebirds on Delaware Bay. These outings, punctuated with vivid stories by the master, will remain one of the most treasured experiences of our lives afield.

After the heady and poignant 1930s, bird study took a backseat to World War II. Attesting to the paucity of observers, there are few records of the thousands of seabirds that probably washed up on our

Roger Tory Peterson photographs spring shorebirds at Reeds Beach in this 1987 image.

shores, victims of the oil spills from the hundreds of ships torpedoed by German submarines off Atlantic beaches. Except for official coastal observers, binoculars were frowned on by authorities who were wary of spies and saboteurs. Clay's mother, Flora, who lived in Sea Isle City while her future husband was overseas, remembered the explosions of torpedoes and the smoke and flames of burning ships off the beaches during the first years of the war, before the tide turned in the desperate Battle of the Atlantic. She remembered, too, the enforced blackouts, which must have been highly beneficial to coastal migrant songbirds—the darkest skies in nearly fifty years and an absence of light pollution that has not occurred since.

One of the few records of oil-killed seabirds from the dark days of the early 1940s came from Dave Cutler (who went on to be a longtime regional editor of the venerable *American Birds*—now *North American Birds*) and some of his DVOC buddies, who picked up dozens of dead alcids on New Jersey beaches during systematic weekend surveys. His brother, Herb Cutler, found the first (dead) Ivory Gull for New Jersey at Island Beach on February 3, 1940, during one of these oiled bird surveys; this specimen is still housed at the Academy of Natural Sciences in Philadelphia. The oil problem was chronic. Even as a kid in the 1950s, Clay remembers getting "tar" (oil) on his bare feet most days at the beach, an enduring legacy of the war. Unrestricted dumping and pumping of tanks and bilges played a role too, as Stone often wrote (prewar) of oiled birds he found on the shores of Cape May. Strict regulations and U.S. Coast Guard enforcement have all but eliminated this threat, but a few oiled birds are still found today; some oil tankers, probably in the dead of night, illegally flush their ballast tanks at the mouth of Delaware Bay or off the coast.

Bird-watchers visited the Cape during the war, as evidenced by the informative brochure for the Witmer Stone Wildlife Sanctuary written by author and conservationist Richard H. Pough (and graced with a Sharp-shinned Hawk illustration by George Miksch Sutton) in about 1942. It invites visitors to enjoy the sanctuary but urges against trespassing on government property—the Cape May Canal and the naval base at Cape May Point. Rebuilding a nation racked first by depression and then by war held sway into the 1950s, but the ornithological record determinedly continued. At this point it was largely the DVOC and its journal *Cassinia* that perpetuated the ornithological history of Cape May. Seasonal reports and summaries in both the NAS's *Audubon Field Notes* and New Jersey Audubon's *New Jersey Nature News* were also important repositories for records from this period. This was when the New Jersey Audubon Society (NJAS), founded in 1897 (making it older than the NAS), began to take an active interest in Cape May. NJAS held its first annual Cape May Autumn Weekend in 1946 and has continued to organize and host this weekend-long offering of bird, butterfly, and botany walks; indoor workshops and pro-grams; boat trips; and celebrated evening programs ever since. (In 1998 THE Bird Show became part of the Cape May Autumn Weekend and fills Cape May Convention Hall with more than fifty nature-focused vendors and exhibits from all over the country, including artists, carvers, gifts and crafts, conservation organizations, and nature tour and optics companies.) This event has played a large role in bringing national awareness and notoriety to Cape May's fall migration. Conservation titan Frank McLaughlin was NJAS executive director from 1952 to 1970 and was instrumental in finally putting a stop to hawk shooting in New Jersey.

Another noteworthy development was the formation in 1946 of the Cape May Geographic Society (CMGS), organized to encourage natural history studies in the vicinity of Cape May. By this time, Cape May's fame had enticed naturalists from all over the country, who congregated there in summer or year-round (often after retirement). Interested in birds, bugs, botany, geology, and history, the CMGS thrived, and its annual bulletin (published from 1947 to 1991) was a wonderful collection of Cape May natural history lore, including the growing bird record. This record was the work of giants: of the ninety-eight charter members of the CMGS, twenty-six were mentioned or quoted in Stone's great works on botany and birds as contributors to his recorded lore. Many of the great naturalists of this period were key players in the CMGS. Dr. Horace Richards, associ-ate curator of geology and paleontology at the Academy of Natural Sci-ences, had a summer home in Cape May Point. When we knew Horace, he was wheelchair bound, and Pat would often spend several evenings each summer looking at slides with Horace and his sister Marie. In the late 1970s, during one of those memorable evenings, Pat quietly said to Horace, "Do you know what you have there?" His slide clearly showed the camouflaged Bunker near the beach on the Point. He'd taken it during one of his aerial surveys of coastal erosion and didn't even know the now exposed Bunker was in the photograph. Horace Richard's historic photo is still prominently displayed at Cape May Point State Park.

Robert Alexander was another key figure in the CMGS. He authored many books, including *Noteworthy Trees of Cape May County, New Jersey,* published in 1950 by the CMGS, and *Ho! For Cape Island!* published in 1956 by the author. Otway Brown, a Cape May resident, was the CMGS's first curator. He earned his living as a gardener, florist's assistant, and clerk; he was the groundskeeper and gardener at the Emlen Physick Estate in Cape May. An active botanist, he capably cataloged the plants of Cape May County from 1893 to 1931. (After his death, the CMGS bound his handwritten manuscript, the "Plants of Cape May County, NJ," and presented it to the Cape May County Library.) Brown was a colleague and close friend of

Pat's mentor, Bill Bailey, shown here in 1983, made invaluable records of Cape May's natural history.

Witmer Stone, and he served as Stone's driver during their many natural history outings together, including fourteen Cape May Christmas Bird Counts. Otway Brown's wife, interestingly, was a descendant of the Bartram family. Other great naturalists involved with the CMGS included Dr. George Clark, J. d'Arcy Northwood, Joseph Jacobs (who diligently monitored nesting Ospreys and Bald Eagles), eminent entomologist C. Brooke Worth, botanist Gilbert Cavileer, and the wonderful William "Bill" Bailey, a compulsive annotator of all things natural and historic and a true keeper of the flame. Bill Bailey (1902–2002)—not the same ornithologist who was a founder of the DVOC—was an accomplished naturalist, botanist, and historian. Bill was Pat's mentor in the 1970s and 1980s, and many of the historical aspects and much of the inspiration for this Cape May book are based on Bill's substantial library and collections, precious archives he generously gathered, shared, and passed down to the next generation of eager young naturalists.

The CMGS was active well into the late 1980s. Both of us played active roles in this group and recall many wonderful evening get-togethers, lectures, and field trips. One fun tradition was the weekly gathering of the CMGS at Roth's Fudge Shop on the Cape May Mall for ice cream after evening lectures in the summer. For two young naturalists to be included with the heavies of the historic and natural world was an awesome experience. We sat around a table feasting on homemade ice cream with the likes of Ernie Choate, Bill Bailey, Bob Alexander, George and Emily Clark, Marie and Horace Richards, Keith Seager, and many others, hanging on every word and gleaning as much as possible. We were listened to as well, and our questions were answered with care.

The aging naturalists were so eager to teach and to share, a lesson for us all. Pat was the editor of the CMGS annual bulletin in 1977 and from 1980 to 1986 and the president of the CMGS from 1986 to 1987. Over time, the society lost many of its older members, and few younger members came along to replace them. In many ways, this "greatest generation" of naturalists could never be replaced. The Cape May Bird Observatory was established in 1976, and as its flame brightened, that of the CMGS flickered. The CMBO sponsored numerous walks and lectures, and as modern birding evolved and grew, fewer people seemed interested in the entire breadth of natural history. (Today, with the keen interest in butterflies, dragonflies, and other aspects of the natural world, the pendulum has clearly swung back.) Conceding the field to the CMBO, the CMGS folded its tent in 1991 but will always be remembered as a major player and a driving force for many years. In much the same way, the Witmer Stone Bird Club in Stone Harbor faded away as the Wetlands Institute grew.

One gentleman whose name will forever stand out from this era is Ernie Choate. Dr. Ernest A. Choate (1900–1980), a student of language and a school principal from Philadelphia, summered and spent many a weekend in Cape May Point from 1938 on, retiring there in 1965. Ernie was the CMGS's first president and became the de facto bird authority at Cape May, chronicling local bird notes for thirty-two years (1947–1979) in the CMGS's annual bulletin. Ernie was a stern taskmaster for bird records (his disciplinarian background served him well here), and he meticulously, if perhaps conservatively, maintained the Cape May avian record. Ernie in many ways kept the fire burning. He penned "Birding at Cape May" in the *Atlantic Naturalist* in 1953—not only the first true site guide to the Cape but also an important update of Stone's 1937 tome. Choate compiled the Cape May Christmas Bird Count for twenty years, from 1952 to 1972. He wrote the delightful and lasting *Dictionary of American Bird Names* (first published in 1973 and revised in 1985), which explores in-depth the language and etymology of bird names. Of note, Ernie also authored the important "Additional Species Recorded (since 1937)" section for the 1965 Dover reprint of *Bird Studies at Old Cape May*. As one of Stone's acolytes, Choate was one of the last links between the old guard and the modern era. He was a great storyteller too. Clay remembers going to his first DVOC meetings, driving up to the Academy of Natural Sciences with Ernie and trying to separate fact from fiction as the older birders entertained the tyro. The trip back from Philadelphia (pre-Route 55) was lengthy, and Ernie always insisted on a break halfway home—not for coffee but for a beer at the Timberdoodle Tavern on Route 50. The Timberdoodle (colloquial for American Woodcock) was a fitting watering hole, but it's now long gone. Memories of Ernie Choate still remain vivid for many today. He was a bit testy in his later years, a description he would have enjoyed and been proud of, but we will always remember his proverbial raised eyebrow fondly.

The DVOC of this era was a feisty group. Since its inception as an all-male club, the DVOC was largely Victorian, aristocratic, and conservative. During the Great Depression, this was the only demographic group that realistically could enjoy birding. In the 1970s the close-knit club began to change. As birding blossomed, many younger members joined, and in 1983, after much contentious discussion (and some hard feelings and bruised male egos), a vote was taken to "allow" women members. Following this monumental (for them) decision, the formerly tight-knit club grew almost exponentially and today is a friendly, lively group that is a driving force in regional ornithological studies (retaining its longtime connection with the Academy of Natural Sciences). Clay will never forget his first DVOC meetings—the gentlemanly irreverence and the testing of newcomers' skills and mettle. They were well-known pranksters—surreptitiously slipping a view of a pinup girl into a novice's slide show to trip him up, a fate that befell Clay several times. The DVOC played a trick on Roger Tory Peterson too, placing a "stuffed" specimen of a Black-necked Stilt on Bunker Pond to fool him as he led a field trip at Cape May Point.

Margaret Shaffer (1891–1995) was a legend to visiting birders from near and far. She ran what was essentially a birders' bed and breakfast in Cape May Point in her home at 507 Pearl Avenue. She first opened her home to boarders during World War II, when she took in workers who were constructing the bunker on the beach near the Cape May Lighthouse. Later, her cottage became the seasonal gathering place of birders, including ornithologists and beginners alike. Some of those who enjoyed her hospitality (as well as hearty breakfasts and dinners) included Richard Pough, Floyd Wolfarth, J. D'Arcy Northwood, Chandler Robbins, Maurice Broun, Rosalie Edge, Ian Sinclair, Don Eckelberry, Guy Coholeach, Arthur Singer, and J. Fenwick Lansdowne. During the 1950s and 1960s, before the proliferation of motels in Cape May, Mrs. Shaffer hosted the spring and fall birding weekends for many bird clubs, finding lodging for members with other homeowners in Cape May Point and preparing breakfasts for great numbers of guests. A young Michael O'Brien was one of the last to stay at Mrs. Shaffer's, on his first trip to Cape May with his father and brother in the mid-1970s. By then, Mrs. Shaffer was in her eighties.

A few other naturalists stand out as well. Keith Seager eagerly birded and botanized the Cape in the early 1970s, at a time when few others were afield. A friend and protégé of Choate, Keith was very active in the CMGS (president from 1980 to 1985) and took over as compiler of the Cape May Christmas Bird Count in 1973 (carrying the baton for twenty years until 1994, when Louise Zemaitis took over). Retired now, Keith is still one of Cape May's most active birders. He's afield almost every day, usually in some out-of-the-way places, and is still making key discoveries, such as the 1990

Lesser Sand Plover (Mongolian Plover) at North Wildwood, one of our rarest birds ever. James F. Akers moved to New Jersey from Ohio in 1959 and soon became a strong force in New Jersey birding and in conservation. In 1981 his *All Year Birding in Southern New Jersey* was published, the first comprehensive handbook and site guide for the southern half of the state. Jim Akers made a major contribution to birding in the region, particularly in the Atlantic County–Forsythe NWR area, and it is only fitting that his son, Fred Akers, is today one of South Jersey's conservation champions as the tireless director of the Great Egg Harbor Watershed Association.

Another character from this era (and we use the word *character* carefully) is Alfred Nicholson. An accomplished landscape artist, he studied birds at Audubon Camp in Maine with Roger Tory Peterson as his instructor. He too vividly remembers his first visit to Cape May, where, as a young boy with an avid interest in birds, he watched an adult Bald Eagle run the gauntlet of gunners along Sunset Boulevard. Every "sportsman" emptied his shotgun at it, yet the eagle somehow kept flying. It was a vision that would help shape Al's lifelong (and sometimes bitter and combative) commitment to conservation and environmental activism. In later years, his focus was always on conservation rather than birding, but he loved his raptors. While hunkered behind the walls of the abandoned buildings at the naval base (now Cape May Point State Park) during November's gray gales, Nicholson discovered that Golden Eagles were, "under the right conditions," regular migrants at Cape May. Later he discovered that Mississippi Kites were annual spring migrants over Pond Creek Marsh (part of Higbee Beach WMA), and he meticulously described in his notebook journal the tame Eskimo Curlew he watched at length at point-blank range in South Cape May's pastureland in September 1960.

Al Nicholson was prominently featured and well captured in Jack Connor's popular book *Season at the Point; The Birds and Birders of Cape May.* For many years Al was a fixture at the Beanery, huddled behind his easel, paintbrush in one hand and binoculars in the other, "waiting for the Golden." He has retreated to neighboring Cumberland County these days, but sometimes, when the wind is just right and if you know where to look,

Al Nicholson works on a painting along the old railroad tracks at the Beanery in this 1982 photo.

you can still find him at his favorite places in Cape May, painting madly and watching the sky, waiting. Like his favorite raptors, he is inexorably drawn to Cape May, and his magnificent, evocative, old-school landscape paintings continue to poignantly capture vistas of Old Cape May and those long-forgotten places and spaces of the Delaware Bayshore.

BIRD STUDIES AT NEW CAPE MAY

The modern era of birding at Cape May began, arguably, on September 1, 1976. That was the day that Pete Dunne climbed the Cape May Hawkwatch for the first time. Following stints as a counter at Hawk Mountain, Pennsylvania, and Raccoon Ridge, New Jersey, Pete was hired by Ernie Choate and Bill Clark to do a full-season hawk count at Cape May. Thus began the renaissance of birding at Cape May. As that autumn season began, the Cape May Bird Observatory was born. From these humble beginnings, the CMBO has become one of the most respected bird observatories in the world—and almost certainly receiving the most visitors and hosting the most natural history programs.

The "hawkwatch platform" that Pete Dunne climbed that first day in 1976 was a homemade picnic table, replaced the next year by a borrowed lifeguard stand. Today's hawkwatch platform is the third to stand in the same spot and can hold several hundred hawkwatchers. A few interim hawk counts had been conducted prior to 1976. Ernie Choate had carried out a full-season hawkwatch in 1965 and repeated that effort in 1970 when he, Fred Tilly, and Al Nicholson carried out an expanded-hours watch under the auspices of the New Jersey State Museum. The 1965 count would be the lowest ever, a mere 3,951 birds, with the lowest number of Peregrine Falcons ever (19). This was the height of the DDT era and also a time when hawks had not yet recovered from the shooting of the first half of the century. Bald Eagle migrants bottomed out at a mere *one* in the 1972 raptor banding station count. See Part I, page 70 for Historical Hawk Counts.

It was on October 16, 1970, though, that the single highest one-day raptor count in Cape May history occurred, when an occluded front and rain created a huge backup of hawks. When a powerful cold front finally pushed through, Choate and Nicholson counted 25,608 hawks, including an astounding 24,875 American Kestrels. Although this count has been questioned because Choate in part extrapolated numbers, one thing is clear—there were an amazing number of kestrels that day! As Nicholson told us recently, "We had to extrapolate—there was simply no way you could count so many birds individually." Although such numbers may be routinely handled today in Texas and Veracruz, with numerous observers and banks of clickers, back in 1970, no one had ever done it before. At the time, it was the largest daily total ever recorded at any autumn hawkwatch in the United States.

Autumn hawk counts were conducted from 1971 to 1975 by William S. Clark as an adjunct to his hawk banding project. Bill Clark, today a world-renowned raptor expert and author, pretty much got his start in Cape May. The Cape May Raptor Banding Project, begun in 1967 and still going strong today, is by far the largest such undertaking in the world; four to five stations attract, trap, band, and release an average

The Cape May Hawkwatch in 1978 consisted of a lifeguard stand and a handful of dedicated observers.

of more than 4,000 hawks each year, resulting in more than 200 recoveries (recaptures and band returns) each year. The Cape May Raptor Banding Project, Inc., is a fully independent effort, a not-for-profit project founded originally by Bill Clark and run locally by veteran bander Sam Orr.

The full-season, full-time, dawn-to-dusk Cape May Hawkwatch that began in 1976 continues to this day, held each year from September 1 to November 30. Skeptics were critical of Pete Dunne's counts in the early years, but visitors soon learned that the counts were solid and real. The hawks were back—the mid-1970s saw the first real recovery of hawks from the ravages of DDT—and Sharp-shinned Hawk, Cooper's Hawk, Osprey, Bald Eagle, and Peregrine Falcon numbers soared. As word got out through Dunne's passionate and eloquent nature writing, the Cape May Bird Observatory began to soar too. The CMBO was formed in August 1976 by Bill Clark and the New Jersey Audubon Society's board of directors. Dunne went from hawk counter to first full-time director of the CMBO, although, for several years, he was the *only* employee.

CMBO will forever be linked and indebted to its first benefactor, Anne Ardrey Northwood. A resident of Cape May Point, Anne was a renaissance woman—an author, poet, and artist. An admitted eccentric, she was a raconteur and enthusiastic patron of the arts as well. Her husband, J. d'Arcy Northwood, was a character in his own right. An Englishman, he was the classic "officer and a gentleman." At age twenty, he served as a pilot in the Royal Flying Corps in World War I and flew dozens of missions against the Germans, including the Red Baron's Flying Circus. He went on to become an adventurer and world traveler—and a prominent ornithologist. At Cape

May, d'Arcy was a warden for NAS, hired to patrol and protect hawks at the Witmer Stone Bird Sanctuary, and he still has the distinction of being the only person ever to see a Swallow-tailed Kite at Cape May during the "official" fall count season, when he watched one over Sunset Boulevard on September 1, 1946 (there have been several August records of southbound swallow-tails in recent years). D'Arcy and Anne married in 1963. From 1954 to 1966, d'Arcy was the first curator at Mill Grove, the first American home of John James Audubon, a 122-acre farm at the mouth of the Perkiomen, near Norristown, Pennsylvania. He was an avid bird-watcher and prominent in the DVOC. Upon retiring from Mill Grove, d'Arcy and Anne moved to a ramshackle cottage that they had purchased in 1965 in Cape May Point. They turned their 2-acre property into a miniature refuge and named it Swan Sea Sanctuary. After d'Arcy Northwood died in 1972, Anne deeded much of her Lily Lake property (four wooded lots) to the NJAS in his memory. She continued to befriend birds and bird-watchers. Her home, like those of Ernie Choate and Margaret Shaffer, was always open.

In 1976 Anne graciously donated space to a fledgling CMBO—first a desk in the atrium, then the whole atrium. When CMBO outgrew those, she offered a second room, and soon fully half her home. She reveled in the success of CMBO and in the attention and friendly faces of those who visited it. Anne, artist and liberal that she was, was also an avid nudist; this, combined with a tendency toward "forgetfulness" in her older years, surprised more than one CMBO visitor in the mid-1980s when Anne greeted them wearing only her warm smile. Anne had her eccentricities, but she was a thoughtful, enlightened, and gracious woman. When she passed away in 1990, she willed her home and remaining property to the NJAS. Then director Paul Kerlinger remodeled CMBO

The Cape May Bird Observatory grew out of the atrium of Anne Northwood's home on Lily Lake.

(mostly with his own hands) into the visitor center and bookstore you can visit today. For those who knew her, every visit to CMBO occasions a quiet remembrance of Anne Northwood and her pivotal role in the CMBO's formation and early history.

The 1980s brought rapid change, both to the region and to the CMBO. By now the observatory was growing in leaps and bounds, expanding its programming into the missions it embraces today—research, education, conservation, and recreation. The

Pete Dunne leads a September seashore bird walk in 1995.

Delaware Bay horseshoe crab–shorebird connection was "discovered" in the early 1980s, and almost overnight, Cape May became a two-season phenomenon, a popular destination in both spring and fall. The CMBO has been supported by a competent, enlightened, and sometimes daring board of directors at the New Jersey Audubon Society (the CMBO's parent organization), hundreds of volunteers, and thousands of members, donors, and patrons, but its meteoric rise, and the concomitant modern fame of Cape May, is unquestionably linked to Pete Dunne.

Pete Dunne's evocative and creative writing, his dynamic and far-reaching vision, and his engaging and affable personality have forever cemented Cape May's place worldwide as a top birding destination. Cape May may have been synonymous with birds since Alexander Wilson's time, but Pete Dunne took the message to the masses. He was more than a birder or even a bard; he was and is a birding entrepreneur, an avian chamber of commerce. Pete Dunne is eponymous with modern birding, and he has helped change bird-watching forever, both at Cape May and elsewhere. He may have stood on the shoulders of the giants who went before, but few would argue that he, more than any other person, has made Cape May the destination that it is today. In his writing, in essence, he demanded that birders come to Cape May, and as disciples of a new, emergent religion—birding—they obeyed. Build it and they will come.

A tour of the local spots where Cape May ornithological history was made would be an interesting panoply of sites: the Somers Mansion, where Audubon allegedly stayed; the 800 block of Queen Street in Cape May City, where Witmer Stone lived (the exact address has been lost); the Choate house on the southeast corner of Lake Drive and Yale Avenue in Cape May

Point; the CMBO Northwood Center; Herbert Mills's Stone Harbor home; maybe Julian Potter's Goshen farm; and probably the Sibley Cottage on the southeast corner of Cape and Cedar Avenues in Cape May Point. It would also include sites such as Pete Dunne's cubbyhole at the Wetlands Institute (a single desk he occupied when Anne Northwood migrated south and closed her unheated home in the winter months) and the C-View Inn on Texas Avenue in Cape May. The latter, a local tavern and a favorite watering hole for Cape May birders for decades, was a place where Cape May ornithological history was made (or at least planned). It was there that the idea for CMBO was first hatched, where *Hawks in Flight* was dreamed up, and even where the World Series of Birding was born—an important location indeed.

But as Cape May birding crested, Pete Dunne stepped back. Pete migrated north; inevitably promoted to vice president of NJAS, he moved to the main office at Bernardsville, New Jersey. There he managed his biggest brainchild ever—the incomparable World Series of Birding, the bird-a-thon fund-raising effort that now raises over $600,000 a year for conservation groups. Back at Cape May, others stepped up to the plate. Pat Sutton was hired in 1986 as the CMBO's first teacher naturalist and began integrating butterflies, dragonflies, and backyard habitat into adult program offerings. In 1987 Paul Kerlinger became CMBO's second director, as well as director of research for NJAS. Change and growth were in the wind, and the Cape May sea breezes boded well.

Birders as Ecotourists

An expert on raptor migration, Kerlinger had been one of the pioneers in the use of radar to study migratory raptors. In the late 1980s, he placed research on an equal footing with education and recreation at CMBO. Research priorities included not only diurnal raptor research but also, for example, owl migration, Black Rail status and distribution, and the importance of the Delaware Bayshore to migrant and wintering birds. In 1988 and 1989 Kerlinger began the first studies of the morning flight at Higbee Beach, the visible reverse migration of neotropical land birds, documenting huge flights under certain conditions in a 1992 paper published in the *Auk*. In 1993 Kerlinger (with Dave Ward, Clay Sutton, and Fred Mears) initiated the now famous Avalon Seawatch, the count of migrating waterbirds passing Avalon in Cape May County each autumn. It was during Kerlinger's tenure at the CMBO that his instant classic *Flight Strategies of Migrating Hawks* (1989) would be published, followed later by his popular *How Birds Migrate* in 1995.

Concern over intense development pressure on the natural areas of Cape May and along the Delaware Bayshore led Kerlinger to perhaps his most significant contribution to Cape May birding. Sensing that traditional tools and methods were falling short in protecting open space, Kerlinger began the first ecotourism studies and surveys at Cape May. In a 1988 landmark study, Kerlinger and CMBO determined that more than 100,000 birders were bringing in more than $10 million each year to Cape May County, a huge economic boost in the relative "off-season" months of spring and fall. (Visitors that year came from thirty-two states and seven foreign countries.) Following the birding boom in the 1990s and the skyrocketing popularity of Delaware Bay in spring, by 1998 the ecotourism value of the shorebird and horseshoe crab gathering alone was assessed at $34 million per year by Kerlinger and his colleague Ted Eubanks. In southern New Jersey, where tourism largely drives the economy, these numbers were real attention-getters, and suddenly birders were no longer a "burden" but a real boon to the year-round economy. Kerlinger and Eubanks have since carried out ecotourism studies throughout the country, but the economic studies at Cape May were a pivotal achievement, a reason why birders are so welcome in Cape May, and an important part of why we still have many places to bird.

Of interest, although ecotourism and its arguments for bird protection are usually thought to be an enlightened issue of the 1990s, economics was a big part of the argument against hawk shooting in the early 1950s. Back then, Burritt Wright, Russel Fowler, and Bennett Matlack of the Audubon Center of South Jersey (a spin-off of NJAS no longer extant) successfully argued "to substantiate the economic value of hawks to the area," writing that "the practical approach to the hawk shooting problem demonstrated to the people of Cape May the dollar value of hawks from the standpoint of the thousands of bird watchers they attract." Such arguments gained unlikely supporters and were in part responsible for ending the annual hawk slaughter, and they are still valid today.

The British Invasion, and a Little Paris

It was in the late 1980s and early 1990s that the second British invasion of Cape May occurred. The first had been in 1812, when British warships in Delaware Bay landed longboats to obtain fresh water from Lily Lake. But the local patriots dug a mile-long trench from Lily Lake to tidal Pond Creek, filling the lake with salt water and rendering the water undrinkable, denying the British a water source. The modern British invasion began when Cape May rapidly became *the* place for British (and other European) birders to see a large number of North American birds during a short holiday. Many visitors from the United Kingdom came to Cape May each fall, and a few stayed. They are known for their intense interest in birding, which in Britain is more driven, more serious, and a more male-dominated pursuit than is generally the case in the United States. In the Old World, birding can often be more a passion than a hobby, a tradition and obsession rather than a pastime.

The British influence on Cape May birding cannot be denied. The focus, skill, knowledge, and field abilities of the visitors, even those who had never visited our shores before, became legendary. A friendly exchange of ideas, data, and identification skills took place, and as a result, the pace and intensity of birding at Cape May changed. For better or worse, the British clearly raised the bar for many Cape May birders. The "better" part of the experience was the focus and pace, the learned skills, and far better documentation of rarities, for example. The "worse" may be less tangible, but the raising of the bar that made birding more intense also made it less leisurely and, for some, a little less fun. It was as if the bird walk had become a bird jog. Call it "birding performance anxiety," perhaps, but with the Brits looking over our shoulders, there seemed to be less of the wide-eyed innocence and wonder that had pervaded Cape May for so many years.

There were many fun aspects of the British influence, including birding vernacular. We all speak the same language, but that didn't preclude a bit of a language barrier. For example, the phrase "I dipped on the Clapper Rail" didn't mean that the birder had fallen overboard trying to see one, merely that he had "missed" seeing it. "Duf gen," at first unfathomable to us, meant that one had received "bad information" about a bird sighting. Soon such terms were in widespread use at Cape May. The barrier worked both ways. When one British gentleman inquired at the CMBO as to where he should begin birding, the staff suggested that he "go to the hawk-watch." "My, that's odd," he countered, "what type of birds would I see at a swine-washing station?" All in all, our British and European friends have been some of our favorite visitors, bringing a wealth of skill, knowledge, and camaraderie to Cape May.

Perhaps in part as a result of the quickened pace, Cape May in the late 1980s and early 1990s became to birding what was 1930s Paris to artists, writers, and poets. Birding was pervasive and all-consuming, and many top birders—writers, artists, photographers, researchers—gravitated to Cape May. By this time, David Sibley was the artist in residence at the CMBO, beginning his *Sibley Guide,* but there were many others, Louise Zemaitis and Shawneen Finnegan among them. Kevin Karlson was rapidly becoming one of the top bird photographers in North America, and nature writer Jack Connor was creating his intimate *Season at the Point: The Birds and Birders of Cape May,* an acclaimed, in-depth look at a single autumn season at the Cape. Other writers included Pete Dunne (who couldn't stay away), Michael O'Brien (pushing the frontiers of sound recording), Richard Crossley (a Brit who came to stay), Paul Lehman (pioneering an understanding of weather and creating a new generation of bird range maps), the Suttons, Paul Kerlinger, and Dick Turner.

These were heady times, and the atmosphere was charged. Rarities were found almost daily, in both good weather and bad, as patterns of vagrancy were discovered. Forever legendary will be Louise Zemaitis's classic Thursday night gatherings (easily as famous as Margaret Shaffer's overnighters in the 1950s and 1960s), where dozens of birders would gather for food, to trade information, for "tercial talk," to learn, and simply to commune. Today, it is not that these halcyon days have ended, but times have changed a bit. Basically, Cape May birding has become big—more diversified and complex. With several hundred resident birders living at Cape May today, they simply won't fit under one roof any longer. And, inevitably, growth has led to more specialization and more focused interests; bird banders, researchers, environmentalists, and butterfly enthusiasts all have their own varied informal alliances, agendas, and schedules. These are not cliques but simply the natural differentiation and organization of growing numbers of birders and naturalists. Be assured that there is still a constant, friendly exchange of information.

Growth inevitably brings change, and if the CMBO can no longer be thought of as a "mom and pop" organization, we can take heart that in its place is a world-class research, education, and conservation organization and, facility. Birds are still an absolute way of life for many at Cape May, but we believe that ornithological history will record the 1980s and early 1990s as the renaissance years for birding at Cape May, a time of revival and renewal. It was an era of vibrant energy, great hopes and dreams, and an unequaled sense of learning, discovery, camaraderie, and celebration.

Into the Future

Several changes led Cape May away from the idyllic years of the late 1980s and early 1990s. One was a physical change, a spreading out. In 1997 the CMBO became two facilities when the Center for Research and Education (CRE) opened its doors in Goshen, 17 miles north of the Northwood Center (which remained open as an information center, bookstore, and gift shop). The CRE, a modern, purpose-built facility, was funded solely and generously by

CMBO's Goshen Center features gardens created specifically as wildlife habitat.

members of the CMBO and NJAS. Today it houses the ever-growing research and education staff, a nature store, classrooms, and the extensive outdoor classroom known as the "Model Backyard Habitat." The other changes were in personnel. After a seven-year tenure, Paul Kerlinger left the CMBO in 1994 for the private sector; he is now an ornithology consultant to the burgeoning wind-power industry, working to ensure safe siting and operation of clean-energy wind turbines. Although he works throughout North America and Europe, he still resides in Cape May. Pete Dunne, who considered his stay in North Jersey almost like living in exile, had returned to his beloved Cape May a few years earlier, working out of the Northwood Center. He resumed the position of CMBO director in 1994, and with that, the modern era at Cape May had come full circle.

Dr. David Mizrahi became the director of research for the NJAS in 2000. Today, the focus of the CMBO's research arm includes the stopover ecology needs of migratory birds, particularly songbirds and shorebirds; selective habitat usage on the Cape May peninsula by songbirds; and both sound recording and radar monitoring of nocturnal migrants (among many other projects). Through its ongoing and important research, the CMBO research division continues to document the ornithological significance of Cape May. In 2006 the hawkwatch and CMBO celebrated their thirtieth anniversary. (On September 12, 1994, in its eighteenth year, the Cape May Hawkwatch had recorded its one millionth autumn raptor migrant, an American Kestrel, tallied by counter Jerry Liguori at 1:46 P.M.)

Today, the CMBO *is* birding at Cape May, offering a plethora of naturalist-led bird and butterfly walks, natural history programs, workshops, and field trips, as well as guides for hire. It offers multiple programs and walks every day of the week from April through early November and numerous weekly programs and walks from mid-November through March, totaling more than 700 offerings for adults each year in southern New Jersey. In addition, the CMBO organizes and hosts two weekend-long events—the Cape May Spring Weekend and the Cape May Autumn Weekend-Bird Show—each including more than ninety different naturalist-led offerings. The Cape May Autumn Weekend/THE Bird Show, which dates back to 1946, is one of the top birding festivals in the world. The World Series of Birding is the biggest birding event in North America.

A second major change in personnel was Cape May's loss of David Allen Sibley when he and his family returned to their New England roots in 2000. David's wife, Joan Walsh, a biologist at the CMBO, had just finished managing a major, five-year effort that culminated in the landmark *Birds of New Jersey,* a complete atlas and compendium of the state's birds; David had just completed the monumental *Sibley Guide to Birds.* David spent parts of nearly twenty years at Cape May, traveling widely and at length, yet calling Cape May home. His artwork graced most of CMBO's publications for many years. In a 2001 interview, David recalled Cape May fondly. "Cape May is easily the best place in eastern North America to watch birds. Nowhere else is there such a variety and number of birds in such a small area. It's amazing, really, that such a postage stamp of an area can have such quality. . . . No other place could have given me what Cape May did for the Sibley Guide. I've always loved Cape May, and I know I'll be returning many times." As David also added, "At Cape May, the birds come to you."

David painted every plate for the *Sibley Guide to Birds* in either a cottage at 607 Cape Avenue in Cape May Point or later in a small studio in West Cape May. With the publication of the *Sibley Guide*, Cape May's role in the major bird

David Sibley, shown here in 1985, called Cape May home for some twenty years.

guides came full circle too. Of the four major guides to the birds of North America that have been completed solely by one author-artist (Wilson's *American Ornithology,* Audubon's *Birds of America,* Peterson's *A Field Guide to the Birds,* and now the *Sibley Guide*), all have been researched or written and painted in part or, in Sibley's case, in whole, at Cape May, New Jersey. The full circle of Cape May birds and birding may be an imperfect sphere—it is really more of a complex and intertwined web—but it makes for a prominent and storied ornithological history.

9

CHANGES THROUGH THE YEARS

Then came the construction of the Harbor, involving the cutting away of part of the meadows and the dredging of the whole area, while the resultant mud and sand were used to fill in the sound.... Where once had been water and marsh there now stretched a vast waste of sand and broken shells.... But in spite of all the changes that we have enumerated, bird life at Cape May is still of abounding interest.... as contrasted with conditions elsewhere in the eastern United States, and without comparison with the glorious days long past, Cape May still proves a worthy Mecca for the ornithologist.
—Witmer Stone, 1937
Bird Studies at Old Cape May

Changes in habitat and the resulting impact on bird life have been dominant themes in bird studies throughout Cape May ornithological history. Monumental changes in the landscape have taken place over time. Witmer Stone in 1937 was already lamenting the major environmental changes he had witnessed during his tenure at Cape May. Little did he know the magnitude of change to come. If Stone were alive today, the development and suburbanization of Cape May County would probably kill him. Besides being an eminent ornithologist, Stone was one of Cape May's first and most passionate conservationists.

The greatest irreversible change has occurred on the barrier islands. These sandy barriers to the Atlantic stretch the length of the New Jersey coast, protecting the rich salt marshes behind them—wetlands that are the most productive ecosystems on earth. In the 1800s farmers from the mainland pastured cattle on the barrier islands during the summer months (there is a wonderful fictional account of this practice, and of the fabled pirates of Cape May, in Steven W. Meader's 1952 *The Fish Hawk's Nest,* Cape May lore at its finest). Wildwood may have been the greatest of all the barrier islands, once holding an immense old-growth maritime forest that is now gone forever. These primeval forests were so big and wild that they held Pileated Woodpeckers. Birds collected there in 1878 and 1879 were the last resident pileates seen in the county until the 1980s, a lengthy time for the call of the "log-cock" to be absent. (Only two or three pairs are present in southern New Jersey even today, a very tenuous and incomplete comeback.)

DISAPPEARING HABITAT

Beginning in the early 1900s, the barrier islands were systematically and relentlessly destroyed for seashore housing. Forests were cut, dunes bulldozed, marshes dredged and filled for basins or lagoons. This continued even into the late 1970s, as the last sections were built up. Today, except for the protected Higbee Beach Wildlife Management Area and the maritime forest at Two Mile Beach, the only vestiges of the dune forests are on private property in Avalon and the Villas. These tiny remnants are still systematically being built on, but conservation groups have no hope of protecting them: A home in the dunes in Avalon (all second and third homes) sells for about $15 million to $20 million. Some habitat is simply too valuable to protect. (In 2005, even average homes in Avalon or Stone Harbor sold for $1.2 million, appreciating about 25 percent every year. The construction industry, fueled by a "tear down and build anew" philosophy, today constitutes over 10 percent of the local economy. Suffice it to say that protecting any open space in modern Cape May County is difficult.)

The impact of the loss of barrier island native vegetation on migratory birds is inestimable. Untold numbers of migrant songbirds once used these dense thickets as stopover habitat to rest and feed on their journey south. The barrier islands are the first landfall for exhausted songbirds blown to sea by the northwest winds of autumn cold fronts. After struggling desperately to reach land, tired and hungry birds are confronted by what is, for them, a barren and inhospitable landscape—akin to us

Rampant development in North Cape May has eliminated much bird habitat, but many coastal communities have seen even greater changes.

Mosquito ditching has resulted in major ecological changes in the salt marsh.

being dropped onto a moonscape. In late October, we watched an exhausted Eastern Phoebe, flying just inches above the water, fight its way in against the wind to a coastal jetty. Its first perch was the last rock at the end of the rock pile, but it was soon forced off, nearly inundated by a wave. It then flew weakly to a support piling at the base of the jetty and remained there for about fifteen minutes until it gathered enough strength to fly to the snow fence at the base of the artificial dunes.

It rested again for about ten minutes and finally flew inland over the dunes. It would have been nice to think that its survival was assured, but we knew that what awaited the bird inland was block after block of wall-to-wall seashore homes, all surrounded by sterile stone lawns and decorative bushes. Probably the nearest habitat that could sustain the phoebe was still miles away—across the causeways to the mainland, and beyond a gauntlet of automobiles, wires, windows, feral cats, and hawks. We'll never know if our phoebe made it.

Historically, New Jersey lost 23 percent of its wetlands between 1950 and 1970. In 1970, after a prolonged and bitter battle, the New Jersey Wetlands Act was passed, finally ending the rampant filling of ecologically priceless coastal tidelands for development. If the proposed Gravens Island Development Project had not been so tirelessly fought by the committed environmentalists of the Izaak Walton League and its eventual successor, the Citizens Allied to Protect the Environment (CAPE), Avalon would be nearly twice as large as it is today. The proposed Plantation Development would have dredged and filled Nummy's Island. A small lagoon (a precursor of a marina) north of the Free Bridge is the only vestige of the failed development. Today, the cedars surrounding the lagoon are a popular heron roost. In 1988, after another epic fight (led by the NJAS), the New Jersey Freshwater Wetlands Protection Act was adopted and gained similar protection for freshwater wetlands, including wooded swamps and wet forests. Another important victory was the passage in 1973 of the Coastal Areas Facilities Review Act (CAFRA), the first coastal zone management law in New Jersey to control land use and development. A hard-fought victory, CAFRA regulates about one-seventh of the state's land area. CAFRA may have its large loopholes, but it is far better than the alternative of no regula-

tion. Also monumental was the enactment in 1979 of federal and state legislation to protect New Jersey's unique Pine Barrens, with more than 1 million acres being designated the New Jersey Pinelands Natural Preserve. A
considerable portion of northern mainland Cape May County is regulated
by the Pinelands Commission's strong land-use requirements, but despite
these controls, water supply remains a major environmental concern in
southern New Jersey, where rampant development and redevelopment continue to deplete available drinking water aquifers.

Major habitat changes have occurred over time on Cape May County's
mainland as well. Although there were once extensive old-growth forests,
it is estimated that precolonial South Jersey forests may have been as much
as 40 percent early successional growth, due to the well-known Pine Barrens
fire ecology. Early settlers immediately began fire suppression, which no
doubt resulted in the first changes in bird life. More important, European
settlers rapidly cleared forests and converted them to farmland, both crop-
land and pastureland. Today, there is far more forested land on the Cape May
peninsula than during the nineteenth century. Even in the twentieth century, early Christmas Bird Counts showed the prevalence of fields and pastures, evidenced by high numbers of grassland birds, including the Northern
Bobwhite and Ring-necked Pheasant—both virtually gone today.

Precolonial old-growth cedar forests must have been magnificent, as
evidenced by the massive preserved stumps that are sometimes uncovered
and by photographs taken of the last surviving giants. The colonial shipbuilding industry, which had its heyday in the late nineteenth century, is
thought to have twice completely clear-cut Atlantic White-cedar from
Cape May and South Jersey swamps. Today, some cedar swamps, such as
those in Belleplain State Forest, have recovered nicely (and some sustainable cedar harvesting continues today). Much of the Cape May peninsula
originally was, and still is, covered by lowland hardwood swamp forest
dominated by Red Maple, Sweet Gum, Sour Gum, and Sweet Bay Magnolia, as well as Pitch Pine, Spanish Oak, Pin Oak, and American Holly.
Such habitats support a rich diversity of breeding birds. Some small remnant sections of fairly old-growth swamp forest still occur in the Cape May
National Wildlife Refuge's Great Cedar Swamp Division and in neighboring Cumberland County's Bear Swamp, where a few hundred acres of
swamp forest contain trees estimated to be more than 500 years old (called
by some the oldest hardwood forest in the northeastern United States).

Some changes have been more subtle. The loss of the American Chestnut led to its replacement by oaks. In the northern Cape May County sections of the Pine Barrens, fire suppression has allowed oaks to gradually
supplant the normally dominant, fire-resistant Pitch Pines. Almost everywhere, observant visitors will notice the characteristic and predominant

American Holly, blueberry, Persimmon, Mountain Laurel, and Sweet Pepperbush understory. Fallow fields quickly grow up in Red Cedar, Black Cherry, and Sweet Gum. South Jersey seemingly has not experienced the well-known acid rain impacts seen throughout much of the East. This is probably because the ground and surface waters and the soils are relatively acidic to begin with. Pine Barrens streams are naturally highly acidic, so plants here show a relative acid tolerance. This may explain the apparently still-healthy forest breeding bird populations, including the Wood Thrush, an abundant breeder in southern New Jersey. Clearly affected by acid rain elsewhere, Wood Thrushes may have become tolerant or have adapted here.

One major impact on the woodlands in Cape May County and throughout southern New Jersey has come from the cyclical Gypsy Moth deforestation. The first major outbreak occurred in 1972, when more than 250,000 acres of forests were defoliated. In 1981 nearly 800,000 acres were consumed, and in 1990 about 430,000. Although some healthy trees easily recover, many of the oaks die—leading to an early successional forest in place of the older trees, as well as a clear replacement of oaks by pines in some areas. Gypsy Moths, native to Europe and Asia, have resulted in a number of changes in bird life. Red-headed Woodpeckers, which prefer an open-understory forest, boomed in the 1970s and 1980s. Yellow-billed and Black-billed Cuckoos, two of the few birds that found Gypsy Moths palatable, exploded as well. All three of these birds declined in the 1990s as the forests grew back and were dominated by dense understory successional growth (and few Gypsy Moths). A more lasting impact on birds was related to the heavy spraying to control the Gypsy Moth—spraying that saved trees but in some areas permanently eliminated a nontarget guild of beneficial lepidoptera on which birds normally fed. An emerging threat to forests is the Southern Pine Bark Beetle, which is rapidly spreading northward as a result of the trend toward warmer winters (climate change). In the early twenty-first century, pine bark beetles killed hundreds of acres of pines in Cape May and Cumberland counties, with an as yet unknown impact on birds. Also of concern is the impact of the enormous deer population on the forest understory. Deer browse is rapidly changing the complexity and makeup of forests throughout New Jersey, and sparser forests with less understory growth can have major effects on birds.

Some of the greatest changes on the mainland occurred in the 1960s and 1970s, when the provision of regional wastewater collection on the lower Cape opened vast areas to development that had previously been off limits due to high water tables and the associated septic system constraints. This period was characterized by poor planning and zoning, small lots, and high density. As a result, thousands of acres of forest were lost forever. However, one beneficial aspect of regional sewerage was the drastically needed upgrades to sewage treatment facilities that occurred in the 1970s and early 1980s. Effluents became much cleaner, and outfall lines were moved from the back bays to the ocean. Today, the ocean, beachfront, and back-bay waters are easily tenfold cleaner than in the 1940–1970 period, and there has been a tremendous beneficial impact on marine life and resources and, in turn, waterbirds. This may be hard to appreciate, but to put this change in perspective, Clay grew up thinking that the back-bay waters were naturally brown in summer. Only in the early 1980s, as regional systems and upgraded treatment plants went on-line (and suspended solids, nutrients, and associated plankton and algae blooms abated), did he realize that summer back-bay waters should be (and were in fact) blue.

Between 1970 and 1980, a 50 percent population growth was recorded in Cape May County. It was a boom-town atmosphere, spurred by both tourism and Atlantic City casino gambling. Casino gambling, approved by referendum in 1976, was touted as the savior for a troubled Atlantic City, but instead it spurred rampant sprawl throughout southern New Jersey, and today, virtually all areas of Cape May County serve as bedroom communities for Atlantic City casino employees. Cape May County's year-round population today is about 105,000, although on a peak holiday weekend in summer, the population may be nearly ten times that. Cape May City's permanent population is about 4,100, and Cape May Point in winter has about 250 people. But although the predominant change in the Cape May landscape has been the loss of field and forest to development, there has been some good news too. Due to septic requirements in non-sewered areas, most zoning now requires large lots, and large lots usually mean that many trees are left. This is good news for the millions of migrants passing through Cape May each year, because many migrant passerines can easily use suburban habitat when lots are left largely wooded.

Considering forests, farms, and fields, the New Jersey Division of Fish and Wildlife estimated a 40 percent habitat loss over twenty years (1972–1992) in southern Cape May County, raising major concerns about the impact on migratory birds that used this acreage as a crucial stopover site. Farmland in particular has dwindled drastically. In southern Cape May County, most farms have

The loss of farms and pasturelands on the Jersey Cape has led to the loss of many grassland species.

become subdivisions—housing developments—with vast green lawns and little available habitat. Today, New Jersey loses an estimated 18,000 acres each year to development, 10,000 of which were once farmland. The loss of farmland has slowed in Cape May County, if only because there is so little farmland left. Farmland preservation programs have protected a number of farms, but modern mechanized agriculture often leaves little for wildlife. The old-fashioned "fallow field" is one of the rarest habitat types on the Cape May peninsula, and as a result, many grassland bird species lack both breeding and migratory habitat. The Upland Sandpiper, Bobolink, Eastern Meadowlark, Grasshopper Sparrow, Vesper Sparrow, and others have all declined drastically in southern New Jersey. For many species, fragmented farmlands cannot provide the contiguous acreage needed for individual territories or for colonies to form. The American Kestrel, as both a breeding bird and a wintering bird, is far rarer than the Bald Eagle in all of southern New Jersey today.

The Effects of Mosquito Control
Other than the general failure of planning and zoning to protect important natural areas and open space, perhaps the greatest adverse impacts to habitat and wildlife have come at the hands of mosquito extermination commissions. For nearly a century, the tourism-driven war waged on mosquitoes by both state and county authorities has had a drastic effect on birds. In *Bird Studies at Old Cape May,* Witmer Stone frequently deplores and grieves the damages done by mosquito control, not only the drainage of all low-lying habitats but also the then common practice of spraying oil on pond surfaces. Roger Tory Peterson would later loudly lament the damage being done by the relentless spraying of DDT at Cape May. DDT use was heavy in Cape May County—measured in tonnage—where it was applied to salt marshes to control mosquitoes from 1944 until it was finally banned in 1972. It is still prevalent in high concentrations in the bottom sediments of coastal bays and is still easily measurable in Osprey and Bald Eagle eggs. (Frequent dredging projects in lagoons and waterways resuspend DDT derivatives by stirring them up from bottom sediments.) Today, most mosquito spraying is done with larvicides—far less harmful than the compounds used in the past—but the adulticide malathion is still used if mosquito numbers are particularly high. Sadly, malathion kills far more than mosquitoes, and this spraying often occurs in late summer, when migrant passerines need all the insects they can get.

Until the late 1960s, in addition to pesticides, mosquitoes were controlled by ditching and draining. These practices have gradually changed, and today mosquitoes are largely controlled by ditching and flooding. This process, known as open marsh water management, floods wetlands with tidal water, with the aim of introducing fish to prey on and control mosquito larvae. It is effective, pervasive, and done on a grand scale. Amphibious heavy machinery can ditch more than a mile of marsh in one day. This alteration of the marshes is somewhat unnoticeable on the ground but is clearly seen on aerial photos. Most salt marshes today no longer have meandering creeks; they are characterized by straight, linear ditches, giving the impression of a crazy patchwork quilt. There is no question that this practice is far better than drainage,

The extent of mosquito ditching is best seen from the air; here high marsh is being flooded in the late 1970s.

and there is no denying that there is a public health aspect to mosquito control, but the net effect has been the alteration of wetlands habitat on a massive scale—and resultant major changes in bird life. Mosquito control activities are remarkably unregulated even on public lands, with little oversight by other agencies or levels of government; mainly, it is a situation of the fox guarding the henhouse. This lack of accountability may slowly change as more independent commissions become county departments or agencies—as occurred in Cape May County in 2005—leading to hope for greater ecological responsibility.

Historically, tidal wetlands were a mixture of Salt Marsh Cordgrass, *Spartina alterniflora* (in low areas flooded daily by the tide), and Saltmeadow Grass or Salt Hay, *S. patens* (in higher-elevation areas flooded intermittently). Open marsh water management opens up areas of high marsh to daily tidal flooding, and in a short time, high marsh vegetation is replaced with low marsh vegetation. *S. alterniflora* rapidly outcompetes *S. patens,* and the area is forever altered. It is a highly effective mosquito control technique, but the diversity of the wetlands complex as a whole suffers dramatically. Low marsh is a highly productive habitat and may have greater diversity than high marsh, but certain species disappear along with the high marsh, and *overall* diversity suffers. As one example, in 1975 our Cape May Christmas Bird Count territory near Goshen contained about 50 percent healthy *S. patens* high marsh, along with Short-eared Owls, Sedge Wrens, and sharp-tailed sparrows. Brackish ponds, known as pans, were filled with American Wigeons, Gadwalls, and (oddly) sometimes Redheads. The mosquito commission began flooding the area in about 1976, and it rapidly filled in with *S. alterniflora.* Today the area is 100 percent low marsh, and the ponds have completely disappeared—now covered with a sea of *S. alterniflora*. Plenty of black ducks and Clapper Rails are still there, but few of the former specialty species. We haven't seen a Short-eared Owl or Rough-legged Hawk there in years. King Rail, Black Rail, Sedge Wren, and Eastern Meadowlark all seem to be victims of a combination of mosquito control activities and rising sea levels.

It seems almost uncanny how the mosquito commission has targeted some of the best bird areas. The last known Cape May County breeding Short-eared Owls were a pair we found (with one fledged young) at Tuckahoe in July 1979. The following spring, the high *S. patens* marsh was ditched and flooded, and breeding Short-eared Owls were never seen there again. In 1993 a pair of Black-necked Stilts found nesting at Goshen Landing provided the first breeding record for New Jersey in more than 100 years. Amazingly, that area was ditched the next winter. The birds returned the following spring but didn't breed in the wet, flooded marsh. There is no vestige of *S. patens* there today. The issue remains current—in 2006, ditching in Forsythe NWR targeted high marsh habitat near Leeds Point and Motts Creek, areas well known to be used by Short-eared Owls and Rough-legged Hawks.

The combination of marsh management, the drainage of woodland pools (extremely damaging to reptile and amphibian populations, and probably a factor in the decline of predators such as the Barred Owl and Red-shouldered Hawk), and heavy DDT use at Cape May means that mosquito control has had a greater impact on birds over time than any other source, program, or agency. We don't mean to be overly critical of the mosquito commissions; after all, it was their public mandate and purpose to kill mosquitoes, not to protect land and birds. And there have been benefits—greatly increased tourism (nobody wants to be bitten by mosquitoes while lying on the beach), economic growth, and public health advantages. But those benefits have come with the irreversible loss of habitat diversity—the mosaic of our natural marshes—and the resultant loss in overall bird species diversity. Simply put, mosquito control has forever and irrevocably changed the bird life of Cape May to a degree that even Witmer Stone never imagined. He wrote with outrage, "And now, in 1936, when one would have supposed that the needs of wildlife had been made sufficiently patent to our Federal Government, we find Civilian Conservation Corps camps established close to the Willets' last stand and hundreds of men, under the plea of finding work for the unemployed, ordered to ditch and drain all the Bayside meadows from Dennisville to Fortescue and unless some way is found to check the outrage, to destroy forever one of our last natural sanctuaries for winter ducks, migrant shore birds, and nesting Willets!" Little did he know that within a few years German prisoners of war would be brought in for these tasks, and following World War II, heavy machinery would accelarate the pace ten-fold. We can only imagine what he might write today.

Related to the changing nature of the tidal salt marsh is the loss of salt hay farms—diked areas of high marsh where the water is kept out for most of the season and S. patens (high marsh) is encouraged. The salt hay is cut several times a season and used not for animal feed (it's too salty) but for construction, landscaping,

Salt hay wagons, shown here in 1977, were once a common sight around Cape May and the Delaware Bayshore.

mulch, and, formerly, furniture and bedding. Today, salt hay is still widely used in casket mattresses. Salt hay farms were once common on the Delaware Bayshore, totaling many thousands of acres in Cape May, Cumberland, and Salem counties. Today, only three or four such farms remain. One is across the creek from the end of Jakes Landing Road, and another is at Turkey Point in nearby Cumberland County; all the others failed economically. In the interest of fish productivity and mosquito control, the dikes have been breached and the areas flooded and returned to tidal flow. As such, these areas produce fewer mosquitoes, lots of black ducks and fish, but few high marsh or grassland-type birds. The salt hay farm at Jakes Landing (private and inaccessible but easily viewed from the parking lot at the end of Jakes Landing Road) remains one of the few places to see hunting Short-eared Owls in winter in Cape May County and one of very few places where Black Rails and Eastern Meadowlarks still breed. As with mosquito management, the loss of salt hay marshes may in fact mean more birds but far less diversity. The loss of S. patens marshes, coupled with the rising sea level attributed to global warming, portends a dim future for many marsh-nesting birds that require higher, drier areas.

Industry and Oil
With both tidal and freshwater wetlands largely protected, new pressures have been placed on uplands—those high and dry areas free of many restrictions. All housing is now routed to uplands and farmlands. In addition, sand and gravel mining for construction fill, cement, and the glass industry is a major land use in upper Cape May and Cumberland counties, consuming large tracts of forest. These strip mines can be a lasting blight

on the landscape, although new regulations now require better reclamation. Major barge ports (and associated dredging and filling), a recurrent spin-off of the sand mining industry, have been proposed but so far have been blocked from all South Jersey rivers. Proposals for offshore oil drilling and related onshore facilities and refineries were prevalent in the 1960s and 1970s, but tourism interests largely defeated them. Today, the specter of off-shore drilling, though unlikely, continues to raise its ugly head due to our country's insatiable dependence on oil.

One major potential threat to birds continues to loom on the horizon, often literally. When standing at Cape May Point, you can usually see up to half a dozen oil tankers traveling up or down Delaware Bay or at anchor in the distance (waiting for high tide or refinery dock space). The combined port of Philadelphia-Camden-Wilmington receives about 70 percent of the oil arriving on the nation's East Coast. About 1 billion barrels of oil per year traverse the Delaware Bay and Delaware River, or a daily average of 2.75 million barrels. Two or three tankers per day pass Cape May on their way upriver, each containing an average of about 1.2 million barrels of oil. Although small off-loading or lightering spills occur with some frequency, the Delaware estuary has never had a major spill. However, in a November 2004 accident, the tanker *Athos I* leaked more than 265,000 gallons of crude oil into the Delaware River near Philadelphia, affecting 126 miles of shoreline and killing as many as 1,000 geese, ducks, and gulls. There are many safeguards in place, but some experts wonder whether a big oil spill, of the *Exxon Valdez* scale, is likely or even inevitable. A major spill would be catastrophic at any season, but perhaps most devastating in May, during Delaware Bay shorebird staging. Oil has not yet drastically impacted birds at Cape May, but it easily could. Mainly, we can be glad that the bay, although shallow, has a sandy or muddy bottom rather than a rocky one.

Cats

Of increasing concern is the growing problem of outdoor cats. The number of outdoor cats continues to grow with the human population, and this is exacerbated by the large number of feral cats on the Jersey Cape—particularly on the barrier islands. This is related to tourism, as vacationers lose or deliberately abandon cats when they depart at the end of the season. Although some municipalities have trap and neuter programs (and others refuse to implement them), most cats are routinely released back into the wild. To say that Cape May and much of Cape May County have a cat problem is an understatement. The director of the county animal shelter recently noted, "The shelter is awash with cats. If you put 100 traps out in Cape May County, seven days a week, you are going to catch 700 cats."

Feral and outdoor cats have had major impacts on nesting Least Tern and Piping Plover colonies. The New Jersey Division of Fish and Wildlife traps cats yearly to protect Piping Plover at Stone Harbor Point. In several areas of the lower Cape they have been implicated in the localized disappearance of House Wrens and Carolina Wrens. One person we know—an avid birder in denial about his own outdoor cats—actually said to us recently, "You know, my cat has brought five Winter Wrens to the doorstep this winter. Who would have imagined there are so many around? I never see Winter Wrens around my house." We don't believe he saw the irony or the cause and effect in his statement. The only good news is that the rapidly growing coyote population on the Cape might soon exert a strong control on feral and outdoor cats.

Sometimes it's hard to remember the hopelessness and resignation of the late 1960s and 1970s, when we feared that all of the Cape would be paved over. That was before land protection efforts and laws finally kicked in. Such feelings occasionally resurface when you come across a brand-new subdivision vulgarly named for what used to be there—such as Whip-poor-will Acres—in some out-of-the-way spot that just weeks before held woods and fields and birds. Once in a while, in some buried, dusty archives, we come across some long-forgotten lines that summon and capture the bleak environmental picture of the 1960s, bringing it back like it was yesterday. Such writings should never be lost or forgotten. The following is from a 1968 column by Dale Rex Coman in the *Philadelphia Evening Bulletin:*

> It was a beautiful day, but the scene that had greeted us at the first platform hung over us as a gloomy black cloud. Even from a distance we could see that something was wrong. The female Osprey, while incubating her eggs, had been shot. Her body was now stiff and cold. Close by, in a little pool, the immaculate white corpse of an American Egret lay sprawled in the water, a bullet hole through its neck and another through one of its legs.
>
> These two senseless killings, slaughter solely for the sake of slaughter, the bodies just left where the birds had expired, attesting to someone's marksmanship, or temporarily appeasing some sort of strange appetite for brutality, aroused a sense of outrage, followed by a feeling of hopelessness and futility.
>
> Just across the tidal creek from the dead Osprey and egret, a dredging barge plodded steadily away at its task of converting lush and life-supporting wet marshland into a dry sandy desert, upon which row after row of summer cottages will soon sprout like weeds.

PROTECTED LANDS

Changing habitats have been an aspect of bird study at Cape May through-out time. Birders today lament the march of homes across farmland and woodland, probably much like the Native Americans regretted the changes brought by European settlers or Witmer Stone deplored the dredging and filling of Cape May Harbor. In the end, habitat and acreage are the bottom line. Today's threats may be more subtle than the shooting of hawks, herons, terns, and songbirds or more imponderable than the ravages of DDT, but they may be even more insidious and long lasting. Habitat loss is forever. As Cape May acreage continues to be developed, it's important to remember that Cape May's remaining undeveloped land has been incon-trovertibly documented as some of the most important migratory bird habitat on earth. Each and every acre counts, and with every acre lost, there is a compelling need to protect the next one and to optimize the value of all remaining habitat, however small the portions may be. There is a crucial need (and a heartening trend) for backyard habitats on the Jersey Cape, rather than the prevalent dead-zone turf and pebble or stone lawns. Clear-ing an acre in Cape May County can impact migratory birds from thou-sands of square miles in the Northeast and rob them of stopover habitat and the fuel necessary to complete their journey. Cape May is that important.

When one considers all the changes in Cape May land use, it would be easy to believe that we've "paved paradise and put up a parking lot." Although it's painfully obvious that much of lower Cape May County has become suburbanized, there is still a good bit of paradise left for birds and birders. There is considerable good news, for the rapid development at Cape May has been paralleled by an urgent rush to preserve and protect

Witmer Stone's namesake sanctuary was created in 1935 to protect migrating hawks from hunters.

land. One can see that there is still a great deal of green on the Cape May County (and neighboring Cumberland and Atlantic Coun-ties) map. And although the pro-tection of open space hasn't quite kept pace with the needs of the birds, the various agencies, orga-nizations, and programs involved have done a miraculous job of preserving land—sometimes just in the nick of time.

The first notable land protec-tion began in reaction to hawk shooting at Cape May. The Wit-mer Stone Wildlife Sanctuary was established in 1935 by the National Association of Audubon Societies (which would become the National Audubon Society) to protect hawk flights from gunners. In much the way that Hawk Mountain was originally leased, the NAS leased about 700 acres straddling Sunset Boulevard, from Cape May Point north to New England Creek (where the Cape May Canal is today), to provide safe passage for the hawks. Wardens patrolled the area to keep shooters out. By 1942 the sanctuary protected approximately 1,000 acres (including government lands). In 1945 management of this leased sanctuary was turned over to the New Jersey Audubon Society, and leases were dropped when all hawk species were finally protected by state law in 1959.

The Northwest Magnesite Plant was built along Sunset Boulevard by Dresser Industries in 1941 to extract magnesite from the salt in seawater. This metal was used on-site in the manufacture of fire bricks—bricks used to line high-temperature furnaces used in steel production—highly important to the war effort. The plant employed more than 175 people. Unfortunately, air pollution controls were not in effect in the 1940s, and the plant, in the midst of the wildlife sanctuary, spewed alkaline plumes from its stacks that soon stunted and killed most of the acid-loving pines and cedars in the vicinity of the plant (along Sunset Boulevard) and in nearby Cape May Point. As a result, much of the Witmer Stone Wildlife Sanctuary was reduced to scrubby growth by 1950. The Magnesite Plant operated until 1983; the facility was demolished in 1989. Today, the factory is completely gone except for the water tower (a favorite peregrine perch), and the site is again protected. In 1999 the state of New Jersey purchased the former 153-acre plant for $1.7 million. The Magnesite Plant property south of Sunset Boulevard is now part of Cape May Point State Park, and the property north of Sunset Boulevard is now part of Higbee Beach WMA. The stunted dune forest along Sunset Boulevard is finally recovering.

Another early conservation success was the protection of the Stone Harbor Bird Sanctuary in 1947. Prior to 1890, a large heronry had been present on Seven Mile Beach, according to Captain William Sutton (as related by Stone in *Bird Studies at Old Cape May*). Decimated by plume hunters, the site was not used again by egrets until 1939. With great fanfare, the town moved swiftly to protect the 21-acre site, and it was dedicated in 1947 in a ceremony that included Charles Lindbergh, radio personality Arthur Godfrey, and Prince Phillip of the Netherlands. At the time, the Stone Harbor Bird Sanctuary and Osaka, Japan, were home to the only two municipally-owned heronries in the world. Seeds sown at this time would later help in the establishment of the Wetlands Institute on Stone Harbor Boulevard in 1969 by conservation visionary Herbert Mills.

A triumph in wildlife protection was the establishment of Brigantine National Wildlife Refuge, north of Cape May near Atlantic City, in 1939.

Brigantine—since 1984 known as the Edwin B. Forsythe National Wildlife Refuge (in honor of Congressman Forsythe, who was a driving force for conservation)—was one of the first national wildlife refuges established in the United States and is still one of the largest in the East. Today the refuge's three management units—Brigantine, Barnegat (added in 1967), and Holgate—encompass more than 46,000 acres, with acquisitions continuing. Its three units are visited by an estimated 250,000 people a year. Forsythe, which will probably always be known as "Brig" to birders, is one of the true jewels of the NWR system.

Concurrent with the establishment of Forsythe was the protection of Belleplain State Forest in Cape May County. Established in 1928, Belleplain now totals over 21,000 acres. Near Dennisville and Woodbine in northern Cape May County, Belleplain State Forest is rural and almost completely forested, with considerable lowland swamp. It is *the* spot for breeding birds in spring and summer and is of inestimable importance for migratory birds as well. Here too, acquisition of additional acreage is ongoing and aggressive, with 2,300 adjacent or contiguous acres added in 2005 alone.

Closer to Cape May City, the first land area protected in perpetuity was Cape May Point State Park. The site was a longtime military base (an army base and a navy and coast guard station used during World War II to protect the Delaware Bay from invasion by enemy forces, and a communication center for the navy's Atlantic Fleet during the Korean War). Damage done by a devastating storm in March 1962 resulted in the military moving out of Cape May Point and transferring the land to the state of New Jersey to be developed for public use. If not for the military occupation of this land until 1964, it likely would have been developed, along with the rest of Cape May Point. Cape May Point State Park, established in 1974, is about 235 acres of woods, wetlands, ponds, and beach, of which 153 acres constitute a state natural area. Because of its location at land's end at the tip of the peninsula, it is as important as any migratory bird habitat anywhere in North America.

Development pressures really began squeezing Cape May's farmlands and woodlands in the early 1970s, and two key sites were nearly lost. Although Higbee Beach today is well known by birders worldwide, in 1970 it was largely abandoned farmland, a dump site, and a nude beach, and American Woodcock were hunted there in numbers well over legal bag limits. It was a lawless place. Off-road vehicles and dune buggies from all over the state descended on the area and enjoyed a free-for-all in the ancient dune system. Huge, gnarled cedar and holly trees were cut for firewood. A large private campground was proposed for the Higbee site, which locals felt was a better alternative than the ongoing abuses. In an eleventh-hour acquisition, however, the New Jersey Division of Fish and Wildlife purchased the area in 1978, using (in part) federal endangered species funds—a purchase made by forward-thinking director Pete McLain at a time when nongame protection was in its infancy. The state immediately limited access, erected barriers, and closed the dunes to all access except for designated walking paths. Recovery of the fragile dunes had begun. Although the state's acquisition of 613-acre Higbee Beach was ostensibly to protect migrant Bald

During the 1960s and '70s, off-road vehicles carved up the fragile dunes of Higbee Beach.

Eagles and Peregrine Falcons (the fledgling CMBO hawk count data were used to support this rationale), it was probably a behind-the-scenes desire by "hook and bullet" Fish and Wildlife officials to preserve (and control) American Woodcock hunting that cemented the state's interest and closed the deal. The motives don't really matter. It was an enlightened move at a crucial time. The end result was the protection of one of the best birding spots in North America.

In 1986 The Nature Conservancy (TNC) purchased Hidden Valley Ranch and transferred this key property, which included Pond Creek Marsh, to the state to be added to Higbee Beach WMA, bringing its total holdings to more than 800 acres. Hidden Valley, a 192-acre farm and the largest privately owned tract remaining at the tip of the Cape May peninsula, was owned by Mary Ellen Dickinson. She had been approached by builders and could have sold the land for many times the price that TNC paid ($900,000), but the ranch had been in the Dickinson family for nearly seventy-five years and she simply didn't want to see it developed. Pond Creek Marsh (apparently, the early settlers couldn't decide what these freshwater wetlands actually were, so they named it all three) is an extensive wetlands area bordered by the upland farm fields and woodlands of the Rea Farm, Higbee Beach, and Hidden Valley Ranch. There are still some nice ponds with cattails and water lilies visible from the trails, but today most of Pond Creek Marsh has been taken over by *Phragmites* or common reed grass, a final result of its drainage for mosquito control. (This is an example of another overwhelming habitat change throughout the Cape May area and all of New Jersey—the takeover of healthy wetlands by the invasive *Phragmites,* which crowds out all other native plants.) With the subsequent addition of the former Magnesite Plant property in 1999, what had been protected by leases, agreements, cooperative landowners, and wardens in the 1930s and 1940s as the Witmer Stone Wildlife Sanctuary was again intact and now permanently protected. Today, total Higbee Beach WMA holdings exceed 1,069 acres.

The South Cape May Meadows was another area developers took aim at. Here too, a campground was proposed in the late 1970s, although this project was unlikely to succeed due to the high water levels and frequent flooding by coastal storms. Again using CMBO data on Peregrine Falcon and Bald Eagle use, TNC stepped up and purchased the property in 1981, thereby protecting it for all time. Today known officially as the Cape May Migratory Bird Refuge, the "Meadows" (as local birders will always call it) is one of TNC's premier refuges. It comprises about 246 acres, a figure that changes constantly due to beach erosion, sand deposition, and beach replenishment. The South Cape May Meadows was originally protected by TNC's Pennsylvania office, but a New Jersey office soon opened, followed by the Delaware Bayshore office in 1994. TNC has been at the forefront of land protection at Cape May ever since. TNC today has eighteen preserves in Cape May, Cumberland, and Salem counties. One of the newest is the Cape Island Creek Preserve northwest of Cape May City, a 179-acre area characterized by exceptional old-field habitat and heavy migratory bird use.

An attempt was made in the late 1970s to establish a Cape May National Wildlife Refuge, but skyrocketing land values south of the Cape May Canal precluded federal purchase. In 1988, armed with emergent data and knowledge that all of the Cape May peninsula was extremely important to migratory birds, the U.S. Fish and Wildlife Service proposed a new plan—protecting the interior of the county and the Delaware Bay beaches and wetlands. At the educated urging of the CMBO's Pat Sutton and advocate Anthony Kopke, federal officials agreed to add Great Cedar Swamp to the proposed boundaries, and in January 1989 the Cape May NWR was established when the first 90 acres were acquired. The proposed acquisition area is about 21,200 acres, and as of 2005, the U.S. Fish and Wildlife Service had purchased more than 11,500 of the targeted acres. Congressman Frank LoBiondo has been an unflagging champion of the project, supporting and procuring appropriations for both the Cape May NWR and Forsythe NWR.

For those of us in the trenches, the establishment of the Cape May NWR was yet another miracle, coming just as Cape May County land development was exploding. The land area covered by the Cape May NWR is both the staging area and the recipient of Cape May Point autumn morning flights (for those birds that don't cross Delaware Bay). It is highly important breeding habitat too. Of interest, just as with Higbee

Beach, American Woodcock were instrumental in tipping the balance in favor of creating the refuge. The Cape May NWR protects myriad American Woodcock—breeders in spring and summer, abundant migrants in spring and fall, and wintering birds. Importantly, Cape May NWR serves as a wildlife corridor to other protected areas: Beaver Swamp WMA, Jakes Landing (Dennis Creek WMA), and Belleplain State Forest. We now have a protected greenbelt stretching the length of Cape May (and neighboring Cumberland) County, routing migratory birds to and from the Cape May and Cape May Point area.

A recent addition to the Cape May NWR is the Two Mile Beach Unit, south of Wildwood Crest and north of Cape May Harbor, accessed off of Ocean Drive. In 1999 this 507-acre tract was declared surplus by the U.S. Coast Guard, transferred to the U.S. Fish and Wildlife Service, and added to the Cape May NWR. A lovely combination of beach, dunes, low maritime forest, tidal salt marsh, and salt ponds, Two Mile is a key addition and provides yet another birding opportunity close to Cape May City. Two Mile provides exceptional migratory bird habitat, as well as a Piping Plover and Least Tern nesting area.

Federal protection efforts in the Cape May region are augmented and supplemented by dedicated state efforts. The New Jersey Green Acres Program is one of the strongest in the nation, and its acquisition efforts are aggressive, targeted, and ongoing, including additions to existing WMAs, state forests, and state parks. In 2006, Green Acres purchased the 239-acre former Ponderlodge Golf Course, including considerable lowland forest, for $8.45 million, during bankruptcy proceedings. The site will be managed for migratory birds as the Villas Wildlife Management Area, in Lower Township. It's tough work—the average per-acre cost of a Green Acres acquisition rose a scary 79 percent between 1998 and 2002. Because these purchases are funded by state taxpayer dollars, ongoing commitment is needed.

Also important was the establishment in 1989 by Cape May County voters (by a two-to-one margin) of a trust fund to preserve open space and agricultural land. The Cape May County Open Space and Farmland Preservation Fund uses dedicated tax revenue to protect open spaces—in urban

Wetland filling destroyed priceless salt marsh for decades until more people put a higher value on preserving wildlife habitat.

areas, but also in rural areas—and the preservation of wildlife habitat is an important goal. The Office of Open Space Protection has been involved in more than seventy-five projects totaling more than 3,000 acres in Cape May County. Purchases and easements on more than 750 acres were planned in 2006, at a cost of nearly $14 million.

In addition, a strong Farmland Preservation Program throughout New Jersey has saved a number of South Jersey farms from development. For birds and birders, the most important of these projects was the protection of the Rea Farm—the famous "Beanery"—long beloved by birders. This 82-acre farm is secure from development for all time, and birders are welcome there. In 1999, in an enlightened move, the CMBO leased the birding rights to the farm—in much the way hunters lease land for hunting. To bird the Rea Farm, you need to be a CMBO or NJAS member or buy a pass at the CMBO Northwood Center. Amazingly, birders have become a "cash crop" for a once beleaguered Cape May farm.

Other exciting news includes the increasing popularity of the transfer of development rights programs in the Pinelands region; Cape May Point's Landscaping and Vegetation Plan Ordinance (passed in 1990), which ensures that the town will remain natural; West Cape May's efforts to study and protect wetlands and endangered species habitat; and Cape May City's serious and long-term efforts to protect and purchase the Sewell Point area at the north end of town (adjacent to the U.S. Coast Guard Training Center). This area, about 110 acres, is part of the Cape May Harbor "fill" that Witmer Stone so lamented, but today, nearly 100 years later, it is dense, brushy coastal forest—an oasis and haven for thousands of migratory birds each year. Sewell Point bird use was documented in the 1980s by an intensive study sponsored by the Environmental Response Network, a Cape May County grassroots effort that, sadly, no longer exists. Although acquisition has not yet been completed, it is anticipated that Sewell Point protection will soon be finalized, providing even more Cape May habitat for birds and opportunities for birders.

Finally, in Cumberland County, the adjacent county north and west of Cape May County, more than 120,000 acres of undeveloped, protected public and private (not-for-profit) land is currently available to birders. These are not second-rate areas for birders; spring shorebirds and songbirds are found throughout the Delaware Bay region, and many fall migrants ultimately go around Delaware Bay rather than cross at Cape May Point. Winter birding on the Delaware Bayshore and along Cumberland County's tidal rivers is second to none, and breeding bird populations are akin to those in the Belleplain State Forest region. The Delaware Bay region was part of Witmer Stone's Old Cape May study area, and we too embrace it in "New Cape May."

Despite major changes to the Cape May landscape and habitats over time, we have managed to preserve some of paradise. There may be a number of parking lots, but many stellar areas are forever off-limits to the despoilers. The various land protection programs have procured a place at Cape May for birds and birders for all time. Much of it happened at the last minute, and sometimes it all seems like a miracle. Maybe that's proof that birders' dreams do come true.

CHANGING BIRD LIFE

Prior to the arrival of the European settlers, Cape May birds probably had achieved some sort of ecological balance or equilibrium. But as the colonial population grew, leading to an unprecedented use of natural resources, the landscape changed rapidly, and the impacts on birds rose exponentially. Since the late seventeenth century, the one constant in the ornithological record is change. Time travel is a favorite fantasy, and one can only wonder what it would have been like to stand at Cape May Point and watch a strong late September or early October cold front pass in the early 1650s. DeVries in 1633 wrote of the "pigeons which obscured the sky," and Evelin in 1648 wrote of the "infinite quantity of bustards, swans, geese and fowls" and "the multitude of pigeons and stores of turkeys." The pigeons were Passenger Pigeons, and the "bustards" were probably Sandhill Cranes and Whooping Cranes, both of which had populations in the East in precolonial times. An observer watching a 1600s flight would see Carolina Parakeets on their southbound migration. A seawatcher would see flocks of Eskimo Curlews passing on September's strong easterly winds, and later in the season,

he would probably count a few Labrador Ducks, which Audubon reported as far south as Maryland. In colder winters, even a Great Auk might be found diving in the rips off the Point, an "accidental" to New Jersey. Because northern Cape May County (near present-day Belleplain State Forest) contained classic Pine Barrens habitat with extensive pine plains (and in the 1600s there was no fire suppression), there were undoubtedly grassy heaths—lek areas—and the time traveler probably would have found Heath Hens among the "stores" of turkeys.

Naturalists visiting Mrs. Shaffer collected these window and wire kills following a heavy nocturnal migration over Cape May Point. The birds are displayed on her front porch in October of 1950.

Change came rapidly and took many forms. Settlers increased and spread throughout New Jersey, claiming dominion over the land and all its wildlife inhabitants. In the way of the era, good species were exploited and bad species were systematically slaughtered. Whether good or bad, the net effect was usually the same, and choices were somewhat arbitrary. As early as 1744, New Jersey passed an "Act to encourage the destruction of crows, blackbirds, squirrels and woodpeckers in the counties of Gloucester, Salem, and Cape May," with bounties to be paid. Just seven years later, New Jersey passed another act to encourage the killing of wolves and panthers—reaffirming bounties paid on wolves dating back to 1675.

Passenger Pigeons were systematically annihilated by early settlers, and Carolina Parakeets, Labrador Ducks, and Great Auks were soon extinct. Eskimo Curlews are probably extinct as well. The eastern populations of Whooping Cranes are long gone, although they are being reintroduced, and Sandhill Cranes are staging a comeback. The Heath Hen, the eastern subspecies of the Greater Prairie Chicken, was an early victim; the leks where they gathered made them highly susceptible to slaughter, and they were gone by 1870. Wild Turkeys had been extirpated by the early 1800s, but reintroduction in the late 1970s was remarkably successful.

As Cape May and all of New Jersey developed, every group of birds would be impacted—some adversely, but others beneficially. Some birds would disappear, but others would boom. Some species experienced several ups and downs. Some changes were slow, occurring over several centuries; others took place in just a few short decades—encompassing only part of the career of a Cape May naturalist—such as the recovery of Common and Least Terns at Stone Harbor Point or the colonization of New Jersey by Glossy Ibis and Black Vultures. And because of Cape May's exceptional ornithological history, we have a rare, exacting record of these changes over time—a baseline and ongoing picture of the status and trends of birds that is available for few other birding locations. It's part of what makes Cape May unique.

Waterbirds

Witmer Stone wrote in 1937 that the Common Loon, "though not the most conspicuous, is probably the most characteristic bird of the harbor and ocean during the winter," and the statement happily remains true today. Indeed, modern studies—Christmas Bird Counts, the Avalon Seawatch count, and pelagic trips—have revealed a substantial autumn loon movement (both common and red-throated) along our coasts. The winter concentration of Common Loons along the beaches and in the Atlantic Ocean off the mouth of Delaware Bay is one of the largest wintering populations known. The spring staging of Red-throated Loons around the mouth of Delaware Bay is unequaled (or unreported) elsewhere.

Many of the top stories of modern-day birding at Cape May relate to great increases in bird populations. Some gains are hard to assess, for what may appear to be an increase might only be a vast gain in our knowledge of the timing and distribution of birds. This has been the case with pelagic birds—shearwaters and storm-petrels—as more and more trips venture offshore to find them. But other increases are true gains in the sheer number of some species, such as Double-crested Cormorants in all seasons.

The Brown Pelican is a recent arrival. Although some assume that the Brown Pelican was "lost" due to DDT, our baseline tells us that they were never here in any numbers. Stone recounts a few records, but he never saw one at Cape May. Today they are an expected and sometimes common sight from spring through fall. Brown Pelicans began to show up in South Jersey in 1982 and now often number in the hundreds—fishing along the coast and loafing on Hereford Inlet sandbars. Though not yet breeding here, they have repeatedly built practice, "starter" nests to the north on Barnegat Bay, so it may be just a matter of time. Although still a vagrant, White Pelicans appear far more frequently today as well.

Casual birders are often quite surprised at the numbers of herons and egrets found in coastal New Jersey, because they associate these wading birds with Florida and the Low Country. New Jersey marshes are a key area for these exquisite birds, but that wasn't always the case. So numerous were most waterbirds in the 1700s that subsistence hunting and egg collecting by local residents had little or no effect on their abundance. But as the human population grew, and improved transportation enabled easier travel from Philadelphia (the first tourists), birds were killed in increasing numbers. Soon, as civilization and society advanced, birds were no longer killed just for food.

Victorian fashion dictated that the plumes of egrets were de rigueur to adorn women's hats, and in the nineteenth century, no birds were hunted so ruthlessly or relentlessly as the herons and egrets. All save the Green Heron and the Black-crowned Night-Heron were virtually exterminated by about 1888. As early as the summer of 1843, William Baird wrote to his brother Spencer that "gunners were so numerous all birds driven off." By 1880, at the height of the millinery trade, whole breeding colonies were wiped out in a few shooting sessions. The birds could not nest or sustain the losses over most of the East. In 1913 the Migratory Bird Treaty was enacted, giving birds their first protection ever. As interest in wildlife conservation grew, and the National Audubon Society's egret protection efforts began to have an effect, wading birds were finally protected by law, albeit more slowly in practice than in theory.

In 1812 Alexander Wilson visited and described a nesting colony of "snowy herons" in what is today Ocean City, but after the slaughter of the late 1800s, it would be 1928 before a Snowy Egret was again recorded in Cape May County. Witmer Stone saw his first in 1930. After new nesting colonies were again wiped out by shooting in 1937 and 1938, the first successful nesting began in 1939 at what would become the Stone Harbor Bird Sanctuary. Recovery would be slow, but it was finally under way.

One of the great stories of Cape May birding is the appearance in 1952 of two Cattle Egrets at McPherson's farm on New England Road—the road to Higbee Beach. This African species (which had apparently crossed the southern Atlantic to establish a colony in Guiana) caused quite a stir among birders, and hundreds came to view them. Thus, the Cattle Egret was the first true rarity of the modern era of Cape May birding. They were soon found to be breeding in Florida (where they had been overlooked); and by 1958, they were breeding near Cape May. Technically, the Cape May Cattle Egrets were the second and third records for North America. Ours were found on May 25, but one was sighted in Massachusetts on April 24. However, Cape May farmer Edgar McPherson said that the first Cattle Egret "came here in April" and claimed, "that bird was here last year too." At least we didn't collect ours; the Massachusetts bird was promptly shot, just before pioneering sight-record advocate Ludlow Griscom arrived

A Cattle Egret in the South Cape May Meadows in the 1970s, when cows were pastured there.

on the scene—although the bird was so rare that even Griscom called for its immediate collection. For many years thereafter, Cattle Egrets became increasingly common around Cape May, but in the 1990s their numbers dwindled drastically, perhaps due to the ongoing loss of farms and livestock in southern New Jersey or changing landfill practices. Cattle Egrets were formerly abundant in Cape May in the vicinity of dumps, but modern sanitation measures (daily covering with soil) eliminated many of the flies and other insects that attracted the birds.

At about the same time, the Glossy Ibis was a new arrival to Cape May from the south. Stone never saw one in New Jersey, but by the early 1950s a few single birds had been seen. In 1953 a flock of nine was seen, and by 1955 they were found breeding. Today, Glossy Ibis are a common breeding bird in southern New Jersey rookeries. White-faced Ibis seem to be following suit, with multiple sightings every spring. "Southern" birds expanding their range north are a recurring and major theme in Cape May ornithology. Nowadays, thousands of herons, egrets, and ibis grace the Cape May County skies daily, often commuting in large flocks from numerous colonies in the back bays on the Atlantic side of the peninsula to prime Delaware Bayshore feeding grounds. At times, huge feeding assemblages form in the salt marshes along the causeways to the barrier beach towns. And although the Stone Harbor Bird Sanctuary is empty of egrets, there are a number of other healthy colonies, many on older, vegetated spoil islands in the vast back bays of Cape May County.

Despite their continued visual abundance, wader numbers have again been dropping in the past two decades. Great Egret nesting populations declined 19 percent from 1978 to 1995; Snowy Egrets declined 58 percent; Cattle Egrets, 94 percent; Black-crowned Night Herons, 85 percent; Yellow-crowned Night-Herons, 17 percent; and Glossy Ibis, 63 percent. Waders may still be a common daily bird around Cape May, but the breeding numbers have dropped precipitously for completely unknown reasons. Only Little Blue Herons and Tricolored Herons posted gains, up 8 and 23 percent respectively, between 1978 and 1995. Black-crowned and Yellow-crowned Night-Herons are now listed as threatened species, requiring monitoring, protection, and vigilance.

Waterfowl

Ducks and geese have been hunted for food for centuries around Cape May. Local subsistence hunters were soon joined first by market hunters and later by out-of-town sportsmen. Although their numbers were no doubt affected, because waterfowl are not colonial nesters (and many nest far to the north and west), they did not suffer the near extirpation of many other birds, such as egrets and terns. Waterfowl numbers were far greater historically than currently. The American Black Duck, a hallmark of the Jersey coastal wetlands, was much more abundant at the turn of the twentieth century. Clay's father remembers a huge morning and evening flight of American Black Ducks over Sea Isle City (and elsewhere, no doubt), as the ducks would leave the salt marsh at dawn and fly to the ocean, where they would spend the day off the beach. This occurred in fall and winter; ducks roosted at sea, where they were safe from hunters. At times they would cover acres of ocean. At dusk, when the "coast was clear," they would return to the marshes to feed. This phenomenon still occurs today during duck hunting season, though in much smaller numbers.

It is hard to comprehend how such a once desirable and nobly regarded bird as the Canada Goose has slipped in stature. Once a trophy among gunners (Clay's father remembered his own father's beaming pride over a brace of big geese—one weighed 13 pounds—as he returned from a day on the water), today Canada Geese are largely disdained by all. Wild Canada Geese from the Arctic taiga and tundra have always migrated through Cape May and still do, albeit in far smaller numbers. In the 1970s, sometimes tens of thousands of migrant geese graced early October cold fronts, heading from natal Arctic areas to mainly Chesapeake Bay wintering grounds. Today, far fewer make the journey. Canadas are still common, but their short-stopped, nonmigratory counterparts have replaced most of the true migrants, and it is these "golf course" geese that have created the problem. Or, more accurately, we have created the problem, for Canada Geese are a prime example of successful wildlife management. The management was *too* successful—protection coupled with habitat alteration led to the skyrocketing of resident Canada Goose numbers, with few solutions in sight. Why migrate to the tundra when they have barren corporate lawn and golf course "tundra" right here? In 2005, it was estimated that 98,000 Canada Geese were resident in New Jersey, where they were virtually absent thirty years ago. But we still anticipate and appreciate the arrival of the true wild migrant Canadas. On that first cool mid-October night, when you have to get out of bed to shut the window on the season's first major cold front, we still relish the music of Canada Geese drifting down from on high, the song of migrants from the far tundra. It is a stirring drama that has played for many centuries at Cape May.

Snow Geese have similarly boomed. In Stone's day, you had to journey to Fortescue on Delaware Bay and hire a boat and guide to take you to Egg Island Point to view New Jersey's only winter flock of about 2,000 Greater Snow Geese. Today, the Delaware Bayshore is still the stronghold for Snow Geese, but now, at peak, there are hundreds of thousands present (greater and lesser)—another example of successful wildlife management. Snow Geese are widely maligned for "eat-outs" in New Jersey, where their heavy

Snow Geese fill the salt marsh, fields, and skies of the Delaware Bayshore today.

grazing on *Spartina* roots denudes the marshes. Wildlife managers often talk of Snow Geese "destroying" the marshes, but we find such eat-outs to be quality mudflat areas used by large numbers of shorebirds in subsequent seasons—a habitat and bounty available only until the *Spartina* reestablishes itself in a few years.

Modern Snow Goose management is characterized by extended hunting seasons and extravagent bag limits, yet one wonders if managers have a good handle on comparative impacts on the far less common Greater Snow Goose as opposed to the booming Lesser Snow Goose populations. Similarly, one might question what impact increased hunting of resident Canada Geese may have had on declining Arctic-breeding migrant Canadas that sometimes share the same habitats in fall and winter. One must trust that these issues are being studied.

Mute Swans have flourished at Cape May as they have everywhere in the northeast. Their introduction in the early twentieth century around New York City led Witmer Stone to write that, in 1937, "we have no record of this bird from Cape May, it may very well occur." He was right. Today hundreds occur at Forsythe NWR, Tuckahoe WMA, and Turkey Point in Cumberland County, always to the detriment of other native waterfowl.

Brant numbers have also seen huge fluctuations over the years. The Brant is a hallmark of our coastal bays. A large percentage of the Atlantic flyway Brant population winters in New Jersey. Although legal game, they escaped heavy hunting pressure because of their strong flavor. Many hunters, including Clay's father and grandfather, considered them inedible. Brant historically fed largely on eelgrass *(Zostera)*, but in the 1930s a severe blight almost completely eliminated eelgrass from the large saltwater bays of New Jersey. In 1925, 80,000 Brant were counted by Ludlow Griscom, J. A. Weber, and Charles Urner from Great Egg Harbor Bay to Manahawkin; by 1933, only 1,800 could be found. Brant survived by "learning" to eat sea lettuce *(Ulva),* something they had not done before, and populations slowly rebounded. Today, eelgrass has made a small comeback, but most Brant still feed on sea lettuce. Brant are also hard hit by harsh winters. If persistent bitter temperatures totally freeze the bays, locking up their submerged food supply, many perish. One of the biggest weather-related Brant die-offs was in February 1977, when thousands starved. Populating Cape May County bays in big numbers, Brant are present from October to mid-May. They leave so late because they breed so far north—from Baffin Island northward—where spring (ice-out) comes very late. A few Brant, perhaps injured individuals or birds that could not make their "takeoff" migratory weight, summer in the Jersey bays. Interestingly, thousands apparently summered in 1953 and 1954, something that had never occurred before (or since). This is when Herb Mills and his friend Marion Glaspey encountered a pair of Brant behind Stone Harbor with a string of fluffy chicks in tow—an unprecedented event several thousand miles south of their normal breeding range. Although common in our winter Atlantic coast marshes and bays, Brant are curiously absent from Delaware Bay marshes, probably due to the lack of large, shallow tidal bays and mudflats. Virtually the only time Brant are seen on the bayshore is when spring migrants put down there at dawn, only to depart northward at dusk.

A major waterfowl trend has been the attraction of species of ducks that prefer brackish and fresh water by the creation of vast impoundments at places such as Forsythe National Wildlife Refuge. For example, Gadwalls, Northern Shovelers, and Ring-necked Ducks were never seen by Witmer Stone in New Jersey, but today all are common migrant and winter ducks, and the Gadwall is a regular breeder. On the other side of the ledger, Ruddy Ducks, once abundant on the Delaware Bay and Delaware River, are far less common today (but experiencing a recent resurgence). Canvasbacks have declined, and the Redhead has become almost a true rarity at Cape May.

Recent counts at the CMBO's Avalon Seawatch have revealed some of the largest numbers of Surf and Black Scoters reported in all of North America passing our Atlantic shores each autumn. Recent fieldwork has revealed that in some winters, when small clams (their principal food source) are abundant, the scoter concentrations at the mouth of Delaware Bay are huge—both regionally and nationally significant. Both scoters and Long-tailed Ducks stage in very large numbers in spring at the mouth of Delaware Bay. The nearshore waters of Cape May have for centuries been highly important to these hardy sea ducks and continue to be so today.

Raptors

Birds of prey at Cape May suffered the direct impacts of shooting, and when this was finally controlled, they were subjected to the effects of DDT. In the nineteenth century, virtually all hawks were considered to be "chicken hawks," and there was a state bounty of 50 cents on these "evil predators." Probably due to the heavy shooting at Cape May and the resultant cost to the state treasury, the bounty was reduced in 1885 to 25 cents a bird. Even then, hawk shooting could be lucrative at a time when weekly salaries were often about $5 a week. In 1903 the bounty was abolished, and certain "beneficial" hawks, such as the Fish Hawk (Osprey) and Sparrowhawk (American Kestrel), were given protection. By 1930, only the Sharp-shinned Hawk, Cooper's Hawk, Northern Goshawk, and Peregrine Falcon were unprotected (it would be another twenty-nine years before all hawks were protected by New Jersey state law, in 1959).

Hawk shooting at Cape May reached its peak in the early 1900s. In 1920 Witmer Stone counted 1,400 hawks killed in a single day along Sunset Boulevard. In 1921 a single gunner killed 140 in one day, and bags of 50 to 60 birds per man were common. Beginning in 1931 the National Audubon Society and later the New Jersey Audubon Society posted wardens in the Cape May area. Mainly, the wardens could only attempt to keep "beneficial" hawks from being shot, but they also leased and posted private property and soon established the Witmer Stone Wildlife Sanctuary, stretching from Cape May Point to Higbee Beach and encompassing much of Sunset Boulevard, the prime killing field. By 1935 the number of hawks killed in a season was reduced to 1,080. Shooting never really resumed after the respite (for hawks) of World War II. Of some note is that at Cape May the hawks were not killed just for target practice and "sport," as was the case at Hawk Mountain and elsewhere. At Cape May the hawks were popular as table fare among certain ethnic groups. Clay's grandfather, who never participated in the hawk shooting, related that most of the shooters were of Italian ancestry, bringing their Old World bird harvesting practices (and recipes) to the New World.

Songbirds were popular table fare too, particularly American

Northern Harriers and Peregrine Falcons are nailed to this early 1900s duck hunter's shack, stark evidence of the attitude towards raptors back then.

Robins and Northern Flickers. Flickers were attracted with poles and fence rails, where the tired migrants would perch, only to be shot. Stone reported two gunners who thus bagged six peach baskets of flickers in one morning. Another hunter shot 400 flickers in an hour and a half.

Roger Tory Peterson, one of the first NJAS wardens, wrote the following poignant words in 1948 in *Birds Over America:*

> The pioneer exploits; later generations conserve. So the hunter has always preceded the aesthete and the ornithologist. At Cape May, as at Hawk Mountain, the hawks were slaughtered for years before anyone became concerned. A concrete highway runs from east to west through the groves of Spanish oaks just north of the town of Cape May Point. Here the local gunners formerly lined the road and waited for the hawks to come over. You could depend on the three boys who lived over the grocery store to be there, and the old Italian who ran the taxi from the railroad station, and the man who owned a boat over on the bay. Sometimes sportsmen came from as far away as Trenton and Camden. One September morning in 1935, I watched 800 sharp-shins try to cross the firing line. Each time a "sharpy" sailed over the treetops it was met by a pattern of lead. Some folded up silently; others, with head wounds, flopped to the ground, chattering shrilly. By noon 254 birds lay on the pavement.
>
> That evening, in a Cape May home, I sat down to a meal of hawks—twenty sharp-shins, broiled like squabs, for a family of six. I tasted the birds, found them good, and wondered what my friends would say if they could see me. Like a spy breaking bread with the enemy, I felt uneasy. I could not tell my hosts I disapproved, for their consciences were clear—weren't they killing the hawks as edible game and at the same time saving all the little song birds? It would have done no good to explain predation, ecology and the natural balance to these folk. Having lived at Cape May all their lives, they had a distorted idea of the abundance of hawks. They did not realize that a single season's sport by the Cape May gunners could drain the sharp-shins from thousands of square miles of northern woodland.

Roger related much the same story to us over dinner one evening, following a day's birding along the same Sunset Boulevard path he had taken so many years before. We asked him if he remembered how the hawks had tasted, and in the lighthearted mood that comes with a few glasses of fine wine after a good day afield, someone offered that they "probably tasted just like chicken," to which Roger chuckled and said simply, "yes." It all seems so far in the past, but it was really only five generations ago for the hawks that now rocket across Sunset Boulevard on crisp autumn mornings. Even today, the forensic ornithological archaeologist can still easily find brass bases of shotgun shells in the dunes. Ten-gauge and sixteen-gauge shotguns are little used today, thereby dating the brass and telling a sordid story of not so long ago.

Although systematic raptor shooting ended in the 1940s, locals still commonly shot "chicken hawks" long after that. In high school, Clay clearly remembers fellow students bragging about their hunting bags on Monday mornings: "I got three black ducks, a mallard, two teal, and two hawks." As before, they thought they were doing the world a favor. Ironically, most of the hawks these duck hunters shot were "marsh hawks," Northern Harriers that would never take a duck. We believe that hunter education, environmental education, and nature programs on television ultimately changed these attitudes in the 1980s.

Hawks had no sooner begun to recover from shooting when they were hit by the effects of DDT. There are few places where these deep impacts were more obvious than at Cape May. Immediately following World War II, the chlorinated hydrocarbons were highly promoted and regarded as the cure-all in terms of insect control, and in the early days, they were used with few or no restrictions. In South Jersey, DDT was massively applied for mosquito control, usually based on the theory that, as a mosquito commission supervisor once told us, "if a little is good, a lot is better."

Bald Eagles were one of the first birds to exhibit the effects of DDT. Historically, there were easily more than sixty nests in New Jersey and at least ten in Cape May County alone. In 1936 there were four active nests in the immediate Cape May area, and they produced a total of nine young that year. In 1956 through 1958, due to DDT-induced eggshell thinning, not a single young eagle was raised in any known nest in South Jersey. Eagles are long-lived, possibly up to thirty years in the wild (which partially masked the decline), but by 1968, only a single nesting pair was left in New Jersey, clinging to their sentinel nest deep in neighboring Cumberland County's old-growth Bear Swamp. For five years

Before reintroduction, these two Bald Eagles, shown here in Bear Swamp in 1976, were the last known nesters in New Jersey.

During a Bald Eagle nest banding in South Jersey, Pat was coerced into holding the young bird—successful hacking has brought them back from the brink of extinction.

they raised no young—defeated by DDT. The nationwide ban on DDT in 1972, followed by intensive reintroduction efforts by the New Jersey Division of Fish and Wildlife's Endangered and Nongame Species Program (between 1982 and 1990, 60 young eagles were hacked into southern New Jersey), allowed Bald Eagles to return from the brink. In 2006, 57 pairs of eagles were resident in New Jersey, with about 40 of them on the Delaware Bayshore and 4 of those in Cape May County. It took nearly fifty years, but Bald Eagles are again a daily sight in Cape May skies. The 2006 Midwinter Bald Eagle Survey found 154 Bald Eagles in southern New Jersey alone. In 1979, the year of the first survey, a paltry 9 Bald Eagles were found.

Osprey have always been a hallmark of Cape May. Like Bald Eagles, they are fish eaters and were similarly ravaged by DDT. Roger Tory Peterson sadly reported in 1964 that "the handsome fish hawk . . . is no longer to be seen wherever one looks in the sky. The big bulky nests are no longer a part of every coastal vista. True, there are local groups such as the colony at Avalon (Cedar Island) which are still producing a fair number of young, but the bird is virtually gone at Cape May." Osprey dwindled to about 50 pairs statewide by the early 1970s before the slow recovery began. In 2003 there were 366 pairs in the state, with about 135 of those in Cape May County. On and near the Maurice River in neighboring Cumberland County, the hardworking group Citizens United to Protect the Maurice River provided artificial nest platforms, and Osprey numbers went from a single pair in 1975 to more than 60 today.

Although 366 pairs seems like a hopeful number, we never will know what the historical Osprey population was. Our birding mentor Al Nicholson relates that when he was young in the 1940s, a single woodlot near Canton in Salem County held a colony of 60 active Osprey nests. There were probably thousands of nests throughout New Jersey. Farmers commonly placed discarded cart wheels on tall cedar posts to serve as artificial nest sites to attract Osprey. Joe Jacobs of Avalon was a dedicated DVOC stalwart who faithfully observed and counted both Osprey and Bald Eagles for decades and documented their decline. Jacobs was one of the most prolific Osprey banders of all time; he died in his seventies after suffering a heart attack while climbing to yet another Osprey nest. In the 1940s, before DDT was introduced, Jacobs knew of 500 active Osprey nests in Cape May County alone; in 1969 he counted only 43 active Osprey nests, and by 1975 there were only 30. As recounted by Arthur Cleveland Bent in his *Life Histories,* the prodigious Major Bendire, a colleague of Witmer Stone who also studied birds at Cape May, mentioned a colony of Osprey on Seven Mile Beach in which "several hundred pairs have nested every season." Also on Seven Mile Beach, between Stone Harbor and Avalon, Clay remembers that when he was a young child there were Osprey nests on almost every telephone pole, and a giant oil tank along Ocean Drive had three nests on the top, with at least the two end nests active. Although they are recovering well, Osprey haven't come all the way back. They still show chemical contamination, and there is strong evidence that overfishing of menhaden or bunker, their principal local prey, has impacted nest success and productivity. Osprey may again grace Cape May skies daily from early March to around Thanksgiving, but we shouldn't ever take our beloved fish hawks for granted.

Peregrine Falcons were another classic victim of DDT, and the entire eastern population was extirpated within twenty years after use of the pesticide began. In 1980 a pair of released peregrines nested on an artificial aerie "hack tower" at Forsythe NWR, the first nesting attempt in New Jersey in nearly a quarter century. Today, the heralded Cornell University–Peregrine Fund Reintroduction Program and the hard work of the state ENSP has returned more than twenty pairs to New Jersey—most of them nesting on buildings and bridges. (In northern New Jersey, three pairs breed on natural cliffs.) At least six pairs breed in Cape May and Cumberland counties. Peregrines are easily viewed on the tower at

A Bald Eagle hacking tower near Dividing Creek, with a pair of young eagles sitting on the crossbar.

SANCTUARY OR SLAUGHTER PEN?

Robert P. Allen
National Association of Audubon Societies

For many years it has been the good fortune of naturalists, and especially bird students, to visit the southernmost tip of New Jersey during the autumn months. There are few places on the continent more ideally situated, geographically, for concentrating and harboring great numbers of migratory birds. But, as is usual with such areas, the woods at Cape May Point have attracted a potent enemy of birds; the man with the gun. This is an example of a situation that seems to be inevitable: a natural phenomenon that is of thrilling and breathtaking dimensions to one man inspires his neighbor to run for a shotgun.

The local residents have always claimed, almost as a birthright, the privilege of taking what birds they pleased from the immense flocks that annually visit their county. Robins, thrushes, flickers, woodcock and various hawks were shot and netted almost without restriction. "Flicker poles" were formerly used, devices for wholesale slaughter that are still operated on the Eastern Shore of Maryland and elsewhere. Most of the kill was taken home for the pot, including the smaller hawks, whose rich breast meat is considered very palatable.

Of course a good many non-edible birds—night herons, crows, vultures and osprey—were shot down "for the fun of seeing them drop," or for "target practice." Many gunners protested to me, on more than one occasion, that it was a shame that they were not allowed to shoot at any hawk that came along, as it was so convenient to get such practice just before the opening of the hunting season!

Protective laws have not been strong enough medicine, and an habitual disregard for them proved contagious.

A solution to this problem has been worked out at Cape May Point during the last five years and is nearing perfection in the Witmer Stone Wildlife Sanctuary, established in the fall of 1935 by the National Association of Audubon Societies.

This essay, originally published in the March 1936 issue of *Nature Magazine*, is included here in its entirety because it so succinctly captures Cape May of the 1930s—the dynamics of the migration and the many obstacles facing a conservation movement in its infancy.

In order that the all-important relationship of the sanctuary to the migratory flights may be understood, the latter should be briefly explained.

The tip of New Jersey may be compared to the mouth of a giant funnel. Under ordinary conditions the fall migrants that journey southward along the coastal strip move towards the bottom of the funnel along its seaward side. Their numbers are large but not overwhelming. More important lanes of travel lie inland in parallel lines along the ridges. A strong wind from the northwest strikes these lines of flight at right angles. If the blow is heavy, all but the strongest flyers are forced to give way, and, like aerial sailing ships, to "run before it."

When this happens in the region north and northwest of New Jersey, it brings immense flocks pouring into the top of our theoretical funnel. Striking the outer edge—the Atlantic Ocean—they struggle southward into the funnel's mouth, often clinging precariously to the outer strips. Doubtless many are carried out to sea, on the tail of a northwester, [and] a few such flocks have actually been observed making their way wearily back to land. It is certain that most of these sea-blown migrants never return to the land.

As these augmented flocks move southward into the neck of the funnel, they are crowded closer and closer together. The farther south they go the greater the density of the flocks. When the jumping-off place is reached, at Cape May Point, this density becomes an amazing concentration of bird life. At this juncture the massed flocks do not pour out of the funnel's mouth to flow serenely onward, fan-wise, across the fifteen-mile width of Delaware Bay. The northwester generally continues to blow throughout the day and an immediate crossing would obviously mean disaster. Instead of making the attempt, the birds round the curve of the Cape and work northward, uncertain as to the next move.

Thus it is that the inviting woods area, which lies directly under this northward flight lane, is so abundantly resorted to by migrants. With its generous cover and food-bearing plants, it is a natural, made-to-order *sanctuary*.

Both legal and illegal gunning have contributed toward making this concentration point a shambles rather than a sanctuary, however. The temptation to shoot more than the limit of woodcock, for

continues on next page

SANCTUARY OR SLAUGHTER PEN? *continued*

example, seems to be irresistible when the birds get up from every available cover. Indeed, the immense numbers of birds appear to have inspired the local nimrods to all sorts of heroic deeds. Close by, in a heavy stand of conifers, migrating Barn Owls gather. I have seen a flock of more than one hundred of these birds in this thicket. One "sportsman," who must have passed half the previous night reading up on the exploits of Daniel Boone and Kit Carson, went into these sheltering pines and slaughtered enough owls "to make a wagonload," according to indignant local people. This was too much for them; but, after all, owls are not good eating!

From time to time a few local and summer residents protested these outrageous practices, chief among them Dr. Witmer Stone, the well-known ornithologist and editor of *The Auk*. These protests, vehement as they were, seemed lost on indifferent and calloused ears. But this was not the case. Others became interested and, finally, alert members of the Delaware Valley Ornithological Club, of Philadelphia, laid the whole matter before the National Association of Audubon Societies.

This was in 1930. The following year the Audubon Association inaugurated a cooperative investigation with the New Jersey Board of Fish and Game Commissioners. Illegal shooting was stopped nearly 100 per cent, food habits of hawks in migration were studied, the flight itself was carefully observed and recorded, and local people were educated in identification of raptors and in general conservation matters.

Finally, in the summer of 1935, plans were made by the Audubon Association to set aside as much of the concentration area as possible. Twenty-five acres of the most strategic part of the wooded section were leased. [Authors' note: This was later increased to approximately 1,000

Forsythe NWR, and they have successfully nested on the Hilton Casino Hotel in Atlantic City for nearly twenty years. Outside the nesting season, they are commonly seen roosting on water towers in Cape May and in all the barrier island communities. To peregrines, water towers are just conveniently located, odd-shaped cliffs.

Peregrines are essentially new arrivals to South Jersey, because historically, they nested only on cliffs and mountain ledges in the northen part of the state. When reintroduction to historic aeries failed, mainly due to Great Horned Owl predation, state wildlife managers "introduced" them to the acres.] Local opposition among the gunners flared, and then subsided before the wholesome nature of the project. In the first week of August a warden, well qualified as an ornithologist, was placed on the job. The area was posted and its limits indicated for the benefit of possible trespassers. The warden kept a detailed record of migrants, making daily reports to the home office.

No serious difficulties were encountered during the fifteen weeks' season. Bisected by a paved county road [authors' note: today known as Sunset Boulevard], whereon gunning is legal under present laws, the inviolate character of the sanctuary area presents a remarkable contrast. The gunners were made to keep strictly within bounds, and air rights vertically above our leased property were maintained.

The sanctuary is more than merely a "no-shooting area," it is a Mecca for bird students and for botanists as well. A total of 198 species and an estimated total of 124,000 individual birds were recorded during the 15 weeks of 1935. Two hundred and fifty species have been known to occur in the immediate region. Typical plants include the prevailing Spanish Oak, the pond pine, holly, purple lady-slipper and slender lycopodium.

What has been accomplished by the establishment of the Witmer Stone Wildlife Sanctuary in New Jersey can be done at other concentration points or along heavy flight lines elsewhere. The Emergency Conservation Committee of New York City pioneered a similar effort at Hawk Mountain in Pennsylvania, with notable success. Investigations are revealing "bird traps" at other points, and every last one of these should be a sanctuary—their natural role—instead of the shameful slaughter pens that man's blundering presence has made of them.

coastal salt marshes, supposedly far from predators. This effort was highly successful, and resident peregrines populated the coast, where previously they had been found only as migrants from the high Arctic. There were some drawbacks and even criticism. For example, near Sea Isle City, one peregrine pair specialized in preying on Least Terns (also an endangered species), decimating an entire colony. In 2005 the Delaware Bay Egg Island tower was moved farther inland to try to prevent peregrine specialization on beleaguered Red Knots on adjacent beaches. The peregrines quickly reoccupied the relocated nest, but the move seems a dubious decision when

A young American Kestrel emerges from a Cape May nest box in this 1994 photo. Today, there are probably no nesting kestrels in the immediate Cape May area.

one considers that a peregrine's home range may be as much as 40 square miles.

Cooper's Hawks and Red-shouldered Hawks are two other species apparently heavily impacted by DDT. Cooper's have now recovered well, but red-shoulders have not and are the rarest of nesters in southern New Jersey. Red-shoulders may also be victimized by other factors, such as loss of preferred reptile and amphibian prey and loss or change of habitat. Whereas Cooper's Hawks and Red-tailed Hawks have clearly adapted to changing landscapes (both species do well in suburban areas in South Jersey and elsewhere), other raptors have not been able to cope so well. Red-shoulders, at least in New Jersey, have not accepted fragmented habitats and breed in only a fraction of their former numbers.

American Kestrels have vanished along with their fallow, old-field habitat. They are one of the many grassland species in steep decline. Today, the American Kestrel is being considered for threatened species status. It is amazing how rapidly the demise of the kestrel has come about. In the 1970s and 1980s, we took them for granted as common breeders and wintering birds. There were three or four pairs that bred on Cape Island alone, and they were an unwanted predator at the South Cape May Meadows Least Tern colony. We remember one dependable pair that nested under the eaves of the Chalfonte Hotel in the late 1970s. Their comings and goings and *killy, killy, killy* calls entertained diners on the veranda. Today, they are long since gone. In 2005, no kestrels bred or wintered on Cape Island, at least to our knowledge. It is a problem that stretches far beyond New Jersey. In 1976 the Cape May Raptor Banding Project banded 1,937 American Kestrel. In 2004 they banded a staggering all-time low of 35.

Among nocturnal birds of prey, the Short-eared Owl has disappeared as a breeder on Cape May's Atlantic coast and Delaware Bay marshes, possibly impacted by DDT but more likely by marsh flooding. Barn Owls have dwindled too around Cape May, no doubt due to a loss of farmland habitat and the concomitant loss of barn and silo nesting structures (Barn Owls are still commonly found as breeders in nearby rural Cumberland and Salem counties).

A final emergent threat to all birds, but apparently of greatest significance to hawks and owls, is West Nile virus. West Nile, vectored by mosquitoes and then carried long distances by migratory birds, is a proven killer of raptors. Short-term impacts have been documented, but it remains to be seen whether long-term declines are occurring. As we have learned from our legacy of ornithological study at Cape May, raptors can never be taken for granted.

Game Birds

Great changes have been seen in game bird populations over time. The Wild Turkey, extirpated by the mid-1840s, has made an almost unbelievable comeback. Reintroduction was begun in 1977 and was hugely successful. In less than two decades after reintroduction, 24,000 birds were estimated present in New Jersey. Today, turkeys are once again a common bird of forests and fields. They are not found immediately around Cape May but are abundant in northern Cape May County, in Belleplain State Forest, for example. In contrast, Ruffed Grouse, historically known as "swamp pheasants" to local hunters, have recently (in the last decade) declined severely in southern New Jersey—the southern limit of their coastal plain range in the United States—perhaps being outcompeted by booming Wild Turkeys. Pat had to stop doing field trips for drumming Ruffed Grouse in 1996 because there were none to be heard, and this is still the case ten years later. A few probably persist in Belleplain and in Cumberland County, and they remain rare but present in the

A Ruffed Grouse on its nest in Goshen in the early 1980s.

Pine Barrens. The Ring-necked Pheasant is an introduced bird, but they were extremely common breeders in the early twentieth century. A few hold on as breeding birds in western Cumberland and Salem Counties, but they have totally disappeared from Cape May County—victims of habitat loss and, possibly, avian encephalitis. Any pheasants seen here today are recently released birds serving as fodder for hunters. An attempted introduction of Gray Partridges in the Woodbine area in the 1950s failed, although a few persisted for a number of years, according to Clay's father. Today, Chukars, released by shooting preserves, are sometimes seen around Woodbine and Belleplain.

The almost total loss of the Northern Bobwhite is a sad tale, but one that is easily understood. They are birds of fallow, weedy fields—a rare habitat type in today's age of mechanized agriculture and the disappearance of farmland to development. The loss of native grasses to nonnative grasses has also been implicated in the demise of quail. In the mid-twentieth century, bobwhites were abundant in southern New Jersey. Clay's father, an avid "quail gunner," would often find more than twenty coveys a day with his English setter bird dogs in the 1950s and 1960s. Early Christmas Bird Counts found hundreds of quail, but today, a bobwhite is almost a red-letter bird, and most that are seen are probably game-farm releases. New Jersey Division of Fish and Wildlife bobwhite survey routes that averaged 25.2 birds per route in the 1970s averaged only 0.3 whistling bobwhites in the spring of 2003. The native Northern Bobwhite, if there are any left, should be listed as an endangered species in New Jersey, but it never will be, because, in the politics of fish and wildlife policies, it is a *game* species (and easily released), not a nongame bird.

During the full-moon high tides of September, Clapper Rails have always been eagerly sought as game in southern New Jersey. These abundant "mud hens" were pursued in purpose-built white cedar skiffs poled across the salt meadows during the highest tides. We still own the 1946 family rail skiff, a classic design built of white cedar with loving care in Sea Isle City, but today it is used only for

Northern Bobwhite were once a common sight in Cape May fields.

photography. Due to their abundance and secretive nature, Clapper Rails were never heavily impacted by gunning and remain a common bird today. The same cannot be said for other rails. King Rail, Black Rail, and (to a lesser extent) Virginia Rail populations have seen severe declines. This is due not to hunting but to the loss of fresh, brackish, and high marsh habitat. Common Moorhen and American Coot populations have dwindled too, due to both drainage and, later, saltwater flooding. Inexplicably, they are still legal game; hunters in 2005 were legally allowed to shoot ten Common Moorhens a day in New Jersey, despite the fact that the species should be listed as endangered here.

The Sora was once a highly representative bird of Delaware Bay tributary marshes. Migrant Soras have avidly been sought by "gentlemen-sportsmen" since the eighteenth century. The famous Philadelphia landscape artist Thomas Eakins painted a number of scenes on Cumberland County's Cohansey River of "gunning for rail." Attesting to the number of birds and also to the abundance of healthy wild rice marshes, 3,720 Soras were shot in 1884 at Tinicum near Philadelphia. Many thousands were shot each year on South Jersey's Cohansey and Maurice rivers, and even into the 1980s, many hundreds were shot by guided parties on the Maurice. Hunters could legally take 25 Soras a day in New Jersey in 2005. Mercifully, however, this strange pastime has almost passed into memory, but not due to regulations, outrage, or even lack of rails. Instead, assaults on the wild rice—due to freshwater withdrawals upstream, the rising sea level, and the herbivory of the booming resident Canada Goose population—doomed first the marsh, then the unusual concentrations of migratory Soras, and finally the gunning (although this could change again as a result of targeted wild rice management and Canada Goose "control").

Shorebirds

Shorebirds, the plovers and sandpipers, may have suffered far more at the hands of humans than any other group of birds. Three, the Black-necked Stilt, the Wilson's Plover, and the American Avocet, were extirpated from New Jersey, and one, the Eskimo Curlew, is probably extinct (although largely from hunting outside of New Jersey). Shorebirds were prime targets first for subsistence hunting, then market gunners, and eventually wealthy sportsmen from the cities. For more than a century they were pursued spring and fall, seasons that for shorebirds virtually overlap.

Shorebird shooting was heavy by as early as the 1840s. One hunter killed 1,200 shorebirds in just a few days' visit to Egg Harbor in the summer of 1843. By 1883 the Black-necked Stilt and American Avocet were gone, and the Wilson's Plover and American Oystercatcher would soon follow. Willet were extirpated from the Atlantic coast marshes, but they managed to hold on in the remote Delaware Bay wetlands. It was natural that the local nesting species would be affected the most; the more highly migratory species such as the Red Knot were impacted less because their numbers were usually more dispersed—with both the breeding (high Arctic) and wintering grounds (Chile and Argentina) largely inaccessible.

With severe population declines clearly evident, shorebirds were finally given protection. In 1926 the Black-bellied Plover and in 1927 the yellowlegs were included under the protection of the Federal Migratory Bird Act. The removal of these larger, more abundant, and popular game species spelled the beginning of the end of shorebird gunning. Years later, Clay's father would fondly remember "whistling in shorebirds" (imitating their calls) in tales twinged with regret that the end had come. They were a challenge and fine eating, he recalled. Today, Clay and his cousin Jon still commonly whistle at Black-bellied Plover flocks pitching in, a handed-down habit that is hard to break, although we have never raised more than our binoculars and cameras at the rushing, wheeling, plaintively whistling flocks of "bullheads."

Recoveries were slow. Piping Plovers gradually returned, yet inexorably they found their nesting beaches covered by people and summer homes. Wilson's Plovers returned only in a few scattered breeding attempts between 1940 and 1963. American Oystercatchers, extirpated in 1896, first bred again in 1947 and since then have continued a slow but steady recolonization. Today there are several hundred pairs in New Jersey, and they nest in good numbers at places such as Stone Harbor Point. In warmer years, approximately 1,000 American Oystercatchers winter in New Jersey, too. (American Oystercatcher is not out of the woods; the entire population is thought to be around 11,000 birds—and rising sea levels could pose a big problem for this beach and marsh nester.)

Willet, listed by both Wilson (1812) and Turnbill (1869) as one of the most common breeding birds in the salt marsh, last nested on the Atlantic coast of New Jersey in 1889 and were first refound as nesters in 1952. Today they are abundant; the Delaware Bay population alone has been estimated at up to 20,000 pairs. We await the return of Black-necked Stilts and American Avocets as breeders. Today, Black-necked Stilts are annual spring visitors (in very small numbers) to southern New Jersey. Since they breed in fair numbers just across the bay in Delaware, we continue to hope that they will eventually return as breeders. Another shorebird has been lost for a reason other than shooting; the Upland Sandpiper disappeared along with farms and pastureland at Cape May, throughout New Jersey, and in much of the East. Today, only a few pairs of uppies remain in southern New Jersey, breeding in remote sections of Atlantic City International Airport and at

The American Avocet has not yet returned to Cape May as a breeder.

Lakehurst Naval Air Station. Far fewer are recorded on migration than formerly.

On the other side of the ledger, Purple Sandpipers, virtually unknown historically, have become common in winter at Cape May. Prior to 1925, Stone recounted only two records for all of New Jersey, but today the Cape May Christmas Bird Count records as many as 250 each year. The reason is obvious—far more so in terms of cause and effect than for most bird species. The building of rock jetties, groins, and breakwaters—a practice that began on a large scale in the 1930s and continued unabated until today—provided artificial but perfect habitat for the rock-loving Purple Sandpiper. These birds are found exclusively on rocky coasts and are virtually never seen on beaches or mudflats. They feed only on the myriad sea life found near the tide line on rocks and boulders. Until jetty building marched down the coast, such rocky habitat occurred only from eastern Canada south to Rhode Island. It is amazing that a bird formerly unknown could now be so abundant at Cape May—thanks solely to our incessant jetty building to control erosion and provide safe passage into inlets and harbors. In one recent year, the Cape May Christmas Bird Count produced the national high count for Purple Sandpipers, with more found here than anywhere else in their range. We anticipate, however, that their numbers will soon be dropping as the ongoing massive beach fill (erosion control) projects work to bury jetties throughout southern New Jersey. Luckily, at

WAVES OF WHIMBRELS

One worthy bird that has long been a hallmark of the Jersey coastal marshes is the Whimbrel. One of our largest shorebirds, the Whimbrel has always been a conspicuous spring and fall wayfarer along the coast. The enigmatic Whimbrel, though, is in a curious, long-term decline for unknown reasons. In 1937 Witmer Stone wrote of the Hudsonian Curlew, as it was then known, as "a wary bird, well able to take care of itself. . . . In spite of the fact that it was a favorite game bird in former days, when the shooting of all shorebirds was permitted, it has not materially decreased in numbers as have many of the small species, and may still be seen in flocks of hundreds and probably thousands at the height of the spring migration. On the vast marshes surrounding Great Sound . . . it is difficult to estimate the number of birds present in these assemblages but there must be several thousand." Clay's father attested to this as well, remembering that in his boyhood gunning days Whimbrels were by far the most wary of the shorebirds and the hardest to fool (and the best eating).

Being a long-distance migrant, the threat to the Whimbrel may be linked to its wintering grounds in South America. Although some Whimbrels winter in Florida and many in Mexico, good numbers go as far south as Argentina, Chile, or even Tierra del Fuego. Some Whimbrels travel down the coast in short flights, but many fly nonstop over the Atlantic to South America, logging up to 2,400 miles, much in the way of American Golden Plovers and Hudsonian Godwits. As always, we question why one individual easily winters in the Carolinas while another goes all the way to the Falkland Islands. With their powerful flight, maybe the reason is just because they can. We've always wondered if Whimbrels heading out on July full-moon tides will soon return to land farther down the coast or if they are leaving land behind for as long as the next forty-eight hours.

Proof that Whimbrels survived the gunning years in large numbers is the report of 1,500 seen at Stone Harbor on August 8, 1953. Nine years later, Whimbrels were still abundant, as Clay's first field note entries attest, concerning an event he witnessed from the back porch of his Stone Harbor home one evening. That evening was a portent of Clay's future. Although it was only about a year after his grandmother had given him his first Peterson guide, and it would be more than a

A flock of Whimbrels is a welcome sight at Shell Bay Landing.

decade before he was an actual wildlife biologist, the seeds had been sown. Some may question the accuracy of a thirteen-year-old's count, but it is important to note that his father identified the birds as "curlew" (a bird well known to him) and helped Clay Jr. with the count.

> On July 17, 1962, came full moon, which brought tides 1'–1½' above normal high water. Over Stone Harbor came large flights of Curlew—unidentified, but probably Hudsonian. They were observed from 7:00 till 9:15 P.M. The high tides had forced them from their feeding grounds in the meadows northward. The Curlew were probably headed for the Stone Harbor Point, for that is where their flight most likely took them. However, they might have gone farther south. At least 3,000 were seen, and possibly more. The flights, often numbering to 100, were numerous till 8:45 P.M. Many singles also passed. A few times their call was heard. I observed them with field glasses. Their flight is extremely fast, and their wing beat is rapid, yet they moved only their wingtips. They are brown, with gray to white on the underside. Their wings are swept back. Their bill is curved downward (just visible with field glasses). They were flying from 150 to 350 feet off the ground. Dad said they would probably fly back tomorrow morning after the tide goes down. The birds do not nest here, this is done on the shores of northern Canada. But after the family is raised, they move southward to feed, and are all past New Jersey by late fall. A

continues on next page

WAVES OF WHIMBRELS *continued*

few smaller birds were observed with the flocks, and Dad said they were most likely Snipe [no doubt Short-billed Dowitcher]. Seeing 4 or 5 flights of 100 of these sleek, fast, birds at almost the same time, was a beautiful sight I'll never forget.

On July 29th, the same thing happened, only not as many were seen. About 150–200 were seen, in ranks up to about 30–40. They were flying lower, and with field glasses I could see them very plainly. Now I am almost sure they are Hudsonian Curlew. It was wet and drizzly.

On July 30th, the same thing happened once again, and this time 1,500–2,000 were seen. The flocks at times contained 150 birds. They were at the same height they were on the 29th. Once there was practically a solid line across the sky.

Modern-era maxima for Whimbrels for Cape May (and for New Jersey) are 500 estimated at Shellbay Landing on May 14, 1984, and again on May 6, 1996; however, normal yearly peak counts are fewer. The Whimbrel is a species of high concern for virtually all national and international shorebird research and conservation groups and agencies. It is often listed at a level of concern behind only the Piping Plover, Red Knot, and Sanderling. Declines may be linked to adverse impacts on their South American wintering grounds, although as high marsh feeders (mainly on fiddler crabs), they could be affected by rising sea levels and the loss of intertidal mudflats. Whimbrels are symbolic of the changes in bird populations over time, but they are an enigma; unlike with most species, we don't know why they have declined. Small groups of Whimbrels are still easily seen at Cape May, particularly on boat trips in the vast sounds or bays. But when you see them, appreciate this waning long-distance flyer—and the tribulations of all our shorebirds. And if you have the fortune to see a July high-tide sunset flight over Stone Harbor Point, with waves of migrating curlews calling as they head out over the darkening Atlantic into a freshening southeast wind, try to marvel at the wondrous Whimbrel with the same wide-eyed awe of a young boy sitting on the back steps with his father in a place that is still there but at a time that is not. ■

least from the Purple Sandpiper's standpoint, coastal storms and erosion continue to expose anew many recently covered jetties.

Also in the black ink in the bird count ledger is the Marbled Godwit. A rare bird in Stone's day (he saw only one at Cape May), they are sometimes seen in large numbers at Brigantine Island and Stone Harbor Point. There are almost always several and often dozens about in fall (July through December), so the Marbled Godwit has certainly lost its former status as a true rarity. The cause is unknown—maybe a shift in the migration route somehow related to climate change. It seems as if all "lingerers" tend to stay far longer and later than in the past. The increase in Marbled Godwit coincides with an increase in "Western" Willets; the reason may be related, as the two species have similar ranges and occupy similar ecological niches in their northern Great Plains breeding range.

Gulls and Terns

Coastal birds such as gulls and terns offer clear examples of what Roger Tory Peterson, in his 1964 introduction to the second edition of *Bird Studies at Old Cape May,* called "debit and credit birds." As if balancing columns in a ledger, some species boomed and others went bust. The local breeding tern species were, along with the egrets, early victims of the millinery trade. With egrets, only the plumes were used in hats, but with terns, often the entire bird—skinned, treated with arsenic, and stuffed—graced a lady's headgear.

As early as 1883, terns were rapidly disappearing from coastal beaches and bays. In 1884 George Spencer Morris wrote a letter to Witmer Stone saying that he could no longer find tern eggs and that he had come across two "professional" gunners for the fashion trade standing beside knee-high piles of terns. Tern carcasses were sold for 12 cents apiece. In 1921 Stone concluded that the Gull-billed Tern, particularly hard hit, was no doubt gone forever, but he noted that the Least Tern, Black Skimmer, and Piping Plover had finally been found nesting again (the Gull-billed Tern was found nesting in 1926 but never regained anywhere near its historical numbers). The Roseate Tern, apparently never numerous, was extirpated; the last Cape May nesting occurred in 1924 on Gull Bar (Champagne Island) in Hereford Inlet. Least and Common Terns were both nearly extirpated from the entire state of New Jersey, but once they were protected from shooting, they slowly returned. We don't have a clear picture of the history of Forster's Terns. Although recorded by early ornithologists in coastal New Jersey, the first confirmed nest was at Brigantine (now Forsythe) NWR in 1955. They have apparently increased and, as salt marsh breeders, haven't been affected nearly as badly as beach-nesting Common and Least Terns. Forster's Terns today are fairly common breeders on the summer coastal marshes.

Terns and Black Skimmers had barely recovered from shooting when the other shoe dropped—the development and loss of much of their barrier island breeding habitat. Even in 1937 Witmer Stone was concerned about the impact of barrier island building on Least Terns. Common Terns may have survived by adopting, in desperation, the breeding strategy of their "cousin" the Forster's Tern—breeding on salt marsh wrack lines, although nesting success for Common Terns is poor in this atypical habitat. Common Terns may also nest on spoil islands (an odd benefit from dredging and filling), and this strategy and location helped save the Black Skimmer too. Skimmers were probably extirpated in the 1890s. Populations of terns and skimmers have rebounded somewhat but will probably never regain their preshooting historical levels. Simply put, there just isn't enough room for them on modern Cape May beaches. Today, the Least Tern and Black Skimmer (and Piping Plover) are listed as endangered species in New Jersey. Colonies are ephemeral and, even when protected, are subject to coastal storms, full-moon high tides, natural predators, feral cats, and, in the bigger picture, coastal erosion and the rising sea level. Successful colonies will probably always require constant and vigilant management and protection.

On a positive note, we now have far more Caspian Terns, Royal Terns, and even Sandwich Terns than ever before. Sandwich Terns, unknown to Stone, are seen annually in late summer in some numbers. Caspian Terns have bred in New Jersey in very small numbers, and a few pairs of Royal Terns at least attempt to breed each year—a valuable and welcome addition to our summer avifauna. Big terns are now abundant in late summer and early fall when Caspians arrive from the north and royals arrive from the south, dispersing from growing nesting colonies in Maryland, Virginia, and the Carolinas. Listen for the relentless food begging calls of juvenile Royal and Caspian Terns as they doggedly follow the adults about.

Quite unlike the terns, gull populations have exploded due to human impacts. Laughing Gulls, which Stone fondly called the "summer gull," are a highly representative bird of Cape May, present in noisy numbers from mid-March through November. Laughing Gulls were persecuted first by egging practices and then by millinery shooting, but under the protection of the Migratory Bird Treaty Act of 1918, their numbers rebounded quickly. New Jersey Laughing Gulls (and all breeding gulls) greatly increased in numbers in the twentieth century. Gulls have exploited the availability of scraps, fishery wastes, and growing landfills to breed in numbers unimaginable in Stone's day. A 1983 targeted survey found nearly 60,000 breeding Laughing Gulls in southern New Jersey—some 30,000 pairs. In 1995 aerial surveys counted fewer, with about 40,000 adult Laughing Gulls present. The marshes north of Cape May are the breeding stronghold; in effect, the entire area along the route of the Intracoastal Waterway, from Cape May to Avalon, is one endless, ongoing Laughing Gull colony (a far cry from Julian Potter's 1910 experience when he estimated 1,500 gulls in this colony, "the larger of the two colonies on the New Jersey coast"). The Laughing Gull colonies in southern New Jersey today are the largest in the world; only the Texas coast has similarly large numbers. Laughing Gulls nest on the marsh on loose, sometimes floating (at high tide) nests constructed of marsh grasses and wrack. The recent decline in nesting may be a result of tidier landfill practices, competition for food and nest sites by expanding Herring and Great Black-backed Gull populations, declining fisheries, or even a lack of horseshoe crab eggs—a key food resource during the early nesting season. The rising sea level could play a role too, as nests are frequently flooded. Predatory Herring and Great Blacked-back Gulls also take many young Laughing Gull chicks.

Herring Gulls, Stone's "winter gull," are actually a fairly recent arrival from the north. Herring Gulls first nested in 1946 (at Stone Harbor), but today more than 7,000 nesters (some 3,500 pairs) are found in southern New Jersey. To contrast the past and current status of the Herring Gull, we offer this anecdote: Sometime around 1920 a taxidermist asked Clay's grandfather, Frank Harold Sutton Sr., to procure a specimen of a Herring Gull for a display. At that time they were so uncommon and wary that it took several months for Frank to fill the order. Today, unwrap a bagel on the beach and it would take you maybe twenty seconds.

Great Black-backed Gulls were quite uncommon in Stone's time; he seldom saw more than 3 or 4 together, and then only in winter. Blackbacks first bred in 1966, and by 1995 there were nearly 400 pairs in South Jersey. The figure is undoubtedly much higher today as they continue to exploit dredge spoil mounds for nesting. The boom in gulls (herring, black-backed, and Laughing) has had a significant impact on other nesting species. Gulls, primarily Laughing Gulls, commonly grab Black Skimmer and tern chicks from nesting colonies. The Great Black-backed Gull is the world's largest gull and a formidable predator. We have seen Great Black-backed Gulls catch and kill Ruddy Duck, Bufflehead, Coot, Pied-billed Grebe, and a nearly fledged Black Skimmer. One frigid winter day we watched a Great Black-backed Gull easily, almost nonchalantly, steal a freshly caught Gadwall from a female Peregrine Falcon. Gull "victims" are often injured or winter-stressed birds, but not always. All gulls prey heavily on tired songbirds that are carried to sea on autumn's northwest winds. Once, near the Cape May Hawkwatch, Great Black-backed Gulls drove a migrant Northern Harrier into the ocean, where they killed and fed on it. Herring Gulls do the same thing to exhausted American Kestrels over the water. Once, a skilled Herring Gull deftly caught several Tree Swallows sitting on the beach at Stone Harbor on an unusually cold late November morning. Gulls are major actors in the ecology of the shore—sometimes beneficial, sometimes maybe not—but they have clearly played a vastly changing role over time at Cape May.

Songbirds

Each group of birds has its own story, but in a group as diverse as pigeons through Old World sparrows, the individual stories are particularly varied, with many actions, reactions, influences, and scenarios involved. Songbirds at Cape May have been impacted over time by local, regional, and international forces. Naturally, the status of neotropical migrants has changed at Cape May, mostly due to situations beyond any local control, such as the destruction of Central and South American rain forest and cloud forest. Although the songbird migration is hard to quantify, many veterans and old-timers commonly relate that it "just isn't *nearly* what it used to be." The loss of migratory stopover habitat at Cape May has had an impact, because fewer birds can rest and feed here. One worry related to the declining acreage of stopover habitat is that less available area will translate into higher concentrations of migrant birds. It is conceivable that passerine populations are lower than we assume, because an increasing concentration in decreasing habitat may mask the true extent of the decline.

The greatest impact of the suburbanization of New Jersey has been the loss of grassland birds, and breeding populations of Grasshopper Sparrow, Vesper Sparrow, "Ipswich" Savannah Sparrow, Eastern Meadowlark, and Horned Lark have declined severely. Henslow's Sparrow is a recent extirpation (about 1970), and the Sedge Wren has nearly been extirpated from New Jersey. Loggerhead Shrike has virtually disappeared as a migrant and wintering bird. Stone reported up to five in a day in the fall; today there is barely one record in a decade. While Eastern Bluebird has recovered well in general terms, it remains uncommon as a breeder in much of southern New Jersey because of the lack of suitable grassland habitat.

As expected, introduced species populations have boomed at Cape May, as they have elsewhere. European Starlings, House Sparrows, and House Finches are all abundant residents. Native Brown-headed Cowbirds continue to boom as forest fragmentation continues unabated through the state and the entire east.

On the plus side, there have been many new arrivals. Perhaps in part related to climate change and global warming, a long-term trend at Cape May and in the entire mid-Atlantic region has been the movement of southern birds to the north. Northern Cardinals and Northern Mockingbirds were two southerners that Stone wrote about; their arrival may have occurred in the 1800s. Since Stone's *Bird Studies at Old Cape May,* Blue

Grosbeak, Indigo Bunting, Boat-tailed Grackle, and Summer Tanager have all expanded north and flourished. Red-headed Woodpecker and Red-bellied Woodpecker have expanded into the northeast since the 1930s. Stone listed the red-bellied as an accidental straggler in New Jersey and never saw one at Cape May. Today it is a common breeder throughout the state and even appears as a fairly common migrant in Cape May. Chuck-will's-widow arrived in 1921 and is now a common bird, although to the apparent detriment of the Whip-poor-will. Although they remain common in the Belleplain area, Whip-poor-wills are now clearly declining in much of Cape May County. Some say they are being outcompeted by the larger Chuck-will's-widow, but more likely are just crowded out by houses and related impacts. Forest succession may play a role, too. Whips tend to use early succession growth and Chucks more mature forest.

The bird life of Cape May keeps changing, even if some of its birding byways never seem to. Here is a scene in Belleplain State Forest.

When we moved to our Goshen home in 1977, on summer evenings we could hear as many as seven Whip-poor-wills calling, but we haven't heard one in nearly a decade. There are, however, at least four Chuck-will's-widows within earshot now, where none were present in 1977. The Pine Barrens remain an important stronghold for the Whip-poor-will.

A nonpasserine southern arrival is the Black Vulture. First found breeding in 1981, there are today many hundreds in South Jersey. Black Vultures are a daily sight year-round in Cape May skies; their rapid expansion may have mirrored the explosion of white-tailed deer (providing vulture food in the form of road-kill and hunters' discarded carcasses). Other southerners that may be following suit are the Eurasian-collared Dove, Mississippi Kite, Brown Pelican, and Royal Tern, all of which have been expanding their range northward. And, as unlikely as it may seem, the Magnificent Frigatebird may be joining this list too. Whether due to climate change, fishery recoveries, or some other reason, frigatebirds have become annual at Cape May in the past few years, with several sightings each summer and fall.

While southern "overshoots" have long been the spice of spring migration, few would dispute that this seems to be an increasing phenomenon. Migration biologists now commonly refer to these southern birds as "overmigrants"—individuals continually attempting to expand, to push their breeding range farther north—and relate the phenomenon to global warming. Painted Bunting, Swainson's Warbler, Mississippi Kite, and White-winged Dove may be classic examples of Cape May overmigrants today, birds seen in far larger numbers than they have in the past.

As at many locations in the east and southeast, Cape May has seen the recent arrival of numerous "western" hummingbirds. *Selasphorus* hummingbirds are annual in fall at the cape, and Rufous, Allen's, Calliope, and Black-chinned Hummingbirds have all been confirmed on the cape within the past decade. Whether because of a shift in migration patterns or as a result of greatly increased numbers of hummingbird feeders and wildlife gardens, western hummers are now avidly sought after.

The Cape May bird ledger has remained pretty well balanced. There have been many documented losses, first from shooting and DDT, and then from habitat degradation and loss, but there have also been significant recoveries and many wonderful success stories. For several centuries of ornithologists, maintaining the Cape May chronicle and ensuring the welfare of Cape May birds have taken a lot of work, but it has been a labor of love, and it has been fruitful. The gains are worth the effort and will continue to be. Change can be for the good or for the bad, but change is the one constant in Cape May birds and birding.

AFTERWORD

You cannot depend on your eyes when your imagination is out of focus.

—Mark Twain

There have been few aspects of birds and birding at Cape May as constant as change. Some changes are sad and irreversible; others are so edifying as to seem magical. Cape May is well known for Merlin Madness, but sometimes it seems as though Merlin the Magician has played a role too.

Yesterday had been gray, blustery, bordering on cold, but now the Indian Summer sun quickly warmed the freshly-turned farm fields and the red and yellow-brown fading forests. Long before the first raptors began to rise from the trees, the sky over the marshes is filled with Tree Swallows, many thousands, looking like swirling smoke as they wash back and forth along the red cedar edge. Not only is the early morning sky filled with birds, it is filled with expectancy for the birders beginning to filter onto the hawkwatch platform.

As the land warms, thermals build along the length of the peninsula, cumulus billowing high into the Cape May autumn sky. These clouds are signposts for soaring, thermal-loving migrating hawks. They are elevators in the sky, and the hawks soon follow them to land's end as inexorably as autos follow the interstate. Over Cape May Point, the hawks begin to appear. Some start to head out over Delaware Bay, but then pause, circling together. Where in yesterday's northwest gale the circling was to summon the courage, in today's gentler wind they circle confidently, to simply gain altitude—altitude that will be converted to distance. The distance for now is just a small portion of their full fall migration, the 10 miles across the water to Cape Henlopen.

The raptors build, the "kettle" growing until the higher hawks peel off, like fighter planes suddenly vectored toward a target, heading for Delaware. Here are 20 Broadwings, there a half-dozen Red-tails, all surrounded by a retinue of Sharp-shinned Hawks. A Merlin cleaves the rising thermal, needless of its assistance. Higher up, following the two harriers, a string of six Osprey, all in a row, line-astern, stream over. None are seen to give even a single flap before they disappear out over the Bay.

Another kettle forms up, and an unkempt, sloppy, wavy line of cormorants crosses through the loose flock of hawks. Higher up a stratospheric skein of Canada Geese passes, some of the first of the still young season, a perfect wedge against the white on blue. The crossbow shape of a Peregrine Falcon arrows through, completing the picture, or so we thought, until someone on the hawkwatch excitedly shouts, "Godwit going left!"

All eyes turn to where the watcher is pointing, and we find the striking Hudsonian Godwit, leading a flock of dowitchers, angling away, heading out to sea on a journey that will end in Chile. It is a brief sighting but one of high drama—a magical view of migration and of a bird that connects the continents, the high arctic to Tierra del Fuego.

Years later, the image is still vivid, indelible in no small part due to David Sibley's masterful drawing of the moment. "Godwit Going Left" hangs in our living room. David well-captured the excitement of that October morning on the hawkwatch in his poster art for the 41st Annual New Jersey Audubon Cape May Autumn Weekend (now known as THE Bird Show), way back in 1987. The pen and ink drawing somehow always evokes the timeless energy that pervades those special autumn days at Cape May. Cape May may have changed over time, but the excitement and the expectation of the gathered faithful have not.

It's hard to imagine Cape May, New Jersey, without its hawkwatch, but of course, it hasn't always been there. Today the Red Cedar edifice of the hawkwatch dominates the landscape at Cape May Point State Park, always beckoning, always looking north, awaiting the specks to materialize, waiting for proximity to overcome distance as the hawks of autumn stream in and overhead. At one of North America's most visited birding destinations, this is a pageant whose acts are played out thousands of times—about 53,000 times each year, the average number of hawks counted per season. It's a daily drama in fall, from sunrises peppered with sharp-shins to the madness of dozens of hunting Merlins near dusk.

Cape May's is a happy hawkwatch, a celebratory and welcoming one, with Cape May Bird Observatory interpretive naturalists on hand to help with identification, provide information, answer questions, or maybe just listen to your birding hopes and dreams. It hasn't always been like this, however. Everything grows and has its roots somewhere in the past, but the momentum, the magnitude of Cape May birds and birding in the present sometimes makes it difficult to remember the depth of the past.

The "official" Cape May Hawkwatch, begun by New Jersey Audubon Society's CMBO on September 1, 1976, has now been running for thirty years. But few birders today remember that the first Cape May count was actually conducted in 1931 by George Saunders of the National Audubon Society, followed in 1932 by Robert P. Allen, a noted ornithologist and writer. These early counts were done as an adjunct to warden duties, in an attempt to silence the guns of autumn—the hawk slaughter that occurred each year as local sportsmen tried not only to make the world safe for songbirds but also to fill the dinner table. The early counts ran until 1937, and the official counters have included James Tanner, of Ivory-billed Woodpecker fame, and a young Roger Tory Peterson, counting at Cape May just a year after the publication of his monumental *Field Guide to the Birds*. Peterson would subsequently return to grace the Cape, and the hawkwatch, many times.

I'm not ancient enough to remember any of that, but I do recall Cape May before the CMBO—a park with no vestige of an "official" hawk count or hawkwatch platform. Cape May Point State Park is a former World War II naval base, and today the omnipresent "bunker" on the beach—a former gun emplacement to protect the entrance to Delaware Bay—is one of the few hints of its military history. My earliest memories of the park are of a mostly abandoned place.

Pete Dunne was the first CMBO counter. He "came down from the mountain," fresh from hawk-counting duties at both Hawk Mountain, Pennsylvania, and Raccoon Ridge, New Jersey, to conduct the first of the modern-day tallies. His first "platform" was a mere concrete pad, the floor of a recently demolished navy building, but he soon appropriated an out-of-season lifeguard's stand for a better view. The rest, as they say, is history. But history should record that today's plush hawkwatch platform is actually the third to have stood on that spot. Each platform that the state park gamely built soon became obsolete due to the growing fame and crowds of Cape May. None was big enough—although today's platform should last a few decades, or at least as long as the hurricanes hold off and the hawks hold out.

Even with this long and solid history, it sometimes seems as if the succession of hawkwatches, culminating in today's bustling operation, appeared as if by magic, in the blink of an eye. It sometimes seems as if the hawks appeared by magic too, that their abundance today is the result of some supernatural power over natural forces. I recently had cause to pull out some of my earliest field notes, looking for some baseline data for a current study of raptor use of South Jersey's river systems. But going back to the beginning (for me), my earliest field notes, was cause for pause (and a couple glasses of wine).

We are all well aware of the ravages of DDT and the near-miraculous recovery of raptors from the dark days of the 1960s and 1970s. But it was sobering to remember, through the looking glass of my early field notes, that I spent two full years hawkwatching at Cape May (1974 and 1975) without seeing a single Bald Eagle. Of course, I wasn't there full time, but it wasn't until November 21, 1976, that I saw my first migrant Bald Eagle at Cape May—a juvenile riding a northwest gale high over the Beanery. Today, Bald Eagles are seen every day, with a high seasonal count of 284 in 1996. The daily high count is 24 (also in 1996), a number that exceeds each seasonal total for the first eight years of the count (balds bottomed at 6 in 1979 at Cape May). It's a well-known story, but for one who saw them dwindle to nearly nothing, the comeback of Bald Eagles seems like nothing short of a miracle.

Similar was the plight of the Peregrine Falcon. Migrant peregrines bottomed at 60 at Cape May in 1977. In 1997, though, 1,793 were counted—another great comeback that seems to be rooted in legerdemain. In 1977 Pete Dunne's count of 60 peregrines was doubted, even questioned in print by one armchair cynic; today, on peak days, 60 are sometimes seen in one hour's counting. Our modern-day daily high count was 298 on October 5, 2002. If you had predicted any such nonsense back in 1976, people would have called you crazy, and that only magic could produce such numbers.

I clearly remember the first day of the first CMBO count on September 1, 1976. Pete Dunne was the new, wet-behind-the-ears counter; I was an environmental planner and water-quality technician taking surf samples on the Cape May Point beach. The peregrine flew right over both of us, on a direct line for Delaware, but we were about a quarter mile apart, separated by houses and dunes. I'll never forget how relieved we both felt when we later compared notes. Peregrines were so rare that this corroboration for this "early" date record was vital, lest we be accused of overexuberance by our sometimes skeptical elders.

But the sleight of hand has worked both ways. In the "now you see it, now you don't" way of a magician, some birds have disappeared just as mysteriously as others have reappeared. The American Kestrel is a species that has declined sharply as a migrant at Cape May and has all but vanished as a breeding and a wintering bird. A seasonal high count of 21,821 kestrels was tallied in 1981, but in 2001 and 2002, counters barely broke 5,000—a precipitous decline. But to really put the kestrel count in perspective, we must remember a hawk count done at Cape May in 1970 by the New Jersey State Museum (a one-year effort only), when an amazing 24,875 American Kestrels were counted in a *single day*. This massive push was precipitated by the "perfect storm" of a cold front following several weeks of rain and stalled fronts. It takes such a historical perspective to realize the degree to which kestrels have diminished; their numbers today are just a trace of their former abundance. This ominous slide is hard to pin on any single cause, with the possibilities including ongoing declines of the kestrel's insect, mammal, and songbird prey base, plus loss and deterioration of its open-country breeding habitats.

One curious aspect of the ebb and flow of Cape May's birds is how some birders seem to find it easier to discredit former numbers than to respect them and confront the reality of the crash. The 24,875 kestrels are now the subject of raised eyebrows, questioned by some because the count technique differed or because some extrapolation was used (Al Nicholson and Ernie Choate were the 1970 counters, and the count seems sound to me). But the point is, or should be, that even though it's an imperfect number, there were a heck of a lot of kestrels that day—a flight of a magnitude not even dreamed of today.

Pete Dunne's early Sharp-shinned Hawk counts are also suspect in the eyes of a few new birders—those who just can't grasp the abundance of old when compared with today's more modest numbers. But I vividly remember in the late 1970s counting over 900 sharp-shins in sight *at once* over the tree line north of the platform—numbers not even hinted at in the past decade. Some consolation is that sharp-shins may not be in the same sort of trouble as the kestrels are. Their decline may be cyclical, and no doubt partly related to short-stopping at northeastern bird feeders.

Magic is predicated on believing—or not—and a magician's act would be useless without a skeptical public, an audience trying to catch him in the act. At Cape May, some of the mysteriously disappearing birds have been historical records of rarities. A healthy, demanding (if not outright skeptical) records committee is important to any birding community, and a strong ornithological record is of paramount importance. It is one of the things that has made Cape May great. It is curious, though, how some key Cape May bird records have now seemingly vanished, as if by the wave of a magician's wand. Some birds have been stricken from the official record, even though they were overwhelmingly accepted by the authorities in charge at the time. The 1979 sight record of Common (Eurasian) Kestrel (a pen-and-ink drawing) even graced the cover of CMBO's journal *Peregrine Observer*, yet today it is gone from the record, not meeting the current stringent standards of the New Jersey Bird Records Committee. The processes of ornithological history are no different from the recording and reanalysis of any historical event, yet I am baffled by how some records have disappeared without a trace, without even a footnote or an asterisk. I'm a great believer in the asterisk (as the reader might guess from the "Hypotheticals" section), and hope that perhaps someday these birds magically reappear.

Another aspect of the ebb and flow of Cape May raptors has been the "standardization" of the season. It may not be from the waving of a magic wand but from the pressing of the "delete" key, that we have lost many birds too. In the early days of the CMBO count, every hawk mattered—from the first dispersing kestrels of early August to the last, late Christmas-week Rough-legged Hawk. Today, the count period begins on September 1 and ends on November 30—period. I know that the relatively few preseason or postseason birds are statistically, scientifically, irrelevant. But I fondly remember some magical early-season days when the Mississippi Kites were circling with broadwings in the hot August haze; and I recall some fine redtail flights punctuated by vibrant adult red-shoulders and Golden Eagles in mid-December. I know these records no longer "count," but the birds were certainly memorable, and I sure miss counting them. Some of the volunteer counters who suffered through the heat and sunburn of the August vigil and nearly froze in December probably miss them too. Of interest, one recent year, both southbound Swallow-tailed and Mississippi Kites were seen on August 15 but didn't even rate a footnote in the season's hawk report. Maybe I'm just too old-fashioned, but in the old days, we would have killed for those birds.

More than birds have disappeared and reappeared at Cape May over the years. The ebb and flow has occurred on other fronts, too. Change has inevitably occurred in physical places. Many former birding hotspots have completely disappeared and been paved over (an issue so immense as to have driven the entire ornithological history of Cape May). Other sites have magically appeared, balancing the endless ledger of good versus evil, with gains of open spaces overcoming losses.

The comings and goings have occurred with people too, and with the same finality as with the loss of open space. There have been, over the past thirty years, several million visitors to the Cape May Hawkwatch (indeed, many thousands each year), but a few stalwart regulars will always remain in my memory, even if they are now gone forever. The late Harold Axtell was a regular at Cape May for many years, and we all learned so much from this great ornithologist. In my impatient youth, his lengthy lectures were exciting but sometimes, in the heat of the hawk flight, interminable. Today, I'd give anything to listen again to just one of his insightful and stirring stories.

The hawkwatch isn't the same today without the late Walter Fritton, a wonderful man who was perhaps the quintessential hawkwatcher, a retired

New York City fireman who migrated to Cape May every year for his fix of "shaaapies" and peregrines. So too, I wait in vain for Fred Mears, the friendly birding ambassador, to amble up onto the platform, the number of his flannel shirt layers foretelling the strength of the cold front. People have been an integral, inseparable part of Cape May magic, and I miss some of them far more than any lost sites or birds.

Though not necessarily a matter of smoke and mirrors, some aspects of Cape May—people, places, and birds—have been so fleeting that now, thirty years down the road, I sometimes wonder, "Did I really see that?" If not pure magic, there were certainly some magical moments. I have been highly privileged to have spent my whole life at Cape May, and I have many wonderful memories of its history, birds, and people. The only problem with the perspective of time (notice I didn't say age) is that some of those memories have become, if not fleeting, somewhat vague—akin to those hot, hazy, seashore summer scenes at Cape May. Yet some days, when the winds are just right, with a flood tide of hawks barreling down the tree line, the memories are crystalline—like the crisp, blue skies of a belting late-October cold front. It is on these days that I still fancifully see yesterday's kestrels mixing with today's peregrines, the sharpies of the old days an attendant retinue around a kettle of Bald Eagles. If you watch long enough and hard enough and with just the right faith in magic, there will always be a veritable sky full of hawks.

And it is on these special days, when the light is just right, that I sometimes think I see Harold Axtell reappear at the end of the hawkwatch platform, smiling, in animated conversation with someone. Why it's Roger Tory Peterson. They're talking about, I think, the most reliable field marks for Cooper's versus Sharp-shinned Hawks. And on the bench over by the pavilion, there's Fred chatting with Walter, reminiscing about the last huge cold front or excitedly predicting the next. And that nattily dressed gentleman in the wide-brimmed hat over at the edge of Bunker Pond—the one smiling and following a flock of Glossy Ibis with his blunderbuss binoculars. He looks just like Witmer Stone.

All are enjoying the enchantment of a fine day at Cape May. A steady stream of fleet and feisty Merlins race by. The Merlins must all be magicians, for they have created a truly magical place indeed.

—C. S.

For More Information

CAPE MAY ON THE WEB
www.capemaytimes.com
www.discovercapemay.com
www.capemaychamber.com/

CAPE MAY BIRD OBSERVATORY (CMBO)
CMBO has two centers:

> Northwood Center
> 701 East Lake Drive
> Cape May Point, NJ 08212
> 609-884-2736
> cmbo1@njaudubon.org

> Center for Research and Education
> 600 Route 47 North (in Goshen)
> Cape May Court House, NJ 08210
> 609-861-0700
> cmbo2@njaudubon.org

www.njaudubon.org/Centers/CMBO/
> *CMBO offers naturalist-led, weekly walks that meet at many of the sites in this book, birding events at peak season (World Series of Birding, Cape May Spring Weekend, Cape May Autumn Weekend/THE Bird Show), and one- to three-day Cape May Birding Workshops.*

www.njaudubon.org/Research/
> *To learn of Avalon Seawatch, Cape May Hawkwatch, Morning Flight, Monarch Monitoring Project, radar studies, and more.*

www.njaudubon.org/Tools.Net/Sightings/CapeMay.aspx
> *The Cape May Birding Hotline (609-898-BIRD/2473) is updated each week and can help you prepare for a visit, including archived hotlines from past years.*

www.njaudubon.org/research/records.html
> *New Jersey Birds includes seasonal bird records and articles of interest. It can now be accessed on NJ Audubon's website.*

www.njaudubon.org/Conservation/HSCrabAlert.html
> *To learn of (and help with) New Jersey Audubon Society's ongoing conservation efforts to protect Delaware Bay shorebirds and horseshoe crabs.*

NEW JERSEY AUDUBON SOCIETY
NJAS has 10 centers in New Jersey, including CMBO's two centers
www.njaudubon.org/Centers/Index.html

Nature Center of Cape May
1600 Delaware Avenue
Cape May, NJ 08204
609-898-8848
nccm@njaudubon.org
www.njaudubon.org/centers/nccm

Sandy Hook Bird Observatory
20 Hartshorne Drive
P.O. Box 553
Fort Hancock, NJ 07732
732-872-2500
shbo@njaudubon.org
www.njaudubon.org/Centers/SHBO

THE WETLANDS INSTITUTE
1075 Stone Harbor Boulevard
Stone Harbor, NJ 08247
609-368-1211
education@wetlandsinstitute.org
www.wetlandsinstitute.org
> *Details educational programs for all ages and the September Wings and Water Festival.*

THE NATURE CONSERVANCY
DELAWARE BAYSHORES CENTER
2350 Route 47
Delmont, NJ 08314
609-861-0600
www.nature.org/wherewework/northamerica/states/newjersey
Details events and preserves.

WEATHER AND BIRD MIGRATION
www.woodcreeper.com/
www.rap.ucar.edu/weather/radar/
NEXRAD radar images (for migration)

NATIONAL WILDLIFE REFUGES (NWR)
managed by U.S. Fish and Wildlife Service

Cape May NWR
24 Kimbles Beach Road
Cape May Court House, NJ 08210
609-463-0994
capemay@fws.gov
www.fws.gov/northeast/capemay

Edwin B. Forsythe NWR (formerly known as Brigantine NWR)
Great Creek Road
Oceanville, NJ 08231
609-652-1665
forsythe@fws.gov
www.fws.gov/northeast/forsythe/

Bombay Hook NWR
2591 Whitehall Neck Road
Smyrna, Delaware 19977
302-653-6872
www.fws.gov/northeast/bombayhook/

WILDLIFE MANAGEMENT AREAS (WMA)
managed by New Jersey Division of Fish and Wildlife
http://www.state.nj.us/dep/fgw/wmaland.htm
- Higbee Beach WMA
- Villas WMA
- Beaver Swamp WMA
- Tuckahoe WMA

- Malibu Beach WMA (Longport Sod Banks)
- Lizard Tail Swamp Preserve
- Heislerville WMA
- Peaslee WMA
- Millville (Bevan) WMA
- Great Bay Boulevard WMA
- Stafford Forge WMA
- Dix WMA
- Salem River WMA

HUNTING SEASONS & REGULATIONS
ON PUBLIC LANDS (WMAS, STATE FORESTS, ETC.)
http://www.nj.gov/dep/fgw/

THREATENED AND ENDANGERED SPECIES
New Jersey Division of Fish and Wildlife
Nongame and Endangered Species Program
www.state.nj.us/dep/fgw/ensphome.htm
> *Site includes statewide reports on beach nesting birds (Black Skimmer, Least Tern, and Piping Plover), Osprey, Bald Eagle, Delaware Bay shorebirds each spring, and other rare, threatened, and endangered species. Extensive information about ENSP's South American expeditions (Red Knot wintering sites) and Arctic searches (Red Knot breeding sites) can be found on this site.*

STATE PARKS AND FORESTS
managed by New Jersey Division of Parks and Forestry
http://www.state.nj.us/dep/parksandforests/parks/

Cape May Point State Park
P.O. Box 107
Cape May Point, NJ 08212
609-884-2159
www.state.nj.us/dep/parksandforests/parks/capemay.html

Belleplain State Forest
County Route 550
P.O. Box 450
Woodbine, NJ 08270
609-861-2404
http://www.state.nj.us/dep/parksandforests/parks/belle.html

Corson's Inlet State Park
c/o Belleplain State Forest
609–861–2404
www.state.nj.us/dep/parksandforests/parks/corsons.html

Barnegat Lighthouse State Park
P.O. Box 167
Barnegat Light, NJ 08006
609–494–2016
http://www.state.nj.us/dep/parksandforests/parks/barnlig.html

Island Beach State Park
P.O. Box 37
Seaside Park, NJ 08752
732–793–0506
www.state.nj.us/dep/parksandforests/parks/island.html

Bass River State Forest
762 Stage Rd
Tuckerton, NJ 08087
609–296–1114
http://www.state.nj.us/dep/parksandforests/parks/bass.html

Wharton State Forest
4110 Nesco Road
Hammonton, NJ 08037
Batsto Office: (609) 561–0024
Atsion Office: (609) 268–0444
http://www.state.nj.us/dep/parksandforests/parks/wharton.html

Brendon T. Byrne State Forest (formerly Lebanon State Forest)
P.O. Box 215
New Lisbon, NJ 08064
609–726–1191
http://www.state.nj.us/dep/parksandforests/parks/byrne.html

Worthington State Forest
HC 62, Box 2
Columbia, NJ 07832
908–841–9575
www.state.nj.us/dep/parksandforests/parks/worthington.html

ADDITIONAL CONTACTS
IN CAPE MAY/CAPE MAY COUNTY AREA:
Back Bay Boat Cruises
aboard *The Skimmer*
with Wildlife Unlimited
Miss Chris Marina
Cape May, NJ 08204
609-884-3100
www.skimmer.com
> *The original "Back Bay Safari."*

Aqua Trails (Kayak tours and rentals)
based at the Nature Center of Cape May
1600 Delaware Ave
Cape May, NJ 08204
http://www.aquatrails.com/
609-884-5600

See Life Paulagics
Paul Guris
P.O. Box 161
Green Lane, PA 18054
215-234-6805
info@paulagics.com
> *To learn of pelagic trip opportunities in New Jersey and beyond.*

Cape May Raptor Banding Project, Inc.
12725 Crystal Lake Ct.
Manassas, VA 20112

Historic Cold Spring Village
720 Route 9
Cape May, NJ 08204
609-898-2300
www.hcsv.org
> *Entrance fee. Seasonally open.*

Mid-Atlantic Center for the Arts
Emlen Physick Estate
1048 Washington Street
Cape May, NJ 08204
800-275-4278
www.capemaymac.org

Hereford Inlet Lighthouse
First and Central Avenues
North Wildwood, NJ 08260
609-522-4520
www.herefordlighthouse.org

CHRISTMAS BIRD COUNT COMPILERS
http://www.audubon.org/bird/cbc/
Cape May CBC, Belleplain CBC, Cumberland CBC, Marmora CBC,
Oceanville CBC

ADDITIONAL CONTACTS IN
ATLANTIC COUNTY AND BEYOND
Estell Manor Park
(part of the Atlantic County Park System)
109 State Highway 50
Mays Landing, NJ 08330
609-645-5960
www.aclink.org/parks

Great Egg Harbor Watershed Association
www.gehwa.org
> *Under "Newsletter" read the results of the regular GEHR bird surveys
> and ongoing research*

Atlantic Audubon Society
(a chapter of National Audubon Society)
PO Box 63
Absecon, NJ 08201
609-272-9656
www.freewebs.com/atlanticaudubonsociety/

New Jersey Conservation Foundation
Bamboo Brook
170 Longview Rd.
Far Hills, NJ 07931
908-234-1225
info@njconservation.org
http://www.njconservation.org/html/gfa-pinebarrens.htm
> *The website shares maps of their Franklin Parker Preserve in the heart of
> the Pine Barrens.*

ADDITIONAL CONTACTS IN CUMBERLAND COUNTY

Public Service Electric and Gas (PSEG)
Estuary Enhancement Program
http://www.pseg.com/environment/estuary/
> *Available on the website (by clicking on "public recreation") are excellent maps to PSEG wetland restoration sites with public access: (1) Commercial Township (Port Norris & Bivalve), (2) Dennis Township (Eldora), (3)Maurice River Township (Heislerville), and others.*

Citizens United to Protect the Maurice River and its Tributaries, Inc.
P.O. Box 474
Millville, NJ 08332
www.cumauriceriver.org
> *Details findings of long-term field work and bird research on the river.*

Natural Lands Trust, Inc.
Harold Peek Preserve
2100 S. 2nd Street
Millville, NJ 08332
856-825-9952
www.natlands.org
> *Details activities at their Delaware Bayshore preserves: Glades Wildlife Preserve, Peek Preserve, Bear Swamp, and others.*

Bayshore Discovery Project
2800 High Street, Bivalve
Port Norris, NJ 08349
856-785-2060
info@bayshorediscoveryproject.org
www.ajmeerwald.org
> *Details educational efforts and the schedule for the A.J. Meerwald, New Jersey's official tall ship.*

Purple Martin Spectacular
Linda Costello at Maurice River Township Hall, 856-785-1120, x-10
> *mid-August event/festival on Maurice River*

Cumberland County Winter Eagle Festival
> *Early February event based at the Mauricetown Firehall, including exhibitors, artists, vendors, presentations, food, and outdoor sites manned by naturalists. For all information, contact Cumberland County's Planning and Development Office at 856-453-2177 or (866) 866-MORE.*

Delaware Valley Ornithological Club
c/o Academy of Natural Sciences
1900 Benjamin Franklin Parkway
Philadelphia, PA 19103
www.dvoc.org
> *Details activities, sightings, bird lists, and much more. DVOC sponsored Witmer Stone's landmark Bird Studies at Old Cape May.*

INJURED BIRDS/REHABILITATION CENTER
Tri-State Bird Rescue
110 Possum Hollow Road
Newark, DE 19711
302-737-9543 (answered from 9 am – 5 pm EST daily)
http://www.tristatebird.org/

INJURED MARINE MAMMALS
Marine Mammal Stranding Center
3625 Atlantic Brigantine Blvd
Brigantine, NJ
609-266-0538
www.marinemammalstrandingcenter.org

CONSERVATION OFFICER
24-hour toll-free number for reporting environmental complaints and abuses, including harassment of shorebirds in spring on the Delaware Bayshore: 1-877-927-6337 or 1-877-WARN-DEP.

CAPE MAY IN PRINT
New Jersey Atlas & Gazetteer, DeLorme. Book of 56 quadrangular state maps covering the entire state and 11 pages of city maps.
The Birds of Cape May, by David Sibley. 1997. Published by Cape May Bird Observatory. Species accounts and bar graphs covering seasonal abundance patterns of each species for the entire county.
Birds of New Jersey, by Joan Walsh, Vince Elia, Rich Kane, and Thomas Halliwell. 1999. Published by Cape May Bird Observatory/New Jersey Audubon Society. This book is the product of a 6-year NJ Audubon research project and includes a breeding bird atlas (210 breeding birds mapped) as well as information on wintering and migrant status for each of the birds known to New Jersey, plus information on New Jersey's rarities (443 species accounts).
Season At The Point: The Birds and Birders of Cape May, by Jack Connor. 1991. The Atlantic Monthly Press. Factual yet evocative saga of one

season's hawk watch and hawk banding at Cape May Point. An introduction to the people and places you may encounter upon visiting Cape May.

Birding Cumberland, a Birder's Guide to Cumberland County, NJ, by Clay Sutton. 2003, Published by Cumberland County, NJ, Department of Planning and Development and Citizens United to Protect the Maurice River and its Tributaries.

New Jersey Birding & Wildlife Trails (Delaware Bayshore: Salem, Cumberland, and Cape May Counties). 2006. This publication was funded by the NJ Department of Transportation, and was created by the New Jersey Audubon Society with assistance from the New Jersey Department of Transportation, Department of Environmental Protection, and the Office of Travel and Tourism. Available (for FREE) at all NJ Audubon centers (including CMBO's two centers). An excellent resource for birding the Delaware Bayshore.

A Guide to Bird Finding in New Jersey, by William J. Boyle, Jr. 2002 (2nd Edition). Published by Rutgers University Press.

Wild Journeys, Migration in New Jersey, by Brian Vernachio, Don Freiday, and Dale Rosselet. 2003. Published by New Jersey Audubon Society. This educational book focuses on the key role New Jersey plays in the lives of the many animals that migrate.

How Birds Migrate, by Paul Kerlinger. 1995. Stackpole Books. An excellent primer on migration, this classic work offers numerous Cape May examples and case studies.

Bird Studies at Old Cape May, by Witmer Stone. 1937. Stackpole Books reprinted this classic two-volume work as one volume in 2000. A fascinating read about the early ornithology of coastal New Jersey; much of it remains remarkably applicable today.

RECENT HAWK COUNTS AT CAPE MAY

	1994	1995	1996	1997	1998
Black Vulture	110	192	161	370	265
Turkey Vulture	2,260	3,230	6,420	5,221	4,282
Osprey	3,257	5,373	6,734	4,631	3,054
Bald Eagle	144	135	284	226	139
Northern Harrier	3,115	2,376	1,860	2,324	2,169
Sharp-shinned Hawk	26,509	26,397	30,741	48,992	22,993
Cooper's Hawk	3,330	5,009	4,742	4,920	3,055
Northern Goshawk	37	54	38	89	15
Red-shouldered Hawk	872	450	572	672	346
Broad-winged Hawk	8,269	1,385	2,844	1,605	1,670
Swainson's Hawk	6	3	4	2	10
Red-tailed Hawk	3,901	3,825	5,135	3,528	2,779
Rough-legged Hawk	2	1	5	0	3
Golden Eagle	12	26	38	18	9
American Kestrel	15,426	8,488	8,044	8,038	7,469
Merlin	2,840	2,065	2,111	2,427	2,040
Peregrine Falcon	741	1,099	1,503	1,793	964
Other			1		2
Total	70,831	60,108	71,237	84,856	51,264

Data courtesy of Cape May Bird Observatory/New Jersey Audubon Society.

1999	2000	2001	2002	2003	2004	2005
190	116	104	150	197	126	345
2,183	776	1,051	1,215	1,241	1,218	3,130
2,557	1,904	1,645	2,038	1,975	1,912	2,446
168	131	229	182	178	210	262
2,028	743	1,203	1,254	2,421	843	1,219
24,625	15,663	12,927	17,165	20,665	14,002	15,305
3,676	2,613	1,874	3,503	4,260	5,037	5,829
69	12	28	28	7	52	23
411	232	343	483	605	573	699
1,234	1,905	1,229	452	1,926	567	580
1	0	1	1	4	2	3
3,484	1,162	1,049	921	1,258	1,948	2,327
13	1	0	2	6	0	1
22	10	10	11	9	11	12
12,600	6,393	5,188	5,405	7,345	2,675	6,163
2,823	1,086	1,380	1,309	1,920	1,543	1,775
833	988	588	1,051	1,024	1,017	1,164
	1		84	155	68	
56,917	33,736	28,849	35,254	45,196	31,804	41,283

AVALON SEAWATCH COUNT 1993–2004
September 22 to December 22

SPECIES	1993	1994	1995	1996	1997
Snow Goose	1,914	5,847	17,146	10,147	5,290
Brant	9,253	11,929	14,552	12,987	16,558
Canada Goose	1,379	12,206	6,979	6,144	6,817
Mute Swan	1	1	12	2	9
Tundra Swan	198	116	146	241	257
Wood Duck	700	831	1,303	984	660
Gadwall	27	3	53	1	25
Am. Wigeon	280	344	1,037	418	284
Am. Black Duck	1,242	2,606	4,422	3,914	2,609
Mallard	322	353	494	312	304
Blue-winged Teal	18	31	84	25	29
Northern Shoveler	31	15	27	25	25
Northern Pintail	694	1,000	2,238	413	584
Green-winged Teal	4,747	7,418	7,995	8,423	3,698
unidentified teal	99	0	12	59	314
Canvasback	5	3	31	3	17
Redhead	7	4	50	8	2
Ring-necked Duck	130	350	104	118	52
Greater Scaup	356	450	872	884	409
Lesser Scaup	538	224	1,355	1,022	455
unidentified scaup	1,644	2,102	3,306	1,773	2,674
King Eider	4	3	12	5	21
Common Eider	12	21	64	106	51
unidentified eider	5	4	9	3	6
Harlequin Duck	9	3	1	1	4
Surf Scoter	64,050	88,492	191,804	182,965	95,415
White-winged Scoter	2,656	3,526	6,126	3,358	4,838
Black Scoter	43,571	56,053	156,005	118,773	119,062
dark-winged (Surf/Black) scoter	47,407	73,135	95,347	160,828	112,909
unidentified scoter	43,030	10,321	1,269	7,504	14,951
Total Scoter	200,714	231,527	450,551	473,428	347,175
Long-tailed Duck	3,051	1,854	3,941	4,159	3,732
Bufflehead	821	1,171	1,350	2,428	1,113

1998	1999	2000	2001	2002	2003	2004
3,250	4,051	10,266	8,252	3,745	4,717	812
8,663	6,494	6,881	7,380	6,445	8,396	5,123
11,864	13,558	2,920	5,255	2,992	8,297	542
14	19	0	0	0	1	0
601	172	127	9	136	57	96
642	757	557	685	580	837	381
14	15	48	44	72	66	22
272	637	374	275	383	270	128
3,172	2,903	2,711	1,563	2,302	2,007	1,277
124	264	318	172	344	223	130
20	77	10	14	6	78	5
22	25	15	8	55	33	6
2,028	694	635	1,528	985	1,865	378
10,729	11,024	7,612	5,483	4,901	9,943	5,399
0	0	126	3	13	0	1
0	2	8	3	1	3	2
6	33	34	4	8	2	1
43	87	99	108	263	112	35
758	1,125	821	642	2,129	2,706	1,058
573	826	546	311	474	1,064	353
3,667	666	470	281	727	1,393	752
4	2	0	2	9	4	2
16	12	14	23	46	173	56
8	0	0	1	0	0	0
6	4	8	1	3	13	6
126,539	208,857	157,123	144,436	150,108	212,008	117,249
5,286	2,943	1,877	2,205	2,036	1,805	2,067
133,337	256,633	134,872	128,669	111,657	153,369	103,525
132,928	36,895	47,041	55,934	88,632	43,901	66,104
125	13,381	20,923	2,590	569	114	5,483
398,215	518,709	361,836	333,834	353,002	411,197	294,428
1,436	2,102	1,250	968	1,976	3,033	1,807
2,260	1,548	1,344	553	1,235	1,364	568

SPECIES	1993	1994	1995	1996	1997
Common Goldeneye	214	179	290	180	210
Hooded Merganser	104	126	371	212	313
Common Merganser	1	10	12	3	9
Red-br Merganser	4,212	3,966	5,577	4,297	4,818
Ruddy Duck	3	13	41	67	61
Red-throated Loon	53,206	53,865	58,881	55,175	65,994
Common Loon	3,231	4,778	4,818	5,026	4,021
unidentified loon	900	264	109	65	253
Pied-billed Grebe	0	1	0	0	1
Horned Grebe	98	141	371	295	388
Red-necked Grebe	9	5	9	15	12
Northern Gannet	24,843	63,498	53,019	49,791	53,387
Brown Pelican	92	76	153	44	130
Double-cr Cormorant	146,387	165,991	209,283	240,670	186,510
Great Cormorant	145	61	108	61	59
American Bittern	0	2	0	0	2
Great Blue Heron	1,026	1,248	1,283	1,376	551
Great Egret	167	175	607	546	354
Snowy Egret	55	318	484	487	319
Little Blue Heron	0	16	83	201	1
Tricolored Heron	0	15	24	7	3
Cattle Egret	0	1	1	0	0
Green Heron	0	0	0	0	0
Black-cr. Night-Heron	1	0	26	121	54
Yellow-cr Night-Heron	0	0	3	3	0
Glossy Ibis	5	0	3	28	12
Common Moorhen	0	1	0	0	0
American Coot	0	2	0	0	2
Pomarine Jaeger	2	3	2	2	1
Parasitic Jaeger	54	146	148	150	224
unidentified jaeger	15	15	5	15	12
Laughing Gull	4,450	10,606	25,487	16,623	9,506
Franklin's Gull	0	0	1	1	0
Little Gull	6	0	3	3	2
Black-headed Gull	0	1	0	2	0
Bonaparte's Gull	3,298	5,061	8,647	6,815	5,998
Ring-billed Gull	12,415	5,565	29,376	23,349	7,143

1998	1999	2000	2001	2002	2003	2004
64	86	215	48	73	151	66
154	76	218	81	128	185	26
3	5	0	2	1	2	0
6,439	4,452	2,523	1,879	3,517	3,995	1,755
20	72	19	60	2	2	4
72,158	38,405	63,558	73,704	54,210	49,294	51,645
5,066	2,599	4,134	3,648	1,815	2,591	1,655
40	1	0	27	0	9	29
1	1	0	0	0	2	0
226	140	63	42	63	81	42
10	3	6	4	3	4	1
76,963	58,726	49,101	30,960	38,951	38,990	34,125
93	96	302	137	242	334	354
179,760	154,358	221,525	169,144	195,473	232,661	157,179
64	94	69	67	101	150	67
0	1	0	1	0	6	0
441	549	550	761	760	1,533	552
215	307	389	717	822	222	203
294	323	86	64	13	243	128
9	2	44	53	41	3	10
0	7	13	27	23	3	3
0	0	0	0	0	0	0
0	1	1	0	0	0	0
0	14	53	35	114	16	17
0	0	0	0	0	0	0
4	3	29	17	4	3	19
0	0	0	0	0	0	0
2	0	0	0	0	0	0
2	4	1	2	1	2	0
135	189	161	162	153	228	120
5	2	9	6	3	2	0
29,380	21,031	33,222	13,742	11,596	20,718	6,513
43	1	0	0	0	0	0
0	5	0	0	1	1	2
0	0	2	0	0	0	0
4,195	2,891	5,324	293	4,088	5,986	5,142
12,871	14,272	8,991	4,990	5,346	25,177	5,327

SPECIES	1993	1994	1995	1996	1997
Herring Gull	1,336	1,203	15,025	24,363	3,508
Iceland Gull	0	2	2	1	1
Lesser Bl-backed Gull	0	1	7	1	2
Great Bl-backed Gull	154	251	2,490	910	454
Bl-legged Kittiwake	8	6	2	201	34
Caspian Tern	31	38	96	55	14
Royal Tern	599	1,728	1,875	2,631	742
Sandwich Tern	0	0	0	0	0
Common Tern	113	1,159	195	2,083	2,803
Forster's Tern	1,959	4,160	14,372	12,167	6,140
Least Tern	0	1	2	0	0
Black Tern	0	0	0	0	0
Black Skimmer	8	174	179	119	169
Dovekie	0	0	2	1	0
Razorbill	13	1	7	5	4
unidentified alcid	10	3	9	3	1
rarities		4	6	11	2
GRAND TOTAL	**487,371**	**605,296**	**951,640**	**976,214**	**747,398**

Data courtesy of Cape May Bird Observatory/New Jersey Audobon Society.

RARITIES

Gr. White–fronted Goose (1 in 1997, 2003), Ross's Goose (1 in 1994, 1999), "Black Brant" (1 in 1994), Pacific Loon (1 in 1999, 2004), Eared Grebe (1 in 1994, 1995), Northern Fulmar (1 in 1996, 1999), Cory's Shearwater (1 in 1995), Sooty Shearwater (1 in 1997), Manx Shearwater (2 in 2003), Wilson's Storm-Petrel (2 in 2003), storm-petrel sp. (1 in 1998, 2003), Am.

1998	1999	2000	2001	2002	2003	2004
8,265	35,169	4,697	2,158	3,980	6,452	2,875
3	0	2	0	2	0	0
3	4	3	2	5	18	1
1,557	2,103	752	566	654	1,057	301
7	15	8	1	4	11	7
13	21	5	8	12	39	9
299	825	327	788	508	1,121	196
0	5	0	0	0	14	0
557	618	29	656	897	1,338	163
1,410	5,353	1,856	5,749	3,941	5,894	6,274
0	0	0	0	0	0	0
0	10	0	2	1	1	0
286	245	48	242	255	148	160
0	1	0	1	0	4	0
5	9	0	7	1	9	78
0	4	0	0	3	4	2
1	4	2	1	0	8	3
849,470	**908,908**	**797,367**	**678,256**	**710,639**	**856,566**	**588,421**

White Pelican (1 in 1994, 5 in 1996), White Ibis (1 in 1996), Wood Stork (1 in 2000), Sandhill Crane (2 in 1996), Long-tailed Jaeger (1 in 1995), California Gull (1 in 1995), Glaucous Gull (1 in 1996, 1999, 2001, 2003), Sabine's Gull (1 in 2000), Arctic Tern (1 in 1995), Bridled Tern (1 in 2003), Thick-billed Murre (1 in 2004), Black Guillemot (1 in 1996, 2004), and Atlantic Puffin (1 in 1995).

Hypotheticals

While regional bird checklists are often highly anecdotal, Cape May's is long-running and solid. The keepers of the list, the chroniclers, have done their work well. The "official" Cape May bird checklist, maintained by CMBO now stands at 412 species recorded for the county—one of the top county lists in the country. Only tropical areas such as south Florida, south Texas, southern California, or southeastern Arizona can boast county bird lists similarly high or higher, and usually the counties are much larger! To our knowledge Cape May has the highest county list on the East Coast north of south Florida.

For ease of reader access, the Cape May County Bird Checklist (and the butterfly checklist) are found at the end of this book. Seasonal occurrence is shown, as well as relative abundance and status. The list is current to May 2006 and includes birds found in Cape May County, the waters of Delaware Bay, and offshore to a distance of 50 miles. Rarities follow the main checklist and are divided into "very rare visitors and vagrants" (those species documented more than four times) and "accidentals" (those birds that have been recorded four or fewer times in Cape May County). Only records accepted by the New Jersey Bird Records Committee are shown in this official list. For more detailed information on specific birds, consult *The Birds of Cape May*, by David Sibley (1997), published by and available at CMBO. Visitors are encouraged to report any rarities or out-of-season birds to CMBO.

While this checklist shows only fully-vetted records, a number of other birds have naturally been reported over time at Cape May. The somewhat old-fashioned category of *hypothetical* has drifted out of the vernacular of modern birding, eclipsed by terms such as *accepted* or *not accepted*—those prime categories in use by records committees throughout North America and the world. And these strong categories make for strong ornithological history—a solid list unsullied by reputation, rumor, politics, or even tall tales.

Cape May has always had a strong list. From the documentation in Audubon's journals to the stern taskmaster attitude of Ernie Choate, sightings records had to measure up. Today, a strong and talented New Jersey Bird Records Committee is the keeper of the record, applying tough standards to all reported sightings and the resultant, requisite write-ups. This is the way it should be, so that, as one records committee stalwart succinctly put it, "there is written evidence for folks seventy-five years from now to look back on." It is how history is not only made but also recorded for posterity. Standards regarding the burden of proof have differed widely over time, from the all-telling nod of the elders' heads in Stone's day to the absolute requirement of an unequivocal image by some conservative committees in today's digital world. Suffice it to say that documentation of rare birds today employs the most demanding standards of any time in ornithological history.

One problem that will never be solved is the lack of written evidence for many historical records. Although some groups use a "historical" category, other records committees do not accept these records without adequate documentation. In some cases, highly intriguing and interesting records have therefore been lost, dropping out of the literature over time because they do not warrant inclusion in modern-day, documented, squeaky-clean lists. In some cases, this is unfortunate, and dropping a record that was, for example, fully acceptable to Witmer Stone because the written proof has been lost is a shame.

For these reasons, we reemploy the archaic *hypothetical* category, believing that it is an aptly descriptive term for some old sightings. To *not* list hypotheticals would in many cases be an injustice, for most of these records were based on strong sightings by qualified individuals that were simply never written up or the written records were lost. We believe that most of the listed hypotheticals have in fact occurred in Cape May. Listing hypotheticals is important for historical continuity, to explain, for example, why a bird may be in an older source, but not in the modern *Birds of New Jersey*. But there is a better reason too, or at least a more evocative one. In a certain sense, some of the amazing hypotheticals are an affirmation of and a testament to the magic and mystery of Cape May—that anything is possible and indeed even probable here. Given time, a positive attitude, and maybe a bit of belief in magic (and the right winds), hypothetically, anything can occur at Cape May.

CAPE MAY COUNTY HYPOTHETICAL LIST
(former published records now retracted are in parenthesis)

Black-browed Albatross
   Storm-related sighting from South Cape May
Fea's Petrel
   Hurricane related, Cape May Point

Neotropic Cormorant
Twice as flyovers with Double-crested Cormorants
Reddish Egret
One record in fall
Barrow's Goldeneye
Several old CBC records without existing documentation
Ferruginous Hawk
Several reports have been withdrawn, but one remains solid—a November 28, 1979, record from Jakes Landing
Eurasian Hobby
One sighting from Cape May Point, from the hawkwatch
(Eurasian Sparrowhawk)
It remains a possibility, but the bird was more likely a melanistic Sharp-shinned Hawk
Whooping Crane
Reported in 1812 by Alexander Wilson
European Golden-Plover
Early fall in South Cape May
Common Ringed Plover
Early fall in South Cape May
(Black Oystercatcher)
Widely disregarded—even individuals present at the brief sighting reportedly disagreed with the identification and posited that the bird was no doubt an oiled or muddy American Oystercatcher; no East Coast records
Eskimo Curlew
Two reports: September 20, 1959, at Cape May Coast Guard Station (written up in The Auk*), and September 30, 1960, at South Cape May Meadows; it's inconceivable that the bird didn't occur at Cape May in the 1800s*
Black-tailed Godwit
One spring report from Jenkins Sound
Great Snipe
One of Cape May's most controversial birds; widely disbelieved today, but Alexander Wetmore reportedly saw photos or film of the bird and agreed with the identification
South Polar Skua
At least 3 reports; occurs annually in offshore canyon waters
Mew Gull
Two October reports
California Gull
Two flybys at Avalon Seawatch

Ross's Gull
Avalon Seawatch in December
Black Swift
Hurricane related, South Cape May
(Brown-crested Flycatcher)
History has proved that the bird was more likely an Ash-throated
Flycatcher
Great Kiskadee
CBC record; identification correct, origin questioned
Black-capped Chickadee
Several mini-invasions were recorded on CBCs in the 1950s and 1960s,
but none was ever documented; several recent records exist too
Kirtland's Warbler
Two early fall records at Higbee Beach
Green-tailed Towhee
October report from Higbee Beach
Bachman's Sparrow
Fall record from Hidden Valley
Cassin's Sparrow
Fall record, Rea Farm
Brewer's Sparrow
Fall record, Rea Farm
Bullock's Oriole
At least 10 reports
Pine Grosbeak
Four fall records from Cape Island
Hoary Redpoll
Winter report at Stone Harbor Point

EXTINCT (?)

The question mark does not relate to whether these birds are extinct, only
to whether they actually occurred at Cape May. Although no actual written records or specimens exist, there is compelling evidence that all these
birds probably occurred at Cape May historically.

Labrador Duck
Records from the New Jersey coast
"Heath Hen" (race of Greater Prairie-Chicken)
Records from Atlantic County 15 miles from Cape May County; Belle-
plain had definite, similar heath "pine plains"

Passenger Pigeon
> The "immense flock of wild pigeons" recorded by De Vries at Cape May
> in 1633 were undoubtedly this species

Carolina Parakeet
> Records from eastern Pennsylvania and Albany, New York

Counting Accepted Records (412), Hypothetical Species (28), and
Extinct Birds (4), but not suspected or possible Escapees, the unofficial
Cape May County Bird list logs in at 444 species as of May 2006.

ESCAPEES (?)

Although some birds that have been seen at Cape May are clearly escapees,
exotics that have either escaped or are the progeny of escapees (birds such
as Black Swan, Blue-crowned Parakeet, Monk Parakeet), others are more
problematic—birds that fall into an ornithological gray area. The hypothetical Hobby could have been a falconer's bird, for example. The Black-
billed Magpie found in the girls' bathroom at Wildwood High School was
probably put there, but from where? (There was a Black-billed Magpie at
the Beanery one fall for a considerable period, but it may have been the
released one from Wildwood. This was sometime in the late 1960s, but the
date was never recorded.) In some cases, we'll never know.

For some birds, origin is always suspect—muddying the water for
record keeping. The resident Cumberland County Common Crane is
probably an escapee, but confirmation has been elusive. Although waterfowl species such as Greylag Goose are probably escapees, others pose
problems. The June 9–15, 1997, Garganey at Forsythe NWR is an accepted
record, yet Cape May's late February–early March 1961 Baikal Teal is not.
Both are long-distance migrants and have similar ranges and possible origins. It is an age-old question, with no easy answer.

Cape May birds can pose additional problems. Cape May lies at the
entrance of Delaware Bay, through which dozens of ships—tankers,
freighters, and container ships—enter daily. Many or most are from foreign
ports—Europe, the Middle East, and even Central America. Any has the
potential to carry birds to the Cape. With modern Atlantic crossings possible in four to five days, it's probably surprising that we don't see more
oddities. Ship-borne birds don't count for some listers, but such possibilities
confuse records that would otherwise be easily relegated to escapee status.
The (Eurasian) Sky Lark at Wildwood in May 1977 was possibly carried by
ship, as was the recent Desert Finch at a Woodbine feeder, which conceiva-
bly hitchhiked on an oil tanker from the Middle East. We'll never know,
but it's fun to contemplate.

Although a Bar-headed Goose with Snow Geese in South Cape May was almost certainly an escapee (because there are no acceptable North American records), a skittish, very wild Ruddy Shelduck with Snow Geese in South Cape May in early winter was intriguing in light of recent proven Ruddy Shelduck vagrancy to Nunavut. Finally, although it defies logic (and some readers will die of laughter), we've always been intrigued by an extremely wild, skittish (it flushed the second it saw us about 75 yards away), slim, sleek male Muscovy we startled from a remote Goshen pond in March a few years back. It rocketed away through the treetops, seemingly wilder than most we've seen in Mexico or Venezuela. Muscovy has no discernible pattern of vagrancy, but with feral ones everywhere and a population widely established in Florida, the origin of a wild individual is anyone's guess.

ON CAPE MAY'S BORDERS

A few species have been found in adjacent counties (Cumberland County to the west and Atlantic County to the north) that have not yet been seen in Cape May County. Many or most of these species are either the provenance (or victims) of the Cape May geographic concentration phenomenon or the effect of the massive drawing power of Forsythe NWR. All might be expected in Cape May County airspace at some point in the near or distant future. (Note: Cape May "hypotheticals" that are *confirmed* in surrounding counties are included here.)

Reddish Egret (Atlantic County)
Greater Flamingo (Atlantic County)—hypothetical, escaped?
Barnacle Goose (Atlantic County)—hypothetical, escaped?
Cinnamon Teal (Atlantic County)
Garganey (Atlantic County)
Tufted Duck (Atlantic County)—hypothetical
Masked Duck (Atlantic County)—hypothetical, escaped?
Ivory Gull (Atlantic County)—hypothetical
Pacific Golden Plover (Cumberland County)
Spotted Redshank (Atlantic County and Cumberland County)
Black-tailed Godwit (Atlantic County)
Pacific Slope/Cordilleran Flycatcher (Atlantic County)
Townsend's Solitaire (Cumberland County)
Varied Thrush (Atlantic County)
Sage Thrasher (Atlantic County)
Sprague's Pipit (Atlantic County)—hypothetical
Black-billed Magpie (Atlantic County)
Pine Grosbeak (Cumberland County)

By adding Atlantic County's and cumberland County's additional birds to the Cape May County list, an amazing 462 species have been seen in "Greater Cape May" (extreme southern New Jersey) as of May 2006.

OFF THE WALL

This final category is one that makes records committees everywhere gnash their teeth, or at least roll their eyes and chuckle, but fun stories of odd birds are part of the Cape May lore and lure—stories that hint at the true depth and scope of the mantra that "anything is possible."

Our favorite story is the one Keith Seager tells about a program he gave years ago to a seashore garden club. After the luncheon and Keith's educational slide show about birds of the salt marsh, it was time for questions and answers. A woman raised her hand and asked, "Mr. Seager, I loved all your heron and egret pictures. Could you tell me if there is an egret with a bill that's shaped like a tablespoon?"

"Why yes," Keith replied, "that would be the Roseate Spoonbill."

"Well, I asked," she said, "because there was one behind my house a few weeks ago. It was with other egrets."

"You must live in Florida," Keith surmised.

"No," came the stunning reply, "I live in Avalon."

It may seem off the wall, but it's pretty good proof that a Roseate Spoonbill has occurred in Cape May County.

Another favorite anecdote came by way of Clay's uncle, Frank Sutton Jr. (and it bears mentioning that until he died at age eighty-seven, he was, as they say, sharp as a tack). In about 2000, while he and Clay were talking about birds (a frequent topic), he told Clay, "I know we only have one kingfisher here—the 'regular' kingfisher. But I remember when I was a boy, a little green-colored kingfisher spent most of one summer along the canal [dredged lagoon] in Sea Isle. Now, what bird would that have been?"

When quizzed, he remembered it as half the size of a Belted Kingfisher and that it wasn't turquoise colored but dark green. Although a Green Kingfisher in Cape May County would certainly fit both the off-the-wall category and the escapee one, it's a fun story about a really odd bird that once graced a Cape May waterway.

Everyone has stories about the one that got away, and Cape May has its fair share of those. Early one day at the hawkwatch, an in-depth and lengthy discussion ensued about whether an eagle that had just passed out over Delaware Bay was a bald or a golden. This doesn't happen too often with a bird as well seen as this eagle was, and by as many raptorphiles as there were on the hawkwatch that day. It went back and forth until someone posed a scenario that stopped the lively conversation dead: "Well, I'm convinced it was an *Aquila,* but which *Aquila* is the question." When the conversation restarted, several agreed that we had probably just witnessed one of the (Eurasion) Spotted Eagles. We'll never know. Though crazy and totally improbable, it's a fun record nonetheless, and to us, a great example of what makes Cape May great.

Acknowledgments

In a place such as Cape May, it can be hard to remember just where all one's influences and inspirations came from. This is not in any way meant to imply ingratitude or lack of recognition of all that has been passed down to us. It is simply that, in our thirty years together, working as naturalists here at the Cape, we have had the privilege of meeting and working with many wonderful people—both residents and visitors, seasoned naturalists and beginners alike.

We have learned incalculable lessons from all of them. All our visitors here at Cape May bring so much energy and enthusiasm, as well as varied backgrounds and experiences. Much of our own education, our natural history knowledge, has been learned from them, gleaned from the questions they ask. As George Spencer Morris, one of our great Victorian-era ornithologists said in an 1894 presentation to the venerable Delaware Valley Ornithological Club, "In our attempts to enlighten others, we have learned far more ourselves than we could ever hope to [humbly] teach them." Likewise, much of our love for Cape May has come from the wonder we have seen on the faces of visitors—whether veterans or first-timers. As educators, we have met thousands of people. We may not recognize each and every one individually, but we thank them all deeply.

Our parents and grandparents had a deep influence on our love for the outdoors and natural history. They gave us roots that continue to grow and nourish us, even today, and we lovingly remember Clay and Flora Sutton and George and Mary Taylor, our parents.

Mentoring can be the most important aspect in the passing down of natural history lessons and lore. We deeply thank our own mentors, not only for the lessons they taught us that we could never learn from books but also for their profound influence on how we perceive the natural world—the perception of what is important and what is not. We thank the late Bill Bailey, Al Nicholson, and the late Ed Manners for their tireless, effortless, and lasting guidance, and for caring. We will always cherish those early days afield, the vision, the energy, the dreams, and the pure fun too.

So often in a life afield, lines cross and blend. Mentor becomes friend, friend becomes colleague, coworker becomes teacher. Rather than try to sort it all out, we'll just say that the following folks are all of the above and are our very favorite people to be afield with: Wendy and Dennis Allen, Jack and Jesse Connor, Sheri Williamson and Tom Wood, Jorge Montejo Diaz, Bob Barber, Jane and the late Bill Ruffin, Michael Male and Judy Fieth, David Sibley and Joan Walsh, Jon Sutton, Jim and Dale Watson, Les and Tony Ficcaglia, Jim Dowdell, Louise Zemaitis and Michael O'Brien, and Ward and Diane Dasey. Thank you for sharing your boundless knowledge and for some awesome memories, too.

There are other friends—some near, some far—who may not join us often in the field but are fellow travelers nevertheless. They have all been an inspiration for this book and beyond: Gary Patterson, John Winklemann, Frank Nicoletti, Dave Ward, Sharon Taylor, BJ Pinnock, Pete and Linda Dunne, Paul Kerlinger and Jane Kashlak, Karen Williams and Paul Kosten, Jerry and Sherry Liguori, Else and Wayne Greenstone, Rick Radis, Mark Garland and Paige Cunningham, Brett and Sheryl Ewald, Dave and Kathy Tetlow, Dick Turner, Jeff Bouton, Pete Plage, Robert Michael Pyle, Ken Soltesz, David Wright, Shawneen Finnegan, Chris Vogel, Gail Dwyer, George Myers, Mike Fritz, Virginia Rettig, Katharine Patterson, Jane Morton Galetto, Bob and Linda Carlough, Bruce Luepke, Bob Dittrick and Lisa Moorhead, Victor Emanuel, Andy Wraithmell, Bob Zappalorti, Steve Eisenhauer, Paul and Anita Guris, and Karen and Brian Johnson. We thank you for your support over all the years.

Another tier of friends and colleagues consists of the dozens of birders and naturalists who now live here at Cape May (or almost do). We wish to thank them for all their contributions to both the Cape May Bird Observatory's educational programs and to our own knowledge of Cape May birds. They are way too numerous to list, but they know who they are. We fondly remember the late Sandy Sherman and the late Fred Mears as two very important and irreplaceable members of this group. Fred, by way of his remarkable enthusiasm and selfless teaching, was in many ways a mentor too.

We graciously thank the following people for their specific contributions to *Cape May Birds:* Pete Dunne, Director of the Cape May Bird Observatory (CMBO), for his longtime support and encouragement; David Mizrahi, Vice President of Research, New Jersey Audubon Society, for sharing research findings, data, and figures; Sam Orr for sharing raptor banding information and insights; Kathy Clark for the latest New Jersey Fish and Wildlife updates; Paul Lehman for his input regarding weather patterns, migration, and so much more; Paul Kerlinger for reviewing the migration section; and Michael O'Brien and Louise Zemaitis for both reviewing the draft manuscript and for innumerable pleasant discussions about the dynamics of Cape May migration. We particularly thank Michael O'Brien and Dave Ward for their contributions to the seawatch section. Colleagues David Sibley, Vince Elia, Chris Vogel, Richard Crossley, Bill Clark, and Jim Dowdell have shared many thoughts and insights on Cape May birds and birding over the years. We also thank Gail Dwyer for her terrific efforts (and always smiling face) during innumerable manuscript revisions, and our wonderfully patient editors, Mark Allison and Ken Krawchuk, for their always valuable input and guidance and, more importantly, their vision.

Another special group are the dedicated chroniclers who have documented the ornithological records, and thus the significance of Cape May, over time. We remember those who followed Witmer Stone: the late Dr. Ernie Choate, the late Dave Cutler (longtime regional editor of *American Birds*), Keith Seager, and Rich Kane (longtime editor of *Records of New Jersey Birds* and a titan in New Jersey conservation). In 1976 the CMBO assumed the mantle and, in turn, Pete Dunne, David Sibley, Vince Elia, Tom Halliwell, Bill Boyle, and Paul Lehman have ably maintained the record. Alan Brady and Kevin Karlson have been key keepers of the photographic record. Thanks to all.

We have many to thank for our knowledge of the world beyond birds and the other things that make Cape May sparkle: David Wright for the first checklist of the butterflies of Cape May County in 1989 and for each revision since, Ken Soltesz for the first annotated checklist of the dragonflies and damselflies of Cape May County in 1991, Bob Barber for the annotated checklist to the dragonflies and damselflies of Cumberland County in 1991, and Jim Dowdell, Dale Schweitzer, and others for strengthening each of these lists over the years.

We offer a final tribute to the group of people who have worked so tirelessly (and sometimes at odds) to protect Cape May and Delaware Bay habitats and birds. Many came before them, but on our watch, the following need to be recognized: the late Frank McLaughlin, the late George Clark, Al Nicholson, Ruth Fisher, Dan O'Connor, Larry Niles, Pete McLain, Kathy Clark, Tony Petrangolo, Rich and Pat Kane, Eric Stiles, Tom Gilmore, Dale Rosselet, Charlotte Todd, Ray Sayre, David Rutherford, Bill Noe, Bud Cook, Sara Davison, Fred and Julie Akers, Willi de Camp, Jane Morton Galetto, Leslie and Tony Ficcaglia, Steve and Janet Eisenhauer, Bruce Luepke, and Hillary Pritchard. There have been many others, but these are those we have been privileged to work with most closely. We thank them all from the heart, along with the many who supported them, their organizations, and their agencies. Keep up the good work, friends. Birds and birding would be far the poorer without your efforts. We will remember you every time we stroll Higbee Beach, Cape May Migratory Bird Refuge, or our favorite Delaware Bayshore haunts.

Last but not least, we recognize some stalwart, and different, Cape May farmers. Because of Mary Ellen Dickinson, we will be able to bird Hidden Valley Ranch today and always. In 1986 she sold the ranch to The Nature Conservancy, even though she had been offered millions by developers who wanted to build as many as 235 units on the site. The property had been in her family for seventy-five years, with both her father and her husband farming it and raising horses there. At the time, she said simply but poignantly, "The land has always been farmed. There is a need for it [as open space]." Similarly, we recognize and thank Les and Diane Rea, the owners of The Beanery. Faced with a declining market for agriculture and a changing landscape and economy, and relentlessly pressured by developers, they could have "sold the farm" for millions. Many others have done just that. Instead, they battled to keep the land as a farm and open space. They persevered in gaining farmland preservation status and today lease (for a nominal fee) the birding rights to the CMBO. Birds and birders can now enjoy the Rea Farm in perpetuity. Few have made such selfless contributions to birds and birding and the preservation of a bit of Old Cape May as the Dickinsons and the Reas.

Seasonal Checklist of the Butterflies of Cape May County

by David Wright, Pat Sutton, and James Dowdell

Cape May County is blessed with a wide variety of butterflies, 107 species to be exact. Although this number is considerably lower than the total number of birds recorded in the county, it is still quite impressive when you consider that butterflies migrate far less than birds and most are permanent "breeders" in the county. Habitat diversity is the key to a large butterfly fauna, and the Cape May area provides a quality blend of salt and freshwater wetlands, bogs, oak and pine woodlands, natural grasslands, old fields, and wildlife gardens.

Historically, Cape May is of special interest to lepidopterists. It was here that Dr. Henry Skinner of Philadelphia discovered Aaron's Skipper in 1890. This skipper of the salt marsh is common in Cape May County, one of the few places it is still found in New Jersey. Also, studies on the life history of the Red-banded Hairstreak were carried out near Reed's Beach by Sid Hessel in the late 1940's. Hessel gained considerable prominence in the field of butterfly science and in 1950 a newly discovered hairstreak from Lakehurst (Ocean County) was named after him. This striking and somewhat rare species, now known as Hessel's Hairstreak, also occurs in the Atlantic white cedar swamps of Cape May County.

The Monarch migration through Cape May each fall (mid–August through November) is as dramatic and wondrous as the bird migration. Cape May is a link in the chain of critical habitats for Monarchs, a chain that reaches all the way to the Monarch winter roosts in the mountains of Mexico. In good years, the Monarch migration can be breathtaking, not only near Cape May, but throughout the county. Large evening Monarch roosts often form near the dunes at Cape May Point and Stone Harbor Point and other vegetated oceanfront areas that have been spared development. Sometimes many hundreds or even a thousand or more can be seen in these migratory roosts. On good flight days in late September and early October, generally warm days with light westerly or northerly winds, thousands of migrant Monarchs can be seen streaming over—some skimming the dunes and others high overhead as mere specks in binoculars. In an amazing conjunction of migrants, on October 1, 1999 an astonishing 44,281 Monarchs were counted at the Avalon Seawatch, with 10,700 counted in a single hour—when it seemed as if the sky was filled with flickering orange confetti. The Monarch record season total at Avalon that year was 85,664. The Cape May Bird Observatory's Monarch Monitoring Project (MMP) is carried out at Cape May each autumn, guided by Dr. Lincoln Brower, MMP Director Dick Walton, and N.J. Audubon Research Director Dr. David Mizrahi. Counts and tagging are coordinated by MMP Field Coordinator Louise Zemaitis and conducted by Louise, MMP field technicians, and key volunteers.

Other butterflies are numerous southbound fall migrants as well, with many Common Buckeyes, Red Admirals, American Ladies, Painted Ladies, Mourning Cloaks, Question Marks, and Eastern Commas frequently seen zipping by at the hawkwatch, the Meadows, and at many locations throughout the Cape. Northbound spring butterfly migration occurs too among these species. On one memorable day in May, many thousands of Red Admirals streamed over the Cape, a massive movement as dramatic as the Monarchs of autumn. Finally, in late summer and fall many immigrants from southern locations head north and appear in Cape May County gardens and meadows, mixing with the traditional southbound migrants in a kaleidoscope of color and movement. Large and showy Cloudless Sulphurs are by far the most conspicuous of this group.

Until recently, there was no popular source that detailed Cape May's butterfly fauna. The first checklist was prepared by David Wright and published in the *Cape May Geographic Society 39th Annual Bulletin, June 1985*. From this paper the first CMBO checklist was prepared by David Wright in 1989. David Wright and Pat Sutton annotated the checklist with seasonal information in the 1993 edition and since then the checklist has been continually updated by Wright and Sutton, particularly with the help of Jim Dowdell and TNC entomologist Dr. Dale Schweitzer. This checklist is current to May 2006, and includes 107 species that have been recorded in Cape May County. It is a compilation of records appearing in private collections, museums, and entomology literature (historic and recent), as well as extensive field work since the first CMBO-sponsored checklist was published in 1989. This checklist is intended to represent the most up-to-date catalog of the region's special butterfly fauna and follows the common names in the *Checklist & English Names of North American Butterflies,* 2nd Edition (2001), published by the North American Butterfly Association, Inc. (NABA).

Many of Cape May's butterflies have not been well studied, especially the skippers (Hesperiidae), and for this reason new species should be expected to turn up from time to time. A suppositional list of "species to look for" is provided following the main checklist; all have occured on Cape May County's borders, in some cases, such as Edward's Hairstreak, just a mile or two away. Small Tortoiseshell and Queen may be of suspect origin, possibly deliberate releases or carried to our region as chrysalids aboard vehicles or ships. Also shown is a list of documented historically occurring species now thought to be extirpated. Sightings of butterflies from either the suppositional or historical lists, as well as sightings of current special concern species such as Checkered White, Bronze Copper, Frosted Elfin, Hessel's Hairstreak, Silver-bordered Fritillary, and Two-spotted Skipper should be brought to the attention of Pat Sutton c/o CMBO, 600 Rt. 47 N, Cape May Court House, NJ 08210.

RELATIVE ABUNDANCE AND STATUS

Abundance and status shown are average numbers in suitable habitat in proper season (and in warm, sunny weather). For many butterflies, flight periods may be brief; a butterfly can be abundant one week and virtually absent the next. Some species, White M Hairstreak for example, are always of extreme low density, and others, such as Bog Copper, never stray even a few feet from preferred natural cranberry bogs. Some immigrants, such as Cloudless Sulphur, can be abundant one year and nearly absent the next.

a	abundant	species observable in great numbers
c	common	should be seen in proper habitat
u	uncommon	present in limited numbers and not certain to be seen
r	rare	seen only at intervals of several years
l	local	only found in very localized/specialized habitat
s	stray/vagrant	irregular immigrant into area; does not breed; rare and not seen most years
★	migratory	some are regular migrants and not considered to be permanent residents; for others, temporary breeding possible, but most cannot survive here for multiple seasons

SEASONS

Early Spring	Late March to Mid-May
Late Spring	Mid-May to Mid-June
Early Summer	Mid-June to Mid-July
Mid-Summer	Mid-July to Late-August
Late Summer/Fall	September to October (November)

SEASONS	Early Spring	Late Spring	Early Summer	Mid Summer	Late Summer/ Fall
Swallowtails (Papilionidae)					
Pipevine Swallowtail, u*			X	X	X
Zebra Swallowtail, s	X	X	X	X	
Black Swallowtail, c	X	X	X	X	X
Eastern Tiger Swallowtail, c	X	X	X	X	X
Spicebush Swallowtail, c	X	X	X	X	X
Palamedes Swallowtail, s*					X
Whites & Sulphurs (Pieridae)					
Checkered White, r*	X	X	X	X	X
Cabbage White, a	X	X	X	X	X
Falcate Orangetip, c	X				
Clouded Sulphur, c	X	X	X	X	X
Orange Sulphur, a	X	X	X	X	X
Cloudless Sulphur, c*		X	X	X	X
Little Yellow, u*				X	X
Sleepy Orange, r*				X	X
Harvesters, Coppers, Hairstreaks, & Blues (Lycaenidae)					
Harvester, r		X	X	X	X
American Copper, c	X	X	X	X	X
Bronze Copper, r			X	X	X
Bog Copper, l/u			X		
Coral Hairstreak, c			X		
Banded Hairstreak, c			X		
Striped Hairstreak, u			X		
"Northern" Oak Hairstreak, r			X		
Brown Elfin, c	X				
Frosted Elfin, l/u	X	X			
Henry's Elfin, c	X				
Eastern Pine Elfin, c	X	X			
'Olive' Juniper Hairstreak, c	X		X	X	
Hessel's Hairstreak, l/u	X				
White M Hairstreak, u	X	X		X	X
Gray Hairstreak, c	X	X	X	X	X
Red-banded Hairstreak, c	X	X	X	X	X

SEASONS	Early Spring	Late Spring	Early Summer	Mid Summer	Late Summer/ Fall
Eastern Tailed-blue, a	X	X	X	X	X
Blueberry Spring Azure, c	X				
Holly Spring Azure, a	X	X			
Summer Azure, c		X	X	X	X
Snouts (Libytheinae: Nymphalidae)					
American Snout, c*		X	X	X	X
Brushfoots **(Nymphalinae: Nymphalidae)**					
Gulf Fritillary, s*				X	X
Variegated Fritillary, c*		X	X	X	X
Great Spangled Fritillary, u			X	X	X
Silver-bordered Fritillary, r	X		X		X
Pearl Crescent, a	X	X	X	X	X
Question Mark, c	X	X	X	X	X
Eastern Comma, u	X	X	X	X	X
Gray Comma, s				X	X
Compton Tortoiseshell, s*	X		X		X
Mourning Cloak, c	X	X	X	X	X
American Lady, c-a*	X	X	X	X	X
Painted Lady, u-c*	X	X	X	X	X
Red Admiral, c-a*	X	X	X	X	X
Common Buckeye, c-a*		X	X	X	X
Red-spotted Purple, c		X	X	X	X
White Admiral, r/s			X	X	
Viceroy, u		X	X	X	X
Hackberry Butterflies **(Apaturinae: Nymphalidae)**					
Hackberry Emperor, u-c		X	X	X	X
Tawny Emperor, u		X	X	X	X
Satyrs & Wood Nymphs **(Satyrinae: Nymphalidae)**					
Appalachian Brown, l/c			X	X	
Little Wood-satyr, c		X	X	X	
Common Wood-nymph, c-a			X	X	X

SEASONS	Early Spring	Late Spring	Early Summer	Mid Summer	Late Summer/ Fall
Milkweed Butterflies (Danainae: Nymphalidae)					
Monarch, a*	X	X	X	X	X
Skippers (Hesperiidae)					
Silver-spotted Skipper, c	X	X	X	X	X
Long-tailed Skipper, u*				X	X
Hoary Edge, u		X	X		
Southern Cloudywing, c		X	X	X	X
Northern Cloudywing, c		X	X		
Hayhurst's Scallopwing, u		X	X	X	X
Sleepy Duskywing, u	X	X			
Juvenal's Duskywing, c-a	X	X			
Horace's Duskywing, c	X	X	X	X	X
Wild Indigo Duskywing, u	X	X	X	X	X
Common Checkered-skipper, u*			X	X	X
Common Sootywing, c		X	X	X	X
Swarthy Skipper, c		X	X	X	X
Clouded Skipper, u*				X	X
Least Skipper, c		X	X	X	X
European Skipper, u		X	X		
Fiery Skipper, c*		X	X	X	X
Leonard's Skipper, u					X
Cobweb Skipper, c	X				
Peck's Skipper, u		X		X	X
Tawny-edged Skipper, u		X	X	X	X
Crossline Skipper, c		X	X	X	X
Whirlabout, s*				X	X
Northern Broken-dash, c				X	
Little Glassywing, u		X	X		
Sachem, c-a*		X	X	X	X
Delaware Skipper, c		X	X	X	
Rare Skipper, l/u			X	X	
Mulberrywing, l/c			X		
Zabulon Skipper, c		X	X	X	X
Aaron's Skipper, l/c-a		X	X	X	X
Broad-winged Skipper, c-a			X	X	

SEASONS	Early Spring	Late Spring	Early Summer	Mid Summer	Late Summer/ Fall
Dion Skipper, l/c				X	
Black Dash, l/u			X		
Two-spotted Skipper, u			X		
Dun Skipper, u		X	X	X	
Dusted Skipper, u		X			
Common Roadside-skipper, u		X		X	
Eufala Skipper, s*					X
Brazilian Skipper, s*					X
Salt Marsh Skipper, c		X	X	X	X
Ocola Skipper, u*				X	X

Historical List
(Past records, but thought to be extirpated)

	Early Spring	Late Spring	Early Summer	Mid Summer	Late Summer/ Fall
Great Purple Hairstreak					X
Aphrodite Fritillary			X	X	
Regal Fritillary				X	X
Meadow Fritillary	X		X		X
Baltimore Checkerspot			X		
Eyed Brown			X	X	
Georgia Satyr			X	X	

Suppositional List
(Species to look for; might be expected to occur)

	Early Spring	Late Spring	Early Summer	Mid Summer	Late Summer/ Fall
Giant Swallowtail*					X
Southern Dogface*					X
Orange-barred Sulphur*					X
Edward's Hairstreak			X		
Hoary Elfin	X				
Small Tortoiseshell* (Eurasian)	X				X
White Peacock				X	X
Queen*				X	X
Golden-banded Skipper		X			
Confused Cloudywing		X	X	X	X
Dotted Skipper			X	X	
Indian Skipper		X			
Arogos Skipper			X	X	
Hobomok Skipper		X	X		

Index

Cape May Chronology—Through the Seasons

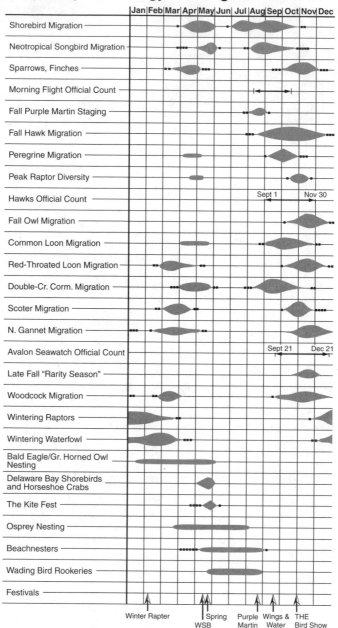

CAPE MAY CHRONOLOGY

Dates shown are composites or averages for the phenomena or the group of
birds. Within a group, species can exhibit very different timetables. Dunlin
return north in April, Red Knot in late May. Cape May's most common
Warbler, the Yellow-rumped Warbler, migrates south mainly at the same
time as sparrows, not the other warblers that move far earlier. For more
exacting species dates, consult Sibley, 1997.

Seasonal Checklist
of the Birds
# of Cape May County

This checklist treats birds found in Cape May County, the waters of Delaware Bay, and offshore to a distance of 50 miles. It contains sightings of 412 species that have been observed here through May 2006, and *excludes* hypotheticals and known or suspected escapes. Key subspecies and color morphs are shown in *italics*. For an annotated checklist and more detailed information please refer to *The Birds of Cape May* (1997) by David Sibley.

Note that this checklist covers not just the Cape May Point area, but all of Cape May County, and therefore status can vary; for example Wild Turkey has never been seen at Cape May Point, yet can be common in the Belleplain area. Likewise, status may not be applicable to the "greater Cape May" region that includes Cumberland and Atlantic Counties and beyond. Harlequin Duck may be common at Barnegat Inlet in winter, and Bald Eagle can be common on the Delaware Bayshore. On the other hand, many neotropical migrant songbirds become less concentrated and less findable away from Cape May, and may have a lesser status in adjacent counties.

SEASONAL OCCURRENCE

W	Winter	December–mid-March
Sp	Spring	mid-March–May
Su	Summer	June–mid-July
EF	Early Fall	mid-July–mid-September
LF	Late Fall	mid-September–November

RELATIVE ABUNDANCE AND STATUS

Note that these are *average* numbers in suitable habitat.

c	common	should not miss; more than 20 individuals per day
f	fairly common	usually seen; 5 to 20 individuals per day
u	uncommon	seen in limited numbers; 1 to 4 per day

s	scarce	usually present, but not seen daily
r	rare	seen only a few times per season
v	very rare	very infrequent; averages 1 or fewer records per season
p	pelagic	found primarily at sea; listed status is that from *shore*
i	introduced	not native to New Jersey
★	regular breeder	
★★	irregular, presumed, or recent former breeder	

	W	Sp	Su	EF	LF
Waterfowl					
Snow Goose	c	c	v	v	c
Brant	c	c	r	v	c
Cackling Goose	v	v			v
Canada Goose*	c	c	f	f	c
Mute Swan* (i)	f	f	f	f	f
Tundra Swan	s	s			f
Wood Duck*	s	u	u	u	u
Gadwall**	c	c	s	u	c
Eurasian Wigeon	r	r		v	r
American Wigeon	c	c		u	c
American Black Duck*	c	c	f	f	c
Mallard*	c	c	c	c	c
Blue-winged Teal**	r	u	s	u	u
Northern Shoveler	f	f		s	f
Northern Pintail	f	c		u	f
Green-winged Teal	f	c	r	f	c
Canvasback	s	s			s
Redhead	r	r			r
Ring-necked Duck	u	u			u
Greater Scaup	f	f			f
Lesser Scaup	f	f			f
King Eider	r	r		v	r
Common Eider	s	r	v	v	s
Harlequin Duck	r	r			r
Surf Scoter	c	c	r	r	c

	W	Sp	Su	EF	LF
White-winged Scoter	f	u	v	v	f
Black Scoter	c	c	r	r	c
Long-tailed Duck	c	c			f
Bufflehead	c	c			c
Common Goldeneye	u	u			u
Hooded Merganser**	c	u	v	v	c
Common Merganser	s	s			s
Red-breasted Merganser	c	c	r	s	c
Ruddy Duck	u	s	v		u

Upland Game Birds

	W	Sp	Su	EF	LF
Ring-necked Pheasant**(i)	r	r	r	r	r
Ruffed Grouse**	r	r	r	r	r
Wild Turkey*	u	f	f	u	u
Northern Bobwhite*	s	s	s	s	s

Loons to Cormorants

	W	Sp	Su	EF	LF
Red-throated Loon	c	c	v	v	c
Common Loon	f	c	r	s	c
Pied-billed Grebe**	f	u	r	s	f
Horned Grebe	f	f			u
Red-necked Grebe	v	v			r
Cory's Shearwater (p)			r	v	
Greater Shearwater (p)		v	v		
Sooty Shearwater (p)		s	r		
Audubon's Shearwater (p)				v	
Wilson's Storm-Petrel (p)		r	s	s	v
Northern Gannet	f	c	s	r	c
American White Pelican	v	v		v	r
Brown Pelican	v	s	u	f	s
Double-crested Cormorant	u	c	c	c	c
Great Cormorant	u	u	v	v	u

Bitterns to Vultures

	W	Sp	Su	EF	LF
American Bittern	s	s	v	u	u
Least Bittern*	v	u	u	u	s
Great Blue Heron**	f	f	s	f	c

	W	Sp	Su	EF	LF
Great Egret*	s	c	c	c	u
Snowy Egret*	r	c	c	c	f
Little Blue Heron*	r	u	u	f	u
Tricolored Heron*	r	u	u	f	u
Cattle Egret**		u	u	u	u
Green Heron*	v	u	f	f	u
Black-crowned Night-Heron*	u	f	f	f	f
Yellow-crowned Night-Heron*		u	u	u	u
White Ibis		r	v	r	v
Glossy Ibis*	v	c	c	c	u
White-faced Ibis		r		v	
Black Vulture*	f	f	u	f	f
Turkey Vulture*	c	c	f	c	c

Diurnal Raptors

	W	Sp	Su	EF	LF
Osprey*	v	f	f	c	c
Swallow-tailed Kite		r	v	v	
Mississippi Kite		s	r	v	
Bald Eagle*	u	s	s	u	u
Northern Harrier*	f	f	s	f	c
Sharp-shinned Hawk	u	u		u	c
Cooper's Hawk*	u	u	s	u	c
Northern Goshawk	r	v			s
Red-shouldered Hawk**	u	u	r	u	c
Broad-winged Hawk*		f	s	f	f
Swainson's Hawk				v	r
Red-tailed Hawk*	f	f	u	f	c
Rough-legged Hawk	s	r			s
Golden Eagle	r				s
American Kestrel**	s	u	r	c	c
Merlin	s	u		f	c
Peregrine Falcon*	s	s	s	f	c

Rails to Cranes

	W	Sp	Su	EF	LF
Black Rail*		s	s	v	v
Clapper Rail*	u	c	c	c	u
King Rail**		s	s	s	v

	W	Sp	Su	EF	LF
Virginia Rail*	s	u	u	u	f
Sora**	v	u	v	u	u
Common Moorhen**	v	u	u	u	u
American Coot**	u	u	r	s	f
Sandhill Crane	v	r			r
Shorebirds					
Black-bellied Plover	f	c	u	c	c
American Golden-Plover		r		s	s
Semipalmated Plover	r	c	u	c	c
Piping Plover*	v	u	u	u	s
Killdeer*	f	f	u	f	c
American Oystercatcher*	f	f	f	f	f
Black-necked Stilt		r	v	v	
American Avocet			v	v	v
Greater Yellowlegs	u	c	u	c	c
Lesser Yellowlegs	s	f	u	c	c
Solitary Sandpiper		u	s	u	s
Willet*		c	c	f	r
"Western" Willet	r	v	v	f	f
Spotted Sandpiper**		f	u	f	u
Upland Sandpiper		r	r	s	v
Whimbrel	v	c	s	f	u
Hudsonian Godwit		v	v	r	r
Marbled Godwit	r	r	v	s	s
Ruddy Turnstone	c	c	u	f	c
Red Knot	s	c	f	u	u
Sanderling	c	c	f	c	c
Semipalmated Sandpiper		c	u	c	c
Western Sandpiper	f	r	r	f	f
Least Sandpiper	r	c	u	c	f
White-rumped Sandpiper		u	u	u	u
Baird's Sandpiper				r	r
Pectoral Sandpiper		u	s	f	f
Purple Sandpiper	c	c			c
Dunlin	c	c	r	u	c
Stilt Sandpiper		r	s	f	u

	W	Sp	Su	EF	LF
Buff-breasted Sandpiper				r	r
Ruff		v	v	v	
Short-billed Dowitcher	r	c	f	c	u
Long-billed Dowitcher	r	v		u	u
Wilson's Snipe	u	c		u	f
American Woodcock*	u	u	u	u	f
Wilson's Phalarope		r	r	s	r
Red-necked Phalarope (p)		v	v	v	v
Red Phalarope (p)	v	v	v	v	v
Jaegers to Alcids					
Pomarine Jaeger (p)		v		v	r
Parasitic Jaeger (p)		s	v	s	u
Laughing Gull*	r	c	c	c	c
Little Gull	r	s	v	v	r
Black-headed Gull	r	r			r
Bonaparte's Gull	c	c	r	r	f
Ring-billed Gull	c	c	s	f	c
Herring Gull*	c	c	c	c	c
Iceland Gull	r	r	v		v
Lesser Black-backed Gull	s	s	v	r	s
Glaucous Gull	r	r			
Great Black-backed Gull*	c	c	c	c	c
Black-legged Kittiwake (p)	r	v			r
Gull-billed Tern*		u	u	u	
Caspian Tern		r	v	u	f
Royal Tern	r	f	u	c	c
Sandwich Tern		v	r	s	v
Roseate Tern		s	r	r	
Common Tern*		c	c	c	f
Arctic Tern (p)		v	v	v	v
Forster's Tern*	s	c	c	c	c
Least Tern*		f	f	f	
Black Tern		r	r	s	r
Black Skimmer*	v	f	f	c	f
Dovekie (p)	v				v
Razorbill (p)	r	v			r

	W	Sp	Su	EF	LF
Pigeons to Woodpeckers					
Rock Pigeon (Feral Pigeon)*(i)	c	c	c	c	c
White-winged Dove		v		v	v
Mourning Dove*	c	c	c	c	c
Black-billed Cuckoo*		u	s	u	s
Yellow-billed Cuckoo*		u	u	u	s
Barn Owl**	s	s	s	s	u
Eastern Screech-Owl*	f	f	f	f	f
Great Horned Owl*	u	u	u	u	u
Snowy Owl	v				v
Barred Owl*	u	u	u	u	u
Long-eared Owl	s	s			u
Short-eared Owl	u	u			u
Northern Saw-whet Owl	s	s			u
Common Nighthawk		s	v	u	s
Chuck-will's-widow*		f	f	f	
Whip-poor-will*		f	f	f	s
Chimney Swift*		c	c	c	f
Ruby-throated Hummingbird*	v	f	f	f	s
Belted Kingfisher*	u	u	s	u	u
Red-headed Woodpecker**	r	s	r	s	s
Red-bellied Woodpecker*	f	f	f	f	f
Yellow-bellied Sapsucker	r	s			u
Downy Woodpecker*	f	f	f	f	f
Hairy Woodpecker*	u	u	u	u	u
Northern Flicker*	f	c	f	c	c
Flycatchers to Vireos					
Olive-sided Flycatcher		r		r	v
Eastern Wood-Pewee*		f	f	c	f
Yellow-bellied Flycatcher		r		u	r
Acadian Flycatcher*		u	u	u	r
Alder Flycatcher		v		u	s
Willow Flycatcher*		s	u	u	
Least Flycatcher		s		f	s
Eastern Phoebe*	r	f	s	s	c
Ash-throated Flycatcher					r

	W	Sp	Su	EF	LF
Great Crested Flycatcher*		f	f	f	u
Western Kingbird	v	v	v	r	r
Eastern Kingbird*		f	f	c	s
Scissor-tailed Flycatcher		v		v	v
White-eyed Vireo*	v	f	f	f	s
Yellow-throated Vireo*		u	s	u	s
Blue-headed Vireo	v	u		s	u
Warbling Vireo		s		u	s
Philadelphia Vireo		v		u	u
Red-eyed Vireo*		c	f	c	f

Jays to Wrens

	W	Sp	Su	EF	LF
Blue Jay*	c	c	f	c	c
American Crow*	c	c	c	c	c
Fish Crow*	f	c	c	c	c
Horned Lark*	u	s	s	s	u
Purple Martin*		c	c	c	r
Tree Swallow*	s	c	c	c	c
No. Rough-winged Swallow*		u	u	f	s
Bank Swallow**		f	s	f	s
Cliff Swallow		u	r	u	u
Cave Swallow	v	v			r
Barn Swallow*		c	c	c	u
Carolina Chickadee*	c	c	c	c	c
Tufted Titmouse*	f	f	f	f	f
Red-breasted Nuthatch**	u	s	v	u	u
White-breasted Nuthatch*	u	u	u	u	u
Brown Creeper**	s	u			u
Carolina Wren*	c	c	c	c	c
House Wren*	r	f	f	f	f
Winter Wren	u	u		r	u
Sedge Wren**	r	r		v	r
Marsh Wren*	u	c	c	c	f

Kinglets to Waxwings

	W	Sp	Su	EF	LF
Golden-crowned Kinglet	u	f		v	c
Ruby-crowned Kinglet	s	f		r	c

	W	Sp	Su	EF	LF
Blue-gray Gnatcatcher*	v	f	f	c	u
Eastern Bluebird*	u	u	u	u	c
Veery		u		c	u
Gray-cheeked Thrush		s		r	u
Bicknell's Thrush		s		v	s
Swainson's Thrush		u		u	f
Hermit Thrush	u	f		v	c
Wood Thrush*		f	f	f	s
American Robin*	c	c	c	c	c
Gray Catbird*	u	c	c	c	c
Northern Mockingbird*	c	c	c	c	c
Brown Thrasher*	u	f	u	u	f
European Starling*(i)	c	c	c	c	c
American Pipit	s	s		v	f
Cedar Waxwing*	u	f	f	c	c

Warblers

	W	Sp	Su	EF	LF
Blue-winged Warbler*		f	f	f	u
Golden-winged Warbler		r		s	r
Tennessee Warbler		s		u	u
Orange-crowned Warbler	r	r			s
Nashville Warbler	v	u		f	u
Northern Parula**		f	r	f	f
Yellow Warbler*		c	f	c	s
Chestnut-sided Warbler		u		f	u
Magnolia Warbler		f		f	f
Cape May Warbler		u		f	f
Black-throated Blue Warbler		f		f	f
Yellow-rumped Warbler	c	c		s	c
Black-throated Green Warbler		f		f	f
Blackburnian Warbler		u		f	u
Yellow-throated Warbler*		f	f	f	r
Pine Warbler*	r	c	c	c	f
Prairie Warbler*	v	f	f	f	s
Palm Warbler	s	u		u	c
Bay-breasted Warbler		u		u	s
Blackpoll Warbler		f	v	u	f

	W	Sp	Su	EF	LF
Cerulean Warbler		r		r	v
Black-and-white Warbler*		c	f	c	f
American Redstart*		c	u	c	f
Prothonotary Warbler*		f	f	u	r
Worm-eating Warbler*		f	f	u	s
Ovenbird*		c	c	c	u
Northern Waterthrush		u		c	f
Louisiana Waterthrush*		u	u	u	
Kentucky Warbler*		u	s	s	
Connecticut Warbler				u	u
Mourning Warbler		r		u	r
Common Yellowthroat*	r	c	c	c	f
Hooded Warbler*		u	u	u	r
Wilson's Warbler		s		u	r
Canada Warbler		u		f	s
Yellow-breasted Chat*	v	f	f	u	s
Tanagers to Buntings					
Summer Tanager*		u	u	u	r
Scarlet Tanager*		f	f	f	c
Eastern Towhee*	u	c	c	c	f
American Tree Sparrow	s	r			s
Chipping Sparrow*	s	c	c	c	c
Clay-colored Sparrow	v	v		r	s
Field Sparrow*	f	f	f	f	c
Vesper Sparrow	v	v			s
Lark Sparrow	v	v		r	r
Savannah Sparrow	f	f		u	c
"Ipswich" Savannah Sparrow	u				s
Grasshopper Sparrow**	v	r	v	v	s
Nelson's Sharp-tailed Sparrow	s	s			u
Saltmarsh Sharp-tailed Sparrow*	u	f	f	f	u
Seaside Sparrow*	u	c	c	c	f
Fox Sparrow	f	u			f
Song Sparrow*	c	c	c	c	c
Lincoln's Sparrow	v	r			u
Swamp Sparrow*	f	f	f	f	c

	W	Sp	Su	EF	LF
White-throated Sparrow	c	c	v	v	c
White-crowned Sparrow	r	s			u
Dark-eyed Junco	c	f			c
Lapland Longspur	r	r			r
Snow Bunting	s	r			u
Northern Cardinal*	c	c	c	c	c
Rose-breasted Grosbeak		f	v	f	f
Blue Grosbeak*		f	f	f	u
Indigo Bunting*		c	c	f	f
Dickcissel	r	r		s	s

Blackbirds to Old World Sparrows

	W	Sp	Su	EF	LF
Bobolink		f	u	c	f
Red-winged Blackbird*	c	c	c	c	c
Eastern Meadowlark*	u	u	u	u	f
Yellow-headed Blackbird	v	v	v	r	v
Rusty Blackbird	u	u			f
Common Grackle*	c	c	c	c	c
Boat-tailed Grackle*	f	f	f	f	f
Brown-headed Cowbird*	c	c	c	c	c
Orchard Oriole*		f	f	f	v
Baltimore Oriole*	r	f	u	c	u
Purple Finch	u	s		r	f
House Finch*(i)	c	c	c	c	c
Red Crossbill**	v	v	v	v	r
Common Redpoll	r	v			r
Pine Siskin	u	s			u
American Goldfinch*	f	c	f	c	c
Evening Grosbeak	v	v			v
House Sparrow*(i)	c	c	c	c	c

RARITIES

Observers lucky enough to encounter any of the species on these two lists (or species marked "v" on the main list) should document the record with careful notes, sketches, and photographs. Please contact CMBO (609-884-2736) and other birders as soon as possible.

Very Rare Visitors and Vagrants

This is a list of species that have been adequately documented *more than four times* in Cape May County, but less than annually since 1985.

Fulvous Whistling-Duck, Greater White-fronted Goose, *Common (Eurasian) Green-winged Teal*, Eared Grebe, Northern Fulmar, Manx Shearwater, Magnificent Frigatebird, Wood Stork, Yellow Rail, Purple Gallinule, Wilson's Plover, Curlew Sandpiper, Long-tailed Jaeger, Franklin's Gull, Sabine's Gull, Bridled Tern, Sooty Tern, Common Murre, Thick-billed Murre, Atlantic Puffin, Eurasian Collared-Dove (i), Rufous Hummingbird, Pileated Woodpecker, Say's Phoebe, Fork-tailed Flycatcher, Loggerhead Shrike, Northern Shrike, Common Raven, Northern Wheatear, *Audubon's Yellow-rumped Warbler*, Black-throated Gray Warbler, Swainson's Warbler, Western Tanager, Henslow's Sparrow, Le Conte's Sparrow, *Gambel's White-crowned Sparrow*, *Oregon Dark-eyed Junco*, Black-headed Grosbeak, Painted Bunting, Brewer's Blackbird, White-winged Crossbill.

Accidentals

These species have been adequately documented *four or fewer times* in Cape May County.

Black-bellied Whistling Duck, Ross's Goose, *Black Brant*, Pacific Loon, Western Grebe, Yellow-nosed Albatross, Black-capped Petrel, White-faced Storm-Petrel, Leach's Storm-Petrel, Band-rumped Storm-Petrel, Brown Booby, Anhinga, *Great White Heron*, White-tailed Kite, *Krider's Hawk*, Eurasian Kestrel, Gyrfalcon, Corn Crake, Northern Lapwing, Lesser Sand-Plover (Mongolian Plover), *Eurasian Whimbrel*, Long-billed Curlew, Bar-tailed Godwit, Red-necked Stint, Little Stint, Sharp-tailed Sandpiper, Common (Eurasian) Woodcock, Great Skua, Black-tailed Gull, Thayer's Gull, White-winged Tern, Whiskered Tern, Brown Noddy, Black Guillemot, Common Ground-Dove, Black-chinned Hummingbird, Calliope Hummingbird, Allen's Hummingbird, Black-backed Woodpecker, Vermilion Flycatcher, Gray Kingbird, Bell's Vireo, Brown-chested Martin, Violet-green Swallow, Brown-headed Nuthatch, Rock Wren, Bewick's Wren, Mountain Bluebird, Bohemian Waxwing, Townsend's Warbler, MacGillivray's Warbler, Spotted Towhee, Lark Bunting, Harris's Sparrow, Golden-crowned Sparrow, Smith's Longspur, Chestnut-collared Longspur.